SPECIAL EDUCATION LAW: STATUTES AND REGULATIONS

Second Edition

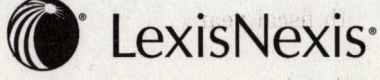

LEXISNEXIS MATTHEW BENDER LAW SCHOOL ADVISORY BOARD

Charles P. Craver
Freda H. Alverson Professor of Law
The George Washington University Law School

Richard D. Freer
Robert Howell Hall Professor of Law
Emory University School of Law

Craig Joyce
Andrews Kurth Professor of Law &
Co-Director, Institute for Intellectual Property and Information Law
University of Houston Law Center

Ellen S. Podgor
Professor of Law
Stetson University College of Law

Paul F. Rothstein
Professor of Law
Georgetown University Law Center

Robin Wellford Slocum
Professor of Law & Director,
Legal Research and Writing Program
Chapman University School of Law

Charles J. Tabb
Alice Curtis Campbell Professor of Law
University of Illinois College of Law

Judith Welch Wegner
Professor of Law
University of North Carolina School of Law

SPECIAL EDUCATION LAW: STATUTES AND REGULATIONS

Second Edition

MARK C. WEBER
Vincent dePaul Professor of Law
DePaul University College of Law

RALPH MAWDSLEY
Professor of Education Administration
Cleveland State University College of Education

SARAH REDFIELD
Professor of Law Franklin Pierce Law Center

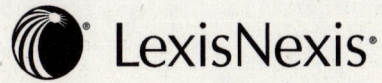

Library of Congress Card Number:
ISBN: 978-1-4224-2073-7

This publication is designed to provide accurate and authoritative information in regard to the subject matter covered. It is sold with the understanding that the publisher is not engaged in rendering legal, accounting, or other professional services. If legal advice or other expert assistance is required, the services of a competent professional should be sought.

LexisNexis, the knowledge burst logo, and Michie are trademarks of Reed Elsevier Properties Inc, used under license. Matthew Bender is a registered trademark of Matthew Bender Properties Inc.

Copyright © 2008 Matthew Bender & Company, Inc., a member of the LexisNexis Group.
Originally published in: 2008.
All Rights Reserved.

No copyright is claimed in the text of statutes, regulations, and excerpts from court opinions quoted within this work. Permission to copy material exceeding fair use, 17 U.S.C. § 107, may be licensed for a fee of 25¢ per page per copy from the Copyright Clearance Center, 222 Rosewood Drive, Danvers, Mass. 01923, telephone (978) 750-8400.

Editorial Offices
744 Broad Street, Newark, NJ 07102 (973) 820-2000
201 Mission St., San Francisco, CA 94105-1831 (415) 908-3200
www.lexis.com

(Pub.03189)

TABLE OF CONTENTS

TITLE 20. EDUCATION 1

CHAPTER 33. EDUCATION OF INDIVIDUALS WITH DISABILITIES 1

§1400.	Short title; table of contents; findings; purposes	1
§1401.	Definitions	4
§1402.	Office of Special Education Programs	10
§1403.	Abrogation of State sovereign immunity	10
§1404.	Acquisition of equipment; construction or alteration of facilities	10
§1405.	Employment of individuals with disabilities	10
§1406.	Requirements for prescribing regulations	10
§1407.	State administration	12
§1408.	Paperwork reduction	12
§1409.	Freely associated States	13
§1411.	Authorization; allotment; use of funds; authorization of appropriations	13
§1412.	State eligibility	25
§1413.	Local educational agency eligibility	39
§1414.	Evaluations, eligibility determinations, individualized education programs, and educational placements	45
§1414a.	[Omitted]	56
§1415.	Procedural safeguards	56
§1416.	Monitoring, technical assistance, and enforcement	69
§1417.	Administration	75
§1418.	Program information	76
§1419.	Preschool grants	78
§1420.	[Omitted]	81
§1421.	[Repealed]	81
§1422.	[Repealed]	81
§1423.	[Repealed]	81
§1424.	[Repealed]	81
§1424a.	[Repealed]	81
§1425.	[Repealed]	81
§1426.	[Repealed]	81

TABLE OF CONTENTS

§ 1427.	[Repealed]	81
§ 1431.	Findings and policy	81
§ 1432.	Definitions	82
§ 1433.	General authority	84
§ 1434.	Eligibility	84
§ 1435.	Requirements for statewide system	84
§ 1436.	Individualized family service plan	88
§ 1437.	State application and assurances	89
§ 1438.	Uses of funds	92
§ 1439.	Procedural safeguards	92
§ 1440.	Payor of last resort	94
§ 1441.	State interagency coordinating council	95
§ 1442.	Federal administration	96
§ 1443.	Allocation of funds	97
§ 1444.	Authorization of appropriations	99
§ 1445.	[Omitted]	99
§ 1450.	Findings	99
§ 1451.	Purpose; definition of personnel; program authority	101
§ 1452.	Eligibility and collaborative process	102
§ 1453.	Applications	104
§ 1454.	Use of funds	105
§ 1455.	Authorization of appropriations	109
§ 1456.	[Omitted]	109
§ 1461.	Purpose; definition of eligible entity	109
§ 1462.	Personnel development to improve services and results for children with disabilities	110
§ 1463.	Technical assistance, demonstration projects, dissemination of information, and implementation of scientifically based research	115
§ 1464.	Studies and evaluations	117
§ 1465.	Interim alternative educational settings, behavioral supports, and systemic school interventions	120
§ 1466.	Authorization of appropriations	121
§ 1470.	Purposes	122
§ 1471.	Parent training and information centers	122
§ 1472.	Community parent resource centers	125
§ 1473.	Technical assistance for parent training and information centers	125
§ 1474.	Technology development, demonstration, and utilization; media services; and instructional materials	126

§1475. Authorization of appropriations	128
§1476. [Omitted]	128
§1477. [Omitted]	128
§1478. [Omitted]	128
§1479. [Omitted]	129
§1480. [Omitted]	129
§1481. Comprehensive plan for subparts 2 and 3	129
§1482. Administrative provisions	131

TITLE 34 EDUCATION 135

SUBTITLE B. REGULATIONS OF THE OFFICES OF THE DEPARTMENT OF EDUCATION 135

CHAPTER III OFFICE OF SPECIAL EDUCATION AND REHABILITATIVE SERVICES, DEPARTMENT OF EDUCATION 135

PART 300 ASSISTANCE TO STATES FOR THE EDUCATION OF CHILDREN WITH DISABILITIES 135

SUBPART A GENERAL 135

§300.1 Purposes.	135
§300.2 Applicability of this part to State and local agencies	135
§300.3 [This section was removed. See 71 FR 46540, 46753, Aug. 14, 2006.]	136
§300.4 Act.	136
§300.5 Assistive technology device.	136
§300.6 Assistive technology service.	136
§300.7 Charter school.	136
§300.8 Child with a disability.	136
§300.9 Consent.	139
§300.10 Core academic subjects.	139
§300.11 Day; business day; school day.	139
§300.12 Educational service agency.	139
§300.13 Elementary school.	140
§300.14 Equipment.	140
§300.15 Evaluation.	140
§300.16 Excess costs.	140
§300.17 Free appropriate public education.	140
§300.18 Highly qualified special education teachers.	141

§ 300.19	Homeless children.	143
§ 300.20	Include.	143
§ 300.21	Indian and Indian tribe.	143
§ 300.22	Individualized education program.	143
§ 300.23	Individualized education program team.	143
§ 300.24	Individualized family service plan.	143
§ 300.25	Infant or toddler with a disability.	143
§ 300.26	Institution of higher education.	144
§ 300.27	Limited English proficient.	144
§ 300.28	Local educational agency.	144
§ 300.29	Native language.	144
§ 300.30	Parent.	145
§ 300.31	Parent training and information center.	145
§ 300.32	Personally identifiable.	145
§ 300.33	Public agency.	145
§ 300.34	Related services.	146
§ 300.35	Scientifically based research.	149
§ 300.36	Secondary school.	149
§ 300.37	Services plan.	149
§ 300.38	Secretary.	149
§ 300.39	Special education.	149
§ 300.40	State.	150
§ 300.41	State educational agency.	150
§ 300.42	Supplementary aids and services.	150
§ 300.43	Transition services.	150
§ 300.44	Universal design.	151
§ 300.45	Ward of the State.	151
SUBPART B STATE ELIGIBILITY		151
§ 300.100	Eligibility for assistance.	151
§ 300.101	Free appropriate public education (FAPE).	151
§ 300.102	Limitation — exception to FAPE for certain ages.	152
§ 300.103	FAPE — methods and payments.	153
§ 300.104	Residential placement.	153
§ 300.105	Assistive technology.	153
§ 300.106	Extended school year services.	153
§ 300.107	Nonacademic services.	154
§ 300.108	Physical education.	154
§ 300.109	Full educational opportunity goal (FEOG).	155
§ 300.110	Program options.	155

§300.111	Child find.	155
§300.112	Individualized education programs (IEP).	156
§300.113	Routine checking of hearing aids and external components of surgically implanted medical devices.	156
§300.114	LRE requirements.	156
§300.115	Continuum of alternative placements.	157
§300.116	Placements.	157
§300.117	Nonacademic settings.	157
§300.118	Children in public or private institutions.	158
§300.119	Technical assistance and training activities.	158
§300.120	Monitoring activities.	158
§300.121	Procedural safeguards.	158
§300.122	Evaluation.	158
§300.123	Confidentiality of personally identifiable information.	158
§300.124	Transition of children from the Part C program to preschool programs.	159
§300.125	[This section was removed and reserved. See 71 FR 46540, 46753, Aug. 14, 2006.]	159
§300.126	[This section was removed and reserved. See 71 FR 46540, 46753, Aug. 14, 2006.]	159
§300.127	[This section was removed and reserved. See 71 FR 46540, 46753, Aug. 14, 2006.]	159
§300.128	[This section was removed and reserved. See 71 FR 46540, 46753, Aug. 14, 2006.]	159
§300.129	State responsibility regarding children in private schools.	159
§300.130	Definition of parentally-placed private school children with disabilities.	159
§300.131	Child find for parentally-placed private school children with disabilities.	160
§300.132	Provision of services for parentally-placed private school children with disabilities—basic requirement.	160
§300.133	Expenditures.	161
§300.134	Consultation.	162
§300.135	Written affirmation.	162
§300.136	Compliance.	163
§300.137	Equitable services determined.	163
§300.138	Equitable services provided.	163
§300.139	Location of services and transportation.	164
§300.140	Due process complaints and State complaints.	164
§300.141	Requirement that funds not benefit a private school.	165
§300.142	Use of personnel.	165

§ 300.143	Separate classes prohibited.	165
§ 300.144	Property, equipment, and supplies.	166
§ 300.145	Applicability of §§ 300.146 through 300.147.	166
§ 300.146	Responsibility of SEA.	166
§ 300.147	Implementation by SEA.	167
§ 300.148	Placement of children by parents when FAPE is at issue.	167
§ 300.149	SEA responsibility for general supervision.	168
§ 300.150	SEA implementation of procedural safeguards.	169
§ 300.151	Adoption of State complaint procedures.	169
§ 300.152	Minimum State complaint procedures.	169
§ 300.153	Filing a complaint.	171
§ 300.154	Methods of ensuring services.	171
§ 300.155	Hearings relating to LEA eligibility.	174
§ 300.156	Personnel qualifications.	174
§ 300.157	Performance goals and indicators.	174
§§ 300.158–300.159	[Reserved]	175
§ 300.160	Participation in assessments.	175
§ 300.161	[Reserved]	176
§ 300.162	Supplementation of State, local, and other Federal funds.	176
§ 300.163	Maintenance of State financial support.	177
§ 300.164	Waiver of requirement regarding supplementing and not supplanting with Part B funds.	177
§ 300.165	Public participation.	179
§ 300.166	Rule of construction.	179
§ 300.167	State advisory panel.	179
§ 300.168	Membership.	179
§ 300.169	Duties.	180
§ 300.170	Suspension and expulsion rates.	180
§ 300.171	Annual description of use of Part B funds.	181
§ 300.172	Access to instructional materials.	181
§ 300.173	Overidentification and disproportionality.	182
§ 300.174	Prohibition on mandatory medication.	182
§ 300.175	SEA as provider of FAPE or direct services.	183
§ 300.176	Exception for prior State plans.	183
§ 300.177	States' sovereign immunity.	183
§ 300.178	Determination by the Secretary that a State is eligible to receive a grant.	184
§ 300.179	Notice and hearing before determining that a State is not eligible to receive a grant.	184
§ 300.180	Hearing official or panel.	184

§300.181	Hearing procedures.	184
§300.182	Initial decision; final decision.	186
§300.183	Filing requirements.	187
§300.184	Judicial review.	187
§300.185	[This section was removed and reserved. See 71 FR 46540, 46753, Aug. 14, 2006.]	188
§300.186	Assistance under other Federal programs.	188
§300.190	By-pass — general.	188
§300.191	Provisions for services under a by-pass.	188
§300.192	Notice of intent to implement a by-pass.	189
§300.193	Request to show cause.	189
§300.194	Show cause hearing.	189
§300.195	Decision.	190
§300.196	Filing requirements.	190
§300.197	Judicial review.	190
§300.198	Continuation of a by-pass.	190
§300.199	State administration.	191
SUBPART C LOCAL EDUCATIONAL AGENCY ELIGIBILITY		191
§300.200	Condition of assistance.	191
§300.201	Consistency with State policies.	191
§300.202	Use of amounts.	191
§300.203	Maintenance of effort.	192
§300.204	Exception to maintenance of effort.	192
§300.205	Adjustment to local fiscal efforts in certain fiscal years.	193
§300.206	Schoolwide programs under title I of the ESEA.	193
§300.207	Personnel development.	194
§300.208	Permissive use of funds.	194
§300.209	Treatment of charter schools and their students.	194
§300.210	Purchase of instructional materials.	195
§300.211	Information for SEA.	196
§300.212	Public information.	196
§300.213	Records regarding migratory children with disabilities.	196
§§300.214–300.219	[Reserved]	196
§300.220	Exception for prior local plans.	196
§300.221	Notification of LEA or State agency in case of ineligibility.	196
§300.222	LEA and State agency compliance.	197
§300.223	Joint establishment of eligibility.	197
§300.224	Requirements for establishing eligibility.	197
§300.225	[Reserved]	198

§ 300.226	Early intervening services.	198
§ 300.227	Direct services by the SEA.	198
§ 300.228	State agency eligibility.	199
§ 300.229	Disciplinary information.	199
§ 300.230	SEA flexibility.	199
§ 300.231	[This section was removed. See 71 FR 46540, 46753, Aug. 14, 2006.]	200
§ 300.232	[This section was removed. See 71 FR 46540, 46753, Aug. 14, 2006.]	200
§ 300.233	[This section was removed. See 71 FR 46540, 46753, Aug. 14, 2006.]	200
§ 300.234	[This section was removed. See 71 FR 46540, 46753, Aug. 14, 2006.]	200
§ 300.235	[This section was removed. See 71 FR 46540, 46753, Aug. 14, 2006.]	200
§§ 300.236 – 300.239	[These sections were removed. See 71 FR 46540, 46753, Aug. 14, 2006.]	200
§ 300.240	[This section was removed. See 71 FR 46540, 46753, Aug. 14, 2006.]	200
§ 300.241	[This section was removed. See 71 FR 46540, 46753, Aug. 14, 2006.]	201
§ 300.242	[This section was removed. See 71 FR 46540, 46753, Aug. 14, 2006.]	201
§ 300.243	[This section was removed. See 71 FR 46540, 46753, Aug. 14, 2006.]	201
§ 300.244	[This section was removed. See 71 FR 46540, 46753, Aug. 14, 2006.]	201
§ 300.245	[This section was removed. See 71 FR 46540, 46753, Aug. 14, 2006.]	201
§ 300.246	[This section was removed. See 71 FR 46540, 46753, Aug. 14, 2006.]	201
§ 300.247	[This section was removed. See 71 FR 46540, 46753, Aug. 14, 2006.]	201
§ 300.248	[This section was removed. See 71 FR 46540, 46753, Aug. 14, 2006.]	201
§ 300.249	[This section was removed. See 71 FR 46540, 46753, Aug. 14, 2006.]	201
§ 300.250	[This section was removed. See 71 FR 46540, 46753, Aug. 14, 2006.]	201
§ 300.260	[This section was removed. See 71 FR 46540, 46753, Aug. 14, 2006.]	201

TABLE OF CONTENTS

§300.261	[This section was removed. See 71 FR 46540, 46753, Aug. 14, 2006.]	201
§300.262	[This section was removed. See 71 FR 46540, 46753, Aug. 14, 2006.]	201
§300.263	[This section was removed. See 71 FR 46540, 46753, Aug. 14, 2006.]	201
§300.264	[This section was removed. See 71 FR 46540, 46753, Aug. 14, 2006.]	201
§300.265	[This section was removed. See 71 FR 46540, 46753, Aug. 14, 2006.]	201
§300.266	[This section was removed. See 71 FR 46540, 46753, Aug. 14, 2006.]	202
§300.267	[This section was removed. See 71 FR 46540, 46753, Aug. 14, 2006.]	202
§300.280	[This section was removed. See 71 FR 46540, 46753, Aug. 14, 2006.]	202
§300.281	[This section was removed. See 71 FR 46540, 46753, Aug. 14, 2006.]	202
§300.282	[This section was removed. See 71 FR 46540, 46753, Aug. 14, 2006.]	202
§300.283	[This section was removed. See 71 FR 46540, 46753, Aug. 14, 2006.]	202
§300.284	[This section was removed. See 71 FR 46540, 46753, Aug. 14, 2006.]	202
SUBPART D	EVALUATIONS, ELIGIBILITY DETERMINATIONS, INDIVIDUALIZED EDUCATION PROGRAMS, AND EDUCATIONAL PLACEMENTS	202
§300.300	Parental consent.	202
§300.301	Initial evaluations.	204
§300.302	Screening for instructional purposes is not evaluation.	205
§300.303	Reevaluations.	205
§300.304	Evaluation procedures.	205
§300.305	Additional requirements for evaluations and reevaluations.	206
§300.306	Determination of eligibility.	207
§300.307	Specific learning disabilities.	208
§300.308	Additional group members.	208
§300.309	Determining the existence of a specific learning disability.	209
§300.310	Observation.	210
§300.311	Specific documentation for the eligibility determination.	210
§300.312	[This section was removed. See 71 FR 46540, 46753, Aug. 14, 2006.]	211

§300.313	[This section was removed. See 71 FR 46540, 46753, Aug. 14, 2006.]	211
§300.320	Definition of individualized education program.	211
§300.321	IEP Team.	213
§300.322	Parent participation.	214
§300.323	When IEPs must be in effect.	215
§300.324	Development, review, and revision of IEP.	216
§300.325	Private school placements by public agencies.	218
§300.326	[Reserved]	219
§300.327	Educational placements.	219
§300.328	Alternative means of meeting participation.	219
§300.340	[This section was removed. See 71 FR 46540, 46753, Aug. 14, 2006.]	219
§300.341	[This section was removed. See 71 FR 46540, 46753, Aug. 14, 2006.]	219
§300.342	[This section was removed. See 71 FR 46540, 46753, Aug. 14, 2006.]	219
§300.343	[This section was removed. See 71 FR 46540, 46753, Aug. 14, 2006.]	219
§300.344	[This section was removed. See 71 FR 46540, 46753, Aug. 14, 2006.]	219
§300.345	[This section was removed. See 71 FR 46540, 46753, Aug. 14, 2006.]	219
§300.346	[This section was removed. See 71 FR 46540, 46753, Aug. 14, 2006.]	219
§300.347	[This section was removed. See 71 FR 46540, 46753, Aug. 14, 2006.]	219
§300.348	[This section was removed. See 71 FR 46540, 46753, Aug. 14, 2006.]	219
§300.349	[This section was removed. See 71 FR 46540, 46753, Aug. 14, 2006.]	220
§300.350	[This section was removed. See 71 FR 46540, 46753, Aug. 14, 2006.]	220
§300.360	[This section was removed. See 71 FR 46540, 46753, Aug. 14, 2006.]	220
§300.361	[This section was removed. See 71 FR 46540, 46753, Aug. 14, 2006.]	220
§§300.362–300.369	[These sections were removed. See 71 FR 46540, 46753, Aug. 14, 2006.]	220
§300.370	[This section was removed. See 71 FR 46540, 46753, Aug. 14, 2006.]	220

TABLE OF CONTENTS

§ 300.371 [This section was removed. See 71 FR 46540, 46753, Aug. 14, 2006.] 220

§ 300.372 [This section was removed. See 71 FR 46540, 46753, Aug. 14, 2006.] 220

§ 300.380 [This section was removed. See 71 FR 46540, 46753, Aug. 14, 2006.] 220

§ 300.381 [This section was removed. See 71 FR 46540, 46753, Aug. 14, 2006.] 220

§ 300.382 [This section was removed. See 71 FR 46540, 46753, Aug. 14, 2006.] 220

§§ 300.383 – 300.387 [These sections were removed. See 71 FR 46540, 46753, Aug. 14, 2006.] 220

§ 300.400 [This section was removed. See 71 FR 46540, 46753, Aug. 14, 2006.] 220

§ 300.401 [This section was removed. See 71 FR 46540, 46753, Aug. 14, 2006.] 220

§ 300.402 [This section was removed. See 71 FR 46540, 46753, Aug. 14, 2006.] 220

§ 300.403 [This section was removed. See 71 FR 46540, 46753, Aug. 14, 2006.] 220

§ 300.450 [This section was removed. See 71 FR 46540, 46753, Aug. 14, 2006.] 221

§ 300.451 [This section was removed. See 71 FR 46540, 46753, Aug. 14, 2006.] 221

§ 300.452 [This section was removed. See 71 FR 46540, 46753, Aug. 14, 2006.] 221

§ 300.453 [This section was removed. See 71 FR 46540, 46753, Aug. 14, 2006.] 221

§ 300.454 [This section was removed. See 71 FR 46540, 46753, Aug. 14, 2006.] 221

§ 300.455 [This section was removed. See 71 FR 46540, 46753, Aug. 14, 2006.] 221

§ 300.456 [This section was removed. See 71 FR 46540, 46753, Aug. 14, 2006.] 221

§ 300.457 [This section was removed. See 71 FR 46540, 46753, Aug. 14, 2006.] 221

§ 300.458 [This section was removed. See 71 FR 46540, 46753, Aug. 14, 2006.] 221

§ 300.459 [This section was removed. See 71 FR 46540, 46753, Aug. 14, 2006.] 221

§ 300.460 [This section was removed. See 71 FR 46540, 46753, Aug. 14, 2006.] 221

§ 300.461	[This section was removed. See 71 FR 46540, 46753, Aug. 14, 2006.]	221
§ 300.462	[This section was removed. See 71 FR 46540, 46753, Aug. 14, 2006.]	221
§ 300.480	[This section was removed. See 71 FR 46540, 46753, Aug. 14, 2006.]	221
§ 300.481	[This section was removed. See 71 FR 46540, 46753, Aug. 14, 2006.]	221
§ 300.482	[This section was removed. See 71 FR 46540, 46753, Aug. 14, 2006.]	222
§ 300.483	[This section was removed. See 71 FR 46540, 46753, Aug. 14, 2006.]	222
§ 300.484	[This section was removed. See 71 FR 46540, 46753, Aug. 14, 2006.]	222
§ 300.485	[This section was removed. See 71 FR 46540, 46753, Aug. 14, 2006.]	222
§ 300.486	[This section was removed. See 71 FR 46540, 46753, Aug. 14, 2006.]	222
§ 300.487	[This section was removed. See 71 FR 46540, 46753, Aug. 14, 2006.]	222

SUBPART E PROCEDURAL SAFEGUARDS DUE PROCESS PROCEDURES FOR PARENTS AND CHILDREN 222

§ 300.500	Responsibility of SEA and other public agencies.	222
§ 300.501	Opportunity to examine records; parent participation in meetings.	222
§ 300.502	Independent educational evaluation.	223
§ 300.503	Prior notice by the public agency; content of notice.	224
§ 300.504	Procedural safeguards notice.	225
§ 300.505	Electronic mail.	226
§ 300.506	Mediation.	226
§ 300.507	Filing a due process complaint.	227
§ 300.508	Due process complaint.	227
§ 300.509	Model forms.	229
§ 300.510	Resolution process.	229
§ 300.511	Impartial due process hearing.	230
§ 300.512	Hearing rights.	231
§ 300.513	Hearing decisions.	232
§ 300.514	Finality of decision; appeal; impartial review.	232
§ 300.515	Timelines and convenience of hearings and reviews.	233
§ 300.516	Civil action.	233
§ 300.517	Attorneys' fees.	234

§300.518	Child's status during proceedings.	235
§300.519	Surrogate parents.	236
§300.520	Transfer of parental rights at age of majority.	236
§300.521	[This section was removed and reserved. See 71 FR 46540, 46753, Aug. 14, 2006.]	237
§300.522	[This section was removed and reserved. See 71 FR 46540, 46753, Aug. 14, 2006.]	237
§300.523	[This section was removed and reserved. See 71 FR 46540, 46753, Aug. 14, 2006.]	237
§300.524	[This section was removed and reserved. See 71 FR 46540, 46753, Aug. 14, 2006.]	237
§300.525	[This section was removed and reserved. See 71 FR 46540, 46753, Aug. 14, 2006.]	237
§300.526	[This section was removed and reserved. See 71 FR 46540, 46753, Aug. 14, 2006.]	237
§300.527	[This section was removed and reserved. See 71 FR 46540, 46753, Aug. 14, 2006.]	237
§300.528	[This section was removed and reserved. See 71 FR 46540, 46753, Aug. 14, 2006.]	237
§300.529	[This section was removed and reserved. See 71 FR 46540, 46753, Aug. 14, 2006.]	237
§300.530	Authority of school personnel.	238
§300.531	Determination of setting.	240
§300.532	Appeal.	240
§300.533	Placement during appeals.	241
§300.534	Protections for children not determined eligible for special education and related services.	241
§300.535	Referral to and action by law enforcement and judicial authorities.	242
§300.536	Change of placement because of disciplinary removals.	242
§300.537	State enforcement mechanisms.	242
§§300.538–300.599	[Reserved]	242

SUBPART F MONITORING, ENFORCEMENT, CONFIDENTIALITY, AND PROGRAM INFORMATION 243

§300.600	State monitoring and enforcement.	243
§300.601	State performance plans and data collection.	243
§300.602	State use of targets and reporting.	244
§300.603	Secretary's review and determination regarding State performance.	244
§300.604	Enforcement.	245
§300.605	Withholding funds.	246

§ 300.606	Public attention.	247
§ 300.607	Divided State agency responsibility.	247
§ 300.608	State enforcement.	247
§ 300.609	Rule of construction.	247
§ 300.610	Confidentiality.	247
§ 300.611	Definitions.	247
§ 300.612	Notice to parents.	248
§ 300.613	Access rights.	248
§ 300.614	Record of access.	248
§ 300.615	Records on more than one child.	249
§ 300.616	List of types and locations of information.	249
§ 300.617	Fees.	249
§ 300.618	Amendment of records at parent's request.	249
§ 300.619	Opportunity for a hearing.	249
§ 300.620	Result of hearing.	249
§ 300.621	Hearing procedures.	250
§ 300.622	Consent.	250
§ 300.623	Safeguards.	250
§ 300.624	Destruction of information.	250
§ 300.625	Children's rights.	250
§ 300.626	Enforcement.	251
§ 300.627	Department use of personally identifiable information.	251
§ 300.640	Annual report of children served — report requirement.	251
§ 300.641	Annual report of children served — information required in the report.	251
§ 300.642	Data reporting.	252
§ 300.643	Annual report of children served — certification.	252
§ 300.644	Annual report of children served — criteria for counting children.	252
§ 300.645	Annual report of children served — other responsibilities of the SEA.	252
§ 300.646	Disproportionality.	253
§ 300.650	[This section was removed. See 71 FR 46540, 46753, Aug. 14, 2006.]	253
§ 300.651	[This section was removed. See 71 FR 46540, 46753, Aug. 14, 2006.]	253
§ 300.652	[This section was removed. See 71 FR 46540, 46753, Aug. 14, 2006.]	253
§ 300.653	[This section was removed. See 71 FR 46540, 46753, Aug. 14, 2006.]	253

§300.660	[This section was removed. See 71 FR 46540, 46753, Aug. 14, 2006.]	253
§300.661	[This section was removed. See 71 FR 46540, 46753, Aug. 14, 2006.]	253
§300.662	[This section was removed. See 71 FR 46540, 46753, Aug. 14, 2006.]	254

SUBPART G AUTHORIZATION, ALLOTMENT, USE OF FUNDS, AND AUTHORIZATION OF APPROPRIATIONS 254

§300.700	Grants to States.	254
§300.701	Outlying areas, freely associated States, and the Secretary of the Interior.	254
§300.702	Technical assistance.	255
§300.703	Allocations to States.	255
§300.704	State-level activities.	257
§300.705	Subgrants to LEAs.	261
§300.706	[This section was removed and reserved. See 71 FR 46540, 46753, Aug. 14, 2006.]	262
§300.707	Use of amounts by Secretary of the Interior.	262
§300.708	Submission of information.	263
§300.709	Public participation.	264
§300.710	Use of funds under Part B of the Act.	264
§300.711	Early intervening services.	264
§300.712	Payments for education and services for Indian children with disabilities aged three through five.	264
§300.713	Plan for coordination of services.	265
§300.714	Establishment of advisory board.	265
§300.715	Annual reports.	266
§300.716	Applicable regulations.	266
§300.717	Definitions applicable to allotments, grants, and use of funds.	266
§300.718	Acquisition of equipment and construction or alteration of facilities.	267
§300.719	[This section was removed. See 71 FR 46540, 46753, Aug. 14, 2006.]	267
§300.720	[This section was removed. See 71 FR 46540, 46753, Aug. 14, 2006.]	267
§300.721	[This section was removed. See 71 FR 46540, 46753, Aug. 14, 2006.]	267
§300.722	Definition [This section was removed. See 71 FR 46540, 46753, Aug. 14, 2006.]	267
§300.750	[This section was removed. See 71 FR 46540, 46753, Aug. 14, 2006.]	267

§ 300.751 [This section was removed. See 71 FR 46540, 46753, Aug. 14, 2006.] 267
§ 300.752 [This section was removed. See 71 FR 46540, 46753, Aug. 14, 2006.] 267
§ 300.753 [This section was removed. See 71 FR 46540, 46753, Aug. 14, 2006.] 267
§ 300.754 [This section was removed. See 71 FR 46540, 46753, Aug. 14, 2006.] 267
§ 300.755 [This section was removed. See 71 FR 46540, 46753, Aug. 14, 2006.] 268
§ 300.756 [This section was removed. See 71 FR 46540, 46753, Aug. 14, 2006.] 268

SUBPART H PRESCHOOL GRANTS FOR CHILDREN WITH DISABILITIES 268

§ 300.800 In general. 268
§§ 300.801–300.802 [Reserved] 268
§ 300.803 Definition of State. 268
§ 300.804 Eligibility. 268
§ 300.805 [Reserved] 268
§ 300.806 Eligibility for financial assistance. 268
§ 300.807 Allocations to States. 268
§ 300.808 Increase in funds. 268
§ 300.809 Limitations. 269
§ 300.810 Decrease in funds. 269
§ 300.811 [Reserved] 270
§ 300.812 Reservation for State activities. 270
§ 300.813 State administration. 270
§ 300.814 Other State-level activities. 270
§ 300.815 Subgrants to LEAs. 271
§ 300.816 Allocations to LEAs. 271
§ 300.817 Reallocation of LEA funds. 271
§ 300.818 Part C of the Act inapplicable. 272
Appendix A to Part 300 Excess Costs Calculation 272
Appendix B to Part 300 Proportionate Share Calculation 274
Appendix C to Part 300 National Instructional Materials Accessibility Standard (NIMAS) 275
Appendix D to Part 300 Maintenance of Effort and Early Intervening Services 275
Appendix E to Part 300 Index for IDEA — Part B Regulations (34 CFR Part 300) 276

TITLE 34 EDUCATION 321

SUBTITLE B REGULATIONS OF THE OFFICES OF THE DEPARTMENT OF EDUCATION 321

CHAPTER III OFFICE OF SPECIAL EDUCATION AND REHABILITATIVE SERVICES, DEPARTMENT OF EDUCATION 321

PART 303 EARLY INTERVENTION PROGRAM FOR INFANTS AND TODDLERS WITH DISABILITIES 321

SUBPART A GENERAL PURPOSE, ELIGIBILITY, AND OTHER GENERAL PROVISIONS 321

§ 303.1   Purpose of the early intervention program for infants and toddlers with disabilities. 321
§ 303.2   Eligible recipients of an award. 321
§ 303.3   Activities that may be supported under this part. 321
§ 303.4   Limitation on eligible children. 322
§ 303.5   Applicable regulations. 322
§ 303.6   Act. 323
§ 303.7   Children. 323
§ 303.8   Council. 323
§ 303.9   Days. 323
§ 303.10 Developmental delay. 323
§ 303.11 Early intervention program. 323
§ 303.12 Early intervention services. 323
§ 303.13 Health services. 327
§ 303.14 IFSP. 328
§ 303.15 Include; including. 328
§ 303.16 Infants and toddlers with disabilities. 328
§ 303.17 Multidisciplinary. 328
§ 303.18 Natural environments. 328
§ 303.19 Parent. 328
§ 303.20 Policies. 329
§ 303.21 Public agency. 329
§ 303.22 Qualified. 329
§ 303.23 Service coordination (case management). 329
§ 303.24 State. 330
§ 303.25 EDGAR definitions that apply. 331

SUBPART B STATE APPLICATION FOR A GRANT 331

§303.100	Conditions of assistance.	331
§303.101	How the Secretary disapproves a State's application or statement of assurances.	332
§303.110	General requirements and timelines for public participation.	332
§303.111	Notice of public hearings and opportunity to comment.	332
§303.112	Public hearings.	332
§303.113	Reviewing public comments received.	332
§303.120	General.	333
§303.121	Reports and records.	333
§303.122	Control of funds and property.	333
§303.123	Prohibition against commingling.	333
§303.124	Prohibition against supplanting.	333
§303.125	Fiscal control.	334
§303.126	Payor of last resort.	334
§303.127	Assurance regarding expenditure of funds.	334
§303.128	Traditionally underserved groups.	334
§303.140	General.	334
§303.141	Information about the Council.	335
§303.142	Designation of lead agency.	335
§303.143	Designation regarding financial responsibility.	335
§303.144	Assurance regarding use of funds.	335
§303.145	Description of use of funds.	335
§303.146	Information about public participation.	336
§303.147	Services to all geographic areas.	336
§303.148	Transition to preschool programs. [For effective date, see Publisher's Note.]	336
§303.148	Transition to preschool programs. [For effective date see Publisher's Note.]	337
§303.160	Minimum components of a statewide system.	338
§303.161	State definition of developmental delay.	338
§303.162	Central directory.	338
§303.163	[Reserved]	338
§303.164	Public awareness program.	338
§303.165	Comprehensive child find system.	338
§303.166	Evaluation, assessment, and nondiscriminatory procedures.	339
§303.167	Individualized family service plans.	339
§303.168	Comprehensive system of personnel development (CSPD).	339
§303.169	Personnel standards.	339

§303.170	Procedural safeguards.	339
§303.171	Supervision and monitoring of programs.	340
§303.172	Lead agency procedures for resolving complaints.	340
§303.173	Policies and procedures related to financial matters.	340
§303.174	Interagency agreements; resolution of individual disputes.	340
§303.175	Policy for contracting or otherwise arranging for services.	340
§303.176	Data collection.	340
§303.180	Payments to the Secretary of the Interior for Indian tribes and tribal organizations.	341

SUBPART C PROCEDURES FOR MAKING GRANTS TO STATES 341

§303.200	Formula for State allocations.	341
§303.201	Distribution of allotments from non-participating States.	342
§303.202	Minimum grant that a State may receive.	342
§303.203	Payments to the Secretary of the Interior.	342
§303.204	Payments to the jurisdictions.	342

SUBPART D PROGRAM AND SERVICE COMPONENTS OF A STATEWIDE SYSTEM OF EARLY INTERVENTION SERVICES 342

§303.300	State eligibility criteria and procedures.	342
§303.301	Central directory.	342
§303.320	Public awareness program.	343
§303.321	Comprehensive child find system.	343
§303.322	Evaluation and assessment.	345
§303.323	Nondiscriminatory procedures.	346
§303.340	General.	347
§303.341	[Reserved]	347
§303.342	Procedures for IFSP development, review, and evaluation.	347
§303.343	Participants in IFSP meetings and periodic reviews.	348
§303.344	Content of an IFSP.	349
§303.345	Provision of services before evaluation and assessment are completed.	350
§303.346	Responsibility and accountability.	351
§303.360	Comprehensive system of personnel development.	351
§303.361	Personnel standards.	351

SUBPART E PROCEDURAL SAFEGUARDS 353

§303.400	General responsibility of lead agency for procedural safeguards.	353

§ 303.401	Definitions of consent, native language, and personally identifiable information.	353
§ 303.402	Opportunity to examine records.	354
§ 303.403	Prior notice; native language.	354
§ 303.404	Parent consent.	354
§ 303.405	Parent right to decline service.	355
§ 303.406	Surrogate parents.	355
§ 303.419	Mediation.	356
§ 303.420	Due process procedures.	356
§ 303.421	Appointment of an impartial person.	357
§ 303.422	Parent rights in administrative proceedings.	357
§ 303.423	Convenience of proceedings; timelines.	358
§ 303.424	Civil action.	358
§ 303.425	Status of a child during proceedings.	358
§ 303.460	Confidentiality of information.	358
SUBPART F STATE ADMINISTRATION		358
§ 303.500	Lead agency establishment or designation.	358
§ 303.501	Supervision and monitoring of programs.	359
§ 303.510	Adopting complaint procedures.	359
§ 303.511	An organization or individual may file a complaint.	360
§ 303.512	Minimum State complaint procedures.	360
§ 303.520	Policies related to payment for services.	361
§ 303.521	Fees.	362
§ 303.522	Identification and coordination of resources.	362
§ 303.523	Interagency agreements.	362
§ 303.524	Resolution of disputes.	363
§ 303.525	Delivery of services in a timely manner.	364
§ 303.526	Policy for contracting or otherwise arranging for services.	364
§ 303.527	Payor of last resort.	364
§ 303.528	Reimbursement procedure.	364
§ 303.540	Data collection.	365
§ 303.560	Use of funds by the lead agency.	365
SUBPART G STATE INTERAGENCY COORDINATING COUNCIL		365
§ 303.600	Establishment of Council.	365
§ 303.601	Composition.	365
§ 303.602	Use of funds by the Council.	366
§ 303.603	Meetings.	367
§ 303.604	Conflict of interest.	367

§303.650	General.	367
§303.651	Advising and assisting the lead agency in its administrative duties.	368
§303.652	Applications.	368
§303.653	Transitional services.	368
§303.654	Annual report to the Secretary.	368

TITLE 20. EDUCATION **369**

CHAPTER 70 STRENGTHENING AND IMPROVEMENT OF ELEMENTARY AND SECONDARY SCHOOLS 369

§6301.	Statement of purpose	369
§6302.	Authorization of appropriations	370
§6303.	School improvement	371
§6304.	State administration	373
§6311.	State plans	373
§6312.	Local educational agency plans	388
§6313.	Eligible school attendance areas	394
§6314.	Schoolwide programs	396
§6315.	Targeted assistance schools	399
§6316.	Academic assessment and local educational agency and school improvement	402
§6317.	School support and recognition	418
§6318.	Parental involvement	421
§6319.	Qualifications for teachers and paraprofessionals	424
§6320.	Participation of children enrolled in private schools	427
§6321.	Fiscal requirements	430
§6322.	Coordination requirements	431
§7801.	Definitions	432
§7802.	Applicability of title	440
§7803.	Applicability to Bureau of Indian Affairs operated schools	440

TITLE 29. LABOR **441**

CHAPTER 16 VOCATIONAL REHABILITATION AND OTHER REHABILITATION SERVICES 441

§705	Definitions	441
§794	Nondiscrimination under Federal grants and programs	451
§794a	Nondiscrimination under Federal grants and programs Remedies and attorney's fees	452

TITLE 34. EDUCATION ... 455

SUBTITLE B REGULATIONS OF THE OFFICES OF THE DEPARTMENT OF EDUCATION ... 455

CHAPTER I OFFICE FOR CIVIL RIGHTS, DEPARTMENT OF EDUCATION ... 455

PART 104 NONDISCRIMINATION ON THE BASIS OF HANDICAP IN PROGRAMS OR ACTIVITIES RECEIVING FEDERAL FINANCIAL ASSISTANCE ... 455

SUBPART A GENERAL PROVISIONS ... 455

§ 104.1   Purpose. ... 455
§ 104.2   Application. ... 455
§ 104.3   Definitions. ... 455
§ 104.4   Discrimination prohibited. ... 457
§ 104.5   Assurances required. ... 458
§ 104.6   Remedial action, voluntary action, and self-evaluation. ... 459
§ 104.7   Designation of responsible employee and adoption of grievance procedures. ... 460
§ 104.8   Notice. ... 460
§ 104.9   Administrative requirements for small recipients. ... 460
§ 104.10 Effect of state or local law or other requirements and effect of employment opportunities. ... 461

SUBPART B EMPLOYMENT PRACTICES ... 461

§ 104.11 Discrimination prohibited. ... 461
§ 104.12 Reasonable accommodation. ... 462
§ 104.13 Employment criteria. ... 462
§ 104.14 Preemployment inquiries. ... 462

SUBPART C ACCESSIBILITY ... 463

§ 104.21 Discrimination prohibited. ... 463
§ 104.22 Existing facilities. ... 463
§ 104.23 New construction. ... 464

SUBPART D PRESCHOOL, ELEMENTARY, AND SECONDARY EDUCATION ... 465

§ 104.31 Application of this subpart. ... 465
§ 104.32 Location and notification. ... 465
§ 104.33 Free appropriate public education. ... 465
§ 104.34 Educational setting. ... 466

§104.35	Evaluation and placement.	467
§104.36	Procedural safeguards.	467
§104.37	Nonacademic services.	467
§104.38	Preschool and adult education.	468
§104.39	Private education.	468

SUBPART E POSTSECONDARY EDUCATION 468

§104.41	Application of this subpart.	468
§104.42	Admissions and recruitment.	469
§104.43	Treatment of students; general.	470
§104.44	Academic adjustments.	470
§104.45	Housing.	471
§104.46	Financial and employment assistance to students.	471
§104.47	Nonacademic services.	471

TITLE 42. THE PUBLIC HEALTH AND WELFARE 473

CHAPTER 126 473

§12101.	Congressional findings and purposes	473
§12102.	Definitions	474

TITLE 42. THE PUBLIC HEALTH AND WELFARE 475

CHAPTER 126 EQUAL OPPORTUNITY FOR INDIVIDUALS WITH DISABILITIES 475

§12131	Definition	475
§12132	Discrimination.	475
§12133	Enforcement.	475
§12134	Regulations.	475
§12141	Definitions.	476
§12142	Public entities operating fixed route systems.	476
§12143	Paratransit as a complement to fixed route service.	477
§12144	Public entity operating a demand responsive system	480
§12145	Temporary relief where lifts are unavailable.	480
§12146	New facilities	480
§12147	Alterations of existing facilities	480
§12148	Public transportation programs and activities in existing facilities and one car per train rule	481
§12149	Regulations	482
§12150	Interim accessibility requirements	482

TITLE 28. JUDICIAL ADMINISTRATION 485

CHAPTER I   DEPARTMENT OF JUSTICE 485

PART 35   NONDISCRIMINATION ON THE BASIS OF DISABILITY IN STATE AND LOCAL GOVERNMENT SERVICES 485

SUBPART A   GENERAL 485

§ 35.101 Purpose. 485
§ 35.102 Application. 485
§ 35.103 Relationship to other laws. 485
§ 35.104 Definitions. 485
§ 35.105 Self-evaluation. 488
§ 35.106 Notice. 488

SUBPART B   GENERAL REQUIREMENTS 488

§ 35.130 General prohibitions against discrimination. 488
§ 35.131 Illegal use of drugs. 490
§ 35.132 Smoking. 490
§ 35.133 Maintenance of accessible features. 491
§ 35.134 Retaliation or coercion. 491
§ 35.135 Personal devices and services. 491

SUBPART C   EMPLOYMENT 491

§ 35.140 Employment discrimination prohibited. 491

SUBPART D   PROGRAM ACCESSIBILITY 491

§ 35.149 Discrimination prohibited. 491
§ 35.150 Existing facilities. 492
§ 35.151 New construction and alterations. 493

SUBPART E   COMMUNICATIONS 494

§ 35.160 General. 494
§ 35.161 Telecommunication devices for the deaf (TDD's). 494
§ 35.162 Telephone emergency services. 494
§ 35.163 Information and signage. 494
§ 35.164 Duties. 494

SUBPART F   COMPLIANCE PROCEDURES 495

§ 35.170 Complaints. 495
§ 35.171 Acceptance of complaints. 495
§ 35.172 Resolution of complaints. 496

§ 35.173	Voluntary compliance agreements.	496
§ 35.174	Referral.	496
§ 35.175	Attorney's fees.	497
§ 35.176	Alternative means of dispute resolution.	497
§ 35.177	Effect of unavailability of technical assistance.	497
§ 35.178	State immunity.	497

TITLE 42. THE PUBLIC HEALTH AND WELFARE 499

CHAPTER 126. EQUAL OPPORTUNITY FOR INDIVIDUALS WITH DISABILITIES 499

§ 12181.	Definitions.	499
§ 12182.	Prohibition of discrimination by public accommodations	500
§ 12183.	New construction and alterations in public accommodations and commercial facilities	503
§ 12184.	Prohibition of discrimination in specified public transportation services provided by private entities	503
§ 12185.	Study.	505
§ 12186.	Regulations	506
§ 12187.	Exemptions for private clubs and religious organizations	507
§ 12188.	Enforcement	508
§ 12189.	Examinations and courses.	509

TITLE 28 JUDICIAL ADMINISTRATION 511

CHAPTER I DEPARTMENT OF JUSTICE 511

PART 36 NONDISCRIMINATION ON THE BASIS OF DISABILITY BY PUBLIC ACCOMMODATIONS AND IN COMMERCIAL FACILITIES 511

SUBPART A GENERAL 511

§ 36.104	Definitions.	511

SUBPART B GENERAL REQUIREMENTS 514

§ 36.201	General.	514
§ 36.202	Activities.	515
§ 36.203	Integrated settings.	515
§ 36.204	Administrative methods.	515
§ 36.205	Association.	515
§ 36.206	Retaliation or coercion.	516

§36.207	Places of public accommodation located in private residences.	516
§36.208	Direct threat.	516
§36.209	Illegal use of drugs.	517
§36.210	Smoking.	517
§36.211	Maintenance of accessible features.	517
§36.212	Insurance.	517

SUBPART C SPECIFIC REQUIREMENTS ... 518

§36.301	Eligibility criteria.	518
§36.302	Modifications in policies, practices, or procedures.	518
§36.303	Auxiliary aids and services.	519
§36.304	Removal of barriers.	520
§36.305	Alternatives to barrier removal.	521
§36.306	Personal devices and services.	522
§36.307	Accessible or special goods.	522
§36.308	Seating in assembly areas.	522
§36.309	Examinations and courses.	523

SUBPART D NEW CONSTRUCTION AND ALTERATIONS ... 524

§36.401	New construction.	524
§36.402	Alterations.	526
§36.403	Alterations: Path of travel.	526
§36.404	Alterations: Elevator exemption.	528
§36.405	Alterations: Historic preservation.	529
§36.406	Standards for new construction and alterations.	529

SUBPART E ENFORCEMENT ... 530

§36.501	Private suits.	530
§36.502	Investigations and compliance reviews.	531
§36.503	Suit by the Attorney General.	531
§36.504	Relief.	531
§36.505	Attorneys fees.	532

TITLE 42. THE PUBLIC HEALTH AND WELFARE ... 533

CHAPTER 126. EQUAL OPPORTUNITY FOR INDIVIDUALS WITH DISABILITIES ... 533

§12201.	Construction.	533
§12202.	State immunity.	533
§12203.	Prohibition against retaliation and coercion.	534

§ 12204.	Regulations by the Architectural and Transportation Barriers Compliance Board	534
§ 12205.	Attorney's fees	534
§ 12206.	Technical assistance	535
§ 12207.	Federal wilderness areas	536
§ 12208.	Transvestites	536
§ 12209.	Instrumentalities of the Congress	536
§ 12210.	Illegal use of drugs	537
§ 12211.	Definitions	538
§ 12212.	Alternative means of dispute resolution	538
§ 12213.	Severability	538

TITLE 20.
EDUCATION

CHAPTER 33. EDUCATION OF INDIVIDUALS WITH DISABILITIES

GENERAL PROVISIONS

§ 1400. Short title; table of contents; findings; purposes

(a) Short title. This *title [20 USCS §§ 1400* et seq.] may be cited as the "Individuals with Disabilities Education Act".

(b) [Omitted]

(c) Findings. Congress finds the following:

(1) Disability is a natural part of the human experience and in no way diminishes the right of individuals to participate in or contribute to society. Improving educational results for children with disabilities is an essential element of our national policy of ensuring equality of opportunity, full participation, independent living, and economic self-sufficiency for individuals with disabilities.

(2) Before the date of enactment of the Education for All Handicapped Children Act of 1975 (Public Law 94-142) [enacted Nov. 29, 1975], the educational needs of millions of children with disabilities were not being fully met because—

(A) the children did not receive appropriate educational services;

(B) the children were excluded entirely from the public school system and from being educated with their peers;

(C) undiagnosed disabilities prevented the children from having a successful educational experience; or

(D) a lack of adequate resources within the public school system forced families to find services outside the public school system.

(3) Since the enactment and implementation of the Education for All Handicapped Children Act of 1975 [enacted Nov. 29, 1975], this *title [20 USCS §§ 1400* et seq.] has been successful in ensuring children with disabilities and the families of such children access to a free appropriate public education and in improving educational results for children with disabilities.

(4) However, the implementation of this *title [20 USCS §§ 1400* et seq.] has been impeded by low expectations, and an insufficient focus on applying replicable research on proven methods of teaching and learning for children with disabilities.

(5) Almost 30 years of research and experience has demonstrated that the education of children with disabilities can be made more effective by—

(A) having high expectations for such children and ensuring their access to the general education curriculum in the regular classroom, to the maximum extent possible, in order to—

(i) meet developmental goals and, to the maximum extent possible, the challenging expectations that have been established for all children; and

(ii) be prepared to lead productive and independent adult lives, to the maximum extent possible;

(B) strengthening the role and responsibility of parents and ensuring that families of such children have meaningful opportunities to participate in the education of their children at school and at home;

(C) coordinating this *title [20 USCS §§ 1400 et seq.]* with other local, educational service agency, State, and Federal school improvement efforts, including improvement efforts under the Elementary and Secondary Education Act of 1965, in order to ensure that such children benefit from such efforts and that special education can become a service for such children rather than a place where such children are sent;

(D) providing appropriate special education and related services, and aids and supports in the regular classroom, to such children, whenever appropriate;

(E) supporting high-quality, intensive preservice preparation and professional development for all personnel who work with children with disabilities in order to ensure that such personnel have the skills and knowledge necessary to improve the academic achievement and functional performance of children with disabilities, including the use of scientifically based instructional practices, to the maximum extent possible;

(F) providing incentives for whole-school approaches, scientifically based early reading programs, positive behavioral interventions and supports, and early intervening services to reduce the need to label children as disabled in order to address the learning and behavioral needs of such children;

(G) focusing resources on teaching and learning while reducing paperwork and requirements that do not assist in improving educational results; and

(H) supporting the development and use of technology, including assistive technology devices and assistive technology services, to maximize accessibility for children with disabilities.

(6) While States, local educational agencies, and educational service agencies are primarily responsible for providing an education for all children with disabilities, it is in the national interest that the Federal Government have a supporting role in assisting State and local efforts to educate children with disabilities in order to improve results for such children and to ensure equal protection of the law.

(7) A more equitable allocation of resources is essential for the Federal Government to meet its responsibility to provide an equal educational opportunity for all individuals.

(8) Parents and schools should be given expanded opportunities to resolve their disagreements in positive and constructive ways.

(9) Teachers, schools, local educational agencies, and States should be relieved of irrelevant and unnecessary paperwork burdens that do not lead to improved educational outcomes.

(10) (A) The Federal Government must be responsive to the growing needs of an increasingly diverse society.

(B) America's ethnic profile is rapidly changing. In 2000, 1 of every 3 persons in the United States was a member of a minority group or was limited English proficient.

(C) Minority children comprise an increasing percentage of public school students.

(D) With such changing demographics, recruitment efforts for special education personnel should focus on increasing the participation of minorities in the teaching profession in order to provide appropriate role models with sufficient knowledge to address the special education needs of these students.

(11) (A) The limited English proficient population is the fastest growing in our Nation, and the growth is occurring in many parts of our Nation.

(B) Studies have documented apparent discrepancies in the levels of referral and placement of limited English proficient children in special education.

(C) Such discrepancies pose a special challenge for special education in the referral of, assessment of, and provision of services for, our Nation's students from non-English language backgrounds.

(12) (A) Greater efforts are needed to prevent the intensification of problems connected with mislabeling and high dropout rates among minority children with disabilities.

(B) More minority children continue to be served in special education than would be expected from the percentage of minority students in the general school population.

(C) African-American children are identified as having mental retardation and emotional disturbance at rates greater than their White counterparts.

(D) In the 1998-1999 school year, African-American children represented just 14.8 percent of the population aged 6 through 21, but comprised 20.2 percent of all children with disabilities.

(E) Studies have found that schools with predominately White students and teachers have placed disproportionately high numbers of their minority students into special education.

(13) (A) As the number of minority students in special education increases, the number of minority teachers and related services personnel produced in colleges and universities continues to decrease.

(B) The opportunity for full participation by minority individuals, minority organizations, and Historically Black Colleges and Universities in awards for grants and contracts, boards of organizations receiving assistance under this *title [20 USCS §§ 1400 et seq.]*, peer review panels, and training of professionals in the area of special education is essential to obtain greater success in the education of minority children with disabilities.

(14) As the graduation rates for children with disabilities continue to climb, providing effective transition services to promote successful post-school employment or education is an important measure of accountability for children with disabilities.

(d) Purposes. The purposes of this *title [20 USCS §§ 1400 et seq.]* are—

(1) (A) to ensure that all children with disabilities have available to them a free appropriate public education that emphasizes special education and related services designed to meet their unique needs and prepare them for further education, employment, and independent living;

(B) to ensure that the rights of children with disabilities and parents of such children are protected; and

(C) to assist States, localities, educational service agencies, and Federal agencies to provide for the education of all children with disabilities;

(2) to assist States in the implementation of a statewide, comprehensive, coordinated, multidisciplinary, interagency system of early intervention services for infants and toddlers with disabilities and their families;

(3) to ensure that educators and parents have the necessary tools to improve educational results for children with disabilities by supporting system improvement activities; coordinated research and personnel preparation; coordinated technical assistance, dissemination, and support; and technology development and media services; and

(4) to assess, and ensure the effectiveness of, efforts to educate children with disabilities.

§ 1401. Definitions

Except as otherwise provided, in this *title [20 USCS §§ 1400 et seq.]*:

(1) Assistive technology device.

(A) In general. The term "assistive technology device" means any item, piece of equipment, or product system, whether acquired commercially off the shelf, modified, or customized, that is used to increase, maintain, or improve functional capabilities of a child with a disability.

(B) Exception. The term does not include a medical device that is surgically implanted, or the replacement of such device.

(2) Assistive technology service. The term "assistive technology service" means any service that directly assists a child with a disability in the selection, acquisition, or use of an assistive technology device. Such term includes—

(A) the evaluation of the needs of such child, including a functional evaluation of the child in the child's customary environment;

(B) purchasing, leasing, or otherwise providing for the acquisition of assistive technology devices by such child;

(C) selecting, designing, fitting, customizing, adapting, applying, maintaining, repairing, or replacing assistive technology devices;

(D) coordinating and using other therapies, interventions, or services with assistive technology devices, such as those associated with existing education and rehabilitation plans and programs;

(E) training or technical assistance for such child, or, where appropriate, the family of such child; and

(F) training or technical assistance for professionals (including individuals providing education and rehabilitation services), employers, or other individuals who provide services to, employ, or are otherwise substantially involved in the major life functions of such child.

(3) Child with a disability.

(A) In general. The term "child with a disability" means a child—

(i) with mental retardation, hearing impairments (including deafness), speech or language impairments, visual impairments (including blindness), serious emotional disturbance (referred to in this *title [20 USCS §§ 1400 et seq.]* as "emotional disturbance"), orthopedic impairments, autism, traumatic brain injury, other health impairments, or specific learning disabilities; and

(ii) who, by reason thereof, needs special education and related services.

(B) Child aged 3 through 9. The term "child with a disability" for a child aged 3 through 9 (or any subset of that age range, including ages 3 through 5), may, at the discretion of the State and the local educational agency, include a child—

(i) experiencing developmental delays, as defined by the State and as measured by appropriate diagnostic instruments and procedures, in 1 or more of the following areas: physical development; cognitive development; communication development; social or emotional development; or adaptive development; and

(ii) who, by reason thereof, needs special education and related services.

(4) Core academic subjects. The term "core academic subjects" has the meaning given

the term in section 9101 of the Elementary and Secondary Education Act of 1965 [*20 USCS § 7801*].

(5) Educational service agency. The term "educational service agency"—

(A) means a regional public multiservice agency—

(i) authorized by State law to develop, manage, and provide services or programs to local educational agencies; and

(ii) recognized as an administrative agency for purposes of the provision of special education and related services provided within public elementary schools and secondary schools of the State; and

(B) includes any other public institution or agency having administrative control and direction over a public elementary school or secondary school.

(6) Elementary school. The term "elementary school" means a nonprofit institutional day or residential school, including a public elementary charter school, that provides elementary education, as determined under State law.

(7) Equipment. The term "equipment" includes—

(A) machinery, utilities, and built-in equipment, and any necessary enclosures or structures to house such machinery, utilities, or equipment; and

(B) all other items necessary for the functioning of a particular facility as a facility for the provision of educational services, including items such as instructional equipment and necessary furniture; printed, published, and audio-visual instructional materials; telecommunications, sensory, and other technological aids and devices; and books, periodicals, documents, and other related materials.

(8) Excess costs. The term "excess costs" means those costs that are in excess of the average annual per-student expenditure in a local educational agency during the preceding school year for an elementary school or secondary school student, as may be appropriate, and which shall be computed after deducting—

(A) amounts received—

(i) under part B [*20 USCS §§ 1411* et seq.];

(ii) under part A of title I of the Elementary and Secondary Education Act of 1965 [*20 USCS §§ 6311* et seq.]; and

(iii) under parts A and B of title III of that Act [*20 USCS §§ 6811* et seq. and *6891* et seq.]; and

(B) any State or local funds expended for programs that would qualify for assistance under any of those parts.

(9) Free appropriate public education. The term "free appropriate public education" means special education and related services that—

(A) have been provided at public expense, under public supervision and direction, and without charge;

(B) meet the standards of the State educational agency;

(C) include an appropriate preschool, elementary school, or secondary school education in the State involved; and

(D) are provided in conformity with the individualized education program required under section 614(d) [*20 USCS § 1414(d)*].

(10) Highly qualified.

(A) In general. For any special education teacher, the term "highly qualified" has the meaning given the term in section 9101 of the Elementary and Secondary Education Act of 1965 [20 USCS § 7801], except that such term also—

(i) includes the requirements described in subparagraph (B); and

(ii) includes the option for teachers to meet the requirements of section 9101 of such Act [20 USCS § 7801] by meeting the requirements of subparagraph (C) or (D).

(B) Requirements for special education teachers. When used with respect to any public elementary school or secondary school special education teacher teaching in a State, such term means that—

(i) the teacher has obtained full State certification as a special education teacher (including certification obtained through alternative routes to certification), or passed the State special education teacher licensing examination, and holds a license to teach in the State as a special education teacher, except that when used with respect to any teacher teaching in a public charter school, the term means that the teacher meets the requirements set forth in the State's public charter school law;

(ii) the teacher has not had special education certification or licensure requirements waived on an emergency, temporary, or provisional basis; and

(iii) the teacher holds at least a bachelor's degree.

(C) Special education teachers teaching to alternate achievement standards. When used with respect to a special education teacher who teaches core academic subjects exclusively to children who are assessed against alternate achievement standards established under the regulations promulgated under section 1111(b)(1) of the Elementary and Secondary Education Act of 1965 [20 USCS § 6311(b)(1)], such term means the teacher, whether new or not new to the profession, may either—

(i) meet the applicable requirements of section 9101 of such Act [20 USCS § 7801] for any elementary, middle, or secondary school teacher who is new or not new to the profession; or

(ii) meet the requirements of subparagraph (B) or (C) of section 9101(23) of such Act [20 USCS § 7801(23)] as applied to an elementary school teacher, or, in the case of instruction above the elementary level, has subject matter knowledge appropriate to the level of instruction being provided, as determined by the State, needed to effectively teach to those standards.

(D) Special education teachers teaching multiple subjects. When used with respect to a special education teacher who teaches 2 or more core academic subjects exclusively to children with disabilities, such term means that the teacher may either—

(i) meet the applicable requirements of section 9101 of the Elementary and Secondary Education Act of 1965 [20 USCS § 7801] for any elementary, middle, or secondary school teacher who is new or not new to the profession;

(ii) in the case of a teacher who is not new to the profession, demonstrate competence in all the core academic subjects in which the teacher teaches in the same manner as is required for an elementary, middle, or secondary school teacher who is not new to the profession under section 9101(23)(C)(ii) [20 USCS § 7801(23)(C)(ii)] of such Act, which may include a single, high objective uniform State standard of evaluation covering multiple subjects; or

(iii) in the case of a new special education teacher who teaches multiple subjects and who is highly qualified in mathematics, language arts, or science, demonstrate competence in the other core academic subjects in which the teacher teaches in the same manner as is required for an elementary, middle, or secondary school teacher under section 9101(23)(C)(ii) of such Act [20 USCS § 7801(23)(C)(ii)], which may include a single, high objective uniform State standard of evaluation covering multiple subjects, not later than 2 years after the date of employment.

(E) Rule of construction. Notwithstanding any other individual right of action that a parent or student may maintain under this part, nothing in this section or part shall be construed to create a right of action on behalf of an individual student or class of students for the failure of a particular State educational agency or local educational agency employee to be highly qualified.

(F) Definition for purposes of the ESEA. A teacher who is highly qualified under this paragraph shall be considered highly qualified for purposes of the Elementary and Secondary Education Act of 1965.

(11) Homeless children. The term "homeless children" has the meaning given the term "homeless children and youths" in section 725 of the McKinney-Vento Homeless Assistance Act (*42 U.S.C. 11434a*).

(12) Indian. The term "Indian" means an individual who is a member of an Indian tribe.

(13) Indian tribe. The term "Indian tribe" means any Federal or State Indian tribe, band, rancheria, pueblo, colony, or community, including any Alaska Native village or regional village corporation (as defined in or established under the Alaska Native Claims Settlement Act (*43 U.S.C. 1601* et seq.)).

(14) Individualized education program; IEP. The term "individualized education program" or "IEP" means a written statement for each child with a disability that is developed, reviewed, and revised in accordance with section 614(d) [*20 USCS § 1414(d)*].

(15) Individualized family service plan. The term "individualized family service plan" has the meaning given the term in section 636 [*20 USCS § 1436*].

(16) Infant or toddler with a disability. The term "infant or toddler with a disability" has the meaning given the term in section 632 [*20 USCS § 1432*].

(17) Institution of higher education. The term "institution of higher education"—

(A) has the meaning given the term in section 101 of the Higher Education Act of 1965 [*20 USCS § 1001*]; and

(B) also includes any community college receiving funding from the Secretary of the Interior under the Tribally Controlled College or University Assistance Act of 1978.

(18) Limited English proficient. The term "limited English proficient" has the meaning given the term in section 9101 of the Elementary and Secondary Education Act of 1965 [*20 USCS § 7801*].

(19) Local educational agency.

(A) In general. The term "local educational agency" means a public board of education or other public authority legally constituted within a State for either administrative control or direction of, or to perform a service function for, public elementary schools or secondary schools in a city, county, township, school district, or other political subdivision of a State, or for such combination of school districts or counties as are recognized in a State as an administrative agency for its public elementary schools or secondary schools.

(B) Educational service agencies and other public institutions or agencies. The term includes—

(i) an educational service agency; and

(ii) any other public institution or agency having administrative control and direction of a public elementary school or secondary school.

(C) BIA funded schools. The term includes an elementary school or secondary school funded by the Bureau of Indian Affairs, but only to the extent that such inclusion makes the school eligible for programs for which specific eligibility is not provided to the school in another provision of law and the school does not have a student population that is smaller than the student population of the local educational agency receiving assistance under this *title [20 USCS §§ 1400* et seq.] with the smallest student population, except that the school shall not be subject to the jurisdiction of any State educational agency other than the Bureau of Indian Affairs.

(20) Native language. The term "native language", when used with respect to an individual who is limited English proficient, means the language normally used by the individual or, in the case of a child, the language normally used by the parents of the child.

(21) Nonprofit. The term "nonprofit", as applied to a school, agency, organization, or institution, means a school, agency, organization, or institution owned and operated by 1 or more nonprofit corporations or associations no part of the net earnings of which inures, or may lawfully inure, to the benefit of any private shareholder or individual.

(22) Outlying area. The term "outlying area" means the United States Virgin Islands, Guam, American Samoa, and the Commonwealth of the Northern Mariana Islands.

(23) Parent. The term "parent" means—

(A) a natural, adoptive, or foster parent of a child (unless a foster parent is prohibited by State law from serving as a parent);

(B) a guardian (but not the State if the child is a ward of the State);

(C) an individual acting in the place of a natural or adoptive parent (including a grandparent, stepparent, or other relative) with whom the child lives, or an individual who is legally responsible for the child's welfare; or

(D) except as used in sections 615(b)(2) and 639(a)(5) [*20 USCS §§ 1415(b)(2)* and *1439(a)(5)*], an individual assigned under either of those sections to be a surrogate parent.

(24) Parent organization. The term "parent organization" has the meaning given the term in section 671(g) [*20 USCS § 1471(g)*].

(25) Parent training and information center. The term "parent training and information center" means a center assisted under section 671 or 672 [*20 USCS § 1471* or *1472*].

(26) Related services.

(A) In general. The term "related services" means transportation, and such developmental, corrective, and other supportive services (including speech-language pathology and audiology services, interpreting services, psychological services, physical and occupational therapy, recreation, including therapeutic recreation, social work services, school nurse services designed to enable a child with a disability to receive a free appropriate public education as described in the individualized education program of the child, counseling services, including rehabilitation counseling, orientation and mobility services, and medical services, except that such medical services shall be for diagnostic and evaluation purposes only) as may be required to assist a child with a disability to benefit from special education, and includes the early identification and assessment of disabling conditions in children.

(B) Exception. The term does not include a medical device that is surgically implanted, or the replacement of such device.

(27) Secondary school. The term "secondary school" means a nonprofit institutional day or residential school, including a public secondary charter school, that provides secondary education, as determined under State law, except that it does not include any education beyond grade 12.

(28) Secretary. The term "Secretary" means the Secretary of Education.

(29) Special education. The term "special education" means specially designed instruction, at no cost to parents, to meet the unique needs of a child with a disability, including—

(A) instruction conducted in the classroom, in the home, in hospitals and institutions, and in other settings; and

(B) instruction in physical education.

(30) Specific learning disability.

(A) In general. The term "specific learning disability" means a disorder in 1 or more of the basic psychological processes involved in understanding or in using language, spoken or written, which disorder may manifest itself in the imperfect ability to listen, think, speak, read, write, spell, or do mathematical calculations.

(B) Disorders included. Such term includes such conditions as perceptual disabilities, brain injury, minimal brain dysfunction, dyslexia, and developmental aphasia.

(C) Disorders not included. Such term does not include a learning problem that is primarily the result of visual, hearing, or motor disabilities, of mental retardation, of emotional disturbance, or of environmental, cultural, or economic disadvantage.

(31) State. The term "State" means each of the 50 States, the District of Columbia, the Commonwealth of Puerto Rico, and each of the outlying areas.

(32) State educational agency. The term "State educational agency" means the State board of education or other agency or officer primarily responsible for the State supervision of public elementary schools and secondary schools, or, if there is no such officer or agency, an officer or agency designated by the Governor or by State law.

(33) Supplementary aids and services. The term "supplementary aids and services" means aids, services, and other supports that are provided in regular education classes or other education-related settings to enable children with disabilities to be educated with nondisabled children to the maximum extent appropriate in accordance with section 612(a)(5) [*20 USCS § 1412(a)(5)*].

(34) Transition services. The term "transition services" means a coordinated set of activities for a child with a disability that—

(A) is designed to be within a results-oriented process, that is focused on improving the academic and functional achievement of the child with a disability to facilitate the child's movement from school to post-school activities, including post-secondary education, vocational education, integrated employment (including supported employment), continuing and adult education, adult services, independent living, or community participation;

(B) is based on the individual child's needs, taking into account the child's strengths, preferences, and interests; and

(C) includes instruction, related services, community experiences, the development of employment and other post-school adult living objectives, and, when appropriate, acquisition of daily living skills and functional vocational evaluation.

(35) Universal design. The term "universal design" has the meaning given the term in section 3 of the Assistive Technology Act of 1998 (*29 U.S.C. 3002*).

(36) Ward of the State.

(A) In general. The term "ward of the State" means a child who, as determined by the State where the child resides, is a foster child, is a ward of the State, or is in the custody of a public child welfare agency.

(B) Exception. The term does not include a foster child who has a foster parent who meets the definition of a parent in paragraph (23).

§ 1402. Office of Special Education Programs

(a) Establishment. There shall be, within the Office of Special Education and Rehabilitative Services in the Department of Education, an Office of Special Education Programs, which shall be the principal agency in the Department for administering and carrying out this *title [20 USCS §§ 1400* et seq.] and other programs and activities concerning the education of children with disabilities.

(b) Director. The Office established under subsection (a) shall be headed by a Director who shall be selected by the Secretary and shall report directly to the Assistant Secretary for Special Education and Rehabilitative Services.

(c) Voluntary and uncompensated services. Notwithstanding *section 1342 of title 31, United States Code*, the Secretary is authorized to accept voluntary and uncompensated services in furtherance of the purposes of this *title [20 USCS §§ 1400* et seq.].

§ 1403. Abrogation of State sovereign immunity

(a) In general. A State shall not be immune under the *11th amendment to the Constitution of the United States* from suit in Federal court for a violation of this *title [20 USCS §§ 1400* et seq.].

(b) Remedies. In a suit against a State for a violation of this *title [20 USCS §§ 1400* et seq.], remedies (including remedies both at law and in equity) are available for such a violation to the same extent as those remedies are available for such a violation in the suit against any public entity other than a State.

(c) Effective date. Subsections (a) and (b) apply with respect to violations that occur in whole or part after the date of enactment of the Education of the Handicapped Act Amendments of 1990 [enacted Oct. 30, 1990].

§ 1404. Acquisition of equipment; construction or alteration of facilities

(a) In general. If the Secretary determines that a program authorized under this *title [20 USCS §§ 1400* et seq.] will be improved by permitting program funds to be used to acquire appropriate equipment, or to construct new facilities or alter existing facilities, the Secretary is authorized to allow the use of those funds for those purposes.

(b) Compliance with certain regulations. Any construction of new facilities or alteration of existing facilities under subsection (a) shall comply with the requirements of—

(1) appendix A of part 36 of title 28, Code of Federal Regulations (commonly known as the "Americans with Disabilities Accessibility Guidelines for Buildings and Facilities"); or

(2) appendix A of subpart 101-19.6 of title 41, Code of Federal Regulations (commonly known as the "Uniform Federal Accessibility Standards").

§ 1405. Employment of individuals with disabilities

The Secretary shall ensure that each recipient of assistance under this *title [20 USCS §§ 1400* et seq.] makes positive efforts to employ and advance in employment qualified individuals with disabilities in programs assisted under this *title [20 USCS §§ 1400* et seq.].

§ 1406. Requirements for prescribing regulations

(a) In general. In carrying out the provisions of this *title [20 USCS §§ 1400* et seq.], the Secretary shall issue regulations under this *title [20 USCS §§ 1400* et seq.] only to the extent that such regulations are necessary to ensure that there is compliance with the specific requirements of this *title [20 USCS §§ 1400* et seq.].

(b) Protections provided to children. The Secretary may not implement, or publish in final form, any regulation prescribed pursuant to this *title [20 USCS §§ 1400* et seq.] that—

(1) violates or contradicts any provision of this *title [20 USCS §§ 1400* et seq.]; or

(2) procedurally or substantively lessens the protections provided to children with disabilities under this *title [20 USCS §§ 1400* et seq.], as embodied in regulations in effect on July 20, 1983 (particularly as such protections related to parental consent to initial evaluation or initial placement in special education, least restrictive environment, related services, timelines, attendance of evaluation personnel at individualized education program meetings, or qualifications of personnel), except to the extent that such regulation reflects the clear and unequivocal intent of Congress in legislation.

(c) Public comment period. The Secretary shall provide a public comment period of not less than 75 days on any regulation proposed under part B or part C *[20 USCS §§ 1411* et seq. or *1431* et seq.] on which an opportunity for public comment is otherwise required by law.

(d) Policy letters and statements. The Secretary may not issue policy letters or other statements (including letters or statements regarding issues of national significance) that—

(1) violate or contradict any provision of this *title [20 USCS §§ 1400* et seq.]; or

(2) establish a rule that is required for compliance with, and eligibility under, this *title [20 USCS §§ 1400* et seq.] without following the requirements of *section 553 of title 5, United States Code [5 USCS § 553]*.

(e) Explanation and assurances. Any written response by the Secretary under subsection (d) regarding a policy, question, or interpretation under part B *[20 USCS §§ 1411* et seq.] shall include an explanation in the written response that—

(1) such response is provided as informal guidance and is not legally binding;

(2) when required, such response is issued in compliance with the requirements of *section 553 of title 5, United States Code [5 USCS § 553]*; and

(3) such response represents the interpretation by the Department of Education of the applicable statutory or regulatory requirements in the context of the specific facts presented.

(f) Correspondence from Department of Education describing interpretations of this title.

(1) In general. The Secretary shall, on a quarterly basis, publish in the Federal Register, and widely disseminate to interested entities through various additional forms of communication, a list of correspondence from the Department of Education received by individuals during the previous quarter that describes the interpretations of the Department of Education of this *title [20 USCS §§ 1400* et seq.] or the regulations implemented pursuant to this *title [20 USCS §§ 1400* et seq.].

(2) Additional information. For each item of correspondence published in a list under paragraph (1), the Secretary shall—

(A) identify the topic addressed by the correspondence and shall include such other summary information as the Secretary determines to be appropriate; and

(B) ensure that all such correspondence is issued, where applicable, in compliance with the requirements of *section 553 of title 5, United States Code.*

§ 1407. State administration

(a) Rulemaking. Each State that receives funds under this *title [20 USCS §§ 1400 et seq.]* shall—

(1) ensure that any State rules, regulations, and policies relating to this *title [20 USCS §§ 1400 et seq.]* conform to the purposes of this *title [20 USCS §§ 1400 et seq.]*;

(2) identify in writing to local educational agencies located in the State and the Secretary any such rule, regulation, or policy as a State-imposed requirement that is not required by this *title [20 USCS §§ 1400 et seq.]* and Federal regulations; and

(3) minimize the number of rules, regulations, and policies to which the local educational agencies and schools located in the State are subject under this *title [20 USCS §§ 1400 et seq.]*.

(b) Support and facilitation. State rules, regulations, and policies under this *title [20 USCS §§ 1400 et seq.]* shall support and facilitate local educational agency and school-level system improvement designed to enable children with disabilities to meet the challenging State student academic achievement standards.

§ 1408. Paperwork reduction

(a) Pilot program.

(1) Purpose. The purpose of this section is to provide an opportunity for States to identify ways to reduce paperwork burdens and other administrative duties that are directly associated with the requirements of this *title [20 USCS §§ 1400 et seq.]*, in order to increase the time and resources available for instruction and other activities aimed at improving educational and functional results for children with disabilities.

(2) Authorization.

(A) In general. In order to carry out the purpose of this section, the Secretary is authorized to grant waivers of statutory requirements of, or regulatory requirements relating to, part B *[20 USCS §§ 1411 et seq.]* for a period of time not to exceed 4 years with respect to not more than 15 States based on proposals submitted by States to reduce excessive paperwork and noninstructional time burdens that do not assist in improving educational and functional results for children with disabilities.

(B) Exception. The Secretary shall not waive under this section any statutory requirements of, or regulatory requirements relating to, applicable civil rights requirements.

(C) Rule of construction. Nothing in this section shall be construed to—

(i) affect the right of a child with a disability to receive a free appropriate public education under part B *[20 USCS §§ 1411 et seq.]*; and

(ii) permit a State or local educational agency to waive procedural safeguards under section 615 *[20 USCS § 1415]*.

(3) Proposal.

(A) In general. A State desiring to participate in the program under this section shall submit a proposal to the Secretary at such time and in such manner as the Secretary may reasonably require.

(B) Content. The proposal shall include—

(i) a list of any statutory requirements of, or regulatory requirements relating to, part B *[20 USCS §§ 1411 et seq.]* that the State desires the Secretary to waive, in whole or in part; and

(ii) a list of any State requirements that the State proposes to waive or change, in whole or in part, to carry out a waiver granted to the State by the Secretary.

(4) Termination of waiver. The Secretary shall terminate a State's waiver under this section if the Secretary determines that the State—

(A) needs assistance under section 616(d)(2)(A)(ii) [20 USCS § 1416(d)(2)(A)(ii)] and that the waiver has contributed to or caused such need for assistance;

(B) needs intervention under section 616(d)(2)(A)(iii) [20 USCS § 1416(d)(2)(A)(iii)] or needs substantial intervention under section 616(d)(2)(A)(iv) [20 USCS § 1416(d)(2)(A)(iv)]; or

(C) failed to appropriately implement its waiver.

(b) Report. Beginning 2 years after the date of enactment of the Individuals with Disabilities Education Improvement Act of 2004 [enacted Dec. 3, 2004], the Secretary shall include in the annual report to Congress submitted pursuant to section 426 of the Department of Education Organization Act [20 USCS § 3486] information related to the effectiveness of waivers granted under subsection (a), including any specific recommendations for broader implementation of such waivers, in—

(1) reducing—

(A) the paperwork burden on teachers, principals, administrators, and related service providers; and

(B) noninstructional time spent by teachers in complying with part B [20 USCS §§ 1411 et seq.];

(2) enhancing longer-term educational planning;

(3) improving positive outcomes for children with disabilities;

(4) promoting collaboration between IEP Team members; and

(5) ensuring satisfaction of family members.

§ 1409. Freely associated States

The Republic of the Marshall Islands, the Federated States of Micronesia, and the Republic of Palau shall continue to be eligible for competitive grants administered by the Secretary under this *title [20 USCS §§ 1400* et seq.] to the extent that such grants continue to be available to States and local educational agencies under this *title [20 USCS §§ 1400* et seq.].

ASSISTANCE FOR EDUCATION OF ALL CHILDREN WITH DISABILITIES

§ 1411. Authorization; allotment; use of funds; authorization of appropriations

(a) Grants to States.

(1) Purpose of grants. The Secretary shall make grants to States, outlying areas, and freely associated States, and provide funds to the Secretary of the Interior, to assist them to provide special education and related services to children with disabilities in accordance with this part.

(2) Maximum amount. The maximum amount of the grant a State may receive under this section—

(A) for fiscal years 2005 and 2006 is—

(i) the number of children with disabilities in the State who are receiving special education and related services—

(I) aged 3 through 5 if the State is eligible for a grant under section 619 [*20 USCS § 1419*]; and

(II) aged 6 through 21; multiplied by

(ii) 40 percent of the average per-pupil expenditure in public elementary schools and secondary schools in the United States; and

(B) for fiscal year 2007 and subsequent fiscal years is—

(i) the number of children with disabilities in the 2004-2005 school year in the State who received special education and related services—

(I) aged 3 through 5 if the State is eligible for a grant under section 619 [*20 USCS § 1419*]; and

(II) aged 6 through 21; multiplied by

(ii) 40 percent of the average per-pupil expenditure in public elementary schools and secondary schools in the United States; adjusted by

(iii) the rate of annual change in the sum of—

(I) 85 percent of such State's population described in subsection (d)(3)(A)(i)(II); and

(II) 15 percent of such State's population described in subsection (d)(3)(A)(i)(III).

(b) Outlying areas and freely associated States; Secretary of the Interior.

(1) Outlying areas and freely associated States.

(A) Funds reserved. From the amount appropriated for any fiscal year under subsection (i), the Secretary shall reserve not more than 1 percent, which shall be used—

(i) to provide assistance to the outlying areas in accordance with their respective populations of individuals aged 3 through 21; and

(ii) to provide each freely associated State a grant in the amount that such freely associated State received for fiscal year 2003 under this part [*20 USCS §§ 1411 et seq.*], but only if the freely associated State meets the applicable requirements of this part [*20 USCS §§ 1411 et seq.*], as well as the requirements of section 611(b)(2)(C) [*20 USCS § 1411(b)(2)(C)*] as such section was in effect on the day before the date of enactment of the Individuals with Disabilities Education Improvement Act of 2004.

(B) Special rule. The provisions of Public Law 95-134, permitting the consolidation of grants by the outlying areas, shall not apply to funds provided to the outlying areas or the freely associated States under this section.

(C) Definition. In this paragraph, the term "freely associated States" means the Republic of the Marshall Islands, the Federated States of Micronesia, and the Republic of Palau.

(2) Secretary of the Interior. From the amount appropriated for any fiscal year under subsection (i), the Secretary shall reserve 1.226 percent to provide assistance to the Secretary of the Interior in accordance with subsection (h).

(c) Technical assistance.

(1) In general. The Secretary may reserve not more than 1/2 of 1 percent of the amounts appropriated under this part [*20 USCS §§ 1411 et seq.*] for each fiscal year to provide technical assistance activities authorized under section 616(i) [*20 USCS § 1416(i)*].

(2) Maximum amount. The maximum amount the Secretary may reserve under paragraph (1) for any fiscal year is $ 25,000,000, cumulatively adjusted by the rate of inflation as measured by the percentage increase, if any, from the preceding fiscal year

in the Consumer Price Index For All Urban Consumers, published by the Bureau of Labor Statistics of the Department of Labor.

(d) Allocations to States.

(1) In general. After reserving funds for technical assistance, and for payments to the outlying areas, the freely associated States, and the Secretary of the Interior under subsections (b) and (c) for a fiscal year, the Secretary shall allocate the remaining amount among the States in accordance with this subsection.

(2) Special rule for use of fiscal year 1999 amount. If a State received any funds under this section for fiscal year 1999 on the basis of children aged 3 through 5, but does not make a free appropriate public education available to all children with disabilities aged 3 through 5 in the State in any subsequent fiscal year, the Secretary shall compute the State's amount for fiscal year 1999, solely for the purpose of calculating the State's allocation in that subsequent year under paragraph (3) or (4), by subtracting the amount allocated to the State for fiscal year 1999 on the basis of those children.

(3) Increase in funds. If the amount available for allocations to States under paragraph (1) for a fiscal year is equal to or greater than the amount allocated to the States under this paragraph for the preceding fiscal year, those allocations shall be calculated as follows:

(A) Allocation of increase.

(i) In general. Except as provided in subparagraph (B), the Secretary shall allocate for the fiscal year—

(I) to each State the amount the State received under this section for fiscal year 1999;

(II) 85 percent of any remaining funds to States on the basis of the States' relative populations of children aged 3 through 21 who are of the same age as children with disabilities for whom the State ensures the availability of a free appropriate public education under this part [20 USCS §§ 1411 et seq.]; and

(III) 15 percent of those remaining funds to States on the basis of the States' relative populations of children described in subclause (II) who are living in poverty.

(ii) Data. For the purpose of making grants under this paragraph, the Secretary shall use the most recent population data, including data on children living in poverty, that are available and satisfactory to the Secretary.

(B) Limitations. Notwithstanding subparagraph (A), allocations under this paragraph shall be subject to the following:

(i) Preceding year allocation. No State's allocation shall be less than its allocation under this section for the preceding fiscal year.

(ii) Minimum. No State's allocation shall be less than the greatest of—

(I) the sum of—

(aa) the amount the State received under this section for fiscal year 1999; and

(bb) 1/3 of 1 percent of the amount by which the amount appropriated under subsection (i) for the fiscal year exceeds the amount appropriated for this section for fiscal year 1999;

(II) the sum of—

(aa) the amount the State received under this section for the preceding fiscal year; and

(bb) that amount multiplied by the percentage by which the increase in the funds appropriated for this section from the preceding fiscal year exceeds 1.5 percent; or

(III) the sum of—

(aa) the amount the State received under this section for the preceding fiscal year; and

(bb) that amount multiplied by 90 percent of the percentage increase in the amount appropriated for this section from the preceding fiscal year.

(iii) Maximum. Notwithstanding clause (ii), no State's allocation under this paragraph shall exceed the sum of—

(I) the amount the State received under this section for the preceding fiscal year; and

(II) that amount multiplied by the sum of 1.5 percent and the percentage increase in the amount appropriated under this section from the preceding fiscal year.

(C) Ratable reduction. If the amount available for allocations under this paragraph is insufficient to pay those allocations in full, those allocations shall be ratably reduced, subject to subparagraph (B)(i).

(4) Decrease in funds. If the amount available for allocations to States under paragraph (1) for a fiscal year is less than the amount allocated to the States under this section for the preceding fiscal year, those allocations shall be calculated as follows:

(A) Amounts greater than fiscal year 1999 allocations. If the amount available for allocations is greater than the amount allocated to the States for fiscal year 1999, each State shall be allocated the sum of—

(i) the amount the State received under this section for fiscal year 1999; and

(ii) an amount that bears the same relation to any remaining funds as the increase the State received under this section for the preceding fiscal year over fiscal year 1999 bears to the total of all such increases for all States.

(B) Amounts equal to or less than fiscal year 1999 allocations.

(i) In general. If the amount available for allocations under this paragraph is equal to or less than the amount allocated to the States for fiscal year 1999, each State shall be allocated the amount the State received for fiscal year 1999.

(ii) Ratable reduction. If the amount available for allocations under this paragraph is insufficient to make the allocations described in clause (i), those allocations shall be ratably reduced.

(e) State-level activities.

(1) State administration.

(A) In general. For the purpose of administering this part [20 USCS §§ 1411 et seq.], including paragraph (3), section 619 [20 USCS § 1419], and the coordination of activities under this part [20 USCS §§ 1411 et seq.] with, and providing technical assistance to, other programs that provide services to children with disabilities—

(i) each State may reserve for each fiscal year not more than the maximum amount the State was eligible to reserve for State administration under this section for fiscal year 2004 or $ 800,000 (adjusted in accordance with subparagraph (B)), whichever is greater; and

(ii) each outlying area may reserve for each fiscal year not more than 5 percent of the amount the outlying area receives under subsection (b)(1) for the fiscal year or $ 35,000, whichever is greater.

(B) Cumulative annual adjustments. For each fiscal year beginning with fiscal year 2005, the Secretary shall cumulatively adjust—

(i) the maximum amount the State was eligible to reserve for State administration under this part [20 USCS §§ 1411 et seq.] for fiscal year 2004; and

(ii) $ 800,000, by the rate of inflation as measured by the percentage increase, if any, from the preceding fiscal year in the Consumer Price Index For All Urban Consumers, published by the Bureau of Labor Statistics of the Department of Labor.

(C) Certification. Prior to expenditure of funds under this paragraph, the State shall certify to the Secretary that the arrangements to establish responsibility for services pursuant to section 612(a)(12)(A) [20 USCS § 1412(a)(12)(A)] are current.

(D) Part C. Funds reserved under subparagraph (A) may be used for the administration of part C [20 USCS §§ 1431 et seq.], if the State educational agency is the lead agency for the State under such part.

(2) Other State-level activities.

(A) State-level activities.

(i) In general. Except as provided in clause (iii), for the purpose of carrying out State-level activities, each State may reserve for each of the fiscal years 2005 and 2006 not more than 10 percent from the amount of the State's allocation under subsection (d) for each of the fiscal years 2005 and 2006, respectively. For fiscal year 2007 and each subsequent fiscal year, the State may reserve the maximum amount the State was eligible to reserve under the preceding sentence for fiscal year 2006 (cumulatively adjusted by the rate of inflation as measured by the percentage increase, if any, from the preceding fiscal year in the Consumer Price Index For All Urban Consumers, published by the Bureau of Labor Statistics of the Department of Labor).

(ii) Small State adjustment. Notwithstanding clause (i) and except as provided in clause (iii), in the case of a State for which the maximum amount reserved for State administration is not greater than $ 850,000, the State may reserve for the purpose of carrying out State-level activities for each of the fiscal years 2005 and 2006, not more than 10.5 percent from the amount of the State's allocation under subsection (d) for each of the fiscal years 2005 and 2006, respectively. For fiscal year 2007 and each subsequent fiscal year, such State may reserve the maximum amount the State was eligible to reserve under the preceding sentence for fiscal year 2006 (cumulatively adjusted by the rate of inflation as measured by the percentage increase, if any, from the preceding fiscal year in the Consumer Price Index For All Urban Consumers, published by the Bureau of Labor Statistics of the Department of Labor).

(iii) Exception. If a State does not reserve funds under paragraph (3) for a fiscal year, then—

(I) in the case of a State that is not described in clause (ii), for fiscal year 2005 or 2006, clause (i) shall be applied by substituting "9.0 percent" for "10 percent"; and

(II) in the case of a State that is described in clause (ii), for fiscal year 2005 or 2006, clause (ii) shall be applied by substituting "9.5 percent" for "10.5 percent".

(B) Required activities. Funds reserved under subparagraph (A) shall be used to carry out the following activities:

(i) For monitoring, enforcement, and complaint investigation.

(ii) To establish and implement the mediation process required by section 615(e) [20 USCS § 1415(e)], including providing for the cost of mediators and support personnel.

(C) Authorized activities. Funds reserved under subparagraph (A) may be used to carry out the following activities:

(i) For support and direct services, including technical assistance, personnel preparation, and professional development and training.

(ii) To support paperwork reduction activities, including expanding the use of technology in the IEP process.

(iii) To assist local educational agencies in providing positive behavioral interventions and supports and appropriate mental health services for children with disabilities.

(iv) To improve the use of technology in the classroom by children with disabilities to enhance learning.

(v) To support the use of technology, including technology with universal design principles and assistive technology devices, to maximize accessibility to the general education curriculum for children with disabilities.

(vi) Development and implementation of transition programs, including coordination of services with agencies involved in supporting the transition of children with disabilities to postsecondary activities.

(vii) To assist local educational agencies in meeting personnel shortages.

(viii) To support capacity building activities and improve the delivery of services by local educational agencies to improve results for children with disabilities.

(ix) Alternative programming for children with disabilities who have been expelled from school, and services for children with disabilities in correctional facilities, children enrolled in State-operated or State-supported schools, and children with disabilities in charter schools.

(x) To support the development and provision of appropriate accommodations for children with disabilities, or the development and provision of alternate assessments that are valid and reliable for assessing the performance of children with disabilities, in accordance with sections 1111(b) and 6111 of the Elementary and Secondary Education Act of 1965 [*20 USCS §§ 6311(b) and 7301*].

(xi) To provide technical assistance to schools and local educational agencies, and direct services, including supplemental educational services as defined in 1116(e) of the Elementary and Secondary Education Act of 1965 [*20 USCS § 6317(e)*] to children with disabilities, in schools or local educational agencies identified for improvement under section 1116 of the Elementary and Secondary Education Act of 1965 [*20 USCS § 6317*] on the sole basis of the assessment results of the disaggregated subgroup of children with disabilities, including providing professional development to special and regular education teachers, who teach children with disabilities, based on scientifically based research to improve educational instruction, in order to improve academic achievement to meet or exceed the objectives established by the State under section 1111(b)(2)(G) the Elementary and Secondary Education Act of 1965 [*20 USCS § 6311(b)(2)(G)*].

(3) Local educational agency risk pool.

(A) In general.

(i) Reservation of funds. For the purpose of assisting local educational agencies (including a charter school that is a local educational agency or a consortium of local educational agencies) in addressing the needs of high need children with disabilities, each State shall have the option to reserve for each fiscal year 10 percent of the amount of funds the State reserves for State-level activities under paragraph (2)(A)—

(I) to establish and make disbursements from the high cost fund to local educational agencies in accordance with this paragraph during the first and succeeding fiscal years of the high cost fund; and

(II) to support innovative and effective ways of cost sharing by the State, by a local educational agency, or among a consortium of local educational agencies, as determined by the State in coordination with representatives from local educational agencies, subject to subparagraph (B)(ii).

(ii) Definition of local educational agency. In this paragraph the term "local educational agency" includes a charter school that is a local educational agency, or a consortium of local educational agencies.

(B) Limitation on uses of funds.

(i) Establishment of high cost fund. A State shall not use any of the funds the State reserves pursuant to subparagraph (A)(i), but may use the funds the State reserves under paragraph (1), to establish and support the high cost fund.

(ii) Innovative and effective cost sharing. A State shall not use more than 5 percent of the funds the State reserves pursuant to subparagraph (A)(i) for each fiscal year to support innovative and effective ways of cost sharing among consortia of local educational agencies.

(C) State plan for high cost fund.

(i) Definition. The State educational agency shall establish the State's definition of a high need child with a disability, which definition shall be developed in consultation with local educational agencies.

(ii) State plan. The State educational agency shall develop, not later than 90 days after the State reserves funds under this paragraph, annually review, and amend as necessary, a State plan for the high cost fund. Such State plan shall—

(I) establish, in coordination with representatives from local educational agencies, a definition of a high need child with a disability that, at a minimum—

(aa) addresses the financial impact a high need child with a disability has on the budget of the child's local educational agency; and

(bb) ensures that the cost of the high need child with a disability is greater than 3 times the average per pupil expenditure (as defined in section 9101 of the Elementary and Secondary Education Act of 1965 [*20 USCS § 7801*]) in that State;

(II) establish eligibility criteria for the participation of a local educational agency that, at a minimum, takes into account the number and percentage of high need children with disabilities served by a local educational agency;

(III) develop a funding mechanism that provides distributions each fiscal year to local educational agencies that meet the criteria developed by the State under subclause (II); and

(IV) establish an annual schedule by which the State educational agency shall make its distributions from the high cost fund each fiscal year.

(iii) Public availability. The State shall make its final State plan publicly available not less than 30 days before the beginning of the school year, including dissemination of such information on the State website.

(D) Disbursements from the high cost fund.

(i) In general. Each State educational agency shall make all annual disbursements from the high cost fund established under subparagraph (A)(i) in accordance with the State plan published pursuant to subparagraph (C).

(ii) Use of disbursements. Each State educational agency shall make annual disbursements to eligible local educational agencies in accordance with its State plan under subparagraph (C)(ii).

(iii) Appropriate costs. The costs associated with educating a high need child with a disability under subparagraph (C)(i) are only those costs associated with providing direct special education and related services to such child that are identified in such child's IEP.

(E) Legal fees. The disbursements under subparagraph (D) shall not support legal fees, court costs, or other costs associated with a cause of action brought on behalf of a child with a disability to ensure a free appropriate public education for such child.

(F) Assurance of a free appropriate public education. Nothing in this paragraph shall be construed—

(i) to limit or condition the right of a child with a disability who is assisted under this part [20 USCS §§ 1411 et seq.] to receive a free appropriate public education pursuant to section 612(a)(1) [20 USCS § 1412(a)(1)] in the least restrictive environment pursuant to section 612(a)(5) [20 USCS § 1412(a)(5)]; or

(ii) to authorize a State educational agency or local educational agency to establish a limit on what may be spent on the education of a child with a disability.

(G) Special rule for risk pool and high need assistance programs in effect as of January 1, 2004. Notwithstanding the provisions of subparagraphs (A) through (F), a State may use funds reserved pursuant to this paragraph for implementing a placement neutral cost sharing and reimbursement program of high need, low incidence, catastrophic, or extraordinary aid to local educational agencies that provides services to high need students based on eligibility criteria for such programs that were created not later than January 1, 2004, and are currently in operation, if such program serves children that meet the requirement of the definition of a high need child with a disability as described in subparagraph (C)(ii)(I).

(H) Medicaid services not affected. Disbursements provided under this paragraph shall not be used to pay costs that otherwise would be reimbursed as medical assistance for a child with a disability under the State medicaid program under title XIX of the Social Security Act [42 USCS §§ 1396 et seq.].

(I) Remaining funds. Funds reserved under subparagraph (A) in any fiscal year but not expended in that fiscal year pursuant to subparagraph (D) shall be allocated to local educational agencies for the succeeding fiscal year in the same manner as funds are allocated to local educational agencies under subsection (f) for the succeeding fiscal year.

(4) Inapplicability of certain prohibitions. A State may use funds the State reserves under paragraphs (1) and (2) without regard to—

(A) the prohibition on commingling of funds in section 612(a)(17)(B) [20 USCS § 1412(a)(17)(B)]; and

(B) the prohibition on supplanting other funds in section 612(a)(17)(C) [20 USCS § 1412(a)(17)(C)].

(5) Report on use of funds. As part of the information required to be submitted to the Secretary under section 612 [20 USCS § 1412], each State shall annually describe how amounts under this section—

(A) will be used to meet the requirements of this *title [20 USCS §§ 1400 et seq.]*; and

(B) will be allocated among the activities described in this section to meet State priorities based on input from local educational agencies.

(6) Special rule for increased funds. A State may use funds the State reserves under paragraph (1)(A) as a result of inflationary increases under paragraph (1)(B) to carry out activities authorized under clause (i), (iii), (vii), or (viii) of paragraph (2)(C).

(7) Flexibility in using funds for part c. Any State eligible to receive a grant under section 619 [20 USCS § 1419] may use funds made available under paragraph (1)(A), subsection (f)(3), or section 619(f)(5) [20 USCS § 1419(f)(5)] to develop and implement a State policy jointly with the lead agency under part C [20 USCS §§ 1431 et seq.] and the State educational agency to provide early intervention services (which shall include an educational component that promotes school readiness and incorporates preliteracy, language, and numeracy skills) in accordance with part C [20 USCS §§ 1431 et seq.] to

children with disabilities who are eligible for services under section 619 [20 USCS § 1419] and who previously received services under part C [20 USCS §§ 1431 et seq.] until such children enter, or are eligible under State law to enter, kindergarten, or elementary school as appropriate.

(f) Subgrants to local educational agencies.

(1) Subgrants required. Each State that receives a grant under this section for any fiscal year shall distribute any funds the State does not reserve under subsection (e) to local educational agencies (including public charter schools that operate as local educational agencies) in the State that have established their eligibility under section 613 [20 USCS § 1413] for use in accordance with this part [20 USCS §§ 1411 et seq.].

(2) Procedure for allocations to local educational agencies. For each fiscal year for which funds are allocated to States under subsection (d), each State shall allocate funds under paragraph (1) as follows:

(A) Base payments. The State shall first award each local educational agency described in paragraph (1) the amount the local educational agency would have received under this section for fiscal year 1999, if the State had distributed 75 percent of its grant for that year under section 611(d) [20 USCS § 1411(d)] as section 611(d) was then in effect.

(B) Allocation of remaining funds. After making allocations under subparagraph (A), the State shall—

(i) allocate 85 percent of any remaining funds to those local educational agencies on the basis of the relative numbers of children enrolled in public and private elementary schools and secondary schools within the local educational agency's jurisdiction; and

(ii) allocate 15 percent of those remaining funds to those local educational agencies in accordance with their relative numbers of children living in poverty, as determined by the State educational agency.

(3) Reallocation of funds. If a State educational agency determines that a local educational agency is adequately providing a free appropriate public education to all children with disabilities residing in the area served by that local educational agency with State and local funds, the State educational agency may reallocate any portion of the funds under this part [20 USCS §§ 1411 et seq.] that are not needed by that local educational agency to provide a free appropriate public education to other local educational agencies in the State that are not adequately providing special education and related services to all children with disabilities residing in the areas served by those other local educational agencies.

(g) Definitions. In this section:

(1) Average per-pupil expenditure in public elementary schools and secondary schools in the united states. The term "average per-pupil expenditure in public elementary schools and secondary schools in the United States" means—

(A) without regard to the source of funds—

(i) the aggregate current expenditures, during the second fiscal year preceding the fiscal year for which the determination is made (or, if satisfactory data for that year are not available, during the most recent preceding fiscal year for which satisfactory data are available) of all local educational agencies in the 50 States and the District of Columbia; plus

(ii) any direct expenditures by the State for the operation of those agencies; divided by

(B) the aggregate number of children in average daily attendance to whom those agencies provided free public education during that preceding year.

(2) State. The term "State" means each of the 50 States, the District of Columbia, and the Commonwealth of Puerto Rico.

(h) Use of amounts by Secretary of the Interior.

(1) Provision of amounts for assistance.

(A) In general. The Secretary of Education shall provide amounts to the Secretary of the Interior to meet the need for assistance for the education of children with disabilities on reservations aged 5 to 21, inclusive, enrolled in elementary schools and secondary schools for Indian children operated or funded by the Secretary of the Interior. The amount of such payment for any fiscal year shall be equal to 80 percent of the amount allotted under subsection (b)(2) for that fiscal year. Of the amount described in the preceding sentence—

(i) 80 percent shall be allocated to such schools by July 1 of that fiscal year; and

(ii) 20 percent shall be allocated to such schools by September 30 of that fiscal year.

(B) Calculation of number of children. In the case of Indian students aged 3 to 5, inclusive, who are enrolled in programs affiliated with the Bureau of Indian Affairs (referred to in this subsection as the "BIA") schools and that are required by the States in which such schools are located to attain or maintain State accreditation, and which schools have such accreditation prior to the date of enactment of the Individuals with Disabilities Education Act Amendments of 1991 [enacted Oct. 7, 1991], the school shall be allowed to count those children for the purpose of distribution of the funds provided under this paragraph to the Secretary of the Interior. The Secretary of the Interior shall be responsible for meeting all of the requirements of this part [20 USCS §§ 1411 et seq.] for those children, in accordance with paragraph (2).

(C) Additional requirement. With respect to all other children aged 3 to 21, inclusive, on reservations, the State educational agency shall be responsible for ensuring that all of the requirements of this part [20 USCS §§ 1411 et seq.] are implemented.

(2) Submission of information. The Secretary of Education may provide the Secretary of the Interior amounts under paragraph (1) for a fiscal year only if the Secretary of the Interior submits to the Secretary of Education information that—

(A) demonstrates that the Department of the Interior meets the appropriate requirements, as determined by the Secretary of Education, of sections 612 [20 USCS § 1412] (including monitoring and evaluation activities) and 613 [20 USCS § 1413];

(B) includes a description of how the Secretary of the Interior will coordinate the provision of services under this part [20 USCS §§ 1411 et seq.] with local educational agencies, tribes and tribal organizations, and other private and Federal service providers;

(C) includes an assurance that there are public hearings, adequate notice of such hearings, and an opportunity for comment afforded to members of tribes, tribal governing bodies, and affected local school boards before the adoption of the policies, programs, and procedures related to the requirements described in subparagraph (A);

(D) includes an assurance that the Secretary of the Interior will provide such information as the Secretary of Education may require to comply with section 618 [20 USCS § 1418];

(E) includes an assurance that the Secretary of the Interior and the Secretary of Health and Human Services have entered into a memorandum of agreement, to be provided to the Secretary of Education, for the coordination of services, resources, and personnel between their respective Federal, State, and local offices and with State and local educational agencies and other entities to facilitate the provision of services to Indian children with disabilities residing on or near reservations (such agreement shall provide for the apportionment of responsibilities and costs, including child find, evaluation, diagnosis, remediation or therapeutic measures, and (where appropriate) equipment and medical or personal supplies as needed for a child to remain in school or a program); and

(F) includes an assurance that the Department of the Interior will cooperate with the Department of Education in its exercise of monitoring and oversight of this application, and any agreements entered into between the Secretary of the Interior and other entities under this part [20 USCS §§ 1411 et seq.], and will fulfill its duties under this part [20 USCS §§ 1411 et seq.].

(3) Applicability. The Secretary shall withhold payments under this subsection with respect to the information described in paragraph (2) in the same manner as the Secretary withholds payments under section 616(e)(6) [20 USCS § 1416(e)(6)].

(4) Payments for education and services for indian children with disabilities aged 3 through 5.

(A) In general. With funds appropriated under subsection (i), the Secretary of Education shall make payments to the Secretary of the Interior to be distributed to tribes or tribal organizations (as defined under section 4 of the Indian Self-Determination and Education Assistance Act [25 USCS § 450b]) or consortia of tribes or tribal organizations to provide for the coordination of assistance for special education and related services for children with disabilities aged 3 through 5 on reservations served by elementary schools and secondary schools for Indian children operated or funded by the Department of the Interior. The amount of such payments under subparagraph (B) for any fiscal year shall be equal to 20 percent of the amount allotted under subsection (b)(2).

(B) Distribution of funds. The Secretary of the Interior shall distribute the total amount of the payment under subparagraph (A) by allocating to each tribe, tribal organization, or consortium an amount based on the number of children with disabilities aged 3 through 5 residing on reservations as reported annually, divided by the total of those children served by all tribes or tribal organizations.

(C) Submission of information. To receive a payment under this paragraph, the tribe or tribal organization shall submit such figures to the Secretary of the Interior as required to determine the amounts to be allocated under subparagraph (B). This information shall be compiled and submitted to the Secretary of Education.

(D) Use of funds. The funds received by a tribe or tribal organization shall be used to assist in child find, screening, and other procedures for the early identification of children aged 3 through 5, parent training, and the provision of direct services. These activities may be carried out directly or through contracts or cooperative agreements with the BIA, local educational agencies, and other public or private nonprofit organizations. The tribe or tribal organization is encouraged to involve Indian parents in the development and implementation of these activities. The tribe or tribal organization shall, as appropriate, make referrals to local, State, or Federal entities for the provision of services or further diagnosis.

(E) Biennial report. To be eligible to receive a grant pursuant to subparagraph (A), the tribe or tribal organization shall provide to the Secretary of the Interior a biennial report of activities undertaken under this paragraph, including the number of contracts and cooperative agreements entered into, the number of children contacted and receiving services for each year, and the estimated number of children needing services during the 2 years following the year in which the report is made. The Secretary of the Interior shall include a summary of this information on a biennial basis in the report to the Secretary of Education required under this subsection. The Secretary of Education may require any additional information from the Secretary of the Interior.

(F) Prohibitions. None of the funds allocated under this paragraph may be used by the

Secretary of the Interior for administrative purposes, including child count and the provision of technical assistance.

(5) Plan for coordination of services. The Secretary of the Interior shall develop and implement a plan for the coordination of services for all Indian children with disabilities residing on reservations covered under this *title [20 USCS §§ 1400* et seq.]. Such plan shall provide for the coordination of services benefiting those children from whatever source, including tribes, the Indian Health Service, other BIA divisions, and other Federal agencies. In developing the plan, the Secretary of the Interior shall consult with all interested and involved parties. The plan shall be based on the needs of the children and the system best suited for meeting those needs, and may involve the establishment of cooperative agreements between the BIA, other Federal agencies, and other entities. The plan shall also be distributed upon request to States, State educational agencies and local educational agencies, and other agencies providing services to infants, toddlers, and children with disabilities, to tribes, and to other interested parties.

(6) Establishment of advisory board. To meet the requirements of section 612(a)(21) [*20 USCS § 1412(a)(21)*], the Secretary of the Interior shall establish, under the BIA, an advisory board composed of individuals involved in or concerned with the education and provision of services to Indian infants, toddlers, children, and youth with disabilities, including Indians with disabilities, Indian parents or guardians of such children, teachers, service providers, State and local educational officials, representatives of tribes or tribal organizations, representatives from State Interagency Coordinating Councils under section 641 [*20 USCS § 1441*] in States having reservations, and other members representing the various divisions and entities of the BIA. The chairperson shall be selected by the Secretary of the Interior. The advisory board shall—

(A) assist in the coordination of services within the BIA and with other local, State, and Federal agencies in the provision of education for infants, toddlers, and children with disabilities;

(B) advise and assist the Secretary of the Interior in the performance of the Secretary of the Interior's responsibilities described in this subsection;

(C) develop and recommend policies concerning effective inter- and intra-agency collaboration, including modifications to regulations, and the elimination of barriers to inter- and intra-agency programs and activities;

(D) provide assistance and disseminate information on best practices, effective program coordination strategies, and recommendations for improved early intervention services or educational programming for Indian infants, toddlers, and children with disabilities; and

(E) provide assistance in the preparation of information required under paragraph (2)(D).

(7) Annual reports.

(A) In general. The advisory board established under paragraph (6) shall prepare and submit to the Secretary of the Interior and to Congress an annual report containing a description of the activities of the advisory board for the preceding year.

(B) Availability. The Secretary of the Interior shall make available to the Secretary of Education the report described in subparagraph (A).

(i) Authorization of appropriations. For the purpose of carrying out this part [*20 USCS §§ 1411* et seq.], other than section 619 [*20 USCS § 1419*], there are authorized to be appropriated—

(1) $ 12,358,376,571 for fiscal year 2005;

(2) $ 14,648,647,143 for fiscal year 2006;

(3) $ 16,938,917,714 for fiscal year 2007;

(4) $ 19,229,188,286 for fiscal year 2008;

(5) $ 21,519,458,857 for fiscal year 2009;

(6) $ 23,809,729,429 for fiscal year 2010;

(7) $ 26,100,000,000 for fiscal year 2011; and

(8) such sums as may be necessary for fiscal year 2012 and each succeeding fiscal year.

§ 1412. State eligibility

(a) In general. A State is eligible for assistance under this part [20 USCS §§ 1411 et seq.] for a fiscal year if the State submits a plan that provides assurances to the Secretary that the State has in effect policies and procedures to ensure that the State meets each of the following conditions:

(1) Free appropriate public education.

(A) In general. A free appropriate public education is available to all children with disabilities residing in the State between the ages of 3 and 21, inclusive, including children with disabilities who have been suspended or expelled from school.

(B) Limitation. The obligation to make a free appropriate public education available to all children with disabilities does not apply with respect to children—

(i) aged 3 through 5 and 18 through 21 in a State to the extent that its application to those children would be inconsistent with State law or practice, or the order of any court, respecting the provision of public education to children in those age ranges; and

(ii) aged 18 through 21 to the extent that State law does not require that special education and related services under this part [20 USCS §§ 1411 et seq.] be provided to children with disabilities who, in the educational placement prior to their incarceration in an adult correctional facility—

(I) were not actually identified as being a child with a disability under section 602 [20 USCS § 1401]; or

(II) did not have an individualized education program under this part [20 USCS §§ 1411 et seq.].

(C) State flexibility. A State that provides early intervention services in accordance with part C [20 USCS §§ 1431 et seq.] to a child who is eligible for services under section 619, is not required to provide such child with a free appropriate public education.

(2) Full educational opportunity goal. The State has established a goal of providing full educational opportunity to all children with disabilities and a detailed timetable for accomplishing that goal.

(3) Child find.

(A) In general. All children with disabilities residing in the State, including children with disabilities who are homeless children or are wards of the State and children with disabilities attending private schools, regardless of the severity of their disabilities, and who are in need of special education and related services, are identified, located, and evaluated and a practical method is developed and implemented to determine which children with disabilities are currently receiving needed special education and related services.

(B) Construction. Nothing in this *title [20 USCS §§ 1400 et seq.]* requires that children be classified by their disability so long as each child who has a disability listed in section 602 [*20 USCS § 1401*] and who, by reason of that disability, needs special education and related services is regarded as a child with a disability under this part [20 USCS §§ 1411 et seq.].

(4) Individualized education program. An individualized education program, or an individualized family service plan that meets the requirements of section 636(d) [20 USCS § 1436(d)], is developed, reviewed, and revised for each child with a disability in accordance with section 614(d) [20 USCS § 1414(d)].

(5) Least restrictive environment.

(A) In general. To the maximum extent appropriate, children with disabilities, including children in public or private institutions or other care facilities, are educated with children who are not disabled, and special classes, separate schooling, or other removal of children with disabilities from the regular educational environment occurs only when the nature or severity of the disability of a child is such that education in regular classes with the use of supplementary aids and services cannot be achieved satisfactorily.

(B) Additional requirement.

(i) In general. A State funding mechanism shall not result in placements that violate the requirements of subparagraph (A), and a State shall not use a funding mechanism by which the State distributes funds on the basis of the type of setting in which a child is served that will result in the failure to provide a child with a disability a free appropriate public education according to the unique needs of the child as described in the child's IEP.

(ii) Assurance. If the State does not have policies and procedures to ensure compliance with clause (i), the State shall provide the Secretary an assurance that the State will revise the funding mechanism as soon as feasible to ensure that such mechanism does not result in such placements.

(6) Procedural safeguards.

(A) In general. Children with disabilities and their parents are afforded the procedural safeguards required by section 615 [20 USCS § 1415].

(B) Additional procedural safeguards. Procedures to ensure that testing and evaluation materials and procedures utilized for the purposes of evaluation and placement of children with disabilities for services under this *title [20 USCS §§ 1400* et seq.] will be selected and administered so as not to be racially or culturally discriminatory. Such materials or procedures shall be provided and administered in the child's native language or mode of communication, unless it clearly is not feasible to do so, and no single procedure shall be the sole criterion for determining an appropriate educational program for a child.

(7) Evaluation. Children with disabilities are evaluated in accordance with subsections (a) through (c) of section 614 [20 USCS § 1414].

(8) Confidentiality. Agencies in the State comply with section 617(c) [20 USCS § 1417(c)] (relating to the confidentiality of records and information).

(9) Transition from part C to preschool programs. Children participating in early intervention programs assisted under part C [20 USCS §§ 1431 et seq.], and who will participate in preschool programs assisted under this part [20 USCS §§ 1411 et seq.], experience a smooth and effective transition to those preschool programs in a manner consistent with section 637(a)(9) [20 USCS § 1437(a)(9)]. By the third birthday of such a child, an individualized education program or, if consistent with sections 614(d)(2)(B) and 636(d) [20 USCS §§ 1414(d)(2)(B) and 1436(d)], an individualized family service plan, has been developed and is being implemented for the child. The local educational agency will participate in transition planning conferences arranged by the designated lead agency under section 635(a)(10) [20 USCS § 1435(a)(10)].

(10) Children in private schools.

(A) Children enrolled in private schools by their parents.

(i) In general. To the extent consistent with the number and location of children with disabilities in the State who are enrolled by their parents in private elementary schools and secondary schools in the school district served by a local educational agency, provision is made for the participation of those children in the program assisted or carried out under this part [20 USCS §§ 1411 et seq.] by providing for such children special education and related services in accordance with the following requirements, unless the Secretary has arranged for services to those children under subsection (f):

(I) Amounts to be expended for the provision of those services (including direct services to parentally placed private school children) by the local educational agency shall be equal to a proportionate amount of Federal funds made available under this part [20 USCS §§ 1411 et seq.].

(II) In calculating the proportionate amount of Federal funds, the local educational agency, after timely and meaningful consultation with representatives of private schools as described in clause (iii), shall conduct a thorough and complete child find process to determine the number of parentally placed children with disabilities attending private schools located in the local educational agency.

(III) Such services to parentally placed private school children with disabilities may be provided to the children on the premises of private, including religious, schools, to the extent consistent with law.

(IV) State and local funds may supplement and in no case shall supplant the proportionate amount of Federal funds required to be expended under this subparagraph.

(V) Each local educational agency shall maintain in its records and provide to the State educational agency the number of children evaluated under this subparagraph, the number of children determined to be children with disabilities under this paragraph, and the number of children served under this paragraph.

(ii) Child find requirement.

(I) In general. The requirements of paragraph (3) (relating to child find) shall apply with respect to children with disabilities in the State who are enrolled in private, including religious, elementary schools and secondary schools.

(II) Equitable participation. The child find process shall be designed to ensure the equitable participation of parentally placed private school children with disabilities and an accurate count of such children.

(III) Activities. In carrying out this clause, the local educational agency, or where applicable, the State educational agency, shall undertake activities similar to those activities undertaken for the agency's public school children.

(IV) Cost. The cost of carrying out this clause, including individual evaluations, may not be considered in determining whether a local educational agency has met its obligations under clause (i).

(V) Completion period. Such child find process shall be completed in a time period comparable to that for other students attending public schools in the local educational agency.

(iii) Consultation. To ensure timely and meaningful consultation, a local educational agency, or where appropriate, a State educational agency, shall consult with private school representatives and representatives of parents of parentally placed private school children with disabilities during the design and development of special education and related services for the children, including regarding—

(I) the child find process and how parentally placed private school children suspected of having a disability can participate equitably, including how parents, teachers, and private school officials will be informed of the process;

(II) the determination of the proportionate amount of Federal funds available to serve parentally placed private school children with disabilities under this subparagraph, including the determination of how the amount was calculated;

(III) the consultation process among the local educational agency, private school officials, and representatives of parents of parentally placed private school children with disabilities, including how such process will operate throughout the school year to ensure that parentally placed private school children with disabilities identified through the child find process can meaningfully participate in special education and related services;

(IV) how, where, and by whom special education and related services will be provided for parentally placed private school children with disabilities, including a discussion of types of services, including direct services and alternate service delivery mechanisms, how such services will be apportioned if funds are insufficient to serve all children, and how and when these decisions will be made; and

(V) how, if the local educational agency disagrees with the views of the private school officials on the provision of services or the types of services, whether provided directly or through a contract, the local educational agency shall provide to the private school officials a written explanation of the reasons why the local educational agency chose not to provide services directly or through a contract.

(iv) Written affirmation. When timely and meaningful consultation as required by clause (iii) has occurred, the local educational agency shall obtain a written affirmation signed by the representatives of participating private schools, and if such representatives do not provide such affirmation within a reasonable period of time, the local educational agency shall forward the documentation of the consultation process to the State educational agency.

(v) Compliance.

(I) In general. A private school official shall have the right to submit a complaint to the State educational agency that the local educational agency did not engage in consultation that was meaningful and timely, or did not give due consideration to the views of the private school official.

(II) Procedure. If the private school official wishes to submit a complaint, the official shall provide the basis of the noncompliance with this subparagraph by the local educational agency to the State educational agency, and the local educational agency shall forward the appropriate documentation to the State educational agency. If the private school official is dissatisfied with the decision of the State educational agency, such official may submit a complaint to the Secretary by providing the basis of the noncompliance with this subparagraph by the local educational agency to the Secretary, and the State educational agency shall forward the appropriate documentation to the Secretary.

(vi) Provision of equitable services.

(I) Directly or through contracts. The provision of services pursuant to this subparagraph shall be provided—

(aa) by employees of a public agency; or

(bb) through contract by the public agency with an individual, association, agency, organization, or other entity.

(II) Secular, neutral, nonideological. Special education and related services provided to parentally placed private school children with disabilities, including materials and equipment, shall be secular, neutral, and nonideological.

(vii) Public control of funds. The control of funds used to provide special education and related services under this subparagraph, and title to materials, equipment, and property purchased with those funds, shall be in a public agency for the uses and purposes provided in this *title [20 USCS §§ 1400* et seq.], and a public agency shall administer the funds and property.

(B) Children placed in, or referred to, private schools by public agencies.

(i) In general. Children with disabilities in private schools and facilities are provided special education and related services, in accordance with an individualized education program, at no cost to their parents, if such children are placed in, or referred to, such schools or facilities by the State or appropriate local educational agency as the means of carrying out the requirements of this part [*20 USCS §§ 1411* et seq.] or any other applicable law requiring the provision of special education and related services to all children with disabilities within such State.

(ii) Standards. In all cases described in clause (i), the State educational agency shall determine whether such schools and facilities meet standards that apply to State educational agencies and local educational agencies and that children so served have all the rights the children would have if served by such agencies.

(C) Payment for education of children enrolled in private schools without consent of or referral by the public agency.

(i) In general. Subject to subparagraph (A), this part [*20 USCS §§ 1411* et seq.] does not require a local educational agency to pay for the cost of education, including special education and related services, of a child with a disability at a private school or facility if that agency made a free appropriate public education available to the child and the parents elected to place the child in such private school or facility.

(ii) Reimbursement for private school placement. If the parents of a child with a disability, who previously received special education and related services under the authority of a public agency, enroll the child in a private elementary school or secondary school without the consent of or referral by the public agency, a court or a hearing officer may require the agency to reimburse the parents for the cost of that enrollment if the court or hearing officer finds that the agency had not made a free appropriate public education available to the child in a timely manner prior to that enrollment.

(iii) Limitation on reimbursement. The cost of reimbursement described in clause (ii) may be reduced or denied—

(I) if—

(aa) at the most recent IEP meeting that the parents attended prior to removal of the child from the public school, the parents did not inform the IEP Team that they were rejecting the placement proposed by the public agency to provide a free appropriate public education to their child, including stating their concerns and their intent to enroll their child in a private school at public expense; or

(bb) 10 business days (including any holidays that occur on a business day) prior to the removal of the child from the public school, the parents did not give written notice to the public agency of the information described in item (aa);

(II) if, prior to the parents' removal of the child from the public school, the public agency informed the parents, through the notice requirements described in section 615(b)(3) [*20 USCS § 1415(b)(3)*], of its intent to evaluate the child (including a statement of the purpose of the evaluation that was appropriate and reasonable), but the parents did not make the child available for such evaluation; or

(III) upon a judicial finding of unreasonableness with respect to actions taken by the parents.

(iv) Exception. Notwithstanding the notice requirement in clause (iii)(I), the cost of reimbursement—

(I) shall not be reduced or denied for failure to provide such notice if—

(aa) the school prevented the parent from providing such notice;

(bb) the parents had not received notice, pursuant to section 615 [20 USCS § 1415], of the notice requirement in clause (iii)(I); or

(cc) compliance with clause (iii)(I) would likely result in physical harm to the child; and

(II) may, in the discretion of a court or a hearing officer, not be reduced or denied for failure to provide such notice if—

(aa) the parent is illiterate or cannot write in English; or

(bb) compliance with clause (iii)(I) would likely result in serious emotional harm to the child.

(11) State educational agency responsible for general supervision.

(A) In general. The State educational agency is responsible for ensuring that—

(i) the requirements of this part [20 USCS §§ 1411 et seq.] are met;

(ii) all educational programs for children with disabilities in the State, including all such programs administered by any other State agency or local agency—

(I) are under the general supervision of individuals in the State who are responsible for educational programs for children with disabilities; and

(II) meet the educational standards of the State educational agency; and

(iii) in carrying out this part [20 USCS §§ 1411 et seq.] with respect to homeless children, the requirements of subtitle B of title VII of the McKinney-Vento Homeless Assistance Act (42 U.S.C. 11431 et seq.) are met.

(B) Limitation. Subparagraph (A) shall not limit the responsibility of agencies in the State other than the State educational agency to provide, or pay for some or all of the costs of, a free appropriate public education for any child with a disability in the State.

(C) Exception. Notwithstanding subparagraphs (A) and (B), the Governor (or another individual pursuant to State law), consistent with State law, may assign to any public agency in the State the responsibility of ensuring that the requirements of this part [20 USCS §§ 1411 et seq.] are met with respect to children with disabilities who are convicted as adults under State law and incarcerated in adult prisons.

(12) Obligations related to and methods of ensuring services.

(A) Establishing responsibility for services. The Chief Executive Officer of a State or designee of the officer shall ensure that an interagency agreement or other mechanism for interagency coordination is in effect between each public agency described in subparagraph (B) and the State educational agency, in order to ensure that all services described in subparagraph (B)(i) that are needed to ensure a free appropriate public education are provided, including the provision of such services during the pendency of any dispute under clause (iii). Such agreement or mechanism shall include the following:

(i) Agency financial responsibility. An identification of, or a method for defining, the financial responsibility of each agency for providing services described in subparagraph (B)(i) to ensure a free appropriate public education to children with disabilities, provided that the financial responsibility of each public agency described in subparagraph (B), including the State medicaid agency and other public insurers of children with disabilities, shall precede the financial responsibility of the local educational agency (or the State agency responsible for developing the child's IEP).

(ii) Conditions and terms of reimbursement. The conditions, terms, and procedures under which a local educational agency shall be reimbursed by other agencies.

(iii) Interagency disputes. Procedures for resolving interagency disputes (including procedures under which local educational agencies may initiate proceedings) under the agreement or other mechanism to secure reimbursement from other agencies or otherwise implement the provisions of the agreement or mechanism.

(iv) Coordination of services procedures. Policies and procedures for agencies to determine and identify the interagency coordination responsibilities of each agency to promote the coordination and timely and appropriate delivery of services described in subparagraph (B)(i).

(B) Obligation of public agency.

(i) In general. If any public agency other than an educational agency is otherwise obligated under Federal or State law, or assigned responsibility under State policy pursuant to subparagraph (A), to provide or pay for any services that are also considered special education or related services (such as, but not limited to, services described in section 602(1) [20 USCS § 1401(1)] relating to assistive technology devices, 602(2) [20 USCS § 1401(2)] relating to assistive technology services, 602(26) [20 USCS § 1401(26)] relating to related services, 602(33) [20 USCS § 1401(33)] relating to supplementary aids and services, and 602(34) [20 USCS § 1401(34)] relating to transition services) that are necessary for ensuring a free appropriate public education to children with disabilities within the State, such public agency shall fulfill that obligation or responsibility, either directly or through contract or other arrangement pursuant to subparagraph (A) or an agreement pursuant to subparagraph (C).

(ii) Reimbursement for services by public agency. If a public agency other than an educational agency fails to provide or pay for the special education and related services described in clause (i), the local educational agency (or State agency responsible for developing the child's IEP) shall provide or pay for such services to the child. Such local educational agency or State agency is authorized to claim reimbursement for the services from the public agency that failed to provide or pay for such services and such public agency shall reimburse the local educational agency or State agency pursuant to the terms of the interagency agreement or other mechanism described in subparagraph (A)(i) according to the procedures established in such agreement pursuant to subparagraph (A)(ii).

(C) Special rule. The requirements of subparagraph (A) may be met through—

(i) State statute or regulation;

(ii) signed agreements between respective agency officials that clearly identify the responsibilities of each agency relating to the provision of services; or

(iii) other appropriate written methods as determined by the Chief Executive Officer of the State or designee of the officer and approved by the Secretary.

(13) Procedural requirements relating to local educational agency eligibility. The State educational agency will not make a final determination that a local educational agency is not eligible for assistance under this part [20 USCS §§ 1411 et seq.] without first affording that agency reasonable notice and an opportunity for a hearing.

(14) Personnel qualifications.

(A) In general. The State educational agency has established and maintains qualifications to ensure that personnel necessary to carry out this part [20 USCS §§ 1411 et seq.] are appropriately and adequately prepared and trained, including that those personnel have the content knowledge and skills to serve children with disabilities.

(B) Related services personnel and paraprofessionals. The qualifications under subparagraph (A) include qualifications for related services personnel and paraprofessionals that—

(i) are consistent with any State-approved or State-recognized certification, licensing, registration, or other comparable requirements that apply to the professional discipline in which those personnel are providing special education or related services;

(ii) ensure that related services personnel who deliver services in their discipline or profession meet the requirements of clause (i) and have not had certification or licensure requirements waived on an emergency, temporary, or provisional basis; and

(iii) allow paraprofessionals and assistants who are appropriately trained and supervised, in accordance with State law, regulation, or written policy, in meeting the requirements of this part [20 USCS §§ 1411 et seq.] to be used to assist in the provision of special education and related services under this part [20 USCS §§ 1411 et seq.] to children with disabilities.

(C) Qualifications for special education teachers. The qualifications described in subparagraph (A) shall ensure that each person employed as a special education teacher in the State who teaches elementary school, middle school, or secondary school is highly qualified by the deadline established in section 1119(a)(2) of the Elementary and Secondary Education Act of 1965 [20 USCS § 6319(a)(2)].

(D) Policy. In implementing this section, a State shall adopt a policy that includes a requirement that local educational agencies in the State take measurable steps to recruit, hire, train, and retain highly qualified personnel to provide special education and related services under this part [20 USCS §§ 1411 et seq.] to children with disabilities.

(E) Rule of construction. Notwithstanding any other individual right of action that a parent or student may maintain under this part [20 USCS §§ 1411 et seq.], nothing in this paragraph shall be construed to create a right of action on behalf of an individual student for the failure of a particular State educational agency or local educational agency staff person to be highly qualified, or to prevent a parent from filing a complaint about staff qualifications with the State educational agency as provided for under this part [20 USCS §§ 1411 et seq.].

(15) Performance goals and indicators. The State—

(A) has established goals for the performance of children with disabilities in the State that—

(i) promote the purposes of this *title* [20 USCS §§ 1400 et seq.], as stated in section 601(d) [20 USCS § 1400(d)];

(ii) are the same as the State's definition of adequate yearly progress, including the State's objectives for progress by children with disabilities, under section 1111(b)(2)(C) of the Elementary and Secondary Education Act of 1965 [20 USCS § 6311(b)(2)(C)];

(iii) address graduation rates and dropout rates, as well as such other factors as the State may determine; and

(iv) are consistent, to the extent appropriate, with any other goals and standards for children established by the State;

(B) has established performance indicators the State will use to assess progress toward achieving the goals described in subparagraph (A), including measurable annual objectives for progress by children with disabilities under section 1111(b)(2)(C)(v)(II)(cc) of the Elementary and Secondary Education Act of 1965 [20 USCS § 6311(b)(2)(C)(v)(II)(cc)]; and

(C) will annually report to the Secretary and the public on the progress of the State, and of children with disabilities in the State, toward meeting the goals established under subparagraph (A), which may include elements of the reports required under section

1111(h) of the Elementary and Secondary Education Act of 1965 [*20 USCS § 6311(h)*].

(16) Participation in assessments.

(A) In general. All children with disabilities are included in all general State and districtwide assessment programs, including assessments described under section 1111 of the Elementary and Secondary Education Act of 1965 [*20 USCS § 6311*], with appropriate accommodations and alternate assessments where necessary and as indicated in their respective individualized education programs.

(B) Accommodation guidelines. The State (or, in the case of a districtwide assessment, the local educational agency) has developed guidelines for the provision of appropriate accommodations.

(C) Alternate assessments.

(i) In general. The State (or, in the case of a districtwide assessment, the local educational agency) has developed and implemented guidelines for the participation of children with disabilities in alternate assessments for those children who cannot participate in regular assessments under subparagraph (A) with accommodations as indicated in their respective individualized education programs.

(ii) Requirements for alternate assessments. The guidelines under clause (i) shall provide for alternate assessments that—

(I) are aligned with the State's challenging academic content standards and challenging student academic achievement standards; and

(II) if the State has adopted alternate academic achievement standards permitted under the regulations promulgated to carry out section 1111(b)(1) of the Elementary and Secondary Education Act of 1965 [*20 USCS § 6311(b)(1)*], measure the achievement of children with disabilities against those standards.

(iii) Conduct of alternate assessments. The State conducts the alternate assessments described in this subparagraph.

(D) Reports. The State educational agency (or, in the case of a districtwide assessment, the local educational agency) makes available to the public, and reports to the public with the same frequency and in the same detail as it reports on the assessment of nondisabled children, the following:

(i) The number of children with disabilities participating in regular assessments, and the number of those children who were provided accommodations in order to participate in those assessments.

(ii) The number of children with disabilities participating in alternate assessments described in subparagraph (C)(ii)(I).

(iii) The number of children with disabilities participating in alternate assessments described in subparagraph (C)(ii)(II).

(iv) The performance of children with disabilities on regular assessments and on alternate assessments (if the number of children with disabilities participating in those assessments is sufficient to yield statistically reliable information and reporting that information will not reveal personally identifiable information about an individual student), compared with the achievement of all children, including children with disabilities, on those assessments.

(E) Universal design. The State educational agency (or, in the case of a districtwide assessment, the local educational agency) shall, to the extent feasible, use universal design principles in developing and administering any assessments under this paragraph.

(17) Supplementation of State, local, and other Federal funds.

(A) Expenditures. Funds paid to a State under this part [20 USCS §§ 1411 et seq.] will be expended in accordance with all the provisions of this part [20 USCS §§ 1411 et seq.].

(B) Prohibition against commingling. Funds paid to a State under this part [20 USCS §§ 1411 et seq.] will not be commingled with State funds.

(C) Prohibition against supplantation and conditions for waiver by Secretary. Except as provided in section 613 [20 USCS § 1413], funds paid to a State under this part [20 USCS §§ 1411 et seq.] will be used to supplement the level of Federal, State, and local funds (including funds that are not under the direct control of State or local educational agencies) expended for special education and related services provided to children with disabilities under this part [20 USCS §§ 1411 et seq.] and in no case to supplant such Federal, State, and local funds, except that, where the State provides clear and convincing evidence that all children with disabilities have available to them a free appropriate public education, the Secretary may waive, in whole or in part, the requirements of this subparagraph if the Secretary concurs with the evidence provided by the State.

(18) Maintenance of State financial support.

(A) In general. The State does not reduce the amount of State financial support for special education and related services for children with disabilities, or otherwise made available because of the excess costs of educating those children, below the amount of that support for the preceding fiscal year.

(B) Reduction of funds for failure to maintain support. The Secretary shall reduce the allocation of funds under section 611 [20 USCS § 1411] for any fiscal year following the fiscal year in which the State fails to comply with the requirement of subparagraph (A) by the same amount by which the State fails to meet the requirement.

(C) Waivers for exceptional or uncontrollable circumstances. The Secretary may waive the requirement of subparagraph (A) for a State, for 1 fiscal year at a time, if the Secretary determines that—

(i) granting a waiver would be equitable due to exceptional or uncontrollable circumstances such as a natural disaster or a precipitous and unforeseen decline in the financial resources of the State; or

(ii) the State meets the standard in paragraph (17)(C) for a waiver of the requirement to supplement, and not to supplant, funds received under this part [20 USCS §§ 1411 et seq.].

(D) Subsequent years. If, for any year, a State fails to meet the requirement of subparagraph (A), including any year for which the State is granted a waiver under subparagraph (C), the financial support required of the State in future years under subparagraph (A) shall be the amount that would have been required in the absence of that failure and not the reduced level of the State's support.

(19) Public participation. Prior to the adoption of any policies and procedures needed to comply with this section (including any amendments to such policies and procedures), the State ensures that there are public hearings, adequate notice of the hearings, and an opportunity for comment available to the general public, including individuals with disabilities and parents of children with disabilities.

(20) Rule of construction. In complying with paragraphs (17) and (18), a State may not use funds paid to it under this part [20 USCS §§ 1411 et. seq.] to satisfy State-law mandated funding obligations to local educational agencies, including funding based on student attendance or enrollment, or inflation.

(21) State advisory panel.

(A) In general. The State has established and maintains an advisory panel for the purpose of providing policy guidance with respect to special education and related services for children with disabilities in the State.

(B) Membership. Such advisory panel shall consist of members appointed by the Governor, or any other official authorized under State law to make such appointments, be representative of the State population, and be composed of individuals involved in, or concerned with, the education of children with disabilities, including—

(i) parents of children with disabilities (ages birth through 26);

(ii) individuals with disabilities;

(iii) teachers;

(iv) representatives of institutions of higher education that prepare special education and related services personnel;

(v) State and local education officials, including officials who carry out activities under subtitle B of title VII of the McKinney-Vento Homeless Assistance Act (*42 U.S.C. 11431 et seq.*);

(vi) administrators of programs for children with disabilities;

(vii) representatives of other State agencies involved in the financing or delivery of related services to children with disabilities;

(viii) representatives of private schools and public charter schools;

(ix) not less than 1 representative of a vocational, community, or business organization concerned with the provision of transition services to children with disabilities;

(x) a representative from the State child welfare agency responsible for foster care; and

(xi) representatives from the State juvenile and adult corrections agencies.

(C) Special rule. A majority of the members of the panel shall be individuals with disabilities or parents of children with disabilities (ages birth through 26).

(D) Duties. The advisory panel shall—

(i) advise the State educational agency of unmet needs within the State in the education of children with disabilities;

(ii) comment publicly on any rules or regulations proposed by the State regarding the education of children with disabilities;

(iii) advise the State educational agency in developing evaluations and reporting on data to the Secretary under section 618 [*20 USCS § 1418*];

(iv) advise the State educational agency in developing corrective action plans to address findings identified in Federal monitoring reports under this part [*20 USCS §§ 1411 et seq.*]; and

(v) advise the State educational agency in developing and implementing policies relating to the coordination of services for children with disabilities.

(22) Suspension and expulsion rates.

(A) In general. The State educational agency examines data, including data disaggregated by race and ethnicity, to determine if significant discrepancies are occurring in the rate of long-term suspensions and expulsions of children with disabilities—

(i) among local educational agencies in the State; or

(ii) compared to such rates for nondisabled children within such agencies.

(B) Review and revision of policies. If such discrepancies are occurring, the State educational agency reviews and, if appropriate, revises (or requires the affected State or local educational agency to revise) its policies, procedures, and practices relating to the development and implementation of IEPs, the use of positive behavioral interventions and supports, and procedural safeguards, to ensure that such policies, procedures, and practices comply with this *title [20 USCS §§ 1400* et seq.].

(23) Access to instructional materials.

(A) In general. The State adopts the National Instructional Materials Accessibility Standard for the purposes of providing instructional materials to blind persons or other persons with print disabilities, in a timely manner after the publication of the National Instructional Materials Accessibility Standard in the Federal Register.

(B) Rights of State educational agency. Nothing in this paragraph shall be construed to require any State educational agency to coordinate with the National Instructional Materials Access Center. If a State educational agency chooses not to coordinate with the National Instructional Materials Access Center, such agency shall provide an assurance to the Secretary that the agency will provide instructional materials to blind persons or other persons with print disabilities in a timely manner.

(C) Preparation and delivery of files. If a State educational agency chooses to coordinate with the National Instructional Materials Access Center, not later than 2 years after the date of enactment of the Individuals with Disabilities Education Improvement Act of 2004 [enacted Dec. 3, 2004], the agency, as part of any print instructional materials adoption process, procurement contract, or other practice or instrument used for purchase of print instructional materials, shall enter into a written contract with the publisher of the print instructional materials to—

(i) require the publisher to prepare and, on or before delivery of the print instructional materials, provide to the National Instructional Materials Access Center electronic files containing the contents of the print instructional materials using the National Instructional Materials Accessibility Standard; or

(ii) purchase instructional materials from the publisher that are produced in, or may be rendered in, specialized formats.

(D) Assistive technology. In carrying out this paragraph, the State educational agency, to the maximum extent possible, shall work collaboratively with the State agency responsible for assistive technology programs.

(E) Definitions. In this paragraph:

(i) National Instructional Materials Access Center. The term "National Instructional Materials Access Center" means the center established pursuant to section 674(e) [*20 USCS § 1474(e)*].

(ii) National Instructional Materials Accessibility Standard. The term "National Instructional Materials Accessibility Standard" has the meaning given the term in section 674(e)(3)(A) [*20 USCS § 1474(e)(3)(A)*].

(iii) Specialized formats. The term "specialized formats" has the meaning given the term in section 674(e)(3)(D) [*20 USCS § 1474(e)(3)(D)*].

(24) Overidentification and disproportionality. The State has in effect, consistent with the purposes of this *title [20 USCS §§ 1400* et seq.] and with section 618(d) [*20 USCS § 1418(d)*], policies and procedures designed to prevent the inappropriate overidentification or disproportionate representation by race and ethnicity of children as children with disabilities, including children with disabilities with a particular impairment described in section 602 [*20 USCS § 1401*].

(25) Prohibition on mandatory medication.

(A) In general. The State educational agency shall prohibit State and local educational agency personnel from requiring a child to obtain a prescription for a substance covered by the Controlled Substances Act (*21 U.S.C. 801* et seq.) as a condition of attending school, receiving an evaluation under subsection (a) or (c) of section 614 [*20 USCS § 1414*], or receiving services under this *title [20 USCS §§ 1400* et seq.].

(B) Rule of construction. Nothing in subparagraph (A) shall be construed to create a Federal prohibition against teachers and other school personnel consulting or sharing classroom-based observations with parents or guardians regarding a student's academic and functional performance, or behavior in the classroom or school, or regarding the need for evaluation for special education or related services under paragraph (3).

(b) State educational agency as provider of free appropriate public education or direct services. If the State educational agency provides free appropriate public education to children with disabilities, or provides direct services to such children, such agency—

(1) shall comply with any additional requirements of section 613(a) [*20 USCS § 1413(a)*], as if such agency were a local educational agency; and

(2) may use amounts that are otherwise available to such agency under this part [*20 USCS §§ 1411* et seq.] to serve those children without regard to section 613(a)(2)(A)(i) [*20 USCS § 1413(a)(2)(A)(i)*] (relating to excess costs).

(c) Exception for prior State plans.

(1) In general. If a State has on file with the Secretary policies and procedures that demonstrate that such State meets any requirement of subsection (a), including any policies and procedures filed under this part [*20 USCS §§ 1411* et seq.] as in effect before the effective date of the Individuals with Disabilities Education Improvement Act of 2004, the Secretary shall consider such State to have met such requirement for purposes of receiving a grant under this part [*20 USCS §§ 1411* et seq.].

(2) Modifications made by State. Subject to paragraph (3), an application submitted by a State in accordance with this section shall remain in effect until the State submits to the Secretary such modifications as the State determines necessary. This section shall apply to a modification to an application to the same extent and in the same manner as this section applies to the original plan.

(3) Modifications required by the Secretary. If, after the effective date of the Individuals with Disabilities Education Improvement Act of 2004, the provisions of this *title [20 USCS §§ 1400* et seq.] are amended (or the regulations developed to carry out this *title [20 USCS §§ 1400* et seq.] are amended), there is a new interpretation of this *title [20 USCS §§ 1400* et seq.] by a Federal court or a State's highest court, or there is an official finding of noncompliance with Federal law or regulations, then the Secretary may require a State to modify its application only to the extent necessary to ensure the State's compliance with this part [*20 USCS §§ 1411* et seq.].

(d) Approval by the Secretary.

(1) In general. If the Secretary determines that a State is eligible to receive a grant under this part [*20 USCS §§ 1411* et seq.], the Secretary shall notify the State of that determination.

(2) Notice and hearing. The Secretary shall not make a final determination that a State is not eligible to receive a grant under this part [*20 USCS §§ 1411* et seq.] until after providing the State—

(A) with reasonable notice; and

(B) with an opportunity for a hearing.

(e) Assistance under other Federal programs. Nothing in this *title [20 USCS §§ 1400* et seq.] permits a State to reduce medical and other assistance available, or to alter eligibility, under titles V and XIX of the Social Security Act [*42 USCS §§ 701* et seq. and

1396 et seq.] with respect to the provision of a free appropriate public education for children with disabilities in the State.

(f) By-pass for children in private schools.

(1) In general. If, on the date of enactment of the Education of the Handicapped Act Amendments of 1983 [enacted Dec. 2, 1983], a State educational agency was prohibited by law from providing for the equitable participation in special programs of children with disabilities enrolled in private elementary schools and secondary schools as required by subsection (a)(10)(A), or if the Secretary determines that a State educational agency, local educational agency, or other entity has substantially failed or is unwilling to provide for such equitable participation, then the Secretary shall, notwithstanding such provision of law, arrange for the provision of services to such children through arrangements that shall be subject to the requirements of such subsection.

(2) Payments.

(A) Determination of amounts. If the Secretary arranges for services pursuant to this subsection, the Secretary, after consultation with the appropriate public and private school officials, shall pay to the provider of such services for a fiscal year an amount per child that does not exceed the amount determined by dividing—

(i) the total amount received by the State under this part [20 USCS §§ 1411 et seq.] for such fiscal year; by

(ii) the number of children with disabilities served in the prior year, as reported to the Secretary by the State under section 618 [20 USCS § 1418].

(B) Withholding of certain amounts. Pending final resolution of any investigation or complaint that may result in a determination under this subsection, the Secretary may withhold from the allocation of the affected State educational agency the amount the Secretary estimates will be necessary to pay the cost of services described in subparagraph (A).

(C) Period of payments. The period under which payments are made under subparagraph (A) shall continue until the Secretary determines that there will no longer be any failure or inability on the part of the State educational agency to meet the requirements of subsection (a)(10)(A).

(3) Notice and hearing.

(A) In general. The Secretary shall not take any final action under this subsection until the State educational agency affected by such action has had an opportunity, for not less than 45 days after receiving written notice thereof, to submit written objections and to appear before the Secretary or the Secretary's designee to show cause why such action should not be taken.

(B) Review of action. If a State educational agency is dissatisfied with the Secretary's final action after a proceeding under subparagraph (A), such agency may, not later than 60 days after notice of such action, file with the United States court of appeals for the circuit in which such State is located a petition for review of that action. A copy of the petition shall be forthwith transmitted by the clerk of the court to the Secretary. The Secretary thereupon shall file in the court the record of the proceedings on which the Secretary based the Secretary's action, as provided in section 2112 of title 28, United States Code [28 USCS § 2112].

(C) Review of findings of fact. The findings of fact by the Secretary, if supported by substantial evidence, shall be conclusive, but the court, for good cause shown, may remand the case to the Secretary to take further evidence, and the Secretary may thereupon make new or modified findings of fact and may modify the Secretary's previous action, and shall file in the court the record of the further proceedings. Such new or modified findings of fact shall likewise be conclusive if supported by substantial evidence.

(D) Jurisdiction of court of appeals; review by United States Supreme Court. Upon the filing of a petition under subparagraph (B), the United States court of appeals shall have jurisdiction to affirm the action of the Secretary or to set it aside, in whole or in part. The judgment of the court shall be subject to review by the Supreme Court of the United States upon certiorari or certification as provided in section 1254 of title 28, United States Code [*28 USCS § 1254*].

§ 1413. Local educational agency eligibility

(a) In general. A local educational agency is eligible for assistance under this part [*20 USCS §§ 1411 et seq.*] for a fiscal year if such agency submits a plan that provides assurances to the State educational agency that the local educational agency meets each of the following conditions:

(1) Consistency with State policies. The local educational agency, in providing for the education of children with disabilities within its jurisdiction, has in effect policies, procedures, and programs that are consistent with the State policies and procedures established under section 612 [*20 USCS § 1412*].

(2) Use of amounts.

(A) In general. Amounts provided to the local educational agency under this part [*20 USCS §§ 1411 et seq.*] shall be expended in accordance with the applicable provisions of this part [*20 USCS §§ 1411 et seq.*] and—

(i) shall be used only to pay the excess costs of providing special education and related services to children with disabilities;

(ii) shall be used to supplement State, local, and other Federal funds and not to supplant such funds; and

(iii) shall not be used, except as provided in subparagraphs (B) and (C), to reduce the level of expenditures for the education of children with disabilities made by the local educational agency from local funds below the level of those expenditures for the preceding fiscal year.

(B) Exception. Notwithstanding the restriction in subparagraph (A)(iii), a local educational agency may reduce the level of expenditures where such reduction is attributable to—

(i) the voluntary departure, by retirement or otherwise, or departure for just cause, of special education personnel;

(ii) a decrease in the enrollment of children with disabilities;

(iii) the termination of the obligation of the agency, consistent with this part [*20 USCS §§ 1411 et seq.*], to provide a program of special education to a particular child with a disability that is an exceptionally costly program, as determined by the State educational agency, because the child—

(I) has left the jurisdiction of the agency;

(II) has reached the age at which the obligation of the agency to provide a free appropriate public education to the child has terminated; or

(III) no longer needs such program of special education; or

(iv) the termination of costly expenditures for long-term purchases, such as the acquisition of equipment or the construction of school facilities.

(C) Adjustment to local fiscal effort in certain fiscal years.

(i) Amounts in excess. Notwithstanding clauses (ii) and (iii) of subparagraph (A), for any fiscal year for which the allocation received by a local educational agency under section 611(f) [20 USCS § 1411(f)] exceeds the amount the local educational agency received for the previous fiscal year, the local educational agency may reduce the level of expenditures otherwise required by subparagraph (A)(iii) by not more than 50 percent of the amount of such excess.

(ii) Use of amounts to carry out activities under ESEA. If a local educational agency exercises the authority under clause (i), the agency shall use an amount of local funds equal to the reduction in expenditures under clause (i) to carry out activities authorized under the Elementary and Secondary Education Act of 1965.

(iii) State prohibition. Notwithstanding clause (i), if a State educational agency determines that a local educational agency is unable to establish and maintain programs of free appropriate public education that meet the requirements of subsection (a) or the State educational agency has taken action against the local educational agency under section 616 [20 USCS § 1416], the State educational agency shall prohibit the local educational agency from reducing the level of expenditures under clause (i) for that fiscal year.

(iv) Special rule. The amount of funds expended by a local educational agency under subsection (f) shall count toward the maximum amount of expenditures such local educational agency may reduce under clause (i).

(D) Schoolwide programs under Title I of the ESEA. Notwithstanding subparagraph (A) or any other provision of this part [20 USCS §§ 1411 et seq.], a local educational agency may use funds received under this part [20 USCS §§ 1411 et seq.] for any fiscal year to carry out a schoolwide program under section 1114 of the Elementary and Secondary Education Act of 1965 [20 USCS § 6314], except that the amount so used in any such program shall not exceed—

(i) the number of children with disabilities participating in the schoolwide program; multiplied by

(ii) (I) the amount received by the local educational agency under this part [20 USCS §§ 1411 et seq.] for that fiscal year; divided by

(II) the number of children with disabilities in the jurisdiction of that agency.

(3) Personnel development. The local educational agency shall ensure that all personnel necessary to carry out this part [20 USCS §§ 1411 et seq.] are appropriately and adequately prepared, subject to the requirements of section 612(a)(14) [20 USCS § 1412(a)(14)] and section 2122 of the Elementary and Secondary Education Act of 1965 [20 USCS § 6612].

(4) Permissive use of funds.

(A) Uses. Notwithstanding paragraph (2)(A) or section 612(a)(17)(B) [20 USCS § 1412(a)(17)(B)] (relating to commingled funds), funds provided to the local educational agency under this part [20 USCS §§ 1411 et seq.] may be used for the following activities:

(i) Services and aids that also benefit nondisabled children. For the costs of special education and related services, and supplementary aids and services, provided in a regular class or other education-related setting to a child with a disability in accordance with the individualized education program of the child, even if 1 or more nondisabled children benefit from such services.

(ii) Early intervening services. To develop and implement coordinated, early intervening educational services in accordance with subsection (f).

(iii) High cost education and related services. To establish and implement cost or risk sharing funds, consortia, or cooperatives for the local educational agency itself, or for local educational agencies working in a consortium of which the local educational agency is a part, to pay for high cost special education and related services.

(B) Administrative case management. A local educational agency may use funds received under this part [20 USCS §§ 1411 et seq.] to purchase appropriate technology for recordkeeping, data collection, and related case management activities of teachers and related services personnel providing services described in the individualized education program of children with disabilities, that is needed for the implementation of such case management activities.

(5) Treatment of charter schools and their students. In carrying out this part [20 USCS §§ 1411 et seq.] with respect to charter schools that are public schools of the local educational agency, the local educational agency—

(A) serves children with disabilities attending those charter schools in the same manner as the local educational agency serves children with disabilities in its other schools, including providing supplementary and related services on site at the charter school to the same extent to which the local educational agency has a policy or practice of providing such services on the site to its other public schools; and

(B) provides funds under this part [20 USCS §§ 1411 et seq.] to those charter schools—

(i) on the same basis as the local educational agency provides funds to the local educational agency's other public schools, including proportional distribution based on relative enrollment of children with disabilities; and

(ii) at the same time as the agency distributes other Federal funds to the agency's other public schools, consistent with the State's charter school law.

(6) Purchase of instructional materials.

(A) In general. Not later than 2 years after the date of enactment of the Individuals with Disabilities Education Improvement Act of 2004 [enacted Dec. 3, 2004], a local educational agency that chooses to coordinate with the National Instructional Materials Access Center, when purchasing print instructional materials, shall acquire the print instructional materials in the same manner and subject to the same conditions as a State educational agency acquires print instructional materials under section 612(a)(23) [20 USCS § 1412(a)(23)].

(B) Rights of local educational agency. Nothing in this paragraph shall be construed to require a local educational agency to coordinate with the National Instructional Materials Access Center. If a local educational agency chooses not to coordinate with the National Instructional Materials Access Center, the local educational agency shall provide an assurance to the State educational agency that the local educational agency will provide instructional materials to blind persons or other persons with print disabilities in a timely manner.

(7) Information for State educational agency. The local educational agency shall provide the State educational agency with information necessary to enable the State educational agency to carry out its duties under this part [20 USCS §§ 1411 et seq.], including, with respect to paragraphs (15) and (16) of section 612(a) [20 USCS § 1412(a)], information relating to the performance of children with disabilities participating in programs carried out under this part [20 USCS §§ 1411 et seq.].

(8) Public information. The local educational agency shall make available to parents of children with disabilities and to the general public all documents relating to the eligibility of such agency under this part [20 USCS §§ 1411 et seq.].

(9) Records regarding migratory children with disabilities. The local educational agency shall cooperate in the Secretary's efforts under section 1308 of the Elementary and Secondary Education Act of 1965 [20 USCS § 6398] to ensure the linkage of records pertaining to migratory children with a disability for the purpose of electronically exchanging, among the States, health and educational information regarding such children.

(b) Exception for prior local plans.

(1) In general. If a local educational agency or State agency has on file with the State educational agency policies and procedures that demonstrate that such local educational agency, or such State agency, as the case may be, meets any requirement of subsection (a), including any policies and procedures filed under this part [20 USCS §§ 1411 et seq.] as in effect before the effective date of the Individuals with Disabilities Education Improvement Act of 2004, the State educational agency shall consider such local educational agency or State agency, as the case may be, to have met such requirement for purposes of receiving assistance under this part [20 USCS §§ 1411 et seq.].

(2) Modification made by local educational agency. Subject to paragraph (3), an application submitted by a local educational agency in accordance with this section shall remain in effect until the local educational agency submits to the State educational agency such modifications as the local educational agency determines necessary.

(3) Modifications required by State educational agency. If, after the effective date of the Individuals with Disabilities Education Improvement Act of 2004, the provisions of this *title [20 USCS §§ 1400* et seq.] are amended (or the regulations developed to carry out this *title [20 USCS §§ 1400* et seq.] are amended), there is a new interpretation of this *title [20 USCS §§ 1400* et seq.] by Federal or State courts, or there is an official finding of noncompliance with Federal or State law or regulations, then the State educational agency may require a local educational agency to modify its application only to the extent necessary to ensure the local educational agency's compliance with this part [20 USCS §§ 1411 et seq.] or State law.

(c) Notification of local educational agency or State agency in case of ineligibility. If the State educational agency determines that a local educational agency or State agency is not eligible under this section, then the State educational agency shall notify the local educational agency or State agency, as the case may be, of that determination and shall provide such local educational agency or State agency with reasonable notice and an opportunity for a hearing.

(d) Local educational agency compliance.

(1) In general. If the State educational agency, after reasonable notice and an opportunity for a hearing, finds that a local educational agency or State agency that has been determined to be eligible under this section is failing to comply with any requirement described in subsection (a), the State educational agency shall reduce or shall not provide any further payments to the local educational agency or State agency until the State educational agency is satisfied that the local educational agency or State agency, as the case may be, is complying with that requirement.

(2) Additional requirement. Any State agency or local educational agency in receipt of a notice described in paragraph (1) shall, by means of public notice, take such measures as may be necessary to bring the pendency of an action pursuant to this subsection to the attention of the public within the jurisdiction of such agency.

(3) Consideration. In carrying out its responsibilities under paragraph (1), the State educational agency shall consider any decision made in a hearing held under section 615 [20 USCS § 1415] that is adverse to the local educational agency or State agency involved in that decision.

(e) Joint establishment of eligibility.

(1) Joint establishment.

(A) In general. A State educational agency may require a local educational agency to establish its eligibility jointly with another local educational agency if the State educational agency determines that the local educational agency will be ineligible under this section because the local educational agency will not be able to establish and maintain programs of sufficient size and scope to effectively meet the needs of children with disabilities.

(B) Charter school exception. A State educational agency may not require a charter school that is a local educational agency to jointly establish its eligibility under subparagraph (A) unless the charter school is explicitly permitted to do so under the State's charter school law.

(2) Amount of payments. If a State educational agency requires the joint establishment of eligibility under paragraph (1), the total amount of funds made available to the affected local educational agencies shall be equal to the sum of the payments that each such local educational agency would have received under section 611(f) [20 USCS § 1411(f)] if such agencies were eligible for such payments.

(3) Requirements. Local educational agencies that establish joint eligibility under this subsection shall—

(A) adopt policies and procedures that are consistent with the State's policies and procedures under section 612(a) [20 USCS § 1412(a)]; and

(B) be jointly responsible for implementing programs that receive assistance under this part [20 USCS §§ 1411 et seq.].

(4) Requirements for educational service agencies.

(A) In general. If an educational service agency is required by State law to carry out programs under this part [20 USCS §§ 1411 et seq.], the joint responsibilities given to local educational agencies under this subsection shall—

(i) not apply to the administration and disbursement of any payments received by that educational service agency; and

(ii) be carried out only by that educational service agency.

(B) Additional requirement. Notwithstanding any other provision of this subsection, an educational service agency shall provide for the education of children with disabilities in the least restrictive environment, as required by section 612(a)(5) [20 USCS § 1412(a)(5)].

(f) Early intervening services.

(1) In general. A local educational agency may not use more than 15 percent of the amount such agency receives under this part [20 USCS §§ 1411 et seq.] for any fiscal year, less any amount reduced by the agency pursuant to subsection (a)(2)(C), if any, in combination with other amounts (which may include amounts other than education funds), to develop and implement coordinated, early intervening services, which may include interagency financing structures, for students in kindergarten through grade 12 (with a particular emphasis on students in kindergarten through grade 3) who have not been identified as needing special education or related services but who need additional academic and behavioral support to succeed in a general education environment.

(2) Activities. In implementing coordinated, early intervening services under this subsection, a local educational agency may carry out activities that include—

(A) professional development (which may be provided by entities other than local educational agencies) for teachers and other school staff to enable such personnel to deliver scientifically based academic instruction and behavioral interventions, including scientifically based literacy instruction, and, where appropriate, instruction on the use of adaptive and instructional software; and

(B) providing educational and behavioral evaluations, services, and supports, including scientifically based literacy instruction.

(3) Construction. Nothing in this subsection shall be construed to limit or create a

right to a free appropriate public education under this part [20 USCS §§ 1411 et seq.].

(4) Reporting. Each local educational agency that develops and maintains coordinated, early intervening services under this subsection shall annually report to the State educational agency on—

(A) the number of students served under this subsection; and

(B) the number of students served under this subsection who subsequently receive special education and related services under this *title [20 USCS §§ 1400* et seq.] during the preceding 2-year period.

(5) Coordination with Elementary and Secondary Education Act of 1965. Funds made available to carry out this subsection may be used to carry out coordinated, early intervening services aligned with activities funded by, and carried out under, the Elementary and Secondary Education Act of 1965 if such funds are used to supplement, and not supplant, funds made available under the Elementary and Secondary Education Act of 1965 for the activities and services assisted under this subsection.

(g) Direct services by the State educational agency.

(1) In general. A State educational agency shall use the payments that would otherwise have been available to a local educational agency or to a State agency to provide special education and related services directly to children with disabilities residing in the area served by that local educational agency, or for whom that State agency is responsible, if the State educational agency determines that the local educational agency or State agency, as the case may be—

(A) has not provided the information needed to establish the eligibility of such local educational agency or State agency under this section;

(B) is unable to establish and maintain programs of free appropriate public education that meet the requirements of subsection (a);

(C) is unable or unwilling to be consolidated with 1 or more local educational agencies in order to establish and maintain such programs; or

(D) has 1 or more children with disabilities who can best be served by a regional or State program or service delivery system designed to meet the needs of such children.

(2) Manner and location of education and services. The State educational agency may provide special education and related services under paragraph (1) in such manner and at such locations (including regional or State centers) as the State educational agency considers appropriate. Such education and services shall be provided in accordance with this part [*20 USCS §§ 1411* et seq.].

(h) State agency eligibility. Any State agency that desires to receive a subgrant for any fiscal year under section 611(f) [*20 USCS § 1411(f)*] shall demonstrate to the satisfaction of the State educational agency that—

(1) all children with disabilities who are participating in programs and projects funded under this part [*20 USCS §§ 1411* et seq.] receive a free appropriate public education, and that those children and their parents are provided all the rights and procedural safeguards described in this part [*20 USCS §§ 1411* et seq.]; and

(2) the agency meets such other conditions of this section as the Secretary determines to be appropriate.

(i) Disciplinary information. The State may require that a local educational agency include in the records of a child with a disability a statement of any current or previous disciplinary action that has been taken against the child and transmit such statement to the same extent that such disciplinary information is included in, and transmitted with, the student records of nondisabled children. The statement may include a description of any behavior engaged in by the child that required disciplinary action, a description of the disciplinary action taken, and any other information that is relevant to the safety of the child and other individuals involved with the child. If the State adopts such a policy, and the child transfers from 1 school to another, the transmission of any of the child's records shall include both the child's current individualized education program and any such statement of current or previous disciplinary action that has been taken against the child.

(j) State agency flexibility.

(1) Adjustment to State fiscal effort in certain fiscal years. For any fiscal year for which the allotment received by a State under section 611 [20 USCS § 1411] exceeds the amount the State received for the previous fiscal year and if the State in school year 2003-2004 or any subsequent school year pays or reimburses all local educational agencies within the State from State revenue 100 percent of the non-Federal share of the costs of special education and related services, the State educational agency, notwithstanding paragraphs (17) and (18) of section 612(a) [20 USCS § 1412(a)] and *section 612(b)* [20 USCS § 1412(b)], may reduce the level of expenditures from State sources for the education of children with disabilities by not more than 50 percent of the amount of such excess.

(2) Prohibition. Notwithstanding paragraph (1), if the Secretary determines that a State educational agency is unable to establish, maintain, or oversee programs of free appropriate public education that meet the requirements of this part [20 USCS §§ 1411 et seq.], or that the State needs assistance, intervention, or substantial intervention under section 616(d)(2)(A) [20 USCS § 1416(d)(2)(A)], the Secretary shall prohibit the State educational agency from exercising the authority in paragraph (1).

(3) Education activities. If a State educational agency exercises the authority under paragraph (1), the agency shall use funds from State sources, in an amount equal to the amount of the reduction under paragraph (1), to support activities authorized under the Elementary and Secondary Education Act of 1965 or to support need based student or teacher higher education programs.

(4) Report. For each fiscal year for which a State educational agency exercises the authority under paragraph (1), the State educational agency shall report to the Secretary the amount of expenditures reduced pursuant to such paragraph and the activities that were funded pursuant to paragraph (3).

(5) Limitation. Notwithstanding paragraph (1), a State educational agency may not reduce the level of expenditures described in paragraph (1) if any local educational agency in the State would, as a result of such reduction, receive less than 100 percent of the amount necessary to ensure that all children with disabilities served by the local educational agency receive a free appropriate public education from the combination of Federal funds received under this *title* [20 USCS §§ 1400 et seq.] and State funds received from the State educational agency.

§ 1414. Evaluations, eligibility determinations, individualized education programs, and educational placements

(a) Evaluations, parental consent, and reevaluations.

(1) Initial evaluations.

(A) In general. A State educational agency, other State agency, or local educational agency shall conduct a full and individual initial evaluation in accordance with this paragraph and subsection (b), before the initial provision of special education and related services to a child with a disability under this part [20 USCS §§ 1411 et seq.].

(B) Request for initial evaluation. Consistent with subparagraph (D), either a parent of a child, or a State educational agency, other State agency, or local educational agency may initiate a request for an initial evaluation to determine if the child is a child with a disability.

(C) Procedures.

(i) In general. Such initial evaluation shall consist of procedures—

(I) to determine whether a child is a child with a disability (as defined in section 602 [20 USCS § 1401]) within 60 days of receiving parental consent for the evaluation, or, if the State establishes a timeframe within which the evaluation must be conducted, within such timeframe; and

(II) to determine the educational needs of such child.

(ii) Exception. The relevant timeframe in clause (i)(I) shall not apply to a local educational agency if—

(I) a child enrolls in a school served by the local educational agency after the relevant timeframe in clause (i)(I) has begun and prior to a determination by the child's previous local educational agency as to whether the child is a child with a disability (as defined in section 602 [20 USCS § 1401]), but only if the subsequent local educational agency is making sufficient progress to ensure a prompt completion of the evaluation, and the parent and subsequent local educational agency agree to a specific time when the evaluation will be completed; or

(II) the parent of a child repeatedly fails or refuses to produce the child for the evaluation.

(D) Parental consent.

(i) In general.

(I) Consent for initial evaluation. The agency proposing to conduct an initial evaluation to determine if the child qualifies as a child with a disability as defined in section 602 [20 USCS § 1401] shall obtain informed consent from the parent of such child before conducting the evaluation. Parental consent for evaluation shall not be construed as consent for placement for receipt of special education and related services.

(II) Consent for services. An agency that is responsible for making a free appropriate public education available to a child with a disability under this part [20 USCS §§ 1411 et seq.] shall seek to obtain informed consent from the parent of such child before providing special education and related services to the child.

(ii) Absence of consent.

(I) For initial evaluation. If the parent of such child does not provide consent for an initial evaluation under clause (i)(I), or the parent fails to respond to a request to provide the consent, the local educational agency may pursue the initial evaluation of the child by utilizing the procedures described in section 615 [20 USCS § 1415], except to the extent inconsistent with State law relating to such parental consent.

(II) For services. If the parent of such child refuses to consent to services under clause (i)(II), the local educational agency shall not provide special education and related services to the child by utilizing the procedures described in section 615 [20 USCS § 1415].

(III) Effect on agency obligations. If the parent of such child refuses to consent to the receipt of special education and related services, or the parent fails to respond to a request to provide such consent—

(aa) the local educational agency shall not be considered to be in violation of the requirement to make available a free appropriate public education to the child for the failure to provide such child with the special education and related services for which the local educational agency requests such consent; and (bb) the local educational agency shall not be required to convene an IEP meeting or develop an IEP under this section for the child for the special education and related services for which the local educational agency requests such consent.

(iii) Consent for wards of the State.

(I) In general. If the child is a ward of the State and is not residing with the child's parent, the agency shall make reasonable efforts to obtain the informed consent from the parent (as defined in section 602 [20 USCS § 1401]) of the child for an initial evaluation to determine whether the child is a child with a disability.

(II) Exception. The agency shall not be required to obtain informed consent from the parent of a child for an initial evaluation to determine whether the child is a child with a disability if—

(aa) despite reasonable efforts to do so, the agency cannot discover the whereabouts of the parent of the child;

(bb) the rights of the parents of the child have been terminated in accordance with State law; or

(cc) the rights of the parent to make educational decisions have been subrogated by a judge in accordance with State law and consent for an initial evaluation has been given by an individual appointed by the judge to represent the child.

(E) Rule of construction. The screening of a student by a teacher or specialist to determine appropriate instructional strategies for curriculum implementation shall not be considered to be an evaluation for eligibility for special education and related services.

(2) Reevaluations.

(A) In general. A local educational agency shall ensure that a reevaluation of each child with a disability is conducted in accordance with subsections (b) and (c)—

(i) if the local educational agency determines that the educational or related services needs, including improved academic achievement and functional performance, of the child warrant a reevaluation; or

(ii) if the child's parents or teacher requests a reevaluation.

(B) Limitation. A reevaluation conducted under subparagraph (A) shall occur—

(i) not more frequently than once a year, unless the parent and the local educational agency agree otherwise; and

(ii) at least once every 3 years, unless the parent and the local educational agency agree that a reevaluation is unnecessary.

(b) Evaluation procedures.

(1) Notice. The local educational agency shall provide notice to the parents of a child with a disability, in accordance with subsections (b)(3), (b)(4), and (c) of section 615 [20 USCS § 1415], that describes any evaluation procedures such agency proposes to conduct.

(2) Conduct of evaluation. In conducting the evaluation, the local educational agency shall—

(A) use a variety of assessment tools and strategies to gather relevant functional, developmental, and academic information, including information provided by the parent, that may assist in determining—

(i) whether the child is a child with a disability; and

(ii) the content of the child's individualized education program, including information related to enabling the child to be involved in and progress in the general education curriculum, or, for preschool children, to participate in appropriate activities;

(B) not use any single measure or assessment as the sole criterion for determining whether a child is a child with a disability or determining an appropriate educational program for the child; and

(C) use technically sound instruments that may assess the relative contribution of cognitive and behavioral factors, in addition to physical or developmental factors.

(3) Additional requirements. Each local educational agency shall ensure that—

(A) assessments and other evaluation materials used to assess a child under this section—

(i) are selected and administered so as not to be discriminatory on a racial or cultural basis;

(ii) are provided and administered in the language and form most likely to yield accurate information on what the child knows and can do academically, developmentally, and functionally, unless it is not feasible to so provide or administer;

(iii) are used for purposes for which the assessments or measures are valid and reliable;

(iv) are administered by trained and knowledgeable personnel; and

(v) are administered in accordance with any instructions provided by the producer of such assessments;

(B) the child is assessed in all areas of suspected disability;

(C) assessment tools and strategies that provide relevant information that directly assists persons in determining the educational needs of the child are provided; and

(D) assessments of children with disabilities who transfer from 1 school district to another school district in the same academic year are coordinated with such children's prior and subsequent schools, as necessary and as expeditiously as possible, to ensure prompt completion of full evaluations.

(4) Determination of eligibility and educational need. Upon completion of the administration of assessments and other evaluation measures—

(A) the determination of whether the child is a child with a disability as defined in section 602(3) [*20 USCS § 1401(3)*] and the educational needs of the child shall be made by a team of qualified professionals and the parent of the child in accordance with paragraph (5); and

(B) a copy of the evaluation report and the documentation of determination of eligibility shall be given to the parent.

(5) Special rule for eligibility determination. In making a determination of eligibility under paragraph (4)(A), a child shall not be determined to be a child with a disability if the determinant factor for such determination is—

(A) lack of appropriate instruction in reading, including in the essential components of reading instruction (as defined in section 1208(3) of the Elementary and Secondary Education Act of 1965 [*20 USCS § 6368(3)*]);

(B) lack of instruction in math; or

(C) limited English proficiency.

(6) Specific learning disabilities.

(A) In general. Notwithstanding section 607(b) [*20 USCS § 1406(b)*], when determining whether a child has a specific learning disability as defined in section 602 [*20 USCS § 1401*], a local educational agency shall not be required to take into consideration whether a child has a severe discrepancy between achievement and intellectual ability in oral expression, listening comprehension, written expression, basic reading skill, reading comprehension, mathematical calculation, or mathematical reasoning.

(B) Additional authority. In determining whether a child has a specific learning disability, a local educational agency may use a process that determines if the child responds to scientific, research-based intervention as a part of the evaluation procedures described in paragraphs (2) and (3).

(c) Additional requirements for evaluation and reevaluations.

(1) Review of existing evaluation data. As part of an initial evaluation (if appropriate) and as part of any reevaluation under this section, the IEP Team and other qualified professionals, as appropriate, shall—

(A) review existing evaluation data on the child, including—

(i) evaluations and information provided by the parents of the child;

(ii) current classroom-based, local, or State assessments, and classroom-based observations; and

(iii) observations by teachers and related services providers; and

(B) on the basis of that review, and input from the child's parents, identify what additional data, if any, are needed to determine—

(i) whether the child is a child with a disability as defined in section 602(3) [*20 USCS § 1401(3)*], and the educational needs of the child, or, in case of a reevaluation of a child, whether the child continues to have such a disability and such educational needs;

(ii) the present levels of academic achievement and related developmental needs of the child;

(iii) whether the child needs special education and related services, or in the case of a reevaluation of a child, whether the child continues to need special education and related services; and

(iv) whether any additions or modifications to the special education and related services are needed to enable the child to meet the measurable annual goals set out in the individualized education program of the child and to participate, as appropriate, in the general education curriculum.

(2) Source of data. The local educational agency shall administer such assessments and other evaluation measures as may be needed to produce the data identified by the IEP Team under paragraph (1)(B).

(3) Parental consent. Each local educational agency shall obtain informed parental consent, in accordance with subsection (a)(1)(D), prior to conducting any reevaluation of a child with a disability, except that such informed parental consent need not be obtained if the local educational agency can demonstrate that it had taken reasonable measures to obtain such consent and the child's parent has failed to respond.

(4) Requirements if additional data are not needed. If the IEP Team and other qualified professionals, as appropriate, determine that no additional data are needed to determine whether the child continues to be a child with a disability and to determine the child's educational needs, the local educational agency—

(A) shall notify the child's parents of—

(i) that determination and the reasons for the determination; and

(ii) the right of such parents to request an assessment to determine whether the child continues to be a child with a disability and to determine the child's educational needs; and

(B) shall not be required to conduct such an assessment unless requested to by the child's parents.

(5) Evaluations before change in eligibility.

(A) In general. Except as provided in subparagraph (B), a local educational agency shall evaluate a child with a disability in accordance with this section before determining that the child is no longer a child with a disability.

(B) Exception.

(i) In general. The evaluation described in subparagraph (A) shall not be required before the termination of a child's eligibility under this part [20 USCS §§ 1411 et seq.] due to graduation from secondary school with a regular diploma, or due to exceeding the age eligibility for a free appropriate public education under State law.

(ii) Summary of performance. For a child whose eligibility under this part [20 USCS §§ 1411 et seq.] terminates under circumstances described in clause (i), a local educational agency shall provide the child with a summary of the child's academic achievement and functional performance, which shall include recommendations on how to assist the child in meeting the child's postsecondary goals.

(d) Individualized education programs.

(1) Definitions. In this *title [20 USCS §§ 1400 et seq.]*:

(A) Individualized education program.

(i) In general. The term "individualized education program" or "IEP" means a written statement for each child with a disability that is developed, reviewed, and revised in accordance with this section and that includes—

(I) a statement of the child's present levels of academic achievement and functional performance, including—

(aa) how the child's disability affects the child's involvement and progress in the general education curriculum;

(bb) for preschool children, as appropriate, how the disability affects the child's participation in appropriate activities; and

(cc) for children with disabilities who take alternate assessments aligned to alternate achievement standards, a description of benchmarks or short-term objectives;

(II) a statement of measurable annual goals, including academic and functional goals, designed to—

(aa) meet the child's needs that result from the child's disability to enable the child to be involved in and make progress in the general education curriculum; and

(bb) meet each of the child's other educational needs that result from the child's disability;

(III) a description of how the child's progress toward meeting the annual goals described in subclause (II) will be measured and when periodic reports on the progress the child is making toward meeting the annual goals (such as through the use of quarterly or other periodic reports, concurrent with the issuance of report cards) will be provided;

(IV) a statement of the special education and related services and supplementary aids and services, based on peer-reviewed research to the extent practicable, to be provided to the child, or on behalf of the child, and a statement of the program modifications or supports for school personnel that will be provided for the child—

(aa) to advance appropriately toward attaining the annual goals;

(bb) to be involved in and make progress in the general education curriculum in accordance with subclause (I) and to participate in extracurricular and other nonacademic activities; and

(cc) to be educated and participate with other children with disabilities and nondisabled children in the activities described in this subparagraph;

(V) an explanation of the extent, if any, to which the child will not participate with nondisabled children in the regular class and in the activities described in subclause (IV)(cc);

(VI) (aa) a statement of any individual appropriate accommodations that are necessary to measure the academic achievement and functional performance of the child on State and districtwide assessments consistent with section 612(a)(16)(A) [20 USCS § 1412(a)(16)(A)]; and

(bb) if the IEP Team determines that the child shall take an alternate assessment on a particular State or districtwide assessment of student achievement, a statement of why—

(AA) the child cannot participate in the regular assessment; and

(BB) the particular alternate assessment selected is appropriate for the child;

(VII) the projected date for the beginning of the services and modifications described in subclause (IV), and the anticipated frequency, location, and duration of those services and modifications; and

(VIII) beginning not later than the first IEP to be in effect when the child is 16, and updated annually thereafter—

(aa) appropriate measurable postsecondary goals based upon age appropriate transition assessments related to training, education, employment, and, where appropriate, independent living skills;

(bb) the transition services (including courses of study) needed to assist the child in reaching those goals; and

(cc) beginning not later than 1 year before the child reaches the age of majority under State law, a statement that the child has been informed of the child's rights under this *title [20 USCS §§ 1400* et seq.], if any, that will transfer to the child on reaching the age of majority under section 615(m) [*20 USCS § 1415(m)*].

(ii) Rule of construction. Nothing in this section shall be construed to require—

(I) that additional information be included in a child's IEP beyond what is explicitly required in this section; and

(II) the IEP Team to include information under 1 component of a child's IEP that is already contained under another component of such IEP.

(B) Individualized education program team. The term "individualized education program team" or "IEP Team" means a group of individuals composed of—

(i) the parents of a child with a disability;

(ii) not less than 1 regular education teacher of such child (if the child is, or may be, participating in the regular education environment);

(iii) not less than 1 special education teacher, or where appropriate, not less than 1 special education provider of such child;

(iv) a representative of the local educational agency who—

(I) is qualified to provide, or supervise the provision of, specially designed instruction to meet the unique needs of children with disabilities;

(II) is knowledgeable about the general education curriculum; and

(III) is knowledgeable about the availability of resources of the local educational agency;

(v) an individual who can interpret the instructional implications of evaluation results, who may be a member of the team described in clauses (ii) through (vi);

(vi) at the discretion of the parent or the agency, other individuals who have knowledge or special expertise regarding the child, including related services personnel as appropriate; and

(vii) whenever appropriate, the child with a disability.

(C) IEP team attendance.

(i) Attendance not necessary. A member of the IEP Team shall not be required to attend an IEP meeting, in whole or in part, if the parent of a child with a disability and the local educational agency agree that the attendance of such member is not necessary because the member's area of the curriculum or related services is not being modified or discussed in the meeting.

(ii) Excusal. A member of the IEP Team may be excused from attending an IEP meeting, in whole or in part, when the meeting involves a modification to or discussion of the member's area of the curriculum or related services, if—

(I) the parent and the local educational agency consent to the excusal; and

(II) the member submits, in writing to the parent and the IEP Team, input into the development of the IEP prior to the meeting.

(iii) Written agreement and consent required. A parent's agreement under clause (i) and consent under clause (ii) shall be in writing.

(D) IEP team transition. In the case of a child who was previously served under part C [20 USCS §§ 1431 et seq.], an invitation to the initial IEP meeting shall, at the request of the parent, be sent to the part C service coordinator or other representatives of the part C system to assist with the smooth transition of services.

(2) Requirement that program be in effect.

(A) In general. At the beginning of each school year, each local educational agency, State educational agency, or other State agency, as the case may be, shall have in effect, for each child with a disability in the agency's jurisdiction, an individualized education program, as defined in paragraph (1)(A).

(B) Program for child aged 3 through 5. In the case of a child with a disability aged 3 through 5 (or, at the discretion of the State educational agency, a 2-year-old child with a disability who will turn age 3 during the school year), the IEP Team shall consider the individualized family service plan that contains the material described in section 636 [20 USCS § 1436], and that is developed in accordance with this section, and the individualized family service plan may serve as the IEP of the child if using that plan as the IEP is—

(i) consistent with State policy; and

(ii) agreed to by the agency and the child's parents.

(C) Program for children who transfer school districts.

(i) In general.

(I) Transfer within the same State. In the case of a child with a disability who transfers school districts within the same academic year, who enrolls in a new school, and who had an IEP that was in effect in the same State, the local educational agency shall provide such child with a free appropriate public education, including services comparable to those described in the previously held IEP, in consultation with the parents until such time as the local educational agency adopts the previously held IEP or develops, adopts, and implements a new IEP that is consistent with Federal and State law.

(II) Transfer outside State. In the case of a child with a disability who transfers school districts within the same academic year, who enrolls in a new school, and who had an IEP that was in effect in another State, the local educational agency shall provide such child with a free appropriate public education, including services comparable to those described in the previously held IEP, in consultation with the parents until such time as the local educational agency conducts an evaluation pursuant to subsection (a)(1), if determined to be necessary by such agency, and develops a new IEP, if appropriate, that is consistent with Federal and State law.

(ii) Transmittal of records. To facilitate the transition for a child described in clause (i)—

(I) the new school in which the child enrolls shall take reasonable steps to promptly obtain the child's records, including the IEP and supporting documents and any other records relating to the provision of special education or related services to the child, from the previous school in which the child was enrolled, pursuant to *section 99.31(a)(2) of title 34, Code of Federal Regulations*; and

(II) the previous school in which the child was enrolled shall take reasonable steps to promptly respond to such request from the new school.

(3) Development of IEP.

(A) In general. In developing each child's IEP, the IEP Team, subject to subparagraph (C), shall consider—

(i) the strengths of the child;

(ii) the concerns of the parents for enhancing the education of their child;

(iii) the results of the initial evaluation or most recent evaluation of the child; and

(iv) the academic, developmental, and functional needs of the child.

(B) Consideration of special factors. The IEP Team shall—

(i) in the case of a child whose behavior impedes the child's learning or that of others, consider the use of positive behavioral interventions and supports, and other strategies, to address that behavior;

(ii) in the case of a child with limited English proficiency, consider the language needs of the child as such needs relate to the child's IEP;

(iii) in the case of a child who is blind or visually impaired, provide for instruction in Braille and the use of Braille unless the IEP Team determines, after an evaluation of the child's reading and writing skills, needs, and appropriate reading and writing media (including an evaluation of the child's future needs for instruction in Braille or the use of Braille), that instruction in Braille or the use of Braille is not appropriate for the child;

(iv) consider the communication needs of the child, and in the case of a child who is deaf or hard of hearing, consider the child's language and communication needs, opportunities for direct communications with peers and professional personnel in the child's language and communication mode, academic level, and full range of needs, including opportunities for direct instruction in the child's language and communication mode; and

(v) consider whether the child needs assistive technology devices and services.

(C) Requirement with respect to regular education teacher. A regular education teacher of the child, as a member of the IEP Team, shall, to the extent appropriate, participate in the development of the IEP of the child, including the determination of appropriate positive behavioral interventions and supports, and other strategies, and the determination of supplementary aids and services, program modifications, and support for school personnel consistent with paragraph (1)(A)(i)(IV).

(D) Agreement. In making changes to a child's IEP after the annual IEP meeting for a school year, the parent of a child with a disability and the local educational agency may agree not to convene an IEP meeting for the purposes of making such changes, and instead may develop a written document to amend or modify the child's current IEP.

(E) Consolidation of IEP team meetings. To the extent possible, the local educational agency shall encourage the consolidation of reevaluation meetings for the child and other IEP Team meetings for the child.

(F) Amendments. Changes to the IEP may be made either by the entire IEP Team or, as provided in subparagraph (D), by amending the IEP rather than by redrafting the entire IEP. Upon request, a parent shall be provided with a revised copy of the IEP with the amendments incorporated.

(4) Review and revision of IEP.

(A) In general. The local educational agency shall ensure that, subject to subparagraph (B), the IEP Team—

(i) reviews the child's IEP periodically, but not less frequently than annually, to determine whether the annual goals for the child are being achieved; and

(ii) revises the IEP as appropriate to address—

(I) any lack of expected progress toward the annual goals and in the general education curriculum, where appropriate;

(II) the results of any reevaluation conducted under this section;

(III) information about the child provided to, or by, the parents, as described in subsection (c)(1)(B);

(IV) the child's anticipated needs; or

(V) other matters.

(B) Requirement with respect to regular education teacher. A regular education teacher of the child, as a member of the IEP Team, shall, consistent with paragraph (1)(C), participate in the review and revision of the IEP of the child.

(5) Multi-year IEP demonstration.

(A) Pilot program.

(i) Purpose. The purpose of this paragraph is to provide an opportunity for States to allow parents and local educational agencies the opportunity for long-term planning by offering the option of developing a comprehensive multi-year IEP, not to exceed 3 years, that is designed to coincide with the natural transition points for the child.

(ii) Authorization. In order to carry out the purpose of this paragraph, the Secretary is authorized to approve not more than 15 proposals from States to carry out the activity described in clause (i).

(iii) Proposal.

(I) In general. A State desiring to participate in the program under this paragraph shall submit a proposal to the Secretary at such time and in such manner as the Secretary may reasonably require.

(II) Content. The proposal shall include—

(aa) assurances that the development of a multi-year IEP under this paragraph is optional for parents;

(bb) assurances that the parent is required to provide informed consent before a comprehensive multi-year IEP is developed;

(cc) a list of required elements for each multi-year IEP, including—

(AA) measurable goals pursuant to paragraph (1)(A)(i)(II), coinciding with natural transition points for the child, that will enable the child to be involved in and make progress in the general education curriculum and that will meet the child's other needs that result from the child's disability; and

(BB) measurable annual goals for determining progress toward meeting the goals described in subitem (AA); and

(dd) a description of the process for the review and revision of each multi-year IEP, including—

(AA) a review by the IEP Team of the child's multi-year IEP at each of the child's natural transition points;

(BB) in years other than a child's natural transition points, an annual review of the child's IEP to determine the child's current levels of progress and whether the annual goals for the child are being achieved, and a requirement to amend the IEP, as appropriate, to enable the child to continue to meet the measurable goals set out in the IEP;

(CC) if the IEP Team determines on the basis of a review that the child is not making sufficient progress toward the goals described in the multi-year IEP, a requirement that the local educational agency shall ensure that the IEP Team carries out a more thorough review of the IEP in accordance with paragraph (4) within 30 calendar days; and

(DD) at the request of the parent, a requirement that the IEP Team shall conduct a review of the child's multi-year IEP rather than or subsequent to an annual review.

(B) Report. Beginning 2 years after the date of enactment of the Individuals with Disabilities Education Improvement Act of 2004 [enacted Dec. 3, 2004], the Secretary shall submit an annual report to the Committee on Education and the Workforce of the House of Representatives and the Committee on Health, Education, Labor, and Pensions of the Senate regarding the effectiveness of the program under this paragraph and any specific recommendations for broader implementation of such program, including—

(i) reducing—

(I) the paperwork burden on teachers, principals, administrators, and related service providers; and

(II) noninstructional time spent by teachers in complying with this part [20 USCS §§ 1411 et seq.];

(ii) enhancing longer-term educational planning;

(iii) improving positive outcomes for children with disabilities;

(iv) promoting collaboration between IEP Team members; and

(v) ensuring satisfaction of family members.

(C) Definition. In this paragraph, the term "natural transition points" means those periods that are close in time to the transition of a child with a disability from preschool to elementary grades, from elementary grades to middle or junior high school grades, from middle or junior high school grades to secondary school grades, and from secondary school grades to post-secondary activities, but in no case a period longer than 3 years.

(6) Failure to meet transition objectives. If a participating agency, other than the local educational agency, fails to provide the transition services described in the IEP in accordance with paragraph (1)(A)(i)(VIII), the local educational agency shall reconvene the IEP Team to identify alternative strategies to meet the transition objectives for the child set out in the IEP.

(7) Children with disabilities in adult prisons.

(A) In general. The following requirements shall not apply to children with disabilities who are convicted as adults under State law and incarcerated in adult prisons:

(i) The requirements contained in section 612(a)(16) [20 USCS § 1412(a)(16)] and paragraph (1)(A)(i)(VI) (relating to participation of children with disabilities in general assessments).

(ii) The requirements of items (aa) and (bb) of paragraph (1)(A)(i)(VIII) (relating to transition planning and transition services), do not apply with respect to such children whose eligibility under this part [20 USCS §§ 1411 et seq.] will end, because of such children's age, before such children will be released from prison.

(B) Additional requirement. If a child with a disability is convicted as an adult under State law and incarcerated in an adult prison, the child's IEP Team may modify the child's IEP or placement notwithstanding the requirements of sections 612(a)(5)(A) [20 USCS § 1412(a)(5)(A)] and paragraph (1)(A) if the State has demonstrated a bona fide security or compelling penological interest that cannot otherwise be accommodated.

(e) Educational placements. Each local educational agency or State educational agency shall ensure that the parents of each child with a disability are members of any group that makes decisions on the educational placement of their child.

(f) Alternative means of meeting participation. When conducting IEP team meetings and placement meetings pursuant to this section, section 615(e) [20 USCS § 1415(e)], and *section 615(f)(1)(B)* [20 USCS § 1415(f)(1)(B)], and carrying out administrative matters under section 615 [20 USCS § 1415] (such as scheduling, exchange of witness lists, and status conferences), the parent of a child with a disability and a local educational agency may agree to use alternative means of meeting participation, such as video conferences and conference calls.

§ 1414a.   [Omitted]

§ 1415.   Procedural safeguards

(a) Establishment of procedures. Any State educational agency, State agency, or local educational agency that receives assistance under this part [20 USCS §§ 1411 et seq.] shall establish and maintain procedures in accordance with this section to ensure that children with disabilities and their parents are guaranteed procedural safeguards with respect to the provision of a free appropriate public education by such agencies.

(b) Types of procedures. The procedures required by this section shall include the following:

(1) An opportunity for the parents of a child with a disability to examine all records relating to such child and to participate in meetings with respect to the identification,

evaluation, and educational placement of the child, and the provision of a free appropriate public education to such child, and to obtain an independent educational evaluation of the child.

(2)

(A) Procedures to protect the rights of the child whenever the parents of the child are not known, the agency cannot, after reasonable efforts, locate the parents, or the child is a ward of the State, including the assignment of an individual to act as a surrogate for the parents, which surrogate shall not be an employee of the State educational agency, the local educational agency, or any other agency that is involved in the education or care of the child. In the case of—

(i) a child who is a ward of the State, such surrogate may alternatively be appointed by the judge overseeing the child's care provided that the surrogate meets the requirements of this paragraph; and

(ii) an unaccompanied homeless youth as defined in section 725(6) of the McKinney-Vento Homeless Assistance Act (*42 U.S.C. 11434a(6)*), the local educational agency shall appoint a surrogate in accordance with this paragraph.

(B) The State shall make reasonable efforts to ensure the assignment of a surrogate not more than 30 days after there is a determination by the agency that the child needs a surrogate.

(3) Written prior notice to the parents of the child, in accordance with subsection (c)(1), whenever the local educational agency—

(A) proposes to initiate or change; or

(B) refuses to initiate or change, the identification, evaluation, or educational placement of the child, or the provision of a free appropriate public education to the child.

(4) Procedures designed to ensure that the notice required by paragraph (3) is in the native language of the parents, unless it clearly is not feasible to do so.

(5) An opportunity for mediation, in accordance with subsection (e).

(6) An opportunity for any party to present a complaint—

(A) with respect to any matter relating to the identification, evaluation, or educational placement of the child, or the provision of a free appropriate public education to such child; and

(B) which sets forth an alleged violation that occurred not more than 2 years before the date the parent or public agency knew or should have known about the alleged action that forms the basis of the complaint, or, if the State has an explicit time limitation for presenting such a complaint under this part [*20 USCS §§ 1411* et seq.], in such time as the State law allows, except that the exceptions to the timeline described in subsection (f)(3)(D) shall apply to the timeline described in this subparagraph.

(7)

(A) Procedures that require either party, or the attorney representing a party, to provide due process complaint notice in accordance with subsection (c)(2) (which shall remain confidential)—

(i) to the other party, in the complaint filed under paragraph (6), and forward a copy of such notice to the State educational agency; and

(ii) that shall include—

(I) the name of the child, the address of the residence of the child (or available contact information in the case of a homeless child), and the name of the school the child is attending;

(II) in the case of a homeless child or youth (within the meaning of section 725(2) of the McKinney-Vento Homeless Assistance Act (*42 U.S.C. 11434a(2)*)), available contact information for the child and the name of the school the child is attending;

(III) a description of the nature of the problem of the child relating to such proposed initiation or change, including facts relating to such problem; and

(IV) a proposed resolution of the problem to the extent known and available to the party at the time.

(B) A requirement that a party may not have a due process hearing until the party, or the attorney representing the party, files a notice that meets the requirements of subparagraph (A)(ii).

(8) Procedures that require the State educational agency to develop a model form to assist parents in filing a complaint and due process complaint notice in accordance with paragraphs (6) and (7), respectively.

(c) Notification requirements.

(1) Content of prior written notice. The notice required by subsection (b)(3) shall include—

(A) a description of the action proposed or refused by the agency;

(B) an explanation of why the agency proposes or refuses to take the action and a description of each evaluation procedure, assessment, record, or report the agency used as a basis for the proposed or refused action;

(C) a statement that the parents of a child with a disability have protection under the procedural safeguards of this part [*20 USCS §§ 1411* et seq.] and, if this notice is not an initial referral for evaluation, the means by which a copy of a description of the procedural safeguards can be obtained;

(D) sources for parents to contact to obtain assistance in understanding the provisions of this part [*20 USCS §§ 1411* et seq.];

(E) a description of other options considered by the IEP Team and the reason why those options were rejected; and

(F) a description of the factors that are relevant to the agency's proposal or refusal.

(2) Due process complaint notice.

(A) Complaint. The due process complaint notice required under subsection (b)(7)(A) shall be deemed to be sufficient unless the party receiving the notice notifies the hearing officer and the other party in writing that the receiving party believes the notice has not met the requirements of subsection (b)(7)(A).

(B) Response to complaint.

(i) Local educational agency response.

(I) In general. If the local educational agency has not sent a prior written notice to the parent regarding the subject matter contained in the parent's due process complaint notice, such local educational agency shall, within 10 days of receiving the complaint, send to the parent a response that shall include—

(aa) an explanation of why the agency proposed or refused to take the action raised in the complaint;

(bb) a description of other options that the IEP Team considered and the reasons why those options were rejected;

(cc) a description of each evaluation procedure, assessment, record, or report the agency used as the basis for the proposed or refused action; and

(dd) a description of the factors that are relevant to the agency's proposal or refusal.

(II) Sufficiency. A response filed by a local educational agency pursuant to subclause (I) shall not be construed to preclude such local educational agency from asserting that the parent's due process complaint notice was insufficient where appropriate.

(ii) Other party response. Except as provided in clause (i), the non-complaining party shall, within 10 days of receiving the complaint, send to the complaint a response that specifically addresses the issues raised in the complaint.

(C) Timing. The party providing a hearing officer notification under subparagraph (A) shall provide the notification within 15 days of receiving the complaint.

(D) Determination. Within 5 days of receipt of the notification provided under subparagraph (C), the hearing officer shall make a determination on the face of the notice of whether the notification meets the requirements of subsection (b)(7)(A), and shall immediately notify the parties in writing of such determination.

(E) Amended complaint notice.

(i) In general. A party may amend its due process complaint notice only if—

(I) the other party consents in writing to such amendment and is given the opportunity to resolve the complaint through a meeting held pursuant to subsection (f)(1)(B); or

(II) the hearing officer grants permission, except that the hearing officer may only grant such permission at any time not later than 5 days before a due process hearing occurs.

(ii) Applicable timeline. The applicable timeline for a due process hearing under this part [*20 USCS §§ 1411* et seq.] shall recommence at the time the party files an amended notice, including the timeline under subsection (f)(1)(B).

(d) Procedural safeguards notice.

(1) In general.

(A) Copy to parents. A copy of the procedural safeguards available to the parents of a child with a disability shall be given to the parents only 1 time a year, except that a copy also shall be given to the parents—

(i) upon initial referral or parental request for evaluation;

(ii) upon the first occurrence of the filing of a complaint under subsection (b)(6); and

(iii) upon request by a parent.

(B) Internet website. A local educational agency may place a current copy of the procedural safeguards notice on its Internet website if such website exists.

(2) Contents. The procedural safeguards notice shall include a full explanation of the procedural safeguards, written in the native language of the parents (unless it clearly is not feasible to do so) and written in an easily understandable manner, available under this section and under regulations promulgated by the Secretary relating to—

(A) independent educational evaluation;

(B) prior written notice;

(C) parental consent;

(D) access to educational records;

(E) the opportunity to present and resolve complaints, including—

(i) the time period in which to make a complaint;

(ii) the opportunity for the agency to resolve the complaint; and

(iii) the availability of mediation;

(F) the child's placement during pendency of due process proceedings;

(G) procedures for students who are subject to placement in an interim alternative educational setting;

(H) requirements for unilateral placement by parents of children in private schools at public expense;

(I) due process hearings, including requirements for disclosure of evaluation results and recommendations;

(J) State-level appeals (if applicable in that State);

(K) civil actions, including the time period in which to file such actions; and

(L) attorneys' fees.

(e) Mediation.

(1) In general. Any State educational agency or local educational agency that receives assistance under this part [20 USCS §§ 1411 et seq.] shall ensure that procedures are established and implemented to allow parties to disputes involving any matter, including matters arising prior to the filing of a complaint pursuant to subsection (b)(6), to resolve such disputes through a mediation process.

(2) Requirements. Such procedures shall meet the following requirements:

(A) The procedures shall ensure that the mediation process—

(i) is voluntary on the part of the parties;

(ii) is not used to deny or delay a parent's right to a due process hearing under subsection (f), or to deny any other rights afforded under this part [20 USCS §§ 1411 et seq.]; and

(iii) is conducted by a qualified and impartial mediator who is trained in effective mediation techniques.

(B) Opportunity to meet with a disinterested party. A local educational agency or a State agency may establish procedures to offer to parents and schools that choose not to use the mediation process, an opportunity to meet, at a time and location convenient to the parents, with a disinterested party who is under contract with—

(i) a parent training and information center or community parent resource center in the State established under section 671 or 672 [20 USCS § 1471 or 1472]; or

(ii) an appropriate alternative dispute resolution entity, to encourage the use, and explain the benefits, of the mediation process to the parents.

(C) List of qualified mediators. The State shall maintain a list of individuals who are qualified mediators and knowledgeable in laws and regulations relating to the provision of special education and related services.

(D) Costs. The State shall bear the cost of the mediation process, including the costs of meetings described in subparagraph (B).

(E) Scheduling and location. Each session in the mediation process shall be scheduled in a timely manner and shall be held in a location that is convenient to the parties to the dispute.

(F) Written agreement. In the case that a resolution is reached to resolve the complaint through the mediation process, the parties shall execute a legally binding agreement that sets forth such resolution and that—

(i) states that all discussions that occurred during the mediation process shall be confidential and may not be used as evidence in any subsequent due process hearing or civil proceeding;

(ii) is signed by both the parent and a representative of the agency who has the authority to bind such agency; and

(iii) is enforceable in any State court of competent jurisdiction or in a district court of the United States.

(G) Mediation discussions. Discussions that occur during the mediation process shall be confidential and may not be used as evidence in any subsequent due process hearing or civil proceeding.

(f) Impartial due process hearing.

(1) In general.

(A) Hearing. Whenever a complaint has been received under subsection (b)(6) or (k), the parents or the local educational agency involved in such complaint shall have an opportunity for an impartial due process hearing, which shall be conducted by the State educational agency or by the local educational agency, as determined by State law or by the State educational agency.

(B) Resolution session.

(i) Preliminary meeting. Prior to the opportunity for an impartial due process hearing under subparagraph (A), the local educational agency shall convene a meeting with the parents and the relevant member or members of the IEP Team who have specific knowledge of the facts identified in the complaint—

(I) within 15 days of receiving notice of the parents' complaint;

(II) which shall include a representative of the agency who has decisionmaking authority on behalf of such agency;

(III) which may not include an attorney of the local educational agency unless the parent is accompanied by an attorney; and

(IV) where the parents of the child discuss their complaint, and the facts that form the basis of the complaint, and the local educational agency is provided the opportunity to resolve the complaint, unless the parents and the local educational agency agree in writing to waive such meeting, or agree to use the mediation process described in subsection (e).

(ii) Hearing. If the local educational agency has not resolved the complaint to the satisfaction of the parents within 30 days of the receipt of the complaint, the due process hearing may occur, and all of the applicable timelines for a due process hearing under this part [20 USCS §§ 1411 et seq.] shall commence.

(iii) Written settlement agreement. In the case that a resolution is reached to resolve the complaint at a meeting described in clause (i), the parties shall execute a legally binding agreement that is—

(I) signed by both the parent and a representative of the agency who has the authority to bind such agency; and

(II) enforceable in any State court of competent jurisdiction or in a district court of the United States.

(iv) Review period. If the parties execute an agreement pursuant to clause (iii), a party may void such agreement within 3 business days of the agreement's execution.

(2) Disclosure of evaluations and recommendations.

(A) In general. Not less than 5 business days prior to a hearing conducted pursuant to paragraph (1), each party shall disclose to all other parties all evaluations completed by that date, and recommendations based on the offering party's evaluations, that the party intends to use at the hearing.

(B) Failure to disclose. A hearing officer may bar any party that fails to comply with subparagraph (A) from introducing the relevant evaluation or recommendation at the hearing without the consent of the other party.

(3) Limitations on hearing.

(A) Person conducting hearing. A hearing officer conducting a hearing pursuant to paragraph (1)(A) shall, at a minimum—

(i) not be—

(I) an employee of the State educational agency or the local educational agency involved in the education or care of the child; or

(II) a person having a personal or professional interest that conflicts with the person's objectivity in the hearing;

(ii) possess knowledge of, and the ability to understand, the provisions of this *title [20 USCS §§ 1400* et seq.], Federal and State regulations pertaining to this *title [20 USCS §§ 1400* et seq.], and legal interpretations of this *title [20 USCS §§ 1400* et seq.] by Federal and State courts;

(iii) possess the knowledge and ability to conduct hearings in accordance with appropriate, standard legal practice; and

(iv) possess the knowledge and ability to render and write decisions in accordance with appropriate, standard legal practice.

(B) Subject matter of hearing. The party requesting the due process hearing shall not be allowed to raise issues at the due process hearing that were not raised in the notice filed under subsection (b)(7), unless the other party agrees otherwise.

(C) Timeline for requesting hearing. A parent or agency shall request an impartial due process hearing within 2 years of the date the parent or agency knew or should have known about the alleged action that forms the basis of the complaint, or, if the State has an explicit time limitation for requesting such a hearing under this part [*20 USCS §§ 1411* et seq.], in such time as the State law allows.

(D) Exceptions to the timeline. The timeline described in subparagraph (C) shall not apply to a parent if the parent was prevented from requesting the hearing due to—

(i) specific misrepresentations by the local educational agency that it had resolved the problem forming the basis of the complaint; or

(ii) the local educational agency's withholding of information from the parent that was required under this part [*20 USCS §§ 1411* et seq.] to be provided to the parent.

(E) Decision of hearing officer.

(i) In general. Subject to clause (ii), a decision made by a hearing officer shall be made on substantive grounds based on a determination of whether the child received a free appropriate public education.

(ii) Procedural issues. In matters alleging a procedural violation, a hearing officer may find that a child did not receive a free appropriate public education only if the procedural inadequacies—

(I) impeded the child's right to a free appropriate public education;

(II) significantly impeded the parents' opportunity to participate in the decisionmaking process regarding the provision of a free appropriate public education to the parents' child; or

(III) caused a deprivation of educational benefits.

(iii) Rule of construction. Nothing in this subparagraph shall be construed to preclude a hearing officer from ordering a local educational agency to comply with procedural requirements under this section.

(F) Rule of construction. Nothing in this paragraph shall be construed to affect the right of a parent to file a complaint with the State educational agency.

(g) Appeal.

(1) In general. If the hearing required by subsection (f) is conducted by a local educational agency, any party aggrieved by the findings and decision rendered in such a hearing may appeal such findings and decision to the State educational agency.

(2) Impartial review and independent decision. The State educational agency shall conduct an impartial review of the findings and decision appealed under paragraph (1). The officer conducting such review shall make an independent decision upon completion of such review.

(h) Safeguards. Any party to a hearing conducted pursuant to subsection (f) or (k), or an appeal conducted pursuant to subsection (g), shall be accorded—

(1) the right to be accompanied and advised by counsel and by individuals with special knowledge or training with respect to the problems of children with disabilities;

(2) the right to present evidence and confront, cross-examine, and compel the attendance of witnesses;

(3) the right to a written, or, at the option of the parents, electronic verbatim record of such hearing; and

(4) the right to written, or, at the option of the parents, electronic findings of fact and decisions, which findings and decisions—

(A) shall be made available to the public consistent with the requirements of section 617(b) [*20 USCS § 1417(b)*] (relating to the confidentiality of data, information, and records); and

(B) shall be transmitted to the advisory panel established pursuant to section 612(a)(21) [*20 USCS § 1412(a)(21)*].

(i) Administrative procedures.

(1) In general.

(A) Decision made in hearing. A decision made in a hearing conducted pursuant to subsection (f) or (k) shall be final, except that any party involved in such hearing may appeal such decision under the provisions of subsection (g) and paragraph (2).

(B) Decision made at appeal. A decision made under subsection (g) shall be final, except that any party may bring an action under paragraph (2).

(2) Right to bring civil action.

(A) In general. Any party aggrieved by the findings and decision made under subsection (f) or (k) who does not have the right to an appeal under subsection (g), and any party aggrieved by the findings and decision made under this subsection, shall have the right to bring a civil action with respect to the complaint presented pursuant to this section, which action may be brought in any State court of competent jurisdiction or in a district court of the United States, without regard to the amount in controversy.

(B) Limitation. The party bringing the action shall have 90 days from the date of the decision of the hearing officer to bring such an action, or, if the State has an explicit time limitation for bringing such action under this part [20 USCS §§ 1411 et seq.], in such time as the State law allows.

(C) Additional requirements. In any action brought under this paragraph, the court—

(i) shall receive the records of the administrative proceedings;

(ii) shall hear additional evidence at the request of a party; and

(iii) basing its decision on the preponderance of the evidence, shall grant such relief as the court determines is appropriate.

(3) Jurisdiction of district courts; attorneys' fees.

(A) In general. The district courts of the United States shall have jurisdiction of actions brought under this section without regard to the amount in controversy.

(B) Award of attorneys' fees.

(i) In general. In any action or proceeding brought under this section, the court, in its discretion, may award reasonable attorneys' fees as part of the costs—

(I) to a prevailing party who is the parent of a child with a disability;

(II) to a prevailing party who is a State educational agency or local educational agency against the attorney of a parent who files a complaint or subsequent cause of action that is frivolous, unreasonable, or without foundation, or against the attorney of a parent who continued to litigate after the litigation clearly became frivolous, unreasonable, or without foundation; or

(III) to a prevailing State educational agency or local educational agency against the attorney of a parent, or against the parent, if the parent's complaint or subsequent cause of action was presented for any improper purpose, such as to harass, to cause unnecessary delay, or to needlessly increase the cost of litigation.

(ii) Rule of construction. Nothing in this subparagraph shall be construed to affect section 327 of the District of Columbia Appropriations Act, 2005.

(C) Determination of amount of attorneys' fees. Fees awarded under this paragraph shall be based on rates prevailing in the community in which the action or proceeding arose for the kind and quality of services furnished. No bonus or multiplier may be used in calculating the fees awarded under this subsection.

(D) Prohibition of attorneys' fees and related costs for certain services.

(i) In general. Attorneys' fees may not be awarded and related costs may not be reimbursed in any action or proceeding under this section for services performed subsequent to the time of a written offer of settlement to a parent if—

(I) the offer is made within the time prescribed by *Rule 68 of the Federal Rules of Civil Procedure* or, in the case of an administrative proceeding, at any time more than 10 days before the proceeding begins;

(II) the offer is not accepted within 10 days; and

(III) the court or administrative hearing officer finds that the relief finally obtained by the parents is not more favorable to the parents than the offer of settlement.

(ii) IEP team meetings. Attorneys' fees may not be awarded relating to any meeting of the IEP Team unless such meeting is convened as a result of an administrative proceeding or judicial action, or, at the discretion of the State, for a mediation described in subsection (e).

(iii) Opportunity to resolve complaints. A meeting conducted pursuant to subsection (f)(1)(B)(i) shall not be considered—

(I) a meeting convened as a result of an administrative hearing or judicial action; or

(II) an administrative hearing or judicial action for purposes of this paragraph.

(E) Exception to prohibition on attorneys' fees and related costs. Notwithstanding subparagraph (D), an award of attorneys' fees and related costs may be made to a parent who is the prevailing party and who was substantially justified in rejecting the settlement offer.

(F) Reduction in amount of attorneys' fees. Except as provided in subparagraph (G), whenever the court finds that—

(i) the parent, or the parent's attorney, during the course of the action or proceeding, unreasonably protracted the final resolution of the controversy;

(ii) the amount of the attorneys' fees otherwise authorized to be awarded unreasonably exceeds the hourly rate prevailing in the community for similar services by attorneys of reasonably comparable skill, reputation, and experience;

(iii) the time spent and legal services furnished were excessive considering the nature of the action or proceeding; or

(iv) the attorney representing the parent did not provide to the local educational agency the appropriate information in the notice of the complaint described in subsection (b)(7)(A), the court shall reduce, accordingly, the amount of the attorneys' fees awarded under this section.

(G) Exception to reduction in amount of attorneys' fees. The provisions of subparagraph (F) shall not apply in any action or proceeding if the court finds that the State or local educational agency unreasonably protracted the final resolution of the action or proceeding or there was a violation of this section.

(j) Maintenance of current educational placement. Except as provided in subsection (k)(4), during the pendency of any proceedings conducted pursuant to this section, unless the State or local educational agency and the parents otherwise agree, the child shall remain in the then-current educational placement of the child, or, if applying for initial admission to a public school, shall, with the consent of the parents, be placed in the public school program until all such proceedings have been completed.

(k) Placement in alternative educational setting.

(1) Authority of school personnel.

(A) Case-by-case determination. School personnel may consider any unique circumstances on a case-by-case basis when determining whether to order a change in placement for a child with a disability who violates a code of student conduct.

(B) Authority. School personnel under this subsection may remove a child with a disability who violates a code of student conduct from their current placement to an appropriate interim alternative educational setting, another setting, or suspension, for not more than 10 school days (to the extent such alternatives are applied to children without disabilities).

(C) Additional authority. If school personnel seek to order a change in placement that would exceed 10 school days and the behavior that gave rise to the violation of the school code is determined not to be a manifestation of the child's disability pursuant to subparagraph (E), the relevant disciplinary procedures applicable to children without disabilities may be applied to the child in the same manner and for the same duration in which the procedures would be applied to children without disabilities, except as provided in section 612(a)(1) [*20 USCS § 1412(a)(1)*] although it may be provided in an interim alternative educational setting.

(D) Services. A child with a disability who is removed from the child's current placement under subparagraph (G) (irrespective of whether the behavior is determined to be a manifestation of the child's disability) or subparagraph (C) shall—

(i) continue to receive educational services, as provided in section 612(a)(1) [*20 USCS § 1412(a)(1)*], so as to enable the child to continue to participate in the general education curriculum, although in another setting, and to progress toward meeting the goals set out in the child's IEP; and

(ii) receive, as appropriate, a functional behavioral assessment, behavioral intervention services and modifications, that are designed to address the behavior violation so that it does not recur.

(E) Manifestation determination.

(i) In general. Except as provided in subparagraph (B), within 10 school days of any decision to change the placement of a child with a disability because of a violation of a code of student conduct, the local educational agency, the parent, and relevant members of the IEP Team (as determined by the parent and the local educational agency) shall review all relevant information in the student's file, including the child's IEP, any teacher observations, and any relevant information provided by the parents to determine—

(I) if the conduct in question was caused by, or had a direct and substantial relationship to, the child's disability; or

(II) if the conduct in question was the direct result of the local educational agency's failure to implement the IEP.

(ii) Manifestation. If the local educational agency, the parent, and relevant members of the IEP Team determine that either subclause (I) or (II) of clause (i) is applicable for the child, the conduct shall be determined to be a manifestation of the child's disability.

(F) Determination that behavior was a manifestation. If the local educational agency, the parent, and relevant members of the IEP Team make the determination that the conduct was a manifestation of the child's disability, the IEP Team shall—

(i) conduct a functional behavioral assessment, and implement a behavioral intervention plan for such child, provided that the local educational agency had not conducted such assessment prior to such determination before the behavior that resulted in a change in placement described in subparagraph (C) or (G);

(ii) in the situation where a behavioral intervention plan has been developed, review the behavioral intervention plan if the child already has such a behavioral intervention plan, and modify it, as necessary, to address the behavior; and

(iii) except as provided in subparagraph (G), return the child to the placement from which the child was removed, unless the parent and the local educational agency agree to a change of placement as part of the modification of the behavioral intervention plan.

(G) Special circumstances. School personnel may remove a student to an interim alternative educational setting for not more than 45 school days without regard to whether the behavior is determined to be a manifestation of the child's disability, in cases where a child—

(i) carries or possesses a weapon to or at school, on school premises, or to or at a school function under the jurisdiction of a State or local educational agency;

(ii) knowingly possesses or uses illegal drugs, or sells or solicits the sale of a controlled substance, while at school, on school premises, or at a school function under the jurisdiction of a State or local educational agency; or

(iii) has inflicted serious bodily injury upon another person while at school, on school premises, or at a school function under the jurisdiction of a State or local educational agency.

(H) Notification. Not later than the date on which the decision to take disciplinary action is made, the local educational agency shall notify the parents of that decision, and of all procedural safeguards accorded under this section.

(2) Determination of setting. The interim alternative educational setting in subparagraphs (C) and (G) of paragraph (1) shall be determined by the IEP Team.

(3) Appeal.

(A) In general. The parent of a child with a disability who disagrees with any decision regarding placement, or the manifestation determination under this subsection, or a local educational agency that believes that maintaining the current placement of the child is substantially likely to result in injury to the child or to others, may request a hearing.

(B) Authority of hearing officer.

(i) In general. A hearing officer shall hear, and make a determination regarding, an appeal requested under subparagraph (A).

(ii) Change of placement order. In making the determination under clause (i), the hearing officer may order a change in placement of a child with a disability. In such situations, the hearing officer may—

(I) return a child with a disability to the placement from which the child was removed; or

(II) order a change in placement of a child with a disability to an appropriate interim alternative educational setting for not more than 45 school days if the hearing officer determines that maintaining the current placement of such child is substantially likely to result in injury to the child or to others.

(4) Placement during appeals. When an appeal under paragraph (3) has been requested by either the parent or the local educational agency—

(A) the child shall remain in the interim alternative educational setting pending the decision of the hearing officer or until the expiration of the time period provided for in paragraph (1)(C), whichever occurs first, unless the parent and the State or local educational agency agree otherwise; and

(B) the State or local educational agency shall arrange for an expedited hearing, which shall occur within 20 school days of the date the hearing is requested and shall result in a determination within 10 school days after the hearing.

(5) Protections for children not yet eligible for special education and related services.

(A) In general. A child who has not been determined to be eligible for special education and related services under this part [20 USCS §§ 1411 et seq.] and who has engaged in behavior that violates a code of student conduct, may assert any of the protections provided for in this part [20 USCS §§ 1411 et seq.] if the local educational agency had knowledge (as determined in accordance with this paragraph) that the child was a child with a disability before the behavior that precipitated the disciplinary action occurred.

(B) Basis of knowledge. A local educational agency shall be deemed to have knowledge that a child is a child with a disability if, before the behavior that precipitated the disciplinary action occurred—

(i) the parent of the child has expressed concern in writing to supervisory or administrative personnel of the appropriate educational agency, or a teacher of the child, that the child is in need of special education and related services;

(ii) the parent of the child has requested an evaluation of the child pursuant to section 614(a)(1)(B) [20 USCS § 1414(a)(1)(B)]; or

(iii) the teacher of the child, or other personnel of the local educational agency, has expressed specific concerns about a pattern of behavior demonstrated by the child, directly to the director of special education of such agency or to other supervisory personnel of the agency.

(C) Exception. A local educational agency shall not be deemed to have knowledge that the child is a child with a disability if the parent of the child has not allowed an evaluation of the child pursuant to section 614 [20 USCS § 1414] or has refused services under this part [20 USCS §§ 1411 et seq.] or the child has been evaluated and it was determined that the child was not a child with a disability under this part [20 USCS §§ 1411 et seq.].

(D) Conditions that apply if no basis of knowledge.

(i) In general. If a local educational agency does not have knowledge that a child is a child with a disability (in accordance with subparagraph (B) or (C)) prior to taking disciplinary measures against the child, the child may be subjected to disciplinary measures applied to children without disabilities who engaged in comparable behaviors consistent with clause (ii).

(ii) Limitations. If a request is made for an evaluation of a child during the time period in which the child is subjected to disciplinary measures under this subsection, the evaluation shall be conducted in an expedited manner. If the child is determined to be a child with a disability, taking into consideration information from the evaluation conducted by the agency and information provided by the parents, the agency shall provide special education and related services in accordance with this part [20 USCS §§ 1411 et seq.], except that, pending the results of the evaluation, the child shall remain in the educational placement determined by school authorities.

(6) Referral to and action by law enforcement and judicial authorities.

(A) Rule of construction. Nothing in this part [20 USCS §§ 1411 et seq.] shall be construed to prohibit an agency from reporting a crime committed by a child with a disability to appropriate authorities or to prevent State law enforcement and judicial authorities from exercising their responsibilities with regard to the application of Federal and State law to crimes committed by a child with a disability.

(B) Transmittal of records. An agency reporting a crime committed by a child with a disability shall ensure that copies of the special education and disciplinary records of the child are transmitted for consideration by the appropriate authorities to whom the agency reports the crime.

(7) Definitions. In this subsection:

(A) Controlled substance. The term "controlled substance" means a drug or other substance identified under schedule I, II, III, IV, or V in section 202(c) of the Controlled Substances Act (21 U.S.C. 812(c)).

(B) Illegal drug. The term "illegal drug" means a controlled substance but does not include a controlled substance that is legally possessed or used under the supervision of a licensed health-care professional or that is legally possessed or used under any other authority under that Act or under any other provision of Federal law.

(C) Weapon. The term "weapon" has the meaning given the term "dangerous weapon" under *section 930(g)(2) of title 18, United States Code.*

(D) Serious bodily injury. The term "serious bodily injury" has the meaning given the term "serious bodily injury" under paragraph (3) of subsection (h) of *section 1365 of title 18, United States Code.*

(l) Rule of construction. Nothing in this *title [20 USCS §§ 1400 et seq.]* shall be construed to restrict or limit the rights, procedures, and remedies available under the Constitution, the Americans with Disabilities Act of 1990, title V of the Rehabilitation Act of 1973 [*29 USCS §§ 790 et seq.*], or other Federal laws protecting the rights of children with disabilities, except that before the filing of a civil action under such laws seeking relief that is also available under this part [*20 USCS §§ 1411 et seq.*], the procedures under subsections (f) and (g) shall be exhausted to the same extent as would be required had the action been brought under this part [*20 USCS §§ 1411 et seq.*].

(m) Transfer of parental rights at age of majority.

(1) In general. A State that receives amounts from a grant under this part [*20 USCS §§ 1411 et seq.*] may provide that, when a child with a disability reaches the age of majority under State law (except for a child with a disability who has been determined to be incompetent under State law)—

(A) the agency shall provide any notice required by this section to both the individual and the parents;

(B) all other rights accorded to parents under this part [*20 USCS §§ 1411 et seq.*] transfer to the child;

(C) the agency shall notify the individual and the parents of the transfer of rights; and

(D) all rights accorded to parents under this part [*20 USCS §§ 1411 et seq.*] transfer to children who are incarcerated in an adult or juvenile Federal, State, or local correctional institution.

(2) Special rule. If, under State law, a child with a disability who has reached the age of majority under State law, who has not been determined to be incompetent, but who is determined not to have the ability to provide informed consent with respect to the educational program of the child, the State shall establish procedures for appointing the parent of the child, or if the parent is not available, another appropriate individual, to represent the educational interests of the child throughout the period of eligibility of the child under this part [*20 USCS §§ 1411 et seq.*].

(n) Electronic mail. A parent of a child with a disability may elect to receive notices required under this section by an electronic mail (e-mail) communication, if the agency makes such option available.

(o) Separate complaint. Nothing in this section shall be construed to preclude a parent from filing a separate due process complaint on an issue separate from a due process complaint already filed.

§ 1416. Monitoring, technical assistance, and enforcement

(a) Federal and State monitoring.

(1) In general. The Secretary shall—

(A) monitor implementation of this part [*20 USCS §§ 1411 et seq.*] through—

(i) oversight of the exercise of general supervision by the States, as required in section 612(a)(11) [*20 USCS § 1412(a)(11)*]; and

(ii) the State performance plans, described in subsection (b);

(B) enforce this part [*20 USCS §§ 1411 et seq.*] in accordance with subsection (e); and

(C) require States to—

(i) monitor implementation of this part [*20 USCS §§ 1411* et seq.] by local educational agencies; and

(ii) enforce this part [*20 USCS §§ 1411* et seq.] in accordance with paragraph (3) and subsection (e).

(2) Focused monitoring. The primary focus of Federal and State monitoring activities described in paragraph (1) shall be on—

(A) improving educational results and functional outcomes for all children with disabilities; and

(B) ensuring that States meet the program requirements under this part [*20 USCS §§ 1411* et seq.], with a particular emphasis on those requirements that are most closely related to improving educational results for children with disabilities.

(3) Monitoring priorities. The Secretary shall monitor the States, and shall require each State to monitor the local educational agencies located in the State (except the State exercise of general supervisory responsibility), using quantifiable indicators in each of the following priority areas, and using such qualitative indicators as are needed to adequately measure performance in the following priority areas:

(A) Provision of a free appropriate public education in the least restrictive environment.

(B) State exercise of general supervisory authority, including child find, effective monitoring, the use of resolution sessions, mediation, voluntary binding arbitration, and a system of transition services as defined in sections 602(34) and 637(a)(9) [*20 USCS §§ 1401(34)* and *1437(a)(9)*].

(C) Disproportionate representation of racial and ethnic groups in special education and related services, to the extent the representation is the result of inappropriate identification.

(4) Permissive areas of review. The Secretary shall consider other relevant information and data, including data provided by States under section 618 [*20 USCS § 1418*].

(b) State performance plans.

(1) Plan.

(A) In general. Not later than 1 year after the date of enactment of the Individuals with Disabilities Education Improvement Act of 2004 [enacted Dec. 3, 2004], each State shall have in place a performance plan that evaluates that State's efforts to implement the requirements and purposes of this part [*20 USCS §§ 1411* et seq.] and describes how the State will improve such implementation.

(B) Submission for approval. Each State shall submit the State's performance plan to the Secretary for approval in accordance with the approval process described in subsection (c).

(C) Review. Each State shall review its State performance plan at least once every 6 years and submit any amendments to the Secretary.

(2) Targets.

(A) In general. As a part of the State performance plan described under paragraph (1), each State shall establish measurable and rigorous targets for the indicators established under the priority areas described in subsection (a)(3).

(B) Data collection.

(i) In general. Each State shall collect valid and reliable information as needed to report annually to the Secretary on the priority areas described in subsection (a)(3).

(ii) Rule of construction. Nothing in this *title [20 USCS §§ 1400* et seq.] shall be construed to authorize the development of a nationwide database of personally identifiable information on individuals involved in studies or other collections of data under this part [20 USCS §§ 1411 et seq.].

(C) Public reporting and privacy.

(i) In general. The State shall use the targets established in the plan and priority areas described in subsection (a)(3) to analyze the performance of each local educational agency in the State in implementing this part [20 USCS §§ 1411 et seq.].

(ii) Report.

(I) Public report. The State shall report annually to the public on the performance of each local educational agency located in the State on the targets in the State's performance plan. The State shall make the State's performance plan available through public means, including by posting on the website of the State educational agency, distribution to the media, and distribution through public agencies.

(II) State performance report. The State shall report annually to the Secretary on the performance of the State under the State's performance plan.

(iii) Privacy. The State shall not report to the public or the Secretary any information on performance that would result in the disclosure of personally identifiable information about individual children or where the available data is insufficient to yield statistically reliable information.

(c) Approval process.

(1) Deemed approval. The Secretary shall review (including the specific provisions described in subsection (b)) each performance plan submitted by a State pursuant to subsection (b)(1)(B) and the plan shall be deemed to be approved by the Secretary unless the Secretary makes a written determination, prior to the expiration of the 120-day period beginning on the date on which the Secretary received the plan, that the plan does not meet the requirements of this section, including the specific provisions described in subsection (b).

(2) Disapproval. The Secretary shall not finally disapprove a performance plan, except after giving the State notice and an opportunity for a hearing.

(3) Notification. If the Secretary finds that the plan does not meet the requirements, in whole or in part, of this section, the Secretary shall—

(A) give the State notice and an opportunity for a hearing; and

(B) notify the State of the finding, and in such notification shall—

(i) cite the specific provisions in the plan that do not meet the requirements; and

(ii) request additional information, only as to the provisions not meeting the requirements, needed for the plan to meet the requirements of this section.

(4) Response. If the State responds to the Secretary's notification described in paragraph (3)(B) during the 30-day period beginning on the date on which the State received the notification, and resubmits the plan with the requested information described in paragraph (3)(B)(ii), the Secretary shall approve or disapprove such plan prior to the later of—

(A) the expiration of the 30-day period beginning on the date on which the plan is resubmitted; or

(B) the expiration of the 120-day period described in paragraph (1).

(5) Failure to respond. If the State does not respond to the Secretary's notification described in paragraph (3)(B) during the 30-day period beginning on the date on which the State received the notification, such plan shall be deemed to be disapproved.

(d) Secretary's review and determination.

(1) Review. The Secretary shall annually review the State performance report submitted pursuant to subsection (b)(2)(C)(ii)(II) in accordance with this section.

(2) Determination.

(A) In general. Based on the information provided by the State in the State performance report, information obtained through monitoring visits, and any other public information made available, the Secretary shall determine if the State—

(i) meets the requirements and purposes of this part [20 USCS §§ 1411 et seq.];

(ii) needs assistance in implementing the requirements of this part [20 USCS §§ 1411 et seq.];

(iii) needs intervention in implementing the requirements of this part [20 USCS §§ 1411 et seq.]; or

(iv) needs substantial intervention in implementing the requirements of this part [20 USCS §§ 1411 et seq.].

(B) Notice and opportunity for a hearing. For determinations made under clause (iii) or (iv) of subparagraph (A), the Secretary shall provide reasonable notice and an opportunity for a hearing on such determination.

(e) Enforcement.

(1) Needs assistance. If the Secretary determines, for 2 consecutive years, that a State needs assistance under subsection (d)(2)(A)(ii) in implementing the requirements of this part [20 USCS §§ 1411 et seq.], the Secretary shall take 1 or more of the following actions:

(A) Advise the State of available sources of technical assistance that may help the State address the areas in which the State needs assistance, which may include assistance from the Office of Special Education Programs, other offices of the Department of Education, other Federal agencies, technical assistance providers approved by the Secretary, and other federally funded nonprofit agencies, and require the State to work with appropriate entities. Such technical assistance may include—

(i) the provision of advice by experts to address the areas in which the State needs assistance, including explicit plans for addressing the area for concern within a specified period of time;

(ii) assistance in identifying and implementing professional development, instructional strategies, and methods of instruction that are based on scientifically based research;

(iii) designating and using distinguished superintendents, principals, special education administrators, special education teachers, and other teachers to provide advice, technical assistance, and support; and

(iv) devising additional approaches to providing technical assistance, such as collaborating with institutions of higher education, educational service agencies, national centers of technical assistance supported under part D [20 USCS §§ 1450 et seq.], and private providers of scientifically based technical assistance.

(B) Direct the use of State-level funds under section 611(e) [20 USCS § 1411(e)] on the area or areas in which the State needs assistance.

(C) Identify the State as a high-risk grantee and impose special conditions on the State's grant under this part [20 USCS §§ 1411 et seq.].

(2) Needs intervention. If the Secretary determines, for 3 or more consecutive years, that a State needs intervention under subsection (d)(2)(A)(iii) in implementing the requirements of this part [20 USCS §§ 1411 et seq.], the following shall apply:

(A) The Secretary may take any of the actions described in paragraph (1).

(B) The Secretary shall take 1 or more of the following actions:

(i) Require the State to prepare a corrective action plan or improvement plan if the Secretary determines that the State should be able to correct the problem within 1 year.

(ii) Require the State to enter into a compliance agreement under section 457 of the General Education Provisions Act [20 USCS § 1234f], if the Secretary has reason to believe that the State cannot correct the problem within 1 year.

(iii) For each year of the determination, withhold not less than 20 percent and not more than 50 percent of the State's funds under section 611(e) [20 USCS § 1411(e)], until the Secretary determines the State has sufficiently addressed the areas in which the State needs intervention.

(iv) Seek to recover funds under section 452 of the General Education Provisions Act [20 USCS § 1234a].

(v) Withhold, in whole or in part, any further payments to the State under this part [20 USCS §§ 1411 et seq.] pursuant to paragraph (5).

(vi) Refer the matter for appropriate enforcement action, which may include referral to the Department of Justice.

(3) Needs substantial intervention. Notwithstanding paragraph (1) or (2), at any time that the Secretary determines that a State needs substantial intervention in implementing the requirements of this part [20 USCS §§ 1411 et seq.] or that there is a substantial failure to comply with any condition of a State educational agency's or local educational agency's eligibility under this part [20 USCS §§ 1411 et seq.], the Secretary shall take 1 or more of the following actions:

(A) Recover funds under section 452 of the General Education Provisions Act [20 USCS § 1234a].

(B) Withhold, in whole or in part, any further payments to the State under this part [20 USCS §§ 1411 et seq.].

(C) Refer the case to the Office of the Inspector General at the Department of Education.

(D) Refer the matter for appropriate enforcement action, which may include referral to the Department of Justice.

(4) Opportunity for hearing.

(A) Withholding funds. Prior to withholding any funds under this section, the Secretary shall provide reasonable notice and an opportunity for a hearing to the State educational agency involved.

(B) Suspension. Pending the outcome of any hearing to withhold payments under subsection (b), the Secretary may suspend payments to a recipient, suspend the authority of the recipient to obligate funds under this part [20 USCS §§ 1411 et seq.], or both, after such recipient has been given reasonable notice and an opportunity to show cause why future payments or authority to obligate funds under this part [20 USCS §§ 1411 et seq.] should not be suspended.

(5) Report to Congress. The Secretary shall report to the Committee on Education and the Workforce of the House of Representatives and the Committee on Health, Education, Labor, and Pensions of the Senate within 30 days of taking enforcement

action pursuant to paragraph (1), (2), or (3), on the specific action taken and the reasons why enforcement action was taken.

(6) Nature of withholding.

(A) Limitation. If the Secretary withholds further payments pursuant to paragraph (2) or (3), the Secretary may determine—

(i) that such withholding will be limited to programs or projects, or portions of programs or projects, that affected the Secretary's determination under subsection (d)(2); or

(ii) that the State educational agency shall not make further payments under this part [20 USCS §§ 1411 et seq.] to specified State agencies or local educational agencies that caused or were involved in the Secretary's determination under subsection (d)(2).

(B) Withholding until rectified. Until the Secretary is satisfied that the condition that caused the initial withholding has been substantially rectified—

(i) payments to the State under this part [20 USCS §§ 1411 et seq.] shall be withheld in whole or in part; and

(ii) payments by the State educational agency under this part [20 USCS §§ 1411 et seq.] shall be limited to State agencies and local educational agencies whose actions did not cause or were not involved in the Secretary's determination under subsection (d)(2), as the case may be.

(7) Public attention. Any State that has received notice under subsection (d)(2) shall, by means of a public notice, take such measures as may be necessary to bring the pendency of an action pursuant to this subsection to the attention of the public within the State.

(8) Judicial review.

(A) In general. If any State is dissatisfied with the Secretary's action with respect to the eligibility of the State under section 612 [20 USCS § 1412], such State may, not later than 60 days after notice of such action, file with the United States court of appeals for the circuit in which such State is located a petition for review of that action. A copy of the petition shall be transmitted by the clerk of the court to the Secretary. The Secretary thereupon shall file in the court the record of the proceedings upon which the Secretary's action was based, as provided in section 2112 of title 28, United States Code [28 USCS § 2112].

(B) Jurisdiction; review by United States Supreme Court. Upon the filing of such petition, the court shall have jurisdiction to affirm the action of the Secretary or to set it aside, in whole or in part. The judgment of the court shall be subject to review by the Supreme Court of the United States upon certiorari or certification as provided in section 1254 of title 28, United States Code [28 USCS § 1254].

(C) Standard of review. The findings of fact by the Secretary, if supported by substantial evidence, shall be conclusive, but the court, for good cause shown, may remand the case to the Secretary to take further evidence, and the Secretary may thereupon make new or modified findings of fact and may modify the Secretary's previous action, and shall file in the court the record of the further proceedings. Such new or modified findings of fact shall be conclusive if supported by substantial evidence.

(f) State enforcement. If a State educational agency determines that a local educational agency is not meeting the requirements of this part [20 USCS §§ 1411 et seq.], including the targets in the State's performance plan, the State educational agency shall prohibit the local educational agency from reducing the local educational agency's maintenance of effort under section 613(a)(2)(C) [20 USCS § 1413(a)(2)(C)] for any fiscal year.

(g) Rule of construction. Nothing in this section shall be construed to restrict the Secretary from utilizing any authority under the General Education Provisions Act to monitor and enforce the requirements of this *title [20 USCS §§ 1400 et seq.]*.

(h) Divided State agency responsibility. For purposes of this section, where responsibility for ensuring that the requirements of this part *[20 USCS §§ 1411 et seq.]* are met with respect to children with disabilities who are convicted as adults under State law and incarcerated in adult prisons is assigned to a public agency other than the State educational agency pursuant to section 612(a)(11)(C) *[20 USCS § 1412(a)(11)(C)]*, the Secretary, in instances where the Secretary finds that the failure to comply substantially with the provisions of this part *[20 USCS §§ 1411 et seq.]* are related to a failure by the public agency, shall take appropriate corrective action to ensure compliance with this part *[20 USCS §§ 1411 et seq.]*, except that—

(1) any reduction or withholding of payments to the State shall be proportionate to the total funds allotted under section 611 *[20 USCS § 1411]* to the State as the number of eligible children with disabilities in adult prisons under the supervision of the other public agency is proportionate to the number of eligible individuals with disabilities in the State under the supervision of the State educational agency; and

(2) any withholding of funds under paragraph (1) shall be limited to the specific agency responsible for the failure to comply with this part *[20 USCS §§ 1411 et seq.]*.

(i) Data capacity and technical assistance review. The Secretary shall—

(1) review the data collection and analysis capacity of States to ensure that data and information determined necessary for implementation of this section is collected, analyzed, and accurately reported to the Secretary; and

(2) provide technical assistance (from funds reserved under section 611(c) *[20 USCS § 1411(c)]*), where needed, to improve the capacity of States to meet the data collection requirements.

§ 1417. Administration

(a) Responsibilities of Secretary. The Secretary shall—

(1) cooperate with, and (directly or by grant or contract) furnish technical assistance necessary to, a State in matters relating to—

(A) the education of children with disabilities; and

(B) carrying out this part *[20 USCS §§ 1411 et seq.]*; and

(2) provide short-term training programs and institutes.

(b) Prohibition against Federal mandates, direction, or control. Nothing in this *title [20 USCS §§ 1400 et seq.]* shall be construed to authorize an officer or employee of the Federal Government to mandate, direct, or control a State, local educational agency, or school's specific instructional content, academic achievement standards and assessments, curriculum, or program of instruction.

(c) Confidentiality. The Secretary shall take appropriate action, in accordance with section 444 of the General Education Provisions Act *[20 USCS § 1232g]*, to ensure the protection of the confidentiality of any personally identifiable data, information, and records collected or maintained by the Secretary and by State educational agencies and local educational agencies pursuant to this part *[20 USCS §§ 1411 et seq.]*.

(d) Personnel. The Secretary is authorized to hire qualified personnel necessary to carry out the Secretary's duties under subsection (a), under section 618 *[20 USCS § 1418]*, and under subpart 4 of part D *[20 USCS §§ 1481 et seq.]*, without regard to the provisions of title 5, United States Code, relating to appointments in the competitive service and without regard to chapter 51 and subchapter III of chapter 53 of such *title*

[5 USCS §§ 5101 et seq. and 5331 et seq.] relating to classification and general schedule pay rates, except that no more than 20 such personnel shall be employed at any time.

(e) Model forms. Not later than the date that the Secretary publishes final regulations under this *title* [20 USCS §§ 1400 et seq.], to implement amendments made by the Individuals with Disabilities Education Improvement Act of 2004, the Secretary shall publish and disseminate widely to States, local educational agencies, and parent and community training and information centers—

(1) a model IEP form;

(2) a model individualized family service plan (IFSP) form;

(3) a model form of the notice of procedural safeguards described in section 615(d) [20 USCS § 1415(d)]; and

(4) a model form of the prior written notice described in subsections (b)(3) and (c)(1) of section 615 [20 USCS § 1415] that is consistent with the requirements of this part [20 USCS §§ 1411 et seq.] and is sufficient to meet such requirements.

§ 1418. Program information

(a) In general. Each State that receives assistance under this part [20 USCS §§ 1411 et seq.], and the Secretary of the Interior, shall provide data each year to the Secretary of Education and the public on the following:

(1)

(A) The number and percentage of children with disabilities, by race, ethnicity, limited English proficiency status, gender, and disability category, who are in each of the following separate categories:

(i) Receiving a free appropriate public education.

(ii) Participating in regular education.

(iii) In separate classes, separate schools or facilities, or public or private residential facilities.

(iv) For each year of age from age 14 through 21, stopped receiving special education and related services because of program completion (including graduation with a regular secondary school diploma), or other reasons, and the reasons why those children stopped receiving special education and related services.

(v)

(I) Removed to an interim alternative educational setting under section 615(k)(1) [20 USCS § 1415(k)(1)].

(II) The acts or items precipitating those removals.

(III) The number of children with disabilities who are subject to long-term suspensions or expulsions.

(B) The number and percentage of children with disabilities, by race, gender, and ethnicity, who are receiving early intervention services.

(C) The number and percentage of children with disabilities, by race, gender, and ethnicity, who, from birth through age 2, stopped receiving early intervention services because of program completion or for other reasons.

(D) The incidence and duration of disciplinary actions by race, ethnicity, limited English proficiency status, gender, and disability category, of children with disabilities, including suspensions of 1 day or more.

(E) The number and percentage of children with disabilities who are removed to alternative educational settings or expelled as compared to children without disabilities who are removed to alternative educational settings or expelled.

(F) The number of due process complaints filed under section 615 [20 USCS § 1415] and the number of hearings conducted.

(G) The number of hearings requested under section 615(k) [20 USCS § 1415(k)] and the number of changes in placements ordered as a result of those hearings.

(H) The number of mediations held and the number of settlement agreements reached through such mediations.

(2) The number and percentage of infants and toddlers, by race, and ethnicity, who are at risk of having substantial developmental delays (as defined in section 632 [20 USCS § 1432]), and who are receiving early intervention services under part C [20 USCS §§ 1431 et seq.].

(3) Any other information that may be required by the Secretary.

(b) Data reporting.

(1) Protection of identifiable data. The data described in subsection (a) shall be publicly reported by each State in a manner that does not result in the disclosure of data identifiable to individual children.

(2) Sampling. The Secretary may permit States and the Secretary of the Interior to obtain the data described in subsection (a) through sampling.

(c) Technical assistance. The Secretary may provide technical assistance to States to ensure compliance with the data collection and reporting requirements under this *title* [20 USCS §§ 1400 et seq.].

(d) Disproportionality.

(1) In general. Each State that receives assistance under this part [20 USCS §§ 1411 et seq.], and the Secretary of the Interior, shall provide for the collection and examination of data to determine if significant disproportionality based on race and ethnicity is occurring in the State and the local educational agencies of the State with respect to—

(A) the identification of children as children with disabilities, including the identification of children as children with disabilities in accordance with a particular impairment described in section 602(3) [20 USCS § 1401(3)];

(B) the placement in particular educational settings of such children; and

(C) the incidence, duration, and type of disciplinary actions, including suspensions and expulsions.

(2) Review and revision of policies, practices, and procedures. In the case of a determination of significant disproportionality with respect to the identification of children as children with disabilities, or the placement in particular educational settings of such children, in accordance with paragraph (1), the State or the Secretary of the Interior, as the case may be, shall—

(A) provide for the review and, if appropriate, revision of the policies, procedures, and practices used in such identification or placement to ensure that such policies, procedures, and practices comply with the requirements of this *title [20 USCS §§ 1400 et seq.]*;

(B) require any local educational agency identified under paragraph (1) to reserve the maximum amount of funds under section 613(f) [20 USCS § 1413(f)] to provide comprehensive coordinated early intervening services to serve children in the local educational agency, particularly children in those groups that were significantly overidentified under paragraph (1); and

(C) require the local educational agency to publicly report on the revision of policies, practices, and procedures described under subparagraph (A).

§ 1419. Preschool grants

(a) In general. The Secretary shall provide grants under this section to assist States to provide special education and related services, in accordance with this part [20 USCS §§ 1411 et seq.]—

(1) to children with disabilities aged 3 through 5, inclusive; and

(2) at the State's discretion, to 2-year-old children with disabilities who will turn 3 during the school year.

(b) Eligibility. A State shall be eligible for a grant under this section if such State—

(1) is eligible under section 612 [20 USCS § 1412] to receive a grant under this part [20 USCS §§ 1411 et seq.]; and

(2) makes a free appropriate public education available to all children with disabilities, aged 3 through 5, residing in the State.

(c) Allocations to States.

(1) In general. The Secretary shall allocate the amount made available to carry out this section for a fiscal year among the States in accordance with paragraph (2) or (3), as the case may be.

(2) Increase in funds. If the amount available for allocations to States under paragraph (1) for a fiscal year is equal to or greater than the amount allocated to the States under this section for the preceding fiscal year, those allocations shall be calculated as follows:

(A) Allocation.

(i) In general. Except as provided in subparagraph (B), the Secretary shall—

(I) allocate to each State the amount the State received under this section for fiscal year 1997;

(II) allocate 85 percent of any remaining funds to States on the basis of the States' relative populations of children aged 3 through 5; and

(III) allocate 15 percent of those remaining funds to States on the basis of the States' relative populations of all children aged 3 through 5 who are living in poverty.

(ii) Data. For the purpose of making grants under this paragraph, the Secretary shall use the most recent population data, including data on children living in poverty, that are available and satisfactory to the Secretary.

(B) Limitations. Notwithstanding subparagraph (A), allocations under this paragraph shall be subject to the following:

(i) Preceding years. No State's allocation shall be less than its allocation under this section for the preceding fiscal year.

(ii) Minimum. No State's allocation shall be less than the greatest of—

(I) the sum of—

(aa) the amount the State received under this section for fiscal year 1997; and

(bb) 1/3 of 1 percent of the amount by which the amount appropriated under subsection (j) for the fiscal year exceeds the amount appropriated for this section for fiscal year 1997;

(II) the sum of—

(aa) the amount the State received under this section for the preceding fiscal year; and

(bb) that amount multiplied by the percentage by which the increase in the funds appropriated under this section from the preceding fiscal year exceeds 1.5 percent; or

(III) the sum of—

(aa) the amount the State received under this section for the preceding fiscal year; and

(bb) that amount multiplied by 90 percent of the percentage increase in the amount appropriated under this section from the preceding fiscal year.

(iii) Maximum. Notwithstanding clause (ii), no State's allocation under this paragraph shall exceed the sum of—

(I) the amount the State received under this section for the preceding fiscal year; and

(II) that amount multiplied by the sum of 1.5 percent and the percentage increase in the amount appropriated under this section from the preceding fiscal year.

(C) Ratable reductions. If the amount available for allocations under this paragraph is insufficient to pay those allocations in full, those allocations shall be ratably reduced, subject to subparagraph (B)(i).

(3) Decrease in funds. If the amount available for allocations to States under paragraph (1) for a fiscal year is less than the amount allocated to the States under this section for the preceding fiscal year, those allocations shall be calculated as follows:

(A) Allocations. If the amount available for allocations is greater than the amount allocated to the States for fiscal year 1997, each State shall be allocated the sum of—

(i) the amount the State received under this section for fiscal year 1997; and

(ii) an amount that bears the same relation to any remaining funds as the increase the State received under this section for the preceding fiscal year over fiscal year 1997 bears to the total of all such increases for all States.

(B) Ratable reductions. If the amount available for allocations is equal to or less than the amount allocated to the States for fiscal year 1997, each State shall be allocated the amount the State received for fiscal year 1997, ratably reduced, if necessary.

(d) Reservation for State activities.

(1) In general. Each State may reserve not more than the amount described in paragraph (2) for administration and other State-level activities in accordance with subsections (e) and (f).

(2) Amount described. For each fiscal year, the Secretary shall determine and report to the State educational agency an amount that is 25 percent of the amount the State received under this section for fiscal year 1997, cumulatively adjusted by the Secretary for each succeeding fiscal year by the lesser of—

(A) the percentage increase, if any, from the preceding fiscal year in the State's allocation under this section; or

(B) the percentage increase, if any, from the preceding fiscal year in the Consumer Price Index For All Urban Consumers published by the Bureau of Labor Statistics of the Department of Labor.

(e) State administration.

(1) In general. For the purpose of administering this section (including the coordination of activities under this part [20 USCS §§ 1411 et seq.] with, and providing technical assistance to, other programs that provide services to children with disabilities) a State

may use not more than 20 percent of the maximum amount the State may reserve under subsection (d) for any fiscal year.

(2) Administration of part C. Funds described in paragraph (1) may also be used for the administration of part C [20 USCS §§ 1431 et seq.].

(f) Other State-level activities. Each State shall use any funds the State reserves under subsection (d) and does not use for administration under subsection (e)—

(1) for support services (including establishing and implementing the mediation process required by section 615(e) [20 USCS § 1415(e)]), which may benefit children with disabilities younger than 3 or older than 5 as long as those services also benefit children with disabilities aged 3 through 5;

(2) for direct services for children eligible for services under this section;

(3) for activities at the State and local levels to meet the performance goals established by the State under section 612(a)(15) [20 USCS § 1412(a)(15)];

(4) to supplement other funds used to develop and implement a statewide coordinated services system designed to improve results for children and families, including children with disabilities and their families, but not more than 1 percent of the amount received by the State under this section for a fiscal year;

(5) to provide early intervention services (which shall include an educational component that promotes school readiness and incorporates preliteracy, language, and numeracy skills) in accordance with part C [20 USCS §§ 1431 et seq.] to children with disabilities who are eligible for services under this section and who previously received services under part C [20 USCS §§ 1431 et seq.] until such children enter, or are eligible under State law to enter, kindergarten; or

(6) at the State's discretion, to continue service coordination or case management for families who receive services under part C [20 USCS §§ 1431 et seq.].

(g) Subgrants to local educational agencies.

(1) Subgrants required. Each State that receives a grant under this section for any fiscal year shall distribute all of the grant funds that the State does not reserve under subsection (d) to local educational agencies in the State that have established their eligibility under section 613 [20 USCS § 1413], as follows:

(A) Base payments. The State shall first award each local educational agency described in paragraph (1) the amount that agency would have received under this section for fiscal year 1997 if the State had distributed 75 percent of its grant for that year under section 619(c)(3) [20 USCS § 1419(c)(3)], as such section was then in effect.

(B) Allocation of remaining funds. After making allocations under subparagraph (A), the State shall—

(i) allocate 85 percent of any remaining funds to those local educational agencies on the basis of the relative numbers of children enrolled in public and private elementary schools and secondary schools within the local educational agency's jurisdiction; and

(ii) allocate 15 percent of those remaining funds to those local educational agencies in accordance with their relative numbers of children living in poverty, as determined by the State educational agency.

(2) Reallocation of funds. If a State educational agency determines that a local educational agency is adequately providing a free appropriate public education to all children with disabilities aged 3 through 5 residing in the area served by the local educational agency with State and local funds, the State educational agency may reallocate any portion of the funds under this section that are not needed by that local educational agency to provide a free appropriate public education to other local educational agencies in the State that are not adequately providing special education and

related services to all children with disabilities aged 3 through 5 residing in the areas the other local educational agencies serve.

(h) Part C inapplicable. Part C [20 USCS §§ 1431 et seq.] does not apply to any child with a disability receiving a free appropriate public education, in accordance with this part [20 USCS §§ 1411 et seq.], with funds received under this section.

(i) State defined. In this section, the term "State" means each of the 50 States, the District of Columbia, and the Commonwealth of Puerto Rico.

(j) Authorization of appropriations. There are authorized to be appropriated to carry out this section such sums as may be necessary.

§ 1420. [Omitted]

§ 1421. [Repealed]

§ 1422. [Repealed]

§ 1423. [Repealed]

§ 1424. [Repealed]

§ 1424a. [Repealed]

§ 1425. [Repealed]

§ 1426. [Repealed]

§ 1427. [Repealed]

INFANTS AND TODDLERS WITH DISABILITIES

§ 1431. Findings and policy

(a) Findings. Congress finds that there is an urgent and substantial need—

(1) to enhance the development of infants and toddlers with disabilities, to minimize their potential for developmental delay, and to recognize the significant brain development that occurs during a child's first 3 years of life;

(2) to reduce the educational costs to our society, including our Nation's schools, by

minimizing the need for special education and related services after infants and toddlers with disabilities reach school age;

(3) to maximize the potential for individuals with disabilities to live independently in society;

(4) to enhance the capacity of families to meet the special needs of their infants and toddlers with disabilities; and

(5) to enhance the capacity of State and local agencies and service providers to identify, evaluate, and meet the needs of all children, particularly minority, low-income, inner city, and rural children, and infants and toddlers in foster care.

(b) Policy. It is the policy of the United States to provide financial assistance to States—

(1) to develop and implement a statewide, comprehensive, coordinated, multidisciplinary, interagency system that provides early intervention services for infants and toddlers with disabilities and their families;

(2) to facilitate the coordination of payment for early intervention services from Federal, State, local, and private sources (including public and private insurance coverage);

(3) to enhance State capacity to provide quality early intervention services and expand and improve existing early intervention services being provided to infants and toddlers with disabilities and their families; and

(4) to encourage States to expand opportunities for children under 3 years of age who would be at risk of having substantial developmental delay if they did not receive early intervention services.

§ 1432. Definitions

In this part [*20 USCS §§ 1431* et seq.]:

(1) At-risk infant or toddler. The term "at-risk infant or toddler" means an individual under 3 years of age who would be at risk of experiencing a substantial developmental delay if early intervention services were not provided to the individual.

(2) Council. The term "council" means a State interagency coordinating council established under section 641 [*20 USCS § 1441*].

(3) Developmental delay. The term "developmental delay", when used with respect to an individual residing in a State, has the meaning given such term by the State under section 635(a)(1) [*20 USCS § 1435(a)(1)*].

(4) Early intervention services. The term "early intervention services" means developmental services that—

(A) are provided under public supervision;

(B) are provided at no cost except where Federal or State law provides for a system of payments by families, including a schedule of sliding fees;

(C) are designed to meet the developmental needs of an infant or toddler with a disability, as identified by the individualized family service plan team, in any 1 or more of the following areas:

(i) physical development;

(ii) cognitive development;

(iii) communication development;

(iv) social or emotional development; or

(v) adaptive development;

(D) meet the standards of the State in which the services are provided, including the requirements of this part [20 USCS §§ 1431 et seq.];

(E) include—

(i) family training, counseling, and home visits;

(ii) special instruction;

(iii) speech-language pathology and audiology services, and sign language and cued language services;

(iv) occupational therapy;

(v) physical therapy;

(vi) psychological services;

(vii) service coordination services;

(viii) medical services only for diagnostic or evaluation purposes;

(ix) early identification, screening, and assessment services;

(x) health services necessary to enable the infant or toddler to benefit from the other early intervention services;

(xi) social work services;

(xii) vision services;

(xiii) assistive technology devices and assistive technology services; and

(xiv) transportation and related costs that are necessary to enable an infant or toddler and the infant's or toddler's family to receive another service described in this paragraph;

(F) are provided by qualified personnel, including—

(i) special educators;

(ii) speech-language pathologists and audiologists;

(iii) occupational therapists;

(iv) physical therapists;

(v) psychologists;

(vi) social workers;

(vii) nurses;

(viii) registered dietitians;

(ix) family therapists;

(x) vision specialists, including ophthalmologists and optometrists;

(xi) orientation and mobility specialists; and

(xii) pediatricians and other physicians;

(G) to the maximum extent appropriate, are provided in natural environments, including the home, and community settings in which children without disabilities participate; and

(H) are provided in conformity with an individualized family service plan adopted in accordance with section 636 [*20 USCS § 1436*].

(5) Infant or toddler with a disability. The term "infant or toddler with a disability"—

(A) means an individual under 3 years of age who needs early intervention services because the individual—

(i) is experiencing developmental delays, as measured by appropriate diagnostic instruments and procedures in 1 or more of the areas of cognitive development, physical development, communication development, social or emotional development, and adaptive development; or

(ii) has a diagnosed physical or mental condition that has a high probability of resulting in developmental delay; and

(B) may also include, at a State's discretion—

(i) at-risk infants and toddlers; and

(ii) children with disabilities who are eligible for services under section 619 [*20 USCS § 1419*] and who previously received services under this part [*20 USCS §§ 1431 et seq.*] until such children enter, or are eligible under State law to enter, kindergarten or elementary school, as appropriate, provided that any programs under this part [*20 USCS §§ 1431 et seq.*] serving such children shall include—

(I) an educational component that promotes school readiness and incorporates pre-literacy, language, and numeracy skills; and

(II) a written notification to parents of their rights and responsibilities in determining whether their child will continue to receive services under this part [*20 USCS §§ 1431 et seq.*] or participate in preschool programs under section 619 [*20 USCS § 1419*].

§ 1433. General authority

The Secretary shall, in accordance with this part [*20 USCS §§ 1431 et seq.*], make grants to States (from their allotments under section 643 [*20 USCS § 1443*]) to assist each State to maintain and implement a statewide, comprehensive, coordinated, multidisciplinary, interagency system to provide early intervention services for infants and toddlers with disabilities and their families.

§ 1434. Eligibility

In order to be eligible for a grant under section 633 [*20 USCS § 1433*], a State shall provide assurances to the Secretary that the State—

(1) has adopted a policy that appropriate early intervention services are available to all infants and toddlers with disabilities in the State and their families, including Indian infants and toddlers with disabilities and their families residing on a reservation geographically located in the State, infants and toddlers with disabilities who are homeless children and their families, and infants and toddlers with disabilities who are wards of the State; and

(2) has in effect a statewide system that meets the requirements of section 635 [*20 USCS § 1435*].

§ 1435. Requirements for statewide system

(a) In general. A statewide system described in section 633 [*20 USCS § 1433*] shall include, at a minimum, the following components:

(1) A rigorous definition of the term "developmental delay" that will be used by the State in carrying out programs under this part [*20 USCS §§ 1431 et seq.*] in order to appropriately identify infants and toddlers with disabilities that are in need of services

under this part [*20 USCS §§ 1431* et seq.].

(2) A State policy that is in effect and that ensures that appropriate early intervention services based on scientifically based research, to the extent practicable, are available to all infants and toddlers with disabilities and their families, including Indian infants and toddlers with disabilities and their families residing on a reservation geographically located in the State and infants and toddlers with disabilities who are homeless children and their families.

(3) A timely, comprehensive, multidisciplinary evaluation of the functioning of each infant or toddler with a disability in the State, and a family-directed identification of the needs of each family of such an infant or toddler, to assist appropriately in the development of the infant or toddler.

(4) For each infant or toddler with a disability in the State, an individualized family service plan in accordance with section 636 [*20 USCS § 1436*], including service coordination services in accordance with such service plan.

(5) A comprehensive child find system, consistent with part B [*20 USCS §§ 1411* et seq.], including a system for making referrals to service providers that includes timelines and provides for participation by primary referral sources and that ensures rigorous standards for appropriately identifying infants and toddlers with disabilities for services under this part [*20 USCS §§ 1431* et seq.] that will reduce the need for future services.

(6) A public awareness program focusing on early identification of infants and toddlers with disabilities, including the preparation and dissemination by the lead agency designated or established under paragraph (10) to all primary referral sources, especially hospitals and physicians, of information to be given to parents, especially to inform parents with premature infants, or infants with other physical risk factors associated with learning or developmental complications, on the availability of early intervention services under this part [*20 USCS §§ 1431* et seq.] and of services under section 619 [*20 USCS § 1419*], and procedures for assisting such sources in disseminating such information to parents of infants and toddlers with disabilities.

(7) A central directory that includes information on early intervention services, resources, and experts available in the State and research and demonstration projects being conducted in the State.

(8) A comprehensive system of personnel development, including the training of paraprofessionals and the training of primary referral sources with respect to the basic components of early intervention services available in the State that—

(A) shall include—

(i) implementing innovative strategies and activities for the recruitment and retention of early education service providers;

(ii) promoting the preparation of early intervention providers who are fully and appropriately qualified to provide early intervention services under this part [*20 USCS §§ 1431* et seq.]; and

(iii) training personnel to coordinate transition services for infants and toddlers served under this part [*20 USCS §§ 1431* et seq.] from a program providing early intervention services under this part [*20 USCS §§ 1431* et seq.] and under part B [*20 USCS §§ 1411* et seq.] (other than section 619 [*20 USCS § 1419*]), to a preschool program receiving funds under section 619 [*20 USCS § 1419*], or another appropriate program; and

(B) may include—

(i) training personnel to work in rural and inner-city areas; and

(ii) training personnel in the emotional and social development of young children.

(9) Policies and procedures relating to the establishment and maintenance of qualifications to ensure that personnel necessary to carry out this part [20 USCS §§ 1431 et seq.] are appropriately and adequately prepared and trained, including the establishment and maintenance of qualifications that are consistent with any State-approved or recognized certification, licensing, registration, or other comparable requirements that apply to the area in which such personnel are providing early intervention services, except that nothing in this part [20 USCS §§ 1431 et seq.] (including this paragraph) shall be construed to prohibit the use of paraprofessionals and assistants who are appropriately trained and supervised in accordance with State law, regulation, or written policy, to assist in the provision of early intervention services under this part [20 USCS §§ 1431 et seq.] to infants and toddlers with disabilities.

(10) A single line of responsibility in a lead agency designated or established by the Governor for carrying out—

(A) the general administration and supervision of programs and activities receiving assistance under section 633 [20 USCS § 1433], and the monitoring of programs and activities used by the State to carry out this part [20 USCS §§ 1431 et seq.], whether or not such programs or activities are receiving assistance made available under section 633 [20 USCS § 1433], to ensure that the State complies with this part [20 USCS §§ 1431 et seq.];

(B) the identification and coordination of all available resources within the State from Federal, State, local, and private sources;

(C) the assignment of financial responsibility in accordance with section 637(a)(2) [20 USCS § 1437(a)(2)] to the appropriate agencies;

(D) the development of procedures to ensure that services are provided to infants and toddlers with disabilities and their families under this part [20 USCS §§ 1431 et seq.] in a timely manner pending the resolution of any disputes among public agencies or service providers;

(E) the resolution of intra- and interagency disputes; and

(F) the entry into formal interagency agreements that define the financial responsibility of each agency for paying for early intervention services (consistent with State law) and procedures for resolving disputes and that include all additional components necessary to ensure meaningful cooperation and coordination.

(11) A policy pertaining to the contracting or making of other arrangements with service providers to provide early intervention services in the State, consistent with the provisions of this part [20 USCS §§ 1431 et seq.], including the contents of the application used and the conditions of the contract or other arrangements.

(12) A procedure for securing timely reimbursements of funds used under this part [20 USCS §§ 1431 et seq.] in accordance with section 640(a) [20 USCS § 1440(a)].

(13) Procedural safeguards with respect to programs under this part [20 USCS §§ 1431 et seq.], as required by section 639 [20 USCS § 1439].

(14) A system for compiling data requested by the Secretary under section 618 [20 USCS § 1418] that relates to this part [20 USCS §§ 1431 et seq.].

(15) A State interagency coordinating council that meets the requirements of section 641 [20 USCS § 1441].

(16) Policies and procedures to ensure that, consistent with section 636(d)(5) [20 USCS § 1436(d)(5)]—

(A) to the maximum extent appropriate, early intervention services are provided in natural environments; and

(B) the provision of early intervention services for any infant or toddler with a disability occurs in a setting other than a natural environment that is most appropriate, as determined by the parent and the individualized family service plan team, only when early intervention cannot be achieved satisfactorily for the infant or toddler in a natural environment.

(b) Policy. In implementing subsection (a)(9), a State may adopt a policy that includes making ongoing good-faith efforts to recruit and hire appropriately and adequately trained personnel to provide early intervention services to infants and toddlers with disabilities, including, in a geographic area of the State where there is a shortage of such personnel, the most qualified individuals available who are making satisfactory progress toward completing applicable course work necessary to meet the standards described in subsection (a)(9).

(c) Flexibility to serve children 3 years of age until entrance into elementary school.

(1) In general. A statewide system described in section 633 [20 USCS § 1433] may include a State policy, developed and implemented jointly by the lead agency and the State educational agency, under which parents of children with disabilities who are eligible for services under section 619 [20 USCS § 1419] and previously received services under this part [20 USCS §§ 1431 et seq.], may choose the continuation of early intervention services (which shall include an educational component that promotes school readiness and incorporates preliteracy, language, and numeracy skills) for such children under this part [20 USCS §§ 1431 et seq.] until such children enter, or are eligible under State law to enter, kindergarten.

(2) Requirements. If a statewide system includes a State policy described in paragraph (1), the statewide system shall ensure that—

(A) parents of children with disabilities served pursuant to this subsection are provided annual notice that contains—

(i) a description of the rights of such parents to elect to receive services pursuant to this subsection or under part B [20 USCS §§ 1411 et seq.]; and

(ii) an explanation of the differences between services provided pursuant to this subsection and services provided under part B [20 USCS §§ 1411 et seq.], including—

(I) types of services and the locations at which the services are provided;

(II) applicable procedural safeguards; and

(III) possible costs (including any fees to be charged to families as described in section 632(4)(B) [20 USCS § 1432(4)(B)]), if any, to parents of infants or toddlers with disabilities;

(B) services provided pursuant to this subsection include an educational component that promotes school readiness and incorporates preliteracy, language, and numeracy skills;

(C) the State policy will not affect the right of any child served pursuant to this subsection to instead receive a free appropriate public education under part B [20 USCS §§ 1411 et seq.];

(D) all early intervention services outlined in the child's individualized family service plan under section 636 [20 USCS § 1436] are continued while any eligibility determination is being made for services under this subsection;

(E) the parents of infants or toddlers with disabilities (as defined in section 632(5)(A) [20 USCS § 1432(5)(A)]) provide informed written consent to the State, before such infants or toddlers reach 3 years of age, as to whether such parents intend to choose the continuation of early intervention services pursuant to this subsection for such infants or toddlers;

(F) the requirements under section 637(a)(9) [*20 USCS § 1437(a)(9)*] shall not apply with respect to a child who is receiving services in accordance with this subsection until not less than 90 days (and at the discretion of the parties to the conference, not more than 9 months) before the time the child will no longer receive those services; and

(G) there will be a referral for evaluation for early intervention services of a child who experiences a substantiated case of trauma due to exposure to family violence (as defined in section 320 of the Family Violence Prevention and Services Act [*42 USCS § 10421*]).

(3) Reporting requirement. If a statewide system includes a State policy described in paragraph (1), the State shall submit to the Secretary, in the State's report under section 637(b)(4)(A) [*20 USCS § 1437(b)(4)(A)*], a report on the number and percentage of children with disabilities who are eligible for services under section 619 [*20 USCS § 1419*] but whose parents choose for such children to continue to receive early intervention services under this part [*20 USCS §§ 1431 et seq.*].

(4) Available funds. If a statewide system includes a State policy described in paragraph (1), the policy shall describe the funds (including an identification as Federal, State, or local funds) that will be used to ensure that the option described in paragraph (1) is available to eligible children and families who provide the consent described in paragraph (2)(E), including fees (if any) to be charged to families as described in section 632(4)(B) [*20 USCS § 1432(4)(B)*].

(5) Rules of construction.

(A) Services under part B. If a statewide system includes a State policy described in paragraph (1), a State that provides services in accordance with this subsection to a child with a disability who is eligible for services under section 619 [*20 USCS § 1419*] shall not be required to provide the child with a free appropriate public education under part B [*20 USCS §§ 1411 et seq.*] for the period of time in which the child is receiving services under this part [*20 USCS §§ 1431 et seq.*].

(B) Services under this part. Nothing in this subsection shall be construed to require a provider of services under this part [*20 USCS §§ 1431 et seq.*] to provide a child served under this part [*20 USCS §§ 1431 et seq.*] with a free appropriate public education.

§ 1436. Individualized family service plan

(a) Assessment and program development. A statewide system described in section 633 [*20 USCS § 1433*] shall provide, at a minimum, for each infant or toddler with a disability, and the infant's or toddler's family, to receive—

(1) a multidisciplinary assessment of the unique strengths and needs of the infant or toddler and the identification of services appropriate to meet such needs;

(2) a family-directed assessment of the resources, priorities, and concerns of the family and the identification of the supports and services necessary to enhance the family's capacity to meet the developmental needs of the infant or toddler; and

(3) a written individualized family service plan developed by a multidisciplinary team, including the parents, as required by subsection (e), including a description of the appropriate transition services for the infant or toddler.

(b) Periodic review. The individualized family service plan shall be evaluated once a year and the family shall be provided a review of the plan at 6-month intervals (or more often where appropriate based on infant or toddler and family needs).

(c) Promptness after assessment. The individualized family service plan shall be developed within a reasonable time after the assessment required by subsection (a)(1) is completed. With the parents' consent, early intervention services may commence prior to the completion of the assessment.

(d) Content of plan. The individualized family service plan shall be in writing and contain—

(1) a statement of the infant's or toddler's present levels of physical development, cognitive development, communication development, social or emotional development, and adaptive development, based on objective criteria;

(2) a statement of the family's resources, priorities, and concerns relating to enhancing the development of the family's infant or toddler with a disability;

(3) a statement of the measurable results or outcomes expected to be achieved for the infant or toddler and the family, including pre-literacy and language skills, as developmentally appropriate for the child, and the criteria, procedures, and timelines used to determine the degree to which progress toward achieving the results or outcomes is being made and whether modifications or revisions of the results or outcomes or services are necessary;

(4) a statement of specific early intervention services based on peer-reviewed research, to the extent practicable, necessary to meet the unique needs of the infant or toddler and the family, including the frequency, intensity, and method of delivering services;

(5) a statement of the natural environments in which early intervention services will appropriately be provided, including a justification of the extent, if any, to which the services will not be provided in a natural environment;

(6) the projected dates for initiation of services and the anticipated length, duration, and frequency of the services;

(7) the identification of the service coordinator from the profession most immediately relevant to the infant's or toddler's or family's needs (or who is otherwise qualified to carry out all applicable responsibilities under this part) who will be responsible for the implementation of the plan and coordination with other agencies and persons, including transition services; and

(8) the steps to be taken to support the transition of the toddler with a disability to preschool or other appropriate services.

(e) Parental consent. The contents of the individualized family service plan shall be fully explained to the parents and informed written consent from the parents shall be obtained prior to the provision of early intervention services described in such plan. If the parents do not provide consent with respect to a particular early intervention service, then only the early intervention services to which consent is obtained shall be provided.

§ 1437. State application and assurances

(a) Application. A State desiring to receive a grant under section 633 [20 USCS § 1433] shall submit an application to the Secretary at such time and in such manner as the Secretary may reasonably require. The application shall contain—

(1) a designation of the lead agency in the State that will be responsible for the administration of funds provided under section 633 [20 USCS § 1433];

(2) a certification to the Secretary that the arrangements to establish financial responsibility for services provided under this part [20 USCS §§ 1431 et seq.] pursuant to section 640(b) [20 USCS § 1440(b)] are current as of the date of submission of the certification;

(3) information demonstrating eligibility of the State under section 634 [20 USCS § 1434], including—

(A) information demonstrating to the Secretary's satisfaction that the State has in effect the statewide system required by section 633 [20 USCS § 1433]; and

(B) a description of services to be provided to infants and toddlers with disabilities and their families through the system;

(4) if the State provides services to at-risk infants and toddlers through the statewide system, a description of such services;

(5) a description of the uses for which funds will be expended in accordance with this part [20 USCS §§ 1431 et seq.];

(6) a description of the State policies and procedures that require the referral for early intervention services under this part [20 USCS §§ 1431 et seq.] of a child under the age of 3 who—

(A) is involved in a substantiated case of child abuse or neglect; or

(B) is identified as affected by illegal substance abuse, or withdrawal symptoms resulting from prenatal drug exposure;

(7) a description of the procedure used to ensure that resources are made available under this part [20 USCS §§ 1431 et seq.] for all geographic areas within the State;

(8) a description of State policies and procedures that ensure that, prior to the adoption by the State of any other policy or procedure necessary to meet the requirements of this part [20 USCS §§ 1431 et seq.], there are public hearings, adequate notice of the hearings, and an opportunity for comment available to the general public, including individuals with disabilities and parents of infants and toddlers with disabilities;

(9) a description of the policies and procedures to be used—

(A) to ensure a smooth transition for toddlers receiving early intervention services under this part [20 USCS §§ 1431 et seq.] (and children receiving those services under section 635(c) [20 USCS § 1435(c)]) to preschool, school, other appropriate services, or exiting the program, including a description of how—

(i) the families of such toddlers and children will be included in the transition plans required by subparagraph (C); and

(ii) the lead agency designated or established under section 635(a)(10) [20 USCS § 1435(a)(10)] will—

(I) notify the local educational agency for the area in which such a child resides that the child will shortly reach the age of eligibility for preschool services under part B [20 USCS §§ 1411 et seq.], as determined in accordance with State law;

(II) in the case of a child who may be eligible for such preschool services, with the approval of the family of the child, convene a conference among the lead agency, the family, and the local educational agency not less than 90 days (and at the discretion of all such parties, not more than 9 months) before the child is eligible for the preschool services, to discuss any such services that the child may receive; and

(III) in the case of a child who may not be eligible for such preschool services, with the approval of the family, make reasonable efforts to convene a conference among the lead agency, the family, and providers of other appropriate services for children who are not eligible for preschool services under part B [20 USCS §§ 1411 et seq.], to discuss the appropriate services that the child may receive;

(B) to review the child's program options for the period from the child's third birthday through the remainder of the school year; and

(C) to establish a transition plan, including, as appropriate, steps to exit from the program;

(10) a description of State efforts to promote collaboration among Early Head Start programs under section 645A of the Head Start Act [42 USCS § 9840a], early education and child care programs, and services under part C [20 USCS §§ 1431 et seq.]; and

(11) such other information and assurances as the Secretary may reasonably require.

(b) Assurances. The application described in subsection (a)—

(1) shall provide satisfactory assurance that Federal funds made available under section 643 [20 USCS § 1443] to the State will be expended in accordance with this part [20 USCS §§ 1431 et seq.];

(2) shall contain an assurance that the State will comply with the requirements of section 640 [20 USCS § 1440];

(3) shall provide satisfactory assurance that the control of funds provided under section 643 [20 USCS § 1443], and title to property derived from those funds, will be in a public agency for the uses and purposes provided in this part [20 USCS §§ 1431 et seq.] and that a public agency will administer such funds and property;

(4) shall provide for—

(A) making such reports in such form and containing such information as the Secretary may require to carry out the Secretary's functions under this part [20 USCS §§ 1431 et seq.]; and

(B) keeping such reports and affording such access to the reports as the Secretary may find necessary to ensure the correctness and verification of those reports and proper disbursement of Federal funds under this part [20 USCS §§ 1431 et seq.];

(5) provide satisfactory assurance that Federal funds made available under section 643 [20 USCS § 1443] to the State—

(A) will not be commingled with State funds; and

(B) will be used so as to supplement the level of State and local funds expended for infants and toddlers with disabilities and their families and in no case to supplant those State and local funds;

(6) shall provide satisfactory assurance that such fiscal control and fund accounting procedures will be adopted as may be necessary to ensure proper disbursement of, and accounting for, Federal funds paid under section 643 [20 USCS § 1443] to the State;

(7) shall provide satisfactory assurance that policies and procedures have been adopted to ensure meaningful involvement of underserved groups, including minority, low-income, homeless, and rural families and children with disabilities who are wards of the State, in the planning and implementation of all the requirements of this part [20 USCS §§ 1431 et seq.]; and

(8) shall contain such other information and assurances as the Secretary may reasonably require by regulation.

(c) Standard for disapproval of application. The Secretary may not disapprove such an application unless the Secretary determines, after notice and opportunity for a hearing, that the application fails to comply with the requirements of this section.

(d) Subsequent State application. If a State has on file with the Secretary a policy, procedure, or assurance that demonstrates that the State meets a requirement of this section, including any policy or procedure filed under this part [20 USCS §§ 1431 et seq.] (as in effect before the date of enactment of the Individuals with Disabilities Education Improvement Act of 2004 [enacted Dec. 3, 2004]), the Secretary shall consider the State to have met the requirement for purposes of receiving a grant under this part [20 USCS §§ 1431 et seq.].

(e) Modification of application. An application submitted by a State in accordance with this section shall remain in effect until the State submits to the Secretary such modifications as the State determines necessary. This section shall apply to a modification of an application to the same extent and in the same manner as this section applies to the original application.

(f) Modifications required by the Secretary. The Secretary may require a State to modify its application under this section, but only to the extent necessary to ensure the State's compliance with this part [20 USCS §§ 1431 et seq.], if—

(1) an amendment is made to this title [20 USCS §§ 1400 et seq.], or a Federal regulation issued under this title [20 USCS §§ 1400 et seq.];

(2) a new interpretation of this title [20 USCS §§ 1400 et seq.] is made by a Federal court or the State's highest court; or

(3) an official finding of noncompliance with Federal law or regulations is made with respect to the State.

§ 1438. Uses of funds

In addition to using funds provided under section 633 [20 USCS § 1433] to maintain and implement the statewide system required by such section, a State may use such funds—

(1) for direct early intervention services for infants and toddlers with disabilities, and their families, under this part [20 USCS §§ 1431 et seq.] that are not otherwise funded through other public or private sources;

(2) to expand and improve on services for infants and toddlers and their families under this part [20 USCS §§ 1431 et seq.] that are otherwise available;

(3) to provide a free appropriate public education, in accordance with part B [20 USCS §§ 1411 et seq.], to children with disabilities from their third birthday to the beginning of the following school year;

(4) with the written consent of the parents, to continue to provide early intervention services under this part [20 USCS §§ 1431 et seq.] to children with disabilities from their 3rd birthday until such children enter, or are eligible under State law to enter, kindergarten, in lieu of a free appropriate public education provided in accordance with part B [20 USCS §§ 1411 et seq.]; and

(5) in any State that does not provide services for at-risk infants and toddlers under section 637(a)(4) [20 USCS § 1437(a)(4)], to strengthen the statewide system by initiating, expanding, or improving collaborative efforts related to at-risk infants and toddlers, including establishing linkages with appropriate public or private community-based organizations, services, and personnel for the purposes of—

(A) identifying and evaluating at-risk infants and toddlers;

(B) making referrals of the infants and toddlers identified and evaluated under subparagraph (A); and

(C) conducting periodic follow-up on each such referral to determine if the status of the infant or toddler involved has changed with respect to the eligibility of the infant or toddler for services under this part [20 USCS §§ 1431 et seq.].

§ 1439. Procedural safeguards

(a) Minimum procedures. The procedural safeguards required to be included in a statewide system under section 635(a)(13) [*20 USCS § 1435(a)(13)*] shall provide, at a minimum, the following:

(1) The timely administrative resolution of complaints by parents. Any party aggrieved by the findings and decision regarding an administrative complaint shall have the right to bring a civil action with respect to the complaint in any State court of competent jurisdiction or in a district court of the United States without regard to the amount in controversy. In any action brought under this paragraph, the court shall receive the records of the administrative proceedings, shall hear additional evidence at the request of a party, and, basing its decision on the preponderance of the evidence, shall grant such relief as the court determines is appropriate.

(2) The right to confidentiality of personally identifiable information, including the right of parents to written notice of and written consent to the exchange of such information among agencies consistent with Federal and State law.

(3) The right of the parents to determine whether they, their infant or toddler, or other family members will accept or decline any early intervention service under this part [*20 USCS §§ 1431* et seq.] in accordance with State law without jeopardizing other early intervention services under this part [*20 USCS §§ 1431* et seq.].

(4) The opportunity for parents to examine records relating to assessment, screening, eligibility determinations, and the development and implementation of the individualized family service plan.

(5) Procedures to protect the rights of the infant or toddler whenever the parents of the infant or toddler are not known or cannot be found or the infant or toddler is a ward of the State, including the assignment of an individual (who shall not be an employee of the State lead agency, or other State agency, and who shall not be any person, or any employee of a person, providing early intervention services to the infant or toddler or any family member of the infant or toddler) to act as a surrogate for the parents.

(6) Written prior notice to the parents of the infant or toddler with a disability whenever the State agency or service provider proposes to initiate or change, or refuses to initiate or change, the identification, evaluation, or placement of the infant or toddler with a disability, or the provision of appropriate early intervention services to the infant or toddler.

(7) Procedures designed to ensure that the notice required by paragraph (6) fully informs the parents, in the parents' native language, unless it clearly is not feasible to do so, of all procedures available pursuant to this section.

(8) The right of parents to use mediation in accordance with section 615 [*20 USCS § 1415*], except that—

(A) any reference in the section to a State educational agency shall be considered to be a reference to a State's lead agency established or designated under section 635(a)(10) [*20 USCS § 1435(a)(10)*];

(B) any reference in the section to a local educational agency shall be considered to be a reference to a local service provider or the State's lead agency under this part [*20 USCS §§ 1431* et seq.], as the case may be; and

(C) any reference in the section to the provision of a free appropriate public education to children with disabilities shall be considered to be a reference to the provision of appropriate early intervention services to infants and toddlers with disabilities.

(b) Services during pendency of proceedings. During the pendency of any proceeding or action involving a complaint by the parents of an infant or toddler with a disability, unless the State agency and the parents otherwise agree, the infant or toddler shall continue to receive the appropriate early intervention services currently being provided or, if applying for initial services, shall receive the services not in dispute.

§ 1440. Payor of last resort

(a) Nonsubstitution. Funds provided under section 643 [20 USCS § 1443] may not be used to satisfy a financial commitment for services that would have been paid for from another public or private source, including any medical program administered by the Secretary of Defense, but for the enactment of this part [20 USCS §§ 1431 et seq.], except that whenever considered necessary to prevent a delay in the receipt of appropriate early intervention services by an infant, toddler, or family in a timely fashion, funds provided under section 643 [20 USCS § 1443] may be used to pay the provider of services pending reimbursement from the agency that has ultimate responsibility for the payment.

(b) Obligations related to and methods of ensuring services.

(1) Establishing financial responsibility for services.

(A) In general. The Chief Executive Officer of a State or designee of the officer shall ensure that an interagency agreement or other mechanism for interagency coordination is in effect between each public agency and the designated lead agency, in order to ensure—

(i) the provision of, and financial responsibility for, services provided under this part [20 USCS §§ 1431 et seq.]; and

(ii) such services are consistent with the requirements of section 635 [20 USCS § 1435] and the State's application pursuant to section 637 [20 USCS § 1437], including the provision of such services during the pendency of any such dispute.

(B) Consistency between agreements or mechanisms under part B. The Chief Executive Officer of a State or designee of the officer shall ensure that the terms and conditions of such agreement or mechanism are consistent with the terms and conditions of the State's agreement or mechanism under section 612(a)(12) [20 USCS § 1412(a)(12)], where appropriate.

(2) Reimbursement for services by public agency.

(A) In general. If a public agency other than an educational agency fails to provide or pay for the services pursuant to an agreement required under paragraph (1), the local educational agency or State agency (as determined by the Chief Executive Officer or designee) shall provide or pay for the provision of such services to the child.

(B) Reimbursement. Such local educational agency or State agency is authorized to claim reimbursement for the services from the public agency that failed to provide or pay for such services and such public agency shall reimburse the local educational agency or State agency pursuant to the terms of the interagency agreement or other mechanism required under paragraph (1).

(3) Special rule. The requirements of paragraph (1) may be met through—

(A) State statute or regulation;

(B) signed agreements between respective agency officials that clearly identify the responsibilities of each agency relating to the provision of services; or

(C) other appropriate written methods as determined by the Chief Executive Officer of the State or designee of the officer and approved by the Secretary through the review and approval of the State's application pursuant to section 637 [20 USCS § 1437].

(c) Reduction of other benefits. Nothing in this part [20 USCS §§ 1431 et seq.] shall be construed to permit the State to reduce medical or other assistance available or to alter eligibility under title V of the Social Security Act [42 USCS §§ 701 et seq.] (relating to maternal and child health) or title XIX of the Social Security Act [42 USCS §§ 1396 et seq.] (relating to medicaid for infants or toddlers with disabilities) within the State.

§ 1441. State interagency coordinating council

(a) Establishment.

(1) In general. A State that desires to receive financial assistance under this part [20 USCS §§ 1431 et seq.] shall establish a State interagency coordinating council.

(2) Appointment. The council shall be appointed by the Governor. In making appointments to the council, the Governor shall ensure that the membership of the council reasonably represents the population of the State.

(3) Chairperson. The Governor shall designate a member of the council to serve as the chairperson of the council, or shall require the council to so designate such a member. Any member of the council who is a representative of the lead agency designated under section 635(a)(10) [20 USCS § 1435(a)(10)] may not serve as the chairperson of the council.

(b) Composition.

(1) In general. The council shall be composed as follows:

(A) Parents. Not less than 20 percent of the members shall be parents of infants or toddlers with disabilities or children with disabilities aged 12 or younger, with knowledge of, or experience with, programs for infants and toddlers with disabilities. Not less than 1 such member shall be a parent of an infant or toddler with a disability or a child with a disability aged 6 or younger.

(B) Service providers. Not less than 20 percent of the members shall be public or private providers of early intervention services.

(C) State legislature. Not less than 1 member shall be from the State legislature.

(D) Personnel preparation. Not less than 1 member shall be involved in personnel preparation.

(E) Agency for early intervention services. Not less than 1 member shall be from each of the State agencies involved in the provision of, or payment for, early intervention services to infants and toddlers with disabilities and their families and shall have sufficient authority to engage in policy planning and implementation on behalf of such agencies.

(F) Agency for preschool services. Not less than 1 member shall be from the State educational agency responsible for preschool services to children with disabilities and shall have sufficient authority to engage in policy planning and implementation on behalf of such agency.

(G) State medicaid agency. Not less than 1 member shall be from the agency responsible for the State medicaid program.

(H) Head Start agency. Not less than 1 member shall be a representative from a Head Start agency or program in the State.

(I) Child care agency. Not less than 1 member shall be a representative from a State agency responsible for child care.

(J) Agency for health insurance. Not less than 1 member shall be from the agency responsible for the State regulation of health insurance.

(K) Office of the coordinator of education of homeless children and youth. Not less than 1 member shall be a representative designated by the Office of Coordinator for Education of Homeless Children and Youths.

(L) State foster care representative. Not less than 1 member shall be a representative from the State child welfare agency responsible for foster care.

(M) Mental health agency. Not less than 1 member shall be a representative from the State agency responsible for children's mental health.

(2) Other members. The council may include other members selected by the Governor, including a representative from the Bureau of Indian Affairs (BIA), or where there is no BIA-operated or BIA-funded school, from the Indian Health Service or the tribe or tribal council.

(c) Meetings. The council shall meet, at a minimum, on a quarterly basis, and in such places as the council determines necessary. The meetings shall be publicly announced, and, to the extent appropriate, open and accessible to the general public.

(d) Management authority. Subject to the approval of the Governor, the council may prepare and approve a budget using funds under this part [20 USCS §§ 1431 et seq.] to conduct hearings and forums, to reimburse members of the council for reasonable and necessary expenses for attending council meetings and performing council duties (including child care for parent representatives), to pay compensation to a member of the council if the member is not employed or must forfeit wages from other employment when performing official council business, to hire staff, and to obtain the services of such professional, technical, and clerical personnel as may be necessary to carry out its functions under this part [20 USCS §§ 1431 et seq.].

(e) Functions of council.

(1) Duties. The council shall—

(A) advise and assist the lead agency designated or established under section 635(a)(10) [20 USCS § 1435(a)(10)] in the performance of the responsibilities set forth in such section, particularly the identification of the sources of fiscal and other support for services for early intervention programs, assignment of financial responsibility to the appropriate agency, and the promotion of the interagency agreements;

(B) advise and assist the lead agency in the preparation of applications and amendments thereto;

(C) advise and assist the State educational agency regarding the transition of toddlers with disabilities to preschool and other appropriate services; and

(D) prepare and submit an annual report to the Governor and to the Secretary on the status of early intervention programs for infants and toddlers with disabilities and their families operated within the State.

(2) Authorized activity. The council may advise and assist the lead agency and the State educational agency regarding the provision of appropriate services for children from birth through age 5. The council may advise appropriate agencies in the State with respect to the integration of services for infants and toddlers with disabilities and at-risk infants and toddlers and their families, regardless of whether at-risk infants and toddlers are eligible for early intervention services in the State.

(f) Conflict of interest. No member of the council shall cast a vote on any matter that is likely to provide a direct financial benefit to that member or otherwise give the appearance of a conflict of interest under State law.

§ 1442. Federal administration

Sections 616, 617, and 618 [20 USCS §§ 1416, 1417, and 1418] shall, to the extent not inconsistent with this part [20 USCS §§ 1431 et seq.], apply to the program authorized by this part [20 USCS §§ 1431 et seq.], except that—

(1) any reference in such sections to a State educational agency shall be considered to be a reference to a State's lead agency established or designated under section 635(a)(10) [20 USCS § 1435(a)(10)];

(2) any reference in such sections to a local educational agency, educational service agency, or a State agency shall be considered to be a reference to an early intervention service provider under this part [*20 USCS §§ 1431* et seq.]; and

(3) any reference to the education of children with disabilities or the education of all children with disabilities shall be considered to be a reference to the provision of appropriate early intervention services to infants and toddlers with disabilities.

§ 1443. Allocation of funds

(a) Reservation of funds for outlying areas.

(1) In general. From the sums appropriated to carry out this part [*20 USCS §§ 1431* et seq.] for any fiscal year, the Secretary may reserve not more than 1 percent for payments to Guam, American Samoa, the United States Virgin Islands, and the Commonwealth of the Northern Mariana Islands in accordance with their respective needs for assistance under this part [*20 USCS §§ 1431* et seq.].

(2) Consolidation of funds. The provisions of Public Law 95-134, permitting the consolidation of grants to the outlying areas, shall not apply to funds those areas receive under this part [*20 USCS §§ 1431* et seq.].

(b) Payments to Indians.

(1) In general. The Secretary shall, subject to this subsection, make payments to the Secretary of the Interior to be distributed to tribes, tribal organizations (as defined under section 4 of the Indian Self-Determination and Education Assistance Act [*25 USCS § 450b*]), or consortia of the above entities for the coordination of assistance in the provision of early intervention services by the States to infants and toddlers with disabilities and their families on reservations served by elementary schools and secondary schools for Indian children operated or funded by the Department of the Interior. The amount of such payment for any fiscal year shall be 1.25 percent of the aggregate of the amount available to all States under this part [*20 USCS §§ 1431* et seq.] for such fiscal year.

(2) Allocation. For each fiscal year, the Secretary of the Interior shall distribute the entire payment received under paragraph (1) by providing to each tribe, tribal organization, or consortium an amount based on the number of infants and toddlers residing on the reservation, as determined annually, divided by the total of such children served by all tribes, tribal organizations, or consortia.

(3) Information. To receive a payment under this subsection, the tribe, tribal organization, or consortium shall submit such information to the Secretary of the Interior as is needed to determine the amounts to be distributed under paragraph (2).

(4) Use of funds. The funds received by a tribe, tribal organization, or consortium shall be used to assist States in child find, screening, and other procedures for the early identification of Indian children under 3 years of age and for parent training. Such funds may also be used to provide early intervention services in accordance with this part [*20 USCS §§ 1431* et seq.]. Such activities may be carried out directly or through contracts or cooperative agreements with the Bureau of Indian Affairs, local educational agencies, and other public or private nonprofit organizations. The tribe, tribal organization, or consortium is encouraged to involve Indian parents in the development and implementation of these activities. The above entities shall, as appropriate, make referrals to local, State, or Federal entities for the provision of services or further diagnosis.

(5) Reports. To be eligible to receive a payment under paragraph (2), a tribe, tribal organization, or consortium shall make a biennial report to the Secretary of the Interior of activities undertaken under this subsection, including the number of contracts and cooperative agreements entered into, the number of infants and toddlers contacted and receiving services for each year, and the estimated number of infants and toddlers needing services during the 2 years following the year in which the report is made. The

Secretary of the Interior shall include a summary of this information on a biennial basis to the Secretary of Education along with such other information as required under section 611(h)(3)(E) [*20 USCS § 1411(h)(3)(E)*]. The Secretary of Education may require any additional information from the Secretary of the Interior.

(6) Prohibited uses of funds. None of the funds under this subsection may be used by the Secretary of the Interior for administrative purposes, including child count, and the provision of technical assistance.

(c) State allotments.

(1) In general. Except as provided in paragraphs (2) and (3), from the funds remaining for each fiscal year after the reservation and payments under subsections (a), (b), and (e), the Secretary shall first allot to each State an amount that bears the same ratio to the amount of such remainder as the number of infants and toddlers in the State bears to the number of infants and toddlers in all States.

(2) Minimum allotments. Except as provided in paragraph (3), no State shall receive an amount under this section for any fiscal year that is less than the greater of—

(A) 1/2 of 1 percent of the remaining amount described in paragraph (1); or

(B) $ 500,000.

(3) Ratable reduction.

(A) In general. If the sums made available under this part [*20 USCS §§ 1431* et seq.] for any fiscal year are insufficient to pay the full amounts that all States are eligible to receive under this subsection for such year, the Secretary shall ratably reduce the allotments to such States for such year.

(B) Additional funds. If additional funds become available for making payments under this subsection for a fiscal year, allotments that were reduced under subparagraph (A) shall be increased on the same basis the allotments were reduced.

(4) Definitions. In this subsection—

(A) the terms "infants" and "toddlers" mean children under 3 years of age; and

(B) the term "State" means each of the 50 States, the District of Columbia, and the Commonwealth of Puerto Rico.

(d) Reallotment of funds. If a State elects not to receive its allotment under subsection (c), the Secretary shall reallot, among the remaining States, amounts from such State in accordance with such subsection.

(e) Reservation for State incentive grants.

(1) In general. For any fiscal year for which the amount appropriated pursuant to the authorization of appropriations under section 644 [*20 USCS § 1444*] exceeds $ 460,000,000, the Secretary shall reserve 15 percent of such appropriated amount to provide grants to States that are carrying out the policy described in section 635(c) [*20 USCS § 1435(c)*] in order to facilitate the implementation of such policy.

(2) Amount of grant.

(A) In general. Notwithstanding paragraphs (2) and (3) of subsection (c), the Secretary shall provide a grant to each State under paragraph (1) in an amount that bears the same ratio to the amount reserved under such paragraph as the number of infants and toddlers in the State bears to the number of infants and toddlers in all States receiving grants under such paragraph.

(B) Maximum amount. No State shall receive a grant under paragraph (1) for any fiscal year in an amount that is greater than 20 percent of the amount reserved under such paragraph for the fiscal year.

(3) Carryover of amounts.

(A) First succeeding fiscal year. Pursuant to section 421(b) of the General Education Provisions Act [20 USCS § 1225(b)], amounts under a grant provided under paragraph (1) that are not obligated and expended prior to the beginning of the first fiscal year succeeding the fiscal year for which such amounts were appropriated shall remain available for obligation and expenditure during such first succeeding fiscal year.

(B) Second succeeding fiscal year. Amounts under a grant provided under paragraph (1) that are not obligated and expended prior to the beginning of the second fiscal year succeeding the fiscal year for which such amounts were appropriated shall be returned to the Secretary and used to make grants to States under section 633 [20 USCS § 1433] (from their allotments under this section) during such second succeeding fiscal year.

§ 1444. Authorization of appropriations

For the purpose of carrying out this part [20 USCS §§ 1431 et seq.], there are authorized to be appropriated such sums as may be necessary for each of the fiscal years 2005 through 2010.

§ 1445. [Omitted]

NATIONAL ACTIVITIES TO IMPROVE EDUCATION OF CHILDREN WITH DISABILITIES

§ 1450. Findings

Congress finds the following:

(1) The Federal Government has an ongoing obligation to support activities that contribute to positive results for children with disabilities, enabling those children to lead productive and independent adult lives.

(2) Systemic change benefiting all students, including children with disabilities, requires the involvement of States, local educational agencies, parents, individuals with disabilities and their families, teachers and other service providers, and other interested individuals and organizations to develop and implement comprehensive strategies that improve educational results for children with disabilities.

(3) State educational agencies, in partnership with local educational agencies, parents of children with disabilities, and other individuals and organizations, are in the best position to improve education for children with disabilities and to address their special needs.

(4) An effective educational system serving students with disabilities should—

(A) maintain high academic achievement standards and clear performance goals for children with disabilities, consistent with the standards and expectations for all students in the educational system, and provide for appropriate and effective strategies and methods to ensure that all children with disabilities have the opportunity to achieve those standards and goals;

(B) clearly define, in objective, measurable terms, the school and post-school results that children with disabilities are expected to achieve; and

(C) promote transition services and coordinate State and local education, social, health, mental health, and other services, in addressing the full range of student needs, particularly the needs of children with disabilities who need significant levels of support to participate and learn in school and the community.

(5) The availability of an adequate number of qualified personnel is critical—

(A) to serve effectively children with disabilities;

(B) to assume leadership positions in administration and direct services;

(C) to provide teacher training; and

(D) to conduct high quality research to improve special education.

(6) High quality, comprehensive professional development programs are essential to ensure that the persons responsible for the education or transition of children with disabilities possess the skills and knowledge necessary to address the educational and related needs of those children.

(7) Models of professional development should be scientifically based and reflect successful practices, including strategies for recruiting, preparing, and retaining personnel.

(8) Continued support is essential for the development and maintenance of a coordinated and high quality program of research to inform successful teaching practices and model curricula for educating children with disabilities.

(9) Training, technical assistance, support, and dissemination activities are necessary to ensure that parts B and C [20 USCS §§ 1411 et seq. and 1431 et seq.] are fully implemented and achieve high quality early intervention, educational, and transitional results for children with disabilities and their families.

(10) Parents, teachers, administrators, and related services personnel need technical assistance and information in a timely, coordinated, and accessible manner in order to improve early intervention, educational, and transitional services and results at the State and local levels for children with disabilities and their families.

(11) Parent training and information activities assist parents of a child with a disability in dealing with the multiple pressures of parenting such a child and are of particular importance in—

(A) playing a vital role in creating and preserving constructive relationships between parents of children with disabilities and schools by facilitating open communication between the parents and schools; encouraging dispute resolution at the earliest possible point in time; and discouraging the escalation of an adversarial process between the parents and schools;

(B) ensuring the involvement of parents in planning and decisionmaking with respect to early intervention, educational, and transitional services;

(C) achieving high quality early intervention, educational, and transitional results for children with disabilities;

(D) providing such parents information on their rights, protections, and responsibilities under this *title* [20 USCS §§ 1400 et seq.] to ensure improved early intervention, educational, and transitional results for children with disabilities;

(E) assisting such parents in the development of skills to participate effectively in the education and development of their children and in the transitions described in section 673(b)(6) [20 USCS § 1473(b)(6)];

(F) supporting the roles of such parents as participants within partnerships seeking to improve early intervention, educational, and transitional services and results for children with disabilities and their families; and

(G) supporting such parents who may have limited access to services and supports, due to economic, cultural, or linguistic barriers.

(12) Support is needed to improve technological resources and integrate technology, including universally designed technologies, into the lives of children with disabilities, parents of children with disabilities, school personnel, and others through curricula, services, and assistive technologies.

STATE PERSONNEL DEVELOPMENT GRANTS

§ 1451. Purpose; definition of personnel; program authority

(a) Purpose. The purpose of this subpart [20 USCS §§ 1451 et seq.] is to assist State educational agencies in reforming and improving their systems for personnel preparation and professional development in early intervention, educational, and transition services in order to improve results for children with disabilities.

(b) Definition of personnel. In this subpart [20 USCS §§ 1451 et seq.] the term "personnel" means special education teachers, regular education teachers, principals, administrators, related services personnel, paraprofessionals, and early intervention personnel serving infants, toddlers, preschoolers, or children with disabilities, except where a particular category of personnel, such as related services personnel, is identified.

(c) Competitive grants.

(1) In general. Except as provided in subsection (d), for any fiscal year for which the amount appropriated under section 655 [20 USCS § 1455], that remains after the Secretary reserves funds under subsection (e) for the fiscal year, is less than $ 100,000,000, the Secretary shall award grants, on a competitive basis, to State educational agencies to carry out the activities described in the State plan submitted under section 653 [20 USCS § 1453].

(2) Priority. In awarding grants under paragraph (1), the Secretary may give priority to State educational agencies that—

(A) are in States with the greatest personnel shortages; or

(B) demonstrate the greatest difficulty meeting the requirements of section 612(a)(14) [20 USCS § 1412(a)(14)].

(3) Minimum amount. The Secretary shall make a grant to each State educational agency selected under paragraph (1) in an amount for each fiscal year that is—

(A) not less than $ 500,000, nor more than $ 4,000,000, in the case of the 50 States, the District of Columbia, and the Commonwealth of Puerto Rico; and

(B) not less than $ 80,000 in the case of an outlying area.

(4) Increase in amount. The Secretary may increase the amounts of grants under paragraph (4) to account for inflation.

(5) Factors. The Secretary shall determine the amount of a grant under paragraph (1) after considering—

(A) the amount of funds available for making the grants;

(B) the relative population of the State or outlying area;

(C) the types of activities proposed by the State or outlying area;

(D) the alignment of proposed activities with section 612(a)(14) [20 USCS § 1412(a)(14)];

(E) the alignment of proposed activities with the State plans and applications submitted under sections 1111 and 2112, respectively, of the Elementary and Secondary Education Act of 1965 [20 USCS § 6311 and 6612]; and

(F) the use, as appropriate, of scientifically based research activities.

(d) Formula grants.

(1) In general. Except as provided in paragraphs (2) and (3), for the first fiscal year for which the amount appropriated under section 655 [20 USCS § 1455], that remains after the Secretary reserves funds under subsection (e) for the fiscal year, is equal to or greater than $ 100,000,000, and for each fiscal year thereafter, the Secretary shall allot to each State educational agency, whose application meets the requirements of this subpart [20 USCS §§ 1451 et seq.], an amount that bears the same relation to the amount remaining as the amount the State received under section 611(d) [20 USCS § 1411(d)] for that fiscal year bears to the amount of funds received by all States (whose applications meet the requirements of this subpart [20 USCS §§ 1451 et seq.]) under section 611(d) [20 USCS § 1411(d)] for that fiscal year.

(2) Minimum allotments for States that received competitive grants.

(A) In general. The amount allotted under this subsection to any State educational agency that received a competitive multi-year grant under subsection (c) for which the grant period has not expired shall be not less than the amount specified for that fiscal year in the State educational agency's grant award document under that subsection.

(B) Special rule. Each such State educational agency shall use the minimum amount described in subparagraph (A) for the activities described in the State educational agency's competitive grant award document for that year, unless the Secretary approves a request from the State educational agency to spend the funds on other activities.

(3) Minimum allotment. The amount of any State educational agency's allotment under this subsection for any fiscal year shall not be less than—

(A) the greater of $ 500,000 or 1/2 of 1 percent of the total amount available under this subsection for that year, in the case of each of the 50 States, the District of Columbia, and the Commonwealth of Puerto Rico; and

(B) $ 80,000, in the case of an outlying area.

(4) Direct benefit. In using grant funds allotted under paragraph (1), a State educational agency shall, through grants, contracts, or cooperative agreements, undertake activities that significantly and directly benefit the local educational agencies in the State.

(e) Continuation awards.

(1) In general. Notwithstanding any other provision of this subpart [20 USCS §§ 1451 et seq.], from funds appropriated under section 655 [20 USCS § 1455] for each fiscal year, the Secretary shall reserve the amount that is necessary to make a continuation award to any State educational agency (at the request of the State educational agency) that received a multi-year award under this part [20 USCS §§ 1450 et seq.] (as this part was in effect on the day before the date of enactment of the Individuals with Disabilities Education Improvement Act of 2004 [enacted Dec. 3, 2004]), to enable the State educational agency to carry out activities in accordance with the terms of the multi-year award.

(2) Prohibition. A State educational agency that receives a continuation award under paragraph (1) for any fiscal year may not receive any other award under this subpart [20 USCS §§ 1451 et seq.] for that fiscal year.

§ 1452. Eligibility and collaborative process

(a) Eligible applicants. A State educational agency may apply for a grant under this subpart [20 USCS §§ 1451 et seq.] for a grant period of not less than 1 year and not more than 5 years.

(b) Partners.

(1) In general. In order to be considered for a grant under this subpart [20 USCS §§ 1451 et seq.], a State educational agency shall establish a partnership with local educational agencies and other State agencies involved in, or concerned with, the education of children with disabilities, including—

(A) not less than 1 institution of higher education; and

(B) the State agencies responsible for administering part C [20 USCS §§ 1431 et seq.], early education, child care, and vocational rehabilitation programs.

(2) Other partners. In order to be considered for a grant under this subpart [20 USCS §§ 1451 et seq.], a State educational agency shall work in partnership with other persons and organizations involved in, and concerned with, the education of children with disabilities, which may include—

(A) the Governor;

(B) parents of children with disabilities ages birth through 26;

(C) parents of nondisabled children ages birth through 26;

(D) individuals with disabilities;

(E) parent training and information centers or community parent resource centers funded under sections 671 and 672 [20 USCS §§ 1471 and 1472], respectively;

(F) community based and other nonprofit organizations involved in the education and employment of individuals with disabilities;

(G) personnel as defined in section 651(b) [20 USCS § 1451(b)];

(H) the State advisory panel established under part B [20 USCS §§ 1411 et seq.];

(I) the State interagency coordinating council established under part C [20 USCS §§ 1431 et seq.];

(J) individuals knowledgeable about vocational education;

(K) the State agency for higher education;

(L) public agencies with jurisdiction in the areas of health, mental health, social services, and juvenile justice;

(M) other providers of professional development that work with infants, toddlers, preschoolers, and children with disabilities; and

(N) other individuals.

(3) Required partner. If State law assigns responsibility for teacher preparation and certification to an individual, entity, or agency other than the State educational agency, the State educational agency shall—

(A) include that individual, entity, or agency as a partner in the partnership under this subsection; and

(B) ensure that any activities the State educational agency will carry out under this subpart [20 USCS §§ 1451 et seq.] that are within that partner's jurisdiction (which may include activities described in section 654(b) [20 USCS § 1454(b)]) are carried out by that partner.

§ 1453. Applications

(a) In general.

(1) Submission. A State educational agency that desires to receive a grant under this subpart [20 USCS §§ 1451 et seq.] shall submit to the Secretary an application at such time, in such manner, and including such information as the Secretary may require.

(2) State plan. The application shall include a plan that identifies and addresses the State and local needs for the personnel preparation and professional development of personnel, as well as individuals who provide direct supplementary aids and services to children with disabilities, and that—

(A) is designed to enable the State to meet the requirements of section 612(a)(14) [20 USCS § 1412(a)(14)] and section 635(a) (8) and (9);

(B) is based on an assessment of State and local needs that identifies critical aspects and areas in need of improvement related to the preparation, ongoing training, and professional development of personnel who serve infants, toddlers, preschoolers, and children with disabilities within the State, including—

(i) current and anticipated personnel vacancies and shortages; and

(ii) the number of preservice and inservice programs; and

(C) is integrated and aligned, to the maximum extent possible, with State plans and activities under the Elementary and Secondary Education Act of 1965, the Rehabilitation Act of 1973 [29 USCS §§ 701 et seq.], and the Higher Education Act of 1965.

(3) Requirement. The State application shall contain an assurance that the State educational agency will carry out each of the strategies described in subsection (b)(4).

(b) Elements of State personnel development plan. Each State personnel development plan under subsection (a)(2) shall—

(1) describe a partnership agreement that is in effect for the period of the grant, which agreement shall specify—

(A) the nature and extent of the partnership described in section 652(b) [20 USCS § 1452(b)] and the respective roles of each member of the partnership, including the partner described in section 652(b)(3) [20 USCS § 1452(b)(3)] if applicable; and

(B) how the State educational agency will work with other persons and organizations involved in, and concerned with, the education of children with disabilities, including the respective roles of each of the persons and organizations;

(2) describe how the strategies and activities described in paragraph (4) will be coordinated with activities supported with other public resources (including part B and part C [20 USCS §§ 1411 et seq. and 1431 et seq.] funds retained for use at the State level for personnel and professional development purposes) and private resources;

(3) describe how the State educational agency will align its personnel development plan under this subpart [20 USCS §§ 1451 et seq.] with the plan and application submitted under sections 1111 and 2112, respectively, of the Elementary and Secondary Education Act of 1965 [20 USCS §§ 6311 and 6612];

(4) describe those strategies the State educational agency will use to address the professional development and personnel needs identified under subsection (a)(2) and how such strategies will be implemented, including—

(A) a description of the programs and activities to be supported under this subpart [20 USCS §§ 1451 et seq.] that will provide personnel with the knowledge and skills to meet the needs of, and improve the performance and achievement of, infants, toddlers, preschoolers, and children with disabilities; and

(B) how such strategies will be integrated, to the maximum extent possible, with other activities supported by grants funded under section 662 [20 USCS § 1462];

(5) provide an assurance that the State educational agency will provide technical assistance to local educational agencies to improve the quality of professional development available to meet the needs of personnel who serve children with disabilities;

(6) provide an assurance that the State educational agency will provide technical assistance to entities that provide services to infants and toddlers with disabilities to improve the quality of professional development available to meet the needs of personnel serving such children;

(7) describe how the State educational agency will recruit and retain highly qualified teachers and other qualified personnel in geographic areas of greatest need;

(8) describe the steps the State educational agency will take to ensure that poor and minority children are not taught at higher rates by teachers who are not highly qualified; and

(9) describe how the State educational agency will assess, on a regular basis, the extent to which the strategies implemented under this subpart [20 USCS §§ 1451 et seq.] have been effective in meeting the performance goals described in section 612(a)(15) [20 USCS § 1412(a)(15)].

(c) Peer review.

(1) In general. The Secretary shall use a panel of experts who are competent, by virtue of their training, expertise, or experience, to evaluate applications for grants under section 651(c)(1) [20 USCS § 1451(c)(1)].

(2) Composition of panel. A majority of a panel described in paragraph (1) shall be composed of individuals who are not employees of the Federal Government.

(3) Payment of fees and expenses of certain members. The Secretary may use available funds appropriated to carry out this subpart [20 USCS §§ 1451 et seq.] to pay the expenses and fees of panel members who are not employees of the Federal Government.

(d) Reporting procedures. Each State educational agency that receives a grant under this subpart [20 USCS §§ 1451 et seq.] shall submit annual performance reports to the Secretary. The reports shall—

(1) describe the progress of the State educational agency in implementing its plan;

(2) analyze the effectiveness of the State educational agency's activities under this subpart [20 USCS §§ 1451 et seq.] and of the State educational agency's strategies for meeting its goals under section 612(a)(15) [20 USCS § 1412(a)(15)]; and

(3) identify changes in the strategies used by the State educational agency and described in subsection (b)(4), if any, to improve the State educational agency's performance.

§ 1454. Use of funds

(a) Professional development activities. A State educational agency that receives a grant under this subpart [20 USCS §§ 1451 et seq.] shall use the grant funds to support activities in accordance with the State's plan described in section 653 [20 USCS § 1453], including 1 or more of the following:

(1) Carrying out programs that provide support to both special education and regular education teachers of children with disabilities and principals, such as programs that—

(A) provide teacher mentoring, team teaching, reduced class schedules and case loads, and intensive professional development;

(B) use standards or assessments for guiding beginning teachers that are consistent with challenging State student academic achievement and functional standards and with the requirements for professional development, as defined in section 9101 of the Elementary and Secondary Education Act of 1965 [20 USCS § 7801]; and

(C) encourage collaborative and consultative models of providing early intervention, special education, and related services.

(2) Encouraging and supporting the training of special education and regular education teachers and administrators to effectively use and integrate technology—

(A) into curricula and instruction, including training to improve the ability to collect, manage, and analyze data to improve teaching, decisionmaking, school improvement efforts, and accountability;

(B) to enhance learning by children with disabilities; and

(C) to effectively communicate with parents.

(3) Providing professional development activities that—

(A) improve the knowledge of special education and regular education teachers concerning—

(i) the academic and developmental or functional needs of students with disabilities; or

(ii) effective instructional strategies, methods, and skills, and the use of State academic content standards and student academic achievement and functional standards, and State assessments, to improve teaching practices and student academic achievement;

(B) improve the knowledge of special education and regular education teachers and principals and, in appropriate cases, paraprofessionals, concerning effective instructional practices, and that—

(i) provide training in how to teach and address the needs of children with different learning styles and children who are limited English proficient;

(ii) involve collaborative groups of teachers, administrators, and, in appropriate cases, related services personnel;

(iii) provide training in methods of—

(I) positive behavioral interventions and supports to improve student behavior in the classroom;

(II) scientifically based reading instruction, including early literacy instruction;

(III) early and appropriate interventions to identify and help children with disabilities;

(IV) effective instruction for children with low incidence disabilities;

(V) successful transitioning to postsecondary opportunities; and

(VI) using classroom-based techniques to assist children prior to referral for special education;

(iv) provide training to enable personnel to work with and involve parents in their child's education, including parents of low income and limited English proficient children with disabilities;

(v) provide training for special education personnel and regular education personnel in planning, developing, and implementing effective and appropriate IEPs; and

(vi) provide training to meet the needs of students with significant health, mobility, or behavioral needs prior to serving such students;

(C) train administrators, principals, and other relevant school personnel in conducting effective IEP meetings; and

(D) train early intervention, preschool, and related services providers, and other relevant school personnel, in conducting effective individualized family service plan (IFSP) meetings.

(4) Developing and implementing initiatives to promote the recruitment and retention of highly qualified special education teachers, particularly initiatives that have been proven effective in recruiting and retaining highly qualified teachers, including programs that provide—

(A) teacher mentoring from exemplary special education teachers, principals, or superintendents;

(B) induction and support for special education teachers during their first 3 years of employment as teachers; or

(C) incentives, including financial incentives, to retain special education teachers who have a record of success in helping students with disabilities.

(5) Carrying out programs and activities that are designed to improve the quality of personnel who serve children with disabilities, such as—

(A) innovative professional development programs (which may be provided through partnerships that include institutions of higher education), including programs that train teachers and principals to integrate technology into curricula and instruction to improve teaching, learning, and technology literacy, which professional development shall be consistent with the definition of professional development in section 9101 of the Elementary and Secondary Education Act of 1965 [20 USCS § 7801]; and

(B) the development and use of proven, cost effective strategies for the implementation of professional development activities, such as through the use of technology and distance learning.

(6) Carrying out programs and activities that are designed to improve the quality of early intervention personnel, including paraprofessionals and primary referral sources, such as—

(A) professional development programs to improve the delivery of early intervention services;

(B) initiatives to promote the recruitment and retention of early intervention personnel; and

(C) interagency activities to ensure that early intervention personnel are adequately prepared and trained.

(b) Other activities. A State educational agency that receives a grant under this subpart [20 USCS §§ 1451 et seq.] shall use the grant funds to support activities in accordance with the State's plan described in section 653 [20 USCS § 1453], including 1 or more of the following:

(1) Reforming special education and regular education teacher certification (including recertification) or licensing requirements to ensure that—

(A) special education and regular education teachers have—

(i) the training and information necessary to address the full range of needs of children with disabilities across disability categories; and

(ii) the necessary subject matter knowledge and teaching skills in the academic subjects that the teachers teach;

(B) special education and regular education teacher certification (including recertification) or licensing requirements are aligned with challenging State academic content standards; and

(C) special education and regular education teachers have the subject matter knowledge and teaching skills, including technology literacy, necessary to help students with disabilities meet challenging State student academic achievement and functional standards.

(2) Programs that establish, expand, or improve alternative routes for State certification of special education teachers for highly qualified individuals with a baccalaureate or master's degree, including mid-career professionals from other occupations, paraprofessionals, and recent college or university graduates with records of academic distinction who demonstrate the potential to become highly effective special education teachers.

(3) Teacher advancement initiatives for special education teachers that promote professional growth and emphasize multiple career paths (such as paths to becoming a career teacher, mentor teacher, or exemplary teacher) and pay differentiation.

(4) Developing and implementing mechanisms to assist local educational agencies and schools in effectively recruiting and retaining highly qualified special education teachers.

(5) Reforming tenure systems, implementing teacher testing for subject matter knowledge, and implementing teacher testing for State certification or licensing, consistent with title II of the Higher Education Act of 1965 [20 USCS §§ 6601 et seq.].

(6) Funding projects to promote reciprocity of teacher certification or licensing between or among States for special education teachers, except that no reciprocity agreement developed under this paragraph or developed using funds provided under this subpart [20 USCS §§ 1451 et seq.] may lead to the weakening of any State teaching certification or licensing requirement.

(7) Assisting local educational agencies to serve children with disabilities through the development and use of proven, innovative strategies to deliver intensive professional development programs that are both cost effective and easily accessible, such as strategies that involve delivery through the use of technology, peer networks, and distance learning.

(8) Developing, or assisting local educational agencies in developing, merit based performance systems, and strategies that provide differential and bonus pay for special education teachers.

(9) Supporting activities that ensure that teachers are able to use challenging State academic content standards and student academic achievement and functional standards, and State assessments for all children with disabilities, to improve instructional practices and improve the academic achievement of children with disabilities.

(10) When applicable, coordinating with, and expanding centers established under, section 2113(c)(18) of the Elementary and Secondary Education Act of 1965 [20 USCS § 6613(c)(18)] to benefit special education teachers.

(c) Contracts and subgrants. A State educational agency that receives a grant under this subpart [20 USCS §§ 1451 et seq.]—

(1) shall award contracts or subgrants to local educational agencies, institutions of higher education, parent training and information centers, or community parent resource centers, as appropriate, to carry out its State plan under this subpart [20 USCS §§ 1451 et seq.]; and

(2) may award contracts and subgrants to other public and private entities, including the lead agency under part C [20 USCS §§ 1431 et seq.], to carry out the State plan.

(d) Use of funds for professional development. A State educational agency that receives a grant under this subpart [20 USCS §§ 1451 et seq.] shall use—

(1) not less than 90 percent of the funds the State educational agency receives under the grant for any fiscal year for activities under subsection (a); and

(2) not more than 10 percent of the funds the State educational agency receives under the grant for any fiscal year for activities under subsection (b).

(e) Grants to outlying areas. Public Law 95-134, permitting the consolidation of grants to the outlying areas, shall not apply to funds received under this subpart [20 USCS §§ 1451 et seq.].

§ 1455. Authorization of appropriations

There are authorized to be appropriated to carry out this subpart [20 USCS §§ 1451 et seq.] such sums as may be necessary for each of the fiscal years 2005 through 2010.

§ 1456. [Omitted]

PERSONNEL PREPARATION, TECHNICAL ASSISTANCE, MODEL DEMONSTRATION PROJECTS, AND DISSEMINATION OF INFORMATION

§ 1461. Purpose; definition of eligible entity

(a) Purpose. The purpose of this subpart [20 USCS §§ 1461 et seq.] is—

(1) to provide Federal funding for personnel preparation, technical assistance, model demonstration projects, information dissemination, and studies and evaluations, in order to improve early intervention, educational, and transitional results for children with disabilities; and

(2) to assist State educational agencies and local educational agencies in improving their education systems for children with disabilities.

(b) Definition of eligible entity.

(1) In general. In this subpart [20 USCS §§ 1461 et seq.], the term "eligible entity" means—

(A) a State educational agency;

(B) a local educational agency;

(C) a public charter school that is a local educational agency under State law;

(D) an institution of higher education;

(E) a public agency not described in subparagraphs (A) through (D);

(F) a private nonprofit organization;

(G) an outlying area;

(H) an Indian tribe or a tribal organization (as defined under section 4 of the Indian Self-Determination and Education Assistance Act [25 USCS § 450b]); or

(I) a for-profit organization, if the Secretary finds it appropriate in light of the purposes of a particular competition for a grant, contract, or cooperative agreement under this subpart [20 USCS §§ 1461 et seq.].

(2) Special rule. The Secretary may limit which eligible entities described in paragraph (1) are eligible for a grant, contract, or cooperative agreement under this subpart [20 USCS §§ 1461 et seq.] to 1 or more of the categories of eligible entities described in paragraph (1).

§ 1462. Personnel development to improve services and results for children with disabilities

(a) In general. The Secretary, on a competitive basis, shall award grants to, or enter into contracts or cooperative agreements with, eligible entities to carry out 1 or more of the following objectives:

(1) To help address the needs identified in the State plan described in section 653(a)(2) [20 USCS § 1453(a)(2)] for highly qualified personnel, as defined in section 651(b) [20 USCS § 1451(b)], to work with infants or toddlers with disabilities, or children with disabilities, consistent with the qualifications described in section 612(a)(14) [20 USCS § 1412(a)(14)].

(2) To ensure that those personnel have the necessary skills and knowledge, derived from practices that have been determined, through scientifically based research, to be successful in serving those children.

(3) To encourage increased focus on academics and core content areas in special education personnel preparation programs.

(4) To ensure that regular education teachers have the necessary skills and knowledge to provide instruction to students with disabilities in the regular education classroom.

(5) To ensure that all special education teachers are highly qualified.

(6) To ensure that preservice and in-service personnel preparation programs include training in—

(A) the use of new technologies;

(B) the area of early intervention, educational, and transition services;

(C) effectively involving parents; and

(D) positive behavioral supports.

(7) To provide high-quality professional development for principals, superintendents, and other administrators, including training in—

(A) instructional leadership;

(B) behavioral supports in the school and classroom;

(C) paperwork reduction;

(D) promoting improved collaboration between special education and general education teachers;

(E) assessment and accountability;

(F) ensuring effective learning environments; and

(G) fostering positive relationships with parents.

(b) Personnel development; enhanced support for beginning special educators.

(1) In general. In carrying out this section, the Secretary shall support activities—

(A) for personnel development, including activities for the preparation of personnel who will serve children with high incidence and low incidence disabilities, to prepare special education and general education teachers, principals, administrators, and related services personnel (and school board members, when appropriate) to meet the diverse and individualized instructional needs of children with disabilities and improve early intervention, educational, and transitional services and results for children with disabilities, consistent with the objectives described in subsection (a); and

(B) for enhanced support for beginning special educators, consistent with the objectives described in subsection (a).

(2) Personnel development. In carrying out paragraph (1)(A), the Secretary shall support not less than 1 of the following activities:

(A) Assisting effective existing, improving existing, or developing new, collaborative personnel preparation activities undertaken by institutions of higher education, local educational agencies, and other local entities that incorporate best practices and scientifically based research, where applicable, in providing special education and general education teachers, principals, administrators, and related services personnel with the knowledge and skills to effectively support students with disabilities, including—

(i) working collaboratively in regular classroom settings;

(ii) using appropriate supports, accommodations, and curriculum modifications;

(iii) implementing effective teaching strategies, classroom-based techniques, and interventions to ensure appropriate identification of students who may be eligible for special education services, and to prevent the misidentification, inappropriate overidentification, or underidentification of children as having a disability, especially minority and limited English proficient children;

(iv) effectively working with and involving parents in the education of their children;

(v) utilizing strategies, including positive behavioral interventions, for addressing the conduct of children with disabilities that impedes their learning and that of others in the classroom;

(vi) effectively constructing IEPs, participating in IEP meetings, and implementing IEPs;

(vii) preparing children with disabilities to participate in statewide assessments (with or without accommodations) and alternate assessments, as appropriate, and to ensure that all children with disabilities are a part of all accountability systems under the Elementary and Secondary Education Act of 1965; and

(viii) working in high need elementary schools and secondary schools, including urban schools, rural schools, and schools operated by an entity described in section 7113(d)(1)(A)(ii) of the Elementary and Secondary Education Act of 1965 [*20 USCS § 7423(d)(1)(A)(ii)*], and schools that serve high numbers or percentages of limited English proficient children.

(B) Developing, evaluating, and disseminating innovative models for the recruitment, induction, retention, and assessment of new, highly qualified teachers to reduce teacher shortages, especially from groups that are underrepresented in the teaching profession, including individuals with disabilities.

(C) Providing continuous personnel preparation, training, and professional development designed to provide support and ensure retention of special education and general education teachers and personnel who teach and provide related services to children with disabilities.

(D) Developing and improving programs for paraprofessionals to become special education teachers, related services personnel, and early intervention personnel, including interdisciplinary training to enable the paraprofessionals to improve early intervention, educational, and transitional results for children with disabilities.

(E) In the case of principals and superintendents, providing activities to promote instructional leadership and improved collaboration between general educators, special education teachers, and related services personnel.

(F) Supporting institutions of higher education with minority enrollments of not less than 25 percent for the purpose of preparing personnel to work with children with disabilities.

(G) Developing and improving programs to train special education teachers to develop an expertise in autism spectrum disorders.

(H) Providing continuous personnel preparation, training, and professional development designed to provide support and improve the qualifications of personnel who provide related services to children with disabilities, including to enable such personnel to obtain advanced degrees.

(3) Enhanced support for beginning special educators. In carrying out paragraph (1)(B), the Secretary shall support not less than 1 of the following activities:

(A) Enhancing and restructuring existing programs or developing preservice teacher education programs to prepare special education teachers, at colleges or departments of education within institutions of higher education, by incorporating an extended (such as an additional 5th year) clinical learning opportunity, field experience, or supervised practicum into such programs.

(B) Creating or supporting teacher-faculty partnerships (such as professional development schools) that—

(i) consist of not less than—

(I) 1 or more institutions of higher education with special education personnel preparation programs;

(II) 1 or more local educational agencies that serve high numbers or percentages of low-income students; or

(III) 1 or more elementary schools or secondary schools, particularly schools that have failed to make adequate yearly progress on the basis, in whole and in part, of the assessment results of the disaggregated subgroup of students with disabilities;

(ii) may include other entities eligible for assistance under this part; and

(iii) provide—

(I) high-quality mentoring and induction opportunities with ongoing support for beginning special education teachers; or

(II) inservice professional development to beginning and veteran special education teachers through the ongoing exchange of information and instructional strategies with faculty.

(c) Low incidence disabilities; authorized activities.

(1) In general. In carrying out this section, the Secretary shall support activities, consistent with the objectives described in subsection (a), that benefit children with low incidence disabilities.

(2) Authorized activities. Activities that may be carried out under this subsection include activities such as the following:

(A) Preparing persons who—

(i) have prior training in educational and other related service fields; and

(ii) are studying to obtain degrees, certificates, or licensure that will enable the persons to assist children with low incidence disabilities to achieve the objectives set out in their individualized education programs described in section 614(d) [20 USCS § 1414(d)], or to assist infants and toddlers with low incidence disabilities to achieve the outcomes described in their individualized family service plans described in section 636 [20 USCS § 1436].

(B) Providing personnel from various disciplines with interdisciplinary training that will contribute to improvement in early intervention, educational, and transitional results for children with low incidence disabilities.

(C) Preparing personnel in the innovative uses and application of technology, including universally designed technologies, assistive technology devices, and assistive technology services—

(i) to enhance learning by children with low incidence disabilities through early intervention, educational, and transitional services; and

(ii) to improve communication with parents.

(D) Preparing personnel who provide services to visually impaired or blind children to teach and use Braille in the provision of services to such children.

(E) Preparing personnel to be qualified educational interpreters, to assist children with low incidence disabilities, particularly deaf and hard of hearing children in school and school related activities, and deaf and hard of hearing infants and toddlers and preschool children in early intervention and preschool programs.

(F) Preparing personnel who provide services to children with significant cognitive disabilities and children with multiple disabilities.

(G) Preparing personnel who provide services to children with low incidence disabilities and limited English proficient children.

(3) Definition. In this section, the term 'low incidence disability' means—

(A) a visual or hearing impairment, or simultaneous visual and hearing impairments;

(B) a significant cognitive impairment; or

(C) any impairment for which a small number of personnel with highly specialized skills and knowledge are needed in order for children with that impairment to receive early intervention services or a free appropriate public education.

(4) Selection of recipients. In selecting eligible entities for assistance under this subsection, the Secretary may give preference to eligible entities submitting applications that include 1 or more of the following:

(A) A proposal to prepare personnel in more than 1 low incidence disability, such as deafness and blindness.

(B) A demonstration of an effective collaboration between an eligible entity and a local educational agency that promotes recruitment and subsequent retention of highly qualified personnel to serve children with low incidence disabilities.

(5) Preparation in use of Braille. The Secretary shall ensure that all recipients of awards under this subsection who will use that assistance to prepare personnel to provide services to visually impaired or blind children that can appropriately be provided in Braille, will prepare those individuals to provide those services in Braille.

(d) Leadership preparation; authorized activities.

(1) In general. In carrying out this section, the Secretary shall support leadership preparation activities that are consistent with the objectives described in subsection (a).

(2) Authorized activities. Activities that may be carried out under this subsection include activities such as the following:

(A) Preparing personnel at the graduate, doctoral, and postdoctoral levels of training to administer, enhance, or provide services to improve results for children with disabilities.

(B) Providing interdisciplinary training for various types of leadership personnel, including teacher preparation faculty, related services faculty, administrators, researchers, supervisors, principals, and other persons whose work affects early intervention, educational, and transitional services for children with disabilities, including children with disabilities who are limited English proficient children.

(e) Applications.

(1) In general. An eligible entity that wishes to receive a grant, or enter into a contract or cooperative agreement, under this section shall submit an application to the Secretary at such time, in such manner, and containing such information as the Secretary may require.

(2) Identified State needs.

(A) Requirement to address identified needs. An application for assistance under subsection (b), (c), or (d) shall include information demonstrating to the satisfaction of the Secretary that the activities described in the application will address needs identified by the State or States the eligible entity proposes to serve.

(B) Cooperation with State educational agencies. An eligible entity that is not a local educational agency or a State educational agency shall include in the eligible entity's application information demonstrating to the satisfaction of the Secretary that the eligible entity and 1 or more State educational agencies or local educational agencies will cooperate in carrying out and monitoring the proposed project.

(3) Acceptance by States of personnel preparation requirements. The Secretary may require eligible entities to provide in the eligible entities' applications assurances from 1 or more States that such States intend to accept successful completion of the proposed personnel preparation program as meeting State personnel standards or other requirements in State law or regulation for serving children with disabilities or serving infants and toddlers with disabilities.

(f) Selection of recipients.

(1) Impact of project. In selecting eligible entities for assistance under this section, the Secretary shall consider the impact of the proposed project described in the application in meeting the need for personnel identified by the States.

(2) Requirement for eligible entities to meet state and professional qualifications. The Secretary shall make grants and enter into contracts and cooperative agreements under this section only to eligible entities that meet State and professionally recognized qualifications for the preparation of special education and related services personnel, if the purpose of the project is to assist personnel in obtaining degrees.

(3) Preferences. In selecting eligible entities for assistance under this section, the Secretary may give preference to eligible entities that are institutions of higher education that are—

(A) educating regular education personnel to meet the needs of children with disabilities in integrated settings;

(B) educating special education personnel to work in collaboration with regular educators in integrated settings; and

(C) successfully recruiting and preparing individuals with disabilities and individuals from groups that are underrepresented in the profession for which the institution of higher education is preparing individuals.

(g) Scholarships. The Secretary may include funds for scholarships, with necessary stipends and allowances, in awards under subsections (b), (c), and (d).

(h) Service obligation.

(1) In general. Each application for assistance under subsections (b), (c), and (d) shall include an assurance that the eligible entity will ensure that individuals who receive a scholarship under the proposed project agree to subsequently provide special education and related services to children with disabilities, or in the case of leadership personnel to subsequently work in the appropriate field, for a period of 2 years for every year for which the scholarship was received or repay all or part of the amount of the scholarship, in accordance with regulations issued by the Secretary.

(2) Special rule. Notwithstanding paragraph (1), the Secretary may reduce or waive the service obligation requirement under paragraph (1) if the Secretary determines that the service obligation is acting as a deterrent to the recruitment of students into special education or a related field.

(3) Secretary's responsibility. The Secretary—

(A) shall ensure that individuals described in paragraph (1) comply with the requirements of that paragraph; and

(B) may use not more than 0.5 percent of the funds appropriated under subsection (i) for each fiscal year, to carry out subparagraph (A), in addition to any other funds that are available for that purpose.

(i) Authorization of appropriations. There are authorized to be appropriated to carry out this section such sums as may be necessary for each of the fiscal years 2005 through 2010.

§ 1463. Technical assistance, demonstration projects, dissemination of information, and implementation of scientifically based research

(a) In general. The Secretary shall make competitive grants to, or enter into contracts or cooperative agreements with, eligible entities to provide technical assistance, support model demonstration projects, disseminate useful information, and implement activities that are supported by scientifically based research.

(b) Required activities. Funds received under this section shall be used to support activities to improve services provided under this *title [20 USCS §§ 1400* et seq.], including the practices of professionals and others involved in providing such services to children with disabilities, that promote academic achievement and improve results for children with disabilities through—

(1) implementing effective strategies for addressing inappropriate behavior of students with disabilities in schools, including strategies to prevent children with emotional and behavioral problems from developing emotional disturbances that require the provision of special education and related services;

(2) improving the alignment, compatibility, and development of valid and reliable assessments and alternate assessments for assessing adequate yearly progress, as described under section 1111(b)(2)(B) of the Elementary and Secondary Education Act of 1965 [*20 USCS § 6311(b)(2)(B)*];

(3) providing training for both regular education teachers and special education teachers to address the needs of students with different learning styles;

(4) disseminating information about innovative, effective, and efficient curricula

designs, instructional approaches, and strategies, and identifying positive academic and social learning opportunities, that—

(A) provide effective transitions between educational settings or from school to post school settings; and

(B) improve educational and transitional results at all levels of the educational system in which the activities are carried out and, in particular, that improve the progress of children with disabilities, as measured by assessments within the general education curriculum involved; and

(5) applying scientifically based findings to facilitate systemic changes, related to the provision of services to children with disabilities, in policy, procedure, practice, and the training and use of personnel.

(c) Authorized activities. Activities that may be carried out under this section include activities to improve services provided under this *title [20 USCS §§ 1400 et seq.]*, including the practices of professionals and others involved in providing such services to children with disabilities, that promote academic achievement and improve results for children with disabilities through—

(1) applying and testing research findings in typical settings where children with disabilities receive services to determine the usefulness, effectiveness, and general applicability of such research findings in such areas as improving instructional methods, curricula, and tools, such as textbooks and media;

(2) supporting and promoting the coordination of early intervention and educational services for children with disabilities with services provided by health, rehabilitation, and social service agencies;

(3) promoting improved alignment and compatibility of general and special education reforms concerned with curricular and instructional reform, and evaluation of such reforms;

(4) enabling professionals, parents of children with disabilities, and other persons to learn about, and implement, the findings of scientifically based research, and successful practices developed in model demonstration projects, relating to the provision of services to children with disabilities;

(5) conducting outreach, and disseminating information, relating to successful approaches to overcoming systemic barriers to the effective and efficient delivery of early intervention, educational, and transitional services to personnel who provide services to children with disabilities;

(6) assisting States and local educational agencies with the process of planning systemic changes that will promote improved early intervention, educational, and transitional results for children with disabilities;

(7) promoting change through a multistate or regional framework that benefits States, local educational agencies, and other participants in partnerships that are in the process of achieving systemic-change outcomes;

(8) focusing on the needs and issues that are specific to a population of children with disabilities, such as providing single-State and multi-State technical assistance and in-service training—

(A) to schools and agencies serving deaf-blind children and their families;

(B) to programs and agencies serving other groups of children with low incidence disabilities and their families;

(C) addressing the postsecondary education needs of individuals who are deaf or hard-of-hearing; and

(D) to schools and personnel providing special education and related services for children with autism spectrum disorders;

(9) demonstrating models of personnel preparation to ensure appropriate placements and services for all students and to reduce disproportionality in eligibility, placement, and disciplinary actions for minority and limited English proficient children; and

(10) disseminating information on how to reduce inappropriate racial and ethnic disproportionalities identified under section 618 *[20 USCS § 1418]*.

(d) Balance among activities and age ranges. In carrying out this section, the Secretary shall ensure that there is an appropriate balance across all age ranges of children with disabilities.

(e) Linking States to information sources. In carrying out this section, the Secretary shall support projects that link States to technical assistance resources, including special education and general education resources, and shall make research and related products available through libraries, electronic networks, parent training projects, and other information sources, including through the activities of the National Center for Education Evaluation and Regional Assistance established under part D of the Education Sciences Reform Act of 2002 *[20 USCS §§ 9561 et seq.]*.

(f) Applications.

(1) In general. An eligible entity that wishes to receive a grant, or enter into a contract or cooperative agreement, under this section shall submit an application to the Secretary at such time, in such manner, and containing such information as the Secretary may require.

(2) Standards. To the maximum extent feasible, each eligible entity shall demonstrate that the project described in the eligible entity's application is supported by scientifically valid research that has been carried out in accordance with the standards for the conduct and evaluation of all relevant research and development established by the National Center for Education Research.

(3) Priority. As appropriate, the Secretary shall give priority to applications that propose to serve teachers and school personnel directly in the school environment.

§ 1464. Studies and evaluations

(a) Studies and evaluations.

(1) Delegation. The Secretary shall delegate to the Director of the Institute of Education Sciences responsibility to carry out this section, other than subsections (d) and (f).

(2) Assessment. The Secretary shall, directly or through grants, contracts, or cooperative agreements awarded to eligible entities on a competitive basis, assess the progress in the implementation of this *title [20 USCS §§ 1400 et seq.]*, including the effectiveness of State and local efforts to provide—

(A) a free appropriate public education to children with disabilities; and

(B) early intervention services to infants and toddlers with disabilities, and infants and toddlers who would be at risk of having substantial developmental delays if early intervention services were not provided to the infants and toddlers.

(b) Assessment of national activities.

(1) In general. The Secretary shall carry out a national assessment of activities carried out with Federal funds under this *title [20 USCS §§ 1400 et seq.]* in order—

(A) to determine the effectiveness of this *title [20 USCS §§ 1400 et seq.]* in achieving the purposes of this *title [20 USCS §§ 1400 et seq.]*;

(B) to provide timely information to the President, Congress, the States, local educational agencies, and the public on how to implement this *title [20 USCS §§ 1400 et seq.]* more effectively; and

(C) to provide the President and Congress with information that will be useful in developing legislation to achieve the purposes of this *title [20 USCS §§ 1400 et seq.]* more effectively.

(2) Scope of assessment. The national assessment shall assess activities supported under this *title [20 USCS §§ 1400 et seq.],* including—

(A) the implementation of programs assisted under this *title [20 USCS §§ 1400 et seq.]* and the impact of such programs on addressing the developmental needs of, and improving the academic achievement of, children with disabilities to enable the children to reach challenging developmental goals and challenging State academic content standards based on State academic assessments;

(B) the types of programs and services that have demonstrated the greatest likelihood of helping students reach the challenging State academic content standards and developmental goals;

(C) the implementation of the professional development activities assisted under this *title [20 USCS §§ 1400 et seq.]* and the impact on instruction, student academic achievement, and teacher qualifications to enhance the ability of special education teachers and regular education teachers to improve results for children with disabilities; and

(D) the effectiveness of schools, local educational agencies, States, other recipients of assistance under this *title [20 USCS §§ 1400 et seq.],* and the Secretary in achieving the purposes of this *title [20 USCS §§ 1400 et seq.]* by—

(i) improving the academic achievement of children with disabilities and their performance on regular statewide assessments as compared to nondisabled children, and the performance of children with disabilities on alternate assessments;

(ii) improving the participation of children with disabilities in the general education curriculum;

(iii) improving the transitions of children with disabilities at natural transition points;

(iv) placing and serving children with disabilities, including minority children, in the least restrictive environment appropriate;

(v) preventing children with disabilities, especially children with emotional disturbances and specific learning disabilities, from dropping out of school;

(vi) addressing the reading and literacy needs of children with disabilities;

(vii) reducing the inappropriate overidentification of children, especially minority and limited English proficient children, as having a disability;

(viii) improving the participation of parents of children with disabilities in the education of their children; and

(ix) resolving disagreements between education personnel and parents through alternate dispute resolution activities, including mediation.

(3) Interim and final reports. The Secretary shall submit to the President and Congress—

(A) an interim report that summarizes the preliminary findings of the assessment not later than 3 years after the date of enactment of the Individuals with Disabilities Education Improvement Act of 2004 [enacted Dec. 3, 2004]; and

(B) a final report of the findings of the assessment not later than 5 years after the date of enactment of such Act [enacted Dec. 3, 2004].

(c) Study on ensuring accountability for students who are held to alternative achievement standards. The Secretary shall carry out a national study or studies to examine—

(1) the criteria that States use to determine—

(A) eligibility for alternate assessments; and

(B) the number and type of children who take those assessments and are held accountable to alternative achievement standards;

(2) the validity and reliability of alternate assessment instruments and procedures;

(3) the alignment of alternate assessments and alternative achievement standards to State academic content standards in reading, mathematics, and science; and

(4) the use and effectiveness of alternate assessments in appropriately measuring student progress and outcomes specific to individualized instructional need.

(d) Annual report. The Secretary shall provide an annual report to Congress that—

(1) summarizes the research conducted under part E of the Education Sciences Reform Act of 2002 [*20 USCS §§ 9567 et seq.*];

(2) analyzes and summarizes the data reported by the States and the Secretary of the Interior under section 618 [*20 USCS § 1418*];

(3) summarizes the studies and evaluations conducted under this section and the timeline for their completion;

(4) describes the extent and progress of the assessment of national activities; and

(5) describes the findings and determinations resulting from reviews of State implementation of this *title [20 USCS §§ 1400 et seq.]*.

(e) Authorized activities. In carrying out this section, the Secretary may support objective studies, evaluations, and assessments, including studies that—

(1) analyze measurable impact, outcomes, and results achieved by State educational agencies and local educational agencies through their activities to reform policies, procedures, and practices designed to improve educational and transitional services and results for children with disabilities;

(2) analyze State and local needs for professional development, parent training, and other appropriate activities that can reduce the need for disciplinary actions involving children with disabilities;

(3) assess educational and transitional services and results for children with disabilities from minority backgrounds, including—

(A) data on—

(i) the number of minority children who are referred for special education evaluation;

(ii) the number of minority children who are receiving special education and related services and their educational or other service placement;

(iii) the number of minority children who graduated from secondary programs with a regular diploma in the standard number of years; and

(iv) the number of minority children who drop out of the educational system; and

(B) the performance of children with disabilities from minority backgrounds on State assessments and other performance indicators established for all students;

(4) measure educational and transitional services and results for children with disabilities served under this *title [20 USCS §§ 1400 et seq.]*, including longitudinal studies that—

(A) examine educational and transitional services and results for children with disabilities who are 3 through 17 years of age and are receiving special education and related services under this *title [20 USCS §§ 1400 et seq.]*, using a national, representative sample of distinct age cohorts and disability categories; and

(B) examine educational results, transition services, postsecondary placement, and employment status for individuals with disabilities, 18 through 21 years of age, who are receiving or have received special education and related services under this *title [20 USCS §§ 1400 et seq.]*; and

(5) identify and report on the placement of children with disabilities by disability category.

(f) Study. The Secretary shall study, and report to Congress regarding, the extent to which States adopt policies described in section 635(c)(1) *[20 USCS § 1435(c)(1)]* and on the effects of those policies.

§ 1465. Interim alternative educational settings, behavioral supports, and systemic school interventions

(a) Program authorized. The Secretary may award grants, and enter into contracts and cooperative agreements, to support safe learning environments that support academic achievement for all students by—

(1) improving the quality of interim alternative educational settings; and

(2) providing increased behavioral supports and research-based, systemic interventions in schools.

(b) Authorized activities. In carrying out this section, the Secretary may support activities to—

(1) establish, expand, or increase the scope of behavioral supports and systemic interventions by providing for effective, research-based practices, including—

(A) training for school staff on early identification, prereferral, and referral procedures;

(B) training for administrators, teachers, related services personnel, behavioral specialists, and other school staff in positive behavioral interventions and supports, behavioral intervention planning, and classroom and student management techniques;

(C) joint training for administrators, parents, teachers, related services personnel, behavioral specialists, and other school staff on effective strategies for positive behavioral interventions and behavior management strategies that focus on the prevention of behavior problems;

(D) developing or implementing specific curricula, programs, or interventions aimed at addressing behavioral problems;

(E) stronger linkages between school-based services and community-based resources, such as community mental health and primary care providers; or

(F) using behavioral specialists, related services personnel, and other staff necessary to implement behavioral supports; or

(2) improve interim alternative educational settings by—

(A) improving the training of administrators, teachers, related services personnel, behavioral specialists, and other school staff (including ongoing mentoring of new teachers) in behavioral supports and interventions;

(B) attracting and retaining a high quality, diverse staff;

(C) providing for referral to counseling services;

(D) utilizing research-based interventions, curriculum, and practices;

(E) allowing students to use instructional technology that provides individualized instruction;

(F) ensuring that the services are fully consistent with the goals of the individual student's IEP;

(G) promoting effective case management and collaboration among parents, teachers, physicians, related services personnel, behavioral specialists, principals, administrators, and other school staff;

(H) promoting interagency coordination and coordinated service delivery among schools, juvenile courts, child welfare agencies, community mental health providers, primary care providers, public recreation agencies, and community-based organizations; or

(I) providing for behavioral specialists to help students transitioning from interim alternative educational settings reintegrate into their regular classrooms.

(c) Definition of eligible entity. In this section, the term "eligible entity" means—

(1) a local educational agency; or

(2) a consortium consisting of a local educational agency and 1 or more of the following entities:

(A) Another local educational agency.

(B) A community-based organization with a demonstrated record of effectiveness in helping children with disabilities who have behavioral challenges succeed.

(C) An institution of higher education.

(D) A community mental health provider.

(E) An educational service agency.

(d) Applications. Any eligible entity that wishes to receive a grant, or enter into a contract or cooperative agreement, under this section shall—

(1) submit an application to the Secretary at such time, in such manner, and containing such information as the Secretary may require; and

(2) involve parents of participating students in the design and implementation of the activities funded under this section.

(e) Report and evaluation. Each eligible entity receiving a grant under this section shall prepare and submit annually to the Secretary a report on the outcomes of the activities assisted under the grant.

§ 1466. Authorization of appropriations

(a) In general. There are authorized to be appropriated to carry out this subpart [20 USCS §§ 1461 et seq.] (other than section 662 [20 USCS § 1462]) such sums as may be necessary for each of the fiscal years 2005 through 2010.

(b) Reservation. From amounts appropriated under subsection (a) for fiscal year 2005, the Secretary shall reserve $ 1,000,000 to carry out the study authorized in section 664(c)

[*20 USCS § 1464(c)*]. From amounts appropriated under subsection (a) for a succeeding fiscal year, the Secretary may reserve an additional amount to carry out such study if the Secretary determines the additional amount is necessary.

SUPPORTS TO IMPROVE RESULTS FOR CHILDREN WITH DISABILITIES

§ 1470. Purposes

The purposes of this subpart [*20 USCS §§ 1470* et seq.] are to ensure that—

(1) children with disabilities and their parents receive training and information designed to assist the children in meeting developmental and functional goals and challenging academic achievement goals, and in preparing to lead productive independent adult lives;

(2) children with disabilities and their parents receive training and information on their rights, responsibilities, and protections under this *title [20 USCS §§ 1400* et seq.], in order to develop the skills necessary to cooperatively and effectively participate in planning and decision making relating to early intervention, educational, and transitional services;

(3) parents, teachers, administrators, early intervention personnel, related services personnel, and transition personnel receive coordinated and accessible technical assistance and information to assist such personnel in improving early intervention, educational, and transitional services and results for children with disabilities and their families; and

(4) appropriate technology and media are researched, developed, and demonstrated, to improve and implement early intervention, educational, and transitional services and results for children with disabilities and their families.

§ 1471. Parent training and information centers

(a) Program authorized.

(1) In general. The Secretary may award grants to, and enter into contracts and cooperative agreements with, parent organizations to support parent training and information centers to carry out activities under this section.

(2) Definition of parent organization. In this section, the term "parent organization" means a private nonprofit organization (other than an institution of higher education) that—

(A) has a board of directors—

(i) the majority of whom are parents of children with disabilities ages birth through 26;

(ii) that includes—

(I) individuals working in the fields of special education, related services, and early intervention; and

(II) individuals with disabilities; and

(iii) the parent and professional members of which are broadly representative of the population to be served, including low-income parents and parents of limited English proficient children; and

(B) has as its mission serving families of children with disabilities who—

(i) are ages birth through 26; and

(ii) have the full range of disabilities described in section 602(3) [20 USCS § 1401(3)].

(b) Required activities. Each parent training and information center that receives assistance under this section shall—

(1) provide training and information that meets the needs of parents of children with disabilities living in the area served by the center, particularly underserved parents and parents of children who may be inappropriately identified, to enable their children with disabilities to—

(A) meet developmental and functional goals, and challenging academic achievement goals that have been established for all children; and

(B) be prepared to lead productive independent adult lives, to the maximum extent possible;

(2) serve the parents of infants, toddlers, and children with the full range of disabilities described in section 602(3) [20 USCS § 1401(3)];

(3) ensure that the training and information provided meets the needs of low-income parents and parents of limited English proficient children;

(4) assist parents to—

(A) better understand the nature of their children's disabilities and their educational, developmental, and transitional needs;

(B) communicate effectively and work collaboratively with personnel responsible for providing special education, early intervention services, transition services, and related services;

(C) participate in decisionmaking processes and the development of individualized education programs under part B [20 USCS §§ 1411 et seq.] and individualized family service plans under part C [20 USCS §§ 1431 et seq.];

(D) obtain appropriate information about the range, type, and quality of—

(i) options, programs, services, technologies, practices and interventions based on scientifically based research, to the extent practicable; and

(ii) resources available to assist children with disabilities and their families in school and at home;

(E) understand the provisions of this *title [20 USCS §§ 1400 et seq.]* for the education of, and the provision of early intervention services to, children with disabilities;

(F) participate in activities at the school level that benefit their children; and

(G) participate in school reform activities;

(5) in States where the State elects to contract with the parent training and information center, contract with State educational agencies to provide, consistent with subparagraphs (B) and (D) of section 615(e)(2) [20 USCS § 1415(e)(2)], individuals who meet with parents to explain the mediation process to the parents;

(6) assist parents in resolving disputes in the most expeditious and effective way possible, including encouraging the use, and explaining the benefits, of alternative methods of dispute resolution, such as the mediation process described in section 615(e) [20 USCS § 1415(e)];

(7) assist parents and students with disabilities to understand their rights and responsibilities under this *title [20 USCS §§ 1400 et seq.]*, including those under section

615(m) [*20 USCS § 1415(m)*] upon the student's reaching the age of majority (as appropriate under State law);

(8) assist parents to understand the availability of, and how to effectively use, procedural safeguards under this *title [20 USCS §§ 1400* et seq.], including the resolution session described in section 615(e) [*20 USCS § 1415(e)*];

(9) assist parents in understanding, preparing for, and participating in, the process described in section 615(f)(1)(B) [*20 USCS § 1415(f)(1)(B)*];

(10) establish cooperative partnerships with community parent resource centers funded under section 672 [*20 USCS § 1472*];

(11) network with appropriate clearinghouses, including organizations conducting national dissemination activities under section 663 [*20 USCS § 1463*] and the Institute of Education Sciences, and with other national, State, and local organizations and agencies, such as protection and advocacy agencies, that serve parents and families of children with the full range of disabilities described in section 602(3) [*20 USCS § 1401(3)*]; and

(12) annually report to the Secretary on—

(A) the number and demographics of parents to whom the center provided information and training in the most recently concluded fiscal year;

(B) the effectiveness of strategies used to reach and serve parents, including underserved parents of children with disabilities; and

(C) the number of parents served who have resolved disputes through alternative methods of dispute resolution.

(c) Optional activities. A parent training and information center that receives assistance under this section may provide information to teachers and other professionals to assist the teachers and professionals in improving results for children with disabilities.

(d) Application requirements. Each application for assistance under this section shall identify with specificity the special efforts that the parent organization will undertake—

(1) to ensure that the needs for training and information of underserved parents of children with disabilities in the area to be served are effectively met; and

(2) to work with community based organizations, including community based organizations that work with low-income parents and parents of limited English proficient children.

(e) Distribution of funds.

(1) In general. The Secretary shall—

(A) make not less than 1 award to a parent organization in each State for a parent training and information center that is designated as the statewide parent training and information center; or

(B) in the case of a large State, make awards to multiple parent training and information centers, but only if the centers demonstrate that coordinated services and supports will occur among the multiple centers.

(2) Selection requirement. The Secretary shall select among applications submitted by parent organizations in a State in a manner that ensures the most effective assistance to parents, including parents in urban and rural areas, in the State.

(f) Quarterly review.

(1) Meetings. The board of directors of each parent organization that receives an award under this section shall meet not less than once in each calendar quarter to review

the activities for which the award was made.

(2) Continuation award. When a parent organization requests a continuation award under this section, the board of directors shall submit to the Secretary a written review of the parent training and information program conducted by the parent organization during the preceding fiscal year.

§ 1472. Community parent resource centers

(a) Program authorized.

(1) In general. The Secretary may award grants to, and enter into contracts and cooperative agreements with, local parent organizations to support community parent resource centers that will help ensure that underserved parents of children with disabilities, including low income parents, parents of limited English proficient children, and parents with disabilities, have the training and information the parents need to enable the parents to participate effectively in helping their children with disabilities—

(A) to meet developmental and functional goals, and challenging academic achievement goals that have been established for all children; and

(B) to be prepared to lead productive independent adult lives, to the maximum extent possible.

(2) Definition of local parent organization. In this section, the term "local parent organization" means a parent organization, as defined in section 671(a)(2) [*20 USCS § 1471(a)(2)*], that—

(A) has a board of directors the majority of whom are parents of children with disabilities ages birth through 26 from the community to be served; and

(B) has as its mission serving parents of children with disabilities who—

(i) are ages birth through 26; and

(ii) have the full range of disabilities described in section 602(3) [*20 USCS § 1401(3)*].

(b) Required activities. Each community parent resource center assisted under this section shall—

(1) provide training and information that meets the training and information needs of parents of children with disabilities proposed to be served by the grant, contract, or cooperative agreement;

(2) carry out the activities required of parent training and information centers under paragraphs (2) through (9) of section 671(b) [*20 USCS § 1471(b)*];

(3) establish cooperative partnerships with the parent training and information centers funded under section 671 [*20 USCS § 1471*]; and

(4) be designed to meet the specific needs of families who experience significant isolation from available sources of information and support.

§ 1473. Technical assistance for parent training and information centers

(a) Program authorized.

(1) In general. The Secretary may, directly or through awards to eligible entities, provide technical assistance for developing, assisting, and coordinating parent training and information programs carried out by parent training and information centers receiving assistance under section 671 [*20 USCS § 1471*] and community parent resource centers receiving assistance under section 672 [*20 USCS § 1472*].

(2) Definition of eligible entity. In this section, the term "eligible entity" has the

meaning given the term in section 661(b) [*20 USCS § 1461(b)*].

(b) Authorized activities. The Secretary may provide technical assistance to a parent training and information center or a community parent resource center under this section in areas such as—

(1) effective coordination of parent training efforts;

(2) dissemination of scientifically based research and information;

(3) promotion of the use of technology, including assistive technology devices and assistive technology services;

(4) reaching underserved populations, including parents of low-income and limited English proficient children with disabilities;

(5) including children with disabilities in general education programs;

(6) facilitation of transitions from—

(A) early intervention services to preschool;

(B) preschool to elementary school;

(C) elementary school to secondary school; and

(D) secondary school to postsecondary environments; and

(7) promotion of alternative methods of dispute resolution, including mediation.

(c) Collaboration with the resource centers. Each eligible entity receiving an award under subsection (a) shall develop collaborative agreements with the geographically appropriate regional resource center and, as appropriate, the regional educational laboratory supported under section 174 of the Education Sciences Reform Act of 2002 [*20 USCS § 9564*], to further parent and professional collaboration.

§ 1474. Technology development, demonstration, and utilization; media services; and instructional materials

(a) Program authorized.

(1) In general. The Secretary, on a competitive basis, shall award grants to, and enter into contracts and cooperative agreements with, eligible entities to support activities described in subsections (b) and (c).

(2) Definition of eligible entity. In this section, the term "eligible entity" has the meaning given the term in section 661(b) [*20 USCS § 1461(b)*].

(b) Technology development, demonstration, and use.

(1) In general. In carrying out this section, the Secretary shall support activities to promote the development, demonstration, and use of technology.

(2) Authorized activities. The following activities may be carried out under this subsection:

(A) Conducting research on and promoting the demonstration and use of innovative, emerging, and universally designed technologies for children with disabilities, by improving the transfer of technology from research and development to practice.

(B) Supporting research, development, and dissemination of technology with universal design features, so that the technology is accessible to the broadest range of individuals with disabilities without further modification or adaptation.

(C) Demonstrating the use of systems to provide parents and teachers with information and training concerning early diagnosis of, intervention for, and effective teaching strategies for, young children with reading disabilities.

(D) Supporting the use of Internet-based communications for students with cognitive disabilities in order to maximize their academic and functional skills.

(c) Educational media services.

(1) In general. In carrying out this section, the Secretary shall support—

(A) educational media activities that are designed to be of educational value in the classroom setting to children with disabilities;

(B) providing video description, open captioning, or closed captioning, that is appropriate for use in the classroom setting, of—

(i) television programs;

(ii) videos;

(iii) other materials, including programs and materials associated with new and emerging technologies, such as CDs, DVDs, video streaming, and other forms of multimedia; or

(iv) news (but only until September 30, 2006);

(C) distributing materials described in subparagraphs (A) and (B) through such mechanisms as a loan service; and

(D) providing free educational materials, including textbooks, in accessible media for visually impaired and print disabled students in elementary schools and secondary schools, postsecondary schools, and graduate schools.

(2) Limitation. The video description, open captioning, or closed captioning described in paragraph (1)(B) shall be provided only when the description or captioning has not been previously provided by the producer or distributor, or has not been fully funded by other sources.

(d) Applications.

(1) In general. Any eligible entity that wishes to receive a grant, or enter into a contract or cooperative agreement, under subsection (b) or (c) shall submit an application to the Secretary at such time, in such manner, and containing such information as the Secretary may require.

(2) Special rule. For the purpose of an application for an award to carry out activities described in subsection (c)(1)(D), such eligible entity shall—

(A) be a national, nonprofit entity with a proven track record of meeting the needs of students with print disabilities through services described in subsection (c)(1)(D);

(B) have the capacity to produce, maintain, and distribute in a timely fashion, up-to-date textbooks in digital audio formats to qualified students; and

(C) have a demonstrated ability to significantly leverage Federal funds through other public and private contributions, as well as through the expansive use of volunteers.

(e) National Instructional Materials Access Center.

(1) In general. The Secretary shall establish and support, through the American Printing House for the Blind, a center to be known as the "National Instructional Materials Access Center" not later than 1 year after the date of enactment of the Individuals with Disabilities Education Improvement Act of 2004 [enacted Dec. 3, 2004].

(2) Duties. The duties of the National Instructional Materials Access Center are the following:

(A) To receive and maintain a catalog of print instructional materials prepared in the

National Instructional Materials Accessibility Standard, as established by the Secretary, made available to such center by the textbook publishing industry, State educational agencies, and local educational agencies.

(B) To provide access to print instructional materials, including textbooks, in accessible media, free of charge, to blind or other persons with print disabilities in elementary schools and secondary schools, in accordance with such terms and procedures as the National Instructional Materials Access Center may prescribe.

(C) To develop, adopt and publish procedures to protect against copyright infringement, with respect to the print instructional materials provided under sections 612(a)(23) and 613(a)(6) [*20 USCS §§ 1412(a)(23) and 1413(a)(6)*].

(3) Definitions. In this subsection:

(A) Blind or other persons with print disabilities. The term "blind or other persons with print disabilities" means children served under this Act and who may qualify in accordance with the Act entitled "An Act to provide books for the adult blind", approved March 3, 1931 (*2 U.S.C. 135a*; 46 Stat. 1487) to receive books and other publications produced in specialized formats.

(B) National Instructional Materials Accessibility Standard. The term "National Instructional Materials Accessibility Standard" means the standard established by the Secretary to be used in the preparation of electronic files suitable and used solely for efficient conversion into specialized formats.

(C) Print instructional materials. The term "print instructional materials" means printed textbooks and related printed core materials that are written and published primarily for use in elementary school and secondary school instruction and are required by a State educational agency or local educational agency for use by students in the classroom.

(D) Specialized formats. The term "specialized formats" has the meaning given the term in *section 121(d)(3) of title 17, United States Code* [*17 USCS § 121(d)(3)*].

(4) Applicability. This subsection shall apply to print instructional materials published after the date on which the final rule establishing the National Instructional Materials Accessibility Standard was published in the Federal Register.

(5) Liability of the Secretary. Nothing in this subsection shall be construed to establish a private right of action against the Secretary for failure to provide instructional materials directly, or for failure by the National Instructional Materials Access Center to perform the duties of such center, or to otherwise authorize a private right of action related to the performance by such center, including through the application of the rights of children and parents established under this Act.

(6) Inapplicability. Subsections (a) through (d) shall not apply to this subsection.

§ 1475. Authorization of appropriations

There are authorized to be appropriated to carry out this subpart [*20 USCS §§ 1470 et seq.*] such sums as may be necessary for each of the fiscal years 2005 through 2010.

§ 1476. [Omitted]

§ 1477. [Omitted]

§ 1478. [Omitted]

§ 1479. [Omitted]

§ 1480. [Omitted]

GENERAL PROVISIONS

§ 1481. Comprehensive plan for subparts 2 and 3

(a) Comprehensive plan.

(1) In general. After receiving input from interested individuals with relevant expertise, the Secretary shall develop and implement a comprehensive plan for activities carried out under subparts 2 and 3 [20 USCS §§ 1461 et seq. and 1471 et seq.] in order to enhance the provision of early intervention services, educational services, related services, and transitional services to children with disabilities under parts B and C [20 USCS §§ 1411 et seq. and 1431 et seq.]. To the extent practicable, the plan shall be coordinated with the plan developed pursuant to section 178(c) [177(c)] of the Education Sciences Reform Act of 2002 [20 USCS § 9567b(c)] and shall include mechanisms to address early intervention, educational, related service and transitional needs identified by State educational agencies in applications submitted for State personnel development grants under subpart 1 [20 USCS §§ 1451 et seq.] and for grants under subparts 2 and 3 [20 USCS §§ 1461 et seq. and 1471 et seq.].

(2) Public comment. The Secretary shall provide a public comment period of not less than 45 days on the plan.

(3) Distribution of funds. In implementing the plan, the Secretary shall, to the extent appropriate, ensure that funds awarded under subparts 2 and 3 [20 USCS §§ 1461 et seq. and 1471 et seq.] are used to carry out activities that benefit, directly or indirectly, children with the full range of disabilities and of all ages.

(4) Reports to Congress. The Secretary shall annually report to Congress on the Secretary's activities under subparts 2 and 3 [20 USCS §§ 1461 et seq. and 1471 et seq.], including an initial report not later than 12 months after the date of enactment of the Individuals with Disabilities Education Improvement Act of 2004 [enacted Dec. 3, 2004].

(b) Assistance authorized. The Secretary is authorized to award grants to, or enter into contracts or cooperative agreements with, eligible entities to enable the eligible entities to carry out the purposes of such subparts in accordance with the comprehensive plan described in subsection (a).

(c) Special populations.

(1) Application requirement. In making an award of a grant, contract, or cooperative agreement under subpart 2 or 3 [20 USCS §§ 1461 et seq. or 1471 et seq.], the Secretary shall, as appropriate, require an eligible entity to demonstrate how the eligible entity will address the needs of children with disabilities from minority backgrounds.

(2) Required outreach and technical assistance. Notwithstanding any other provision of this title [20 USCS §§ 1400 et seq.], the Secretary shall reserve not less than 2 percent of the total amount of funds appropriated to carry out subparts 2 and 3 [20 USCS §§ 1461 et seq. and 1471 et seq.] for either or both of the following activities:

(A) Providing outreach and technical assistance to historically Black colleges and universities, and to institutions of higher education with minority enrollments of not less than 25 percent, to promote the participation of such colleges, universities, and institutions in activities under this subpart.

(B) Enabling historically Black colleges and universities, and the institutions described in subparagraph (A), to assist other colleges, universities, institutions, and agencies in improving educational and transitional results for children with disabilities, if the historically Black colleges and universities and the institutions of higher education described in subparagraph (A) meet the criteria established by the Secretary under this subpart.

(d) Priorities. The Secretary, in making an award of a grant, contract, or cooperative agreement under subpart 2 or 3 [20 USCS §§ 1461 et seq. or 1471 et seq.], may, without regard to the rulemaking procedures under *section 553 of title 5, United States Code* [5 USCS § 553], limit competitions to, or otherwise give priority to—

(1) projects that address 1 or more—

(A) age ranges;

(B) disabilities;

(C) school grades;

(D) types of educational placements or early intervention environments;

(E) types of services;

(F) content areas, such as reading; or

(G) effective strategies for helping children with disabilities learn appropriate behavior in the school and other community based educational settings;

(2) projects that address the needs of children based on the severity or incidence of their disability;

(3) projects that address the needs of—

(A) low achieving students;

(B) underserved populations;

(C) children from low income families;

(D) limited English proficient children;

(E) unserved and underserved areas;

(F) rural or urban areas;

(G) children whose behavior interferes with their learning and socialization;

(H) children with reading difficulties;

(I) children in public charter schools;

(J) children who are gifted and talented; or

(K) children with disabilities served by local educational agencies that receive payments under title VIII of the Elementary and Secondary Education Act of 1965 [20 USCS §§ 7701 et seq.];

(4) projects to reduce inappropriate identification of children as children with disabilities, particularly among minority children;

(5) projects that are carried out in particular areas of the country, to ensure broad geographic coverage;

(6) projects that promote the development and use of technologies with universal design, assistive technology devices, and assistive technology services to maximize children with disabilities' access to and participation in the general education curriculum; and

(7) any activity that is authorized in subpart 2 or 3 [20 USCS §§ 1461 et seq. or 1471 et seq.].

(e) Eligibility for financial assistance. No State or local educational agency, or other public institution or agency, may receive a grant or enter into a contract or cooperative agreement under subpart 2 or 3 [20 USCS §§ 1461 et seq. or 1471 et seq.] that relates exclusively to programs, projects, and activities pertaining to children aged 3 through 5, inclusive, unless the State is eligible to receive a grant under section 619(b) [20 USCS § 1419(b)].

§ 1482. Administrative provisions

(a) Applicant and recipient responsibilities.

(1) Development and assessment of projects. The Secretary shall require that an applicant for, and a recipient of, a grant, contract, or cooperative agreement for a project under subpart 2 or 3 [20 USCS §§ 1461 et seq. or 1471 et seq.]—

(A) involve individuals with disabilities or parents of individuals with disabilities ages birth through 26 in planning, implementing, and evaluating the project; and

(B) where appropriate, determine whether the project has any potential for replication and adoption by other entities.

(2) Additional responsibilities. The Secretary may require a recipient of a grant, contract, or cooperative agreement under subpart 2 or 3 [20 USCS §§ 1461 et seq. or 1471 et seq.] to—

(A) share in the cost of the project;

(B) prepare any findings and products from the project in formats that are useful for specific audiences, including parents, administrators, teachers, early intervention personnel, related services personnel, and individuals with disabilities;

(C) disseminate such findings and products; and

(D) collaborate with other such recipients in carrying out subparagraphs (B) and (C).

(b) Application management.

(1) Standing panel.

(A) In general. The Secretary shall establish and use a standing panel of experts who are qualified, by virtue of their training, expertise, or experience, to evaluate each application under subpart 2 or 3 [20 USCS §§ 1461 et seq. or 1471 et seq.] that requests more than $ 75,000 per year in Federal financial assistance.

(B) Membership. The standing panel shall include, at a minimum—

(i) individuals who are representatives of institutions of higher education that plan, develop, and carry out high quality programs of personnel preparation;

(ii) individuals who design and carry out scientifically based research targeted to the improvement of special education programs and services;

(iii) individuals who have recognized experience and knowledge necessary to integrate and apply scientifically based research findings to improve educational and transitional results for children with disabilities;

(iv) individuals who administer programs at the State or local level in which children with disabilities participate;

(v) individuals who prepare parents of children with disabilities to participate in making decisions about the education of their children;

(vi) individuals who establish policies that affect the delivery of services to children with disabilities;

(vii) individuals who are parents of children with disabilities ages birth through 26 who are benefiting, or have benefited, from coordinated research, personnel preparation, and technical assistance; and

(viii) individuals with disabilities.

(C) Term. No individual shall serve on the standing panel for more than 3 consecutive years.

(2) Peer-review panels for particular competitions.

(A) Composition. The Secretary shall ensure that each subpanel selected from the standing panel that reviews an application under subpart 2 or 3 [*20 USCS §§ 1461* et seq. or *1471* et seq.] includes—

(i) individuals with knowledge and expertise on the issues addressed by the activities described in the application; and

(ii) to the extent practicable, parents of children with disabilities ages birth through 26, individuals with disabilities, and persons from diverse backgrounds.

(B) Federal employment limitation. A majority of the individuals on each subpanel that reviews an application under subpart 2 or 3 [*20 USCS §§ 1461* et seq. or *1471* et seq.] shall be individuals who are not employees of the Federal Government.

(3) Use of discretionary funds for administrative purposes.

(A) Expenses and fees of non-federal panel members. The Secretary may use funds available under subpart 2 or 3 [*20 USCS §§ 1461* et seq. or *1471* et seq.] to pay the expenses and fees of the panel members who are not officers or employees of the Federal Government.

(B) Administrative support. The Secretary may use not more than 1 percent of the funds appropriated to carry out subpart 2 or 3 [*20 USCS §§ 1461* et seq. or *1471* et seq.] to pay non-Federal entities for administrative support related to management of applications submitted under subpart 2 or 3 [*20 USCS §§ 1461* et seq. or *1471* et seq.], respectively.

(c) Program evaluation. The Secretary may use funds made available to carry out subpart 2 or 3 to evaluate activities carried out under subpart 2 or 3 [*20 USCS §§ 1461* et seq. or *1471* et seq.], respectively.

(d) Minimum funding required.

(1) In general. Subject to paragraph (2), the Secretary shall ensure that, for each fiscal year, not less than the following amounts are provided under subparts 2 and 3 [*20 USCS §§ 1461* et seq. and *1471* et seq.] to address the following needs:

(A) $ 12,832,000 to address the educational, related services, transitional, and early intervention needs of children with deaf-blindness.

(B) $ 4,000,000 to address the postsecondary, vocational, technical, continuing, and adult education needs of individuals with deafness.

(C) $ 4,000,000 to address the educational, related services, and transitional needs of children with an emotional disturbance and those who are at risk of developing an emotional disturbance.

(2) Ratable reduction. If the sum of the amount appropriated to carry out subparts 2 and 3 [*20 USCS §§ 1461* et seq. or *1471* et seq.], and part E of the Education Sciences Reform Act of 2002 [*20 USCS §§ 9567* et seq.] for any fiscal year is less than $ 130,000,000, the amounts listed in paragraph (1) shall be ratably reduced for the fiscal year.

TITLE 34
EDUCATION

SUBTITLE B   REGULATIONS OF THE OFFICES OF THE DEPARTMENT OF EDUCATION

CHAPTER III   OFFICE OF SPECIAL EDUCATION AND REHABILITATIVE SERVICES, DEPARTMENT OF EDUCATION

PART 300   ASSISTANCE TO STATES FOR THE EDUCATION OF CHILDREN WITH DISABILITIES

SUBPART A   GENERAL PURPOSES AND APPLICABILITY

§ 300.1 Purposes.

The purposes of this part are —

(a) To ensure that all children with disabilities have available to them a free appropriate public education that emphasizes special education and related services designed to meet their unique needs and prepare them for further education, employment, and independent living;

(b) To ensure that the rights of children with disabilities and their parents are protected;

(c) To assist States, localities, educational service agencies, and Federal agencies to provide for the education of all children with disabilities; and

(d) To assess and ensure the effectiveness of efforts to educate children with disabilities.

§ 300.2 Applicability of this part to State and local agencies.

(a) *States.* This part applies to each State that receives payments under Part B of the Act, as defined in § 300.4.

(b) *Public agencies within the State.* The provisions of this part —

(1) Apply to all political subdivisions of the State that are involved in the education of children with disabilities, including:

(i) The State educational agency (SEA).

(ii) Local educational agencies (LEAs), educational service agencies (ESAs), and public charter schools that are not otherwise included as LEAs or ESAs and are not a school of an LEA or ESA.

(iii) Other State agencies and schools (such as Departments of Mental Health and Welfare and State schools for children with deafness or children with blindness).

(iv) State and local juvenile and adult correctional facilities; and

(2) Are binding on each public agency in the State that provides special education and related services to children with disabilities, regardless of whether that agency is receiving funds under Part B of the Act.

(c) Private schools and facilities. Each public agency in the State is responsible for ensuring that the rights and protections under Part B of the Act are given to children with disabilities—

(1) Referred to or placed in private schools and facilities by that public agency; or

(2) Placed in private schools by their parents under the provisions of § 300.148.

§ 300.3 [This section was removed. See 71 FR 46540, 46753, Aug. 14, 2006.]

DEFINITIONS USED IN THIS PART

§ 300.4 **Act.**

Act means the Individuals with Disabilities Education Act, as amended.

§ 300.5 **Assistive technology device.**

Assistive technology device means any item, piece of equipment, or product system, whether acquired commercially off the shelf, modified, or customized, that is used to increase, maintain, or improve the functional capabilities of a child with a disability. The term does not include a medical device that is surgically implanted, or the replacement of such device.

§ 300.6 **Assistive technology service.**

Assistive technology service means any service that directly assists a child with a disability in the selection, acquisition, or use of an assistive technology device. The term includes —

(a) The evaluation of the needs of a child with a disability, including a functional evaluation of the child in the child's customary environment;

(b) Purchasing, leasing, or otherwise providing for the acquisition of assistive technology devices by children with disabilities;

(c) Selecting, designing, fitting, customizing, adapting, applying, maintaining, repairing, or replacing assistive technology devices;

(d) Coordinating and using other therapies, interventions, or services with assistive technology devices, such as those associated with existing education and rehabilitation plans and programs;

(e) Training or technical assistance for a child with a disability or, if appropriate, that child's family; and

(f) Training or technical assistance for professionals (including individuals providing education or rehabilitation services), employers, or other individuals who provide services to, employ, or are otherwise substantially involved in the major life functions of that child.

§ 300.7 **Charter school.**

Charter school has the meaning given the term in section 5210(1) of the Elementary and Secondary Education Act of 1965, as amended, *20 U.S.C. 6301* et seq. (ESEA).

§ 300.8 **Child with a disability.**

(a) General. (1) Child with a disability means a child evaluated in accordance with §§ 300.304 through 300.311 as having mental retardation, a hearing impairment (including deafness), a speech or language impairment, a visual impairment (including blindness), a serious emotional disturbance (referred to in this part as "emotional disturbance"), an orthopedic impairment, autism, traumatic brain injury, an other health impairment, a specific learning disability, deaf-blindness, or multiple disabilities, and who, by reason thereof, needs special education and related services.

(2)(i) Subject to paragraph (a)(2)(ii) of this section, if it is determined, through an appropriate evaluation under §§ 300.304 through 300.311, that a child has one of the disabilities identified in paragraph (a)(1) of this section, but only needs a related service and not special education, the child is not a child with a disability under this part.

(ii) If, consistent with § 300.39(a)(2), the related service required by the child is considered special education rather than a related service under State standards, the child would be determined to be a child with a disability under paragraph (a)(1) of this section.

(b) Children aged three through nine experiencing developmental delays. Child with a disability for children aged three through nine (or any subset of that age range, including ages three through five), may, subject to the conditions described in § 300.111(b), include a child —

(1) Who is experiencing developmental delays, as defined by the State and as measured by appropriate diagnostic instruments and procedures, in one or more of the following areas: Physical development, cognitive development, communication development, social or emotional development, or adaptive development; and

(2) Who, by reason thereof, needs special education and related services.

(c) Definitions of disability terms. The terms used in this definition of a child with a disability are defined as follows:

(1)(i) Autism means a developmental disability significantly affecting verbal and nonverbal communication and social interaction, generally evident before age three, that adversely affects a child's educational performance. Other characteristics often associated with autism are engagement in repetitive activities and stereotyped movements, resistance to environmental change or change in daily routines, and unusual responses to sensory experiences.

(ii) Autism does not apply if a child's educational performance is adversely affected primarily because the child has an emotional disturbance, as defined in paragraph (c)(4) of this section.

(iii) A child who manifests the characteristics of autism after age three could be identified as having autism if the criteria in paragraph (c)(1)(i) of this section are satisfied.

(2) Deaf-blindness means concomitant hearing and visual impairments, the combination of which causes such severe communication and other developmental and educational needs that they cannot be accommodated in special education programs solely for children with deafness or children with blindness.

(3) Deafness means a hearing impairment that is so severe that the child is impaired in processing linguistic information through hearing, with or without amplification, that adversely affects a child's educational performance.

(4)(i) Emotional disturbance means a condition exhibiting one or more of the following characteristics over a long period of time and to a marked degree that adversely affects a child's educational performance:

(A) An inability to learn that cannot be explained by intellectual, sensory, or health factors.

(B) An inability to build or maintain satisfactory interpersonal relationships with peers and teachers.

(C) Inappropriate types of behavior or feelings under normal circumstances.

(D) A general pervasive mood of unhappiness or depression.

(E) A tendency to develop physical symptoms or fears associated with personal or school problems.

(ii) Emotional disturbance includes schizophrenia. The term does not apply to children who are socially maladjusted, unless it is determined that they have an emotional disturbance under paragraph (c)(4)(i) of this section.

(5) Hearing impairment means an impairment in hearing, whether permanent or fluctuating, that adversely affects a child's educational performance but that is not included under the definition of deafness in this section.

(6) Mental retardation means significantly subaverage general intellectual functioning, existing concurrently with deficits in adaptive behavior and manifested during the developmental period, that adversely affects a child's educational performance.

(7) Multiple disabilities means concomitant impairments (such as mental retardation-blindness or mental retardation-orthopedic impairment), the combination of which causes such severe educational needs that they cannot be accommodated in special education programs solely for one of the impairments. Multiple disabilities does not include deaf-blindness.

(8) Orthopedic impairment means a severe orthopedic impairment that adversely affects a child's educational performance. The term includes impairments caused by a congenital anomaly, impairments caused by disease (e.g., poliomyelitis, bone tuberculosis), and impairments from other causes (e.g., cerebral palsy, amputations, and fractures or burns that cause contractures).

(9) Other health impairment means having limited strength, vitality, or alertness, including a heightened alertness to environmental stimuli, that results in limited alertness with respect to the educational environment, that —

(i) Is due to chronic or acute health problems such as asthma, attention deficit disorder or attention deficit hyperactivity disorder, diabetes, epilepsy, a heart condition, hemophilia, lead poisoning, leukemia, nephritis, rheumatic fever, sickle cell anemia, and Tourette syndrome; and

(ii) Adversely affects a child's educational performance.

(10) Specific learning disability — (i) General. Specific learning disability means a disorder in one or more of the basic psychological processes involved in understanding or in using language, spoken or written, that may manifest itself in the imperfect ability to listen, think, speak, read, write, spell, or to do mathematical calculations, including conditions such as perceptual disabilities, brain injury, minimal brain dysfunction, dyslexia, and developmental aphasia.

(ii) Disorders not included. Specific learning disability does not include learning problems that are primarily the result of visual, hearing, or motor disabilities, of mental retardation, of emotional disturbance, or of environmental, cultural, or economic disadvantage.

(11) Speech or language impairment means a communication disorder, such as stuttering, impaired articulation, a language impairment, or a voice impairment, that adversely affects a child's educational performance.

(12) Traumatic brain injury means an acquired injury to the brain caused by an external physical force, resulting in total or partial functional disability or psychosocial impairment, or both, that adversely affects a child's educational performance. Traumatic

brain injury applies to open or closed head injuries resulting in impairments in one or more areas, such as cognition; language; memory; attention; reasoning; abstract thinking; judgment; problem-solving; sensory, perceptual, and motor abilities; psychosocial behavior; physical functions; information processing; and speech. Traumatic brain injury does not apply to brain injuries that are congenital or degenerative, or to brain injuries induced by birth trauma.

(13) Visual impairment including blindness means an impairment in vision that, even with correction, adversely affects a child's educational performance. The term includes both partial sight and blindness.

§ 300.9 Consent.

Consent means that —

(a) The parent has been fully informed of all information relevant to the activity for which consent is sought, in his or her native language, or through another mode of communication;

(b) The parent understands and agrees in writing to the carrying out of the activity for which his or her consent is sought, and the consent describes that activity and lists the records (if any) that will be released and to whom; and

(c)(1) The parent understands that the granting of consent is voluntary on the part of the parent and may be revoked at any time.

(2) If a parent revokes consent, that revocation is not retroactive (i.e., it does not negate an action that has occurred after the consent was given and before the consent was revoked).

§ 300.10 Core academic subjects.

Core academic subjects means English, reading or language arts, mathematics, science, foreign languages, civics and government, economics, arts, history, and geography.

§ 300.11 Day; business day; school day.

(a) Day means calendar day unless otherwise indicated as business day or school day.

(b) Business day means Monday through Friday, except for Federal and State holidays (unless holidays are specifically included in the designation of business day, as in § 300.148(d)(1)(ii)).

(c)(1) School day means any day, including a partial day that children are in attendance at school for instructional purposes.

(2) School day has the same meaning for all children in school, including children with and without disabilities.

§ 300.12 Educational service agency.

Educational service agency means —

(a) A regional public multiservice agency —

(1) Authorized by State law to develop, manage, and provide services or programs to LEAs;

(2) Recognized as an administrative agency for purposes of the provision of special education and related services provided within public elementary schools and secondary schools of the State;

(b) Includes any other public institution or agency having administrative control and direction over a public elementary school or secondary school; and

(c) Includes entities that meet the definition of intermediate educational unit in section 602(23) of the Act as in effect prior to June 4, 1997.

§ 300.13 Elementary school.

Elementary school means a nonprofit institutional day or residential school, including a public elementary charter school, that provides elementary education, as determined under State law.

§ 300.14 Equipment.

Equipment means —

(a) Machinery, utilities, and built-in equipment, and any necessary enclosures or structures to house the machinery, utilities, or equipment; and

(b) All other items necessary for the functioning of a particular facility as a facility for the provision of educational services, including items such as instructional equipment and necessary furniture; printed, published and audio-visual instructional materials; telecommunications, sensory, and other technological aids and devices; and books, periodicals, documents, and other related materials.

§ 300.15 Evaluation.

Evaluation means procedures used in accordance with §§ 300.304 through 300.311 to determine whether a child has a disability and the nature and extent of the special education and related services that the child needs.

§ 300.16 Excess costs.

Excess costs means those costs that are in excess of the average annual per-student expenditure in an LEA during the preceding school year for an elementary school or secondary school student, as may be appropriate, and that must be computed after deducting —

(a) Amounts received —

(1) Under Part B of the Act;

(2) Under Part A of title I of the ESEA; and

(3) Under Parts A and B of title III of the ESEA and;

(b) Any State or local funds expended for programs that would qualify for assistance under any of the parts described in paragraph (a) of this section, but excluding any amounts for capital outlay or debt service. (See Appendix A to part 300 for an example of how excess costs must be calculated.)

§ 300.17 Free appropriate public education.

Free appropriate public education or FAPE means special education and related services that —

(a) Are provided at public expense, under public supervision and direction, and without charge;

(b) Meet the standards of the SEA, including the requirements of this part;

(c) Include an appropriate preschool, elementary school, or secondary school education in the State involved; and

(d) Are provided in conformity with an individualized education program (IEP) that meets the requirements of §§ 300.320 through 300.324.

§ 300.18 Highly qualified special education teachers.

(a) *Requirements for special education teachers teaching core academic subjects.* For any public elementary or secondary school special education teacher teaching core academic subjects, the term highly qualified has the meaning given the term in section 9101 of the ESEA and *34 CFR 200.56*, except that the requirements for highly qualified also —

(1) Include the requirements described in paragraph (b) of this section; and

(2) Include the option for teachers to meet the requirements of section 9101 of the ESEA by meeting the requirements of paragraphs (c) and (d) of this section.

(b) *Requirements for special education teachers in general.* (1) When used with respect to any public elementary school or secondary school special education teacher teaching in a State, highly qualified requires that —

(i) The teacher has obtained full State certification as a special education teacher (including certification obtained through alternative routes to certification), or passed the State special education teacher licensing examination, and holds a license to teach in the State as a special education teacher, except that when used with respect to any teacher teaching in a public charter school, highly qualified means that the teacher meets the certification or licensing requirements, if any, set forth in the State's public charter school law;

(ii) The teacher has not had special education certification or licensure requirements waived on an emergency, temporary, or provisional basis; and

(iii) The teacher holds at least a bachelor's degree.

(2) A teacher will be considered to meet the standard in paragraph (b)(1)(i) of this section if that teacher is participating in an alternative route to special education certification program under which —

(i) The teacher —

(A) Receives high-quality professional development that is sustained, intensive, and classroom-focused in order to have a positive and lasting impact on classroom instruction, before and while teaching;

(B) Participates in a program of intensive supervision that consists of structured guidance and regular ongoing support for teachers or a teacher mentoring program;

(C) Assumes functions as a teacher only for a specified period of time not to exceed three years; and

(D) Demonstrates satisfactory progress toward full certification as prescribed by the State; and

(ii) The State ensures, through its certification and licensure process, that the provisions in paragraph (b)(2)(i) of this section are met.

(3) Any public elementary school or secondary school special education teacher teaching in a State, who is not teaching a core academic subject, is highly qualified if the teacher meets the requirements in paragraph (b)(1) or the requirements in (b)(1)(iii) and (b)(2) of this section.

(c) *Requirements for special education teachers teaching to alternate academic achievement standards.* When used with respect to a special education teacher who teaches core academic subjects exclusively to children who are assessed against alternate academic achievement standards established under *34 CFR 200.1(d)*, highly qualified means the teacher, whether new or not new to the profession, may either —

(1) Meet the applicable requirements of section 9101 of the ESEA and *34 CFR 200.56* for any elementary, middle, or secondary school teacher who is new or not new to the profession; or

(2) Meet the requirements of paragraph (B) or (C) of section 9101(23) of the ESEA as applied to an elementary school teacher, or, in the case of instruction above the elementary level, meet the requirements of paragraph (B) or (C) of section 9101(23) of the ESEA as applied to an elementary school teacher and have subject matter knowledge appropriate to the level of instruction being provided and needed to effectively teach to those alternate academic achievement standards, as determined by the State.

(d) Requirements for special education teachers teaching multiple subjects. Subject to paragraph (e) of this section, when used with respect to a special education teacher who teaches two or more core academic subjects exclusively to children with disabilities, highly qualified means that the teacher may either —

(1) Meet the applicable requirements of section 9101 of the ESEA and *34 CFR 200.56(b)* or (c);

(2) In the case of a teacher who is not new to the profession, demonstrate competence in all the core academic subjects in which the teacher teaches in the same manner as is required for an elementary, middle, or secondary school teacher who is not new to the profession under *34 CFR 200.56(c)* which may include a single, high objective uniform State standard of evaluation (HOUSSE) covering multiple subjects; or

(3) In the case of a new special education teacher who teaches multiple subjects and who is highly qualified in mathematics, language arts, or science, demonstrate, not later than two years after the date of employment, competence in the other core academic subjects in which the teacher teaches in the same manner as is required for an elementary, middle, or secondary school teacher under *34 CFR 200.56(c)*, which may include a single HOUSSE covering multiple subjects.

(e) Separate HOUSSE standards for special education teachers. Provided that any adaptations of the State's HOUSSE would not establish a lower standard for the content knowledge requirements for special education teachers and meet all the requirements for a HOUSSE for regular education teachers —

(1) A State may develop a separate HOUSSE for special education teachers; and

(2) The standards described in paragraph (e)(1) of this section may include single HOUSSE evaluations that cover multiple subjects.

(f) Rule of construction. Notwithstanding any other individual right of action that a parent or student may maintain under this part, nothing in this part shall be construed to create a right of action on behalf of an individual student or class of students for the failure of a particular SEA or LEA employee to be highly qualified, or to prevent a parent from filing a complaint under §§ 300.151 through 300.153 about staff qualifications with the SEA as provided for under this part.

(g) Applicability of definition to ESEA; and clarification of new special education teacher. (1) A teacher who is highly qualified under this section is considered highly qualified for purposes of the ESEA.

(2) For purposes of § 300.18(d)(3), a fully certified regular education teacher who subsequently becomes fully certified or licensed as a special education teacher is a new special education teacher when first hired as a special education teacher.

(h) Private school teachers not covered. The requirements in this section do not apply to teachers hired by private elementary schools and secondary schools including private school teachers hired or contracted by LEAs to provide equitable services to parentally-placed private school children with disabilities under § 300.138.

§ 300.19 Homeless children.

Homeless children has the meaning given the term homeless children and youths in section 725 *(42 U.S.C. 11434a)* of the McKinney-Vento Homeless Assistance Act, as amended, *42 U.S.C. 11431* et seq.

§ 300.20 Include.

Include means that the items named are not all of the possible items that are covered, whether like or unlike the ones named.

§ 300.21 Indian and Indian tribe.

(a) Indian means an individual who is a member of an Indian tribe.

(b) Indian tribe means any Federal or State Indian tribe, band, rancheria, pueblo, colony, or community, including any Alaska Native village or regional village corporation (as defined in or established under the Alaska Native Claims Settlement Act, *43 U.S.C. 1601* et seq.).

(c) Nothing in this definition is intended to indicate that the Secretary of the Interior is required to provide services or funding to a State Indian tribe that is not listed in the Federal Register list of Indian entities recognized as eligible to receive services from the United States, published pursuant to Section 104 of the Federally Recognized Indian Tribe List Act of 1994, *25 U.S.C. 479a-1.*

§ 300.22 Individualized education program.

Individualized education program or IEP means a written statement for a child with a disability that is developed, reviewed, and revised in accordance with §§ 300.320 through 300.324.

§ 300.23 Individualized education program team.

Individualized education program team or IEP Team means a group of individuals described in § 300.321 that is responsible for developing, reviewing, or revising an IEP for a child with a disability.

§ 300.24 Individualized family service plan.

Individualized family service plan or IFSP has the meaning given the term in section 636 of the Act.

§ 300.25 Infant or toddler with a disability.

Infant or toddler with a disability —

(a) Means an individual under three years of age who needs early intervention services because the individual —

(1) Is experiencing developmental delays, as measured by appropriate diagnostic instruments and procedures in one or more of the areas of cognitive development, physical development, communication development, social or emotional development, and adaptive development; or

(2) Has a diagnosed physical or mental condition that has a high probability of resulting in developmental delay; and

(b) May also include, at a State's discretion —

(1) At-risk infants and toddlers; and

(2) Children with disabilities who are eligible for services under section 619 and who previously received services under Part C of the Act until such children enter, or are eligible under State law to enter, kindergarten or elementary school, as appropriate, provided that any programs under Part C of the Act serving such children shall include —

(i) An educational component that promotes school readiness and incorporates pre-literacy, language, and numeracy skills; and

(ii) A written notification to parents of their rights and responsibilities in determining whether their child will continue to receive services under Part C of the Act or participate in preschool programs under section 619.

§ 300.26 Institution of higher education.

Institution of higher education —

(a) Has the meaning given the term in section 101 of the Higher Education Act of 1965, as amended, *20 U.S.C. 1021* et seq. (HEA); and

(b) Also includes any community college receiving funds from the Secretary of the Interior under the Tribally Controlled Community College or University Assistance Act of 1978, *25 U.S.C. 1801*, et seq.

§ 300.27 Limited English proficient.

Limited English proficient has the meaning given the term in section 9101(25) of the ESEA.

§ 300.28 Local educational agency.

(a) General. Local educational agency or LEA means a public board of education or other public authority legally constituted within a State for either administrative control or direction of, or to perform a service function for, public elementary or secondary schools in a city, county, township, school district, or other political subdivision of a State, or for a combination of school districts or counties as are recognized in a State as an administrative agency for its public elementary schools or secondary schools.

(b) Educational service agencies and other public institutions or agencies. The term includes —

(1) An educational service agency, as defined in § 300.12; and

(2) Any other public institution or agency having administrative control and direction of a public elementary school or secondary school, including a public nonprofit charter school that is established as an LEA under State law.

(c) BIA funded schools. The term includes an elementary school or secondary school funded by the Bureau of Indian Affairs, and not subject to the jurisdiction of any SEA other than the Bureau of Indian Affairs, but only to the extent that the inclusion makes the school eligible for programs for which specific eligibility is not provided to the school in another provision of law and the school does not have a student population that is smaller than the student population of the LEA receiving assistance under the Act with the smallest student population.

§ 300.29 Native language.

(a) Native language, when used with respect to an individual who is limited English proficient, means the following:

(1) The language normally used by that individual, or, in the case of a child, the language normally used by the parents of the child, except as provided in paragraph (a)(2) of this section.

(2) In all direct contact with a child (including evaluation of the child), the language normally used by the child in the home or learning environment.

(b) For an individual with deafness or blindness, or for an individual with no written language, the mode of communication is that normally used by the individual (such as sign language, Braille, or oral communication).

§ 300.30 Parent.

(a) Parent means —

(1) A biological or adoptive parent of a child;

(2) A foster parent, unless State law, regulations, or contractual obligations with a State or local entity prohibit a foster parent from acting as a parent;

(3) A guardian generally authorized to act as the child's parent, or authorized to make educational decisions for the child (but not the State if the child is a ward of the State);

(4) An individual acting in the place of a biological or adoptive parent (including a grandparent, stepparent, or other relative) with whom the child lives, or an individual who is legally responsible for the child's welfare; or

(5) A surrogate parent who has been appointed in accordance with § 300.519 or section 639(a)(5) of the Act.

(b) (1) Except as provided in paragraph (b)(2) of this section, the biological or adoptive parent, when attempting to act as the parent under this part and when more than one party is qualified under paragraph (a) of this section to act as a parent, must be presumed to be the parent for purposes of this section unless the biological or adoptive parent does not have legal authority to make educational decisions for the child.

(2) If a judicial decree or order identifies a specific person or persons under paragraphs (a)(1) through (4) of this section to act as the "parent" of a child or to make educational decisions on behalf of a child, then such person or persons shall be determined to be the "parent" for purposes of this section.

§ 300.31 Parent training and information center.

Parent training and information center means a center assisted under sections 671 or 672 of the Act.

§ 300.32 Personally identifiable.

Personally identifiable means information that contains —

(a) The name of the child, the child's parent, or other family member;

(b) The address of the child;

(c) A personal identifier, such as the child's social security number or student number; or

(d) A list of personal characteristics or other information that would make it possible to identify the child with reasonable certainty.

§ 300.33 Public agency.

Public agency includes the SEA, LEAs, ESAs, nonprofit public charter schools that are not otherwise included as LEAs or ESAs and are not a school of an LEA or ESA, and any other political subdivisions of the State that are responsible for providing education to children with disabilities.

§ 300.34 Related services.

(a) General. Related services means transportation and such developmental, corrective, and other supportive services as are required to assist a child with a disability to benefit from special education, and includes speech-language pathology and audiology services, interpreting services, psychological services, physical and occupational therapy, recreation, including therapeutic recreation, early identification and assessment of disabilities in children, counseling services, including rehabilitation counseling, orientation and mobility services, and medical services for diagnostic or evaluation purposes. Related services also include school health services and school nurse services, social work services in schools, and parent counseling and training.

(b) Exception; services that apply to children with surgically implanted devices, including cochlear implants.

(1) Related services do not include a medical device that is surgically implanted, the optimization of that device's functioning (e.g., mapping), maintenance of that device, or the replacement of that device.

(2) Nothing in paragraph (b)(1) of this section —

(i) Limits the right of a child with a surgically implanted device (e.g., cochlear implant) to receive related services (as listed in paragraph (a) of this section) that are determined by the IEP Team to be necessary for the child to receive FAPE.

(ii) Limits the responsibility of a public agency to appropriately monitor and maintain medical devices that are needed to maintain the health and safety of the child, including breathing, nutrition, or operation of other bodily functions, while the child is transported to and from school or is at school; or

(iii) Prevents the routine checking of an external component of a surgically implanted device to make sure it is functioning properly, as required in § 300.113(b).

(c) Individual related services terms defined. The terms used in this definition are defined as follows:

(1) Audiology includes —

(i) Identification of children with hearing loss;

(ii) Determination of the range, nature, and degree of hearing loss, including referral for medical or other professional attention for the habilitation of hearing;

(iii) Provision of habilitative activities, such as language habilitation, auditory training, speech reading (lip-reading), hearing evaluation, and speech conservation;

(iv) Creation and administration of programs for prevention of hearing loss;

(v) Counseling and guidance of children, parents, and teachers regarding hearing loss; and

(vi) Determination of children's needs for group and individual amplification, selecting and fitting an appropriate aid, and evaluating the effectiveness of amplification.

(2) Counseling services means services provided by qualified social workers, psychologists, guidance counselors, or other qualified personnel.

(3) Early identification and assessment of disabilities in children means the implementation of a formal plan for identifying a disability as early as possible in a child's life.

(4) Interpreting services includes —

§ 300.34   IDEA REGULATIONS

(i) The following, when used with respect to children who are deaf or hard of hearing: Oral transliteration services, cued language transliteration services, sign language transliteration and interpreting services, and transcription services, such as communication access real-time translation (CART), C-Print, and TypeWell; and

(ii) Special interpreting services for children who are deaf-blind.

(5) Medical services means services provided by a licensed physician to determine a child's medically related disability that results in the child's need for special education and related services.

(6) Occupational therapy —

(i) Means services provided by a qualified occupational therapist; and

(ii) Includes —

(A) Improving, developing, or restoring functions impaired or lost through illness, injury, or deprivation;

(B) Improving ability to perform tasks for independent functioning if functions are impaired or lost; and

(C) Preventing, through early intervention, initial or further impairment or loss of function.

(7) Orientation and mobility services —

(i) Means services provided to blind or visually impaired children by qualified personnel to enable those students to attain systematic orientation to and safe movement within their environments in school, home, and community; and

(ii) Includes teaching children the following, as appropriate:

(A) Spatial and environmental concepts and use of information received by the senses (such as sound, temperature and vibrations) to establish, maintain, or regain orientation and line of travel (e.g., using sound at a traffic light to cross the street);

(B) To use the long cane or a service animal to supplement visual travel skills or as a tool for safely negotiating the environment for children with no available travel vision;

(C) To understand and use remaining vision and distance low vision aids; and

(D) Other concepts, techniques, and tools.

(8)(i) Parent counseling and training means assisting parents in understanding the special needs of their child;

(ii) Providing parents with information about child development; and

(iii) Helping parents to acquire the necessary skills that will allow them to support the implementation of their child's IEP or IFSP.

(9) Physical therapy means services provided by a qualified physical therapist.

(10) Psychological services includes —

(i) Administering psychological and educational tests, and other assessment procedures;

(ii) Interpreting assessment results;

(iii) Obtaining, integrating, and interpreting information about child behavior and conditions relating to learning;

(iv) Consulting with other staff members in planning school programs to meet the special educational needs of children as indicated by psychological tests, interviews, direct observation, and behavioral evaluations;

(v) Planning and managing a program of psychological services, including psychological counseling for children and parents; and

(vi) Assisting in developing positive behavioral intervention strategies.

(11) Recreation includes —

(i) Assessment of leisure function;

(ii) Therapeutic recreation services;

(iii) Recreation programs in schools and community agencies; and

(iv) Leisure education.

(12) Rehabilitation counseling services means services provided by qualified personnel in individual or group sessions that focus specifically on career development, employment preparation, achieving independence, and integration in the workplace and community of a student with a disability. The term also includes vocational rehabilitation services provided to a student with a disability by vocational rehabilitation programs funded under the Rehabilitation Act of 1973, as amended, *29 U.S.C. 701* et seq.

(13) School health services and school nurse services means health services that are designed to enable a child with a disability to receive FAPE as described in the child's IEP. School nurse services are services provided by a qualified school nurse. School health services are services that may be provided by either a qualified school nurse or other qualified person.

(14) Social work services in schools includes —

(i) Preparing a social or developmental history on a child with a disability;

(ii) Group and individual counseling with the child and family;

(iii) Working in partnership with parents and others on those problems in a child's living situation (home, school, and community) that affect the child's adjustment in school;

(iv) Mobilizing school and community resources to enable the child to learn as effectively as possible in his or her educational program; and

(v) Assisting in developing positive behavioral intervention strategies.

(15) Speech-language pathology services includes —

(i) Identification of children with speech or language impairments;

(ii) Diagnosis and appraisal of specific speech or language impairments;

(iii) Referral for medical or other professional attention necessary for the habilitation of speech or language impairments;

(iv) Provision of speech and language services for the habilitation or prevention of communicative impairments; and

(v) Counseling and guidance of parents, children, and teachers regarding speech and language impairments.

(16) Transportation includes —

(i) Travel to and from school and between schools;

(ii) Travel in and around school buildings; and

(iii) Specialized equipment (such as special or adapted buses, lifts, and ramps), if required to provide special transportation for a child with a disability.

§ 300.35 Scientifically based research.

Scientifically based research has the meaning given the term in section 9101(37) of the ESEA.

§ 300.36 Secondary school.

Secondary school means a nonprofit institutional day or residential school, including a public secondary charter school that provides secondary education, as determined under State law, except that it does not include any education beyond grade 12.

§ 300.37 Services plan.

Services plan means a written statement that describes the special education and related services the LEA will provide to a parentally-placed child with a disability enrolled in a private school who has been designated to receive services, including the location of the services and any transportation necessary, consistent with § 300.132, and is developed and implemented in accordance with §§ 300.137 through 300.139.

§ 300.38 Secretary.

Secretary means the Secretary of Education.

§ 300.39 Special education.

(a) *General.* (1) Special education means specially designed instruction, at no cost to the parents, to meet the unique needs of a child with a disability, including —

(i) Instruction conducted in the classroom, in the home, in hospitals and institutions, and in other settings; and

(ii) Instruction in physical education.

(2) Special education includes each of the following, if the services otherwise meet the requirements of paragraph (a)(1) of this section —

(i) Speech-language pathology services, or any other related service, if the service is considered special education rather than a related service under State standards;

(ii) Travel training; and

(iii) Vocational education.

(b) *Individual special education terms defined.* The terms in this definition are defined as follows:

(1) At no cost means that all specially-designed instruction is provided without charge, but does not preclude incidental fees that are normally charged to nondisabled students or their parents as a part of the regular education program.

(2) Physical education means —

(i) The development of —

(A) Physical and motor fitness;

(B) Fundamental motor skills and patterns; and

(C) Skills in aquatics, dance, and individual and group games and sports (including intramural and lifetime sports); and

(ii) Includes special physical education, adapted physical education, movement education, and motor development.

(3) Specially designed instruction means adapting, as appropriate to the needs of an eligible child under this part, the content, methodology, or delivery of instruction —

(i) To address the unique needs of the child that result from the child's disability; and

(ii) To ensure access of the child to the general curriculum, so that the child can meet the educational standards within the jurisdiction of the public agency that apply to all children.

(4) Travel training means providing instruction, as appropriate, to children with significant cognitive disabilities, and any other children with disabilities who require this instruction, to enable them to —

(i) Develop an awareness of the environment in which they live; and

(ii) Learn the skills necessary to move effectively and safely from place to place within that environment (e.g., in school, in the home, at work, and in the community).

(5) Vocational education means organized educational programs that are directly related to the preparation of individuals for paid or unpaid employment, or for additional preparation for a career not requiring a baccalaureate or advanced degree.

§ 300.40 State.

State means each of the 50 States, the District of Columbia, the Commonwealth of Puerto Rico, and each of the outlying areas.

§ 300.41 State educational agency.

State educational agency or SEA means the State board of education or other agency or officer primarily responsible for the State supervision of public elementary schools and secondary schools, or, if there is no such officer or agency, an officer or agency designated by the Governor or by State law.

§ 300.42 Supplementary aids and services.

Supplementary aids and services means aids, services, and other supports that are provided in regular education classes, other education-related settings, and in extracurricular and nonacademic settings, to enable children with disabilities to be educated with nondisabled children to the maximum extent appropriate in accordance with §§ 300.114 through 300.116.

§ 300.43 Transition services.

(a) Transition services means a coordinated set of activities for a child with a disability that —

(1) Is designed to be within a results-oriented process, that is focused on improving the academic and functional achievement of the child with a disability to facilitate the child's movement from school to post-school activities, including postsecondary education, vocational education, integrated employment (including supported employment), continuing and adult education, adult services, independent living, or community participation;

(2) Is based on the individual child's needs, taking into account the child's strengths, preferences, and interests; and includes —

(i) Instruction;

(ii) Related services;

(iii) Community experiences;

(iv) The development of employment and other post-school adult living objectives; and

(v) If appropriate, acquisition of daily living skills and provision of a functional vocational evaluation.

(b) Transition services for children with disabilities may be special education, if provided as specially designed instruction, or a related service, if required to assist a child with a disability to benefit from special education.

§ 300.44 Universal design.

Universal design has the meaning given the term in section 3 of the Assistive Technology Act of 1998, as amended, *29 U.S.C. 3002.*

§ 300.45 Ward of the State.

(a) General. Subject to paragraph (b) of this section, ward of the State means a child who, as determined by the State where the child resides, is —

(1) A foster child;

(2) A ward of the State; or

(3) In the custody of a public child welfare agency.

(b) Exception. Ward of the State does not include a foster child who has a foster parent who meets the definition of a parent in § 300.30.

SUBPART B STATE ELIGIBILITY
GENERAL

§ 300.100 Eligibility for assistance.

A State is eligible for assistance under Part B of the Act for a fiscal year if the State submits a plan that provides assurances to the Secretary that the State has in effect policies and procedures to ensure that the State meets the conditions in §§ 300.101 through 300.176.

(Approved by the Office of Management and Budget under control number 1820-0030)

FAPE REQUIREMENTS

§ 300.101 Free appropriate public education (FAPE).

(a) General. A free appropriate public education must be available to all children residing in the State between the ages of 3 and 21, inclusive, including children with disabilities who have been suspended or expelled from school, as provided for in § 300.530(d).

(b) FAPE for children beginning at age 3. (1) Each State must ensure that—

(i) The obligation to make FAPE available to each eligible child residing in the State begins no later than the child's third birthday; and

(ii) An IEP or an IFSP is in effect for the child by that date, in accordance with § 300.323(b).

(2) If a child's third birthday occurs during the summer, the child's IEP Team shall determine the date when services under the IEP or IFSP will begin.

(c) Children advancing from grade to grade. (1) Each State must ensure that FAPE is available to any individual child with a disability who needs special education and related services, even though the child has not failed or been retained in a course or grade, and is advancing from grade to grade.

(2) The determination that a child described in paragraph (a) of this section is eligible under this part, must be made on an individual basis by the group responsible within the child's LEA for making eligibility determinations.

(Approved by the Office of Management and Budget under control number 1820-0030)

§ 300.102 Limitation — exception to FAPE for certain ages.

(a) General. The obligation to make FAPE available to all children with disabilities does not apply with respect to the following:

(1) Children aged 3, 4, 5, 18, 19, 20, or 21 in a State to the extent that its application to those children would be inconsistent with State law or practice, or the order of any court, respecting the provision of public education to children of those ages.

(2)(i) Children aged 18 through 21 to the extent that State law does not require that special education and related services under Part B of the Act be provided to students with disabilities who, in the last educational placement prior to their incarceration in an adult correctional facility—

(A) Were not actually identified as being a child with a disability under § 300.8; and

(B) Did not have an IEP under Part B of the Act.

(ii) The exception in paragraph (a)(2)(i) of this section does not apply to children with disabilities, aged 18 through 21, who—

(A) Had been identified as a child with a disability under § 300.8 and had received services in accordance with an IEP, but who left school prior to their incarceration; or

(B) Did not have an IEP in their last educational setting, but who had actually been identified as a child with a disability under § 300.8.

(3)(i) Children with disabilities who have graduated from high school with a regular high school diploma.

(ii) The exception in paragraph (a)(3)(i) of this section does not apply to children who have graduated from high school but have not been awarded a regular high school diploma.

(iii) Graduation from high school with a regular high school diploma constitutes a change in placement, requiring written prior notice in accordance with § 300.503.

(iv) As used in paragraphs (a)(3)(i) through (a)(3)(iii) of this section, the term regular high school diploma does not include an alternative degree that is not fully aligned with the State's academic standards, such as a certificate or a general educational development credential (GED).

(4) Children with disabilities who are eligible under subpart H of this part, but who receive early intervention services under Part C of the Act.

(b) Documents relating to exceptions. The State must assure that the information it has provided to the Secretary regarding the exceptions in paragraph (a) of this section, as required by § 300.700 (for purposes of making grants to States under this part), is current and accurate.

(Approved by the Office of Management and Budget under control number 1820-0030)

OTHER FAPE REQUIREMENTS

§ 300.103 FAPE — methods and payments.

(a) Each State may use whatever State, local, Federal, and private sources of support that are available in the State to meet the requirements of this part. For example, if it is necessary to place a child with a disability in a residential facility, a State could use joint agreements between the agencies involved for sharing the cost of that placement.

(b) Nothing in this part relieves an insurer or similar third party from an otherwise valid obligation to provide or to pay for services provided to a child with a disability.

(c) Consistent with § 300.323(c), the State must ensure that there is no delay in implementing a child's IEP, including any case in which the payment source for providing or paying for special education and related services to the child is being determined.

(Approved by the Office of Management and Budget under control number 1820-0030)

§ 300.104 Residential placement

If placement in a public or private residential program is necessary to provide special education and related services to a child with a disability, the program, including non-medical care and room and board, must be at no cost to the parents of the child.

(Approved by the Office of Management and Budget under control number 1820-0030)

§ 300.105 Assistive technology.

(a) Each public agency must ensure that assistive technology devices or assistive technology services, or both, as those terms are defined in §§ 300.5 and 300.6, respectively, are made available to a child with a disability if required as a part of the child's—

(1) Special education under § 300.36;

(2) Related services under § 300.34; or

(3) Supplementary aids and services under §§ 300.38 and 300.114(a)(2)(ii).

(b) On a case-by-case basis, the use of school-purchased assistive technology devices in a child's home or in other settings is required if the child's IEP Team determines that the child needs access to those devices in order to receive FAPE.

(Approved by the Office of Management and Budget under control number 1820-0030)

§ 300.106 Extended school year services.

(a) General. (1) Each public agency must ensure that extended school year services are available as necessary to provide FAPE, consistent with paragraph (a)(2) of this section.

(2) Extended school year services must be provided only if a child's IEP Team determines, on an individual basis, in accordance with §§ 300.320 through 300.324, that the services are necessary for the provision of FAPE to the child.

(3) In implementing the requirements of this section, a public agency may not—

(i) Limit extended school year services to particular categories of disability; or

(ii) Unilaterally limit the type, amount, or duration of those services.

(b) *Definition.* As used in this section, the term extended school year services means special education and related services that—

(1) Are provided to a child with a disability—

(i) Beyond the normal school year of the public agency;

(ii) In accordance with the child's IEP; and

(iii) At no cost to the parents of the child; and

(2) Meet the standards of the SEA.

(Approved by the Office of Management and Budget under control number 1820-0030)

§ 300.107 Nonacademic services.

The State must ensure the following:

(a) Each public agency must take steps, including the provision of supplementary aids and services determined appropriate and necessary by the child's IEP Team, to provide nonacademic and extracurricular services and activities in the manner necessary to afford children with disabilities an equal opportunity for participation in those services and activities.

(b) Nonacademic and extracurricular services and activities may include counseling services, athletics, transportation, health services, recreational activities, special interest groups or clubs sponsored by the public agency, referrals to agencies that provide assistance to individuals with disabilities, and employment of students, including both employment by the public agency and assistance in making outside employment available.

(Approved by the Office of Management and Budget under control number 1820-0030)

§ 300.108 Physical education.

The State must ensure that public agencies in the State comply with the following:

(a) *General.* Physical education services, specially designed if necessary, must be made available to every child with a disability receiving FAPE, unless the public agency enrolls children without disabilities and does not provide physical education to children without disabilities in the same grades.

(b) *Regular physical education.* Each child with a disability must be afforded the opportunity to participate in the regular physical education program available to nondisabled children unless —

(1) The child is enrolled full time in a separate facility; or

(2) The child needs specially designed physical education, as prescribed in the child's IEP.

(c) *Special physical education.* If specially designed physical education is prescribed in a child's IEP, the public agency responsible for the education of that child must provide the services directly or make arrangements for those services to be provided through other public or private programs.

(d) *Education in separate facilities.* The public agency responsible for the education of a child with a disability who is enrolled in a separate facility must ensure that the child receives appropriate physical education services in compliance with this section.

(Approved by the Office of Management and Budget under control number 1820-0030)

§ 300.109 Full educational opportunity goal (FEOG).

The State must have in effect policies and procedures to demonstrate that the State has established a goal of providing full educational opportunity to all children with disabilities, aged birth through 21, and a detailed timetable for accomplishing that goal.

(Approved by the Office of Management and Budget under control number 1820-0030)

§ 300.110 Program options.

The State must ensure that each public agency takes steps to ensure that its children with disabilities have available to them the variety of educational programs and services available to nondisabled children in the area served by the agency, including art, music, industrial arts, consumer and homemaking education, and vocational education.

(Approved by the Office of Management and Budget under control number 1820-0030)

§ 300.111 Child find.

(a) General. (1) The State must have in effect policies and procedures to ensure that—

(i) All children with disabilities residing in the State, including children with disabilities who are homeless children or are wards of the State, and children with disabilities attending private schools, regardless of the severity of their disability, and who are in need of special education and related services, are identified, located, and evaluated; and

(ii) A practical method is developed and implemented to determine which children are currently receiving needed special education and related services.

(b) Use of term developmental delay. The following provisions apply with respect to implementing the child find requirements of this section:

(1) A State that adopts a definition of developmental delay under § 300.8(b) determines whether the term applies to children aged three through nine, or to a subset of that age range (e.g., ages three through five).

(2) A State may not require an LEA to adopt and use the term developmental delay for any children within its jurisdiction.

(3) If an LEA uses the term developmental delay for children described in § 300.8(b), the LEA must conform to both the State's definition of that term and to the age range that has been adopted by the State.

(4) If a State does not adopt the term developmental delay, an LEA may not independently use that term as a basis for establishing a child's eligibility under this part.

(c) Other children in child find. Child find also must include—

(1) Children who are suspected of being a child with a disability under § 300.8 and in need of special education, even though they are advancing from grade to grade; and

(2) Highly mobile children, including migrant children.

(d) Construction. Nothing in the Act requires that children be classified by their disability so long as each child who has a disability that is listed in § 300.8 and who, by reason of that disability, needs special education and related services is regarded as a child with a disability under Part B of the Act.

(Approved by the Office of Management and Budget under control number 1820-0030)

§ 300.112 Individualized education programs (IEP).

The State must ensure that an IEP, or an IFSP that meets the requirements of section 636(d) of the Act, is developed, reviewed, and revised for each child with a disability in accordance with §§ 300.320 through 300.324, except as provided in § 300.300(b)(3)(ii).

(Approved by the Office of Management and Budget under control number 1820-0030)

§ 300.113 Routine checking of hearing aids and external components of surgically implanted medical devices.

(a) Hearing aids. Each public agency must ensure that hearing aids worn in school by children with hearing impairments, including deafness, are functioning properly.

(b) External components of surgically implanted medical devices. (1) Subject to paragraph (b)(2) of this section, each public agency must ensure that the external components of surgically implanted medical devices are functioning properly.

(2) For a child with a surgically implanted medical device who is receiving special education and related services under this part, a public agency is not responsible for the post-surgical maintenance, programming, or replacement of the medical device that has been surgically implanted (or of an external component of the surgically implanted medical device).

(Approved by the Office of Management and Budget under control number 1820-0030)

LEAST RESTRICTIVE ENVIRONMENT (LRE)

§ 300.114 LRE requirements.

(a) General. (1) Except as provided in § 300.324(d)(2) (regarding children with disabilities in adult prisons), the State must have in effect policies and procedures to ensure that public agencies in the State meet the LRE requirements of this section and §§ 300.115 through 300.120.

(2) Each public agency must ensure that—

(i) To the maximum extent appropriate, children with disabilities, including children in public or private institutions or other care facilities, are educated with children who are nondisabled; and

(ii) Special classes, separate schooling, or other removal of children with disabilities from the regular educational environment occurs only if the nature or severity of the disability is such that education in regular classes with the use of supplementary aids and services cannot be achieved satisfactorily.

(b) Additional requirement—State funding mechanism —(1) General. (i) A State funding mechanism must not result in placements that violate the requirements of paragraph (a) of this section; and

(ii) A State must not use a funding mechanism by which the State distributes funds on the basis of the type of setting in which a child is served that will result in the failure to provide a child with a disability FAPE according to the unique needs of the child, as described in the child's IEP.

(2) Assurance. If the State does not have policies and procedures to ensure compliance with paragraph (b)(1) of this section, the State must provide the Secretary an assurance that the State will revise the funding mechanism as soon as feasible to ensure that the mechanism does not result in placements that violate that paragraph.

(Approved by the Office of Management and Budget under control number 1820-0030)

§ 300.115 Continuum of alternative placements.

(a) Each public agency must ensure that a continuum of alternative placements is available to meet the needs of children with disabilities for special education and related services.

(b) The continuum required in paragraph (a) of this section must—

(1) Include the alternative placements listed in the definition of special education under § 300.38 (instruction in regular classes, special classes, special schools, home instruction, and instruction in hospitals and institutions); and

(2) Make provision for supplementary services (such as resource room or itinerant instruction) to be provided in conjunction with regular class placement.

(Approved by the Office of Management and Budget under control number 1820-0030)

§ 300.116 Placements.

In determining the educational placement of a child with a disability, including a preschool child with a disability, each public agency must ensure that —

(a) The placement decision —

(1) Is made by a group of persons, including the parents, and other persons knowledgeable about the child, the meaning of the evaluation data, and the placement options; and

(2) Is made in conformity with the LRE provisions of this subpart, including §§ 300.114 through 300.118;

(b) The child's placement —

(1) Is determined at least annually;

(2) Is based on the child's IEP; and

(3) Is as close as possible to the child's home;

(c) Unless the IEP of a child with a disability requires some other arrangement, the child is educated in the school that he or she would attend if nondisabled;

(d) In selecting the LRE, consideration is given to any potential harmful effect on the child or on the quality of services that he or she needs; and

(e) A child with a disability is not removed from education in age-appropriate regular classrooms solely because of needed modifications in the general education curriculum.

(Approved by the Office of Management and Budget under control number 1820-0030)

§ 300.117 Nonacademic settings.

In providing or arranging for the provision of nonacademic and extracurricular services and activities, including meals, recess periods, and the services and activities set forth in § 300.107, each public agency must ensure that each child with a disability participates with nondisabled children in the extracurricular services and activities to the maximum extent appropriate to the needs of that child. The public agency must ensure that each child with a disability has the supplementary aids and services determined by the child's IEP Team to be appropriate and necessary for the child to participate in nonacademic settings.

(Approved by the Office of Management and Budget under control number 1820-0030)

§ 300.118 Children in public or private institutions.

Except as provided in § 300.149(d) (regarding agency responsibility for general supervision of some individuals in adult prisons), an SEA must ensure that § 300.114 is effectively implemented, including, if necessary, making arrangements with public and private institutions (such as a memorandum of agreement or special implementation procedures).

(Approved by the Office of Management and Budget under control number 1820-0030)

§ 300.119 Technical assistance and training activities.

Each SEA must carry out activities to ensure that teachers and administrators in all public agencies—

(a) Are fully informed about their responsibilities for implementing § 300.114; and

(b) Are provided with technical assistance and training necessary to assist them in this effort.

(Approved by the Office of Management and Budget under control number 1820-0030)

§ 300.120 Monitoring activities.

(a) The SEA must carry out activities to ensure that § 300.114 is implemented by each public agency.

(b) If there is evidence that a public agency makes placements that are inconsistent with § 300.114, the SEA must —

(1) Review the public agency's justification for its actions; and

(2) Assist in planning and implementing any necessary corrective action.

(Approved by the Office of Management and Budget under control number 1820-0030)

ADDITIONAL ELIGIBILITY REQUIREMENTS

§ 300.121 Procedural safeguards.

(a) General. The State must have procedural safeguards in effect to ensure that each public agency in the State meets the requirements of §§ 300.500 through 300.536.

(b) Procedural safeguards identified. Children with disabilities and their parents must be afforded the procedural safeguards identified in paragraph (a) of this section.

(Approved by the Office of Management and Budget under control number 1820-0030)

§ 300.122 Evaluation.

Children with disabilities must be evaluated in accordance with §§ 300.300 through 300.311 of subpart D of this part.

(Approved by the Office of Management and Budget under control number 1820-0030)

§ 300.123 Confidentiality of personally identifiable information.

The State must have policies and procedures in effect to ensure that public agencies in the State comply with §§ 300.610 through 300.626 related to protecting the confidentiality of any personally identifiable information collected, used, or maintained under Part B of the Act.

(Approved by the Office of Management and Budget under control number 1820-0030)

§ 300.124 Transition of children from the Part C program to preschool programs.

The State must have in effect policies and procedures to ensure that—

(a) Children participating in early intervention programs assisted under Part C of the Act, and who will participate in preschool programs assisted under Part B of the Act, experience a smooth and effective transition to those preschool programs in a manner consistent with section 637(a)(9) of the Act;

(b) By the third birthday of a child described in paragraph (a) of this section, an IEP or, if consistent with § 300.323(b) and section 636(d) of the Act, an IFSP, has been developed and is being implemented for the child consistent with § 300.101(b); and

(c) Each affected LEA will participate in transition planning conferences arranged by the designated lead agency under section 635(a)(10) of the Act.

(Approved by the Office of Management and Budget under control number 1820-0030)

§ 300.125

[This section was removed and reserved. See 71 FR 46540, 46753, Aug. 14, 2006.]

§ 300.126

[This section was removed and reserved. See 71 FR 46540, 46753, Aug. 14, 2006.]

§ 300.127

[This section was removed and reserved. See 71 FR 46540, 46753, Aug. 14, 2006.]

§ 300.128

[This section was removed and reserved. See 71 FR 46540, 46753, Aug. 14, 2006.]

CHILDREN IN PRIVATE SCHOOLS

§ 300.129 State responsibility regarding children in private schools.

The State must have in effect policies and procedures that ensure that LEAs, and, if applicable, the SEA, meet the private school requirements in §§ 300.130 through 300.148.

(Approved by the Office of Management and Budget under control number 1820-0030)

CHILDREN WITH DISABILITIES ENROLLED BY THEIR PARENTS IN PRIVATE SCHOOLS

§ 300.130 Definition of parentally-placed private school children with disabilities.

Parentally-placed private school children with disabilities means children with disabilities enrolled by their parents in private, including religious, schools or facilities that meet the definition of elementary school in § 300.13 or secondary school in § 300.36, other than children with disabilities covered under §§ 300.145 through 300.147.

(Approved by the Office of Management and Budget under control number 1820-0030)

§ 300.131 Child find for parentally-placed private school children with disabilities.

(a) General. Each LEA must locate, identify, and evaluate all children with disabilities who are enrolled by their parents in private, including religious, elementary schools and secondary schools located in the school district served by the LEA, in accordance with paragraphs (b) through (e) of this section, and §§ 300.111 and 300.201.

(b) Child find design. The child find process must be designed to ensure—

(1) The equitable participation of parentally-placed private school children; and

(2) An accurate count of those children.

(c) Activities. In carrying out the requirements of this section, the LEA, or, if applicable, the SEA, must undertake activities similar to the activities undertaken for the agency's public school children.

(d) Cost. The cost of carrying out the child find requirements in this section, including individual evaluations, may not be considered in determining if an LEA has met its obligation under § 300.133.

(e) Completion period. The child find process must be completed in a time period comparable to that for students attending public schools in the LEA consistent with § 300.301.

(f) Out-of-State children. Each LEA in which private, including religious, elementary schools and secondary schools are located must, in carrying out the child find requirements in this section, include parentally-placed private school children who reside in a State other than the State in which the private schools that they attend are located.

(Approved by the Office of Management and Budget under control number 1820-0030)

§ 300.132 Provision of services for parentally-placed private school children with disabilities—basic requirement.

(a) General. To the extent consistent with the number and location of children with disabilities who are enrolled by their parents in private, including religious, elementary schools and secondary schools located in the school district served by the LEA, provision is made for the participation of those children in the program assisted or carried out under Part B of the Act by providing them with special education and related services, including direct services determined in accordance with § 300.137, unless the Secretary has arranged for services to those children under the by-pass provisions in §§ 300.190 through 300.198.

(b) Services plan for parentally-placed private school children with disabilities. In accordance with paragraph (a) of this section and §§ 300.137 through 300.139, a services plan must be developed and implemented for each private school child with a disability who has been designated by the LEA in which the private school is located to receive special education and related services under this part.

(c) Record keeping. Each LEA must maintain in its records, and provide to the SEA, the following information related to parentally-placed private school children covered under §§ 300.130 through 300.144:

(1) The number of children evaluated;

(2) The number of children determined to be children with disabilities; and

(3) The number of children served.

(Approved by the Office of Management and Budget under control numbers 1820-0030 and 1820-0600)

§ 300.133 Expenditures.

(a) Formula. To meet the requirement of § 300.132(a), each LEA must spend the following on providing special education and related services (including direct services) to parentally-placed private school children with disabilities:

(1) For children aged 3 through 21, an amount that is the same proportion of the LEA's total subgrant under section 611(f) of the Act as the number of private school children with disabilities aged 3 through 21 who are enrolled by their parents in private, including religious, elementary schools and secondary schools located in the school district served by the LEA, is to the total number of children with disabilities in its jurisdiction aged 3 through 21.

(2)(i) For children aged three through five, an amount that is the same proportion of the LEA's total subgrant under section 619(g) of the Act as the number of parentally-placed private school children with disabilities aged three through five who are enrolled by their parents in a private, including religious, elementary school located in the school district served by the LEA, is to the total number of children with disabilities in its jurisdiction aged three through five.

(ii) As described in paragraph (a)(2)(i) of this section, children aged three through five are considered to be parentally-placed private school children with disabilities enrolled by their parents in private, including religious, elementary schools, if they are enrolled in a private school that meets the definition of elementary school in § 300.13.

(3) If an LEA has not expended for equitable services all of the funds described in paragraphs (a)(1) and (a)(2) of this section by the end of the fiscal year for which Congress appropriated the funds, the LEA must obligate the remaining funds for special education and related services (including direct services) to parentally-placed private school children with disabilities during a carry-over period of one additional year.

(b) Calculating proportionate amount. In calculating the proportionate amount of Federal funds to be provided for parentally-placed private school children with disabilities, the LEA, after timely and meaningful consultation with representatives of private schools under § 300.134, must conduct a thorough and complete child find process to determine the number of parentally-placed children with disabilities attending private schools located in the LEA. (See Appendix B for an example of how proportionate share is calculated).

(c) Annual count of the number of parentally-placed private school children with disabilities. (1) Each LEA must—

(i) After timely and meaningful consultation with representatives of parentally-placed private school children with disabilities (consistent with § 300.134), determine the number of parentally-placed private school children with disabilities attending private schools located in the LEA; and

(ii) Ensure that the count is conducted on any date between October 1 and December 1, inclusive, of each year.

(2) The count must be used to determine the amount that the LEA must spend on providing special education and related services to parentally-placed private school children with disabilities in the next subsequent fiscal year.

(d) Supplement, not supplant. State and local funds may supplement and in no case supplant the proportionate amount of Federal funds required to be expended for parentally-placed private school children with disabilities under this part.

(Approved by the Office of Management and Budget under control number 1820-0030)

§ 300.134 Consultation.

To ensure timely and meaningful consultation, an LEA, or, if appropriate, an SEA, must consult with private school representatives and representatives of parents of parentally-placed private school children with disabilities during the design and development of special education and related services for the children regarding the following:

(a) *Child find.* The child find process, including—

(1) How parentally-placed private school children suspected of having a disability can participate equitably; and

(2) How parents, teachers, and private school officials will be informed of the process.

(b) *Proportionate share of funds.* The determination of the proportionate share of Federal funds available to serve parentally-placed private school children with disabilities under § 300.133(b), including the determination of how the proportionate share of those funds was calculated.

(c) *Consultation process.* The consultation process among the LEA, private school officials, and representatives of parents of parentally-placed private school children with disabilities, including how the process will operate throughout the school year to ensure that parentally-placed children with disabilities identified through the child find process can meaningfully participate in special education and related services.

(d) *Provision of special education and related services.* How, where, and by whom special education and related services will be provided for parentally-placed private school children with disabilities, including a discussion of—

(1) The types of services, including direct services and alternate service delivery mechanisms; and

(2) How special education and related services will be apportioned if funds are insufficient to serve all parentally-placed private school children; and

(3) How and when those decisions will be made;

(e) *Written explanation by LEA regarding services.* How, if the LEA disagrees with the views of the private school officials on the provision of services or the types of services (whether provided directly or through a contract), the LEA will provide to the private school officials a written explanation of the reasons why the LEA chose not to provide services directly or through a contract.

(Approved by the Office of Management and Budget under control numbers 1820-0030 and 1820-0600)

§ 300.135 Written affirmation.

(a) When timely and meaningful consultation, as required by § 300.134, has occurred, the LEA must obtain a written affirmation signed by the representatives of participating private schools.

(b) If the representatives do not provide the affirmation within a reasonable period of time, the LEA must forward the documentation of the consultation process to the SEA.

(Approved by the Office of Management and Budget under control numbers 1820-0030 and 1820-0600)

§ 300.136 Compliance.

(a) General. A private school official has the right to submit a complaint to the SEA that the LEA—

(1) Did not engage in consultation that was meaningful and timely; or

(2) Did not give due consideration to the views of the private school official.

(b) Procedure. (1) If the private school official wishes to submit a complaint, the official must provide to the SEA the basis of the noncompliance by the LEA with the applicable private school provisions in this part; and

(2) The LEA must forward the appropriate documentation to the SEA.

(3)(i) If the private school official is dissatisfied with the decision of the SEA, the official may submit a complaint to the Secretary by providing the information on noncompliance described in paragraph (b)(1) of this section; and

(ii) The SEA must forward the appropriate documentation to the Secretary.

(Approved by the Office of Management and Budget under control numbers 1820-0030 and 1820-0600)

§ 300.137 Equitable services determined.

(a) No individual right to special education and related services. No parentally-placed private school child with a disability has an individual right to receive some or all of the special education and related services that the child would receive if enrolled in a public school.

(b) Decisions. (1) Decisions about the services that will be provided to parentally-placed private school children with disabilities under §§ 300.130 through 300.144 must be made in accordance with paragraph (c) of this section and § 300.134(d).

(2) The LEA must make the final decisions with respect to the services to be provided to eligible parentally-placed private school children with disabilities.

(c) Services plan for each child served under §§ 300.130 through 300.144. If a child with a disability is enrolled in a religious or other private school by the child's parents and will receive special education or related services from an LEA, the LEA must—

(1) Initiate and conduct meetings to develop, review, and revise a services plan for the child, in accordance with § 300.138(b); and

(2) Ensure that a representative of the religious or other private school attends each meeting. If the representative cannot attend, the LEA shall use other methods to ensure participation by the religious or other private school, including individual or conference telephone calls.

(Approved by the Office of Management and Budget under control number 1820-0030)

§ 300.138 Equitable services provided.

(a) General. (1) The services provided to parentally-placed private school children with disabilities must be provided by personnel meeting the same standards as personnel providing services in the public schools, except that private elementary school and secondary school teachers who are providing equitable services to parentally-placed private school children with disabilities do not have to meet the highly qualified special education teacher requirements of § 300.18.

(2) Parentally-placed private school children with disabilities may receive a different amount of services than children with disabilities in public schools.

(b) Services provided in accordance with a services plan. (1) Each parentally-placed private school child with a disability who has been designated to receive services under § 300.132 must have a services plan that describes the specific special education and related services that the LEA will provide to the child in light of the services that the LEA has determined, through the process described in §§ 300.134 and 300.137, it will make available to parentally-placed private school children with disabilities.

(2) The services plan must, to the extent appropriate—

(i) Meet the requirements of § 300.320, or for a child ages three through five, meet the requirements of § 300.323(b) with respect to the services provided; and

(ii) Be developed, reviewed, and revised consistent with §§ 300.321 through 300.324.

(c) Provision of equitable services. (1) The provision of services pursuant to this section and §§ 300.139 through 300.143 must be provided:

(i) By employees of a public agency; or

(ii) Through contract by the public agency with an individual, association, agency, organization, or other entity.

(2) Special education and related services provided to parentally-placed private school children with disabilities, including materials and equipment, must be secular, neutral, and nonideological.

(Approved by the Office of Management and Budget under control number 1820-0030)

§ 300.139 Location of services and transportation.

(a) Services on private school premises. Services to parentally-placed private school children with disabilities may be provided on the premises of private, including religious, schools, to the extent consistent with law.

(b) Transportation —(1) General. (i) If necessary for the child to benefit from or participate in the services provided under this part, a parentally-placed private school child with a disability must be provided transportation—

(A) From the child's school or the child's home to a site other than the private school; and

(B) From the service site to the private school, or to the child's home, depending on the timing of the services.

(ii) LEAs are not required to provide transportation from the child's home to the private school.

(2) Cost of transportation. The cost of the transportation described in paragraph (b)(1)(i) of this section may be included in calculating whether the LEA has met the requirement of § 300.133.

(Approved by the Office of Management and Budget under control number 1820-0030)

§ 300.140 Due process complaints and State complaints.

(a) Due process not applicable, except for child find. (1) Except as provided in paragraph (b) of this section, the procedures in §§ 300.504 through 300.519 do not apply to complaints that an LEA has failed to meet the requirements of §§ 300.132 through 300.139, including the provision of services indicated on the child's services plan.

(b) Child find complaints—to be filed with the LEA in which the private school is located. (1) The procedures in §§ 300.504 through 300.519 apply to complaints that an LEA has failed to meet the child find requirements in § 300.131, including the requirements in §§ 300.300 through 300.311.

(2) Any due process complaint regarding the child find requirements (as described in paragraph (b)(1) of this section) must be filed with the LEA in which the private school is located and a copy must be forwarded to the SEA.

(c) State complaints. (1) Any complaint that an SEA or LEA has failed to meet the requirements in §§ 300.132 through 300.135 and 300.137 through 300.144 must be filed in accordance with the procedures described in §§ 300.151 through 300.153.

(2) A complaint filed by a private school official under § 300.136(a) must be filed with the SEA in accordance with the procedures in § 300.136(b).

(Approved by the Office of Management and Budget under control number 1820-0030)

§ 300.141   Requirement that funds not benefit a private school.

(a) An LEA may not use funds provided under section 611 or 619 of the Act to finance the existing level of instruction in a private school or to otherwise benefit the private school.

(b) The LEA must use funds provided under Part B of the Act to meet the special education and related services needs of parentally-placed private school children with disabilities, but not for meeting—

(1) The needs of a private school; or

(2) The general needs of the students enrolled in the private school.

(Approved by the Office of Management and Budget under control number 1820-0030)

§ 300.142   Use of personnel.

(a) Use of public school personnel. An LEA may use funds available under sections 611 and 619 of the Act to make public school personnel available in other than public facilities—

(1) To the extent necessary to provide services under §§ 300.130 through 300.144 for parentally-placed private school children with disabilities; and

(2) If those services are not normally provided by the private school.

(b) Use of private school personnel. An LEA may use funds available under sections 611 and 619 of the Act to pay for the services of an employee of a private school to provide services under §§ 300.130 through 300.144 if—

(1) The employee performs the services outside of his or her regular hours of duty; and

(2) The employee performs the services under public supervision and control.

(Approved by the Office of Management and Budget under control number 1820-0030)

§ 300.143   Separate classes prohibited.

An LEA may not use funds available under section 611 or 619 of the Act for classes that are organized separately on the basis of school enrollment or religion of the children if—'

(a) The classes are at the same site; and

(b) The classes include children enrolled in public schools and children enrolled in private schools.

(Approved by the Office of Management and Budget under control number 1820-0030)

§ 300.144 Property, equipment, and supplies.

(a) A public agency must control and administer the funds used to provide special education and related services under §§ 300.137 through 300.139, and hold title to and administer materials, equipment, and property purchased with those funds for the uses and purposes provided in the Act.

(b) The public agency may place equipment and supplies in a private school for the period of time needed for the Part B program.

(c) The public agency must ensure that the equipment and supplies placed in a private school—

(1) Are used only for Part B purposes; and

(2) Can be removed from the private school without remodeling the private school facility.

(d) The public agency must remove equipment and supplies from a private school if—

(1) The equipment and supplies are no longer needed for Part B purposes; or

(2) Removal is necessary to avoid unauthorized use of the equipment and supplies for other than Part B purposes.

(e) No funds under Part B of the Act may be used for repairs, minor remodeling, or construction of private school facilities.

(Approved by the Office of Management and Budget under control number 1820-0030)

CHILDREN WITH DISABILITIES IN PRIVATE SCHOOLS PLACED OR REFERRED BY PUBLIC AGENCIES

§ 300.145 Applicability of §§ 300.146 through 300.147.

Sections 300.146 through 300.147 apply only to children with disabilities who are or have been placed in or referred to a private school or facility by a public agency as a means of providing special education and related services.

(Approved by the Office of Management and Budget under control number 1820-0030)

§ 300.146 Responsibility of SEA.

Each SEA must ensure that a child with a disability who is placed in or referred to a private school or facility by a public agency—

(a) Is provided special education and related services—

(1) In conformance with an IEP that meets the requirements of §§ 300.320 through 300.325; and

(2) At no cost to the parents;

(b) Is provided an education that meets the standards that apply to education provided by the SEA and LEAs including the requirements of this part, except for § 300.18 and § 300.156(c); and

(c) Has all of the rights of a child with a disability who is served by a public agency.

(Approved by the Office of Management and Budget under control number 1820-0030)

§ 300.147 Implementation by SEA.

In implementing § 300.146, the SEA must—

(a) Monitor compliance through procedures such as written reports, on-site visits, and parent questionnaires;

(b) Disseminate copies of applicable standards to each private school and facility to which a public agency has referred or placed a child with a disability; and

(c) Provide an opportunity for those private schools and facilities to participate in the development and revision of State standards that apply to them.

(Approved by the Office of Management and Budget under control number 1820-0030)

CHILDREN WITH DISABILITIES ENROLLED BY THEIR PARENTS IN PRIVATE SCHOOLS WHEN FAPE IS AT ISSUE

§ 300.148 Placement of children by parents when FAPE is at issue.

(a) *General.* This part does not require an LEA to pay for the cost of education, including special education and related services, of a child with a disability at a private school or facility if that agency made FAPE available to the child and the parents elected to place the child in a private school or facility. However, the public agency must include that child in the population whose needs are addressed consistent with §§ 300.131 through 300.144.

(b) *Disagreements about FAPE.* Disagreements between the parents and a public agency regarding the availability of a program appropriate for the child, and the question of financial reimbursement, are subject to the due process procedures in §§ 300.504 through 300.520.

(c) *Reimbursement for private school placement.* If the parents of a child with a disability, who previously received special education and related services under the authority of a public agency, enroll the child in a private preschool, elementary school, or secondary school without the consent of or referral by the public agency, a court or a hearing officer may require the agency to reimburse the parents for the cost of that enrollment if the court or hearing officer finds that the agency had not made FAPE available to the child in a timely manner prior to that enrollment and that the private placement is appropriate. A parental placement may be found to be appropriate by a hearing officer or a court even if it does not meet the State standards that apply to education provided by the SEA and LEAs.

(d) *Limitation on reimbursement.* The cost of reimbursement described in paragraph (c) of this section may be reduced or denied—

(1) If—

(i) At the most recent IEP Team meeting that the parents attended prior to removal of the child from the public school, the parents did not inform the IEP Team that they were rejecting the placement proposed by the public agency to provide FAPE to their child, including stating their concerns and their intent to enroll their child in a private school at public expense; or

(ii) At least ten (10) business days (including any holidays that occur on a business day) prior to the removal of the child from the public school, the parents did not give written notice to the public agency of the information described in paragraph (d)(1)(i) of this section;

(2) If, prior to the parents' removal of the child from the public school, the public agency informed the parents, through the notice requirements described in § 300.503(a)(1), of its intent to evaluate the child (including a statement of the purpose of the evaluation that was appropriate and reasonable), but the parents did not make the child available for the evaluation; or

(3) Upon a judicial finding of unreasonableness with respect to actions taken by the parents.

(e) Exception. Notwithstanding the notice requirement in paragraph (d)(1) of this section, the cost of reimbursement—

(1) Must not be reduced or denied for failure to provide the notice if—

(i) The school prevented the parents from providing the notice;

(ii) The parents had not received notice, pursuant to § 300.504, of the notice requirement in paragraph (d)(1) of this section; or

(iii) Compliance with paragraph (d)(1) of this section would likely result in physical harm to the child; and

(2) May, in the discretion of the court or a hearing officer, not be reduced or denied for failure to provide this notice if—

(i) The parents are not literate or cannot write in English; or

(ii) Compliance with paragraph (d)(1) of this section would likely result in serious emotional harm to the child.

(Approved by the Office of Management and Budget under control number 1820-0030)

SEA RESPONSIBILITY FOR GENERAL SUPERVISION AND IMPLEMENTATION OF PROCEDURAL SAFEGUARDS

§ 300.149 SEA responsibility for general supervision.

(a) The SEA is responsible for ensuring—

(1) That the requirements of this part are carried out; and

(2) That each educational program for children with disabilities administered within the State, including each program administered by any other State or local agency (but not including elementary schools and secondary schools for Indian children operated or funded by the Secretary of the Interior)—

(i) Is under the general supervision of the persons responsible for educational programs for children with disabilities in the SEA; and

(ii) Meets the educational standards of the SEA (including the requirements of this part).

(3) In carrying out this part with respect to homeless children, the requirements of subtitle B of title VII of the McKinney-Vento Homeless Assistance Act *(42 U.S.C. 11431 et seq.)* are met.

(b) The State must have in effect policies and procedures to ensure that it complies with the monitoring and enforcement requirements in §§ 300.600 through 300.602 and §§ 300.606 through 300.608.

(c) Part B of the Act does not limit the responsibility of agencies other than educational agencies for providing or paying some or all of the costs of FAPE to children with disabilities in the State.

(d) Notwithstanding paragraph (a) of this section, the Governor (or another individual pursuant to State law) may assign to any public agency in the State the responsibility of ensuring that the requirements of Part B of the Act are met with respect to students with disabilities who are convicted as adults under State law and incarcerated in adult prisons.

(Approved by the Office of Management and Budget under control number 1820-0030)

§ 300.150   SEA implementation of procedural safeguards.

The SEA (and any agency assigned responsibility pursuant to § 300.149(d)) must have in effect procedures to inform each public agency of its responsibility for ensuring effective implementation of procedural safeguards for the children with disabilities served by that public agency.

(Approved by the Office of Management and Budget under control number 1820-0030)

STATE COMPLAINT PROCEDURES

§ 300.151   Adoption of State complaint procedures.

(a) General. Each SEA must adopt written procedures for—

(1) Resolving any complaint, including a complaint filed by an organization or individual from another State, that meets the requirements of § 300.153 by—

(i) Providing for the filing of a complaint with the SEA; and

(ii) At the SEA's discretion, providing for the filing of a complaint with a public agency and the right to have the SEA review the public agency's decision on the complaint; and

(2) Widely disseminating to parents and other interested individuals, including parent training and information centers, protection and advocacy agencies, independent living centers, and other appropriate entities, the State procedures under §§ 300.151 through 300.153.

(b) Remedies for denial of appropriate services. In resolving a complaint in which the SEA has found a failure to provide appropriate services, an SEA, pursuant to its general supervisory authority under Part B of the Act, must address—

(1) The failure to provide appropriate services, including corrective action appropriate to address the needs of the child (such as compensatory services or monetary reimbursement); and

(2) Appropriate future provision of services for all children with disabilities.

(Approved by the Office of Management and Budget under control numbers 1820-0030 and 1820-0600)

§ 300.152   Minimum State complaint procedures.

(a) Time limit; minimum procedures. Each SEA must include in its complaint procedures a time limit of 60 days after a complaint is filed under § 300.153 to—

(1) Carry out an independent on-site investigation, if the SEA determines that an investigation is necessary;

(2) Give the complainant the opportunity to submit additional information, either

orally or in writing, about the allegations in the complaint;

(3) Provide the public agency with the opportunity to respond to the complaint, including, at a minimum—

(i) At the discretion of the public agency, a proposal to resolve the complaint; and

(ii) An opportunity for a parent who has filed a complaint and the public agency to voluntarily engage in mediation consistent with § 300.506;

(4) Review all relevant information and make an independent determination as to whether the public agency is violating a requirement of Part B of the Act or of this part; and

(5) Issue a written decision to the complainant that addresses each allegation in the complaint and contains—

(i) Findings of fact and conclusions; and

(ii) The reasons for the SEA's final decision.

(b) *Time extension; final decision; implementation.* The SEA's procedures described in paragraph (a) of this section also must—

(1) Permit an extension of the time limit under paragraph (a) of this section only if—

(i) Exceptional circumstances exist with respect to a particular complaint; or

(ii) The parent (or individual or organization, if mediation or other alternative means of dispute resolution is available to the individual or organization under State procedures) and the public agency involved agree to extend the time to engage in mediation pursuant to paragraph (a)(3)(ii) of this section, or to engage in other alternative means of dispute resolution, if available in the State; and

(2) Include procedures for effective implementation of the SEA's final decision, if needed, including—

(i) Technical assistance activities;

(ii) Negotiations; and

(iii) Corrective actions to achieve compliance.

(c) *Complaints filed under this section and due process hearings under § 300.507 and §§ 300.530 through 300.532.* (1) If a written complaint is received that is also the subject of a due process hearing under § 300.507 or §§ 300.530 through 300.532, or contains multiple issues of which one or more are part of that hearing, the State must set aside any part of the complaint that is being addressed in the due process hearing until the conclusion of the hearing. However, any issue in the complaint that is not a part of the due process action must be resolved using the time limit and procedures described in paragraphs (a) and (b) of this section.

(2) If an issue raised in a complaint filed under this section has previously been decided in a due process hearing involving the same parties—

(i) The due process hearing decision is binding on that issue; and

(ii) The SEA must inform the complainant to that effect.

(3) A complaint alleging a public agency's failure to implement a due process hearing decision must be resolved by the SEA.

(Approved by the Office of Management and Budget under control numbers 1820-0030 and 1820-0600)

§ 300.153   Filing a complaint.

(a) An organization or individual may file a signed written complaint under the procedures described in §§ 300.151 through 300.152.

(b) The complaint must include—

(1) A statement that a public agency has violated a requirement of Part B of the Act or of this part;

(2) The facts on which the statement is based;

(3) The signature and contact information for the complainant; and

(4) If alleging violations with respect to a specific child—

(i) The name and address of the residence of the child;

(ii) The name of the school the child is attending;

(iii) In the case of a homeless child or youth (within the meaning of section 725(2) of the McKinney-Vento Homeless Assistance Act *(42 U.S.C. 11434a*(2)), available contact information for the child, and the name of the school the child is attending;

(iv) A description of the nature of the problem of the child, including facts relating to the problem; and

(v) A proposed resolution of the problem to the extent known and available to the party at the time the complaint is filed.

(c) The complaint must allege a violation that occurred not more than one year prior to the date that the complaint is received in accordance with § 300.151.

(d) The party filing the complaint must forward a copy of the complaint to the LEA or public agency serving the child at the same time the party files the complaint with the SEA.

(Approved by the Office of Management and Budget under control numbers 1820-0030 and 1820-0600)

METHODS OF ENSURING SERVICES

§ 300.154   Methods of ensuring services.

(a) *Establishing responsibility for services.* The Chief Executive Officer of a State or designee of that officer must ensure that an interagency agreement or other mechanism for interagency coordination is in effect between each noneducational public agency described in paragraph (b) of this section and the SEA, in order to ensure that all services described in paragraph (b)(1) of this section that are needed to ensure FAPE are provided, including the provision of these services during the pendency of any dispute under paragraph (a)(3) of this section. The agreement or mechanism must include the following:

(1) An identification of, or a method for defining, the financial responsibility of each agency for providing services described in paragraph (b)(1) of this section to ensure FAPE to children with disabilities. The financial responsibility of each noneducational public agency described in paragraph (b) of this section, including the State Medicaid agency and other public insurers of children with disabilities, must precede the financial responsibility of the LEA (or the State agency responsible for developing the child's IEP).

(2) The conditions, terms, and procedures under which an LEA must be reimbursed by other agencies.

(3) Procedures for resolving interagency disputes (including procedures under which LEAs may initiate proceedings) under the agreement or other mechanism to secure reimbursement from other agencies or otherwise implement the provisions of the agreement or mechanism.

(4) Policies and procedures for agencies to determine and identify the interagency coordination responsibilities of each agency to promote the coordination and timely and appropriate delivery of services described in paragraph (b)(1) of this section.

(b) Obligation of noneducational public agencies. (1)(i) If any public agency other than an educational agency is otherwise obligated under Federal or State law, or assigned responsibility under State policy or pursuant to paragraph (a) of this section, to provide or pay for any services that are also considered special education or related services (such as, but not limited to, services described in § 300.5 relating to assistive technology devices, § 300.6 relating to assistive technology services, § 300.34 relating to related services, § 300.41 relating to supplementary aids and services, and § 300.42 relating to transition services) that are necessary for ensuring FAPE to children with disabilities within the State, the public agency must fulfill that obligation or responsibility, either directly or through contract or other arrangement pursuant to paragraph (a) of this section or an agreement pursuant to paragraph (c) of this section.

(ii) A noneducational public agency described in paragraph (b)(1)(i) of this section may not disqualify an eligible service for Medicaid reimbursement because that service is provided in a school context.

(2) If a public agency other than an educational agency fails to provide or pay for the special education and related services described in paragraph (b)(1) of this section, the LEA (or State agency responsible for developing the child's IEP) must provide or pay for these services to the child in a timely manner. The LEA or State agency is authorized to claim reimbursement for the services from the noneducational public agency that failed to provide or pay for these services and that agency must reimburse the LEA or State agency in accordance with the terms of the interagency agreement or other mechanism described in paragraph (a) of this section.

(c) Special rule. The requirements of paragraph (a) of this section may be met through—

(1) State statute or regulation;

(2) Signed agreements between respective agency officials that clearly identify the responsibilities of each agency relating to the provision of services; or

(3) Other appropriate written methods as determined by the Chief Executive Officer of the State or designee of that officer and approved by the Secretary.

(d) Children with disabilities who are covered by public benefits or insurance. (1) A public agency may use the Medicaid or other public benefits or insurance programs in which a child participates to provide or pay for services required under this part, as permitted under the public benefits or insurance program, except as provided in paragraph (d)(2) of this section.

(2) With regard to services required to provide FAPE to an eligible child under this part, the public agency—

(i) May not require parents to sign up for or enroll in public benefits or insurance programs in order for their child to receive FAPE under Part B of the Act;

(ii) May not require parents to incur an out-of-pocket expense such as the payment of a deductible or co-pay amount incurred in filing a claim for services provided pursuant to this part, but pursuant to paragraph (g)(2) of this section, may pay the cost that the parents otherwise would be required to pay;

(iii) May not use a child's benefits under a public benefits or insurance program if that use would—

(A) Decrease available lifetime coverage or any other insured benefit;

(B) Result in the family paying for services that would otherwise be covered by the public benefits or insurance program and that are required for the child outside of the time the child is in school;

(C) Increase premiums or lead to the discontinuation of benefits or insurance; or

(D) Risk loss of eligibility for home and community-based waivers, based on aggregate health-related expenditures; and

(iv)(A) Must obtain parental consent, consistent with § 300.9, each time that access to public benefits or insurance is sought; and

(B) Notify parents that the parents' refusal to allow access to their public benefits or insurance does not relieve the public agency of its responsibility to ensure that all required services are provided at no cost to the parents.

(e) Children with disabilities who are covered by private insurance. (1) With regard to services required to provide FAPE to an eligible child under this part, a public agency may access the parents' private insurance proceeds only if the parents provide consent consistent with § 300.9.

(2) Each time the public agency proposes to access the parents' private insurance proceeds, the agency must—

(i) Obtain parental consent in accordance with paragraph (e)(1) of this section; and

(ii) Inform the parents that their refusal to permit the public agency to access their private insurance does not relieve the public agency of its responsibility to ensure that all required services are provided at no cost to the parents.

(f) Use of Part B funds. (1) If a public agency is unable to obtain parental consent to use the parents' private insurance, or public benefits or insurance when the parents would incur a cost for a specified service required under this part, to ensure FAPE the public agency may use its Part B funds to pay for the service.

(2) To avoid financial cost to parents who otherwise would consent to use private insurance, or public benefits or insurance if the parents would incur a cost, the public agency may use its Part B funds to pay the cost that the parents otherwise would have to pay to use the parents' benefits or insurance (e.g., the deductible or co-pay amounts).

(g) Proceeds from public benefits or insurance or private insurance. (1) Proceeds from public benefits or insurance or private insurance will not be treated as program income for purposes of *34 CFR 80.25*.

(2) If a public agency spends reimbursements from Federal funds (e.g., Medicaid) for services under this part, those funds will not be considered "State or local" funds for purposes of the maintenance of effort provisions in §§ 300.163 and 300.203.

(h) Construction. Nothing in this part should be construed to alter the requirements imposed on a State Medicaid agency, or any other agency administering a public benefits or insurance program by Federal statute, regulations or policy under title XIX, or title XXI of the Social Security Act, *42 U.S.C. 1396* through 1396v and *42 U.S.C. 1397aa* through 1397jj, or any other public benefits or insurance program.

(Approved by the Office of Management and Budget under control number 1820-0030)

ADDITIONAL ELIGIBILITY REQUIREMENTS

§ 300.155 Hearings relating to LEA eligibility.

The SEA must not make any final determination that an LEA is not eligible for assistance under Part B of the Act without first giving the LEA reasonable notice and an opportunity for a hearing under *34 CFR 76.401(d)*.

(Approved by the Office of Management and Budget under control number 1820-0030)

§ 300.156 Personnel qualifications.

(a) *General.* The SEA must establish and maintain qualifications to ensure that personnel necessary to carry out the purposes of this part are appropriately and adequately prepared and trained, including that those personnel have the content knowledge and skills to serve children with disabilities.

(b) *Related services personnel and paraprofessionals.* The qualifications under paragraph (a) of this section must include qualifications for related services personnel and paraprofessionals that—

(1) Are consistent with any State-approved or State-recognized certification, licensing, registration, or other comparable requirements that apply to the professional discipline in which those personnel are providing special education or related services; and

(2) Ensure that related services personnel who deliver services in their discipline or profession—

(i) Meet the requirements of paragraph (b)(1) of this section; and

(ii) Have not had certification or licensure requirements waived on an emergency, temporary, or provisional basis; and

(iii) Allow paraprofessionals and assistants who are appropriately trained and supervised, in accordance with State law, regulation, or written policy, in meeting the requirements of this part to be used to assist in the provision of special education and related services under this part to children with disabilities.

(c) *Qualifications for special education teachers.* The qualifications described in paragraph (a) of this section must ensure that each person employed as a public school special education teacher in the State who teaches in an elementary school, middle school, or secondary school is highly qualified as a special education teacher by the deadline established in section 1119(a)(2) of the ESEA.

(d) *Policy.* In implementing this section, a State must adopt a policy that includes a requirement that LEAs in the State take measurable steps to recruit, hire, train, and retain highly qualified personnel to provide special education and related services under this part to children with disabilities.

(e) *Rule of construction.* Notwithstanding any other individual right of action that a parent or student may maintain under this part, nothing in this part shall be construed to create a right of action on behalf of an individual student or a class of students for the failure of a particular SEA or LEA employee to be highly qualified, or to prevent a parent from filing a complaint about staff qualifications with the SEA as provided for under this part.

(Approved by the Office of Management and Budget under control number 1820-0030)

§ 300.157 Performance goals and indicators.

The State must—

(a) Have in effect established goals for the performance of children with disabilities in the State that—

(1) Promote the purposes of this part, as stated in § 300.1;

(2) Are the same as the State's objectives for progress by children in its definition of adequate yearly progress, including the State's objectives for progress by children with disabilities, under section 1111(b)(2)(C) of the ESEA, *20 U.S.C. 6311;*

(3) Address graduation rates and dropout rates, as well as such other factors as the State may determine; and

(4) Are consistent, to the extent appropriate, with any other goals and academic standards for children established by the State;

(b) Have in effect established performance indicators the State will use to assess progress toward achieving the goals described in paragraph (a) of this section, including measurable annual objectives for progress by children with disabilities under section 1111(b)(2)(C)(v)(II)(cc) of the ESEA, *20 U.S.C. 6311;* and

(c) Annually report to the Secretary and the public on the progress of the State, and of children with disabilities in the State, toward meeting the goals established under paragraph (a) of this section, which may include elements of the reports required under section 1111(h) of the ESEA.

(Approved by the Office of Management and Budget under control number 1820-0030)

§§ 300.158–300.159 [Reserved]

§ 300.160 Participation in assessments.

(a) *General.* A State must ensure that all children with disabilities are included in all general State and district-wide assessment programs, including assessments described under section 1111 of the ESEA, *20 U.S.C. 6311,* with appropriate accommodations and alternate assessments, if necessary, as indicated in their respective IEPs.

(b) *Accommodation guidelines.* (1) A State (or, in the case of a district-wide assessment, an LEA) must develop guidelines for the provision of appropriate accommodations.

(2) The State's (or, in the case of a district-wide assessment, the LEA's) guidelines must —

(i) Identify only those accommodations for each assessment that do not invalidate the score; and

(ii) Instruct IEP Teams to select, for each assessment, only those accommodations that do not invalidate the score.

(c) *Alternate assessments.* (1) A State (or, in the case of a district-wide assessment, an LEA) must develop and implement alternate assessments and guidelines for the participation of children with disabilities in alternate assessments for those children who cannot participate in regular assessments, even with accommodations, as indicated in their respective IEPs, as provided in paragraph (a) of this section.

(2) For assessing the academic progress of students with disabilities under Title I of the ESEA, the alternate assessments and guidelines in paragraph (c)(1) of this section must provide for alternate assessments that —

(i) Are aligned with the State's challenging academic content standards and challenging student academic achievement standards;

(ii) If the State has adopted modified academic achievement standards permitted in *34 CFR 200.1(e),* measure the achievement of children with disabilities meeting the State's criteria under § 200.1(e)(2) against those standards; and

(iii) If the State has adopted alternate academic achievement standards permitted in 34 CFR 200.1(d), measure the achievement of children with the most significant cognitive disabilities against those standards.

(d) Explanation to IEP Teams. A State (or in the case of a district-wide assessment, an LEA) must provide IEP Teams with a clear explanation of the differences between assessments based on grade-level academic achievement standards and those based on modified or alternate academic achievement standards, including any effects of State or local policies on the student's education resulting from taking an alternate assessment based on alternate or modified academic achievement standards (such as whether only satisfactory performance on a regular assessment would qualify a student for a regular high school diploma).

(e) Inform parents. A State (or in the case of a district-wide assessment, an LEA) must ensure that parents of students selected to be assessed based on alternate or modified academic achievement standards are informed that their child's achievement will be measured based on alternate or modified academic achievement standards.

(f) Reports. An SEA (or, in the case of a district-wide assessment, an LEA) must make available to the public, and report to the public with the same frequency and in the same detail as it reports on the assessment of nondisabled children, the following:

(1) The number of children with disabilities participating in regular assessments, and the number of those children who were provided accommodations (that did not result in an invalid score) in order to participate in those assessments.

(2) The number of children with disabilities, if any, participating in alternate assessments based on grade-level academic achievement standards.

(3) The number of children with disabilities, if any, participating in alternate assessments based on modified academic achievement standards.

(4) The number of children with disabilities, if any, participating in alternate assessments based on alternate academic achievement standards.

(5) Compared with the achievement of all children, including children with disabilities, the performance results of children with disabilities on regular assessments, alternate assessments based on grade-level academic achievement standards, alternate assessments based on modified academic achievement standards, and alternate assessments based on alternate academic achievement standards if —

(i) The number of children participating in those assessments is sufficient to yield statistically reliable information; and

(ii) Reporting that information will not reveal personally identifiable information about an individual student on those assessments.

(g) Universal design. An SEA (or, in the case of a district-wide assessment, an LEA) must, to the extent possible, use universal design principles in developing and administering any assessments under this section.

§ 300.161 [Reserved]

§ 300.162 Supplementation of State, local, and other Federal funds.

(a) Expenditures. Funds paid to a State under this part must be expended in accordance with all the provisions of this part.

(b) Prohibition against commingling. (1) Funds paid to a State under this part must not be commingled with State funds.

(2) The requirement in paragraph (b)(1) of this section is satisfied by the use of a separate accounting system that includes an audit trail of the expenditure of funds paid to a State under this part. Separate bank accounts are not required. (See *34 CFR 76.702* (Fiscal control and fund accounting procedures).)

(c) *State-level nonsupplanting.* (1) Except as provided in § 300.203, funds paid to a State under Part B of the Act must be used to supplement the level of Federal, State, and local funds (including funds that are not under the direct control of the SEA or LEAs) expended for special education and related services provided to children with disabilities under Part B of the Act, and in no case to supplant those Federal, State, and local funds.

(2) If the State provides clear and convincing evidence that all children with disabilities have available to them FAPE, the Secretary may waive, in whole or in part, the requirements of paragraph (c)(1) of this section if the Secretary concurs with the evidence provided by the State under § 300.164.

(Approved by the Office of Management and Budget under control number 1820-0030)

§ 300.163   Maintenance of State financial support.

(a) *General.* A State must not reduce the amount of State financial support for special education and related services for children with disabilities, or otherwise made available because of the excess costs of educating those children, below the amount of that support for the preceding fiscal year.

(b) *Reduction of funds for failure to maintain support.* The Secretary reduces the allocation of funds under section 611 of the Act for any fiscal year following the fiscal year in which the State fails to comply with the requirement of paragraph (a) of this section by the same amount by which the State fails to meet the requirement.

(c) *Waivers for exceptional or uncontrollable circumstances.* The Secretary may waive the requirement of paragraph (a) of this section for a State, for one fiscal year at a time, if the Secretary determines that—

(1) Granting a waiver would be equitable due to exceptional or uncontrollable circumstances such as a natural disaster or a precipitous and unforeseen decline in the financial resources of the State; or

(2) The State meets the standard in § 300.164 for a waiver of the requirement to supplement, and not to supplant, funds received under Part B of the Act.

(d) *Subsequent years.* If, for any fiscal year, a State fails to meet the requirement of paragraph (a) of this section, including any year for which the State is granted a waiver under paragraph (c) of this section, the financial support required of the State in future years under paragraph (a) of this section shall be the amount that would have been required in the absence of that failure and not the reduced level of the State's support.

(Approved by the Office of Management and Budget under control number 1820-0030)

§ 300.164   Waiver of requirement regarding supplementing and not supplanting with Part B funds.

(a) Except as provided under §§ 300.202 through 300.205, funds paid to a State under Part B of the Act must be used to supplement and increase the level of Federal, State, and local funds (including funds that are not under the direct control of SEAs or LEAs) expended for special education and related services provided to children with disabilities under Part B of the Act and in no case to supplant those Federal, State, and local funds. A State may use funds it retains under § 300.704(a) and (b) without regard to the prohibition on supplanting other funds.

(b) If a State provides clear and convincing evidence that all eligible children with disabilities throughout the State have FAPE available to them, the Secretary may waive for a period of one year in whole or in part the requirement under § 300.162 (regarding State-level nonsupplanting) if the Secretary concurs with the evidence provided by the State.

(c) If a State wishes to request a waiver under this section, it must submit to the Secretary a written request that includes—

(1) An assurance that FAPE is currently available, and will remain available throughout the period that a waiver would be in effect, to all eligible children with disabilities throughout the State, regardless of the public agency that is responsible for providing FAPE to them. The assurance must be signed by an official who has the authority to provide that assurance as it applies to all eligible children with disabilities in the State;

(2) All evidence that the State wishes the Secretary to consider in determining whether all eligible children with disabilities have FAPE available to them, setting forth in detail—

(i) The basis on which the State has concluded that FAPE is available to all eligible children in the State; and

(ii) The procedures that the State will implement to ensure that FAPE remains available to all eligible children in the State, which must include—

(A) The State's procedures under § 300.111 for ensuring that all eligible children are identified, located and evaluated;

(B) The State's procedures for monitoring public agencies to ensure that they comply with all requirements of this part;

(C) The State's complaint procedures under §§ 300.151 through 300.153; and

(D) The State's hearing procedures under §§ 300.511 through 300.516 and §§ 300.530 through 300.536;

(3) A summary of all State and Federal monitoring reports, and State complaint decisions (see §§ 300.151 through 300.153) and hearing decisions (see §§ 300.511 through 300.516 and §§ 300.530 through 300.536), issued within three years prior to the date of the State's request for a waiver under this section, that includes any finding that FAPE has not been available to one or more eligible children, and evidence that FAPE is now available to all children addressed in those reports or decisions; and

(4) Evidence that the State, in determining that FAPE is currently available to all eligible children with disabilities in the State, has consulted with the State advisory panel under § 300.167.

(d) If the Secretary determines that the request and supporting evidence submitted by the State makes a prima facie showing that FAPE is, and will remain, available to all eligible children with disabilities in the State, the Secretary, after notice to the public throughout the State, conducts a public hearing at which all interested persons and organizations may present evidence regarding the following issues:

(1) Whether FAPE is currently available to all eligible children with disabilities in the State.

(2) Whether the State will be able to ensure that FAPE remains available to all eligible children with disabilities in the State if the Secretary provides the requested waiver.

(e) Following the hearing, the Secretary, based on all submitted evidence, will provide a waiver, in whole or in part, for a period of one year if the Secretary finds that the State has provided clear and convincing evidence that FAPE is currently available to all eligible children with disabilities in the State, and the State will be able to ensure that

FAPE remains available to all eligible children with disabilities in the State if the Secretary provides the requested waiver.

(f) A State may receive a waiver of the requirement of section 612(a)(18)(A) of the Act and § 300.164 if it satisfies the requirements of paragraphs (b) through (e) of this section.

(g) The Secretary may grant subsequent waivers for a period of one year each, if the Secretary determines that the State has provided clear and convincing evidence that all eligible children with disabilities throughout the State have, and will continue to have throughout the one-year period of the waiver, FAPE available to them.

(Approved by the Office of Management and Budget under control number 1820-0030)

§ 300.165 Public participation.

(a) Prior to the adoption of any policies and procedures needed to comply with Part B of the Act (including any amendments to those policies and procedures), the State must ensure that there are public hearings, adequate notice of the hearings, and an opportunity for comment available to the general public, including individuals with disabilities and parents of children with disabilities.

(b) Before submitting a State plan under this part, a State must comply with the public participation requirements in paragraph (a) of this section and those in *20 U.S.C. 1232d*(b)(7).

(Approved by the Office of Management and Budget under control number 1820-0030)

§ 300.166 Rule of construction.

In complying with §§ 300.162 and 300.163, a State may not use funds paid to it under this part to satisfy State-law mandated funding obligations to LEAs, including funding based on student attendance or enrollment, or inflation.

(Approved by the Office of Management and Budget under control number 1820-0030)

STATE ADVISORY PANEL

§ 300.167 State advisory panel.

The State must establish and maintain an advisory panel for the purpose of providing policy guidance with respect to special education and related services for children with disabilities in the State.

(Approved by the Office of Management and Budget under control number 1820-0030)

§ 300.168 Membership.

(a) General. The advisory panel must consist of members appointed by the Governor, or any other official authorized under State law to make such appointments, be representative of the State population and be composed of individuals involved in, or concerned with the education of children with disabilities, including—

(1) Parents of children with disabilities (ages birth through 26);

(2) Individuals with disabilities;

(3) Teachers;

(4) Representatives of institutions of higher education that prepare special education and related services personnel;

(5) State and local education officials, including officials who carry out activities under subtitle B of title VII of the McKinney-Vento Homeless Assistance Act, *(42 U.S.C. 11431 et seq.)*;

(6) Administrators of programs for children with disabilities;

(7) Representatives of other State agencies involved in the financing or delivery of related services to children with disabilities;

(8) Representatives of private schools and public charter schools;

(9) Not less than one representative of a vocational, community, or business organization concerned with the provision of transition services to children with disabilities;

(10) A representative from the State child welfare agency responsible for foster care; and

(11) Representatives from the State juvenile and adult corrections agencies.

(b) *Special rule.* A majority of the members of the panel must be individuals with disabilities or parents of children with disabilities (ages birth through 26).

(Approved by the Office of Management and Budget under control number 1820-0030)

§ 300.169 Duties.

The advisory panel must—

(a) Advise the SEA of unmet needs within the State in the education of children with disabilities;

(b) Comment publicly on any rules or regulations proposed by the State regarding the education of children with disabilities;

(c) Advise the SEA in developing evaluations and reporting on data to the Secretary under section 618 of the Act;

(d) Advise the SEA in developing corrective action plans to address findings identified in Federal monitoring reports under Part B of the Act; and

(e) Advise the SEA in developing and implementing policies relating to the coordination of services for children with disabilities.

(Approved by the Office of Management and Budget under control number 1820-0030)

OTHER PROVISIONS REQUIRED FOR STATE ELIGIBILITY

§ 300.170 Suspension and expulsion rates.

(a) *General.* The SEA must examine data, including data disaggregated by race and ethnicity, to determine if significant discrepancies are occurring in the rate of long-term suspensions and expulsions of children with disabilities—

(1) Among LEAs in the State; or

(2) Compared to the rates for nondisabled children within those agencies.

(b) *Review and revision of policies.* If the discrepancies described in paragraph (a) of this section are occurring, the SEA must review and, if appropriate, revise (or require the affected State agency or LEA to revise) its policies, procedures, and practices relating to the development and implementation of IEPs, the use of positive behavioral interventions and supports, and procedural safeguards, to ensure that these policies, procedures, and practices comply with the Act.

(Approved by the Office of Management and Budget under control number 1820-0030)

§ 300.171 Annual description of use of Part B funds.

(a) In order to receive a grant in any fiscal year a State must annually describe—

(1) How amounts retained for State administration and State-level activities under § 300.704 will be used to meet the requirements of this part; and

(2) How those amounts will be allocated among the activities described in § 300.704 to meet State priorities based on input from LEAs.

(b) If a State's plans for use of its funds under § 300.704 for the forthcoming year do not change from the prior year, the State may submit a letter to that effect to meet the requirement in paragraph (a) of this section.

(c) The provisions of this section do not apply to the Virgin Islands, Guam, American Samoa, the Commonwealth of the Northern Mariana Islands, and the freely associated States.

(Approved by the Office of Management and Budget under control number 1820-0030)

§ 300.172 Access to instructional materials.

(a) *General.* The State must—

(1) Adopt the National Instructional Materials Accessibility Standard (NIMAS), published as appendix C to part 300, for the purposes of providing instructional materials to blind persons or other persons with print disabilities, in a timely manner after publication of the NIMAS in the Federal Register on July 19, 2006 *(71 FR 41084);* and

(2) Establish a State definition of "timely manner" for purposes of paragraphs (b)(2) and (b)(3) of this section if the State is not coordinating with the National Instructional Materials Access Center (NIMAC) or (b)(3) and (c)(2) of this section if the State is coordinating with the NIMAC.

(b) *Rights and responsibilities of SEA.* (1) Nothing in this section shall be construed to require any SEA to coordinate with the NIMAC.

(2) If an SEA chooses not to coordinate with the NIMAC, the SEA must provide an assurance to the Secretary that it will provide instructional materials to blind persons or other persons with print disabilities in a timely manner.

(3) Nothing in this section relieves an SEA of its responsibility to ensure that children with disabilities who need instructional materials in accessible formats, but are not included under the definition of blind or other persons with print disabilities in § 300.172(e)(1)(i) or who need materials that cannot be produced from NIMAS files, receive those instructional materials in a timely manner.

(4) In order to meet its responsibility under paragraphs (b)(2), (b)(3), and (c) of this section to ensure that children with disabilities who need instructional materials in accessible formats are provided those materials in a timely manner, the SEA must ensure that all public agencies take all reasonable steps to provide instructional materials in accessible formats to children with disabilities who need those instructional materials at the same time as other children receive instructional materials.

(c) *Preparation and delivery of files.* If an SEA chooses to coordinate with the NIMAC, as of December 3, 2006, the SEA must—

(1) As part of any print instructional materials adoption process, procurement contract, or other practice or instrument used for purchase of print instructional

materials, enter into a written contract with the publisher of the print instructional materials to—

(i) Require the publisher to prepare and, on or before delivery of the print instructional materials, provide to NIMAC electronic files containing the contents of the print instructional materials using the NIMAS; or

(ii) Purchase instructional materials from the publisher that are produced in, or may be rendered in, specialized formats.

(2) Provide instructional materials to blind persons or other persons with print disabilities in a timely manner.

(d) Assistive technology. In carrying out this section, the SEA, to the maximum extent possible, must work collaboratively with the State agency responsible for assistive technology programs.

(e) Definitions. (1) In this section and § 300.210—

(i) Blind persons or other persons with print disabilities means children served under this part who may qualify to receive books and other publications produced in specialized formats in accordance with the Act entitled "An Act to provide books for adult blind," approved March 3, 1931, *2 U.S.C 135a*;

(ii) National Instructional Materials Access Center or NIMAC means the center established pursuant to section 674(e) of the Act;

(iii) National Instructional Materials Accessibility Standard or NIMAS has the meaning given the term in section 674(e)(3)(B) of the Act;

(iv) Specialized formats has the meaning given the term in section 674(e)(3)(D) of the Act.

(2) The definitions in paragraph (e)(1) of this section apply to each State and LEA, whether or not the State or LEA chooses to coordinate with the NIMAC.

(Approved by the Office of Management and Budget under control number 1820-0030)

§ 300.173 Overidentification and disproportionality.

The State must have in effect, consistent with the purposes of this part and with section 618(d) of the Act, policies and procedures designed to prevent the inappropriate overidentification or disproportionate representation by race and ethnicity of children as children with disabilities, including children with disabilities with a particular impairment described in § 300.8.

(Approved by the Office of Management and Budget under control number 1820-0030)

§ 300.174 Prohibition on mandatory medication.

(a) General. The SEA must prohibit State and LEA personnel from requiring parents to obtain a prescription for substances identified under schedules I, II, III, IV, or V in section 202(c) of the Controlled Substances Act *(21 U.S.C. 812(c))* for a child as a condition of attending school, receiving an evaluation under §§ 300.300 through 300.311, or receiving services under this part.

(b) Rule of construction. Nothing in paragraph (a) of this section shall be construed to create a Federal prohibition against teachers and other school personnel consulting or sharing classroom-based observations with parents or guardians regarding a student's academic and functional performance, or behavior in the classroom or school, or regarding the need for evaluation for special education or related services under § 300.111 (related to child find).

(Approved by the Office of Management and Budget under control number 1820-0030)

§ 300.175 SEA as provider of FAPE or direct services.

If the SEA provides FAPE to children with disabilities, or provides direct services to these children, the agency—

(a) Must comply with any additional requirements of §§ 300.201 and 300.202 and §§ 300.206 through 300.226 as if the agency were an LEA; and

(b) May use amounts that are otherwise available to the agency under Part B of the Act to serve those children without regard to § 300.202(b) (relating to excess costs).

(Approved by the Office of Management and Budget under control number 1820-0030)

§ 300.176 Exception for prior State plans.

(a) *General.* If a State has on file with the Secretary policies and procedures approved by the Secretary that demonstrate that the State meets any requirement of § 300.100, including any policies and procedures filed under Part B of the Act as in effect before, December 3, 2004, the Secretary considers the State to have met the requirement for purposes of receiving a grant under Part B of the Act.

(b) *Modifications made by a State.* (1) Subject to paragraph (b)(2) of this section, policies and procedures submitted by a State in accordance with this subpart remain in effect until the State submits to the Secretary the modifications that the State determines necessary.

(2) The provisions of this subpart apply to a modification to an application to the same extent and in the same manner that they apply to the original plan.

(c) *Modifications required by the Secretary.* The Secretary may require a State to modify its policies and procedures, but only to the extent necessary to ensure the State's compliance with this part, if—

(1) After December 3, 2004, the provisions of the Act or the regulations in this part are amended;

(2) There is a new interpretation of this Act by a Federal court or a State's highest court; or

(3) There is an official finding of noncompliance with Federal law or regulations.

(Approved by the Office of Management and Budget under control number 1820-0030)

§ 300.177 States' sovereign immunity.

(a) *General.* A State that accepts funds under this part waives its immunity under the 11th amendment to the Constitution of the United States from suit in Federal court for a violation of this part.

(b) *Remedies.* In a suit against a State for a violation of this part, remedies (including remedies both at law and in equity) are available for such a violation in the suit against a public entity other than a State.

(c) *Effective date.* Paragraphs (a) and (b) of this section apply with respect to violations that occur in whole or part after the date of enactment of the Education of the Handicapped Act Amendments of 1990.

DEPARTMENT PROCEDURES

§ 300.178 Determination by the Secretary that a State is eligible to receive a grant.

If the Secretary determines that a State is eligible to receive a grant under Part B of the Act, the Secretary notifies the State of that determination.

§ 300.179 Notice and hearing before determining that a State is not eligible to receive a grant.

(a) General. (1) The Secretary does not make a final determination that a State is not eligible to receive a grant under Part B of the Act until providing the State—

(i) With reasonable notice; and

(ii) With an opportunity for a hearing.

(2) In implementing paragraph (a)(1)(i) of this section, the Secretary sends a written notice to the SEA by certified mail with return receipt requested.

(b) Content of notice. In the written notice described in paragraph (a)(2) of this section, the Secretary—

(1) States the basis on which the Secretary proposes to make a final determination that the State is not eligible;

(2) May describe possible options for resolving the issues;

(3) Advises the SEA that it may request a hearing and that the request for a hearing must be made not later than 30 days after it receives the notice of the proposed final determination that the State is not eligible; and

(4) Provides the SEA with information about the hearing procedures that will be followed.

§ 300.180 Hearing official or panel.

(a) If the SEA requests a hearing, the Secretary designates one or more individuals, either from the Department or elsewhere, not responsible for or connected with the administration of this program, to conduct a hearing.

(b) If more than one individual is designated, the Secretary designates one of those individuals as the Chief Hearing Official of the Hearing Panel. If one individual is designated, that individual is the Hearing Official.

§ 300.181 Hearing procedures.

(a) As used in §§ 300.179 through 300.184 the term party or parties means the following:

(1) An SEA that requests a hearing regarding the proposed disapproval of the State's eligibility under this part.

(2) The Department official who administers the program of financial assistance under this part.

(3) A person, group or agency with an interest in and having relevant information about the case that has applied for and been granted leave to intervene by the Hearing Official or Hearing Panel.

(b) Within 15 days after receiving a request for a hearing, the Secretary designates a Hearing Official or Hearing Panel and notifies the parties.

(c) The Hearing Official or Hearing Panel may regulate the course of proceedings and the conduct of the parties during the proceedings. The Hearing Official or Hearing Panel takes all steps necessary to conduct a fair and impartial proceeding, to avoid delay, and to maintain order, including the following:

(1) The Hearing Official or Hearing Panel may hold conferences or other types of appropriate proceedings to clarify, simplify, or define the issues or to consider other matters that may aid in the disposition of the case.

(2) The Hearing Official or Hearing Panel may schedule a prehearing conference with the Hearing Official or Hearing Panel and the parties.

(3) Any party may request the Hearing Official or Hearing Panel to schedule a prehearing or other conference. The Hearing Official or Hearing Panel decides whether a conference is necessary and notifies all parties.

(4) At a prehearing or other conference, the Hearing Official or Hearing Panel and the parties may consider subjects such as—

(i) Narrowing and clarifying issues;

(ii) Assisting the parties in reaching agreements and stipulations;

(iii) Clarifying the positions of the parties;

(iv) Determining whether an evidentiary hearing or oral argument should be held; and

(v) Setting dates for—

(A) The exchange of written documents;

(B) The receipt of comments from the parties on the need for oral argument or evidentiary hearing;

(C) Further proceedings before the Hearing Official or Hearing Panel (including an evidentiary hearing or oral argument, if either is scheduled);

(D) Requesting the names of witnesses each party wishes to present at an evidentiary hearing and estimation of time for each presentation; or

(E) Completion of the review and the initial decision of the Hearing Official or Hearing Panel.

(5) A prehearing or other conference held under paragraph (c)(4) of this section may be conducted by telephone conference call.

(6) At a prehearing or other conference, the parties must be prepared to discuss the subjects listed in paragraph (b)(4) of this section.

(7) Following a prehearing or other conference the Hearing Official or Hearing Panel may issue a written statement describing the issues raised, the action taken, and the stipulations and agreements reached by the parties.

(d) The Hearing Official or Hearing Panel may require parties to state their positions and to provide all or part of the evidence in writing.

(e) The Hearing Official or Hearing Panel may require parties to present testimony through affidavits and to conduct cross-examination through interrogatories.

(f) The Hearing Official or Hearing Panel may direct the parties to exchange relevant documents or information and lists of witnesses, and to send copies to the Hearing Official or Panel.

(g) The Hearing Official or Hearing Panel may receive, rule on, exclude, or limit evidence at any stage of the proceedings.

(h) The Hearing Official or Hearing Panel may rule on motions and other issues at any stage of the proceedings.

(i) The Hearing Official or Hearing Panel may examine witnesses.

(j) The Hearing Official or Hearing Panel may set reasonable time limits for submission of written documents.

(k) The Hearing Official or Hearing Panel may refuse to consider documents or other submissions if they are not submitted in a timely manner unless good cause is shown.

(l) The Hearing Official or Hearing Panel may interpret applicable statutes and regulations but may not waive them or rule on their validity.

(m)(1) The parties must present their positions through briefs and the submission of other documents and may request an oral argument or evidentiary hearing. The Hearing Official or Hearing Panel shall determine whether an oral argument or an evidentiary hearing is needed to clarify the positions of the parties.

(2) The Hearing Official or Hearing Panel gives each party an opportunity to be represented by counsel.

(n) If the Hearing Official or Hearing Panel determines that an evidentiary hearing would materially assist the resolution of the matter, the Hearing Official or Hearing Panel gives each party, in addition to the opportunity to be represented by counsel—

(1) An opportunity to present witnesses on the party's behalf; and

(2) An opportunity to cross-examine witnesses either orally or with written questions.

(o) The Hearing Official or Hearing Panel accepts any evidence that it finds is relevant and material to the proceedings and is not unduly repetitious.

(p)(1) The Hearing Official or Hearing Panel—

(i) Arranges for the preparation of a transcript of each hearing;

(ii) Retains the original transcript as part of the record of the hearing; and

(iii) Provides one copy of the transcript to each party.

(2) Additional copies of the transcript are available on request and with payment of the reproduction fee.

(q) Each party must file with the Hearing Official or Hearing Panel all written motions, briefs, and other documents and must at the same time provide a copy to the other parties to the proceedings.

§ 300.182 Initial decision; final decision.

(a) The Hearing Official or Hearing Panel prepares an initial written decision that addresses each of the points in the notice sent by the Secretary to the SEA under § 300.179 including any amendments to or further clarifications of the issues, under § 300.181(c)(7).

(b) The initial decision of a Hearing Panel is made by a majority of Panel members.

(c) The Hearing Official or Hearing Panel mails, by certified mail with return receipt requested, a copy of the initial decision to each party (or to the party's counsel) and to the Secretary, with a notice stating that each party has an opportunity to submit written comments regarding the decision to the Secretary.

(d) Each party may file comments and recommendations on the initial decision with the Hearing Official or Hearing Panel within 15 days of the date the party receives the Panel's decision.

(e) The Hearing Official or Hearing Panel sends a copy of a party's initial comments and recommendations to the other parties by certified mail with return receipt requested. Each party may file responsive comments and recommendations with the Hearing Official or Hearing Panel within seven days of the date the party receives the initial comments and recommendations.

(f) The Hearing Official or Hearing Panel forwards the parties' initial and responsive comments on the initial decision to the Secretary who reviews the initial decision and issues a final decision.

(g) The initial decision of the Hearing Official or Hearing Panel becomes the final decision of the Secretary unless, within 25 days after the end of the time for receipt of written comments and recommendations, the Secretary informs the Hearing Official or Hearing Panel and the parties to a hearing in writing that the decision is being further reviewed for possible modification.

(h) The Secretary rejects or modifies the initial decision of the Hearing Official or Hearing Panel if the Secretary finds that it is clearly erroneous.

(i) The Secretary conducts the review based on the initial decision, the written record, the transcript of the Hearing Official's or Hearing Panel's proceedings, and written comments.

(j) The Secretary may remand the matter to the Hearing Official or Hearing Panel for further proceedings.

(k) Unless the Secretary remands the matter as provided in paragraph (j) of this section, the Secretary issues the final decision, with any necessary modifications, within 30 days after notifying the Hearing Official or Hearing Panel that the initial decision is being further reviewed.

(Approved by the Office of Management and Budget under control number 1820-0030)

§ 300.183   Filing requirements.

(a) Any written submission by a party under §§ 300.179 through 300.184 must be filed by hand delivery, by mail, or by facsimile transmission. The Secretary discourages the use of facsimile transmission for documents longer than five pages.

(b) The filing date under paragraph (a) of this section is the date the document is—

(1) Hand-delivered;

(2) Mailed; or

(3) Sent by facsimile transmission.

(c) A party filing by facsimile transmission is responsible for confirming that a complete and legible copy of the document was received by the Department.

(d) If a document is filed by facsimile transmission, the Secretary, the Hearing Official, or the Hearing Panel, as applicable, may require the filing of a follow-up hard copy by hand delivery or by mail within a reasonable period of time.

(e) If agreed upon by the parties, service of a document may be made upon the other party by facsimile transmission.

§ 300.184   Judicial review.

If a State is dissatisfied with the Secretary's final decision with respect to the eligibility of the State under section 612 of the Act, the State may, not later than 60 days after notice of that decision, file with the United States Court of Appeals for the circuit in which that State is located a petition for review of that decision. A copy of the petition must be transmitted by the clerk of the court to the Secretary. The Secretary then files in the court the record of the proceedings upon which the Secretary's decision was based, as provided in *28 U.S.C. 2112.*

§ 300.185

[This section was removed and reserved. See 71 FR 46540, 46753, Aug. 14, 2006.]

§ 300.186 Assistance under other Federal programs.

Part B of the Act may not be construed to permit a State to reduce medical and other assistance available, or to alter eligibility, under titles V and XIX of the Social Security Act with respect to the provision of FAPE for children with disabilities in the State.

BY-PASS FOR CHILDREN IN PRIVATE SCHOOLS

§ 300.190 By-pass — general.

(a) If, on December 2, 1983, the date of enactment of the Education of the Handicapped Act Amendments of 1983, an SEA was prohibited by law from providing for the equitable participation in special programs of children with disabilities enrolled in private elementary schools and secondary schools as required by section 612(a)(10)(A) of the Act, or if the Secretary determines that an SEA, LEA, or other public agency has substantially failed or is unwilling to provide for such equitable participation then the Secretary shall, notwithstanding such provision of law, arrange for the provision of services to these children through arrangements which shall be subject to the requirements of section 612(a)(10)(A) of the Act.

(b) The Secretary waives the requirement of section 612(a)(10)(A) of the Act and of §§ 300.131 through 300.144 if the Secretary implements a by-pass.

§ 300.191 Provisions for services under a by-pass.

(a) Before implementing a by-pass, the Secretary consults with appropriate public and private school officials, including SEA officials, in the affected State, and as appropriate, LEA or other public agency officials to consider matters such as—

(1) Any prohibition imposed by State law that results in the need for a by-pass; and

(2) The scope and nature of the services required by private school children with disabilities in the State, and the number of children to be served under the by-pass.

(b) After determining that a by-pass is required, the Secretary arranges for the provision of services to private school children with disabilities in the State, LEA or other public agency in a manner consistent with the requirements of section 612(a)(10)(A) of the Act and §§ 300.131 through 300.144 by providing services through one or more agreements with appropriate parties.

(c) For any fiscal year that a by-pass is implemented, the Secretary determines the maximum amount to be paid to the providers of services by multiplying—

(1) A per child amount determined by dividing the total amount received by the State under Part B of the Act for the fiscal year by the number of children with disabilities served in the prior year as reported to the Secretary under section 618 of the Act; by

(2) The number of private school children with disabilities (as defined in §§ 300.8(a) and 300.130) in the State, LEA or other public agency, as determined by the Secretary on the basis of the most recent satisfactory data available, which may include an estimate of the number of those children with disabilities.

(d) The Secretary deducts from the State's allocation under Part B of the Act the amount the Secretary determines is necessary to implement a by-pass and pays that amount to the provider of services. The Secretary may withhold this amount from the State's allocation pending final resolution of any investigation or complaint that could result in a determination that a by-pass must be implemented.

§ 300.192 Notice of intent to implement a by-pass.

(a) Before taking any final action to implement a by-pass, the Secretary provides the SEA and, as appropriate, LEA or other public agency with written notice.

(b) In the written notice, the Secretary—

(1) States the reasons for the proposed by-pass in sufficient detail to allow the SEA and, as appropriate, LEA or other public agency to respond; and

(2) Advises the SEA and, as appropriate, LEA or other public agency that it has a specific period of time (at least 45 days) from receipt of the written notice to submit written objections to the proposed by-pass and that it may request in writing the opportunity for a hearing to show cause why a by-pass should not be implemented.

(c) The Secretary sends the notice to the SEA and, as appropriate, LEA or other public agency by certified mail with return receipt requested.

§ 300.193 Request to show cause.

An SEA, LEA or other public agency in receipt of a notice under § 300.192 that seeks an opportunity to show cause why a by-pass should not be implemented must submit a written request for a show cause hearing to the Secretary, within the specified time period in the written notice in § 300.192(b)(2).

§ 300.194 Show cause hearing.

(a) If a show cause hearing is requested, the Secretary—

(1) Notifies the SEA and affected LEA or other public agency, and other appropriate public and private school officials of the time and place for the hearing;

(2) Designates a person to conduct the show cause hearing. The designee must not have had any responsibility for the matter brought for a hearing; and

(3) Notifies the SEA, LEA or other public agency, and representatives of private schools that they may be represented by legal counsel and submit oral or written evidence and arguments at the hearing.

(b) At the show cause hearing, the designee considers matters such as—

(1) The necessity for implementing a by-pass;

(2) Possible factual errors in the written notice of intent to implement a by-pass; and

(3) The objections raised by public and private school representatives.

(c) The designee may regulate the course of the proceedings and the conduct of parties during the pendency of the proceedings. The designee takes all steps necessary to conduct a fair and impartial proceeding, to avoid delay, and to maintain order.

(d) The designee has no authority to require or conduct discovery.

(e) The designee may interpret applicable statutes and regulations, but may not waive them or rule on their validity.

(f) The designee arranges for the preparation, retention, and, if appropriate, dissemination of the record of the hearing.

(g) Within 10 days after the hearing, the designee—

(1) Indicates that a decision will be issued on the basis of the existing record; or

(2) Requests further information from the SEA, LEA, other public agency, representatives of private schools or Department officials.

§ 300.195 Decision.

(a) The designee who conducts the show cause hearing—

(1) Within 120 days after the record of a show cause hearing is closed, issues a written decision that includes a statement of findings; and

(2) Submits a copy of the decision to the Secretary and sends a copy to each party by certified mail with return receipt requested.

(b) Each party may submit comments and recommendations on the designee's decision to the Secretary within 30 days of the date the party receives the designee's decision.

(c) The Secretary adopts, reverses, or modifies the designee's decision and notifies all parties to the show cause hearing of the Secretary's final action. That notice is sent by certified mail with return receipt requested.

§ 300.196 Filing requirements.

(a) Any written submission under § 300.194 must be filed by hand-delivery, by mail, or by facsimile transmission. The Secretary discourages the use of facsimile transmission for documents longer than five pages.

(b) The filing date under paragraph (a) of this section is the date the document is—

(1) Hand-delivered;

(2) Mailed; or

(3) Sent by facsimile transmission.

(c) A party filing by facsimile transmission is responsible for confirming that a complete and legible copy of the document was received by the Department.

(d) If a document is filed by facsimile transmission, the Secretary or the hearing officer, as applicable, may require the filing of a follow-up hard copy by hand-delivery or by mail within a reasonable period of time.

(e) If agreed upon by the parties, service of a document may be made upon the other party by facsimile transmission.

(f) A party must show a proof of mailing to establish the filing date under paragraph (b)(2) of this section as provided in *34 CFR 75.102(d)*.

§ 300.197 Judicial review.

If dissatisfied with the Secretary's final action, the SEA may, within 60 days after notice of that action, file a petition for review with the United States Court of Appeals for the circuit in which the State is located. The procedures for judicial review are described in section 612(f)(3) (B) through (D) of the Act.

§ 300.198 Continuation of a by-pass.

The Secretary continues a by-pass until the Secretary determines that the SEA, LEA or other public agency will meet the requirements for providing services to private school children.

STATE ADMINISTRATION

§ 300.199 State administration.

(a) Rulemaking. Each State that receives funds under Part B of the Act must—

(1) Ensure that any State rules, regulations, and policies relating to this part conform to the purposes of this part;

(2) Identify in writing to LEAs located in the State and the Secretary any such rule, regulation, or policy as a State-imposed requirement that is not required by Part B of the Act and Federal regulations; and

(3) Minimize the number of rules, regulations, and policies to which the LEAs and schools located in the State are subject under Part B of the Act.

(b) Support and facilitation. State rules, regulations, and policies under Part B of the Act must support and facilitate LEA and school-level system improvement designed to enable children with disabilities to meet the challenging State student academic achievement standards.

(Approved by the Office of Management and Budget under control number 1820-0030)

SUBPART C LOCAL EDUCATIONAL AGENCY ELIGIBILITY

§ 300.200 Condition of assistance.

An LEA is eligible for assistance under Part B of the Act for a fiscal year if the agency submits a plan that provides assurances to the SEA that the LEA meets each of the conditions in §§ 300.201 through 300.213.

§ 300.201 Consistency with State policies.

The LEA, in providing for the education of children with disabilities within its jurisdiction, must have in effect policies, procedures, and programs that are consistent with the State policies and procedures established under §§ 300.101 through 300.163, and §§ 300.165 through 300.174.

(Approved by the Office of Management and Budget under control number 1820-0600)

§ 300.202 Use of amounts.

(a) General. Amounts provided to the LEA under Part B of the Act—

(1) Must be expended in accordance with the applicable provisions of this part;

(2) Must be used only to pay the excess costs of providing special education and related services to children with disabilities, consistent with paragraph (b) of this section; and

(3) Must be used to supplement State, local, and other Federal funds and not to supplant those funds.

(b) Excess cost requirement —(1) General. (i) The excess cost requirement prevents an LEA from using funds provided under Part B of the Act to pay for all of the costs directly attributable to the education of a child with a disability, subject to paragraph (b)(1)(ii) of this section.

(ii) The excess cost requirement does not prevent an LEA from using Part B funds to pay for all of the costs directly attributable to the education of a child with a disability in any of the ages 3, 4, 5, 18, 19, 20, or 21, if no local or State funds are available for nondisabled children of these ages. However, the LEA must comply with the nonsupplanting and other requirements of this part in providing the education and services for these children.

(2)(i) An LEA meets the excess cost requirement if it has spent at least a minimum average amount for the education of its children with disabilities before funds under Part B of the Act are used.

(ii) The amount described in paragraph (b)(2)(i) of this section is determined in accordance with the definition of excess costs in § 300.16. That amount may not include capital outlay or debt service.

(3) If two or more LEAs jointly establish eligibility in accordance with § 300.223, the minimum average amount is the average of the combined minimum average amounts determined in accordance with the definition of excess costs in § 300.16 in those agencies for elementary or secondary school students, as the case may be.

(Approved by the Office of Management and Budget under control number 1820-0600)

§ 300.203   Maintenance of effort.

(a) *General.* Except as provided in §§ 300.204 and 300.205, funds provided to an LEA under Part B of the Act must not be used to reduce the level of expenditures for the education of children with disabilities made by the LEA from local funds below the level of those expenditures for the preceding fiscal year.

(b) *Standard.* (1) Except as provided in paragraph (b)(2) of this section, the SEA must determine that an LEA complies with paragraph (a) of this section for purposes of establishing the LEA's eligibility for an award for a fiscal year if the LEA budgets, for the education of children with disabilities, at least the same total or per capita amount from either of the following sources as the LEA spent for that purpose from the same source for the most recent prior year for which information is available:

(i) Local funds only.

(ii) The combination of State and local funds.

(2) An LEA that relies on paragraph (b)(1)(i) of this section for any fiscal year must ensure that the amount of local funds it budgets for the education of children with disabilities in that year is at least the same, either in total or per capita, as the amount it spent for that purpose in the most recent fiscal year for which information is available and the standard in paragraph (b)(1)(i) of this section was used to establish its compliance with this section.

(3) The SEA may not consider any expenditures made from funds provided by the Federal Government for which the SEA is required to account to the Federal Government or for which the LEA is required to account to the Federal Government directly or through the SEA in determining an LEA's compliance with the requirement in paragraph (a) of this section.

(Approved by the Office of Management and Budget under control number 1820-0600)

§ 300.204   Exception to maintenance of effort.

Notwithstanding the restriction in § 300.203(a), an LEA may reduce the level of expenditures by the LEA under Part B of the Act below the level of those expenditures for the preceding fiscal year if the reduction is attributable to any of the following:

(a) The voluntary departure, by retirement or otherwise, or departure for just cause, of special education or related services personnel.

(b) A decrease in the enrollment of children with disabilities.

(c) The termination of the obligation of the agency, consistent with this part, to provide a program of special education to a particular child with a disability that is an exceptionally costly program, as determined by the SEA, because the child—

(1) Has left the jurisdiction of the agency;

(2) Has reached the age at which the obligation of the agency to provide FAPE to the child has terminated; or

(3) No longer needs the program of special education.

(d) The termination of costly expenditures for long-term purchases, such as the acquisition of equipment or the construction of school facilities.

(e) The assumption of cost by the high cost fund operated by the SEA under § 300.704(c).

(Approved by the Office of Management and Budget under control number 1820-0600)

§ 300.205 Adjustment to local fiscal efforts in certain fiscal years.

(a) *Amounts in excess.* Notwithstanding § 300.202(a)(2) and (b) and § 300.203(a), and except as provided in paragraph (d) of this section and § 300.230(e)(2), for any fiscal year for which the allocation received by an LEA under § 300.705 exceeds the amount the LEA received for the previous fiscal year, the LEA may reduce the level of expenditures otherwise required by § 300.203(a) by not more than 50 percent of the amount of that excess.

(b) *Use of amounts to carry out activities under ESEA.* If an LEA exercises the authority under paragraph (a) of this section, the LEA must use an amount of local funds equal to the reduction in expenditures under paragraph (a) of this section to carry out activities that could be supported with funds under the ESEA regardless of whether the LEA is using funds under the ESEA for those activities.

(c) *State prohibition.* Notwithstanding paragraph (a) of this section, if an SEA determines that an LEA is unable to establish and maintain programs of FAPE that meet the requirements of section 613(a) of the Act and this part or the SEA has taken action against the LEA under section 616 of the Act and subpart F of these regulations, the SEA must prohibit the LEA from reducing the level of expenditures under paragraph (a) of this section for that fiscal year.

(d) *Special rule.* The amount of funds expended by an LEA for early intervening services under § 300.226 shall count toward the maximum amount of expenditures that the LEA may reduce under paragraph (a) of this section.

(Approved by the Office of Management and Budget under control number 1820-0600)

§ 300.206 Schoolwide programs under title I of the ESEA.

(a) *General.* Notwithstanding the provisions of §§ 300.202 and 300.203 or any other provision of Part B of the Act, an LEA may use funds received under Part B of the Act for any fiscal year to carry out a schoolwide program under section 1114 of the ESEA, except that the amount used in any schoolwide program may not exceed—

(1)(i) The amount received by the LEA under Part B of the Act for that fiscal year; divided by

(ii) The number of children with disabilities in the jurisdiction of the LEA; and multiplied by

(2) The number of children with disabilities participating in the schoolwide program.

(b) *Funding conditions.* The funds described in paragraph (a) of this section are subject to the following conditions:

(1) The funds must be considered as Federal Part B funds for purposes of the calculations required by § 300.202(a)(2) and (a)(3).

(2) The funds may be used without regard to the requirements of § 300.202(a)(1).

(c) *Meeting other Part B requirements.* Except as provided in paragraph (b) of this section, all other requirements of Part B of the Act must be met by an LEA using Part B funds in accordance with paragraph (a) of this section, including ensuring that children with disabilities in schoolwide program schools—

(1) Receive services in accordance with a properly developed IEP; and

(2) Are afforded all of the rights and services guaranteed to children with disabilities under the Act.

(Approved by the Office of Management and Budget under control number 1820-0600)

§ 300.207 Personnel development.

The LEA must ensure that all personnel necessary to carry out Part B of the Act are appropriately and adequately prepared, subject to the requirements of § 300.156 (related to personnel qualifications) and section 2122 of the ESEA.

(Approved by the Office of Management and Budget under control number 1820-0600)

§ 300.208 Permissive use of funds.

(a) *Uses.* Notwithstanding §§ 300.202, 300.203(a), and 300.162(b), funds provided to an LEA under Part B of the Act may be used for the following activities:

(1) *Services and aids that also benefit nondisabled children.* For the costs of special education and related services, and supplementary aids and services, provided in a regular class or other education-related setting to a child with a disability in accordance with the IEP of the child, even if one or more nondisabled children benefit from these services.

(2) *Early intervening services.* To develop and implement coordinated, early intervening educational services in accordance with § 300.226.

(3) *High cost special education and related services.* To establish and implement cost or risk sharing funds, consortia, or cooperatives for the LEA itself, or for LEAs working in a consortium of which the LEA is a part, to pay for high cost special education and related services.

(b) *Administrative case management.* An LEA may use funds received under Part B of the Act to purchase appropriate technology for recordkeeping, data collection, and related case management activities of teachers and related services personnel providing services described in the IEP of children with disabilities, that is needed for the implementation of those case management activities.

(Approved by the Office of Management and Budget under control number 1820-0600)

§ 300.209 Treatment of charter schools and their students.

(a) *Rights of children with disabilities.* Children with disabilities who attend public charter schools and their parents retain all rights under this part.

(b) Charter schools that are public schools of the LEA. (1) In carrying out Part B of the Act and these regulations with respect to charter schools that are public schools of the LEA, the LEA must—

(i) Serve children with disabilities attending those charter schools in the same manner as the LEA serves children with disabilities in its other schools, including providing supplementary and related services on site at the charter school to the same extent to which the LEA has a policy or practice of providing such services on the site to its other public schools; and

(ii) Provide funds under Part B of the Act to those charter schools—

(A) On the same basis as the LEA provides funds to the LEA's other public schools, including proportional distribution based on relative enrollment of children with disabilities; and

(B) At the same time as the LEA distributes other Federal funds to the LEA's other public schools, consistent with the State's charter school law.

(2) If the public charter school is a school of an LEA that receives funding under § 300.705 and includes other public schools—

(i) The LEA is responsible for ensuring that the requirements of this part are met, unless State law assigns that responsibility to some other entity; and

(ii) The LEA must meet the requirements of paragraph (b)(1) of this section.

(c) Public charter schools that are LEAs. If the public charter school is an LEA, consistent with § 300.28, that receives funding under § 300.705, that charter school is responsible for ensuring that the requirements of this part are met, unless State law assigns that responsibility to some other entity.

(d) Public charter schools that are not an LEA or a school that is part of an LEA. (1) If the public charter school is not an LEA receiving funding under § 300.705, or a school that is part of an LEA receiving funding under § 300.705, the SEA is responsible for ensuring that the requirements of this part are met.

(2) Paragraph (d)(1) of this section does not preclude a State from assigning initial responsibility for ensuring the requirements of this part are met to another entity. However, the SEA must maintain the ultimate responsibility for ensuring compliance with this part, consistent with § 300.149.

(Approved by the Office of Management and Budget under control number 1820-0600)

§ 300.210 Purchase of instructional materials.

(a) General. Not later than December 3, 2006, an LEA that chooses to coordinate with the National Instructional Materials Access Center (NIMAC), when purchasing print instructional materials, must acquire those instructional materials in the same manner, and subject to the same conditions as an SEA under § 300.172.

(b) Rights of LEA. (1) Nothing in this section shall be construed to require an LEA to coordinate with the NIMAC.

(2) If an LEA chooses not to coordinate with the NIMAC, the LEA must provide an assurance to the SEA that the LEA will provide instructional materials to blind persons or other persons with print disabilities in a timely manner.

(3) Nothing in this section relieves an LEA of its responsibility to ensure that children with disabilities who need instructional materials in accessible formats but are not included under the definition of blind or other persons with print disabilities in § 300.172(e)(1)(i) or who need materials that cannot be produced from NIMAS files, receive those instructional materials in a timely manner.

(Approved by the Office of Management and Budget under control number 1820-0600)

§ 300.211   Information for SEA.

The LEA must provide the SEA with information necessary to enable the SEA to carry out its duties under Part B of the Act, including, with respect to §§ 300.157 and 300.160, information relating to the performance of children with disabilities participating in programs carried out under Part B of the Act.

(Approved by the Office of Management and Budget under control number 1820-0600)

§ 300.212   Public information.

The LEA must make available to parents of children with disabilities and to the general public all documents relating to the eligibility of the agency under Part B of the Act.

(Approved by the Office of Management and Budget under control number 1820-0600)

§ 300.213   Records regarding migratory children with disabilities.

The LEA must cooperate in the Secretary's efforts under section 1308 of the ESEA to ensure the linkage of records pertaining to migratory children with disabilities for the purpose of electronically exchanging, among the States, health and educational information regarding those children.

(Approved by the Office of Management and Budget under control number 1820-0600)

§§ 300.214–300.219   [Reserved]

§ 300.220   Exception for prior local plans.

(a) General. If an LEA or a State agency described in § 300.228 has on file with the SEA policies and procedures that demonstrate that the LEA or State agency meets any requirement of § 300.200, including any policies and procedures filed under Part B of the Act as in effect before December 3, 2004, the SEA must consider the LEA or State agency to have met that requirement for purposes of receiving assistance under Part B of the Act.

(b) Modification made by an LEA or State agency. Subject to paragraph (c) of this section, policies and procedures submitted by an LEA or a State agency in accordance with this subpart remain in effect until the LEA or State agency submits to the SEA the modifications that the LEA or State agency determines are necessary.

(c) Modifications required by the SEA. The SEA may require an LEA or a State agency to modify its policies and procedures, but only to the extent necessary to ensure the LEA's or State agency's compliance with Part B of the Act or State law, if—

(1) After December 3, 2004, the effective date of the Individuals with Disabilities Education Improvement Act of 2004, the applicable provisions of the Act (or the regulations developed to carry out the Act) are amended;

(2) There is a new interpretation of an applicable provision of the Act by Federal or State courts; or

(3) There is an official finding of noncompliance with Federal or State law or regulations.

§ 300.221   Notification of LEA or State agency in case of ineligibility.

If the SEA determines that an LEA or State agency is not eligible under Part B of the Act, then the SEA must—

(a) Notify the LEA or State agency of that determination; and

(b) Provide the LEA or State agency with reasonable notice and an opportunity for a hearing.

§ 300.222 LEA and State agency compliance.

(a) *General.* If the SEA, after reasonable notice and an opportunity for a hearing, finds that an LEA or State agency that has been determined to be eligible under this subpart is failing to comply with any requirement described in §§ 300.201 through 300.213, the SEA must reduce or must not provide any further payments to the LEA or State agency until the SEA is satisfied that the LEA or State agency is complying with that requirement.

(b) *Notice requirement.* Any State agency or LEA in receipt of a notice described in paragraph (a) of this section must, by means of public notice, take the measures necessary to bring the pendency of an action pursuant to this section to the attention of the public within the jurisdiction of the agency.

(c) *Consideration.* In carrying out its responsibilities under this section, each SEA must consider any decision resulting from a hearing held under §§ 300.511 through 300.533 that is adverse to the LEA or State agency involved in the decision.

§ 300.223 Joint establishment of eligibility.

(a) *General.* An SEA may require an LEA to establish its eligibility jointly with another LEA if the SEA determines that the LEA will be ineligible under this subpart because the agency will not be able to establish and maintain programs of sufficient size and scope to effectively meet the needs of children with disabilities.

(b) *Charter school exception.* An SEA may not require a charter school that is an LEA to jointly establish its eligibility under paragraph (a) of this section unless the charter school is explicitly permitted to do so under the State's charter school statute.

(c) *Amount of payments.* If an SEA requires the joint establishment of eligibility under paragraph (a) of this section, the total amount of funds made available to the affected LEAs must be equal to the sum of the payments that each LEA would have received under § 300.705 if the agencies were eligible for those payments.

§ 300.224 Requirements for establishing eligibility.

(a) *Requirements for LEAs in general.* LEAs that establish joint eligibility under this section must—

(1) Adopt policies and procedures that are consistent with the State's policies and procedures under §§ 300.101 through 300.163, and §§ 300.165 through 300.174; and

(2) Be jointly responsible for implementing programs that receive assistance under Part B of the Act.

(b) *Requirements for educational service agencies in general.* If an educational service agency is required by State law to carry out programs under Part B of the Act, the joint responsibilities given to LEAs under Part B of the Act—

(1) Do not apply to the administration and disbursement of any payments received by that educational service agency; and

(2) Must be carried out only by that educational service agency.

(c) *Additional requirement.* Notwithstanding any other provision of §§ 300.223

through 300.224, an educational service agency must provide for the education of children with disabilities in the least restrictive environment, as required by § 300.112.

(Approved by the Office of Management and Budget under control number 1820-0600)

§ 300.225 [Reserved]

§ 300.226 **Early intervening services.**

(a) General. An LEA may not use more than 15 percent of the amount the LEA receives under Part B of the Act for any fiscal year, less any amount reduced by the LEA pursuant to § 300.205, if any, in combination with other amounts (which may include amounts other than education funds), to develop and implement coordinated, early intervening services, which may include interagency financing structures, for students in kindergarten through grade 12 (with a particular emphasis on students in kindergarten through grade three) who are not currently identified as needing special education or related services, but who need additional academic and behavioral support to succeed in a general education environment. (See Appendix D for examples of how § 300.205(d), regarding local maintenance of effort, and § 300.226(a) affect one another.)

(b) Activities. In implementing coordinated, early intervening services under this section, an LEA may carry out activities that include—

(1) Professional development (which may be provided by entities other than LEAs) for teachers and other school staff to enable such personnel to deliver scientifically based academic and behavioral interventions, including scientifically based literacy instruction, and, where appropriate, instruction on the use of adaptive and instructional software; and

(2) Providing educational and behavioral evaluations, services, and supports, including scientifically based literacy instruction.

(c) Construction. Nothing in this section shall be construed to either limit or create a right to FAPE under Part B of the Act or to delay appropriate evaluation of a child suspected of having a disability.

(d) Reporting. Each LEA that develops and maintains coordinated, early intervening services under this section must annually report to the SEA on—

(1) The number of children served under this section who received early intervening services; and

(2) The number of children served under this section who received early intervening services and subsequently receive special education and related services under Part B of the Act during the preceding two year period.

(e) Coordination with ESEA. Funds made available to carry out this section may be used to carry out coordinated, early intervening services aligned with activities funded by, and carried out under the ESEA if those funds are used to supplement, and not supplant, funds made available under the ESEA for the activities and services assisted under this section.

(Approved by the Office of Management and Budget under control number 1820-0600)

§ 300.227 **Direct services by the SEA.**

(a) General. (1) An SEA must use the payments that would otherwise have been available to an LEA or to a State agency to provide special education and related services directly to children with disabilities residing in the area served by that LEA, or for whom that State agency is responsible, if the SEA determines that the LEA or State agency—

(i) Has not provided the information needed to establish the eligibility of the LEA or State agency, or elected not to apply for its Part B allotment, under Part B of the Act;

(ii) Is unable to establish and maintain programs of FAPE that meet the requirements of this part;

(iii) Is unable or unwilling to be consolidated with one or more LEAs in order to establish and maintain the programs; or

(iv) Has one or more children with disabilities who can best be served by a regional or State program or service delivery system designed to meet the needs of these children.

(2) SEA administrative procedures. (i) In meeting the requirements in paragraph (a)(1) of this section, the SEA may provide special education and related services directly, by contract, or through other arrangements.

(ii) The excess cost requirements of § 300.202(b) do not apply to the SEA.

(b) Manner and location of education and services. The SEA may provide special education and related services under paragraph (a) of this section in the manner and at the locations (including regional or State centers) as the SEA considers appropriate. The education and services must be provided in accordance with this part.

§ 300.228 State agency eligibility.

Any State agency that desires to receive a subgrant for any fiscal year under § 300.705 must demonstrate to the satisfaction of the SEA that—

(a) All children with disabilities who are participating in programs and projects funded under Part B of the Act receive FAPE, and that those children and their parents are provided all the rights and procedural safeguards described in this part; and

(b) The agency meets the other conditions of this subpart that apply to LEAs.

§ 300.229 Disciplinary information.

(a) The State may require that a public agency include in the records of a child with a disability a statement of any current or previous disciplinary action that has been taken against the child and transmit the statement to the same extent that the disciplinary information is included in, and transmitted with, the student records of nondisabled children.

(b) The statement may include a description of any behavior engaged in by the child that required disciplinary action, a description of the disciplinary action taken, and any other information that is relevant to the safety of the child and other individuals involved with the child.

(c) If the State adopts such a policy, and the child transfers from one school to another, the transmission of any of the child's records must include both the child's current IEP and any statement of current or previous disciplinary action that has been taken against the child.

§ 300.230 SEA flexibility.

(a) Adjustment to State fiscal effort in certain fiscal years. For any fiscal year for which the allotment received by a State under § 300.703 exceeds the amount the State received for the previous fiscal year and if the State in school year 2003-2004 or any subsequent school year pays or reimburses all LEAs within the State from State revenue 100 percent of the non-Federal share of the costs of special education and related services, the SEA, notwithstanding §§ 300.162 through 300.163 (related to State-level nonsupplanting and maintenance of effort), and § 300.175 (related to direct services by the SEA) may reduce the level of expenditures from State sources for the education of children with disabilities by not more than 50 percent of the amount of such excess.

(b) Prohibition. Notwithstanding paragraph (a) of this section, if the Secretary determines that an SEA is unable to establish, maintain, or oversee programs of FAPE that meet the requirements of this part, or that the State needs assistance, intervention, or substantial intervention under § 300.603, the Secretary prohibits the SEA from exercising the authority in paragraph (a) of this section.

(c) Education activities. If an SEA exercises the authority under paragraph (a) of this section, the agency must use funds from State sources, in an amount equal to the amount of the reduction under paragraph (a) of this section, to support activities authorized under the ESEA, or to support need-based student or teacher higher education programs.

(d) Report. For each fiscal year for which an SEA exercises the authority under paragraph (a) of this section, the SEA must report to the Secretary—

(1) The amount of expenditures reduced pursuant to that paragraph; and

(2) The activities that were funded pursuant to paragraph (c) of this section.

(e) Limitation. (1) Notwithstanding paragraph (a) of this section, an SEA may not reduce the level of expenditures described in paragraph (a) of this section if any LEA in the State would, as a result of such reduction, receive less than 100 percent of the amount necessary to ensure that all children with disabilities served by the LEA receive FAPE from the combination of Federal funds received under Part B of the Act and State funds received from the SEA.

(2) If an SEA exercises the authority under paragraph (a) of this section, LEAs in the State may not reduce local effort under § 300.205 by more than the reduction in the State funds they receive.

§ 300.231

[This section was removed. See 71 FR 46540, 46753, Aug. 14, 2006.]

§ 300.232

[This section was removed. See 71 FR 46540, 46753, Aug. 14, 2006.]

§ 300.233

[This section was removed. See 71 FR 46540, 46753, Aug. 14, 2006.]

§ 300.234

[This section was removed. See 71 FR 46540, 46753, Aug. 14, 2006.]

§ 300.235

[This section was removed. See 71 FR 46540, 46753, Aug. 14, 2006.]

§§ 300.236

— 300.239 [These sections were removed. See 71 FR 46540, 46753, Aug. 14, 2006.]

§ 300.240

[This section was removed. See 71 FR 46540, 46753, Aug. 14, 2006.]

§ 300.241

[This section was removed. See 71 FR 46540, 46753, Aug. 14, 2006.]

§ 300.242

[This section was removed. See 71 FR 46540, 46753, Aug. 14, 2006.]

§ 300.243

[This section was removed. See 71 FR 46540, 46753, Aug. 14, 2006.]

§ 300.244

[This section was removed. See 71 FR 46540, 46753, Aug. 14, 2006.]

§ 300.245

[This section was removed. See 71 FR 46540, 46753, Aug. 14, 2006.]

§ 300.246

[This section was removed. See 71 FR 46540, 46753, Aug. 14, 2006.]

§ 300.247

[This section was removed. See 71 FR 46540, 46753, Aug. 14, 2006.]

§ 300.248

[This section was removed. See 71 FR 46540, 46753, Aug. 14, 2006.]

§ 300.249

[This section was removed. See 71 FR 46540, 46753, Aug. 14, 2006.]

§ 300.250

[This section was removed. See 71 FR 46540, 46753, Aug. 14, 2006.]

§ 300.260

[This section was removed. See 71 FR 46540, 46753, Aug. 14, 2006.]

§ 300.261

[This section was removed. See 71 FR 46540, 46753, Aug. 14, 2006.]

§ 300.262

[This section was removed. See 71 FR 46540, 46753, Aug. 14, 2006.]

§ 300.263

[This section was removed. See 71 FR 46540, 46753, Aug. 14, 2006.]

§ 300.264

[This section was removed. See 71 FR 46540, 46753, Aug. 14, 2006.]

§ 300.265

[This section was removed. See 71 FR 46540, 46753, Aug. 14, 2006.]

§ 300.266

[This section was removed. See 71 FR 46540, 46753, Aug. 14, 2006.]

§ 300.267

[This section was removed. See 71 FR 46540, 46753, Aug. 14, 2006.]

§ 300.280

[This section was removed. See 71 FR 46540, 46753, Aug. 14, 2006.]

§ 300.281

[This section was removed. See 71 FR 46540, 46753, Aug. 14, 2006.]

§ 300.282

[This section was removed. See 71 FR 46540, 46753, Aug. 14, 2006.]

§ 300.283

[This section was removed. See 71 FR 46540, 46753, Aug. 14, 2006.]

§ 300.284

[This section was removed. See 71 FR 46540, 46753, Aug. 14, 2006.]

SUBPART D EVALUATIONS, ELIGIBILITY DETERMINATIONS, INDIVIDUALIZED EDUCATION PROGRAMS, AND EDUCATIONAL PLACEMENTS
PARENTAL CONSENT

§ 300.300 Parental consent.

(a) *Parental consent for initial evaluation.* (1)(i) The public agency proposing to conduct an initial evaluation to determine if a child qualifies as a child with a disability under § 300.8 must, after providing notice consistent with §§ 300.503 and 300.504, obtain informed consent, consistent with § 300.9, from the parent of the child before conducting the evaluation.

(ii) Parental consent for initial evaluation must not be construed as consent for initial provision of special education and related services.

(iii) The public agency must make reasonable efforts to obtain the informed consent from the parent for an initial evaluation to determine whether the child is a child with a disability.

(2) For initial evaluations only, if the child is a ward of the State and is not residing with the child's parent, the public agency is not required to obtain informed consent from the parent for an initial evaluation to determine whether the child is a child with a disability if—

(i) Despite reasonable efforts to do so, the public agency cannot discover the whereabouts of the parent of the child;

(ii) The rights of the parents of the child have been terminated in accordance with State law; or

(iii) The rights of the parent to make educational decisions have been subrogated by a judge in accordance with State law and consent for an initial evaluation has been given by an individual appointed by the judge to represent the child.

(3)(i) If the parent of a child enrolled in public school or seeking to be enrolled in public school does not provide consent for initial evaluation under paragraph (a)(1) of this section, or the parent fails to respond to a request to provide consent, the public agency may, but is not required to, pursue the initial evaluation of the child by utilizing the procedural safeguards in subpart E of this part (including the mediation procedures under § 300.506 or the due process procedures under §§ 300.507 through 300.516), if appropriate, except to the extent inconsistent with State law relating to such parental consent.

(ii) The public agency does not violate its obligation under § 300.111 and §§ 300.301 through 300.311 if it declines to pursue the evaluation.

(b) *Parental consent for services.* (1) A public agency that is responsible for making FAPE available to a child with a disability must obtain informed consent from the parent of the child before the initial provision of special education and related services to the child.

(2) The public agency must make reasonable efforts to obtain informed consent from the parent for the initial provision of special education and related services to the child.

(3) If the parent of a child fails to respond or refuses to consent to services under paragraph (b)(1) of this section, the public agency may not use the procedures in subpart E of this part (including the mediation procedures under § 300.506 or the due process procedures under §§ 300.507 through 300.516) in order to obtain agreement or a ruling that the services may be provided to the child.

(4) If the parent of the child refuses to consent to the initial provision of special education and related services, or the parent fails to respond to a request to provide consent for the initial provision of special education and related services, the public agency—

(i) Will not be considered to be in violation of the requirement to make available FAPE to the child for the failure to provide the child with the special education and related services for which the public agency requests consent; and

(ii) Is not required to convene an IEP Team meeting or develop an IEP under §§ 300.320 and 300.324 for the child for the special education and related services for which the public agency requests such consent.

(c) *Parental consent for reevaluations.* (1) Subject to paragraph (c)(2) of this section, each public agency—

(i) Must obtain informed parental consent, in accordance with § 300.300(a)(1), prior to conducting any reevaluation of a child with a disability.

(ii) If the parent refuses to consent to the reevaluation, the public agency may, but is not required to, pursue the reevaluation by using the consent override procedures described in paragraph (a)(3) of this section.

(iii) The public agency does not violate its obligation under § 300.111 and §§ 300.301 through 300.311 if it declines to pursue the evaluation or reevaluation.

(2) The informed parental consent described in paragraph (c)(1) of this section need not be obtained if the public agency can demonstrate that—

(i) It made reasonable efforts to obtain such consent; and

(ii) The child's parent has failed to respond.

(d) *Other consent requirements.*

(1) Parental consent is not required before—

(i) Reviewing existing data as part of an evaluation or a reevaluation; or

(ii) Administering a test or other evaluation that is administered to all children unless, before administration of that test or evaluation, consent is required of parents of all children.

(2) In addition to the parental consent requirements described in paragraph (a) of this section, a State may require parental consent for other services and activities under this part if it ensures that each public agency in the State establishes and implements effective procedures to ensure that a parent's refusal to consent does not result in a failure to provide the child with FAPE.

(3) A public agency may not use a parent's refusal to consent to one service or activity under paragraphs (a) or (d)(2) of this section to deny the parent or child any other service, benefit, or activity of the public agency, except as required by this part.

(4)(i) If a parent of a child who is home schooled or placed in a private school by the parents at their own expense does not provide consent for the initial evaluation or the reevaluation, or the parent fails to respond to a request to provide consent, the public agency may not use the consent override procedures (described in paragraphs (a)(3) and (c)(1) of this section); and

(ii) The public agency is not required to consider the child as eligible for services under §§ 300.132 through 300.144.

(5) To meet the reasonable efforts requirement in paragraphs (a)(1)(iii), (a)(2)(i), (b)(2), and (c)(2)(i) of this section, the public agency must document its attempts to obtain parental consent using the procedures in § 300.322(d).

EVALUATIONS AND REEVALUATIONS

§ 300.301 Initial evaluations.

(a) *General.* Each public agency must conduct a full and individual initial evaluation, in accordance with §§ 300.304 through 300.306, before the initial provision of special education and related services to a child with a disability under this part.

(b) *Request for initial evaluation.* Consistent with the consent requirements in § 300.300, either a parent of a child or a public agency may initiate a request for an initial evaluation to determine if the child is a child with a disability.

(c) *Procedures for initial evaluation.* The initial evaluation—

(1)(i) Must be conducted within 60 days of receiving parental consent for the evaluation; or

(ii) If the State establishes a timeframe within which the evaluation must be conducted, within that timeframe; and

(2) Must consist of procedures—

(i) To determine if the child is a child with a disability under § 300.8; and

(ii) To determine the educational needs of the child.

(d) *Exception.* The timeframe described in paragraph (c)(1) of this section does not apply to a public agency if—

(1) The parent of a child repeatedly fails or refuses to produce the child for the evaluation; or

(2) A child enrolls in a school of another public agency after the relevant timeframe in paragraph (c)(1) of this section has begun, and prior to a determination by the child's previous public agency as to whether the child is a child with a disability under § 300.8.

(e) The exception in paragraph (d)(2) of this section applies only if the subsequent public agency is making sufficient progress to ensure a prompt completion of the evaluation, and the parent and subsequent public agency agree to a specific time when the evaluation will be completed.

§ 300.302 Screening for instructional purposes is not evaluation.

The screening of a student by a teacher or specialist to determine appropriate instructional strategies for curriculum implementation shall not be considered to be an evaluation for eligibility for special education and related services.

§ 300.303 Reevaluations.

(a) General. A public agency must ensure that a reevaluation of each child with a disability is conducted in accordance with §§ 300.304 through 300.311—

(1) If the public agency determines that the educational or related services needs, including improved academic achievement and functional performance, of the child warrant a reevaluation; or

(2) If the child's parent or teacher requests a reevaluation.

(b) Limitation. A reevaluation conducted under paragraph (a) of this section—

(1) May occur not more than once a year, unless the parent and the public agency agree otherwise; and

(2) Must occur at least once every 3 years, unless the parent and the public agency agree that a reevaluation is unnecessary.

§ 300.304 Evaluation procedures.

(a) Notice. The public agency must provide notice to the parents of a child with a disability, in accordance with § 300.503, that describes any evaluation procedures the agency proposes to conduct.

(b) Conduct of evaluation. In conducting the evaluation, the public agency must—

(1) Use a variety of assessment tools and strategies to gather relevant functional, developmental, and academic information about the child, including information provided by the parent, that may assist in determining—

(i) Whether the child is a child with a disability under § 300.8; and

(ii) The content of the child's IEP, including information related to enabling the child to be involved in and progress in the general education curriculum (or for a preschool child, to participate in appropriate activities);

(2) Not use any single measure or assessment as the sole criterion for determining whether a child is a child with a disability and for determining an appropriate educational program for the child; and

(3) Use technically sound instruments that may assess the relative contribution of cognitive and behavioral factors, in addition to physical or developmental factors.

(c) Other evaluation procedures. Each public agency must ensure that—

(1) Assessments and other evaluation materials used to assess a child under this part—

(i) Are selected and administered so as not to be discriminatory on a racial or cultural basis;

(ii) Are provided and administered in the child's native language or other mode of communication and in the form most likely to yield accurate information on what the child knows and can do academically, developmentally, and functionally, unless it is clearly not feasible to so provide or administer;

(iii) Are used for the purposes for which the assessments or measures are valid and reliable;

(iv) Are administered by trained and knowledgeable personnel; and

(v) Are administered in accordance with any instructions provided by the producer of the assessments.

(2) Assessments and other evaluation materials include those tailored to assess specific areas of educational need and not merely those that are designed to provide a single general intelligence quotient.

(3) Assessments are selected and administered so as best to ensure that if an assessment is administered to a child with impaired sensory, manual, or speaking skills, the assessment results accurately reflect the child's aptitude or achievement level or whatever other factors the test purports to measure, rather than reflecting the child's impaired sensory, manual, or speaking skills (unless those skills are the factors that the test purports to measure).

(4) The child is assessed in all areas related to the suspected disability, including, if appropriate, health, vision, hearing, social and emotional status, general intelligence, academic performance, communicative status, and motor abilities;

(5) Assessments of children with disabilities who transfer from one public agency to another public agency in the same school year are coordinated with those children's prior and subsequent schools, as necessary and as expeditiously as possible, consistent with § 300.301(d)(2) and (e), to ensure prompt completion of full evaluations.

(6) In evaluating each child with a disability under §§ 300.304 through 300.306, the evaluation is sufficiently comprehensive to identify all of the child's special education and related services needs, whether or not commonly linked to the disability category in which the child has been classified.

(7) Assessment tools and strategies that provide relevant information that directly assists persons in determining the educational needs of the child are provided.

§ 300.305 Additional requirements for evaluations and reevaluations.

(a) *Review of existing evaluation data.* As part of an initial evaluation (if appropriate) and as part of any reevaluation under this part, the IEP Team and other qualified professionals, as appropriate, must—

(1) Review existing evaluation data on the child, including—

(i) Evaluations and information provided by the parents of the child;

(ii) Current classroom-based, local, or State assessments, and classroom-based observations; and

(iii) Observations by teachers and related services providers; and

(2) On the basis of that review, and input from the child's parents, identify what additional data, if any, are needed to determine—

(i)(A) Whether the child is a child with a disability, as defined in § 300.8, and the educational needs of the child; or

(B) In case of a reevaluation of a child, whether the child continues to have such a disability, and the educational needs of the child;

(ii) The present levels of academic achievement and related developmental needs of the child;

(iii)(A) Whether the child needs special education and related services; or

(B) In the case of a reevaluation of a child, whether the child continues to need special education and related services; and

(iv) Whether any additions or modifications to the special education and related services are needed to enable the child to meet the measurable annual goals set out in the IEP of the child and to participate, as appropriate, in the general education curriculum.

(b) *Conduct of review.* The group described in paragraph (a) of this section may conduct its review without a meeting.

(c) *Source of data.* The public agency must administer such assessments and other evaluation measures as may be needed to produce the data identified under paragraph (a) of this section.

(d) *Requirements if additional data are not needed.* (1) If the IEP Team and other qualified professionals, as appropriate, determine that no additional data are needed to determine whether the child continues to be a child with a disability, and to determine the child's educational needs, the public agency must notify the child's parents of —

(i) That determination and the reasons for the determination; and

(ii) The right of the parents to request an assessment to determine whether the child continues to be a child with a disability, and to determine the child's educational needs.

(2) The public agency is not required to conduct the assessment described in paragraph (d)(1)(ii) of this section unless requested to do so by the child's parents.

(e) *Evaluations before change in eligibility.* (1) Except as provided in paragraph (e)(2) of this section, a public agency must evaluate a child with a disability in accordance with §§ 300.304 through 300.311 before determining that the child is no longer a child with a disability.

(2) The evaluation described in paragraph (e)(1) of this section is not required before the termination of a child's eligibility under this part due to graduation from secondary school with a regular diploma, or due to exceeding the age eligibility for FAPE under State law.

(3) For a child whose eligibility terminates under circumstances described in paragraph (e)(2) of this section, a public agency must provide the child with a summary of the child's academic achievement and functional performance, which shall include recommendations on how to assist the child in meeting the child's postsecondary goals.

§ 300.306 Determination of eligibility.

(a) *General.* Upon completion of the administration of assessments and other evaluation measures—

(1) A group of qualified professionals and the parent of the child determines whether the child is a child with a disability, as defined in § 300.8, in accordance with paragraph (c) of this section and the educational needs of the child; and

(2) The public agency provides a copy of the evaluation report and the documentation

of determination of eligibility at no cost to the parent.

(b) Special rule for eligibility determination. A child must not be determined to be a child with a disability under this part—

(1) If the determinant factor for that determination is—

(i) Lack of appropriate instruction in reading, including the essential components of reading instruction (as defined in section 1208(3) of the ESEA);

(ii) Lack of appropriate instruction in math; or

(iii) Limited English proficiency; and

(2) If the child does not otherwise meet the eligibility criteria under § 300.8(a).

(c) Procedures for determining eligibility and educational need. (1) In interpreting evaluation data for the purpose of determining if a child is a child with a disability under § 300.8, and the educational needs of the child, each public agency must—

(i) Draw upon information from a variety of sources, including aptitude and achievement tests, parent input, and teacher recommendations, as well as information about the child's physical condition, social or cultural background, and adaptive behavior; and

(ii) Ensure that information obtained from all of these sources is documented and carefully considered.

(2) If a determination is made that a child has a disability and needs special education and related services, an IEP must be developed for the child in accordance with §§ 300.320 through 300.324.

ADDITIONAL PROCEDURES FOR IDENTIFYING CHILDREN WITH SPECIFIC LEARNING DISABILITIES

§ 300.307 Specific learning disabilities.

(a) General. A State must adopt, consistent with § 300.309, criteria for determining whether a child has a specific learning disability as defined in § 300.8(c)(10). In addition, the criteria adopted by the State—

(1) Must not require the use of a severe discrepancy between intellectual ability and achievement for determining whether a child has a specific learning disability, as defined in § 300.8(c)(10);

(2) Must permit the use of a process based on the child's response to scientific, research-based intervention; and

(3) May permit the use of other alternative research-based procedures for determining whether a child has a specific learning disability, as defined in § 300.8(c)(10).

(b) Consistency with State criteria. A public agency must use the State criteria adopted pursuant to paragraph (a) of this section in determining whether a child has a specific learning disability.

§ 300.308 Additional group members.

The determination of whether a child suspected of having a specific learning disability is a child with a disability as defined in § 300.8, must be made by the child's parents and a team of qualified professionals, which must include—

(a)(1) The child's regular teacher; or

(2) If the child does not have a regular teacher, a regular classroom teacher qualified to teach a child of his or her age; or

(3) For a child of less than school age, an individual qualified by the SEA to teach a child of his or her age; and

(b) At least one person qualified to conduct individual diagnostic examinations of children, such as a school psychologist, speech-language pathologist, or remedial reading teacher.

§ 300.309 Determining the existence of a specific learning disability.

(a) The group described in § 300.306 may determine that a child has a specific learning disability, as defined in § 300.8(c)(10), if—

(1) The child does not achieve adequately for the child's age or to meet State-approved grade-level standards in one or more of the following areas, when provided with learning experiences and instruction appropriate for the child's age or State-approved grade-level standards:

(i) Oral expression.

(ii) Listening comprehension.

(iii) Written expression.

(iv) Basic reading skill.

(v) Reading fluency skills.

(vi) Reading comprehension.

(vii) Mathematics calculation.

(viii) Mathematics problem solving.

(2)(i) The child does not make sufficient progress to meet age or State-approved grade-level standards in one or more of the areas identified in paragraph (a)(1) of this section when using a process based on the child's response to scientific, research-based intervention; or

(ii) The child exhibits a pattern of strengths and weaknesses in performance, achievement, or both, relative to age, State-approved grade-level standards, or intellectual development, that is determined by the group to be relevant to the identification of a specific learning disability, using appropriate assessments, consistent with §§ 300.304 and 300.305; and

(3) The group determines that its findings under paragraphs (a)(1) and (2) of this section are not primarily the result of—

(i) A visual, hearing, or motor disability;

(ii) Mental retardation;

(iii) Emotional disturbance;

(iv) Cultural factors;

(v) Environmental or economic disadvantage; or

(vi) Limited English proficiency.

(b) To ensure that underachievement in a child suspected of having a specific learning disability is not due to lack of appropriate instruction in reading or math, the group must consider, as part of the evaluation described in §§ 300.304 through 300.306—

(1) Data that demonstrate that prior to, or as a part of, the referral process, the child

was provided appropriate instruction in regular education settings, delivered by qualified personnel; and

(2) Data-based documentation of repeated assessments of achievement at reasonable intervals, reflecting formal assessment of student progress during instruction, which was provided to the child's parents.

(c) The public agency must promptly request parental consent to evaluate the child to determine if the child needs special education and related services, and must adhere to the timeframes described in §§ 300.301 and 300.303, unless extended by mutual written agreement of the child's parents and a group of qualified professionals, as described in § 300.306(a)(1)—

(1) If, prior to a referral, a child has not made adequate progress after an appropriate period of time when provided instruction, as described in paragraphs (b)(1) and (b)(2) of this section; and

(2) Whenever a child is referred for an evaluation.

§ 300.310 Observation.

(a) The public agency must ensure that the child is observed in the child's learning environment (including the regular classroom setting) to document the child's academic performance and behavior in the areas of difficulty.

(b) The group described in § 300.306(a)(1), in determining whether a child has a specific learning disability, must decide to—

(1) Use information from an observation in routine classroom instruction and monitoring of the child's performance that was done before the child was referred for an evaluation; or

(2) Have at least one member of the group described in § 300.306(a)(1) conduct an observation of the child's academic performance in the regular classroom after the child has been referred for an evaluation and parental consent, consistent with § 300.300(a), is obtained.

(c) In the case of a child of less than school age or out of school, a group member must observe the child in an environment appropriate for a child of that age.

§ 300.311 Specific documentation for the eligibility determination.

(a) For a child suspected of having a specific learning disability, the documentation of the determination of eligibility, as required in § 300.306(a)(2), must contain a statement of—

(1) Whether the child has a specific learning disability;

(2) The basis for making the determination, including an assurance that the determination has been made in accordance with § 300.306(c)(1);

(3) The relevant behavior, if any, noted during the observation of the child and the relationship of that behavior to the child's academic functioning;

(4) The educationally relevant medical findings, if any;

(5) Whether—

(i) The child does not achieve adequately for the child's age or to meet State-approved grade-level standards consistent with § 300.309(a)(1); and

(ii)(A) The child does not make sufficient progress to meet age or State-approved grade-level standards consistent with § 300.309(a)(2)(i); or

(B) The child exhibits a pattern of strengths and weaknesses in performance, achievement, or both, relative to age, State-approved grade level standards or intellectual development consistent with § 300.309(a)(2)(ii);

(6) The determination of the group concerning the effects of a visual, hearing, or motor disability; mental retardation; emotional disturbance; cultural factors; environmental or economic disadvantage; or limited English proficiency on the child's achievement level; and

(7) If the child has participated in a process that assesses the child's response to scientific, research-based intervention—

(i) The instructional strategies used and the student-centered data collected; and

(ii) The documentation that the child's parents were notified about—

(A) The State's policies regarding the amount and nature of student performance data that would be collected and the general education services that would be provided;

(B) Strategies for increasing the child's rate of learning; and

(C) The parents' right to request an evaluation.

(b) Each group member must certify in writing whether the report reflects the member's conclusion. If it does not reflect the member's conclusion, the group member must submit a separate statement presenting the member's conclusions.

§ 300.312

[This section was removed. See 71 FR 46540, 46753, Aug. 14, 2006.]

§ 300.313

[This section was removed. See 71 FR 46540, 46753, Aug. 14, 2006.]

INDIVIDUALIZED EDUCATION PROGRAMS

§ 300.320 Definition of individualized education program.

(a) *General.* As used in this part, the term individualized education program or IEP means a written statement for each child with a disability that is developed, reviewed, and revised in a meeting in accordance with §§ 300.320 through 300.324, and that must include—

(1) A statement of the child's present levels of academic achievement and functional performance, including—

(i) How the child's disability affects the child's involvement and progress in the general education curriculum (i.e., the same curriculum as for nondisabled children); or

(ii) For preschool children, as appropriate, how the disability affects the child's participation in appropriate activities;

(2)(i) A statement of measurable annual goals, including academic and functional goals designed to—

(A) Meet the child's needs that result from the child's disability to enable the child to be involved in and make progress in the general education curriculum; and

(B) Meet each of the child's other educational needs that result from the child's disability;

(ii) For children with disabilities who take alternate assessments aligned to alternate academic achievement standards, a description of benchmarks or short-term objectives;

(3) A description of—

(i) How the child's progress toward meeting the annual goals described in paragraph (2) of this section will be measured; and

(ii) When periodic reports on the progress the child is making toward meeting the annual goals (such as through the use of quarterly or other periodic reports, concurrent with the issuance of report cards) will be provided;

(4) A statement of the special education and related services and supplementary aids and services, based on peer-reviewed research to the extent practicable, to be provided to the child, or on behalf of the child, and a statement of the program modifications or supports for school personnel that will be provided to enable the child—

(i) To advance appropriately toward attaining the annual goals;

(ii) To be involved in and make progress in the general education curriculum in accordance with paragraph (a)(1) of this section, and to participate in extracurricular and other nonacademic activities; and

(iii) To be educated and participate with other children with disabilities and nondisabled children in the activities described in this section;

(5) An explanation of the extent, if any, to which the child will not participate with nondisabled children in the regular class and in the activities described in paragraph (a)(4) of this section;

(6)(i) A statement of any individual appropriate accommodations that are necessary to measure the academic achievement and functional performance of the child on State and districtwide assessments consistent with section 612(a)(16) of the Act; and

(ii) If the IEP Team determines that the child must take an alternate assessment instead of a particular regular State or districtwide assessment of student achievement, a statement of why—

(A) The child cannot participate in the regular assessment; and

(B) The particular alternate assessment selected is appropriate for the child; and

(7) The projected date for the beginning of the services and modifications described in paragraph (a)(4) of this section, and the anticipated frequency, location, and duration of those services and modifications.

(b) *Transition services.* Beginning not later than the first IEP to be in effect when the child turns 16, or younger if determined appropriate by the IEP Team, and updated annually, thereafter, the IEP must include—

(1) Appropriate measurable postsecondary goals based upon age appropriate transition assessments related to training, education, employment, and, where appropriate, independent living skills; and

(2) The transition services (including courses of study) needed to assist the child in reaching those goals.

(c) *Transfer of rights at age of majority.* Beginning not later than one year before the child reaches the age of majority under State law, the IEP must include a statement that the child has been informed of the child's rights under Part B of the Act, if any, that will transfer to the child on reaching the age of majority under § 300.520.

(d) *Construction.* Nothing in this section shall be construed to require—

(1) That additional information be included in a child's IEP beyond what is explicitly required in section 614 of the Act; or

(2) The IEP Team to include information under one component of a child's IEP that is already contained under another component of the child's IEP.

INDIVIDUALIZED EDUCATION PROGRAMS

§ 300.321 IEP Team.

(a) General. The public agency must ensure that the IEP Team for each child with a disability includes—

(1) The parents of the child;

(2) Not less than one regular education teacher of the child (if the child is, or may be, participating in the regular education environment);

(3) Not less than one special education teacher of the child, or where appropriate, not less than one special education provider of the child;

(4) A representative of the public agency who—

(i) Is qualified to provide, or supervise the provision of, specially designed instruction to meet the unique needs of children with disabilities;

(ii) Is knowledgeable about the general education curriculum; and

(iii) Is knowledgeable about the availability of resources of the public agency.

(5) An individual who can interpret the instructional implications of evaluation results, who may be a member of the team described in paragraphs (a)(2) through (a)(6) of this section;

(6) At the discretion of the parent or the agency, other individuals who have knowledge or special expertise regarding the child, including related services personnel as appropriate; and

(7) Whenever appropriate, the child with a disability.

(b) Transition services participants. (1) In accordance with paragraph (a)(7) of this section, the public agency must invite a child with a disability to attend the child's IEP Team meeting if a purpose of the meeting will be the consideration of the postsecondary goals for the child and the transition services needed to assist the child in reaching those goals under § 300.320(b).

(2) If the child does not attend the IEP Team meeting, the public agency must take other steps to ensure that the child's preferences and interests are considered.

(3) To the extent appropriate, with the consent of the parents or a child who has reached the age of majority, in implementing the requirements of paragraph (b)(1) of this section, the public agency must invite a representative of any participating agency that is likely to be responsible for providing or paying for transition services.

(c) Determination of knowledge and special expertise. The determination of the knowledge or special expertise of any individual described in paragraph (a)(6) of this section must be made by the party (parents or public agency) who invited the individual to be a member of the IEP Team.

(d) Designating a public agency representative. A public agency may designate a public agency member of the IEP Team to also serve as the agency representative, if the criteria in paragraph (a)(4) of this section are satisfied.

(e) *IEP Team attendance.* (1) A member of the IEP Team described in paragraphs (a)(2) through (a)(5) of this section is not required to attend an IEP Team meeting, in whole or in part, if the parent of a child with a disability and the public agency agree, in writing, that the attendance of the member is not necessary because the member's area of the curriculum or related services is not being modified or discussed in the meeting.

(2) A member of the IEP Team described in paragraph (e)(1) of this section may be excused from attending an IEP Team meeting, in whole or in part, when the meeting involves a modification to or discussion of the member's area of the curriculum or related services, if—

(i) The parent, in writing, and the public agency consent to the excusal; and

(ii) The member submits, in writing to the parent and the IEP Team, input into the development of the IEP prior to the meeting.

(f) *Initial IEP Team meeting for child under Part C.* In the case of a child who was previously served under Part C of the Act, an invitation to the initial IEP Team meeting must, at the request of the parent, be sent to the Part C service coordinator or other representatives of the Part C system to assist with the smooth transition of services.

§ 300.322 Parent participation.

(a) *Public agency responsibility—general.* Each public agency must take steps to ensure that one or both of the parents of a child with a disability are present at each IEP Team meeting or are afforded the opportunity to participate, including—

(1) Notifying parents of the meeting early enough to ensure that they will have an opportunity to attend; and

(2) Scheduling the meeting at a mutually agreed on time and place.

(b) *Information provided to parents.* (1) The notice required under paragraph (a)(1) of this section must—

(i) Indicate the purpose, time, and location of the meeting and who will be in attendance; and

(ii) Inform the parents of the provisions in § 300.321(a)(6) and (c) (relating to the participation of other individuals on the IEP Team who have knowledge or special expertise about the child), and § 300.321(f) (relating to the participation of the Part C service coordinator or other representatives of the Part C system at the initial IEP Team meeting for a child previously served under Part C of the Act).

(2) For a child with a disability beginning not later than the first IEP to be in effect when the child turns 16, or younger if determined appropriate by the IEP Team, the notice also must—

(i) Indicate—

(A) That a purpose of the meeting will be the consideration of the postsecondary goals and transition services for the child, in accordance with § 300.320(b); and

(B) That the agency will invite the student; and

(ii) Identify any other agency that will be invited to send a representative.

(c) *Other methods to ensure parent participation.* If neither parent can attend an IEP Team meeting, the public agency must use other methods to ensure parent participation, including individual or conference telephone calls, consistent with § 300.328 (related to alternative means of meeting participation).

(d) *Conducting an IEP Team meeting without a parent in attendance.* A meeting may be conducted without a parent in attendance if the public agency is unable to convince the parents that they should attend. In this case, the public agency must keep a record of its attempts to arrange a mutually agreed on time and place, such as—

(1) Detailed records of telephone calls made or attempted and the results of those calls;

(2) Copies of correspondence sent to the parents and any responses received; and

(3) Detailed records of visits made to the parent's home or place of employment and the results of those visits.

(e) Use of interpreters or other action, as appropriate. The public agency must take whatever action is necessary to ensure that the parent understands the proceedings of the IEP Team meeting, including arranging for an interpreter for parents with deafness or whose native language is other than English.

(f) Parent copy of child's IEP. The public agency must give the parent a copy of the child's IEP at no cost to the parent.

§ 300.323 When IEPs must be in effect.

(a) General. At the beginning of each school year, each public agency must have in effect, for each child with a disability within its jurisdiction, an IEP, as defined in § 300.320.

(b) IEP or IFSP for children aged three through five. (1) In the case of a child with a disability aged three through five (or, at the discretion of the SEA, a two-year-old child with a disability who will turn age three during the school year), the IEP Team must consider an IFSP that contains the IFSP content (including the natural environments statement) described in section 636(d) of the Act and its implementing regulations (including an educational component that promotes school readiness and incorporates pre-literacy, language, and numeracy skills for children with IFSPs under this section who are at least three years of age), and that is developed in accordance with the IEP procedures under this part. The IFSP may serve as the IEP of the child, if using the IFSP as the IEP is—

(i) Consistent with State policy; and

(ii) Agreed to by the agency and the child's parents.

(2) In implementing the requirements of paragraph (b)(1) of this section, the public agency must—

(i) Provide to the child's parents a detailed explanation of the differences between an IFSP and an IEP; and

(ii) If the parents choose an IFSP, obtain written informed consent from the parents.

(c) Initial IEPs; provision of services. Each public agency must ensure that—

(1) A meeting to develop an IEP for a child is conducted within 30 days of a determination that the child needs special education and related services; and

(2) As soon as possible following development of the IEP, special education and related services are made available to the child in accordance with the child's IEP.

(d) Accessibility of child's IEP to teachers and others. Each public agency must ensure that—

(1) The child's IEP is accessible to each regular education teacher, special education teacher, related services provider, and any other service provider who is responsible for its implementation; and

(2) Each teacher and provider described in paragraph (d)(1) of this section is informed of—

(i) His or her specific responsibilities related to implementing the child's IEP; and

(ii) The specific accommodations, modifications, and supports that must be provided for the child in accordance with the IEP.

(e) IEPs for children who transfer public agencies in the same State. If a child with a disability (who had an IEP that was in effect in a previous public agency in the same State) transfers to a new public agency in the same State, and enrolls in a new school within the same school year, the new public agency (in consultation with the parents) must provide FAPE to the child (including services comparable to those described in the child's IEP from the previous public agency), until the new public agency either—

(1) Adopts the child's IEP from the previous public agency; or

(2) Develops, adopts, and implements a new IEP that meets the applicable requirements in §§ 300.320 through 300.324.

(f) IEPs for children who transfer from another State. If a child with a disability (who had an IEP that was in effect in a previous public agency in another State) transfers to a public agency in a new State, and enrolls in a new school within the same school year, the new public agency (in consultation with the parents) must provide the child with FAPE (including services comparable to those described in the child's IEP from the previous public agency), until the new public agency—

(1) Conducts an evaluation pursuant to §§ 300.304 through 300.306 (if determined to be necessary by the new public agency); and

(2) Develops, adopts, and implements a new IEP, if appropriate, that meets the applicable requirements in §§ 300.320 through 300.324.

(g) Transmittal of records. To facilitate the transition for a child described in paragraphs (e) and (f) of this section—

(1) The new public agency in which the child enrolls must take reasonable steps to promptly obtain the child's records, including the IEP and supporting documents and any other records relating to the provision of special education or related services to the child, from the previous public agency in which the child was enrolled, pursuant to *34 CFR 99.31(a)(2)*; and

(2) The previous public agency in which the child was enrolled must take reasonable steps to promptly respond to the request from the new public agency.

DEVELOPMENT OF IEP

§ 300.324   Development, review, and revision of IEP.

(a) Development of IEP —(1) General. In developing each child's IEP, the IEP Team must consider—

(i) The strengths of the child;

(ii) The concerns of the parents for enhancing the education of their child;

(iii) The results of the initial or most recent evaluation of the child; and

(iv) The academic, developmental, and functional needs of the child.

(2) Consideration of special factors. The IEP Team must—

(i) In the case of a child whose behavior impedes the child's learning or that of others, consider the use of positive behavioral interventions and supports, and other strategies, to address that behavior;

(ii) In the case of a child with limited English proficiency, consider the language needs of the child as those needs relate to the child's IEP;

(iii) In the case of a child who is blind or visually impaired, provide for instruction in Braille and the use of Braille unless the IEP Team determines, after an evaluation of the child's reading and writing skills, needs, and appropriate reading and writing media (including an evaluation of the child's future needs for instruction in Braille or the use of Braille), that instruction in Braille or the use of Braille is not appropriate for the child;

(iv) Consider the communication needs of the child, and in the case of a child who is deaf or hard of hearing, consider the child's language and communication needs, opportunities for direct communications with peers and professional personnel in the child's language and communication mode, academic level, and full range of needs, including opportunities for direct instruction in the child's language and communication mode; and

(v) Consider whether the child needs assistive technology devices and services.

(3) Requirement with respect to regular education teacher. A regular education teacher of a child with a disability, as a member of the IEP Team, must, to the extent appropriate, participate in the development of the IEP of the child, including the determination of—

(i) Appropriate positive behavioral interventions and supports and other strategies for the child; and

(ii) Supplementary aids and services, program modifications, and support for school personnel consistent with § 300.320(a)(4).

(4) Agreement. (i) In making changes to a child's IEP after the annual IEP Team meeting for a school year, the parent of a child with a disability and the public agency may agree not to convene an IEP Team meeting for the purposes of making those changes, and instead may develop a written document to amend or modify the child's current IEP.

(ii) If changes are made to the child's IEP in accordance with paragraph (a)(4)(i) of this section, the public agency must ensure that the child's IEP Team is informed of those changes.

(5) Consolidation of IEP Team meetings. To the extent possible, the public agency must encourage the consolidation of reevaluation meetings for the child and other IEP Team meetings for the child.

(6) Amendments. Changes to the IEP may be made either by the entire IEP Team at an IEP Team meeting, or as provided in paragraph (a)(4) of this section, by amending the IEP rather than by redrafting the entire IEP. Upon request, a parent must be provided with a revised copy of the IEP with the amendments incorporated.

(b) Review and revision of IEPs —(1) General. Each public agency must ensure that, subject to paragraphs (b)(2) and (b)(3) of this section, the IEP Team—

(i) Reviews the child's IEP periodically, but not less than annually, to determine whether the annual goals for the child are being achieved; and

(ii) Revises the IEP, as appropriate, to address—

(A) Any lack of expected progress toward the annual goals described in § 300.320(a)(2), and in the general education curriculum, if appropriate;

(B) The results of any reevaluation conducted under § 300.303;

(C) Information about the child provided to, or by, the parents, as described under § 300.305(a)(2);

(D) The child's anticipated needs; or

(E) Other matters.

(2) Consideration of special factors. In conducting a review of the child's IEP, the IEP Team must consider the special factors described in paragraph (a)(2) of this section.

(3) Requirement with respect to regular education teacher. A regular education teacher of the child, as a member of the IEP Team, must, consistent with paragraph (a)(3) of this section, participate in the review and revision of the IEP of the child.

(c) Failure to meet transition objectives —(1) Participating agency failure. If a participating agency, other than the public agency, fails to provide the transition services described in the IEP in accordance with § 300.320(b), the public agency must reconvene the IEP Team to identify alternative strategies to meet the transition objectives for the child set out in the IEP.

(2) Construction. Nothing in this part relieves any participating agency, including a State vocational rehabilitation agency, of the responsibility to provide or pay for any transition service that the agency would otherwise provide to children with disabilities who meet the eligibility criteria of that agency.

(d) Children with disabilities in adult prisons —(1) Requirements that do not apply. The following requirements do not apply to children with disabilities who are convicted as adults under State law and incarcerated in adult prisons:

(i) The requirements contained in section 612(a)(16) of the Act and § 300.320(a)(6) (relating to participation of children with disabilities in general assessments).

(ii) The requirements in § 300.320(b) (relating to transition planning and transition services) do not apply with respect to the children whose eligibility under Part B of the Act will end, because of their age, before they will be eligible to be released from prison based on consideration of their sentence and eligibility for early release.

(2) Modifications of IEP or placement. (i) Subject to paragraph (d)(2)(ii) of this section, the IEP Team of a child with a disability who is convicted as an adult under State law and incarcerated in an adult prison may modify the child's IEP or placement if the State has demonstrated a bona fide security or compelling penological interest that cannot otherwise be accommodated.

(ii) The requirements of §§ 300.320 (relating to IEPs), and 300.112 (relating to LRE), do not apply with respect to the modifications described in paragraph (d)(2)(i) of this section.

§ 300.325 Private school placements by public agencies.

(a) Developing IEPs. (1) Before a public agency places a child with a disability in, or refers a child to, a private school or facility, the agency must initiate and conduct a meeting to develop an IEP for the child in accordance with §§ 300.320 and 300.324.

(2) The agency must ensure that a representative of the private school or facility attends the meeting. If the representative cannot attend, the agency must use other methods to ensure participation by the private school or facility, including individual or conference telephone calls.

(b) Reviewing and revising IEPs. (1) After a child with a disability enters a private school or facility, any meetings to review and revise the child's IEP may be initiated and conducted by the private school or facility at the discretion of the public agency.

(2) If the private school or facility initiates and conducts these meetings, the public agency must ensure that the parents and an agency representative—

(i) Are involved in any decision about the child's IEP; and

(ii) Agree to any proposed changes in the IEP before those changes are implemented.

(c) *Responsibility.* Even if a private school or facility implements a child's IEP, responsibility for compliance with this part remains with the public agency and the SEA.

§ 300.326 [Reserved]

§ 300.327 **Educational placements.**

Consistent with § 300.501(c), each public agency must ensure that the parents of each child with a disability are members of any group that makes decisions on the educational placement of their child.

§ 300.328 **Alternative means of meeting participation.**

When conducting IEP Team meetings and placement meetings pursuant to this subpart, and subpart E of this part, and carrying out administrative matters under section 615 of the Act (such as scheduling, exchange of witness lists, and status conferences), the parent of a child with a disability and a public agency may agree to use alternative means of meeting participation, such as video conferences and conference calls.

§ 300.340

[This section was removed. See 71 FR 46540, 46753, Aug. 14, 2006.]

§ 300.341

[This section was removed. See 71 FR 46540, 46753, Aug. 14, 2006.]

§ 300.342

[This section was removed. See 71 FR 46540, 46753, Aug. 14, 2006.]

§ 300.343

[This section was removed. See 71 FR 46540, 46753, Aug. 14, 2006.]

§ 300.344

[This section was removed. See 71 FR 46540, 46753, Aug. 14, 2006.]

§ 300.345

[This section was removed. See 71 FR 46540, 46753, Aug. 14, 2006.]

§ 300.346

[This section was removed. See 71 FR 46540, 46753, Aug. 14, 2006.]

§ 300.347

[This section was removed. See 71 FR 46540, 46753, Aug. 14, 2006.]

§ 300.348

[This section was removed. See 71 FR 46540, 46753, Aug. 14, 2006.]

§ 300.349

[This section was removed. See 71 FR 46540, 46753, Aug. 14, 2006.]

§ 300.350

[This section was removed. See 71 FR 46540, 46753, Aug. 14, 2006.]

§ 300.360

[This section was removed. See 71 FR 46540, 46753, Aug. 14, 2006.]

§ 300.361

[This section was removed. See 71 FR 46540, 46753, Aug. 14, 2006.]

§§ 300.362–300.369

[These sections were removed. See 71 FR 46540, 46753, Aug. 14, 2006.]

§ 300.370

[This section was removed. See 71 FR 46540, 46753, Aug. 14, 2006.]

§ 300.371

[This section was removed. See 71 FR 46540, 46753, Aug. 14, 2006.]

§ 300.372

[This section was removed. See 71 FR 46540, 46753, Aug. 14, 2006.]

§ 300.380

[This section was removed. See 71 FR 46540, 46753, Aug. 14, 2006.]

§ 300.381

[This section was removed. See 71 FR 46540, 46753, Aug. 14, 2006.]

§ 300.382

[This section was removed. See 71 FR 46540, 46753, Aug. 14, 2006.]

§§ 300.383

— 300.387 [These sections were removed. See 71 FR 46540, 46753, Aug. 14, 2006.]

§ 300.400

[This section was removed. See 71 FR 46540, 46753, Aug. 14, 2006.]

§ 300.401

[This section was removed. See 71 FR 46540, 46753, Aug. 14, 2006.]

§ 300.402

[This section was removed. See 71 FR 46540, 46753, Aug. 14, 2006.]

§ 300.403

[This section was removed. See 71 FR 46540, 46753, Aug. 14, 2006.]

§ 300.450

[This section was removed. See 71 FR 46540, 46753, Aug. 14, 2006.]

§ 300.451

[This section was removed. See 71 FR 46540, 46753, Aug. 14, 2006.]

§ 300.452

[This section was removed. See 71 FR 46540, 46753, Aug. 14, 2006.]

§ 300.453

[This section was removed. See 71 FR 46540, 46753, Aug. 14, 2006.]

§ 300.454

[This section was removed. See 71 FR 46540, 46753, Aug. 14, 2006.]

§ 300.455

[This section was removed. See 71 FR 46540, 46753, Aug. 14, 2006.]

§ 300.456

[This section was removed. See 71 FR 46540, 46753, Aug. 14, 2006.]

§ 300.457

[This section was removed. See 71 FR 46540, 46753, Aug. 14, 2006.]

§ 300.458

[This section was removed. See 71 FR 46540, 46753, Aug. 14, 2006.]

§ 300.459

[This section was removed. See 71 FR 46540, 46753, Aug. 14, 2006.]

§ 300.460

[This section was removed. See 71 FR 46540, 46753, Aug. 14, 2006.]

§ 300.461

[This section was removed. See 71 FR 46540, 46753, Aug. 14, 2006.]

§ 300.462

[This section was removed. See 71 FR 46540, 46753, Aug. 14, 2006.]

§ 300.480

[This section was removed. See 71 FR 46540, 46753, Aug. 14, 2006.]

§ 300.481

[This section was removed. See 71 FR 46540, 46753, Aug. 14, 2006.]

§ 300.482

[This section was removed. See 71 FR 46540, 46753, Aug. 14, 2006.]

§ 300.483

[This section was removed. See 71 FR 46540, 46753, Aug. 14, 2006.]

§ 300.484

[This section was removed. See 71 FR 46540, 46753, Aug. 14, 2006.]

§ 300.485

[This section was removed. See 71 FR 46540, 46753, Aug. 14, 2006.]

§ 300.486

[This section was removed. See 71 FR 46540, 46753, Aug. 14, 2006.]

§ 300.487

[This section was removed. See 71 FR 46540, 46753, Aug. 14, 2006.]

SUBPART E PROCEDURAL SAFEGUARDS DUE PROCESS PROCEDURES FOR PARENTS AND CHILDREN
DUE PROCESS PROCEDURES FOR PARENTS AND CHILDREN

§ 300.500 Responsibility of SEA and other public agencies.

Each SEA must ensure that each public agency establishes, maintains, and implements procedural safeguards that meet the requirements of §§ 300.500 through 300.536.

§ 300.501 Opportunity to examine records; parent participation in meetings.

(a) Opportunity to examine records. The parents of a child with a disability must be afforded, in accordance with the procedures of §§ 300.613 through 300.621, an opportunity to inspect and review all education records with respect to—

(1) The identification, evaluation, and educational placement of the child; and

(2) The provision of FAPE to the child.

(b) Parent participation in meetings. (1) The parents of a child with a disability must be afforded an opportunity to participate in meetings with respect to—

(i) The identification, evaluation, and educational placement of the child; and

(ii) The provision of FAPE to the child.

(2) Each public agency must provide notice consistent with § 300.322(a)(1) and (b)(1) to ensure that parents of children with disabilities have the opportunity to participate in meetings described in paragraph (b)(1) of this section.

(3) A meeting does not include informal or unscheduled conversations involving public agency personnel and conversations on issues such as teaching methodology, lesson plans, or coordination of service provision. A meeting also does not include preparatory activities that public agency personnel engage in to develop a proposal or response to a

parent proposal that will be discussed at a later meeting.

(c) Parent involvement in placement decisions. (1) Each public agency must ensure that a parent of each child with a disability is a member of any group that makes decisions on the educational placement of the parent's child.

(2) In implementing the requirements of paragraph (c)(1) of this section, the public agency must use procedures consistent with the procedures described in § 300.322(a) through (b)(1).

(3) If neither parent can participate in a meeting in which a decision is to be made relating to the educational placement of their child, the public agency must use other methods to ensure their participation, including individual or conference telephone calls, or video conferencing.

(4) A placement decision may be made by a group without the involvement of a parent, if the public agency is unable to obtain the parent's participation in the decision. In this case, the public agency must have a record of its attempt to ensure their involvement.

§ 300.502 Independent educational evaluation.

(a) General. (1) The parents of a child with a disability have the right under this part to obtain an independent educational evaluation of the child, subject to paragraphs (b) through (e) of this section.

(2) Each public agency must provide to parents, upon request for an independent educational evaluation, information about where an independent educational evaluation may be obtained, and the agency criteria applicable for independent educational evaluations as set forth in paragraph (e) of this section.

(3) For the purposes of this subpart—

(i) Independent educational evaluation means an evaluation conducted by a qualified examiner who is not employed by the public agency responsible for the education of the child in question; and

(ii) Public expense means that the public agency either pays for the full cost of the evaluation or ensures that the evaluation is otherwise provided at no cost to the parent, consistent with § 300.103.

(b) Parent right to evaluation at public expense.

(1) A parent has the right to an independent educational evaluation at public expense if the parent disagrees with an evaluation obtained by the public agency, subject to the conditions in paragraphs (b)(2) through (4) of this section.

(2) If a parent requests an independent educational evaluation at public expense, the public agency must, without unnecessary delay, either—

(i) File a due process complaint to request a hearing to show that its evaluation is appropriate; or

(ii) Ensure that an independent educational evaluation is provided at public expense, unless the agency demonstrates in a hearing pursuant to §§ 300.507 through 300.513 that the evaluation obtained by the parent did not meet agency criteria.

(3) If the public agency files a due process complaint notice to request a hearing and the final decision is that the agency's evaluation is appropriate, the parent still has the right to an independent educational evaluation, but not at public expense.

(4) If a parent requests an independent educational evaluation, the public agency may ask for the parent's reason why he or she objects to the public evaluation. However, the public agency may not require the parent to provide an explanation and may not unreasonably delay either providing the independent educational evaluation at public

expense or filing a due process complaint to request a due process hearing to defend the public evaluation.

(5) A parent is entitled to only one independent educational evaluation at public expense each time the public agency conducts an evaluation with which the parent disagrees.

(c) *Parent-initiated evaluations.* If the parent obtains an independent educational evaluation at public expense or shares with the public agency an evaluation obtained at private expense, the results of the evaluation—

(1) Must be considered by the public agency, if it meets agency criteria, in any decision made with respect to the provision of FAPE to the child; and

(2) May be presented by any party as evidence at a hearing on a due process complaint under subpart E of this part regarding that child.

(d) *Requests for evaluations by hearing officers.* If a hearing officer requests an independent educational evaluation as part of a hearing on a due process complaint, the cost of the evaluation must be at public expense.

(e) *Agency criteria.* (1) If an independent educational evaluation is at public expense, the criteria under which the evaluation is obtained, including the location of the evaluation and the qualifications of the examiner, must be the same as the criteria that the public agency uses when it initiates an evaluation, to the extent those criteria are consistent with the parent's right to an independent educational evaluation.

(2) Except for the criteria described in paragraph (e)(1) of this section, a public agency may not impose conditions or timelines related to obtaining an independent educational evaluation at public expense.

§ 300.503 Prior notice by the public agency; content of notice.

(a) *Notice.* Written notice that meets the requirements of paragraph (b) of this section must be given to the parents of a child with a disability a reasonable time before the public agency—

(1) Proposes to initiate or change the identification, evaluation, or educational placement of the child or the provision of FAPE to the child; or

(2) Refuses to initiate or change the identification, evaluation, or educational placement of the child or the provision of FAPE to the child.

(b) *Content of notice.* The notice required under paragraph (a) of this section must include—

(1) A description of the action proposed or refused by the agency;

(2) An explanation of why the agency proposes or refuses to take the action;

(3) A description of each evaluation procedure, assessment, record, or report the agency used as a basis for the proposed or refused action;

(4) A statement that the parents of a child with a disability have protection under the procedural safeguards of this part and, if this notice is not an initial referral for evaluation, the means by which a copy of a description of the procedural safeguards can be obtained;

(5) Sources for parents to contact to obtain assistance in understanding the provisions of this part;

(6) A description of other options that the IEP Team considered and the reasons why those options were rejected; and

(7) A description of other factors that are relevant to the agency's proposal or refusal.

(c) *Notice in understandable language.* (1) The notice required under paragraph (a) of this section must be—

(i) Written in language understandable to the general public; and

(ii) Provided in the native language of the parent or other mode of communication used by the parent, unless it is clearly not feasible to do so.

(2) If the native language or other mode of communication of the parent is not a written language, the public agency must take steps to ensure—

(i) That the notice is translated orally or by other means to the parent in his or her native language or other mode of communication;

(ii) That the parent understands the content of the notice; and

(iii) That there is written evidence that the requirements in paragraphs (c)(2)(i) and (ii) of this section have been met.

§ 300.504 Procedural safeguards notice.

(a) *General.* A copy of the procedural safeguards available to the parents of a child with a disability must be given to the parents only one time a school year, except that a copy also must be given to the parents—

(1) Upon initial referral or parent request for evaluation;

(2) Upon receipt of the first State complaint under §§ 300.151 through 300.153 and upon receipt of the first due process complaint under § 300.507 in a school year;

(3) In accordance with the discipline procedures in § 300.530(h); and

(4) Upon request by a parent.

(b) *Internet Web site.* A public agency may place a current copy of the procedural safeguards notice on its Internet Web site if a Web site exists.

(c) *Contents.* The procedural safeguards notice must include a full explanation of all of the procedural safeguards available under § 300.148, §§ 300.151 through 300.153, § 300.300, §§ 300.502 through 300.503, §§ 300.505 through 300.518, §§ 300.530 through 300.536 and §§ 300.610 through 300.625 relating to—

(1) Independent educational evaluations;

(2) Prior written notice;

(3) Parental consent;

(4) Access to education records;

(5) Opportunity to present and resolve complaints through the due process complaint and State complaint procedures, including—

(i) The time period in which to file a complaint;

(ii) The opportunity for the agency to resolve the complaint; and

(iii) The difference between the due process complaint and the State complaint procedures, including the jurisdiction of each procedure, what issues may be raised, filing and decisional timelines, and relevant procedures;

(6) The availability of mediation;

(7) The child's placement during the pendency of any due process complaint;

(8) Procedures for students who are subject to placement in an interim alternative educational setting;

(9) Requirements for unilateral placement by parents of children in private schools at public expense;

(10) Hearings on due process complaints, including requirements for disclosure of evaluation results and recommendations;

(11) State-level appeals (if applicable in the State);

(12) Civil actions, including the time period in which to file those actions; and

(13) Attorneys' fees.

(d) Notice in understandable language. The notice required under paragraph (a) of this section must meet the requirements of § 300.503(c).

(Approved by the Office of Management and Budget under control number 1820-0600)

§ 300.505 Electronic mail.

A parent of a child with a disability may elect to receive notices required by §§ 300.503, 300.504, and 300.508 by an electronic mail communication, if the public agency makes that option available.

§ 300.506 Mediation.

(a) General. Each public agency must ensure that procedures are established and implemented to allow parties to disputes involving any matter under this part, including matters arising prior to the filing of a due process complaint, to resolve disputes through a mediation process.

(b) Requirements. The procedures must meet the following requirements:

(1) The procedures must ensure that the mediation process—

(i) Is voluntary on the part of the parties;

(ii) Is not used to deny or delay a parent's right to a hearing on the parent's due process complaint, or to deny any other rights afforded under Part B of the Act; and

(iii) Is conducted by a qualified and impartial mediator who is trained in effective mediation techniques.

(2) A public agency may establish procedures to offer to parents and schools that choose not to use the mediation process, an opportunity to meet, at a time and location convenient to the parents, with a disinterested party—

(i) Who is under contract with an appropriate alternative dispute resolution entity, or a parent training and information center or community parent resource center in the State established under section 671 or 672 of the Act; and

(ii) Who would explain the benefits of, and encourage the use of, the mediation process to the parents.

(3)(i) The State must maintain a list of individuals who are qualified mediators and knowledgeable in laws and regulations relating to the provision of special education and related services.

(ii) The SEA must select mediators on a random, rotational, or other impartial basis.

(4) The State must bear the cost of the mediation process, including the costs of meetings described in paragraph (b)(2) of this section.

(5) Each session in the mediation process must be scheduled in a timely manner and must be held in a location that is convenient to the parties to the dispute.

(6) If the parties resolve a dispute through the mediation process, the parties must

execute a legally binding agreement that sets forth that resolution and that—

(i) States that all discussions that occurred during the mediation process will remain confidential and may not be used as evidence in any subsequent due process hearing or civil proceeding; and

(ii) Is signed by both the parent and a representative of the agency who has the authority to bind such agency.

(7) A written, signed mediation agreement under this paragraph is enforceable in any State court of competent jurisdiction or in a district court of the United States.

(8) Discussions that occur during the mediation process must be confidential and may not be used as evidence in any subsequent due process hearing or civil proceeding of any Federal court or State court of a State receiving assistance under this part.

(c) *Impartiality of mediator.* (1) An individual who serves as a mediator under this part—

(i) May not be an employee of the SEA or the LEA that is involved in the education or care of the child; and

(ii) Must not have a personal or professional interest that conflicts with the person's objectivity.

(2) A person who otherwise qualifies as a mediator is not an employee of an LEA or State agency described under § 300.228 solely because he or she is paid by the agency to serve as a mediator.

(Approved by the Office of Management and Budget under control number 1820-0600)

§ 300.507 Filing a due process complaint.

(a) *General.* (1) A parent or a public agency may file a due process complaint on any of the matters described in § 300.503(a)(1) and (2) (relating to the identification, evaluation or educational placement of a child with a disability, or the provision of FAPE to the child).

(2) The due process complaint must allege a violation that occurred not more than two years before the date the parent or public agency knew or should have known about the alleged action that forms the basis of the due process complaint, or, if the State has an explicit time limitation for filing a due process complaint under this part, in the time allowed by that State law, except that the exceptions to the timeline described in § 300.511(f) apply to the timeline in this section.

(b) *Information for parents.* The public agency must inform the parent of any free or low-cost legal and other relevant services available in the area if—

(1) The parent requests the information; or

(2) The parent or the agency files a due process complaint under this section.

(Approved by the Office of Management and Budget under control number 1820-0600)

§ 300.508 Due process complaint.

(a) *General.* (1) The public agency must have procedures that require either party, or the attorney representing a party, to provide to the other party a due process complaint (which must remain confidential).

(2) The party filing a due process complaint must forward a copy of the due process complaint to the SEA.

(b) Content of complaint. The due process complaint required in paragraph (a)(1) of this section must include—

(1) The name of the child;

(2) The address of the residence of the child;

(3) The name of the school the child is attending;

(4) In the case of a homeless child or youth (within the meaning of section 725(2) of the McKinney-Vento Homeless Assistance Act *(42 U.S.C. 11434a(2))*, available contact information for the child, and the name of the school the child is attending;

(5) A description of the nature of the problem of the child relating to the proposed or refused initiation or change, including facts relating to the problem; and

(6) A proposed resolution of the problem to the extent known and available to the party at the time.

(c) Notice required before a hearing on a due process complaint. A party may not have a hearing on a due process complaint until the party, or the attorney representing the party, files a due process complaint that meets the requirements of paragraph (b) of this section.

(d) Sufficiency of complaint. (1) The due process complaint required by this section must be deemed sufficient unless the party receiving the due process complaint notifies the hearing officer and the other party in writing, within 15 days of receipt of the due process complaint, that the receiving party believes the due process complaint does not meet the requirements in paragraph (b) of this section.

(2) Within five days of receipt of notification under paragraph (d)(1) of this section, the hearing officer must make a determination on the face of the due process complaint of whether the due process complaint meets the requirements of paragraph (b) of this section, and must immediately notify the parties in writing of that determination.

(3) A party may amend its due process complaint only if—

(i) The other party consents in writing to the amendment and is given the opportunity to resolve the due process complaint through a meeting held pursuant to § 300.510; or

(ii) The hearing officer grants permission, except that the hearing officer may only grant permission to amend at any time not later than five days before the due process hearing begins.

(4) If a party files an amended due process complaint, the timelines for the resolution meeting in § 300.510(a) and the time period to resolve in § 300.510(b) begin again with the filing of the amended due process complaint.

(e) LEA response to a due process complaint. (1) If the LEA has not sent a prior written notice under § 300.503 to the parent regarding the subject matter contained in the parent's due process complaint, the LEA must, within 10 days of receiving the due process complaint, send to the parent a response that includes—

(i) An explanation of why the agency proposed or refused to take the action raised in the due process complaint;

(ii) A description of other options that the IEP Team considered and the reasons why those options were rejected;

(iii) A description of each evaluation procedure, assessment, record, or report the agency used as the basis for the proposed or refused action; and

(iv) A description of the other factors that are relevant to the agency's proposed or refused action.

(2) A response by an LEA under paragraph (e)(1) of this section shall not be construed to preclude the LEA from asserting that the parent's due process complaint was insufficient, where appropriate.

(f) *Other party response to a due process complaint.* Except as provided in paragraph (e) of this section, the party receiving a due process complaint must, within 10 days of receiving the due process complaint, send to the other party a response that specifically addresses the issues raised in the due process complaint.

§ 300.509 Model forms.

(a) Each SEA must develop model forms to assist parents and public agencies in filing a due process complaint in accordance with §§ 300.507(a) and 300.508(a) through (c) and to assist parents and other parties in filing a State complaint under §§ 300.151 through 300.153. However, the SEA or LEA may not require the use of the model forms.

(b) Parents, public agencies, and other parties may use the appropriate model form described in paragraph (a) of this section, or another form or other document, so long as the form or document that is used meets, as appropriate, the content requirements in § 300.508(b) for filing a due process complaint, or the requirements in § 300.153(b) for filing a State complaint.

§ 300.510 Resolution process.

(a) *Resolution meeting.* (1) Within 15 days of receiving notice of the parent's due process complaint, and prior to the initiation of a due process hearing under § 300.511, the LEA must convene a meeting with the parent and the relevant member or members of the IEP Team who have specific knowledge of the facts identified in the due process complaint that—

(i) Includes a representative of the public agency who has decision-making authority on behalf of that agency; and

(ii) May not include an attorney of the LEA unless the parent is accompanied by an attorney.

(2) The purpose of the meeting is for the parent of the child to discuss the due process complaint, and the facts that form the basis of the due process complaint, so that the LEA has the opportunity to resolve the dispute that is the basis for the due process complaint.

(3) The meeting described in paragraph (a)(1) and (2) of this section need not be held if—

(i) The parent and the LEA agree in writing to waive the meeting; or

(ii) The parent and the LEA agree to use the mediation process described in § 300.506.

(4) The parent and the LEA determine the relevant members of the IEP Team to attend the meeting.

(b) *Resolution period.* (1) If the LEA has not resolved the due process complaint to the satisfaction of the parent within 30 days of the receipt of the due process complaint, the due process hearing may occur.

(2) Except as provided in paragraph (c) of this section, the timeline for issuing a final decision under § 300.515 begins at the expiration of this 30-day period.

(3) Except where the parties have jointly agreed to waive the resolution process or to use mediation, notwithstanding paragraphs (b)(1) and (2) of this section, the failure of the parent filing a due process complaint to participate in the resolution meeting will delay the timelines for the resolution process and due process hearing until the meeting is held.

(4) If the LEA is unable to obtain the participation of the parent in the resolution meeting after reasonable efforts have been made (and documented using the procedures in § 300.322(d)), the LEA may, at the conclusion of the 30-day period, request that a hearing officer dismiss the parent's due process complaint.

(5) If the LEA fails to hold the resolution meeting specified in paragraph (a) of this section within 15 days of receiving notice of a parent's due process complaint or fails to participate in the resolution meeting, the parent may seek the intervention of a hearing officer to begin the due process hearing timeline.

(c) Adjustments to 30-day resolution period. The 45-day timeline for the due process hearing in § 300.515(a) starts the day after one of the following events:

(1) Both parties agree in writing to waive the resolution meeting;

(2) After either the mediation or resolution meeting starts but before the end of the 30-day period, the parties agree in writing that no agreement is possible;

(3) If both parties agree in writing to continue the mediation at the end of the 30-day resolution period, but later, the parent or public agency withdraws from the mediation process.

(d) Written settlement agreement. If a resolution to the dispute is reached at the meeting described in paragraphs (a)(1) and (2) of this section, the parties must execute a legally binding agreement that is—

(1) Signed by both the parent and a representative of the agency who has the authority to bind the agency; and

(2) Enforceable in any State court of competent jurisdiction or in a district court of the United States, or, by the SEA, if the State has other mechanisms or procedures that permit parties to seek enforcement of resolution agreements, pursuant to § 300.537.

(e) Agreement review period. If the parties execute an agreement pursuant to paragraph (d) of this section, a party may void the agreement within 3 business days of the agreement's execution.

§ 300.511 Impartial due process hearing.

(a) General. Whenever a due process complaint is received under § 300.507 or § 300.532, the parents or the LEA involved in the dispute must have an opportunity for an impartial due process hearing, consistent with the procedures in §§ 300.507, 300.508, and 300.510.

(b) Agency responsible for conducting the due process hearing. The hearing described in paragraph (a) of this section must be conducted by the SEA or the public agency directly responsible for the education of the child, as determined under State statute, State regulation, or a written policy of the SEA.

(c) Impartial hearing officer. (1) At a minimum, a hearing officer—

(i) Must not be—

(A) An employee of the SEA or the LEA that is involved in the education or care of the child; or

(B) A person having a personal or professional interest that conflicts with the person's objectivity in the hearing;

(ii) Must possess knowledge of, and the ability to understand, the provisions of the Act, Federal and State regulations pertaining to the Act, and legal interpretations of the Act by Federal and State courts;

(iii) Must possess the knowledge and ability to conduct hearings in accordance with appropriate, standard legal practice; and

(iv) Must possess the knowledge and ability to render and write decisions in accordance with appropriate, standard legal practice.

(2) A person who otherwise qualifies to conduct a hearing under paragraph (c)(1) of this section is not an employee of the agency solely because he or she is paid by the agency to serve as a hearing officer.

(3) Each public agency must keep a list of the persons who serve as hearing officers. The list must include a statement of the qualifications of each of those persons.

(d) *Subject matter of due process hearings.* The party requesting the due process hearing may not raise issues at the due process hearing that were not raised in the due process complaint filed under § 300.508(b), unless the other party agrees otherwise.

(e) *Timeline for requesting a hearing.* A parent or agency must request an impartial hearing on their due process complaint within two years of the date the parent or agency knew or should have known about the alleged action that forms the basis of the due process complaint, or if the State has an explicit time limitation for requesting such a due process hearing under this part, in the time allowed by that State law.

(f) *Exceptions to the timeline.* The timeline described in paragraph (e) of this section does not apply to a parent if the parent was prevented from filing a due process complaint due to—

(1) Specific misrepresentations by the LEA that it had resolved the problem forming the basis of the due process complaint; or

(2) The LEA's withholding of information from the parent that was required under this part to be provided to the parent.

(Approved by the Office of Management and Budget under control number 1820-0600)

§ 300.512 Hearing rights.

(a) *General.* Any party to a hearing conducted pursuant to §§ 300.507 through 300.513 or §§ 300.530 through 300.534, or an appeal conducted pursuant to § 300.514, has the right to—

(1) Be accompanied and advised by counsel and by individuals with special knowledge or training with respect to the problems of children with disabilities;

(2) Present evidence and confront, cross-examine, and compel the attendance of witnesses;

(3) Prohibit the introduction of any evidence at the hearing that has not been disclosed to that party at least five business days before the hearing;

(4) Obtain a written, or, at the option of the parents, electronic, verbatim record of the hearing; and

(5) Obtain written, or, at the option of the parents, electronic findings of fact and decisions.

(b) *Additional disclosure of information.* (1) At least five business days prior to a hearing conducted pursuant to § 300.511(a), each party must disclose to all other parties all evaluations completed by that date and recommendations based on the offering party's evaluations that the party intends to use at the hearing.

(2) A hearing officer may bar any party that fails to comply with paragraph (b)(1) of this section from introducing the relevant evaluation or recommendation at the hearing without the consent of the other party.

(c) *Parental rights at hearings.* Parents involved in hearings must be given the right to—

(1) Have the child who is the subject of the hearing present;

(2) Open the hearing to the public; and

(3) Have the record of the hearing and the findings of fact and decisions described in paragraphs (a)(4) and (a)(5) of this section provided at no cost to parents.

§ 300.513   Hearing decisions.

(a) *Decision of hearing officer on the provision of FAPE.* (1) Subject to paragraph (a)(2) of this section, a hearing officer's determination of whether a child received FAPE must be based on substantive grounds.

(2) In matters alleging a procedural violation, a hearing officer may find that a child did not receive a FAPE only if the procedural inadequacies—

(i) Impeded the child's right to a FAPE;

(ii) Significantly impeded the parent's opportunity to participate in the decision-making process regarding the provision of a FAPE to the parent's child; or

(iii) Caused a deprivation of educational benefit.

(3) Nothing in paragraph (a) of this section shall be construed to preclude a hearing officer from ordering an LEA to comply with procedural requirements under §§ 300.500 through 300.536.

(b) *Construction clause.* Nothing in §§ 300.507 through 300.513 shall be construed to affect the right of a parent to file an appeal of the due process hearing decision with the SEA under § 300.514(b), if a State level appeal is available.

(c) *Separate request for a due process hearing.* Nothing in §§ 300.500 through 300.536 shall be construed to preclude a parent from filing a separate due process complaint on an issue separate from a due process complaint already filed.

(d) *Findings and decision to advisory panel and general public.* The public agency, after deleting any personally identifiable information, must—

(1) Transmit the findings and decisions referred to in § 300.512(a)(5) to the State advisory panel established under § 300.167; and

(2) Make those findings and decisions available to the public.

§ 300.514   Finality of decision; appeal; impartial review.

(a) *Finality of hearing decision.* A decision made in a hearing conducted pursuant to §§ 300.507 through 300.513 or §§ 300.530 through 300.534 is final, except that any party involved in the hearing may appeal the decision under the provisions of paragraph (b) of this section and § 300.516.

(b) *Appeal of decisions; impartial review.* (1) If the hearing required by § 300.511 is conducted by a public agency other than the SEA, any party aggrieved by the findings and decision in the hearing may appeal to the SEA.

(2) If there is an appeal, the SEA must conduct an impartial review of the findings and decision appealed. The official conducting the review must—

(i) Examine the entire hearing record;

(ii) Ensure that the procedures at the hearing were consistent with the requirements of due process;

(iii) Seek additional evidence if necessary. If a hearing is held to receive additional evidence, the rights in § 300.512 apply;

(iv) Afford the parties an opportunity for oral or written argument, or both, at the discretion of the reviewing official;

(v) Make an independent decision on completion of the review; and

(vi) Give a copy of the written, or, at the option of the parents, electronic findings of fact and decisions to the parties.

(c) *Findings and decision to advisory panel and general public.* The SEA, after deleting any personally identifiable information, must—

(1) Transmit the findings and decisions referred to in paragraph (b)(2)(vi) of this section to the State advisory panel established under § 300.167; and

(2) Make those findings and decisions available to the public.

(d) *Finality of review decision.* The decision made by the reviewing official is final unless a party brings a civil action under § 300.516.

§ 300.515 Timelines and convenience of hearings and reviews.

(a) The public agency must ensure that not later than 45 days after the expiration of the 30 day period under § 300.510(b), or the adjusted time periods described in § 300.510(c)—

(1) A final decision is reached in the hearing; and

(2) A copy of the decision is mailed to each of the parties.

(b) The SEA must ensure that not later than 30 days after the receipt of a request for a review—

(1) A final decision is reached in the review; and

(2) A copy of the decision is mailed to each of the parties.

(c) A hearing or reviewing officer may grant specific extensions of time beyond the periods set out in paragraphs (a) and (b) of this section at the request of either party.

(d) Each hearing and each review involving oral arguments must be conducted at a time and place that is reasonably convenient to the parents and child involved.

§ 300.516 Civil action.

(a) *General.* Any party aggrieved by the findings and decision made under §§ 300.507 through 300.513 or §§ 300.530 through 300.534 who does not have the right to an appeal under § 300.514(b), and any party aggrieved by the findings and decision under § 300.514(b), has the right to bring a civil action with respect to the due process complaint notice requesting a due process hearing under § 300.507 or §§ 300.530 through 300.532. The action may be brought in any State court of competent jurisdiction or in a district court of the United States without regard to the amount in controversy.

(b) *Time limitation.* The party bringing the action shall have 90 days from the date of the decision of the hearing officer or, if applicable, the decision of the State review official, to file a civil action, or, if the State has an explicit time limitation for bringing civil actions under Part B of the Act, in the time allowed by that State law.

(c) *Additional requirements.* In any action brought under paragraph (a) of this section, the court—

(1) Receives the records of the administrative proceedings;

(2) Hears additional evidence at the request of a party; and

(3) Basing its decision on the preponderance of the evidence, grants the relief that the court determines to be appropriate.

(d) Jurisdiction of district courts. The district courts of the United States have jurisdiction of actions brought under section 615 of the Act without regard to the amount in controversy.

(e) Rule of construction. Nothing in this part restricts or limits the rights, procedures, and remedies available under the Constitution, the Americans with Disabilities Act of 1990, title V of the Rehabilitation Act of 1973, or other Federal laws protecting the rights of children with disabilities, except that before the filing of a civil action under these laws seeking relief that is also available under section 615 of the Act, the procedures under §§ 300.507 and 300.514 must be exhausted to the same extent as would be required had the action been brought under section 615 of the Act.

§ 300.517   Attorneys' fees.

(a) In general. (1) In any action or proceeding brought under section 615 of the Act, the court, in its discretion, may award reasonable attorneys' fees as part of the costs to—

(i) The prevailing party who is the parent of a child with a disability;

(ii) To a prevailing party who is an SEA or LEA against the attorney of a parent who files a complaint or subsequent cause of action that is frivolous, unreasonable, or without foundation, or against the attorney of a parent who continued to litigate after the litigation clearly became frivolous, unreasonable, or without foundation; or

(iii) To a prevailing SEA or LEA against the attorney of a parent, or against the parent, if the parent's request for a due process hearing or subsequent cause of action was presented for any improper purpose, such as to harass, to cause unnecessary delay, or to needlessly increase the cost of litigation.

(2) Nothing in this subsection shall be construed to affect section 327 of the District of Columbia Appropriations Act, 2005.

(b) Prohibition on use of funds. (1) Funds under Part B of the Act may not be used to pay attorneys' fees or costs of a party related to any action or proceeding under section 615 of the Act and subpart E of this part.

(2) Paragraph (b)(1) of this section does not preclude a public agency from using funds under Part B of the Act for conducting an action or proceeding under section 615 of the Act.

(c) Award of fees. A court awards reasonable attorneys' fees under section 615(i)(3) of the Act consistent with the following:

(1) Fees awarded under section 615(i)(3) of the Act must be based on rates prevailing in the community in which the action or proceeding arose for the kind and quality of services furnished. No bonus or multiplier may be used in calculating the fees awarded under this paragraph.

(2)(i) Attorneys' fees may not be awarded and related costs may not be reimbursed in any action or proceeding under section 615 of the Act for services performed subsequent to the time of a written offer of settlement to a parent if—

(A) The offer is made within the time prescribed by *Rule 68 of the Federal Rules of Civil Procedure* or, in the case of an administrative proceeding, at any time more than 10 days before the proceeding begins;

(B) The offer is not accepted within 10 days; and

(C) The court or administrative hearing officer finds that the relief finally obtained by the parents is not more favorable to the parents than the offer of settlement.

(ii) Attorneys' fees may not be awarded relating to any meeting of the IEP Team unless the meeting is convened as a result of an administrative proceeding or judicial action, or at the discretion of the State, for a mediation described in § 300.506.

(iii) A meeting conducted pursuant to § 300.510 shall not be considered—

(A) A meeting convened as a result of an administrative hearing or judicial action; or

(B) An administrative hearing or judicial action for purposes of this section.

(3) Notwithstanding paragraph (c)(2) of this section, an award of attorneys' fees and related costs may be made to a parent who is the prevailing party and who was substantially justified in rejecting the settlement offer.

(4) Except as provided in paragraph (c)(5) of this section, the court reduces, accordingly, the amount of the attorneys' fees awarded under section 615 of the Act, if the court finds that—

(i) The parent, or the parent's attorney, during the course of the action or proceeding, unreasonably protracted the final resolution of the controversy;

(ii) The amount of the attorneys' fees otherwise authorized to be awarded unreasonably exceeds the hourly rate prevailing in the community for similar services by attorneys of reasonably comparable skill, reputation, and experience;

(iii) The time spent and legal services furnished were excessive considering the nature of the action or proceeding; or

(iv) The attorney representing the parent did not provide to the LEA the appropriate information in the due process request notice in accordance with § 300.508.

(5) The provisions of paragraph (c)(4) of this section do not apply in any action or proceeding if the court finds that the State or local agency unreasonably protracted the final resolution of the action or proceeding or there was a violation of section 615 of the Act.

§ 300.518 Child's status during proceedings.

(a) Except as provided in § 300.533, during the pendency of any administrative or judicial proceeding regarding a due process complaint notice requesting a due process hearing under § 300.507, unless the State or local agency and the parents of the child agree otherwise, the child involved in the complaint must remain in his or her current educational placement.

(b) If the complaint involves an application for initial admission to public school, the child, with the consent of the parents, must be placed in the public school until the completion of all the proceedings.

(c) If the complaint involves an application for initial services under this part from a child who is transitioning from Part C of the Act to Part B and is no longer eligible for Part C services because the child has turned three, the public agency is not required to provide the Part C services that the child had been receiving. If the child is found eligible for special education and related services under Part B and the parent consents to the initial provision of special education and related services under § 300.300(b), then the public agency must provide those special education and related services that are not in dispute between the parent and the public agency.

(d) If the hearing officer in a due process hearing conducted by the SEA or a State review official in an administrative appeal agrees with the child's parents that a change of placement is appropriate, that placement must be treated as an agreement between the State and the parents for purposes of paragraph (a) of this section.

§ 300.519 Surrogate parents.

(a) General. Each public agency must ensure that the rights of a child are protected when—

(1) No parent (as defined in § 300.30) can be identified;

(2) The public agency, after reasonable efforts, cannot locate a parent;

(3) The child is a ward of the State under the laws of that State; or

(4) The child is an unaccompanied homeless youth as defined in section 725(6) of the McKinney-Vento Homeless Assistance Act *(42 U.S.C. 11434a(6))*.

(b) Duties of public agency. The duties of a public agency under paragraph (a) of this section include the assignment of an individual to act as a surrogate for the parents. This must include a method—

(1) For determining whether a child needs a surrogate parent; and

(2) For assigning a surrogate parent to the child.

(c) Wards of the State. In the case of a child who is a ward of the State, the surrogate parent alternatively may be appointed by the judge overseeing the child's case, provided that the surrogate meets the requirements in paragraphs (d)(2)(i) and (e) of this section.

(d) Criteria for selection of surrogate parents. (1) The public agency may select a surrogate parent in any way permitted under State law.

(2) Public agencies must ensure that a person selected as a surrogate parent—

(i) Is not an employee of the SEA, the LEA, or any other agency that is involved in the education or care of the child;

(ii) Has no personal or professional interest that conflicts with the interest of the child the surrogate parent represents; and

(iii) Has knowledge and skills that ensure adequate representation of the child.

(e) Non-employee requirement; compensation. A person otherwise qualified to be a surrogate parent under paragraph (d) of this section is not an employee of the agency solely because he or she is paid by the agency to serve as a surrogate parent.

(f) Unaccompanied homeless youth. In the case of a child who is an unaccompanied homeless youth, appropriate staff of emergency shelters, transitional shelters, independent living programs, and street outreach programs may be appointed as temporary surrogate parents without regard to paragraph (d)(2)(i) of this section, until a surrogate parent can be appointed that meets all of the requirements of paragraph (d) of this section.

(g) Surrogate parent responsibilities. The surrogate parent may represent the child in all matters relating to—

(1) The identification, evaluation, and educational placement of the child; and

(2) The provision of FAPE to the child.

(h) SEA responsibility. The SEA must make reasonable efforts to ensure the assignment of a surrogate parent not more than 30 days after a public agency determines that the child needs a surrogate parent.

§ 300.520 Transfer of parental rights at age of majority.

(a) General. A State may provide that, when a child with a disability reaches the age of majority under State law that applies to all children (except for a child with a disability who has been determined to be incompetent under State law)—

(1)(i) The public agency must provide any notice required by this part to both the child and the parents; and

(ii) All rights accorded to parents under Part B of the Act transfer to the child;

(2) All rights accorded to parents under Part B of the Act transfer to children who are incarcerated in an adult or juvenile, State or local correctional institution; and

(3) Whenever a State provides for the transfer of rights under this part pursuant to paragraph (a)(1) or (a)(2) of this section, the agency must notify the child and the parents of the transfer of rights.

(b) Special rule. A State must establish procedures for appointing the parent of a child with a disability, or, if the parent is not available, another appropriate individual, to represent the educational interests of the child throughout the period of the child's eligibility under Part B of the Act if, under State law, a child who has reached the age of majority, but has not been determined to be incompetent, can be determined not to have the ability to provide informed consent with respect to the child's educational program.

§ 300.521

[This section was removed and reserved. See 71 FR 46540, 46753, Aug. 14, 2006.]

§ 300.522

[This section was removed and reserved. See 71 FR 46540, 46753, Aug. 14, 2006.]

§ 300.523

[This section was removed and reserved. See 71 FR 46540, 46753, Aug. 14, 2006.]

§ 300.524

[This section was removed and reserved. See 71 FR 46540, 46753, Aug. 14, 2006.]

§ 300.525

[This section was removed and reserved. See 71 FR 46540, 46753, Aug. 14, 2006.]

§ 300.526

[This section was removed and reserved. See 71 FR 46540, 46753, Aug. 14, 2006.]

§ 300.527

[This section was removed and reserved. See 71 FR 46540, 46753, Aug. 14, 2006.]

§ 300.528

[This section was removed and reserved. See 71 FR 46540, 46753, Aug. 14, 2006.]

§ 300.529

[This section was removed and reserved. See 71 FR 46540, 46753, Aug. 14, 2006.]

DISCIPLINE PROCEDURES

§ 300.530 Authority of school personnel.

(a) *Case-by-case determination.* School personnel may consider any unique circumstances on a case-by-case basis when determining whether a change in placement, consistent with the other requirements of this section, is appropriate for a child with a disability who violates a code of student conduct.

(b) *General.* (1) School personnel under this section may remove a child with a disability who violates a code of student conduct from his or her current placement to an appropriate interim alternative educational setting, another setting, or suspension, for not more than 10 consecutive school days (to the extent those alternatives are applied to children without disabilities), and for additional removals of not more than 10 consecutive school days in that same school year for separate incidents of misconduct (as long as those removals do not constitute a change of placement under § 300.536).

(2) After a child with a disability has been removed from his or her current placement for 10 school days in the same school year, during any subsequent days of removal the public agency must provide services to the extent required under paragraph (d) of this section.

(c) *Additional authority.* For disciplinary changes in placement that would exceed 10 consecutive school days, if the behavior that gave rise to the violation of the school code is determined not to be a manifestation of the child's disability pursuant to paragraph (e) of this section, school personnel may apply the relevant disciplinary procedures to children with disabilities in the same manner and for the same duration as the procedures would be applied to children without disabilities, except as provided in paragraph (d) of this section.

(d) *Services.* (1) A child with a disability who is removed from the child's current placement pursuant to paragraphs (c), or (g) of this section must—

(i) Continue to receive educational services, as provided in § 300.101(a), so as to enable the child to continue to participate in the general education curriculum, although in another setting, and to progress toward meeting the goals set out in the child's IEP; and

(ii) Receive, as appropriate, a functional behavioral assessment, and behavioral intervention services and modifications, that are designed to address the behavior violation so that it does not recur.

(2) The services required by paragraph (d)(1), (d)(3), (d)(4), and (d)(5) of this section may be provided in an interim alternative educational setting.

(3) A public agency is only required to provide services during periods of removal to a child with a disability who has been removed from his or her current placement for 10 school days or less in that school year, if it provides services to a child without disabilities who is similarly removed.

(4) After a child with a disability has been removed from his or her current placement for 10 school days in the same school year, if the current removal is for not more than 10 consecutive school days and is not a change of placement under § 300.536, school personnel, in consultation with at least one of the child's teachers, determine the extent to which services are needed, as provided in § 300.101(a), so as to enable the child to continue to participate in the general education curriculum, although in another setting, and to progress toward meeting the goals set out in the child's IEP.

(5) If the removal is a change of placement under § 300.536, the child's IEP Team determines appropriate services under paragraph (d)(1) of this section.

(e) *Manifestation determination.* (1) Within 10 school days of any decision to change the placement of a child with a disability because of a violation of a code of student conduct, the LEA, the parent, and relevant members of the child's IEP Team (as determined by the parent and the LEA) must review all relevant information in the student's file, including the child's IEP, any teacher observations, and any relevant information provided by the parents to determine—

(i) If the conduct in question was caused by, or had a direct and substantial relationship to, the child's disability; or

(ii) If the conduct in question was the direct result of the LEA's failure to implement the IEP.

(2) The conduct must be determined to be a manifestation of the child's disability if the LEA, the parent, and relevant members of the child's IEP Team determine that a condition in either paragraph (e)(1)(i) or (1)(ii) of this section was met.

(3) If the LEA, the parent, and relevant members of the child's IEP Team determine the condition described in paragraph (e)(1)(ii) of this section was met, the LEA must take immediate steps to remedy those deficiencies.

(f) *Determination that behavior was a manifestation.* If the LEA, the parent, and relevant members of the IEP Team make the determination that the conduct was a manifestation of the child's disability, the IEP Team must—

(1) Either—

(i) Conduct a functional behavioral assessment, unless the LEA had conducted a functional behavioral assessment before the behavior that resulted in the change of placement occurred, and implement a behavioral intervention plan for the child; or

(ii) If a behavioral intervention plan already has been developed, review the behavioral intervention plan, and modify it, as necessary, to address the behavior; and

(2) Except as provided in paragraph (g) of this section, return the child to the placement from which the child was removed, unless the parent and the LEA agree to a change of placement as part of the modification of the behavioral intervention plan.

(g) *Special circumstances.* School personnel may remove a student to an interim alternative educational setting for not more than 45 school days without regard to whether the behavior is determined to be a manifestation of the child's disability, if the child—

(1) Carries a weapon to or possesses a weapon at school, on school premises, or to or at a school function under the jurisdiction of an SEA or an LEA;

(2) Knowingly possesses or uses illegal drugs, or sells or solicits the sale of a controlled substance, while at school, on school premises, or at a school function under the jurisdiction of an SEA or an LEA; or

(3) Has inflicted serious bodily injury upon another person while at school, on school premises, or at a school function under the jurisdiction of an SEA or an LEA.

(h) *Notification.* On the date on which the decision is made to make a removal that constitutes a change of placement of a child with a disability because of a violation of a code of student conduct, the LEA must notify the parents of that decision, and provide the parents the procedural safeguards notice described in § 300.504.

(i) *Definitions.* For purposes of this section, the following definitions apply:

(1) *Controlled substance* means a drug or other substance identified under schedules I, II, III, IV, or V in section (c) of the Controlled Substances Act *(21 U.S.C. 812*(c)).

(2) *Illegal drug* means a controlled substance; but does not include a controlled substance that is legally possessed or used under the supervision of a licensed health-care professional or that is legally possessed or used under any other authority

under that Act or under any other provision of Federal law.

(3) Serious bodily injury has the meaning given the term "serious bodily injury" under paragraph (3) of subsection (h) of section 1365 of title 18, United States Code.

(4) Weapon has the meaning given the term "dangerous weapon" under paragraph (2) of the first subsection (g) of section 930 of title 18, United States Code.

§ 300.531 Determination of setting.

The child's IEP Team determines the interim alternative educational setting for services under § 300.530(c), (d)(5), and (g).

§ 300.532 Appeal.

(a) General. The parent of a child with a disability who disagrees with any decision regarding placement under §§ 300.530 and 300.531, or the manifestation determination under § 300.530(e), or an LEA that believes that maintaining the current placement of the child is substantially likely to result in injury to the child or others, may appeal the decision by requesting a hearing. The hearing is requested by filing a complaint pursuant to §§ 300.507 and 300.508(a) and (b).

(b) Authority of hearing officer. (1) A hearing officer under § 300.511 hears, and makes a determination regarding an appeal under paragraph (a) of this section.

(2) In making the determination under paragraph (b)(1) of this section, the hearing officer may—

(i) Return the child with a disability to the placement from which the child was removed if the hearing officer determines that the removal was a violation of § 300.530 or that the child's behavior was a manifestation of the child's disability; or

(ii) Order a change of placement of the child with a disability to an appropriate interim alternative educational setting for not more than 45 school days if the hearing officer determines that maintaining the current placement of the child is substantially likely to result in injury to the child or to others.

(3) The procedures under paragraphs (a) and (b)(1) and (2) of this section may be repeated, if the LEA believes that returning the child to the original placement is substantially likely to result in injury to the child or to others.

(c) Expedited due process hearing. (1) Whenever a hearing is requested under paragraph (a) of this section, the parents or the LEA involved in the dispute must have an opportunity for an impartial due process hearing consistent with the requirements of §§ 300.507 and 300.508(a) through (c) and §§ 300.510 through 300.514, except as provided in paragraph (c)(2) through (4) of this section.

(2) The SEA or LEA is responsible for arranging the expedited due process hearing, which must occur within 20 school days of the date the complaint requesting the hearing is filed. The hearing officer must make a determination within 10 school days after the hearing.

(3) Unless the parents and LEA agree in writing to waive the resolution meeting described in paragraph (c)(3)(i) of this section, or agree to use the mediation process described in § 300.506—

(i) A resolution meeting must occur within seven days of receiving notice of the due process complaint; and

(ii) The due process hearing may proceed unless the matter has been resolved to the satisfaction of both parties within 15 days of the receipt of the due process complaint.

(4) A State may establish different State-imposed procedural rules for expedited due

process hearings conducted under this section than it has established for other due process hearings, but, except for the timelines as modified in paragraph (c)(3) of this section, the State must ensure that the requirements in §§ 300.510 through 300.514 are met.

(5) The decisions on expedited due process hearings are appealable consistent with § 300.514.

§ 300.533 Placement during appeals.

When an appeal under § 300.532 has been made by either the parent or the LEA, the child must remain in the interim alternative educational setting pending the decision of the hearing officer or until the expiration of the time period specified in § 300.530(c) or (g), whichever occurs first, unless the parent and the SEA or LEA agree otherwise.

§ 300.534 Protections for children not determined eligible for special education and related services.

(a) General. A child who has not been determined to be eligible for special education and related services under this part and who has engaged in behavior that violated a code of student conduct, may assert any of the protections provided for in this part if the public agency had knowledge (as determined in accordance with paragraph (b) of this section) that the child was a child with a disability before the behavior that precipitated the disciplinary action occurred.

(b) Basis of knowledge. A public agency must be deemed to have knowledge that a child is a child with a disability if before the behavior that precipitated the disciplinary action occurred—

(1) The parent of the child expressed concern in writing to supervisory or administrative personnel of the appropriate educational agency, or a teacher of the child, that the child is in need of special education and related services;

(2) The parent of the child requested an evaluation of the child pursuant to §§ 300.300 through 300.311; or

(3) The teacher of the child, or other personnel of the LEA, expressed specific concerns about a pattern of behavior demonstrated by the child directly to the director of special education of the agency or to other supervisory personnel of the agency.

(c) Exception. A public agency would not be deemed to have knowledge under paragraph (b) of this section if—

(1) The parent of the child—

(i) Has not allowed an evaluation of the child pursuant to §§ 300.300 through 300.311; or

(ii) Has refused services under this part; or

(2) The child has been evaluated in accordance with §§ 300.300 through 300.311 and determined to not be a child with a disability under this part.

(d) Conditions that apply if no basis of knowledge. (1) If a public agency does not have knowledge that a child is a child with a disability (in accordance with paragraphs (b) and (c) of this section) prior to taking disciplinary measures against the child, the child may be subjected to the disciplinary measures applied to children without disabilities who engage in comparable behaviors consistent with paragraph (d)(2) of this section.

(2)(i) If a request is made for an evaluation of a child during the time period in which the child is subjected to disciplinary measures under § 300.530, the evaluation must be conducted in an expedited manner.

(ii) Until the evaluation is completed, the child remains in the educational placement determined by school authorities, which can include suspension or expulsion without educational services.

(iii) If the child is determined to be a child with a disability, taking into consideration information from the evaluation conducted by the agency and information provided by the parents, the agency must provide special education and related services in accordance with this part, including the requirements of §§ 300.530 through 300.536 and section 612(a)(1)(A) of the Act.

§ 300.535 Referral to and action by law enforcement and judicial authorities.

(a) Rule of construction. Nothing in this part prohibits an agency from reporting a crime committed by a child with a disability to appropriate authorities or prevents State law enforcement and judicial authorities from exercising their responsibilities with regard to the application of Federal and State law to crimes committed by a child with a disability.

(b) Transmittal of records. (1) An agency reporting a crime committed by a child with a disability must ensure that copies of the special education and disciplinary records of the child are transmitted for consideration by the appropriate authorities to whom the agency reports the crime.

(2) An agency reporting a crime under this section may transmit copies of the child's special education and disciplinary records only to the extent that the transmission is permitted by the Family Educational Rights and Privacy Act.

§ 300.536 Change of placement because of disciplinary removals.

(a) For purposes of removals of a child with a disability from the child's current educational placement under §§ 300.530 through 300.535, a change of placement occurs if—

(1) The removal is for more than 10 consecutive school days; or

(2) The child has been subjected to a series of removals that constitute a pattern—

(i) Because the series of removals total more than 10 school days in a school year;

(ii) Because the child's behavior is substantially similar to the child's behavior in previous incidents that resulted in the series of removals; and

(iii) Because of such additional factors as the length of each removal, the total amount of time the child has been removed, and the proximity of the removals to one another.

(b)(1) The public agency determines on a case-by-case basis whether a pattern of removals constitutes a change of placement.

(2) This determination is subject to review through due process and judicial proceedings.

§ 300.537 State enforcement mechanisms.

Notwithstanding §§ 300.506(b)(7) and 300.510(d)(2), which provide for judicial enforcement of a written agreement reached as a result of mediation or a resolution meeting, there is nothing in this part that would prevent the SEA from using other mechanisms to seek enforcement of that agreement, provided that use of those mechanisms is not mandatory and does not delay or deny a party the right to seek enforcement of the written agreement in a State court of competent jurisdiction or in a district court of the United States.

§§ 300.538–300.599 [Reserved]

SUBPART F MONITORING, ENFORCEMENT, CONFIDENTIALITY, AND PROGRAM INFORMATION
MONITORING, TECHNICAL ASSISTANCE, AND ENFORCEMENT

§ 300.600 State monitoring and enforcement.

(a) The State must monitor the implementation of this part, enforce this part in accordance with § 300.604(a)(1) and (a)(3), (b)(2)(i) and (b)(2)(v), and (c)(2), and annually report on performance under this part.

(b) The primary focus of the State's monitoring activities must be on—

(1) Improving educational results and functional outcomes for all children with disabilities; and

(2) Ensuring that public agencies meet the program requirements under Part B of the Act, with a particular emphasis on those requirements that are most closely related to improving educational results for children with disabilities.

(c) As a part of its responsibilities under paragraph (a) of this section, the State must use quantifiable indicators and such qualitative indicators as are needed to adequately measure performance in the priority areas identified in paragraph (d) of this section, and the indicators established by the Secretary for the State performance plans.

(d) The State must monitor the LEAs located in the State, using quantifiable indicators in each of the following priority areas, and using such qualitative indicators as are needed to adequately measure performance in those areas:

(1) Provision of FAPE in the least restrictive environment.

(2) State exercise of general supervision, including child find, effective monitoring, the use of resolution meetings, mediation, and a system of transition services as defined in § 300.43 and in *20 U.S.C. 1437*(a)(9).

(3) Disproportionate representation of racial and ethnic groups in special education and related services, to the extent the representation is the result of inappropriate identification.

(Approved by the Office of Management and Budget under control number 1820-0624)

§ 300.601 State performance plans and data collection.

(a) *General.* Not later than December 3, 2005, each State must have in place a performance plan that evaluates the State's efforts to implement the requirements and purposes of Part B of the Act, and describes how the State will improve such implementation.

(1) Each State must submit the State's performance plan to the Secretary for approval in accordance with the approval process described in section 616(c) of the Act.

(2) Each State must review its State performance plan at least once every six years, and submit any amendments to the Secretary.

(3) As part of the State performance plan, each State must establish measurable and rigorous targets for the indicators established by the Secretary under the priority areas described in § 300.600(d).

(b) *Data collection.* (1) Each State must collect valid and reliable information as needed to report annually to the Secretary on the indicators established by the Secretary for the State performance plans.

(2) If the Secretary permits States to collect data on specific indicators through State monitoring or sampling, and the State collects the data through State monitoring or

sampling, the State must collect data on those indicators for each LEA at least once during the period of the State performance plan.

(3) Nothing in Part B of the Act shall be construed to authorize the development of a nationwide database of personally identifiable information on individuals involved in studies or other collections of data under Part B of the Act.

(Approved by the Office of Management and Budget under control number 1820-0624)

§ 300.602 State use of targets and reporting.

(a) *General.* Each State must use the targets established in the State's performance plan under § 300.601 and the priority areas described in § 300.600(d) to analyze the performance of each LEA.

(b) *Public reporting and privacy*—(1) *Public report.* (i) Subject to paragraph (b)(1)(ii) of this section, the State must—

(A) Report annually to the public on the performance of each LEA located in the State on the targets in the State's performance plan; and

(B) Make the State's performance plan available through public means, including by posting on the Web site of the SEA, distribution to the media, and distribution through public agencies.

(ii) If the State, in meeting the requirements of paragraph (b)(1)(i) of this section, collects performance data through State monitoring or sampling, the State must include in its report under paragraph (b)(1)(i)(A) of this section the most recently available performance data on each LEA, and the date the data were obtained.

(2) *State performance report.* The State must report annually to the Secretary on the performance of the State under the State's performance plan.

(3) *Privacy.* The State must not report to the public or the Secretary any information on performance that would result in the disclosure of personally identifiable information about individual children, or where the available data are insufficient to yield statistically reliable information.

(Approved by the Office of Management and Budget under control number 1820-0624)

§ 300.603 Secretary's review and determination regarding State performance.

(a) *Review.* The Secretary annually reviews the State's performance report submitted pursuant to § 300.602(b)(2).

(b) *Determination*—(1) *General.* Based on the information provided by the State in the State's annual performance report, information obtained through monitoring visits, and any other public information made available, the Secretary determines if the State—

(i) Meets the requirements and purposes of Part B of the Act;

(ii) Needs assistance in implementing the requirements of Part B of the Act;

(iii) Needs intervention in implementing the requirements of Part B of the Act; or

(iv) Needs substantial intervention in implementing the requirements of Part B of the Act.

(2) *Notice and opportunity for a hearing.* (i) For determinations made under paragraphs (b)(1)(iii) and (b)(1)(iv) of this section, the Secretary provides reasonable notice and an opportunity for a hearing on those determinations.

(ii) The hearing described in paragraph (b)(2) of this section consists of an opportunity to meet with the Assistant Secretary for Special Education and Rehabilitative Services to demonstrate why the Department should not make the determination described in paragraph (b)(1) of this section.

§ 300.604   Enforcement.

(a) Needs assistance. If the Secretary determines, for two consecutive years, that a State needs assistance under § 300.603(b)(1)(ii) in implementing the requirements of Part B of the Act, the Secretary takes one or more of the following actions:

(1) Advises the State of available sources of technical assistance that may help the State address the areas in which the State needs assistance, which may include assistance from the Office of Special Education Programs, other offices of the Department of Education, other Federal agencies, technical assistance providers approved by the Secretary, and other federally funded nonprofit agencies, and requires the State to work with appropriate entities. Such technical assistance may include—

(i) The provision of advice by experts to address the areas in which the State needs assistance, including explicit plans for addressing the area for concern within a specified period of time;

(ii) Assistance in identifying and implementing professional development, instructional strategies, and methods of instruction that are based on scientifically based research;

(iii) Designating and using distinguished superintendents, principals, special education administrators, special education teachers, and other teachers to provide advice, technical assistance, and support; and

(iv) Devising additional approaches to providing technical assistance, such as collaborating with institutions of higher education, educational service agencies, national centers of technical assistance supported under Part D of the Act, and private providers of scientifically based technical assistance.

(2) Directs the use of State-level funds under section 611(e) of the Act on the area or areas in which the State needs assistance.

(3) Identifies the State as a high-risk grantee and imposes special conditions on the State's grant under Part B of the Act.

(b) Needs intervention. If the Secretary determines, for three or more consecutive years, that a State needs intervention under § 300.603(b)(1)(iii) in implementing the requirements of Part B of the Act, the following shall apply:

(1) The Secretary may take any of the actions described in paragraph (a) of this section.

(2) The Secretary takes one or more of the following actions:

(i) Requires the State to prepare a corrective action plan or improvement plan if the Secretary determines that the State should be able to correct the problem within one year.

(ii) Requires the State to enter into a compliance agreement under section 457 of the General Education Provisions Act, as amended, *20 U.S.C. 1221* et seq. (GEPA), if the Secretary has reason to believe that the State cannot correct the problem within one year.

(iii) For each year of the determination, withholds not less than 20 percent and not more than 50 percent of the State's funds under section 611(e) of the Act, until the Secretary determines the State has sufficiently addressed the areas in which the State needs intervention.

(iv) Seeks to recover funds under section 452 of GEPA.

(v) Withholds, in whole or in part, any further payments to the State under Part B of the Act.

(vi) Refers the matter for appropriate enforcement action, which may include referral to the Department of Justice.

(c) Needs substantial intervention. Notwithstanding paragraph (a) or (b) of this section, at any time that the Secretary determines that a State needs substantial intervention in implementing the requirements of Part B of the Act or that there is a substantial failure to comply with any condition of an SEA's or LEA's eligibility under Part B of the Act, the Secretary takes one or more of the following actions:

(1) Recovers funds under section 452 of GEPA.

(2) Withholds, in whole or in part, any further payments to the State under Part B of the Act.

(3) Refers the case to the Office of the Inspector General at the Department of Education.

(4) Refers the matter for appropriate enforcement action, which may include referral to the Department of Justice.

(d) Report to Congress. The Secretary reports to the Committee on Education and the Workforce of the House of Representatives and the Committee on Health, Education, Labor, and Pensions of the Senate within 30 days of taking enforcement action pursuant to paragraph (a), (b), or (c) of this section, on the specific action taken and the reasons why enforcement action was taken.

§ 300.605 Withholding funds.

(a) Opportunity for hearing. Prior to withholding any funds under Part B of the Act, the Secretary provides reasonable notice and an opportunity for a hearing to the SEA involved, pursuant to the procedures in §§ 300.180 through 300.183.

(b) Suspension. Pending the outcome of any hearing to withhold payments under paragraph (a) of this section, the Secretary may suspend payments to a recipient, suspend the authority of the recipient to obligate funds under Part B of the Act, or both, after the recipient has been given reasonable notice and an opportunity to show cause why future payments or authority to obligate funds under Part B of the Act should not be suspended.

(c) Nature of withholding. (1) If the Secretary determines that it is appropriate to withhold further payments under § 300.604(b)(2) or (c)(2), the Secretary may determine—

(i) That the withholding will be limited to programs or projects, or portions of programs or projects, that affected the Secretary's determination under § 300.603(b)(1); or

(ii) That the SEA must not make further payments under Part B of the Act to specified State agencies or LEAs that caused or were involved in the Secretary's determination under § 300.603(b)(1).

(2) Until the Secretary is satisfied that the condition that caused the initial withholding has been substantially rectified—

(i) Payments to the State under Part B of the Act must be withheld in whole or in part; and

(ii) Payments by the SEA under Part B of the Act must be limited to State agencies and LEAs whose actions did not cause or were not involved in the Secretary's determination under § 300.603(b)(1), as the case may be.

§ 300.606   Public attention.

Any State that has received notice under §§ 300.603(b)(1)(ii) through (iv) must, by means of a public notice, take such measures as may be necessary to notify the public within the State of the pendency of an action taken pursuant to § 300.604.

§ 300.607   Divided State agency responsibility.

For purposes of this subpart, if responsibility for ensuring that the requirements of Part B of the Act are met with respect to children with disabilities who are convicted as adults under State law and incarcerated in adult prisons is assigned to a public agency other than the SEA pursuant to § 300.149(d), and if the Secretary finds that the failure to comply substantially with the provisions of Part B of the Act are related to a failure by the public agency, the Secretary takes appropriate corrective action to ensure compliance with Part B of the Act, except that—

(a) Any reduction or withholding of payments to the State under § 300.604 must be proportionate to the total funds allotted under section 611 of the Act to the State as the number of eligible children with disabilities in adult prisons under the supervision of the other public agency is proportionate to the number of eligible individuals with disabilities in the State under the supervision of the SEA; and

(b) Any withholding of funds under § 300.604 must be limited to the specific agency responsible for the failure to comply with Part B of the Act.

§ 300.608   State enforcement.

(a) If an SEA determines that an LEA is not meeting the requirements of Part B of the Act, including the targets in the State's performance plan, the SEA must prohibit the LEA from reducing the LEA's maintenance of effort under § 300.203 for any fiscal year.

(b) Nothing in this subpart shall be construed to restrict a State from utilizing any other authority available to it to monitor and enforce the requirements of Part B of the Act.

§ 300.609   Rule of construction.

Nothing in this subpart shall be construed to restrict the Secretary from utilizing any authority under GEPA, including the provisions in 34 CFR parts 76, 77, 80, and 81 to monitor and enforce the requirements of the Act, including the imposition of special conditions under *34 CFR 80.12*.

CONFIDENTIALITY OF INFORMATION

§ 300.610   Confidentiality.

The Secretary takes appropriate action, in accordance with section 444 of GEPA, to ensure the protection of the confidentiality of any personally identifiable data, information, and records collected or maintained by the Secretary and by SEAs and LEAs pursuant to Part B of the Act, and consistent with §§ 300.611 through 300.627.

§ 300.611   Definitions.

As used in §§ 300.611 through 300.625—

(a) Destruction means physical destruction or removal of personal identifiers from information so that the information is no longer personally identifiable.

(b) Education records means the type of records covered under the definition of "education records" in 34 CFR part 99 (the regulations implementing the Family Educational Rights and Privacy Act of 1974, *20 U.S.C. 1232g* (FERPA)).

(c) Participating agency means any agency or institution that collects, maintains, or uses personally identifiable information, or from which information is obtained, under Part B of the Act.

§ 300.612   Notice to parents.

(a) The SEA must give notice that is adequate to fully inform parents about the requirements of § 300.123, including—

(1) A description of the extent that the notice is given in the native languages of the various population groups in the State;

(2) A description of the children on whom personally identifiable information is maintained, the types of information sought, the methods the State intends to use in gathering the information (including the sources from whom information is gathered), and the uses to be made of the information;

(3) A summary of the policies and procedures that participating agencies must follow regarding storage, disclosure to third parties, retention, and destruction of personally identifiable information; and

(4) A description of all of the rights of parents and children regarding this information, including the rights under FERPA and implementing regulations in 34 CFR part 99.

(b) Before any major identification, location, or evaluation activity, the notice must be published or announced in newspapers or other media, or both, with circulation adequate to notify parents throughout the State of the activity.

§ 300.613   Access rights.

(a) Each participating agency must permit parents to inspect and review any education records relating to their children that are collected, maintained, or used by the agency under this part. The agency must comply with a request without unnecessary delay and before any meeting regarding an IEP, or any hearing pursuant to § 300.507 or §§ 300.530 through 300.532, or resolution session pursuant to § 300.510, and in no case more than 45 days after the request has been made.

(b) The right to inspect and review education records under this section includes—

(1) The right to a response from the participating agency to reasonable requests for explanations and interpretations of the records;

(2) The right to request that the agency provide copies of the records containing the information if failure to provide those copies would effectively prevent the parent from exercising the right to inspect and review the records; and

(3) The right to have a representative of the parent inspect and review the records.

(c) An agency may presume that the parent has authority to inspect and review records relating to his or her child unless the agency has been advised that the parent does not have the authority under applicable State law governing such matters as guardianship, separation, and divorce.

§ 300.614   Record of access.

Each participating agency must keep a record of parties obtaining access to education records collected, maintained, or used under Part B of the Act (except access by parents and authorized employees of the participating agency), including the name of the party, the date access was given, and the purpose for which the party is authorized to use the records.

§ 300.615   Records on more than one child.

If any education record includes information on more than one child, the parents of those children have the right to inspect and review only the information relating to their child or to be informed of that specific information.

§ 300.616   List of types and locations of information.

Each participating agency must provide parents on request a list of the types and locations of education records collected, maintained, or used by the agency.

§ 300.617   Fees.

(a) Each participating agency may charge a fee for copies of records that are made for parents under this part if the fee does not effectively prevent the parents from exercising their right to inspect and review those records.

(b) A participating agency may not charge a fee to search for or to retrieve information under this part.

§ 300.618   Amendment of records at parent's request.

(a) A parent who believes that information in the education records collected, maintained, or used under this part is inaccurate or misleading or violates the privacy or other rights of the child may request the participating agency that maintains the information to amend the information.

(b) The agency must decide whether to amend the information in accordance with the request within a reasonable period of time of receipt of the request.

(c) If the agency decides to refuse to amend the information in accordance with the request, it must inform the parent of the refusal and advise the parent of the right to a hearing under § 300.619.

§ 300.619   Opportunity for a hearing.

The agency must, on request, provide an opportunity for a hearing to challenge information in education records to ensure that it is not inaccurate, misleading, or otherwise in violation of the privacy or other rights of the child.

§ 300.620   Result of hearing.

(a) If, as a result of the hearing, the agency decides that the information is inaccurate, misleading or otherwise in violation of the privacy or other rights of the child, it must amend the information accordingly and so inform the parent in writing.

(b) If, as a result of the hearing, the agency decides that the information is not inaccurate, misleading, or otherwise in violation of the privacy or other rights of the child, it must inform the parent of the parent's right to place in the records the agency maintains on the child a statement commenting on the information or setting forth any reasons for disagreeing with the decision of the agency.

(c) Any explanation placed in the records of the child under this section must—

(1) Be maintained by the agency as part of the records of the child as long as the record or contested portion is maintained by the agency; and

(2) If the records of the child or the contested portion is disclosed by the agency to any party, the explanation must also be disclosed to the party.

§ 300.621 Hearing procedures.

A hearing held under § 300.619 must be conducted according to the procedures in *34 CFR 99.22.*

§ 300.622 Consent.

(a) Parental consent must be obtained before personally identifiable information is disclosed to parties, other than officials of participating agencies in accordance with paragraph (b)(1) of this section, unless the information is contained in education records, and the disclosure is authorized without parental consent under 34 CFR part 99. (b)(1) Except as provided in paragraphs (b)(2) and (b)(3) of this section, parental consent is not required before personally identifiable information is released to officials of participating agencies for purposes of meeting a requirement of this part.

(2) Parental consent, or the consent of an eligible child who has reached the age of majority under State law, must be obtained before personally identifiable information is released to officials of participating agencies providing or paying for transition services in accordance with § 300.321(b)(3).

(3) If a child is enrolled, or is going to enroll in a private school that is not located in the LEA of the parent's residence, parental consent must be obtained before any personally identifiable information about the child is released between officials in the LEA where the private school is located and officials in the LEA of the parent's residence.

§ 300.623 Safeguards.

(a) Each participating agency must protect the confidentiality of personally identifiable information at collection, storage, disclosure, and destruction stages.

(b) One official at each participating agency must assume responsibility for ensuring the confidentiality of any personally identifiable information.

(c) All persons collecting or using personally identifiable information must receive training or instruction regarding the State's policies and procedures under § 300.123 and 34 CFR part 99.

(d) Each participating agency must maintain, for public inspection, a current listing of the names and positions of those employees within the agency who may have access to personally identifiable information.

§ 300.624 Destruction of information.

(a) The public agency must inform parents when personally identifiable information collected, maintained, or used under this part is no longer needed to provide educational services to the child.

(b) The information must be destroyed at the request of the parents. However, a permanent record of a student's name, address, and phone number, his or her grades, attendance record, classes attended, grade level completed, and year completed may be maintained without time limitation.

§ 300.625 Children's rights.

(a) The SEA must have in effect policies and procedures regarding the extent to which children are afforded rights of privacy similar to those afforded to parents, taking into consideration the age of the child and type or severity of disability.

(b) Under the regulations for FERPA in *34 CFR 99.5(a)*, the rights of parents regarding education records are transferred to the student at age 18.

(c) If the rights accorded to parents under Part B of the Act are transferred to a student who reaches the age of majority, consistent with § 300.520, the rights regarding educational records in §§ 300.613 through 300.624 must also be transferred to the student. However, the public agency must provide any notice required under section 615 of the Act to the student and the parents.

§ 300.626 Enforcement.

The SEA must have in effect the policies and procedures, including sanctions that the State uses, to ensure that its policies and procedures consistent with §§ 300.611 through 300.625 are followed and that the requirements of the Act and the regulations in this part are met.

§ 300.627 Department use of personally identifiable information.

If the Department or its authorized representatives collect any personally identifiable information regarding children with disabilities that is not subject to the Privacy Act of 1974, *5 U.S.C. 552a*, the Secretary applies the requirements of *5 U.S.C.* 552a(b)(1) and (b)(2), 552a(b)(4) through (b)(11); 552a(c) through 552a(e)(3)(B); 552a(e)(3)(D); 552a(e)(5) through (e)(10); 552a(h); 552a(m); and 552a(n); and the regulations implementing those provisions in 34 CFR part 5b.

REPORTS — PROGRAM INFORMATION

§ 300.640 Annual report of children served — report requirement.

(a) The SEA must annually report to the Secretary on the information required by section 618 of the Act at the times specified by the Secretary.

(b) The SEA must submit the report on forms provided by the Secretary.

(Approved by the Office of Management and Budget under control numbers 1820-0030, 1820-0043, 1820-0659, 1820-0621, 1820-0518, 1820-0521, 1820-0517, and 1820-0677)

§ 300.641 Annual report of children served — information required in the report.

(a) For purposes of the annual report required by section 618 of the Act and § 300.640, the State and the Secretary of the Interior must count and report the number of children with disabilities receiving special education and related services on any date between October 1 and December 1 of each year.

(b) For the purpose of this reporting provision, a child's age is the child's actual age on the date of the child count.

(c) The SEA may not report a child under more than one disability category.

(d) If a child with a disability has more than one disability, the SEA must report that child in accordance with the following procedure:

(1) If a child has only two disabilities and those disabilities are deafness and blindness, and the child is not reported as having a developmental delay, that child must be reported under the category "deaf-blindness."

(2) A child who has more than one disability and is not reported as having deaf-blindness or as having a developmental delay must be reported under the category "multiple disabilities."

(Approved by the Office of Management and Budget under control numbers 1820-0030, 1820-0043, 1820-0621, 1820-0521, and 1820-0517)

§ 300.642 Data reporting.

(a) Protection of personally identifiable data. The data described in section 618(a) of the Act and in § 300.641 must be publicly reported by each State in a manner that does not result in disclosure of data identifiable to individual children.

(b) Sampling. The Secretary may permit States and the Secretary of the Interior to obtain data in section 618(a) of the Act through sampling.

(Approved by the Office of Management and Budget under control numbers 1820-0030, 1820-0043, 1820-0518, 1820-0521, and 1820-0517)

§ 300.643 Annual report of children served — certification.

The SEA must include in its report a certification signed by an authorized official of the agency that the information provided under § 300.640 is an accurate and unduplicated count of children with disabilities receiving special education and related services on the dates in question.

(Approved by the Office of Management and Budget under control numbers 1820-0030 and 1820-0043)

§ 300.644 Annual report of children served — criteria for counting children.

The SEA may include in its report children with disabilities who are enrolled in a school or program that is operated or supported by a public agency, and that—

(a) Provides them with both special education and related services that meet State standards;

(b) Provides them only with special education, if a related service is not required, that meets State standards; or

(c) In the case of children with disabilities enrolled by their parents in private schools, counts those children who are eligible under the Act and receive special education or related services or both that meet State standards under §§ 300.132 through 300.144.

(Approved by the Office of Management and Budget under control numbers 1820-0030, 1820-0043, 1820-0659, 1820-0621, 1820-0521, and 1820-0517)

§ 300.645 Annual report of children served — other responsibilities of the SEA.

In addition to meeting the other requirements of §§ 300.640 through 300.644, the SEA must —

(a) Establish procedures to be used by LEAs and other educational institutions in counting the number of children with disabilities receiving special education and related services;

(b) Set dates by which those agencies and institutions must report to the SEA to ensure that the State complies with § 300.640(a);

(c) Obtain certification from each agency and institution that an unduplicated and accurate count has been made;

(d) Aggregate the data from the count obtained from each agency and institution, and prepare the reports required under §§ 300.640 through 300.644; and

(e) Ensure that documentation is maintained that enables the State and the Secretary to audit the accuracy of the count.

(Approved by the Office of Management and Budget under control numbers 1820-0030, 1820-0043, 1820-0659, 1820-0621, 1820-0518, 1820-0521, and 1820-0517)

§ 300.646   Disproportionality.

(a) General. Each State that receives assistance under Part B of the Act, and the Secretary of the Interior, must provide for the collection and examination of data to determine if significant disproportionality based on race and ethnicity is occurring in the State and the LEAs of the State with respect to—

(1) The identification of children as children with disabilities, including the identification of children as children with disabilities in accordance with a particular impairment described in section 602(3) of the Act;

(2) The placement in particular educational settings of these children; and

(3) The incidence, duration, and type of disciplinary actions, including suspensions and expulsions.

(b) Review and revision of policies, practices, and procedures. In the case of a determination of significant disproportionality with respect to the identification of children as children with disabilities, or the placement in particular educational settings of these children, in accordance with paragraph (a) of this section, the State or the Secretary of the Interior must—

(1) Provide for the review and, if appropriate revision of the policies, procedures, and practices used in the identification or placement to ensure that the policies, procedures, and practices comply with the requirements of the Act.

(2) Require any LEA identified under paragraph (a) of this section to reserve the maximum amount of funds under section 613(f) of the Act to provide comprehensive coordinated early intervening services to serve children in the LEA, particularly, but not exclusively, children in those groups that were significantly overidentified under paragraph (a) of this section; and

(3) Require the LEA to publicly report on the revision of policies, practices, and procedures described under paragraph (b)(1) of this section.

§ 300.650

[This section was removed. See 71 FR 46540, 46753, Aug. 14, 2006.]

§ 300.651

[This section was removed. See 71 FR 46540, 46753, Aug. 14, 2006.]

§ 300.652

[This section was removed. See 71 FR 46540, 46753, Aug. 14, 2006.]

§ 300.653

[This section was removed. See 71 FR 46540, 46753, Aug. 14, 2006.]

§ 300.660

[This section was removed. See 71 FR 46540, 46753, Aug. 14, 2006.]

§ 300.661

[This section was removed. See 71 FR 46540, 46753, Aug. 14, 2006.]

§ 300.662

[This section was removed. See 71 FR 46540, 46753, Aug. 14, 2006.]

SUBPART G AUTHORIZATION, ALLOTMENT, USE OF FUNDS, AND AUTHORIZATION OF APPROPRIATIONS
ALLOTMENTS, GRANTS, AND USE OF FUNDS

§ 300.700 Grants to States.

(a) Purpose of grants. The Secretary makes grants to States, outlying areas, and freely associated States (as defined in § 300.717), and provides funds to the Secretary of the Interior, to assist them to provide special education and related services to children with disabilities in accordance with Part B of the Act.

(b) Maximum amount. The maximum amount of the grant a State may receive under section 611 of the Act is—

(1) For fiscal years 2005 and 2006—

(i) The number of children with disabilities in the State who are receiving special education and related services—

(A) Aged three through five, if the State is eligible for a grant under section 619 of the Act; and

(B) Aged 6 through 21; multiplied by—

(ii) Forty (40) percent of the average per-pupil expenditure in public elementary schools and secondary schools in the United States (as defined in § 300.717); and

(2) For fiscal year 2007 and subsequent fiscal years—

(i) The number of children with disabilities in the 2004-2005 school year in the State who received special education and related services—

(A) Aged three through five if the State is eligible for a grant under section 619 of the Act; and

(B) Aged 6 through 21; multiplied by

(ii) Forty (40) percent of the average per-pupil expenditure in public elementary schools and secondary schools in the United States (as defined in § 300.717);

(iii) Adjusted by the rate of annual change in the sum of—

(A) Eighty-five (85) percent of the State's population of children aged 3 through 21 who are of the same age as children with disabilities for whom the State ensures the availability of FAPE under Part B of the Act; and

(B) Fifteen (15) percent of the State's population of children described in paragraph (b)(2)(iii)(A) of this section who are living in poverty.

§ 300.701 Outlying areas, freely associated States, and the Secretary of the Interior.

(a) Outlying areas and freely associated States. (1) Funds reserved. From the amount appropriated for any fiscal year under section 611(i) of the Act, the Secretary reserves not more than one percent, which must be used—

(i) To provide assistance to the outlying areas in accordance with their respective populations of individuals aged 3 through 21; and

(ii) To provide each freely associated State a grant in the amount that the freely associated State received for fiscal year 2003 under Part B of the Act, but only if the freely associated State—

(A) Meets the applicable requirements of Part B of the Act that apply to States.

(B) Meets the requirements in paragraph (a)(2) of this section.

(2) Application. Any freely associated State that wishes to receive funds under Part B of the Act must include, in its application for assistance—

(i) Information demonstrating that it will meet all conditions that apply to States under Part B of the Act.

(ii) An assurance that, notwithstanding any other provision of Part B of the Act, it will use those funds only for the direct provision of special education and related services to children with disabilities and to enhance its capacity to make FAPE available to all children with disabilities;

(iii) The identity of the source and amount of funds, in addition to funds under Part B of the Act, that it will make available to ensure that FAPE is available to all children with disabilities within its jurisdiction; and

(iv) Such other information and assurances as the Secretary may require.

(3) Special rule. The provisions of Public Law 95-134, permitting the consolidation of grants by the outlying areas, do not apply to funds provided to the outlying areas or to the freely associated States under Part B of the Act.

(b) Secretary of the Interior. From the amount appropriated for any fiscal year under section 611(i) of the Act, the Secretary reserves 1.226 percent to provide assistance to the Secretary of the Interior in accordance with §§ 300.707 through 300.716.

§ 300.702 Technical assistance.

(a) In general. The Secretary may reserve not more than one-half of one percent of the amounts appropriated under Part B of the Act for each fiscal year to support technical assistance activities authorized under section 616(i) of the Act.

(b) Maximum amount. The maximum amount the Secretary may reserve under paragraph (a) of this section for any fiscal year is $ 25,000,000, cumulatively adjusted by the rate of inflation as measured by the percentage increase, if any, from the preceding fiscal year in the Consumer Price Index For All Urban Consumers, published by the Bureau of Labor Statistics of the Department of Labor.

§ 300.703 Allocations to States.

(a) General. After reserving funds for technical assistance under § 300.702, and for payments to the outlying areas, the freely associated States, and the Secretary of the Interior under § 300.701 (a) and (b) for a fiscal year, the Secretary allocates the remaining amount among the States in accordance with paragraphs (b), (c), and (d) of this section.

(b) Special rule for use of fiscal year 1999 amount. If a State received any funds under section 611 of the Act for fiscal year 1999 on the basis of children aged three through five, but does not make FAPE available to all children with disabilities aged three through five in the State in any subsequent fiscal year, the Secretary computes the State's amount for fiscal year 1999, solely for the purpose of calculating the State's allocation in that subsequent year under paragraph (c) or (d) of this section, by subtracting the amount allocated to the State for fiscal year 1999 on the basis of those children.

(c) Increase in funds. If the amount available for allocations to States under paragraph (a) of this section for a fiscal year is equal to or greater than the amount allocated to the

States under section 611 of the Act for the preceding fiscal year, those allocations are calculated as follows:

(1) Allocation of increase. —(i) General. Except as provided in paragraph (c)(2) of this section, the Secretary allocates for the fiscal year—

(A) To each State the amount the State received under this section for fiscal year 1999;

(B) Eighty-five (85) percent of any remaining funds to States on the basis of the States' relative populations of children aged 3 through 21 who are of the same age as children with disabilities for whom the State ensures the availability of FAPE under Part B of the Act; and

(C) Fifteen (15) percent of those remaining funds to States on the basis of the States' relative populations of children described in paragraph (c)(1)(i)(B) of this section who are living in poverty.

(ii) Data. For the purpose of making grants under this section, the Secretary uses the most recent population data, including data on children living in poverty, that are available and satisfactory to the Secretary.

(2) Limitations. Notwithstanding paragraph (c)(1) of this section, allocations under this section are subject to the following:

(i) Preceding year allocation. No State's allocation may be less than its allocation under section 611 of the Act for the preceding fiscal year.

(ii) Minimum. No State's allocation may be less than the greatest of—

(A) The sum of—

(1) The amount the State received under section 611 of the Act for fiscal year 1999; and

(2) One third of one percent of the amount by which the amount appropriated under section 611(i) of the Act for the fiscal year exceeds the amount appropriated for section 611 of the Act for fiscal year 1999;

(B) The sum of—

(1) The amount the State received under section 611 of the Act for the preceding fiscal year; and

(2) That amount multiplied by the percentage by which the increase in the funds appropriated for section 611 of the Act from the preceding fiscal year exceeds 1.5 percent; or

(C) The sum of—

(1) The amount the State received under section 611 of the Act for the preceding fiscal year; and

(2) That amount multiplied by 90 percent of the percentage increase in the amount appropriated for section 611 of the Act from the preceding fiscal year.

(iii) Maximum. Notwithstanding paragraph (c)(2)(ii) of t his section, no State's allocation under paragraph (a) of this section may exceed the sum of—

(A) The amount the State received under section 611 of the Act for the preceding fiscal year; and

(B) That amount multiplied by the sum of 1.5 percent and the percentage increase in the amount appropriated under section 611 of the Act from the preceding fiscal year.

(3) Ratable reduction. If the amount available for allocations to States under paragraph (c) of this section is insufficient to pay those allocations in full, those allocations are ratably reduced, subject to paragraph (c)(2)(i) of this section.

(d) *Decrease in funds.* If the amount available for allocations to States under paragraph (a) of this section for a fiscal year is less than the amount allocated to the States under section 611 of the Act for the preceding fiscal year, those allocations are calculated as follows:

(1) *Amounts greater than fiscal year 1999 allocations.* If the amount available for allocations under paragraph (a) of this section is greater than the amount allocated to the States for fiscal year 1999, each State is allocated the sum of—

(i) *1999 amount.* The amount the State received under section 611 of the Act for fiscal year 1999; and

(ii) *Remaining funds.* An amount that bears the same relation to any remaining funds as the increase the State received under section 611 of the Act for the preceding fiscal year over fiscal year 1999 bears to the total of all such increases for all States.

(2) *Amounts equal to or less than fiscal year 1999 allocations.* —(i) *General.* If the amount available for allocations under paragraph (a) of this section is equal to or less than the amount allocated to the States for fiscal year 1999, each State is allocated the amount it received for fiscal year 1999.

(ii) *Ratable reduction.* If the amount available for allocations under paragraph (d) of this section is insufficient to make the allocations described in paragraph (d)(2)(i) of this section, those allocations are ratably reduced.

§ 300.704 State-level activities.

(a) *State administration.* (1) For the purpose of administering Part B of the Act, including paragraph (c) of this section, section 619 of the Act, and the coordination of activities under Part B of the Act with, and providing technical assistance to, other programs that provide services to children with disabilities—

(i) Each State may reserve for each fiscal year not more than the maximum amount the State was eligible to reserve for State administration under section 611 of the Act for fiscal year 2004 or $ 800,000 (adjusted in accordance with paragraph (a)(2) of this section), whichever is greater; and

(ii) Each outlying area may reserve for each fiscal year not more than five percent of the amount the outlying area receives under § 300.701(a) for the fiscal year or $ 35,000, whichever is greater.

(2) For each fiscal year, beginning with fiscal year 2005, the Secretary cumulatively adjusts—

(i) The maximum amount the State was eligible to reserve for State administration under section 611 of the Act for fiscal year 2004; and

(ii) $ 800,000, by the rate of inflation as measured by the percentage increase, if any, from the preceding fiscal year in the Consumer Price Index for All Urban Consumers, published by the Bureau of Labor Statistics of the Department of Labor.

(3) Prior to expenditure of funds under paragraph (a) of this section, the State must certify to the Secretary that the arrangements to establish responsibility for services pursuant to section 612(a)(12)(A) of the Act are current.

(4) Funds reserved under paragraph (a)(1) of this section may be used for the administration of Part C of the Act, if the SEA is the lead agency for the State under that Part.

(b) *Other State-level activities.* (1) States may reserve a portion of their allocations for other State-level activities. The maximum amount that a State may reserve for other State-level activities is as follows:

(i) If the amount that the State sets aside for State administration under paragraph

(a) of this section is greater than $ 850,000 and the State opts to finance a high cost fund under paragraph (c) of this section:

(A) For fiscal years 2005 and 2006, 10 percent of the State's allocation under § 300.703.

(B) For fiscal year 2007 and subsequent fiscal years, an amount equal to 10 percent of the State's allocation for fiscal year 2006 under § 300.703 adjusted cumulatively for inflation.

(ii) If the amount that the State sets aside for State administration under paragraph (a) of this section is greater than $ 850,000 and the State opts not to finance a high cost fund under paragraph (c) of this section—

(A) For fiscal years 2005 and 2006, nine percent of the State's allocation under § 300.703.

(B) For fiscal year 2007 and subsequent fiscal years, an amount equal to nine percent of the State's allocation for fiscal year 2006 adjusted cumulatively for inflation.

(iii) If the amount that the State sets aside for State administration under paragraph (a) of this section is less than or equal to $ 850,000 and the State opts to finance a high cost fund under paragraph (c) of this section:

(A) For fiscal years 2005 and 2006, 10.5 percent of the State's allocation under § 300.703.

(B) For fiscal year 2007 and subsequent fiscal years, an amount equal to 10.5 percent of the State's allocation for fiscal year 2006 under § 300.703 adjusted cumulatively for inflation.

(iv) If the amount that the State sets aside for State administration under paragraph (a) of this section is equal to or less than $ 850,000 and the State opts not to finance a high cost fund under paragraph (c) of this section:

(A) For fiscal years 2005 and 2006, nine and one-half percent of the State's allocation under § 300.703.

(B) For fiscal year 2007 and subsequent fiscal years, an amount equal to nine and one-half percent of the State's allocation for fiscal year 2006 under § 300.703 adjusted cumulatively for inflation.

(2) The adjustment for inflation is the rate of inflation as measured by the percentage of increase, if any, from the preceding fiscal year in the Consumer Price Index for All Urban Consumers, published by the Bureau of Labor Statistics of the Department of Labor.

(3) Some portion of the funds reserved under paragraph (b)(1) of this section must be used to carry out the following activities:

(i) For monitoring, enforcement, and complaint investigation; and

(ii) To establish and implement the mediation process required by section 615(e) of the Act, including providing for the costs of mediators and support personnel;

(4) Funds reserved under paragraph (b)(1) of this section also may be used to carry out the following activities:

(i) For support and direct services, including technical assistance, personnel preparation, and professional development and training;

(ii) To support paperwork reduction activities, including expanding the use of technology in the IEP process;

(iii) To assist LEAs in providing positive behavioral interventions and supports and mental health services for children with disabilities;

(iv) To improve the use of technology in the classroom by children with disabilities to enhance learning;

(v) To support the use of technology, including technology with universal design principles and assistive technology devices, to maximize accessibility to the general education curriculum for children with disabilities;

(vi) Development and implementation of transition programs, including coordination of services with agencies involved in supporting the transition of students with disabilities to postsecondary activities;

(vii) To assist LEAs in meeting personnel shortages;

(viii) To support capacity building activities and improve the delivery of services by LEAs to improve results for children with disabilities;

(ix) Alternative programming for children with disabilities who have been expelled from school, and services for children with disabilities in correctional facilities, children enrolled in State-operated or State-supported schools, and children with disabilities in charter schools;

(x) To support the development and provision of appropriate accommodations for children with disabilities, or the development and provision of alternate assessments that are valid and reliable for assessing the performance of children with disabilities, in accordance with sections 1111(b) and 6111 of the ESEA; and

(xi) To provide technical assistance to schools and LEAs, and direct services, including supplemental educational services as defined in section 1116(e) of the ESEA to children with disabilities, in schools or LEAs identified for improvement under section 1116 of the ESEA on the sole basis of the assessment results of the disaggregated subgroup of children with disabilities, including providing professional development to special and regular education teachers, who teach children with disabilities, based on scientifically based research to improve educational instruction, in order to improve academic achievement to meet or exceed the objectives established by the State under section 1111(b)(2)(G) of the ESEA.

(c) *Local educational agency high cost fund.* (1) *In general*—

(i) For the purpose of assisting LEAs (including a charter school that is an LEA or a consortium of LEAs) in addressing the needs of high need children with disabilities, each State has the option to reserve for each fiscal year 10 percent of the amount of funds the State reserves for other State-level activities under paragraph (b)(1) of this section—

(A) To finance and make disbursements from the high cost fund to LEAs in accordance with paragraph (c) of this section during the first and succeeding fiscal years of the high cost fund; and

(B) To support innovative and effective ways of cost sharing by the State, by an LEA, or among a consortium of LEAs, as determined by the State in coordination with representatives from LEAs, subject to paragraph (c)(2)(ii) of this section.

(ii) For purposes of paragraph (c) of this section, local educational agency includes a charter school that is an LEA, or a consortium of LEAs.

(2)(i) A State must not use any of the funds the State reserves pursuant to paragraph (c)(1)(i) of this section, which are solely for disbursement to LEAs, for costs associated with establishing, supporting, and otherwise administering the fund. The State may use funds the State reserves under paragraph (a) of this section for those administrative costs.

(ii) A State must not use more than 5 percent of the funds the State reserves pursuant to paragraph (c)(1)(i) of this section for each fiscal year to support innovative and effective ways of cost sharing among consortia of LEAs.

(3)(i) The SEA must develop, not later than 90 days after the State reserves funds under paragraph (c)(1)(i) of this section, annually review, and amend as necessary, a State plan for the high cost fund. Such State plan must—

(A) Establish, in consultation and coordination with representatives from LEAs, a definition of a high need child with a disability that, at a minimum—

(1) Addresses the financial impact a high need child with a disability has on the budget of the child's LEA; and

(2) Ensures that the cost of the high need child with a disability is greater than 3 times the average per pupil expenditure (as defined in section 9101 of the ESEA) in that State;

(B) Establish eligibility criteria for the participation of an LEA that, at a minimum, take into account the number and percentage of high need children with disabilities served by an LEA;

(C) Establish criteria to ensure that placements supported by the fund are consistent with the requirements of §§ 300.114 through 300.118;

(D) Develop a funding mechanism that provides distributions each fiscal year to LEAs that meet the criteria developed by the State under paragraph(c)(3)(i)(B) of this section;

(E) Establish an annual schedule by which the SEA must make its distributions from the high cost fund each fiscal year; and

(F) If the State elects to reserve funds for supporting innovative and effective ways of cost sharing under paragraph (c)(1)(i)(B) of this section, describe how these funds will be used.

(ii) The State must make its final State plan available to the public not less than 30 days before the beginning of the school year, including dissemination of such information on the State Web site.

(4)(i) Each SEA must make all annual disbursements from the high cost fund established under paragraph (c)(1)(i) of this section in accordance with the State plan published pursuant to paragraph (c)(3) of this section.

(ii) The costs associated with educating a high need child with a disability, as defined under paragraph (c)(3)(i)(A) of this section, are only those costs associated with providing direct special education and related services to the child that are identified in that child's IEP, including the cost of room and board for a residential placement determined necessary, consistent with § 300.114, to implement a child's IEP.

(iii) The funds in the high cost fund remain under the control of the State until disbursed to an LEA to support a specific child who qualifies under the State plan for the high cost funds or distributed to LEAs, consistent with paragraph (c)(9) of this section.

(5) The disbursements under paragraph (c)(4) of this section must not be used to support legal fees, court costs, or other costs associated with a cause of action brought on behalf of a child with a disability to ensure FAPE for such child.

(6) Nothing in paragraph (c) of this section—

(i) Limits or conditions the right of a child with a disability who is assisted under Part B of the Act to receive FAPE pursuant to section 612(a)(1) of the Act in the least restrictive environment pursuant to section 612(a)(5) of the Act; or

(ii) Authorizes an SEA or LEA to establish a limit on what may be spent on the education of a child with a disability.

(7) Notwithstanding the provisions of paragraphs (c)(1) through (6) of this section, a

State may use funds reserved pursuant to paragraph (c)(1)(i) of this section for implementing a placement neutral cost sharing and reimbursement program of high need, low incidence, catastrophic, or extraordinary aid to LEAs that provides services to high need children based on eligibility criteria for such programs that were created not later than January 1, 2004, and are currently in operation, if such program serves children that meet the requirement of the definition of a high need child with a disability as described in paragraph (c)(3)(i)(A) of this section.

(8) Disbursements provided under paragraph (c) of this section must not be used to pay costs that otherwise would be reimbursed as medical assistance for a child with a disability under the State Medicaid program under Title XIX of the Social Security Act.

(9) Funds reserved under paragraph (c)(1)(i) of this section from the appropriation for any fiscal year, but not expended pursuant to paragraph (c)(4) of this section before the beginning of their last year of availability for obligation, must be allocated to LEAs in the same manner as other funds from the appropriation for that fiscal year are allocated to LEAs under § 300.705 during their final year of availability.

(d) *Inapplicability of certain prohibitions.* A State may use funds the State reserves under paragraphs (a) and (b) of this section without regard to—

(1) The prohibition on commingling of funds in § 300.162(b).

(2) The prohibition on supplanting other funds in § 300.162(c).

(e) *Special rule for increasing funds.* A State may use funds the State reserves under paragraph (a)(1) of this section as a result of inflationary increases under paragraph (a)(2) of this section to carry out activities authorized under paragraph(b)(4)(i), (iii), (vii), or (viii) of this section.

(f) *Flexibility in using funds for Part C.* Any State eligible to receive a grant under section 619 of the Act may use funds made available under paragraph (a)(1) of this section, § 300.705(c), or § 300.814(e) to develop and implement a State policy jointly with the lead agency under Part C of the Act and the SEA to provide early intervention services (which must include an educational component that promotes school readiness and incorporates preliteracy, language, and numeracy skills) in accordance with Part C of the Act to children with disabilities who are eligible for services under section 619 of the Act and who previously received services under Part C of the Act until the children enter, or are eligible under State law to enter, kindergarten, or elementary school as appropriate.

(Approved by the Office of Management and Budget under control number 1820-0600)

§ 300.705 Subgrants to LEAs.

(a) *Subgrants required.* Each State that receives a grant under section 611 of the Act for any fiscal year must distribute any funds the State does not reserve under § 300.704 to LEAs (including public charter schools that operate as LEAs) in the State that have established their eligibility under section 613 of the Act for use in accordance with Part B of the Act.

(b) *Allocations to LEAs.* For each fiscal year for which funds are allocated to States under § 300.703, each State shall allocate funds as follows:

(1) *Base payments.* The State first must award each LEA described in paragraph (a) of this section the amount the LEA would have received under section 611 of the Act for fiscal year 1999, if the State had distributed 75 percent of its grant for that year under section 611(d) of the Act, as that section was then in effect.

(2) *Base payment adjustments.* For any fiscal year after 1999—

(i) If a new LEA is created, the State must divide the base allocation determined under paragraph (b)(1) of this section for the LEAs that would have been responsible for serving children with disabilities now being served by the new LEA, among the new LEA and affected LEAs based on the relative numbers of children with disabilities ages 3 through 21, or ages 6 through 21 if a State has had its payment reduced under § 300.703(b), currently provided special education by each of the LEAs;

(ii) If one or more LEAs are combined into a single new LEA, the State must combine the base allocations of the merged LEAs; and

(iii) If, for two or more LEAs, geographic boundaries or administrative responsibility for providing services to children with disabilities ages 3 through 21 change, the base allocations of affected LEAs must be redistributed among affected LEAs based on the relative numbers of children with disabilities ages 3 through 21, or ages 6 through 21 if a State has had its payment reduced under § 300.703(b), currently provided special education by each affected LEA.

(3) Allocation of remaining funds. After making allocations under paragraph (b)(1) of this section, as adjusted by paragraph (b)(2) of this section, the State must—

(i) Allocate 85 percent of any remaining funds to those LEAs on the basis of the relative numbers of children enrolled in public and private elementary schools and secondary schools within the LEA's jurisdiction; and

(ii) Allocate 15 percent of those remaining funds to those LEAs in accordance with their relative numbers of children living in poverty, as determined by the SEA.

(c) Reallocation of funds. If an SEA determines that an LEA is adequately providing FAPE to all children with disabilities residing in the area served by that agency with State and local funds, the SEA may reallocate any portion of the funds under this part that are not needed by that LEA to provide FAPE to other LEAs in the State that are not adequately providing special education and related services to all children with disabilities residing in the areas served by those other LEAs.

(Approved by the Office of Management and Budget under control number 1820-0030)

§ 300.706

[This section was removed and reserved. See 71 FR 46540, 46753, Aug. 14, 2006.]

SECRETARY OF THE INTERIOR

§ 300.707 Use of amounts by Secretary of the Interior.

(a) Definitions. For purposes of §§ 300.707 through 300.716, the following definitions apply:

(1) Reservation means Indian Country as defined in *18 U.S.C. 1151*.

(2) Tribal governing body has the definition given that term in *25 U.S.C. 2021*(19).

(b) Provision of amounts for assistance. The Secretary provides amounts to the Secretary of the Interior to meet the need for assistance for the education of children with disabilities on reservations aged 5 to 21, inclusive, enrolled in elementary schools and secondary schools for Indian children operated or funded by the Secretary of the Interior. The amount of the payment for any fiscal year is equal to 80 percent of the amount allotted under section 611(b)(2) of the Act for that fiscal year. Of the amount described in the preceding sentence, after the Secretary of the Interior reserves funds for administration under § 300.710, 80 percent must be allocated to such schools by July 1 of that fiscal year and 20 percent must be allocated to such schools by September 30 of that fiscal year.

(c) *Additional requirement.* With respect to all other children aged 3 to 21, inclusive, on reservations, the SEA of the State in which the reservation is located must ensure that all of the requirements of Part B of the Act are implemented.

§ 300.708　Submission of information.

The Secretary may provide the Secretary of the Interior amounts under § 300.707 for a fiscal year only if the Secretary of the Interior submits to the Secretary information that—

(a) Meets the requirements of section 612(a)(1), (3) through (9), (10)(B) through (C), (11) through (12), (14) through (16), (19), and (21) through (25) of the Act (including monitoring and evaluation activities);

(b) Meets the requirements of section 612(b) and (e) of the Act;

(c) Meets the requirements of section 613(a)(1), (2)(A)(i), (7) through (9) and section 613(i) of the Act (references to LEAs in these sections must be read as references to elementary schools and secondary schools for Indian children operated or funded by the Secretary of the Interior);

(d) Meets the requirements of section 616 of the Act that apply to States (references to LEAs in section 616 of the Act must be read as references to elementary schools and secondary schools for Indian children operated or funded by the Secretary of the Interior).

(e) Meets the requirements of this part that implement the sections of the Act listed in paragraphs (a) through (d) of this section;

(f) Includes a description of how the Secretary of the Interior will coordinate the provision of services under Part B of the Act with LEAs, tribes and tribal organizations, and other private and Federal service providers;

(g) Includes an assurance that there are public hearings, adequate notice of the hearings, and an opportunity for comment afforded to members of tribes, tribal governing bodies, and affected local school boards before the adoption of the policies, programs, and procedures related to the requirements described in paragraphs (a) through (d) of this section;

(h) Includes an assurance that the Secretary of the Interior provides the information that the Secretary may require to comply with section 618 of the Act;

(i)(1) Includes an assurance that the Secretary of the Interior and the Secretary of Health and Human Services have entered into a memorandum of agreement, to be provided to the Secretary, for the coordination of services, resources, and personnel between their respective Federal, State, and local offices and with the SEAs and LEAs and other entities to facilitate the provision of services to Indian children with disabilities residing on or near reservations.

(2) The agreement must provide for the apportionment of responsibilities and costs, including child find, evaluation, diagnosis, remediation or therapeutic measures, and (where appropriate) equipment and medical or personal supplies, as needed for a child with a disability to remain in a school or program; and

(j) Includes an assurance that the Department of the Interior will cooperate with the Department in its exercise of monitoring and oversight of the requirements in this section and §§ 300.709 through 300.711 and §§ 300.713 through 300.716, and any agreements entered into between the Secretary of the Interior and other entities under Part B of the Act, and will fulfill its duties under Part B of the Act. The Secretary withholds payments under § 300.707 with respect to the requirements described in this section in the same manner as the Secretary withholds payments under section 616(e)(6) of the Act.

§ 300.709 Public participation.

In fulfilling the requirements of § 300.708 the Secretary of the Interior must provide for public participation consistent with § 300.165.

§ 300.710 Use of funds under Part B of the Act.

(a) The Secretary of the Interior may reserve five percent of its payment under § 300.707(b) in any fiscal year, or $500,000, whichever is greater, for administrative costs in carrying out the provisions of §§ 300.707 through 300.709, 300.711, and 300.713 through 300.716.

(b) Payments to the Secretary of the Interior under § 300.712 must be used in accordance with that section.

§ 300.711 Early intervening services.

(a) The Secretary of the Interior may allow each elementary school and secondary school for Indian children operated or funded by the Secretary of the Interior to use not more than 15 percent of the amount the school receives under § 300.707(b) for any fiscal year, in combination with other amounts (which may include amounts other than education funds), to develop and implement coordinated, early intervening services, which may include interagency financing structures, for children in kindergarten through grade 12 (with a particular emphasis on children in kindergarten through grade three) who have not been identified as needing special education or related services but who need additional academic and behavioral support to succeed in a general education environment, in accordance with section 613(f) of the Act.

(b) Each elementary school and secondary school for Indian children operated or funded by the Secretary of the Interior that develops and maintains coordinated early intervening services in accordance with section 613(f) of the Act and § 300.226 must annually report to the Secretary of the Interior in accordance with section 613(f) of the Act.

§ 300.712 Payments for education and services for Indian children with disabilities aged three through five.

(a) *General.* With funds appropriated under section 611(i) of the Act, the Secretary makes payments to the Secretary of the Interior to be distributed to tribes or tribal organizations (as defined under section 4 of the Indian Self-Determination and Education Assistance Act) or consortia of tribes or tribal organizations to provide for the coordination of assistance for special education and related services for children with disabilities aged three through five on reservations served by elementary schools and secondary schools for Indian children operated or funded by the Department of the Interior. The amount of the payments under paragraph (b) of this section for any fiscal year is equal to 20 percent of the amount allotted under § 300.701(b).

(b) *Distribution of funds.* The Secretary of the Interior must distribute the total amount of the payment under paragraph (a) of this section by allocating to each tribe, tribal organization, or consortium an amount based on the number of children with disabilities aged three through five residing on reservations as reported annually, divided by the total of those children served by all tribes or tribal organizations.

(c) *Submission of information.* To receive a payment under this section, the tribe or tribal organization must submit the figures to the Secretary of the Interior as required to determine the amounts to be allocated under paragraph (b) of this section. This information must be compiled and submitted to the Secretary.

(d) *Use of funds.* (1) The funds received by a tribe or tribal organization must be used to assist in child find, screening, and other procedures for the early identification of children aged three through five, parent training, and the provision of direct services. These activities may be carried out directly or through contracts or cooperative agreements with the BIA, LEAs, and other public or private nonprofit organizations. The tribe or tribal organization is encouraged to involve Indian parents in the development and implementation of these activities.

(2) The tribe or tribal organization, as appropriate, must make referrals to local, State, or Federal entities for the provision of services or further diagnosis.

(e) Biennial report. To be eligible to receive a grant pursuant to paragraph (a) of this section, the tribe or tribal organization must provide to the Secretary of the Interior a biennial report of activities undertaken under this section, including the number of contracts and cooperative agreements entered into, the number of children contacted and receiving services for each year, and the estimated number of children needing services during the two years following the year in which the report is made. The Secretary of the Interior must include a summary of this information on a biennial basis in the report to the Secretary required under section 611(h) of the Act. The Secretary may require any additional information from the Secretary of the Interior.

(f) Prohibitions. None of the funds allocated under this section may be used by the Secretary of the Interior for administrative purposes, including child count and the provision of technical assistance.

§ 300.713 Plan for coordination of services.

(a) The Secretary of the Interior must develop and implement a plan for the coordination of services for all Indian children with disabilities residing on reservations served by elementary schools and secondary schools for Indian children operated or funded by the Secretary of the Interior.

(b) The plan must provide for the coordination of services benefiting those children from whatever source, including tribes, the Indian Health Service, other BIA divisions, other Federal agencies, State educational agencies, and State, local, and tribal juvenile and adult correctional facilities.

(c) In developing the plan, the Secretary of the Interior must consult with all interested and involved parties.

(d) The plan must be based on the needs of the children and the system best suited for meeting those needs, and may involve the establishment of cooperative agreements between the BIA, other Federal agencies, and other entities.

(e) The plan also must be distributed upon request to States; to SEAs, LEAs, and other agencies providing services to infants, toddlers, and children with disabilities; to tribes; and to other interested parties.

§ 300.714 Establishment of advisory board.

(a) To meet the requirements of section 612(a)(21) of the Act, the Secretary of the Interior must establish, under the BIA, an advisory board composed of individuals involved in or concerned with the education and provision of services to Indian infants, toddlers, children, and youth with disabilities, including Indians with disabilities, Indian parents or guardians of such children, teachers, service providers, State and local educational officials, representatives of tribes or tribal organizations, representatives from State Interagency Coordinating Councils under section 641 of the Act in States having reservations, and other members representing the various divisions and entities of the BIA. The chairperson must be selected by the Secretary of the Interior.

(b) The advisory board must—

(1) Assist in the coordination of services within the BIA and with other local, State,

and Federal agencies in the provision of education for infants, toddlers, and children with disabilities;

(2) Advise and assist the Secretary of the Interior in the performance of the Secretary of the Interior's responsibilities described in section 611(h) of the Act;

(3) Develop and recommend policies concerning effective inter- and intra-agency collaboration, including modifications to regulations, and the elimination of barriers to inter- and intra-agency programs and activities;

(4) Provide assistance and disseminate information on best practices, effective program coordination strategies, and recommendations for improved early intervention services or educational programming for Indian infants, toddlers, and children with disabilities; and

(5) Provide assistance in the preparation of information required under § 300.708(h).

§ 300.715   Annual reports.

(a) *In general.* The advisory board established under § 300.714 must prepare and submit to the Secretary of the Interior and to Congress an annual report containing a description of the activities of the advisory board for the preceding year.

(b) *Availability.* The Secretary of the Interior must make available to the Secretary the report described in paragraph (a) of this section.

§ 300.716   Applicable regulations.

The Secretary of the Interior must comply with the requirements of §§ 300.103 through 300.108, 300.110 through 300.124, 300.145 through 300.154, 300.156 through 300.160, 300.165, 300.170 through 300.186, 300.226, 300.300 through 300.606, 300.610 through 300.646, and 300.707 through 300.716.

DEFINITIONS THAT APPLY TO THIS SUBPART

§ 300.717   Definitions applicable to allotments, grants, and use of funds.

As used in this subpart—

(a) *Freely associated States* means the Republic of the Marshall Islands, the Federated States of Micronesia, and the Republic of Palau;

(b) *Outlying areas* means the United States Virgin Islands, Guam, American Samoa, and the Commonwealth of the Northern Mariana Islands;

(c) *State* means each of the 50 States, the District of Columbia, and the Commonwealth of Puerto Rico; and

(d) *Average per-pupil expenditure in public elementary schools and secondary schools in the United States* means—

(1) Without regard to the source of funds—

(i) The aggregate current expenditures, during the second fiscal year preceding the fiscal year for which the determination is made (or, if satisfactory data for that year are not available, during the most recent preceding fiscal year for which satisfactory data are available) of all LEAs in the 50 States and the District of Columbia); plus

(ii) Any direct expenditures by the State for the operation of those agencies; divided by (2) The aggregate number of children in average daily attendance to whom those agencies provided free public education during that preceding year.

ACQUISITION OF EQUIPMENT AND CONSTRUCTION OR ALTERATION OF FACILITIES

§ 300.718 Acquisition of equipment and construction or alteration of facilities.

(a) General. If the Secretary determines that a program authorized under Part B of the Act will be improved by permitting program funds to be used to acquire appropriate equipment, or to construct new facilities or alter existing facilities, the Secretary may allow the use of those funds for those purposes.

(b) Compliance with certain regulations. Any construction of new facilities or alteration of existing facilities under paragraph (a) of this section must comply with the requirements of—

(1) Appendix A of part 36 of title 28, Code of Federal Regulations (commonly known as the "Americans with Disabilities Accessibility Standards for Buildings and Facilities"); or

(2) Appendix A of subpart 101-19.6 of title 41, Code of Federal Regulations (commonly known as the "Uniform Federal Accessibility Standards").

§ 300.719

[This section was removed. See 71 FR 46540, 46753, Aug. 14, 2006.]

§ 300.720

[This section was removed. See 71 FR 46540, 46753, Aug. 14, 2006.]

§ 300.721

[This section was removed. See 71 FR 46540, 46753, Aug. 14, 2006.]

§ 300.722

Definition [This section was removed. See 71 FR 46540, 46753, Aug. 14, 2006.]

§ 300.750

[This section was removed. See 71 FR 46540, 46753, Aug. 14, 2006.]

§ 300.751

[This section was removed. See 71 FR 46540, 46753, Aug. 14, 2006.]

§ 300.752

[This section was removed. See 71 FR 46540, 46753, Aug. 14, 2006.]

§ 300.753

[This section was removed. See 71 FR 46540, 46753, Aug. 14, 2006.]

§ 300.754

[This section was removed. See 71 FR 46540, 46753, Aug. 14, 2006.]

§ 300.755

[This section was removed. See 71 FR 46540, 46753, Aug. 14, 2006.]

§ 300.756

[This section was removed. See 71 FR 46540, 46753, Aug. 14, 2006.]

SUBPART H   PRESCHOOL GRANTS FOR CHILDREN WITH DISABILITIES

§ 300.800   In general.

The Secretary provides grants under section 619 of the Act to assist States to provide special education and related services in accordance with Part B of the Act—

(a) To children with disabilities aged three through five years; and

(b) At a State's discretion, to two-year-old children with disabilities who will turn three during the school year.

§§ 300.801–300.802   [Reserved]

§ 300.803   Definition of State.

As used in this subpart, State means each of the 50 States, the District of Columbia, and the Commonwealth of Puerto Rico.

§ 300.804   Eligibility.

A State is eligible for a grant under section 619 of the Act if the State—

(a) Is eligible under section 612 of the Act to receive a grant under Part B of the Act; and

(b) Makes FAPE available to all children with disabilities, aged three through five, residing in the State.

(Approved by the Office of Management and Budget under control number 1820-0030)

§ 300.805   [Reserved]

§ 300.806   Eligibility for financial assistance.

No State or LEA, or other public institution or agency, may receive a grant or enter into a contract or cooperative agreement under subpart 2 or 3 of Part D of the Act that relates exclusively to programs, projects, and activities pertaining to children aged three through five years, unless the State is eligible to receive a grant under section 619(b) of the Act.

§ 300.807   Allocations to States.

The Secretary allocates the amount made available to carry out section 619 of the Act for a fiscal year among the States in accordance with §§ 300.808 through 300.810.

§ 300.808   Increase in funds.

If the amount available for allocation to States under § 300.807 for a fiscal year is equal to or greater than the amount allocated to the States under section 619 of the Act for the preceding fiscal year, those allocations are calculated as follows:

(a) Except as provided in § 300.809, the Secretary—

(1) Allocates to each State the amount the State received under section 619 of the Act for fiscal year 1997;

(2) Allocates 85 percent of any remaining funds to States on the basis of the States' relative populations of children aged three through five; and

(3) Allocates 15 percent of those remaining funds to States on the basis of the States' relative populations of all children aged three through five who are living in poverty.

(b) For the purpose of making grants under this section, the Secretary uses the most recent population data, including data on children living in poverty, that are available and satisfactory to the Secretary.

§ 300.809   Limitations.

(a) Notwithstanding § 300.808, allocations under that section are subject to the following:

(1) No State's allocation may be less than its allocation under section 619 of the Act for the preceding fiscal year.

(2) No State's allocation may be less than the greatest of—

(i) The sum of—

(A) The amount the State received under section 619 of the Act for fiscal year 1997; and

(B) One-third of one percent of the amount by which the amount appropriated under section 619(j) of the Act for the fiscal year exceeds the amount appropriated for section 619 of the Act for fiscal year 1997;

(ii) The sum of—

(A) The amount the State received under section 619 of the Act for the preceding fiscal year; and

(B) That amount multiplied by the percentage by which the increase in the funds appropriated under section 619 of the Act from the preceding fiscal year exceeds 1.5 percent; or

(iii) The sum of—

(A) The amount the State received under section 619 of the Act for the preceding fiscal year; and

(B) That amount multiplied by 90 percent of the percentage increase in the amount appropriated under section 619 of the Act from the preceding fiscal year.

(b) Notwithstanding paragraph (a)(2) of this section, no State's allocation under § 300.808 may exceed the sum of—

(1) The amount the State received under section 619 of the Act for the preceding fiscal year; and

(2) That amount multiplied by the sum of 1.5 percent and the percentage increase in the amount appropriated under section 619 of the Act from the preceding fiscal year.

(c) If the amount available for allocation to States under § 300.808 and paragraphs (a) and (b) of this section is insufficient to pay those allocations in full, those allocations are ratably reduced, subject to paragraph (a)(1) of this section.

§ 300.810   Decrease in funds.

If the amount available for allocations to States under § 300.807 for a fiscal year is less than the amount allocated to the States under section 619 of the Act for the preceding fiscal year, those allocations are calculated as follows:

(a) If the amount available for allocations is greater than the amount allocated to the States for fiscal year 1997, each State is allocated the sum of—

(1) The amount the State received under section 619 of the Act for fiscal year 1997; and

(2) An amount that bears the same relation to any remaining funds as the increase the State received under section 619 of the Act for the preceding fiscal year over fiscal year 1997 bears to the total of all such increases for all States.

(b) If the amount available for allocations is equal to or less than the amount allocated to the States for fiscal year 1997, each State is allocated the amount the State received for fiscal year 1997, ratably reduced, if necessary.

§ 300.811 [Reserved]

§ 300.812 Reservation for State activities.

(a) Each State may reserve not more than the amount described in paragraph (b) of this section for administration and other State-level activities in accordance with §§ 300.813 and 300.814.

(b) For each fiscal year, the Secretary determines and reports to the SEA an amount that is 25 percent of the amount the State received under section 619 of the Act for fiscal year 1997, cumulatively adjusted by the Secretary for each succeeding fiscal year by the lesser of—

(1) The percentage increase, if any, from the preceding fiscal year in the State's allocation under section 619 of the Act; or

(2) The rate of inflation, as measured by the percentage increase, if any, from the preceding fiscal year in the Consumer Price Index for All Urban Consumers, published by the Bureau of Labor Statistics of the Department of Labor.

§ 300.813 State administration.

(a) For the purpose of administering section 619 of the Act (including the coordination of activities under Part B of the Act with, and providing technical assistance to, other programs that provide services to children with disabilities), a State may use not more than 20 percent of the maximum amount the State may reserve under § 300.812 for any fiscal year.

(b) Funds described in paragraph (a) of this section may also be used for the administration of Part C of the Act.

§ 300.814 Other State-level activities.

Each State must use any funds the State reserves under § 300.812 and does not use for administration under § 300.813—

(a) For support services (including establishing and implementing the mediation process required by section 615(e) of the Act), which may benefit children with disabilities younger than three or older than five as long as those services also benefit children with disabilities aged three through five;

(b) For direct services for children eligible for services under section 619 of the Act;

(c) For activities at the State and local levels to meet the performance goals established by the State under section 612(a)(15) of the Act;

(d) To supplement other funds used to develop and implement a statewide coordinated services system designed to improve results for children and families, including children with disabilities and their families, but not more than one percent of the amount received by the State under section 619 of the Act for a fiscal year;

(e) To provide early intervention services (which must include an educational component that promotes school readiness and incorporates preliteracy, language, and numeracy skills) in accordance with Part C of the Act to children with disabilities who are eligible for services under section 619 of the Act and who previously received services under Part C of the Act until such children enter, or are eligible under State law to enter, kindergarten; or

(f) At the State's discretion, to continue service coordination or case management for families who receive services under Part C of the Act, consistent with § 300.814(e).

§ 300.815 Subgrants to LEAs.

Each State that receives a grant under section 619 of the Act for any fiscal year must distribute all of the grant funds that the State does not reserve under § 300.812 to LEAs in the State that have established their eligibility under section 613 of the Act.

§ 300.816 Allocations to LEAs.

(a) *Base payments.* The State must first award each LEA described in § 300.815 the amount that agency would have received under section 619 of the Act for fiscal year 1997 if the State had distributed 75 percent of its grant for that year under section 619(c)(3), as such section was then in effect.

(b) *Base payment adjustments.* For fiscal year 1998 and beyond—

(1) If a new LEA is created, the State must divide the base allocation determined under paragraph (a) of this section for the LEAs that would have been responsible for serving children with disabilities now being served by the new LEA, among the new LEA and affected LEAs based on the relative numbers of children with disabilities ages three through five currently provided special education by each of the LEAs;

(2) If one or more LEAs are combined into a single new LEA, the State must combine the base allocations of the merged LEAs; and

(3) If for two or more LEAs, geographic boundaries or administrative responsibility for providing services to children with disabilities ages three through five changes, the base allocations of affected LEAs must be redistributed among affected LEAs based on the relative numbers of children with disabilities ages three through five currently provided special education by each affected LEA.

(c) *Allocation of remaining funds.* After making allocations under paragraph (a) of this section, the State must—

(1) Allocate 85 percent of any remaining funds to those LEAs on the basis of the relative numbers of children enrolled in public and private elementary schools and secondary schools within the LEA's jurisdiction; and

(2) Allocate 15 percent of those remaining funds to those LEAs in accordance with their relative numbers of children living in poverty, as determined by the SEA.

(d) *Use of best data.* For the purpose of making grants under this section, States must apply on a uniform basis across all LEAs the best data that are available to them on the numbers of children enrolled in public and private elementary and secondary schools and the numbers of children living in poverty.

§ 300.817 Reallocation of LEA funds.

If an SEA determines that an LEA is adequately providing FAPE to all children with disabilities aged three through five residing in the area served by the LEA with State and local funds, the SEA may reallocate any portion of the funds under section 619 of the Act that are not needed by that LEA to provide FAPE to other LEAs in the State that are not adequately providing special education and related services to all children with disabilities aged three through five residing in the areas the other LEAs serve.

§ 300.818 Part C of the Act inapplicable.

Part C of the Act does not apply to any child with a disability receiving FAPE, in accordance with Part B of the Act, with funds received under section 619 of the Act.

Appendix A to Part 300   Excess Costs Calculation

Except as otherwise provided, amounts provided to an LEA under Part B of the Act may be used only to pay the excess costs of providing special education and related services to children with disabilities. Excess costs are those costs for the education of an elementary school or secondary school student with a disability that are in excess of the average annual per student expenditure in an LEA during the preceding school year for an elementary school or secondary school student, as may be appropriate. An LEA must spend at least the average annual per student expenditure on the education of an elementary school or secondary school child with a disability before funds under Part B of the Act are used to pay the excess costs of providing special education and related services.

Section 602(8) of the Act and § 300.16 require the LEA to compute the minimum average amount separately for children with disabilities in its elementary schools and for children with disabilities in its secondary schools. LEAs may not compute the minimum average amount it must spend on the education of children with disabilities based on a combination of the enrollments in its elementary schools and secondary schools.

The following example shows how to compute the minimum average amount an LEA must spend for the education of each of its elementary school children with disabilities under section 602(3) of the Act before it may use funds under Part B of the Act.

a. First the LEA must determine the total amount of its expenditures for elementary school students from all sources — local, State, and Federal (including Part B) — in the preceding school year. Only capital outlay and debt services are excluded.

Example: The following is an example of a computation for children with disabilities enrolled in an LEA's elementary schools. In this example, the LEA had an average elementary school enrollment for the preceding school year of 800 (including 100 children with disabilities). The LEA spent the following amounts last year for elementary school students (including its elementary school children with disabilities):

   (1) From State and local tax funds: $6,500,000
   (2) From Federal funds: $600,000

   Total expenditures: $7,100,000   Of this total, $ 60,000 was for capital outlay and debt service relating to the education of elementary school students. This must be subtracted from total expenditures.

   (1) Total Expenditures: $7,100,000
   (2) Less capital outlay and debt: – $60,000

   Total expenditures for elementary school students less capital outlay and debt:: $7,040,000

b. Next, the LEA must subtract from the total expenditures amounts spent for:

(1) IDEA, Part B allocation,

(2) ESEA, Title I, Part A allocation,

(3) ESEA, Title III, Parts A and B allocation,

(4) State and local funds for children with disabilities, and

(5) State or local funds for programs under ESEA, Title I, Part A, and Title III, Parts A and B.

These are funds that the LEA actually spent, not funds received last year but carried over for the current school year.

Example: The LEA spent the following amounts for elementary school students last year:

(1) From funds under IDEA, Part B allocation: $200,000

(2) From funds under ESEA, Title I, Part A allocation: $250,000

(3) From funds under ESEA, Title III, Parts A and B allocation: $50,000

(4) From State funds and local funds for children with disabilities: $500,000

(5) From State and local funds for programs under ESEA, Title I, Part A, and Title III, Parts A and B: $150,000

Total: $1,150,000

(1) Total expenditures less capital outlay and debt: $7,040,000

(2) Other deductions: –$1,150,000

Total: $5890,000

c. Except as otherwise provided, the LEA next must determine the average annual per student expenditure for its elementary schools dividing the average number of students enrolled in the elementary schools of the agency during the preceding year (including its children with disabilities) into the amount computed under the above paragraph. The amount obtained through this computation is the minimum amount the LEA must spend (on the average) for the education of each of its elementary school children with disabilities. Funds under Part B of the Act may be used only for costs over and above this minimum.

(1) Amount from Step fnb: $5,890,000

(2) Average number of students enrolled: $800

(3) $5,890,000/800 Average annual per student expenditure: $7,362

d. Except as otherwise provided, to determine the total minimum amount of funds the LEA must spend for the education of its elementary school children with disabilities in the LEA (not including capital outlay and debt service), the LEA must multiply the number of elementary school children with disabilities in the LEA times the average annual per student expenditure obtained in paragraph c above. Funds under Part B of the Act can only be used for excess costs over and above this minimum.

(1) Number of children with disabilities in the LEA's elementary schools: 100

(2) Average annual per student expenditure: $7,362

(3) $7,362 x 100

Total minimum amount of funds the LEA must spend for the education of children with disabilities enrolled in the LEA's elementary schools before using Part B funds: $736,200

Appendix B to Part 300 Proportionate Share Calculation

Each LEA must expend, during the grant period, on the provision of special education and related services for the parentally-placed private school children with disabilities enrolled in private elementary schools and secondary schools located in the LEA an amount that is equal to—

(1) A proportionate share of the LEA's subgrant under section 611(f) of the Act for children with disabilities aged 3 through 21. This is an amount that is the same proportion of the LEA's total subgrant under section 611(f) of the Act as the number of parentally-placed private school children with disabilities aged 3 through 21 enrolled in private elementary schools and secondary schools located in the LEA is to the total number of children with disabilities enrolled in public and private elementary schools and secondary schools located in the LEA aged 3 through 21; and

(2) A proportionate share of the LEA's subgrant under section 619(g) of the Act for children with disabilities aged 3 through 5. This is an amount that is the same proportion of the LEA's total subgrant under section 619(g) of the Act as the total number of parentally-placed private school children with disabilities aged 3 through 5 enrolled in private elementary schools located in the LEA is to the total number of children with disabilities enrolled in public and private elementary schools located in the LEA aged 3 through 5.

Consistent with section 612(a)(10)(A)(i) of the Act and § 300.133 of these regulations, annual expenditures for parentally-placed private school children with disabilities are calculated based on the total number of children with disabilities enrolled in public and private elementary schools and secondary schools located in the LEA eligible to receive special education and related services under Part B, as compared with the total number of eligible parentally-placed private school children with disabilities enrolled in private elementary schools located in the LEA. This ratio is used to determine the proportion of the LEA's total Part B subgrants under section 611(f) of the Act for children aged 3 through 21, and under section 619(g) of the Act for children aged 3 through 5, that is to be expended on services for parentally-placed private school children with disabilities enrolled in private elementary schools and secondary schools located in the LEA.

The following is an example of how the proportionate share is calculated:

There are 300 eligible children with disabilities enrolled in the Flintstone School District and 20 eligible parentally-placed private school children with disabilities enrolled in private elementary schools and secondary schools located in the LEA for a total of 320 eligible public and private school children with disabilities (note: proportionate share for parentally-placed private school children is based on total children eligible, not children served). The number of eligible parentally-placed private school children with disabilities (20) divided by the total number of eligible public and private school children with disabilities (320) indicates that 6.25 percent of the LEA's subgrant must be spent for the group of eligible parentally-placed children with disabilities enrolled in private elementary schools and secondary schools located in the LEA. Flintstone School District receives $ 152,500 in Federal flow through funds. Therefore, the LEA must spend $ 9,531.25 on special education or related services to the group of parentally-placed private school children with disabilities enrolled in private elementary schools and secondary schools located in the LEA. (Note: The LEA must calculate the proportionate share of IDEA funds before earmarking funds for any early intervening activities in § 300.226).

The following outlines the calculations for the example of how the proportionate share is calculated.
Proportionate Share Calculation for Parentally-Placed Private School Children with Disabilities For Flintstone School District:

Number of eligible children with disabilities in public schools in the LEA: 300

Number of parentally-placed eligible children with disabilities in private elementary schools and secondary schools located in the LEA: <u>20</u>

Total number of eligible children: 320

Federal Flow-Through Funds to Flintstone School District

Total allocation to Flintstone: $152,500

Calculating Proportionate Share:

Total allocation to Flinstone: $152,500

Divided by total number of eligible children: 320

Average allocation per eligible child: 476.5625

Multiplied by the number of parentally placed children with disabilities: 20

Amount to be expended for parentally-placed children with disabilities: $9,531.25

Appendix C to Part 300 National Instructional Materials Accessibility Standard (NIMAS)

[Omitted.]

Appendix D to Part 300 Maintenance of Effort and Early Intervening Services

LEAs that seek to reduce their local maintenance of effort in accordance with § 300.205(d) and use some of their Part B funds for early intervening services under § 300.226 must do so with caution because the local maintenance of effort reduction provision and the authority to use Part B funds for early intervening services are interconnected. The decisions that an LEA makes about the amount of funds that it uses for one purpose affect the amount that it may use for the other. Below are examples that illustrate how §§ 300.205(d) and 300.226(a) affect one another.

Example 1: In this example, the amount that is 15 percent of the LEA's total grant (see § 300.226(a)), which is the maximum amount that the LEA may use for early intervening services (EIS), is greater than the amount that may be used for local maintenance of effort (MOE) reduction (50 percent of the increase in the LEA's grant from the prior year's grant) (see § 300.205(a)).

Prior Year's Allocation: $900,000

Current Year's Allocation: $1,000,000

Increase: $100,000

Maximum Available for MOE Reduction: $50,000

Maximum Available for EIS: $150,000 If the LEA chooses to set aside $ 150,000 for EIS, it may not reduce its MOE (MOE maximum $ 50,000 less $ 150,000 for EIS means $ 0 can be used for MOE).

If the LEA chooses to set aside $ 100,000 for EIS, it may not reduce its MOE (MOE maximum $ 50,000 less $ 100,000 for EIS means $ 0 can be used for MOE).

If the LEA chooses to set aside $ 50,000 for EIS, it may not reduce its MOE (MOE maximum $ 50,000 less $ 50,000 for EIS means $ 0 can be used for MOE).

If the LEA chooses to set aside $ 30,000 for EIS, it may reduce its MOE by $ 20,000 (MOE maximum $ 50,000 less $ 30,000 for EIS means $ 20,000 can be used for MOE).

If the LEA chooses to set aside $ 0 for EIS, it may reduce its MOE by $ 50,000 (MOE maximum $ 50,000 less $ 0 for EIS means $ 50,000 can be used for MOE).

Example 2: In this example, the amount that is 15 percent of the LEA's total grant (see § 300.226(a)), which is the maximum amount that the LEA may use for EIS, is less than the amount that may be used for MOE reduction (50 percent of the increase in the LEA's grant from the prior year's grant) (see § 300.205(a)).

Prior Year's Allocation: $1,000,000

Current Year's Allocation: $2,000,000

Increase: $1,000,000

Maximum Available for MOE Reduction: $500,000

Maximum Available for EIS: $300,000   If the LEA chooses to use no funds for MOE, it may set aside $ 300,000 for EIS (EIS maximum $ 300,000 less $ 0 means $ 300,000 for EIS).

If the LEA chooses to use $ 100,000 for MOE, it may set aside $ 200,000 for EIS (EIS maximum $ 300,000 less $ 100,000 means $ 200,000 for EIS).

If the LEA chooses to use $ 150,000 for MOE, it may set aside $ 150,000 for EIS (EIS maximum $ 300,000 less $ 150,000 means $ 150,000 for EIS).

If the LEA chooses to use $ 300,000 for MOE, it may not set aside anything for EIS (EIS maximum $ 300,000 less $ 300,000 means $ 0 for EIS).

If the LEA chooses to use $ 500,000 for MOE, it may not set aside anything for EIS (EIS maximum $ 300,000 less $ 500,000 means $ 0 for EIS).

Appendix E to Part 300   Index for IDEA — Part B Regulations (34 CFR Part 300)

ACCESS TO
. Access rights (Parents) . . .300.613.
. Assistive technology devices in child's home . . .300.105(b).
. Disciplinary records . . .300.229.
. Education records (Procedural safeguards notice) . . .300.504(c)(4).
. General curriculum (Ensure access to) . . .300.39(b)(3)(ii).
. Instructional materials (see §§ 300.172, 300.210).
. List of employees who may have access to records . . .300.623(d).
. Parent's private insurance proceeds . . .300.154(e).
. Record of access (Confidentiality) . . .300.614.
ACCESSIBILITY STANDARDS (Regarding construction)
. Americans with Disabilities Accessibility Standards for Buildings and Facilities . . .300.718(b)(1).
. Uniform Federal Accessibility Standards . . .300.718(b)(2).
ACCOMMODATIONS
. In assessments . . .300.320(a)(6)(i).
. State level activities in support of . . .300.704(b)(4)(x).
ACT (Definition) . . .300.4.
ADD AND ADHD (See "Attention deficit disorder" and "Attention deficit hyperactivity disorder")
ADDITIONAL DISCLOSURE OF INFORMATION REQUIREMENT . . .300.512(b).
ADULT CORRECTIONAL FACILITIES (See "Correctional facilities")
ADULT PRISONS (Children with disabilities in)
. Divided State agency responsibility . . .300.607.
. FAPE requirements:
. Exception to FAPE . . .300.102(a)(2).

. Modifications of IEP or placement . . . 300.324(d)(2).
. Requirements that do not apply . . .300.324(d)(1).
. Governor . . .300.149(d).
. Other public agency responsibility . . .300.149(d).
ADVERSELY AFFECTS EDUCATIONAL PERFORMANCE (See "Child with a disability," § 300.8(c)(1)(i), (c)(3), (c)(4)(i), (c)(5), (c)(6), (c)(8), (c)(9)(ii), (c)(11), (c)(12))
ADVISORY BOARD
(Secretary of the Interior) . . .300.714.
ADVISORY PANEL (See "State advisory panel")
AGE-APPROPRIATE CLASSROOM . . .300.116(e).
ALLOCATION(S)
. By-pass for private school children (see§ 300.191(d)).
. To LEAs (see §§ 300.705(b), 300.816)
. To Outlying areas . . .300.701(a).
. To Secretary of the Interior . . .300.707.
. To States (see §§ 300.703, 300.807 through 300.810)
ALLOWABLE COSTS
(By SEA for State administration) . . .300.704(a).
ALTERATION OF FACILITIES . . .300.718(b).
ALTERNATE ASSESSMENTS . . .
. Aligned with alternate academic achievement standards . . .300.320(a)(2)(ii).
. Development and provision of in accordance with ESEA . . .300.704(b)(4)(x).
. Participation determined by IEP Team . . .300.320(a)(6)(ii).
ALTERNATIVE PLACEMENTS (Continuum) . . .300.115.
ALTERNATIVE STRATEGIES to meet transition objectives . . .300.324(c)(1).
AMENDMENTS
. To LEA policies and procedures . . .300.220(b).
. To State policies and procedures:
. Made by State . . .300.176(b).
. Required by the Secretary . . .300.176(c).
ANNUAL GOALS (IEPs)
. FAPE for children suspended or expelled (see §§ 300.101(a), 300.530(d))
. IEP content:
. How progress will be measured . . .300.320(a)(3).
. Special education and related services. . .300.320(a)(4).
. Statement of measurable annual goals. . .300.320(a)(2)(i).
. Review and revision of IEP. . .300.324(b)(1).
. Review of existing evaluation data. . .300.305(a).
ANNUAL REPORT
Of children served (see §§ 300.640 through 300.646)
On education of Indian children . . .300.715.
APPENDICES TO PART 300 (A through E)
Excess Costs Calculation (see Appendix A)
Proportionate Share Calculation (see Appendix B)
National Instructional Materials Accessibility Standard (NIMAS) (see Appendix C)
Maintenance of Effort and Early Intervening Services (see Appendix D)
Index for IDEA—Part B Regulations (This Appendix E)
APPLICABILITY OF THIS PART to State, local, and private agencies. . .300.2.

APPLICATION
. Initial admission to public school. . .300.518(b).
. Initial services. . .300.518(c).
ASSESSMENT(S)
. For specific learning disability (see § 300.309(a)(2)(ii), (b)(2))
. Functional behavioral assessment (see § 300.530(d)(1)(ii), (f)(1)(i))
. In evaluation (see §§ 300.304(b), (c), 300.305(a)(1)(ii), (c), (d))
. Of leisure function (in "Recreation"). . .300.34(c)(11)(i).
ASSESSMENTS—STATE and DISTRICT-WIDE
Alternate assessments (see § 300.320 (a)(2)(ii), (a)(6)(ii))
Performance indicators. . .300.157.
ASSISTANCE UNDER OTHER FEDERAL PROGRAMS. . .300.186.
ASSISTIVE TECHNOLOGY (AT)
. AT devices. . .300.5.
. AT services. . .300.6.
. Consideration of special factors. . .300.324(a)(2)(v).
. Hearing aids. . .300.113.
. Requirement:
. Ensure availability of. . .300.105(a).
. Surgically implanted medical devices (see §§ 300.5, 300.34(b), 300.113(b))
ASTHMA. . .300.8(c)(9).
ATTENTION DEFICIT DISORDER (ADD). . .300.8(c)(9).
ATTENTION DEFICIT HYPERACTIVITY DISORDER (ADHD). . .300.8(c)(9).
ATTORNEYS' FEES. . .300.517.
. Award of fees. . .300.517(c).
. Prohibition on use of funds for. . . . . .300.517(b).
. When court reduces fee awards. . .300.517(c)(4).
AUDIOLOGY. . .300.34(c)(1).
AUTHORITY (A-O)
. Of guardian. . .300.30(a)(3).
. Of hearing officer (Discipline). . .300.532(b).
. Of school personnel (Discipline). . .300.530.
. Of Secretary to monitor and enforce. . .300.609.
AUTHORITY (P-Z)
. Parental authority to inspect and review
records. . .300.613.
. State complaint procedures. . .300.151(b).
. Waiver request (Signed by person with
authority). . .300.164(c)(1).
AUTISM. . .300.8(c)(1).
AVERAGE PER-PUPIL EXPENDITURE
(Definition). . .300.717(d).
BASE PAYMENTS (to LEAs) (See § 300.705(b)(1), (b)(2))
BASIS OF KNOWLEDGE: Protection for children not yet eligible. . .300.534(b).
BEHAVIORAL ASSESSMENT (See "Functional behavioral assessment"). . .
BEHAVIORAL INTERVENTION(S). . .300.530(f).
. Assist in developing. . .300.34(c)(10)(vi).
. Behavioral intervention plan. . .300.530(f).
. Consideration of by IEP Team. . .300.324(a)(2)(i).
. Not a manifestation of disability. . .300.530(d).
. Regular education teacher (Determination of). . .300.324(a)(3).
. Suspension and expulsion rates. . .300.170(b).
BENCHMARKS OR SHORT TERM OBJECTIVES. . .300.320(a)(2)(ii).

BENEFITS TO NONDISABLED (Permissive use of funds)...300.208(a)(1).
BIA (See "Bureau of Indian Affairs")
BLIND(NESS): Under "Visual impairment"
. Access to instructional materials (see §§ 300.172, 300.210(b)(3))
. Consideration of special factors by IEP Team...300.324(a)(2).
. Definition...300.8(c)(13).
BRAILLE (see §§ 300.29(b), 300.324(a)(2)(iii))
BUREAU OF INDIAN AFFAIRS (BIA)
. BIA funded schools...300.28(c).
. In definition of "LEA"...300.28(c).
. See also §§ 300.21(c), 300.713(b), (d),...300.714
. Use of funds...300.712(d).
BUSINESS DAY
. Definition...300.11(b).
. See "Timelines," "Timelines—Discipline"
BY-PASS: Private school children with disabilities (see §§ 300.190 through 300.198)
CALENDAR DAY
. Definition...300.11(a).
. See "Timelines," "Timelines—Discipline"
CERTIFICATION
. Annual report of children served...300.643.
CHANGE OF PLACEMENT BECAUSE OF DISCIPLINARY...300.536.
REMOVALS
CHARTER SCHOOLS
. Applicability of this part to...300.2(b)(1)(ii).
. Definition...300.7.
. Exception: joint establishment of eligibility...300.223(b).
. In definition of "Elementary school"...300.13.
. In definition of "LEA"...300.28(b)(2).
. In definition of "Public agency"...300.33.
. In definition of "Secondary school"...300.36.
. State-level activities regarding charter schools...300.704(b)(4)(ix).
. Treatment of charter schools and their students...300.209.
CHIEF EXECUTIVE OFFICER (CEO)
. Adult prisons (Assigned by Governor)...300.149(d).
. Methods of ensuring services (see § 300.154(a), (c))
CHILD COUNT
. Annual report of children served (see §§ 300.640 through 300.646)
. Certification...300.643.
. Criteria for...300.644.
. Dates for count...300.641(a).
. Indian children...300.712(b).
. LEA records of private school children...300.132(c).
. Procedures for counting children served...300.645(a).
CHILD FIND
. Basic requirement...300.111(a).
. Children advancing from grade to grade...300.111(c)(1).
. Developmental delay...300.111(b).
. Highly mobile children...300.111(c)(2).

. Homeless children . . .300.111(a)(1)(i).
. Indian children aged 3 through 5 . . .300.712(d)(1).
. Migrant children . . .300.111(c)(2).
. Private school children . . .300.131(b).
. Protections for children not determined
eligible . . .300.534.
. Secretaries of the Interior and Health and . . .300.708(i)(2).
Human Services (Memo of agreement)
CHILD WITH A DISABILITY (CWD)
. Adversely affects educational performance (see § 300.8(c)(1)(i), (c)(3), (c)(4)(i), (c)(5), (c)(6), (c)(8), (c)(9)(ii), (c)(11), (c)(12), (c)(13))
. Children experiencing developmental delay(s) . . .300.8(b)(1).
. Children who need only a related service . . .300.8(a)(2).
. Definition . . .300.8(a)(1).
. Individual disability terms (Defined) . . .300.8(c).
. Requirement . . .300.111(b).
. See "Developmental delay(s)"
CHILD'S STATUS DURING PROCEEDINGS
. Discipline (see §§ 300.530(f)(2), 300.533)
. Pendency (Stay put) . . .300.518.
CHILDREN ADVANCING FROM GRADE TO GRADE
. Child find . . .300.111(c)(1).
. FAPE . . .300.101(c).
CHILDREN EXPERIENCING DEVELOPMENTAL DELAY(S)
(See "Developmental delay(s)")
CHILDREN'S RIGHTS (Confidentiality) . . .300.625.
CIVIL ACTION—PROCEEDINGS . . .300.516.
. Finality of review decision . . .300.514(d).
. Mediation . . .300.506(b)(6)(i).
. Procedural safeguards notice . . .300.504(c)(12).
. See "Court(s)"
COCHLEAR IMPLANT (See "Surgically implanted medical device") . . .300.34(b).
CODE OF CONDUCT
. Case-by-case determination . . .300.530(a).
. Manifestation determination review . . .300.530(e).
. Protections for children not determined
eligible . . .300.534(a).
COMMINGLING—PROHIBITION AGAINST . . .300.162(b).
COMMUNITY-BASED WAIVERS (Public benefits or
insurance) . . .300.154(d)(2)(iii).
COMPLAINT(S): DUE PROCESS
. Attorneys' fees . . .300.517(a)(1).
. Civil action . . .300.516(a).
. Pendency . . .300.518(a).
. Private school children (Complaints) . . .300.140(c).
. See "Due process hearing(s) and reviews"
COMPLAINT(S): STATE COMPLAINT PROCEDURES (A-P)
. Adoption of State complaint procedures . . .300.151(a).
. Complaint investigations (SEA allocations
for) . . .300.704(b)(3)(i).
. Filing a complaint . . .300.153(a).
. Minimum State complaint procedures . . .300.152.
. Private schools (State complaints) . . .300.140.

. Procedural safeguards notice . . . 300.504(c).
. Provisions for services under by-pass . . . 300.191(d).
. Public agency failure to implement hearing
decision . . . 300.152(c)(3).
COMPLAINT(S): STATE COMPLAINT PROCEDURES (Q-Z)
. See also §§ 300.151 through 300.153
. Time limit . . . 300.152(a).
. Waiver of nonsupplanting requirement . . . 300.163(c)(2).
COMPLIANCE—COMPLY (A-M)
. Child find requirements . . . 300.111(a).
. Department procedures (If failure to comply) . . . 300.604(c).
. FAPE requirement . . . 300.101(a).
. LEA and State agency compliance . . . 300.222(a).
. LRE (State funding mechanism) . . . 300.114(b).
. Modifications of policies:
. Made by LEA or State agency . . . 300.176(b).
. Required by SEA . . . 300.220(c).
. Required by Secretary . . . 300.176(c).
. Monitoring (See "Monitor; Monitoring activities");
COMPLIANCE—COMPLY (N-Z)
. Physical education . . . 300.108.
. Private school placement by parents . . . 300.148(e).
. Private school placements by public agencies:
. IEP requirement . . . 300.325(c).
. SEA (Monitor compliance) . . . 300.147(a)
. Public participation requirements . . . 300.165.
. SEA responsibility if LEA does not comply . . . 300.227(a).
. State funding mechanism (LRE) . . . 300.114(b).
. COMPREHENSIVE EVALUATION . . . 300.304(c)(6).
CONDITION OF ASSISTANCE
. LEA eligibility . . . 300.200.
. State eligibility . . . 300.100.
CONFIDENTIALITY (A-C)
. Access rights . . . 300.613.
. Children's rights . . . 300.625.
. Consent . . . . . . 300.622.
CONFIDENTIALITY (D-E)
Definitions:
. Destruction of information . . . 300.611(a).
. Education records . . . 300.611(b).
. Participating agency . . . 300.611(c).
. Department use of personally identifiable
information . . . 300.627.
. Disciplinary information . . . 300.229.
. Enforcement by SEA . . . 300.626.
CONFIDENTIALITY (F-Z)
. Family Educational Rights and Privacy Act:
. Children's rights . . . 300.625.
. Disciplinary records . . . 300.535(b)(2).
. In definition of "Education records" . . . 300.611(b).
. Notice to parents . . . 300.612(a)(3).
. Fees . . . . . . 300.617.
. Hearing procedures . . . 300.621.

. List of types and location of information . . .300.616.
. Notice to parents . . .300.612(a).
. Opportunity for a hearing . . .300.619.
. Parental authority to inspect and review records . . .300.613(b).
. Record of access . . .300.614.
. Records on more than one child . . .300.615.
. Result of hearing . . .300.620.
. Safeguards . . .300.623.
. State eligibility requirement . . .300.123.
CONSENT (A-I)
. Confidentiality (Records to non-agency officials) . . .300.622(a).
. Definition . . .300.9.
. IEP vs. IFSP . . .300.323(b)(2)(ii).
. Initial evaluations . . .300.300(a).
. Initial provision of services . . .300.300(b).
CONSENT (J-Z)
. Not required:
. Before administering a test or other evaluation to all children existing data 300.300(d)(1)(i). . . .300.300(d)(1)(ii).
. When screening for instructional purposes . . .300.302.
. Private insurance (Accessing) . . .300.154(e)(1).
. Reasonable efforts to obtain consent:
. For initial evaluation . . .300.300(a)(1)(iii).
. For initial evaluations for wards of the State . . .300.300(a)(2).
. For initial provision of services . . .300.300(b)(2).
. Reasonable efforts requirements . . .300.300(d)(5).
. Reevaluations . . .. . .300.300(c)(2).
. Release of information from education records . . .300.622.
CONSIDERATION OF SPECIAL FACTORS (by IEP Team) . . .. . .300.324(a)(2).
CONSISTENCY WITH STATE POLICIES: LEA . . .300.201.
CONSTRUCTION
. Accessibility standards . . .300.718(b).
. Exception to maintenance of effort . . .300.204(d). (Termination of costly expenditures for construction) . . .
. Private schools (No funds may be used for) . . .300.144(e).
CONSTRUCTION CLAUSES (A-I)
. Child find (Nothing requires classifying children by disability) . . .300.111(d).
. Civil action (Exhaust administrative remedies under Part B before filing a civil action) . . .300.516(e).
. Early intervening services . . .300.226(c).
. Funding mandated by State law . . .300.166.
. Hearing: right of parent to appeal decision . . .300.513(b).
. Highly qualified SEA or LEA staff . . .. . .300.156(e).
. Highly qualified teacher . . .300.18(f).
. IEP (Inclusion of additional information beyond explicit requirements) . . .300.320(d)(1).
. IEP (Information in more than one component not required) . . .300.320(d)(2).
CONSTRUCTION CLAUSES (J-Z)

. Prohibition on mandatory medication . . .300.174(b).
. Referral to and action by law enforcement and judicial authorities . . .300.535(a).
. Secretary's authority to monitor enforcement under GEPA . . .300.609.
. State Medicaid agency (Nothing alters requirements imposed under Titles XIX or XXI or other public benefits or insurance program) . . .300.154(h).
. Transition service . . .300.324(c)(2).
CONSUMER PRICE INDEX For All Urban Consumers (regarding rate of inflation) (See §§ 300.702(b), 300.704(a)(2)(ii), (b)(2), 300.812(b)(2))
CONTENT OF IEP . . .300.320(a).
CONTINUUM OF ALTERNATIVE PLACEMENTS (See "Least restrictive environment") . . .300.115.
CONTROLLED SUBSTANCE (Definition) . . .300.530(i)(1).
COORDINATION OF SERVICES
. Methods of ensuring services . . .300.154(a).
. Secretary of the Interior . . .300.708(i)(1).
. Advisory board (Service coordination within BIA) . . .. . .300.714(b)(1).
. Payments for children aged 3 through 5 . . .300.712(a).
. See "Interagency agreements," "Interagency coordination"
. State advisory panel (Advise SEA on) . . .300.169(e).
. Use of LEA funds for early intervening services . . .300.208(a)(2).
. Use of SEA allocations for transition . . .300.704(b)(4)(vi).
CO-PAY OR DEDUCTIBLE (Public benefits or insurance) . . .300.154(d)(2)(ii).
CORE ACADEMIC SUBJECTS
. Definition . . .300.10.
. See "Highly qualified special education teachers" . . .300.18.
CORRECTIONAL FACILITIES
. Applicability of this part to . . .300.2(b)(1)(iv).
. Divided State agency responsibility . . .300.607.
. Exception to FAPE (Children in adult facilities) . . .300.102(a)(2).
. See also "Adult prisons"
. State advisory panel (Representatives on) . . .300.168(a)(11).
. State juvenile-adult correctional facilities . . .300.2(b)(1)(iv).
. Transfer of rights to children in . . .300.520(a)(2).
CORRECTIVE ACTION (PLAN)
. Corrective actions to achieve compliance (see §§ 300.152(b)(2)(iii), 300.607)
. Monitoring activities . . .300.120(b)(2).
. Needs intervention by Secretary . . .300.604(b)(2)(i).
. State advisory panel (Advise SEA on) . . .300.169(d).
COUNSELING SERVICES (Definition) . . .300.34(c)(2).
COUNT (See "Child count")
COURT(S)
. Attorneys' fees . . .300.517.
. Civil action . . .300.516.
. Court order:
. Exception to FAPE for certain ages . . .300.102(a)(1).
. Judicial review:
. By-pass . . .300.197.

. Department procedures . . .300.184.
. New interpretation of Act by courts requiring modification . . .300.176(c)(2).
. Reimbursement for private school placement
(see § 300.148(b) through (e))
CRIME (See "Reporting a crime") . . .300.535.
CRITERIA (A-I)
. Child count . . .300.644.
. Child eligibility (Determinant factor) . . .300.306(b)(1).
. IEP Team (Public agency representative) . . .300.321(a)(4).
. Independent educational evaluation . . .300.502.
CRITERIA (J-Z)
. Specific learning disability (see §§ 300.307, 300.309)
. Surrogate parents . . .300.519(d).
CURRENT PLACEMENT (Discipline)
. Authority of hearing officer . . .300.532(b).
. Placement during appeals . . .300.533.
DATA (A-L)
. Allocation of remaining funds to LEAs . . .300.816(d).
. Average per-pupil expenditure (Definition) . . .300.717(d).
. By-pass (Provision of services under) . . .300.191(c)(2).
. Determination of needed evaluation data . . .300.305(c).
. Disaggregated data . . .300.704(b)(4)(xi).
. Evaluation data:
. Procedures for determining eligibility and
placement . . .300.306(c).
. Review of existing data . . .300.305(a)(1).
. Grants to States most recent data . . .300.703(c)(1)(ii).
. LRE (Placements—meaning of evaluation data . . .300.116(a)(1).
DATA (M-Z)
. Parental consent (Not required for reviewing existing evaluation data) . . .300.300(d)(1)(i).
. State advisory council (Advise SEA on) . . .300.169(c).
. Suspension and expulsion rates . . .300.170(a).
DAY
. Business day (Definition) . . .300.11(b).
. Day (Calendar) . . .300.11(a).
. Discipline (See "Timelines—Discipline")
. School day (Definition) . . .300.11(c).
. . See "Timelines"
DECREASE IN ENROLLMENT (Exception to LEA
maintenance of effort) . . .300.204(b).
DECREASE IN FUNDS (To States) . . .300.703(d).
DEDUCTIBLE OR CO-PAY (Public benefits or
insurance) . . .300.154(d)(2)(ii).
DEFINITIONS (A-D)
. Act . . .300.4.
. Assistive technology device . . .300.5.
. Assistive technology service . . .300.6.
. At no cost . . .300.39(b)(1).
. Audiology . . .300.34(c)(1).
. Autism . . .300.8(c)(1).
. Average per-pupil expenditure in public elementary and secondary schools in the United States . . .300.717(d).

. Business day . . .300.11(b).
. Charter school . . .300.7.
. Child with a disability . . .300.8(a)(1).
. Consent . . .300.9.
. Controlled substance . . .300.530(i)(1).
. Core academic subjects . . .300.10.
. Counseling services . . .300.34(c)(2).
. Day; business day; school day . . .300.11.
. Deaf-blindness . . .300.8(c)(2).
. Deafness . . .300.8(c)(3).
. Destruction (Of information) . . .300.611(a).
. Developmental delays(s) . . .300.8(b).
DEFINITIONS (E-H)
. Early identification and assessment . . .300.34(c)(3).
. Education records . . .300.611(b).
. Educational service agency . . .300.12.
. Elementary school . . .300.13.
. Emotional disturbance . . .300.8(c)(4).
. Equipment . . .300.14.
. Evaluation . . .300.15.
. Excess costs . . .300.16.
. Extended school year services . . .300.106(b).
. Free appropriate public education . . .300.17.
. Freely associated States . . .300.717(a).
. Hearing impairment . . .300.8(c)(5).
. Highly qualified special education teacher . . .300.18(b).
. Homeless children . . .300.19.
DEFINITIONS (I)
. IEP Team . . .300.23.
. Illegal drug . . .300.530(i)(2).
. Include . . .300.20.
. Independent educational evaluation . . .300.502(a)(3)(i).
. Indian . . .300.21(a).
. Indian tribe . . .300.21(b).
. Individualized education program (IEP) . . .300.22.
. Individualized family service plan . . .300.24.
. Infant or toddler with a disability . . .300.25.
. Institution of higher education . . . . .300.26.
. Interpreting services . . .300.34(c)(4).
DEFINITIONS (J-O)
. Limited English proficient (LEP) . . .300.27.
. Local educational agency (LEA) . . .300.28.
. Medical services . . .300.34(c)(5).
. Mental retardation . . .300.8(c)(6).
. Multiple disabilities . . .300.8(c)(7).
. Native language . . .300.29(a).
. Occupational therapy . . . . .300.34(c)(6).
. Orientation and mobility services . . .300.34(c)(7).
. Orthopedic impairment . . .300.8(c)(8).
. Other health impairment . . .300.8(c)(9).
. Outlying areas . . .300.717(b).
DEFINITIONS (P-R)
. Parent . . .300.30(a).

. Parent counseling and training . . . .300.34(c)(8).
. Parent training and information center . . . .300.31.
. Parentally-placed private school children
with disabilities . . .. . .300.130.
. Participating agency (as used in "Confidentiality") . . . .300.611(c).
. Party or parties (Regarding procedures) . . . .300.181(a).
. Personally identifiable . . . .300.32.
. Physical education . . . .300.39(b)(2).
. Physical therapy . . . .300.34(c)(9).
. Psychological services . . . .300.34(c)(10).
. Public agency . . .. . .300.33.
. Public expense . . . .300.502(a)(3)(ii).
. Recreation . . . .300.34(c)(11).
. Rehabilitation counseling services . . . .300.34(c)(12).
. Related services . . . .300.34(a).
DEFINITIONS (S)
. School day . . . .300.11(c).
. School health services . . . .300.34(c)(13).
. School nurse services . . . .300.34(c)(13).
. Scientifically based research . . . .300.35.
. Secondary school . . . .300.36.
. Secretary . . . .300.38.
. Serious bodily injury . . . .300.530(i)(3).
. Services plan . . . .300.37.
. Social work services in schools . . . .300.34(c)(14).
. Special education . . . .300.39(a).
. Specially designed instruction . . . .300.39(b)(3).
. Specific learning disability . . . .300.8(c)(10).
. Speech-language pathology services . . . .300.34(c)(15).
. Speech or language impairment . . . .300.8(c)(11).
. State . . . .300.40.
. State (Special definition) . . . .300.717(c).
. State educational agency (SEA) . . . .300.41.
. Supplementary aids and services . . . .300.42.
DEFINITIONS (T-Z)
. Transition services . . . .300.43.
. Transportation . . . .300.34(c)(16).
. Traumatic brain injury . . . .300.8(c)(12).
. Travel training . . . .300.38(b)(4).
. Universal design . . . .300.44.
. Visual impairment including blindness . . . .300.8(c)(13).
. Vocational education . . . .300.39(b)(5).
. Ward of the State . . . .300.45.
. Weapon . . . .300.530(i)(4).
DEPARTMENT OF LABOR, Bureau of Labor Statistics
(Regarding rate of inflation) (see §§ 300.702(b), 300.704(a)(2)(ii), (b)(2), 300.812(b)(2))
DEPARTMENT (U.S. Department of Education)
. Enforcement: hearing procedures (see §§ 300.178 through 300.184)
. Monitoring (Regarding Secretary of the
Interior) . . . .300.708(a).
. Personally identifiable information (Use of) . . . .300.627.
DESTRUCTION OF INFORMATION . . . .300.624(b).
. Definition . . . .300.611(a).

DETERMINANT FACTOR for eligibility determination
. Lack of instruction in reading or math (see § 300.306(b)(1)(i), (b)(1)(ii))
. Limited English proficiency . . .300.306(b)(1)(iii).
DEVELOPMENT, REVIEW, AND REVISION OF IEP . . .300.324.
DEVELOPMENTAL DELAY(S)
. In definition of "Child with a disability" . . .300.8(b).
. Requirements for using "Developmental delay" . . .300.111(b).
. State definition . . .300.111(b).
. Using specified disability categories . . .300.111(d).
DIABETES . . .300.8(c)(9)(i).
DIRECT SERVICES
. For children in private schools (see§§ 300.132(a); 300.133(a); 300.134(d)(1))
. Nature and location of services . . .300.227(b).
. Payment by Secretary of the Interior . . .300.712(d).
. SEA (Additional information) . . .300.175(a).
. State-level activities . . .300.704(b)(4)(i).
. Use of LEA allocations for . . .300.227(a).
DISABILITY: ADVERSELY AFFECTS EDUCATIONAL PERFORMANCE (See "Adversely affects educational performance")
DISAGGREGATED DATA
. Assessment results for subgroup of children with disabilities . . .300.704(b)(4)(xi).
. For suspension and expulsion by race and ethnicity . . .300.170(a).
DISCIPLINE (A-B)
. Alternative educational setting (see §§ 300.530(d)(1), (d)(2), (d)(4), (g), 300.531, 300.533)
. Appeal . . .300.532(a).
. Behavioral interventions—intervention plan . . .300.530(f).
DISCIPLINE (C-H)
. Change of placements for disciplinary removals . . .300.536.
. Child's status during due process hearings . . .300.518.
. Determination of setting . . .300.531.
. Expedited due process hearings . . .300.532(c).
. Functional behavioral assessment (see § 300.530(d)(1)(ii), (f)(1)(i))
. Hearing officer (authority of) (see §§ 300.532(b), 300.533)
DISCIPLINE (I-Z)
. IEP Team (relevant members) (see §§ 300.530(e)(1), (f), 300.531)
. Interim alternative educational setting (see §§ 300.530(b), (d)(2), (g), 300.531, 300.532(b)(2)(ii), 300.533)
. Manifestation determination . . .300.530(e).
. Placement during appeals . . .300.533.
. Protections for children not determined eligible . . .300.534.
. Referral to and action by law enforcement and judicial authorities . . .300.535.
. School personnel (Authority of) . . .300.530(b).
. See "Timelines—Discipline"
DISCLOSURE
. Additional disclosure of information requirement . . .300.512(b).
. Consent required before disclosing:
. Education records to public benefits or

insurance agencies . . .300.154(d)(2)(iv).
. Personal information to non-agency officials . . .300.622(a).
. Notice on disclosure of evaluation results . . .300.504(c)(10).
. Policies on disclosing information to 3rd
parties . . .300.612(a)(3).
. Prohibit evidence not disclosed . . .300.512(a)(3).
DISPROPORTIONALITY . . .300.646.
DISPUTES
. Interagency disputes (Methods of ensuring services):
. Ensure services during pendency of dispute . . .300.154(a).
. Procedures for resolving . . .300.154(a)(3).
. Mediation (see also § 300.532(c)(3)) . . .300.506.
. Attorneys' fees for . . .300.517(c)(2)(ii).
. During discipline appeal process . . .300.532(c)(3).
. During resolution process (see § 300.510(b)(3), (c)(3))
. Enforcement of agreement (see §§ 300.506(b)(7), 300.510(d)(2), 300.537)
DIVIDED STATE AGENCY RESPONSIBILITY (Adult
prisons) . . .300.607.
DIVORCE—SEPARATION (Authority to review
records) . . .300.613(c).
DROPOUT RATES (Performance indicators) . . .300.157(a)(3).
DUE PROCESS HEARING(S) AND REVIEWS (A-E)
. Agency responsible for conducting hearing . . .300.511(b).
. Appeal of decisions; impartial review . . .300.514(b).
. Attorneys' fees . . .300.517(a).
. Basic requirements (see §§ 300.507 through 300.514)
. Child's status during proceedings (Pendency) . . .300.518.
. Parent request for hearing (Discipline) . . .300.532(a).
. Civil action . . .300.516(a).
. Evaluations disclosed at least 5 business
days before hearing . . .300.512(a)(3).
. Expedited due process hearings (Discipline) . . .300.532(c).
DUE PROCESS HEARING(S) AND REVIEWS (F-I)
. Failure to implement a due process hearing
decision . . .300.152(c)(3).
. Finality of decision; appeal; impartial
review . . .300.514.
. Findings of fact and decisions (see § 300.512(a)(5), (c)(3)):
. To State advisory panel (see §§ 300.513(d), 300.514(c))
. Hearing rights . . .300.512(a).
. Impartial hearing officer . . .300.511(c).
. See "Hearing officer(s)"
DUE PROCESS HEARING(S) AND REVIEWS (J-Z)
. Parental rights at hearings . . .300.512(c).
. Party notice to other party . . .300.508(c).
. Model form to assist parents . . .300.509.
. Party request for hearing (Discipline) . . .300.532(a).
. Pendency (Stay put) . . .300.518.
. Prohibit evidence not introduced 5 business
days before hearing . . .300.512(a)(3).
. Record of hearing . . .300.512(c)(3).
. See "Civil action—proceedings," "Court(s)" "Procedural safeguards," "Timelines" . . .
. Timelines and convenience of hearings— reviews (see §§ 300.506(b)(5), 300.511(e),

Appendix E to Part 300 IDEA REGULATIONS 289

300.516(b))
EARLY IDENTIFICATION AND ASSESSMENT
(Definition) . . .300.34(c)(3).
EARLY INTERVENING SERVICES . . .300.226.
. Adjustment to local fiscal efforts . . .300.205(d).
. Do not limit/create right to FAPE . . .300.226(c).
. For children not currently identified as needing special education or related services . . .300.226(a).
. Permissive use of funds . . .300.208(a)(2).
. Scientifically based literacy instruction . . .300.226(b).
. Use of funds:
. By LEA . . .300.226(a).
. By Secretary of the Interior . . .300.711.
EDUCATION RECORDS (Definition) . . .300.611(b).
EDUCATIONAL PLACEMENTS (LRE) . . .300.114.
EDUCATIONAL SERVICE AGENCY (ESA)
. Definition . . .300.12.
. In definition of "LEA" . . .300.28(b)(1).
. Joint establishment of eligibility (Regarding ESAs) . . .300.224(b).
. Additional requirements (Regarding LRE) . . .300.224(c).
ELEMENTARY AND SECONDARY EDUCATION ACT OF 1965 (ESEA)
. Coordination of early intervening services . . .300.226(e).
. Excess cost requirement . . .300.202(b).
. Schoolwide programs . . . . .300.206(a).
ELIGIBILITY (CHILD—STUDENT) (A-G)
. Additional eligibility requirements (see §§ 300.121 through 300.124, 300.307 through 300.311)
. Children with disabilities in adult prisons . . .300.324(d).
. Children with specific learning disabilities (Documentation of eligibility determination) . . .300.311(a).
. Determinant factor for . . .300.306(b)(1).
. Determination of eligibility . . .300.306.
. Developmental delay (Non-use of term by LEA if not adopted by State) . . .300.111(b)(iv).
. Documentation of eligibility (To parent) . . .300.306(a)(2).
. Graduation with regular diploma: termination (see §§ 300.102(a)(3), 300.305(e)(2)).
ELIGIBILITY (CHILD—STUDENT) (H-Z)
. Lack of instruction in reading or math . . .300.306(b).
. Limited English proficiency . . .300.306(b).
. Public benefits or insurance (Risk loss of eligibility) . . .§ 300.154(d)(2)(iii).
. Termination of eligibility (see §§ 300.204(c), 300.305(e)(2))
. Transfer of rights (Special rule) . . .300.520(b).
ELIGIBILITY (PUBLIC AGENCIES)
. Hearings related to (See "Hearings—Hearing procedures")
. Joint establishment of (see §§ 300.202(b)(3), 300.223(a), 300.224(a))
. LEA (See "LEA eligibility") Secretary of the Interior . . .300.712(e).
. State (See "State eligibility")
. State agency eligibility . . .300.228.
. See "State agencies"
EMOTIONAL DISTURBANCE (Definition) . . .300.8(c)(4).
ENFORCEMENT

. Department procedures (see §§ 300.600, 300.604, 300.605)
. Referral to law enforcement authorities . . . 300.535.
. State policies and procedures:
. Enforcement mechanisms . . . 300.537.
. LEA not meeting requirements . . . 300.608.
. Regarding confidentiality . . . 300.626.
EPILEPSY . . . 300.8(c)(9)(i).
EQUIPMENT
. Acquisition of . . . . . . 300.718(a).
. Definition . . . 300.14.
. Exception to maintenance of effort . . . 300.204(d).
. Placement in private school . . . 300.144.
EVALUATION (A-G)
. Assessments in (see §§ 300.304(b), (c) . . . 300.305(c)).
. Basic requirements (see §§ 300.301, 300.303, 00.324)
. Comprehensive (Identify all special
education needs) . . . 300.304(c)(6).
. Definition of . . . 300.15.
. Evaluation procedures . . . 300.304.
. Evaluation report to parents . . . 300.306(a)(2).
. Existing evaluation data (Review of) . . . 300.305(a)(1).
. Graduation (Evaluation not required for) . . . 300.305(e)(2).
EVALUATION (H-Z)
. Independent educational evaluation (IEE) . . . 300.502.
. Initial evaluation (see §§ 300.301, 300.305)
. Observation in determining SLD . . . 300.310.
. Parent consent . . . 300.300.
. Parent right to evaluation at public expense . . . 300.502(b).
. Reevaluation . . . 300.303.
EXCEPTION
. Charter schools exception (Joint
eligibility) . . . . . . 300.223(b).
. For prior local policies and procedures . . . 300.220.
. For prior State policies and procedures . . . 300.176(a).
. To FAPE:
. For certain ages . . . 300.102.
. For graduating with a regular diploma . . . 300.102 (a)(3)(i).
. For children in adult prisons (see §§ 300.102(a)(2), 300.324(d)).
. To maintenance of effort . . . 300.204.
. To reimbursement for parental placement . . . 300.148(e).
EXCESS COSTS
. Calculation of (see Appendix A—Excess Costs Calculation)
. Definition . . . 300.16.
. Excess cost requirement . . . 300.202(b)
. Joint establishment of eligibility . . . 300.202(b)(3)
. LEA requirement . . . 300.202(b)
. Limitation on use of Part B funds . . . 300.202(b)
. Meeting the excess cost requirement . . . 300.202(b)(2)
. See also §§ 300.163(a), 300.175(b), 300.202(a), 300.227(a)(2)(ii)
EXISTING EVALUATION DATA (Review of) . . . 300.305(a)(1).
EXPEDITED DUE PROCESS HEARINGS . . . 300.532(c).
. Authority of hearing officer . . . 300.532(b).
. Party appeal (Hearing requested by parents) . . . 300.532(a).

EXPULSION (See "Suspension and expulsion")
EXTENDED SCHOOL YEAR SERVICES . . .300.106.
EXTRACURRICULAR
. IEP content . . .300.320(a)(4)(ii).
. In supplementary aids and services . . .300.42.
. Nonacademic services . . .300.107.
. Nonacademic settings . . .300.117.
FACILITIES
. Alteration of . . .300.718.
. Children in private schools or facilities (see §§ 300.130, 300.142(a), 300.144(b), (c), . . .300.147(c))
. Construction of . . .300.718.
. Physical education (In separate facilities) . . .300.108(d).
. Private schools and facilities . . .300.2(c).
. See also "Correctional facilities"
. Termination of expenses for construction of . . .300.204(d).
FAMILY EDUCATIONAL RIGHTS AND PRIVACY ACT (FERPA) (See "Confidentiality")
FAPE (A-G)
. Definition . . .300.17.
. Documentation of exceptions . . .300.102(b).
. Exception to FAPE:
. For certain ages . . .300.102(a).
. For children receiving early intervention services . . .300.102(a)(4).
. For children graduating with a regular diploma . . .300.102(a)(3).
. For children in adult correctional facilities . . .300.102(a)(2).
. For children:
. Advancing from grade to grade . . .300.101(c).
. Beginning at age 3 . . .300.101(b).
. On Indian reservations . . .300.707(c).
. Suspended or expelled from school . . .300.101(a).
. General requirement . . .300.101(a).
FAPE (H-Z)
. Methods and payments . . .300.103.
. Private school children with disabilities:
. Placed by parents when FAPE is at issue . . .300.148.
. Placed in or referred by public agencies (see §§ 300.145 through 300.147)
. Reallocation of LEA funds (FAPE adequately provided) . . .300.705(c).
. Services (and placement) for FAPE:
. Based on child's needs (Not disability category) . . .300.304(c)(6).
. State eligibility condition . . .300.100.
FAS (Freely associated States) . . .300.717(a).
FAX (FACSIMILE TRANSMISSION)
. Department procedures (see §§ 300.183,300.196(a) through (e))
FERPA (Family Educational Rights and Privacy Act) (See "Confidentiality")
FILING A CLAIM (Private insurance) . . .300.154(e).
FILING A COMPLAINT (State complaint procedures) . . .300.153.
FILING REQUIREMENTS

. By-pass (Regarding private school children) . . .300.196.
. Department procedures . . .300.183.
. See §§ 300.178 through 300.186.
FINALITY OF DECISION . . .300.514.
FORMULA
. Allocations to LEAs . . .300.705(b).
. Allocations to States . . .300.703.
. Allocation to States when by-pass is implemented . . .300.191.
. Allocation to States regarding section 619 (see §§ 300.807, 300.810).
. Parentally-placed private school children . . .300.133.
. SEA set aside funds . . .300.704(b).
. See also § 300.171(a).
FOSTER PARENT . . .300.30(a)(2).
. See also § 300.45(b).
FREELY ASSOCIATED STATES AND OUTLYING AREAS
. Funding for . . .300.701(a).
. Purpose of grants . . .300.700(a).
FULL EDUCATIONAL OPPORTUNITY GOAL . . .300.109.
FUNCTIONAL BEHAVIORAL ASSESSMENT (see § 300.530(d)(1)(ii), (f)(1)(i))
FUNDING MECHANISM: LRE . . .300.114(b).
FUNDS (See "Use of funds")
GENERAL CURRICULUM
. Discipline (Continue participating in) . . .300.530(d)(1)(i).
. Evaluation procedures:
. Be involved and progress in . . .300.304(b)(1)(ii).
. Review of existing evaluation data . . .300.305(a)(1).
. IEPs:
. Measurable annual goals . . .300.320(a)(2)(i).
. Present levels of educational performance . . .300.320(a)(1).
. Review and revision of IEPs . . .300.324(b)(1)(ii).
. Special education and related services . . .300.320(a)(4)(ii).
. IEP Team . . .300.321(a)(4)(ii).
. Specially designed instruction (Definition) . . .300.39(b)(3).
GOALS
Annual goals (See "IEP" and "Annual goals").
. Performance goals and indicators . . .300.157.
. State and local activities to meet . . .300.814(c).
. Use of State-level funds to meet . . .300.704(b)(4)(x).
GOVERNOR (Adult prisons) . . .300.149(d).
. See also "Chief executive officer".
GRADUATION
. Evaluation not required for . . .300.305(e)(2).
. Exception to FAPE . . .300.102(a)(3)(i).
. Graduation rates as performance indicators . . . 300.157(a)(3).
. Written prior notice required . . .300.102(a)(3)(iii).
GRANDPARENT OR STEPPARENT (In definition of "Parent") . . .300.30(a)(4).
GRANTS
. Grants to States: . . .300.700. 300.700(b).
. Maximum amount
. Purpose of . . .300.700(a).
. See "Subgrants".
GUARDIAN (In definition of "Parent"). . .300.30(a)(3).

GUARDIANSHIP, SEPARATION, AND DIVORCE. . .300.613(c).
(Regarding parent's authority to review records)
HEALTH AND HUMAN SERVICES (Secretary of). . .300.708(i)(1).
HEARING AIDS: Proper functioning of. . .300.113(a).
HEARING IMPAIRMENT
. Definition. . .300.8(c)(5).
. Related services, audiology. . .300.34(c)(1).
HEARING OFFICER(S) (A-B)
. Additional disclosure of information requirement. . .300.512(b).
. Attorneys' fees. . .300.517(c)(2)(i).
. Authority of (Discipline). . .300.532(b).
. Basis of decisions. . .300.513(a).
HEARING OFFICER(S) (C-Z)
. Change of placement:
. Hearing officer decision agrees with parents. . .300.518(d).
. Hearing officer may order. . .300.532(b)(2)(ii).
. Expedited due process hearing (Discipline). . .300.532(c).
. Impartial hearing officer. . .300.511(c).
. Parent appeal (Discipline). . .300.532(a).
. Placement during appeals. . .300.533.
. Private school placement when FAPE is at
issue. . .300.148(b).
. Reimbursement for private school placement
by parents. . .300.148(c).
. Requests for evaluations by. . .300.502(d).
HEARING RIGHTS. . .300.512.
HEARINGS—HEARING PROCEDURES
. Due process (See "Due process hearings").
. Public hearings on policies and procedures. . .300.165(a).
. State and local eligibility:
. LEA eligibility. . .300.155.
. Notification in case of LEA or State
ineligibility. . .300.221.
. State eligibility (Notice and hearing) (see §§ 300.178, 300.179, 300.181).
HEART CONDITION. . .300.8(c)(9)(i).
HEIGHTENED ALERTNESS TO ENVIRONMENTAL STIMULI (In "Other health impairment"). . .300.8(c)(9).
HIGH COST FUND (LEA). . .300.704(c).
HIGHLY MOBILE CHILDREN (e.g., homeless and migrant children). . .300.111(c)(2).
HIGHLY QUALIFIED TEACHER (A-Q)
. Alternative route to certification. . .300.18(b)(2).
. Definition of. . .300.18.
. Private school teachers. . .300.18(h).
HIGHLY QUALIFIED TEACHER (R-Z)
. Requirements for in general. . .300.18(b).
. Requirements for teaching to alternate academic achievement standards. . . .. .300.18(c).
. Requirements for teaching multiple subjects. . .300.18(d).
. Personnel qualifications. . .300.156(c).
HIGH NEED CHILD. . .300.704(c)(3)(i).
HOMELESS CHILDREN
. Child find. . .300.111(a)(1)(i).

. Definition of. . .300.19.
. McKinney-Vento Homeless Assistance Act (see §§ 300.19, 300.149(a)(3), 300.153(b)(4)(iii), 300.168(a)(5), 300.508(b)(4)).
. Surrogate parents for. . .300.519(a)(4).
HYPERACTIVITY (Attention deficit hyperactivity disorder). . .300.8(c)(9)(i).
INAPPLICABILITY (Of requirements that prohibit commingling and supplanting of funds). . .300.704(d).
IEE (See "Independent educational evaluation")
IEP (A-I)
. Agency responsibilities for transition services. . .300.324(c)(1).
. Basic requirements (see §§ 300.320 through 300.324).
. Child participation when considering transition. . .300.321(b)(1).
. Consideration of special factors. . .300.324(a)(2).
. Consolidation of IEP Team meetings. . .300.324(a)(5).
. Content of IEPs. . .300.320(a).
. Definition (see §§ 300.22, 300.320).
. Development, review, and revision of. . .300.324.
. IEP or IFSP for children aged 3 through 5. . .300.323(b).
. IEP Team. . .300.321.
IEP (J-Z)
. Modifications of IEP or placement (FAPE for children in adult prisons). . .300.324(d)(2)(i).
. Modify/Amend without convening meeting (see § 300.324(a)(4), (a)(6)).
. Parent participation. . .300.322.
. Alternative means. . .300.328.
. Part C coordinator involvement. . .300.321(f).
. Private school placements by public agencies. . .300.325(a)(1).
. Regular education teacher (See "IEP Team").
. Review and revision of IEPs. . .300.324(b).
. SEA responsibility regarding private school. . .300.325(c).
. State eligibility requirement. . .300.112.
. Transition services. . .300.320(b).
. When IEPs must be in effect. . .300.323.
IEP TEAM. . .300.321.
. Alternative educational setting (Determined by). . .300.531.
. Consideration of special factors. . .300.324(a)(2).
. Assistive technology. . .300.324(a)(2)(v).
. Behavioral interventions. . .300.324(a)(2)(i).
. Braille needs. . .300.324(a)(2)(iii).
. Communication needs (Deafness and other needs). . .300.324(a)(2)(iv).
. Limited English proficiency. . .300.324(a)(2)(ii).
. Determination of knowledge or special expertise. . .300.321(c).
. Discipline procedures (see §§ 300.530(e),. . .300.531).
. Manifestation determination. . .300.530(e).
. Other individuals who have knowledge or special expertise (At parent or agency discretion). . .300.321(a)(6).
. Participation by private school (public

agency placement). . .300.325(a).
. Regular education teacher (see §§ 300.321(a)(2), 300.324(a)(3)).
IFSP (INDIVIDUALIZED FAMILY SERVICE PLAN)
. Definition. . .300.24.
. Transition from Part C. . .300.124.
. IFSP vs. IEP. . .300.323(b).
ILLEGAL DRUG (Definition—discipline). . .300.530(i)(2).
IMPARTIAL DUE PROCESS HEARING. . .300.511.
. See "Due process hearings and reviews".
IMPARTIAL HEARING OFFICER. . .300.511(c).
IMPARTIALITY OF MEDIATOR. . .300.506(b)(1).
INCIDENTAL BENEFITS (Permissive use of funds). . .300.208.
INCIDENTAL FEES (In definition of "at no cost" under "Special education"). . .300.39(b)(1).
INCLUDE (Definition). . .300.20.
INDEPENDENT EDUCATIONAL EVALUATION (IEE). . .300.502.
. Agency criteria (see § 300.502(a)(2), (b)(2)(ii), (c)(1), (e)).
. Definition. . .300.502(a)(3)(i).
. Parent-initiated evaluations. . .300.502(c).
. Parent right to. . .300.502(a)(1).
. Procedural safeguards notice. . .300.504(c)(1).
. Public expense (Definition under IEE). . .. . .300.502(a)(3)(ii).
. Request by hearing officers. . .300.502(d).
. Use as evidence at hearing. . .300.502(c)(2).
INDIAN; INDIAN CHILDREN
. Child find for Indian children aged 3
through 5. . .300.712(d).
. Definition of "Indian". . .300.21(a).
. Definition of "Indian tribe". . .300.21(b).
. Early intervening services. . .300.711.
. Payments and use of amounts for:
. Education and services for children aged 3
through 5. . .300.712(a).
. Education of Indian children. . .300.707.
. Plan for coordination of services. . .300.713.
. Submission of information by Secretary of
Interior. . .300.708.
INDICATORS. . .300.157(b).
. See "Performance goals and indicators".
INDIVIDUALIZED EDUCATION PROGRAM (See "IEP")
INDIVIDUALIZED FAMILY SERVICE PLAN (See "IFSP")
INFORMED CONSENT (See "Consent")
INITIAL EVALUATION. . .300.301.
. Consent before conducting. . .300.300(a)(1)(i).
. For ward of State. . .300.300(a)(2).
. Not construed as consent for initial
placement. . .300.300(a)(1)(ii).
. When not required. . .300.300(a)(2).
. Review of existing evaluation data. . .300.305(a).
INSTITUTION OF HIGHER EDUCATION
. Definition. . .300.26.
INSTRUCTIONAL MATERIALS
. Access to. . .300.172.

. Audio-visual materials. . .300.14(b).
. LEA purchase of. . .300.210.
. NIMAC:
. SEA coordination with. . .300.172(c).
. SEA rights and responsibilities if not coordinating. . .300.172(b).
INSURANCE
. Community-based waivers (see. . .§ 300.154(d)(2)(iii)(D)).
. Financial costs. . .300.154(f)(2).
. Financial responsibility of LEA/SEA. . .300.154(a)(1).
. Out-of-pocket expense. . .300.154(d)(2)(ii).
. Private insurance. . .300.154(e).
. Public benefits or insurance. . .300.154(d).
. Risk of loss of eligibility (see § 300.154(d)(2)(iii)(D)).
INTERAGENCY AGREEMENTS
. FAPE methods and payments (Joint agreements). . .300.103(a).
. LRE (Children in public/private
institutions). . .300.114(a)(2)(i).
. Methods of ensuring services. . .300.154(a).
. SEA responsibility for general supervision. . .300.149.
. Secretary of Interior—with Health and Human Services Secretary. . .300.708(i)(1).
. Cooperative agreements (BIA and other
agencies). . .300.712(d).
INTERAGENCY COORDINATION (See "Coordination of services," "Interagency agreements")
INTERAGENCY DISPUTES. . .300.154(a)(3).
INTERAGENCY RESPONSIBILITIES (Transition
services). . .300.320(b).
INTERIM ALTERNATIVE EDUCATIONAL SETTING (See §§ 300.530(b), 300.531, 300.532(b)(2)(ii), 300.533)
INTERPRETING SERVICES
. As a related service. . .300.34(a).
. Definition. . .300.34(c)(4).
JOINT ESTABLISHMENT OF ELIGIBILITY (LEAs). . .300.223.
. See also §§ 300.202(b)(3), 300.224.
JUDICIAL
. Authorities (Referral to). . .300.535.
. Finding of unreasonableness. . .300.148(d)(3).
. Proceeding (During pendency). . .300.518(a).
. Review. . .300.197.
. See also:
. Civil action (see §§ 300.504(c)(12),. . .300.514(d), 300.516)
. Court(s) (see §§ 300.102(a)(1), 300.184, 300.148(c), (d)(3), 300.197, 300.516(a), (c), (d), 300.517(a), (c))
JUVENILE-ADULT CORRECTIONS FACILITIES (See "Correctional facilities")
LAW ENFORCEMENT AND JUDICIAL AUTHORITIES
. Referral to. . .300.535.
LEA (LOCAL EDUCATIONAL AGENCY) (A-C)
. Allocations to LEAs. . .300.705(b).
. Reallocation of funds (If LEA is adequately providing FAPE). . .300.705(c).
. Charter schools and LEAs (See "Charter schools").
. Child count—LEAs:
. Parentally-placed private school children
with disabilities. . .300.133(c).

. Procedures for counting all children served (Annual report). . .300.645.
. See also "Child count".
. Child find—LEAs:
. Parentally-placed private school children
with disabilities. . .300.131.
. See also "Child find"
. Compliance (LEA and State agency). . .300.222.
. Consistency of LEA policies with State policies. . .300.201.

LEA (D-G)
. Definition of LEA. . .300.28.
. Developmental delay: Use of term by LEAs (see § 300.111(b)(2) through (b)(4)).
. Direct services by SEA (If LEA is unable or unwilling to serve CWDs, etc.). . .300.227.
. Discipline and LEAs (See "Discipline").
. Eligibility of LEA:
. Condition of assistance (see §§ 300.200 through 300.213)
. Exception for prior local plans.. . .300.220.
. Ineligibility of LEA (Notice by SEA). . .300.221.
. SEA hearings on LEA eligibility. . .300.155.
. Excess cost requirement—LEA:. . .300.202(b).
. Use of amounts for excess costs. . .300.202(a)(2).
. See also "Excess costs".

LEA (H-L)
. Hearings relating to LEA eligibility. . .300.155.
. Information for SEA. . .. . .300.211.
. Instructional materials (Purchase of). . .300.210.
. Joint establishment of eligibility (By two
or more LEAs). . .300.202(b)(3).
. See also §§ 300.223, 300.224
. LEA and State agency compliance. . .300.222.
. LEA policies (Modification of). . .300.220(b).
. See "LEA eligibility," "Eligibility of LEA".

LEA (M-P)
. Maintenance of effort regarding LEAs (See "Maintenance of effort").
. Methods of ensuring services—LEAs (see § 300.154(a)(1) through (a)(4), (b)).
. Migratory children with disabilities
(Linkage with records under ESEA). . .300.213.
. Modification of policies by LEA. . .300.220(b).
. Noncompliance of LEA (SEA determination). . .300.222(a).
. Notice requirement (On LEA). . .300.222(b).
. Purchase of instructional materials. . .300.210.
. Personnel shortages (Use of funds to assist
LEAs in meeting). . .300.704(b)(4)(vii).
. Public information (By LEA). . .300.212.

LEA (R-T)
. Reallocation of LEA funds (If LEA is adequately providing FAPE). . .300.705(c).
. Reimbursement of LEAs by other agencies (See "Methods of ensuring services," § 300.154(a)(2) through (a)(3), (b)(2)).
. Review and revision of policies. . .300.170(b).
. SEA reduction in payments to LEA. . .300.222(a).
. SEA use of LEA allocations for direct
services. . .300.227.
. Show cause hearing (By-pass requirement). . .300.194.
. State-level nonsupplanting. . .300.162(c).

. Subgrants to LEAs. . .300.705(a).
. Suspension and expulsion rates—LEAs. . .300.170(a)(1).
. Transition planning conferences (Part C to B). . .300.124(c).

LEA (U-Z)
. Use of amounts (by LEA). . .300.202.
. (See "Permissive use of funds").
. Use of SEA allocations (Regarding LEAs). . .300.704.
. For capacity-building, etc. (see § 300.704(b)(4)(viii)).
. To assist in meeting personnel shortages (see § 300.704(b)(4)(vii)).

LEA ELIGIBILITY (A-I)
. Adjustment to local fiscal efforts in certain fiscal years. . .300.205.
. Charter schools—public:
. Rights of children with disabilities who attend public charter schools. . .300.209(a).
. That are public schools of the LEA. . .300.209(b).
. That are LEAs. . .300.209(c).
. That are not an LEA or a school that is part of an LEA. . .300.209(d).
. Treatment of charter schools and their students. . .300.209.
. See also "Charter schools".
. Condition of assistance. . .300.200.
. See §§ 300.201 through 300.213.
. Consistency with State policies. . .300.201.
. Information for SEA. . .300.211.

LEA ELIGIBILITY (M-Z)
. Maintenance of effort. . .300.203.
. Exception to. . .300.204.
. Migratory children with disabilities—records regarding 300.213.
. Permissive use of funds. . .300.208.
. Administrative case management. . .300.208(b).
. Early intervening services. . .300.208(a)(2).
. High cost special education and related services. . .300.208(a)(3).
. Services and aids that also benefit nondisabled children. . .300.208(a)(1).
. Personnel development. . .300.207.
. Records regarding migratory children with disabilities. . .300.213.
. State prohibition (If LEA is unable to establish/maintain programs of FAPE). . .300.205(c).
. Treatment of charter schools and their students. . .300.209.

LEAD POISONING (Other health impairment). . .300.8(c)(9)(i).

LEAST RESTRICTIVE ENVIRONMENT (LRE)
. Children in public or private institutions. . .300.118.
. Continuum of alternative placements. . .300.115.
. Educational service agency (Additional requirement regarding LRE). . .300.224(c).
. Monitoring activities. . .300.120.
. Nonacademic settings. . .300.117.
. Placements. . .300.116.
. State eligibility requirements. . .300.114.

. Additional requirement: State funding mechanism. . .300.114(b).
. Technical assistance and training. . .300.119.
LEISURE EDUCATION (Recreation). . .300.34(c)(11)(iv).
LEP (See "Limited English proficient")
LEUKEMIA (Other health impairment). . .300.8(c)(9)(i).
LIMITED ENGLISH PROFICIENT (LEP)
. Definition of. . .300.27.
. Determinant factor in eligibility determination. . .300.306(b)(1)(iii).
. In development, review, and revision of IEP. . .300.324(a)(2)(ii).
. In "native language" (Definition). . .300.29(a).
. Special rule—LEP not determinant factor. . .300.306(b)(1)(iii).
LOCAL EDUCATIONAL AGENCY (See "LEA")
LRE (See "Least restrictive environment")
MAINTENANCE OF EFFORT (MOE-LEA) (A-R)
. Amounts in excess (Reduce level). . .300.205(a).
. Exception to. . .300.204.
. Maintenance of effort and early intervening services (see Appendix D)
. Maintenance of effort—LEA. . .300.203.
. Non-reduction of (State enforcement). . .300.608.
. Public benefits or insurance proceeds are not MOE. . .300.154(g)(2).
. See "Methods of ensuring services".
MAINTENANCE OF EFFORT (MOE-LEA) (S-Z)
. SEA flexibility. . .300.230(a).
. State enforcement (SEA must prohibit LEA from reducing MOE). . .300.608.
MAINTENANCE OF STATE FINANCIAL SUPPORT. . .300.163.
. Reduction of funds for failure to maintain support. . .300.163(b).
. Subsequent years (Regarding a waiver). . .300.163(d).
. Waivers: Exceptional or uncontrollable circumstances. . .300.163(c).
MANIFESTATION DETERMINATION (See "Discipline"). . .300.530(e).
McKINNEY-VENTO HOMELESS ASSISTANCE ACT
. In definition of "Homeless children". . .300.19.
. In filing a State complaint. . .300.153(b)(4)(iii).
. SEA responsibility for general supervision (Regarding homeless children). . .300.149(a)(3).
. State advisory panel (Membership). . .300.168(a)(5).
. Surrogate parents (Homeless child's rights protected. . .300.519(a)(4).
MEDIATION (A-O)
. Benefits of (Meeting to explain). . .300.506(b)(2)(ii).
. Confidential discussions. . .300.506(b)(6)(i).
. Cost of (Borne by State). . .300.506(b)(4).
. Disinterested party (To meet with parents and schools. . .300.506(b)(2).
. Disputes (Resolve through mediation). . .300.506(a).
. Legally binding agreement. . .300.506(b)(6).
. Mediation procedures (By public agency to allow parties to resolve disputes). . .300.506(a).
. Mediators:

. Impartiality of. . .300.506(c).
. List of. . .300.506(b)(3)(i).
. Qualified and impartial (see § 300.506(b)(1)(iii)).
. Meeting to explain benefits of. . .300.506(b)(2)(ii).
. Not used as evidence in hearing. . .300.506(b)(8).
. Not used to deny/delay right to hearing. . .300.506(b)(1)(ii),
. Opportunity to meet. . .30.506(b)(2).

MEDIATION (P-Z)
. Parent training and information center. . .300.506(b)(2)(i). 300.504(c)(6).
. Procedural safeguards notice
. Random selection of mediators. . .300.506(b)(3)(ii).
. Use of SEA allocations to establish. . .300.704(b)(3)(ii).
. Voluntary. . .300.506(b)(1)(i).
. Written mediation agreement. . .300.506(b)(7).

MEDICAID
. Children covered by public benefits or insurance. . .300.154(d)(1).
. Construction (Nothing alters requirements imposed under Titles XIX or XXI). . .300.154(h).
. Financial responsibility of each non-educational public agency (e.g., State Medicaid). . .300.154(a)(1).
. LEA high cost fund (Disbursements not medical assistance under State Medicaid). . .300.704(c)(8).
. Medicaid reimbursement not disqualified because service in school context. . .300.154(b)(1)(ii).
. Methods of ensuring services (see§ 300.154(a)(1), (b)(1)(ii), (d), (g)(2), (h))
. Proceeds from public or private insurance. . .300.154(g)(1).
. Public agency may use Medicaid. . .300.154(a)(1).
. State Medicaid, etc., must precede financial responsibility of LEA. . .300.154(a)(1).

MEDICAL (A-L)
. Assistance under other Federal programs. . .300.186.
. Assistive technology device (Does not include a surgically implanted medical device). . .. . .300.5.
. LEA high cost fund (Disbursements not medical assistance under State Medicaid). . .300.704(c)(8).

MEDICAL (M-Q)
. Medical services in ("Related services"):
. Audiology (Referral for). . .300.34(c)(1)(ii).
. Definition of. . .300.34(c)(5).
. For diagnostic purposes. . .300.34(a).
. Speech-language pathology (Referral for). . .300.34(c)(15)(iii).
. Medical supplies, etc. (Memo of agreement between HHS and Interior). . .300.708(i)(2).
. Non-medical (Residential placement). . .300.104.

MEDICAL (R-Z)
. Referral for medical services:
. Audiology. . .300.34(c)(1)(ii).
. Speech-language pathology services. . .300.34(c)(15)(iii).
. Related services: Exception; surgically implanted devices ("Cochlear implants"). . .300.34(b).
. Routine checking of hearing aids and other devices. . .300.113.

. SLD: Educationally relevant medical findings, if any. . .300.311(a)(4).
MEDICATION
. Prohibition on mandatory medication. . .300.174.
MEETING(S)
. Alternative means of meeting participation. . .300.328.
. Consolidation of IEP Team meetings. . .300.324(a)(5).
. Equitable services determined (Parentally- placed private school CWDs). . .300.137.
. IEP Team meetings (See "IEP").
. Mediation (Opportunity to meet). . .300.506(b)(2).
. Opportunity to examine records; participation in IEP Team meetings. . .300.501.
. Parent participation in meetings (see § 300.506(b)(2), (b)(4)).
. Private school placements by public agencies. . .300.325.
. Reviewing and revising IEPs (Private school placements). . .300.325(b).
. Services plan for private school children
(Meetings). . .300.137(c)(1).
MENTAL RETARDATION (Definition). . .300.8(c)(6).
METHODS OF ENSURING SERVICES. . .300.154.
MIGRANT CHILDREN
. Child find. . .300.111(c)(2).
. Records regarding migratory children
(Linkage with ESEA). . .300.213.
MINIMUM STATE COMPLAINT PROCEDURES. . .300.152.
. See "Complaints," "State complaint procedures".
MONITOR; MONITORING ACTIVITIES (A-N)
. Allowable costs for monitoring. . .300.704(b)(3)(i).
. Children placed in private schools by public
agencies. . .300.147(a).
. Implementation by SEA. . .300.147(a).
. LRE (SEA monitoring activities). . .300.120.
. Monitoring activities (LRE). . .300.120.
. Monitoring—Enforcement (Subpart F). . .300.600.
. Rule of construction (Use any authority under GEPA to monitor). . .300.609.
. Secretary's review and determination
regarding State performance. . .300.603(b)(1).
. State exercise of general supervision. . .300.600(d)(2).
. State use of targets and reporting. . .300.602(a), (b)(1).
MONITOR; MONITORING ACTIVITIES (O-Z)
. Outlying areas, etc. (see § 300.701(a)(1)(ii)).
. Private school children: SEA monitoring. . .300.147(a).
. SEA responsibility for general supervision. . .300.149(b).
. Secretary of the Interior. . .300.708.
. State advisory panel functions (Advise SEA on corrective action plans). . .300.169(d).
. Use of SEA allocations for monitoring. . .300.704(b)(3)(i).
. Waiver (State's procedures for monitoring). . .300.164(c)(2)(ii)(B).
. Summary of monitoring reports. . .300.164(c)(3).
MULTIPLE DISABILITIES (Definition). . .300.8(c)(7).
NATIONAL INSTRUCTIONAL MATERIALS ACCESS CENTER
(NIMAC). . .300.172(e)(1)(ii).
NATIONAL INSTRUCTIONAL MATERIALS ACCESSIBILITY . . . 300.172(e)(1)(iii).
STANDARDS (NIMAS)
. See also Appendix C.
NATIVE LANGUAGE

. Confidentiality (Notice to parents). . .300.612(a)(1).
. Definition. . .300.29.
. Definition of "Consent". . .300.9.
. Evaluation procedures (Tests in native language). . .. . .300.304(c)(1)(ii).
. Notice to parents: Confidentiality (In native language). . .300.612(a)(1).
. Prior notice:
. Notice in native language. . .300.503(c)(1)(ii).
. Notice translated orally. . .300.503(c)(2)(i).
. Steps if not a written language. . .300.503(c)(2).
NATURE/LOCATION OF SERVICES (Direct services by SEA). . .300.227.
NEPHRITIS (In "Other health impairment"). . .300.8(c)(9)(i).
NIMAC (See "National Instructional Materials Access Center")
NIMAS (See "National Instructional Materials Accessibility Standard")
NONACADEMIC
. Activities: Participate in (IEP content). . .300.320(a)(4)(ii).
. Services and extracurricular activities (Equal opportunity to participate in). . .300.107(a).
. Settings. . .300.117.
NONCOMMINGLING. . .300.162(b).
NONDISABLED (Children; students) (A-P)
. At no cost (In definition of "special education"). . .300.39(b)(1).
. Disciplinary information. . .300.229(a).
. Excess cost requirement. . .300.202(b).
. IEP (definition) (see § 300.320(a)(1)(i), (a)(4)(iii), (a)(5))
. LRE (General requirement). . .300.114.
. Nonacademic settings. . .300.117.
. Placement. . .300.116.
. Program options. . .300.110.
NONDISABLED (Children; students) (R-Z)
. Regular physical education. . .300.108(b).
. Services and aids that also benefit nondisabled children. . .300.208(a)(1).
. Special education (Definition: In definition of "at no cost"). . .300.39(b)(1).
. Supplementary aids and services. . .300.42.
. Suspension and expulsion rates. . .300.170(a)(2).
NONEDUCATIONAL (Public agency)
. Medicaid service (May not be disqualified because in school context) . . . 300.154(b)(1)(ii).
. Methods of ensuring services (see § 300.154(a), (b))
. Obligation of. . .300.154(b).
. Reimbursement for services by. . .300.154(b)(2).
NON-MEDICAL CARE (Residential placement). . .300.104.
NONSUPPLANTING
. Excess cost requirement (Regarding children aged 3 through 5 and 18 through 21). . .300.202(b)(1)(ii).
. LEA nonsupplanting. . .300.202(b)(1)(ii).
. SEA flexibility. . .300.230(a).
. State-level activities (Inapplicability of certain provisions). . .300.704(d).
. State-level nonsupplanting. . .300.162(c).
. Waiver of requirement. . .300.164.

NOTICES: By parents or parties
. Attorneys' fees: When court reduces fee award regarding due process request notice. . .300.517(c)(4)(iv).
. Children enrolled by parents in private schools when FAPE is at issue. . .300.148(d)(1)(i).
. Due process complaint (Notice before a hearing on a complaint). . .300.508(c).
. Private school placement by parents (When
FAPE is at issue). . .300.148(d)(1)(i).
NOTICES: Public agency (A-M)
. By-pass (Judicial review). . .300.197.
. Children's rights (Transfer of rights). . .300.625(c).
. Confidentiality (Notice to parents). . .300.612.
. Department procedures (Notice to States). . .300.179.
. See "Judicial review". . .300.184.
. Discipline (Notification). . .300.530(h).
. Exception to FAPE (Graduation). . .300.102(a)(3).
. Hearings relating to LEA eligibility. . .300.155.
. IEP meetings (Parent participation). . .300.322(b).
. Judicial review: If State dissatisfied with
eligibility determination. . .300.184.
. LEA and State agency compliance. . .300.222.
. Notification in case of ineligibility. . .300.221(b).
NOTICES: Public agency (N-P)
. Notice before a hearing on a due process
complaint. . .300.508(c).
. Notice and hearing before State ineligible. . .300.179.
. Notice in understandable language. . .300.503(c).
. Notification of LEA in case of ineligibility. . .300.221(b).
. Parent participation in meetings. . .300.501(b)(2).
. Prior notice by public agency. . .300.503.
. Private school placement by parents when FAPE is at issue (Public agency notice). . .300.148(d)(2).
. Procedural safeguards notice. . .300.504.
. Public attention. . .300.606.
. Public participation (Notice of hearings). . .300.165(a).
NOTICES: Public agency (Q-Z)
. Secretary of the Interior (Submission of
information). . .300.708(g).
. Secretary's review and determination of
State performance. . .300.603(b)(2).
. Transfer of parental rights. . .300.520(a)(1)(i).
. Use of electronic mail. . .300.505.
. Withholding funds. . .300.605.
OCCUPATIONAL THERAPY. . .300.34(c)(6).
OPPORTUNITY TO EXAMINE RECORDS. . .300.501.
ORIENTATION AND MOBILITY SERVICES. . .300.34(c)(7).
ORTHOPEDIC IMPAIRMENT. . .300.8(c)(8).
OTHER HEALTH IMPAIRMENT. . .300.8(c)(9).
OTHER INDIVIDUALS ON IEP TEAM. . .300.321(a)(6).
OUTLYING AREAS—FREELY ASSOCIATED STATES
. Allocations to States (General)300.703(a).
. Annual description of use of funds300.171(c).
. Definitions applicable to allotments, grants and use of funds:

. Freely associated States. . .300.717(a).
. Outlying areas. . .300.717(b).
. Definition of "State" (Includes "Outlying areas"). . .300.40.
. Outlying areas and freely associated States. . .300.701.
. Purpose of grants. . .300.700(a).
OUT-OF-POCKET EXPENSE (Public benefits or insurance). . .300.154(d)(2)(ii).
PARAPROFESSIONALS
. "Personnel qualifications" 3. . .00.156(b). (a)(a)
PARENT (Definition). . .300.30.
PARENT: RIGHTS AND PROTECTIONS (A-G)
. Appeal (Manifestation determination). . .300.532.
. Confidentiality (Authority to inspect and review records). . .300.613(c).
. Consent (See "Consent")
. Counseling and training (Definition). . .300.34(c)(8).
. Definition of "Parent". . .300.30.
. Foster parent. . .300.30(a)(2).
. Grandparent or stepparent. . .300.30(a)(4).
. Guardian. . .300.30(a)(3).
PARENT: RIGHTS AND PROTECTIONS (H-N)
. Independent educational evaluation. . .300.502.
. Parent-initiated evaluations. . .300.502(c).
. Parent right to evaluation at public expense. . .300.502(b).
. IEP and parent involvement:
. Copy of child's IEP. . .300.322(f).
. Informed of child's progress. . .300.320(a)(3)(ii).
. Option to invite other individuals. . .300.321(a)(6).
. Participation in meetings. . .300.322.
. Team member. . .300.321(a)(1).
. Informed consent (Accessing private insurance). . .300.154(e)(1).
. Involvement in placement decisions. . .300.501(c).
. Meetings (Participation in). . .300.501(b).
. Notice to public agency:
. Before a hearing on a due process complaint. . .300.508(c).
. Before removing child from public school. . .300.148(d)(1)(ii).
. Timeline for requesting a hearing. . .300.511(e).
. Opportunity to examine records. . .300.501(a).
PARENT: RIGHTS AND PROTECTIONS (O-Z)
. Parent counseling and training. . .300.34(c)(8).
. Placement decisions (Involvement in). . .300.501(c).
. Request for hearing (Discipline). . .300.532(a).
. Right to an independent educational evaluation. . .300.502(b).
PARENTAL CONSENT (See "Consent")
PARENTALLY-PLACED PRIVATE SCHOOL CHILDREN WITH DISABILITIES (A-E)
. Annual count of the number of. . .300.133(c).
. Bypass (see §§ 300.190 through 300.198)
. Child find for. . .300.131.
. Calculating proportionate amount. . .300.133(b).
. Compliance. . .300.136.

Appendix E to Part 300   IDEA REGULATIONS   305

. Consultation with private schools. . .300.134.
. Written affirmation. . .300.135.
. Definition of. . .300.130.
. Due process complaints and State complaints. . .300.140.
. Equitable services determined. . .300.137.
. Equitable services provided. . .300.138.
. Expenditures. . .300.133.
. Formula. . .300.133(a).

PARENTALLY-PLACED PRIVATE SCHOOL CHILDREN WITH DISABILITIES (F-R)

. No individual right to special education and related services. . .300.137(a).
. Property, equipment, and supplies. . .300.144.
. Proportionate share of funds. . .300.134(b).
. See "Appendix B—Proportionate Share Calculation"
. Provision of equitable services. . .300.138(c).
. Religious schools (see §§ 300.131(a),. . .300.137(c), 300.139(a))
. Requirement that funds not benefit a private school. . .300.141.

PARENTALLY-PLACED PRIVATE SCHOOL CHILDREN WITH DISABILITIES (S-T)

. Separate classes prohibited. . .300.143.
. Services on private school premises. . .300.139(a).
. Services plan (Definition). . .300.37.
. For each child served under §§ 300.130 through 300.144. . .300.137(c).
. See also §§ 300.132(b), 300.138(b),. . .300.140(a)
. State eligibility requirement. . .300.129.
. Transportation (Cost of). . .300.139(b)(2).

PARENTALLY-PLACED PRIVATE SCHOOL CHILDREN WITH DISABILITIES (U-Z)

. Use of personnel:
. Private school personnel. . .300.142(b).
. Public school personnel. . .300.142(a).
. Written affirmation. . .300.135.
. Written explanation by LEA regarding services. . .300.134(e).

PARTICIPATING AGENCY

. Confidentiality provisions:
. Definition of participating agency. . .300.611(c).
. See also §§ 300.613(c), 300.614, 300.616, 300.618, 300.623
. IEP requirements (Transition services). . .300.324(c).

PENDENCY (Stay put)

. Child's status during due process proceedings. . .300.518.
. Placement during appeals (Discipline). . .300.533.
. Procedural safeguards notice. . .300.504(c)(7).

PERFORMANCE GOALS AND INDICATORS

. Assess progress toward achieving goals. . .300.157(c).
. Establishment of goals. . .300.157.
. Other State level activities. . .300.814(c).
. Performance goals and indicators. . .300.157.
. State monitoring and enforcement. . .300.600(c).
. State performance plans and data collection. . .300.601.

PERFORMANCE; PERFORMANCE PLANS (STATE)
. Enforcement. . .300.604.
. Public reporting and privacy. . .300.602(b).
. Secretary's review and determination regarding State performance. . .300.603.
. State performance plans and data collection. . .300.601.
. State performance report. . .300.602(b)(2).
. State use of targets and reporting. . .300.602.
. Public reporting. . .300.602(b)(1).
. State performance report. . .300.602(b)(2).

PERMISSIVE USE OF FUNDS (LEAs)
. Administrative case management. . .300.208(b).
. Early intervening services. . .300.208(a)(2).
. High cost education and related services. . .300.208(a)(3).
. Permissive use of funds. . .300.208.
. Services and aids that also benefit nondisabled children. . .300.208(a)(1).

PERSONALLY IDENTIFIABLE (PI) INFORMATION (A-H)
. Confidentiality of (State eligibility requirement). . .300.123.
. Consent (confidentiality). . .300.622(a).
. Data collection (State performance plans). . .300.601(b)(3).
. Definition of "personally identifiable". . .300.32.
. Department use of information. . .300.627.
. Destruction:
. Definition of. . .300.611(a).
. Destruction of information. . .300.624.
. Hearing decisions to advisory panel and the public. . .300.513(d).

PERSONALLY IDENTIFIABLE (PI) INFORMATION (I-Z)
. Notice to parents (Confidentiality):
. Children on whom PI information is maintained. . .300.612(a)(2).
. Policies and procedures regarding disclosure to third parties, etc. . .300.612(a)(3).
. Participating agency (Definition). . .300.611(c).
. Protection of PI information. . .300.642(a).
. See also § 300.610
. Safeguards (Protect PI information). . .300.623.

PERSONNEL QUALIFICATIONS. . .300.156.

PERSONNEL SHORTAGES
. Use of SEA allocations to meet. . .300.704(b)(4)(vii).

PHYSICAL EDUCATION
. Definition. . .300.39(b)(2).
. State eligibility requirement. . .300.108.

PHYSICAL THERAPY (Definition). . .300.34(c)(9).

PLACEMENT(S) (A-Co)
. Adult prisons (CWDs in):
. Last educational placement before incarceration. . .300.102(a)(2)(i).
. Modifications to IEPs and placements. . .300.324(d)(2).
. Alternative means of meeting participation (Regarding "Placement meetings"). . .300.328.
. Change in placement: Graduation. . .300.102(a)(3)(iii).

. Child's placement during pendency of any complaint. . .300.504(c)(7).
. See also "Pendency" (Child's status during proceedings). . .300.518.
. Children with disabilities in adult prisons: Placements regarding (see §§ 300.102(a)(2)(i),300.324(d)(2))
. Continuum of alternative placements (Continuum—LRE). . .300.115.

PLACEMENT(S) (Cu-L)
. Current placement (see § 300.530(b)((2), (d))
. Current "Educational placement:"
. Change of placements because of disciplinary removals. . .300.536.
. Child's status during proceedings. . .300.518(a).
. Disciplinary changes in placement. . .300.530(c).
. Discipline procedures and placements (see §§ 300.530 through 300.536)
. Educational placements (Parents in any group that makes placement decisions). . .300.327.
. Graduation: A change in placement (Exception to FAPE). . .300.102(a)(3)(iii).
. Last educational placement (Before incarceration). . .300.102(a)(2)(i).
. Least restrictive environment (LRE) (see §§ 300.114 through 300.120)
. Notification: LEA must notify parents of decision to change placement. . .300.530(h).

PLACEMENT(S) (O-Z)
. Pendency (Child's status during proceedings). . .300.518.
Placement of children by parents if FAPE is at issue. . .300.148.
. Placements (LRE). . .300.116.
. Requirements for unilateral placement by parents of CWDs in private schools (In . . .300.504(c)(9). "Procedural safeguards notice")
. State funding mechanism (Must not result in placements that violate LRE). . .300.114(b)(1).

POLICY: POLICIES AND PROCEDURES
. Condition of assistance (LEA eligibility). . .300.200.
. Consistency with State policies. . .300.201.
. See also §§ 300.200 through 300.213
. Eligibility for assistance (State). . .300.100.
. Exception for prior policies on file:
. With the SEA. . .300.220.
. With the Secretary. . .300.176(a).
. FAPE policy. . .300.101(a).
. Joint establishment of eligibility (Requirements). . .300.223.
. Modifications of:
. LEA or State agency policies. . .300.220(b).
. Required by Secretary. . .300.176(c).
. State policies (By a State). . .300.176(b).
. Public participation. . .300.165.
. Secretary of the Interior. . .300.708.
. Public participation. . .300.709.
. Submission of information. . .300.708.

PREPONDERANCE OF EVIDENCE

. Civil action. . .300.516(c)(3).
PRESCHOOL GRANTS
. Allocations to LEAs. . .300.816.
. Subgrants to LEAs. . .300.815.
. Other State-level activities. . .300.814.
. Provide early intervention services in accordance with Part C of the Act. . .300.814(e).
. Service coordination or case management. . .300.814(f).
. State administration. . .300.813.
. Use of funds for administration of Part C. . .300.813(b).
PRIOR NOTICE
. By public agency. . .300.503.
. Notice required before a hearing on a due process complaint. . .300.508(c).
. Procedural safeguards notice. . .300.504.
PRISONS (See "Adult prisons")
PRIVATE INSURANCE
. Children with disabilities who are covered by. . .300.154(e).
. Proceeds from public benefits or insurance or private insurance. . .300.154(g).
. Use of Part B funds. . .300.154(f).
PRIVATE SCHOOLS AND FACILITIES
. Applicability of this part to State and local agencies:
. CWDs placed in private schools by parents under § 300.148. . .300.2(c)(2).
. CWDs referred to or placed in private schools by public agency. . .300.2(c)(1).
PRIVATE SCHOOL CHILDREN ENROLLED BY THEIR PARENTS
. Placement of children by parents when FAPE is at issue. . .300.148.
. See "Parentally-placed private school children with disabilities"
PRIVATE SCHOOL PLACEMENTS BY PUBLIC AGENCIES (A-D)
. Applicability of this part to private schools. . .300.2(c)(1).
. Applicable standards (SEA to disseminate to private schools involved). . .300.147(b).
PRIVATE SCHOOL PLACEMENTS BY PUBLIC AGENCIES (E-Z)
. Implementation by SEA (Must monitor, provide standards, etc.). . .300.147.
. Monitor compliance. . .300.147(a).
. Input by private schools (Provide for). . .300.147(c).
. Responsibility of SEA. . .300.146.
PROCEDURAL SAFEGUARDS: DUE PROCESS PROCEDURES (A-C)
. Additional disclosure of information (5 business days before hearing). . .300.512(b).
. Agency responsible for conducting hearing. . .300.511(b).
. Appeal of hearing decisions; impartial review. . .300.514(b).
. Attorneys' fees. . .300.517.
. Child's status during proceedings. . .300.518.
. Civil action. . .300.516.
. Consent (Definition). . .300.9.
. Court (See "Court(s)")
PROCEDURAL SAFEGUARDS: DUE PROCESS PROCEDURES (D-H). . .300.505.

. Electronic mail (Parent may elect to receive notices by)
. Evaluation (Definition). . .300.15.
. Evaluations: Hearing officer requests for. . .300.502(d).
. Finality of decision; appeal; impartial
review. . .300.514.
. Findings and decision to advisory panel and
public. . .300.513(d).
. Hearing rights. . .300.512.
PROCEDURAL SAFEGUARDS: DUE PROCESS PROCEDURES (I-Pa)
. Impartial due process hearing. . .300.511.
. Impartial hearing officer. . .300.511(c).
. Impartiality of mediator. . .300.506(c).
. Independent educational evaluation. . .300.502.
. Definition. . .300.502(a)(3)(i).
. Jurisdiction of district courts. . .300.516(d).
. See "Court(s)"
. Mediation. . .300.506.
. Opportunity to meet with a disinterested
party. . .300.506(b)(2).
. Model form to assist parties in filing a due
process or State complaint. . .300.509.
. Notice required before a hearing on a due
process complaint. . .300.508(c).
. Opportunity to examine records. . .300.501(a).
. Parental consent300.300.
. Parent-initiated evaluations300.502(c).
. Parent involvement in placement decisions300.501(c).
. Parent participation in meetings300.501(b).
. Parental rights at hearings300.512(c).
. Parent right to evaluation at public expense. . .300.502(b).
. Public expense (Definition). . .300.502(a)(3)(ii).
PROCEDURAL SAFEGUARDS: DUE PROCESS PROCEDURES (Pe-Z)
. Pendency300.518.
. Personally identifiable (Definition)300.32.
. Prior notice by public agency300.503.
. Procedural safeguards notice300.504.
. Prohibition on introduction of undisclosed evidence 5 business days before hearing300.512(a)(3).
. Record of hearing300.512(a)(4).
. Resolution process. . .300.510.
. SEA implementation of. . .300.150.
. See "Civil Action Proceedings," "Court(s)," "Hearing Officer(s)," "Timelines"
. Surrogate parents. . .300.519.
. Timelines and convenience of hearings. . .300.515.
. Transfer of parental rights at age of majority. . .300.520.
PROCEDURAL SAFEGUARDS NOTICE. . .300.504.
. Internet Web site (Notice on). . .300.504(b).
PROCEEDS FROM PUBLIC BENEFITS OR INSURANCE OR. . .300.154(g).
PRIVATE INSURANCE
PROGRAM INCOME (Not treated as proceeds from
insurance). . .300.154(g.)
PROGRAM MODIFICATIONS OR SUPPORTS (IEP content). . .300.320(a)(4).
PROPORTIONATE SHARE CALCULATION (See Appendix B)

PROTECTIONS FOR CHILDREN NOT DETERMINED. . .300.534.
ELIGIBLE (Discipline)s
PSYCHOLOGICAL SERVICES (Definition). . .300.34(c)(10).
PUBLIC AGENCY (Definition). . .300.33.
PUBLIC BENEFITS OR INSURANCE. . .300.154(d).
PUBLIC BENEFITS OR INSURANCE OR PRIVATE. . .300.154(g).
INSURANCE (Proceeds from)
PUBLIC CHARTER SCHOOLS (See "Charter schools")
PUBLIC EXPENSE (Definition under IEE). . .300.502(a)(3)(ii).
PUBLIC HEARINGS (On policies)
. State eligibility. . .300.165(a).
. Secretary of the Interior. . .300.708(g).
PUBLIC INFORMATION (LEA). . .300.212.
PUBLIC NOTICE
. LEA and State agency compliance. . .300.222(b).
. Public attention (If State has received a
notice under § 300.603). . .300.606.
PURPOSES (Of this Part 300). . .300.1.
QUALIFIED PERSONNEL. . .300.156.
. Related services definitions (see § 300.34(c)(2), (c)(5), (c)(6), (c)(7), (c)(9), (c)(12), (c)(13)).
RATE OF INFLATION (In the Consumer Price Index for All Urban Consumers) (see §§ 300.702(b), 300.704(a)(2)(ii), 300.704(b)(2), 300.812(b)(2)).
REALLOCATION OF LEA FUNDS (If SEA determines LEA adequately providing FAPE) (see § 300.705(c), 300.817)).
RECORDS (A-D)
. Access rights (Parents' right to inspect). . .300.613.
. Fees for records. . .300.617.
. Records on more than one child. . .300.615.
. Civil action (Court shall receive records). . .300.516(c)(1).
. Conducting IEP Team meetings without parents (Records of attempts to convince parents). . .300.322(d).
Confidentiality (See "Confidentiality")
. Consent to release records. . .300.622(b).
Disciplinary records:
. Determination that behavior not manifestation. . .300.530(e).
. Disciplinary information. . .300.229(c).
. Referral to and action by law enforcement
and judicial authorities. . .300.535.
RECORDS (E-Z)
. Education records (Definition). . .300.611(b).
. Of parentally-placed private school CWDs
(LEA to SEA). . .300.132(c).
. Opportunity to examine records. . .300.501(a).
. Procedural safeguards notice (Access to
education records). . .300.504(c)(4).
. Record of access. . .300.614.
. See also "Transfer during academic year"
RECREATION (Definition). . .300.34(c)(11).
REDUCTION OF FUNDS FOR FAILURE TO MAINTAIN. . .300.163(b).
SUPPORT
REEVALUATION
. Frequency of occurrence . . .300.303(b).
. Parental consent required before conducting . . .300.300(c)(1).

. If parent fails to consent . . .300.300(c)(1)(ii).
. Parental consent not required for:
. Administering a test that all children take . . .300.300(d)(1)(ii).
. Reviewing existing data . . .300.300(d)(1)(i).
. Parent refusal to consent . . .300.300(c)(1)(ii).
. Review of existing evaluation data . . .300.305(a).
. Revision of IEP (To address reevaluation) . . .300.324(b)(1)(ii).
REFERRAL (A-M)
. Discipline:
. Referral to and action by law enforcement
and judicial authorities . . .300.535.
. Protections for children not determined
eligible . . .300.534.
. Enforcement (Referral for) . . .300.604(b)(2)(vi).
. Indian children (Referral for services or further diagnosis) . . .300.712(d)(2).
. Medical attention (Referral for):
. Audiology . . .300.34(c)(1)(ii).
. Speech-language pathology services . . .300.34(c)(15)(iii).
REFERRAL (N-Z)
. Nonacademic and extracurricular services . . .300.107(b).
Referral to agencies regarding assistance to individuals with disabilities)
. Prior notice (If not initial referral for
evaluation) . . .300.503(b)(4).
. Private school placement when FAPE is at issue (Reimbursement when no referral by public agency) . . .300.148(c).
. Procedural safeguards notice (Upon initial referral for evaluation) . . .300.504(a)(1).
. Referral to and action by law enforcement
and judicial authorities . . .300.535.
REGULAR EDUCATION TEACHER
. Access to IEP . . .300.323(d).
. IEP Team member . . .300.321(a)(2).
. Participate in IEP development . . .300.324(a)(3).
. Behavioral interventions . . .300.324(a)(3)(i).
. Supplementary aids and services . . .300.324(a)(3)(ii).
REGULATIONS
. Applicable regulations (Secretary of the
Interior) . . .300.716.
. Applicability of this part to State, local,
and private agencies . . .300.2.
REHABILITATION
. Assistive technology service (see § 300.6(d), (f))
. Rehabilitation Act of 1973 (see §§ 300.34(c)(12), 300.516(e))
. Rehabilitation counseling services:
. Definition . . .300.34(c)(12).
. In vocational rehabilitation (VR) programs . . .300.34(c)(12).
. Transition services (State VR agency
responsibility) . . .300.324(c)(2).
REHABILITATION COUNSELING SERVICES . . .300.34(c)(12).
REIMBURSEMENT
. Methods of ensuring services (see § 300.154(a)(3), (b)(1)(ii), (b)(2), (g)(2))
. Private school placement when FAPE is at issue:
. Limitation on reimbursement . . .300.148(d).
. Reimbursement for private school placement . . .300.148(c).

. Subject to due process procedures . . .300.148(b).
. Reimbursement by non-educational public
agency . . .300.154(b)(2).
. Reimbursement by SEA to LEA . . .300.704(c)(7).
RELATED SERVICES
. Definition . . .300.34.
. Observations by teachers and related services providers regarding existing evaluation data . . .300.305(a)(1)(iii).
RELATION OF PART B TO OTHER FEDERAL PROGRAMS . . .300.186.
RELIGIOUS SCHOOLS
. Child find for parentally-placed private
school children . . .300.131(a).
. Child find for out-of-State children . . .300.131(f).
. Formula for LEA expenditures on . . .300.133(a).
. See "Parentally-placed private school children with disabilities"
. Services plan for each child served . . .300.137(c).
. Services provided on-site . . .300.139(a).
REMEDIES FOR DENIAL OF APPROPRIATE SERVICES . . .300.151(b).
REPORTS (A-C)
. Annual report of children
served . . .300.640.
. See also §§ 300.641 through 300.646
. Annual report to Secretary of Interior by advisory board on Indian children . . .300.715(a).
. Biennial report (Indian tribes) . . .300.712(e).
. Child count (Annual report of children served) . . .300.641.
REPORTS (D-Z)
. Evaluation reports to parents . . .300.306(a)(2).
. Monitoring compliance of publicly placed children in private schools (e.g., written reports) . . .300.147(a).
Monitoring reports (Waiver of nonsupplanting
requirement) . . .300.164(c)(3).
. Performance goals (Progress reports) . . .300.157(c).
. Secretary's report to States regarding 25%
of funds . . .300.812(b).
REPORT CARDS . . .300.320(a)(3)(ii).
REPORTING A CRIME to law enforcement and
judicial authorities . . .300.535.
RESIDENTIAL PLACEMENTS . . .300.104.
REVOKE CONSENT AT ANY TIME (In definition of
"Consent") . . .300.9(c)(1).
RHEUMATIC FEVER . . .300.8(c)(9)(i).
RISK OF LOSS OF ELIGIBILITY FOR INSURANCE . . .300.154(d)(2)(iii)(D).
SCHOOL DAY
. Definition . . .300.11(c).
. See "Timelines," "Timelines—Discipline"
SCHOOL HEALTH SERVICES AND SCHOOL NURSE . . .300.34(c)(13).
SERVICES
SCHOOL PERSONNEL
. Content of IEP . . .300.320(a)(4).
. Development, review, and revision of IEP . . .300.324(a)(4).
. Disciplinary authority . . .300.530.
. Use of private school personnel . . .300.142(b).

. Use of public school personnel . . .300.142(a).
SCHOOLWIDE PROGRAMS . . .300.206.
SEA RESPONSIBILITY
. For all education programs . . .300.149.
. For direct services . . .300.227.
. For each parentally-placed private school child designated to receive services . . .300.132(b).
. For impartial review . . .300.514(b)(2).
. Prohibition of LEA from reducing maintenance of effort . . .300.608.
SECRETARY
. Determination that a State is eligible . . .300.178.
. Notice and hearing before determining that a State is not eligible . . .300.179.
. Waiver of nonsupplanting requirement . . .300.164.
SECRETARY OF THE INTERIOR
. Advisory board establishment . . .300.714.
. Annual report by advisory board . . .300.715.
. Biennial report (By tribe or tribal organization) . . .300.712(e).
. Eligibility (see §§ 300.708 through 300.716)
. Payments for:
. Children aged 3 through 5 . . .300.712.
. Child find and screening . . .300.712(d).
. Plan for coordination of services . . .300.713.
. Use of funds for early intervening services . . .300.711.
SEPARATION—DIVORCE (Authority to review records) . . .300.613(c).
SERVICES PLAN for parentally-placed private school children (see §§ 300.132(b), 300.137(c) 300.138(b))
SERVICES THAT ALSO BENEFIT NONDISABLED CHILDREN . . .300.208(a)(1).
SHORTAGE OF PERSONNEL (Policy to address) . . .300.704(b)(4)(vii).
SHORT TERM OBJECTIVES OR BENCHMARKS . . .300.320(a)(2)(ii).
SHOULD HAVE KNOWN (Regarding due process complaint) . . .300.511(e).
SHOW CAUSE HEARING . . .300.194.
. Decision . . .300.195.
. Implementation of by-pass (see §§ 300.192(b)(2), 300.193)
. Right to legal counsel . . .300.194(a)(3).
SICKLE CELL ANEMIA . . .300.8(c)(9)(i).
SLD (See "Specific Learning Disability")
SOCIAL WORK SERVICES IN SCHOOLS (Definition) . . .300.34(b)(14).
SPECIAL FACTORS (IEP Team) . . .300.324(a)(2).
SPECIAL EDUCATION (Definition) . . .300.39.
SPECIAL EDUCATION PROVIDER . . .300.321(a)(3).
SPECIAL EDUCATION TEACHER
. IEP accessible to . . .300.323(d).
. On IEP Team . . .300.321(a)(3).
. Requirements regarding highly qualified . . .300.18.
SPECIAL RULE
. Adjustments to local efforts . . .300.205(d).
. For child's eligibility determination . . .300.306(b).
. For increasing funds . . .300.704(e).

. Methods of ensuring services . . .300.154(c).
. LEA high cost fund . . .300.704(c).
. Regarding outlying areas and freely associated States . . .300.701(a)(3).
. Regarding transfer of rights . . .300.520(b).
. Regarding use of FY 1999 amount . . .300.703(b).
. State advisory panel (Parent members) . . .300.168(b).
SPECIFIC LEARNING DISABILITY
. Definition . . .300.8(c)(10).
. Evaluation requirements and report (see §§ 300.306(a), 300.307 through 300.311)
. Other alternative research-based procedures . . .300.307(a)(3).
. Response to scientific, research-based intervention (see §§ 300.307(a)(2), 300.309(a)(2)(i), 300.311(a)(7))
. Scientifically based research:
. Definition . . .300.35.
. Enforcement . . .300.604(a)(1)(ii).
. Severe discrepancy . . .300.307(a)(1).
SPEECH-LANGUAGE PATHOLOGY SERVICES
. Definition . . .300.34(b)(15).
. Speech or language impairment (Definition) . . .300.8(c)(11).
STATE
. Definition . . .300.40.
. Special definition for grants . . .300.717(c).
. Sovereign immunity . . .300.177.
STATE ADMINISTRATION (Use of funds for) (see §§ 300.704(a), 300.812(a)).
STATE ADVISORY PANEL . . .300.167
. Due process hearings (Findings and decisions to State advisory panel) (see §§ 300.513(d)(1), 300.514(c)(1))
. Duties . . .300.169.
. Establishment . . .300.167.
. Membership . . .300.168.
. Waiver of nonsupplant requirement (State has consulted with advisory panel regarding provision of FAPE) . . .300.164(c)(4).
STATE AGENCIES
. Applicability of Part B to other State
agencies . . .300.2(b)(1)(iii).
. Compliance (LEA and State agency) . . .300.222.
. Eligibility (LEA and State agency): . . .
. General conditions (see §§ 300.200 through . . .300.213)
. Notification of LEA or State agency in case
of ineligibility . . .300.221.
. State advisory panel (Membership) . . .300.168.
. State agency eligibility . . .300.228.
. State Medicaid agency . . .300.154(a)(1), (h).
STATE COMPLAINT PROCEDURES (see §§ 300.151 through 300.153)
. See "Complaint(s): State complaint procedures"
STATE ELIGIBILITY
. Condition of assistance . . .300.100.
. Department procedures (see §§ 300.178 through 300.186)
. Determination of eligibility (By the Secretary) . . .300.178.
. General conditions . . .300.100.
. Notice and hearing before determining that a
State is not eligible . . .300.179.
. Specific conditions (see §§ 300.101 through 300.176)

STATE JUVENILE AND ADULT CORRECTIONAL . . .300.2(b)(1)(iv).
FACILITIES
. See also "Correctional facilities," "Adult prisons"
STATE-LEVEL ACTIVITIES (With Part B funds) . . .300.704.
STATE-LEVEL NONSUPPLANTING . . .300.162(c).
. Waiver by Secretary . . .300.162(c)(2).
. Waiver of requirement . . .300.164.
STATE MAINTENANCE OF EFFORT . . .300.163.
SUBGRANT(S)
. State agency eligibility . . .300.228.
. To LEAs . . .300.705(a).
STATE MEDICAID AGENCY
. Methods of ensuring services . . .300.154(a)(1).
. See also "Medicaid"
STATE SCHOOLS
. Applicability of this part to schools for children with deafness or blindness . . .300.2(b)(1)(iii).
STATE VOCATIONAL REHABILITATION AGENCY (See "Rehabilitation")
STATES' SOVEREIGN IMMUNITY . . .300.177.
STAY-PUT (Child's status during proceedings) . . .300.518.
. See also "Pendency" . . .
SUBSTANTIAL LIKELIHOOD OF INJURY (Discipline) . . .300.532(a).
SUPPLEMENTARY AIDS AND SERVICES
. Definition . . .300.42.
. IEP content . . .300.320(a)(4).
. In "assistive technology" . . .300.105(a)(3).
. LRE requirements . . .300.114(a)(2)(ii).
. Methods of ensuring services . . .300.154(b).
. Requirement regarding regular education
teacher (IEP) . . .300.324(a)(3)(ii).
. Services that also benefit nondisabled
children . . .300.208(a)(1).
SUPPLEMENT—NOT SUPPLANT
. LEA requirement . . .300.202(a)(3).
. State level nonsupplanting . . .300.162(c).
. See "Nonsupplanting"
SUPPORT SERVICES (see §§ 300.704(b)(4)(i)), 300.814(a))
SURGICALLY IMPLANTED MEDICAL DEVICE (see §§ 300.5, 300.34(b), 300.113(b))
SURROGATE PARENTS . . .300.519.
. Appointed for homeless youth . . .300.519(f).
. In definition of "Parent" . . .300.30(a)(5).
. Timeline for assignment . . .300.519(h).
SUSPENSION (EXPULSION)
. Alternative programming for children
expelled . . .300.704(b)(4)(ix).
. Provision of FAPE . . .300.101(a).
. Suspension and expulsion rates . . .300.170(a).
. Suspension or expulsion without services . . .300.534(d)(2)(ii).
TEACHERS
See "Regular education teacher"
See "Special education teacher"
TECHNICAL ASSISTANCE (Amounts to support) . . .300.702.

TECHNICALLY SOUND INSTRUMENTS (Evaluation)...300.304(b)(3).
TERMINATION OF AGENCY OBLIGATION to provide special education to a particular child (Exception to MOE)...300.204(c).
THERAPEUTIC RECREATION...300.34(b)(11)(ii).
TIMELINES (A-D)
. Access rights (Confidentiality: 45 days)...300.613(a).
. Annual report of children served (Between Oct. 1 and Dec. 1)...300.641(a).
. Annual count of parentally-placed private school children (Between Oct. 1 and Dec. 1)...300.133(c).
. Assignment of surrogate parent (Not more than 30 days)...300.519(h).
. Attorneys' fees (10 days prohibition)...300.517(c)(2)(i).
. Complaint procedures (State: 60 days)...300.152(a).
. Department hearing procedures (30 days)...300.179(b)(3).
. See also §§ 300.181 through 300.184
. Due process hearings and reviews (see §§ 300.510(b)(2), 300.511(e), (f)):
. Conducted within 20 school days; decision within 10 school days...300.532(c)(2).
. Decision within 45 days after expiration of 30 day period...300.515(a).
. Disclose evaluations before hearings (5 business days)...300.512(a)(3).
TIMELINES (E-H)
. Hearing procedures (State eligibility: 30 days)...300.179(b)(3).
. Hearing rights:
. Disclosure of evaluations (At least 5 business days before hearing)...300.512(b)(1).
. Prohibit introduction of evidence not disclosed (At least 5 business days before hearing)...300.512(a)(3).
. Reviews (Decision not later than 30 days)...300.515(b).
TIMELINES (I-Z)
. IEP (Initial meeting: 30 days)...300.323(c)(1).
. Initial evaluation (60 days)...300.301(c)(1).
. Parent notice before private placement (At least 10 business days)...300.148(d)(2).
. Show cause hearing...300.194(g).
. Decision...300.195(a)(1).
. State eligibility: Department hearing procedures (see §§ 300.179(b)(3), 300.181(b), 300.182(d), (e), (g), (k), 300.184)
. Timelines and convenience of hearings and reviews...300.515.
TIMELINES—DISCIPLINE (A-P)
. Authority of hearing officer (May order change of placement for not more than 45 school days)...300.532(b)(2)(ii).
. Authority of school personnel:
. Change of placement for not more than 45 consecutive days for weapons or drugs...300.530(g).
. Removal of a child for not more than 10 school days...300.530(b).
. Change of placement for disciplinary removals:
. Of more than 10 consecutive school days...300.536(a)(1).
. Because series of removals total more than 10 school days...300.536(a)(2)(i).
. Due process hearing request...300.507(a)(2).

- Expedited due process hearings:
- Conducted within 20 days . . .300.532(c)(2).
- Decision within 10 days . . .300.532(c)(3)(i).
- Hearing officer (Order change of placement for not more than 45 days) . . .300.532(b)(2)(ii).
- Manifestation determination review (Conducted in no more than 10 school days) . . .300.530(e).
- Placement during appeals (Not longer than 45 days) . . .300.532(b)(2)(ii).

TIMELINES—DISCIPLINE (Q-Z)
- Removals for not more than:
- 10 school days (By school personnel) . . .300.530(b).
- 45 days (To interim alternative educational setting) . . .300.532(b)(2)(ii).

By hearing officer (For substantial likelihood of injury to child or others) . . .300.532(b)(2)(ii).
By school personnel (For weapons or drugs) (see § 300.530(g)(1), (g)(2))

TIMETABLE: Full educational opportunity goal (FEOG) . . .300.109.

TRAINING
- Assistive technology services (see § 300.6(e), (f))
- Confidentiality procedures (Personnel using personally identifiable information must receive training) . . .300.623(c).
- Parent counseling and training . . .300.34(b)(8).
- Technical assistance and training for teachers and administrators . . .300.119.
- Travel training (see § 300.39(a)(2)(ii), (b)(4))

TRANSFER DURING ACADEMIC YEAR
- Assessments coordinated between public agencies . . .300.304(c)(5).
- New school district responsibilities (see § 300.323(e), (f))
- Transmittal of records . . .300.323(g).

TRANSFER OF PARENTAL RIGHTS . . .300.520.
- IEP requirement . . .300.320(c).
- Special rule . . .300.520(b).
- To children in correctional institutions . . .300.520(a)(2).

TRANSITION FROM PART C TO PART B . . .300.124.

TRANSITION SERVICES (NEEDS)
- Agency responsibilities for (see §§ 300.321(b)(3), 300.324(c)(2))
- Alternative strategies . . .300.324(c)(1).
- Child participation in IEP Team meetings . . .300.321(b)(1).
- Definition . . .300.43.
- IEP requirement (Statement of)
- Transition service needs . . .300.320(b).
- Needed transition services . . .300.43(b).
- State rehabilitation agency . . .300.324(c)(2).

TRANSMITTAL OF RECORDS TO LAW ENFORCEMENT AND . . .300.535(b).
JUDICIAL AUTHORITIES

TRANSPORTATION
- Definition . . .300.34(c)(16).
- Nonacademic services . . .300.107(b).
- Of private school children . . .300.139(b).

TRAUMATIC BRAIN INJURY (Definition) . . .300.8(c)(12).
TRAVEL TRAINING (see § 300.39(a)(2)(ii), (b)(4))

. Definition . . .300.39(b)(4).
TREATMENT OF CHARTER SCHOOLS AND THEIR STUDENTS . . .300.209.
TREATMENT OF FEDERAL FUNDS IN CERTAIN YEARS . . .300.205.
UNIVERSAL DESIGN
. Definition . . .300.44.
. Support technology with universal design
principles . . .300.704(b)(4)(v).
USE OF AMOUNTS (LEA) . . .300.202.
USE OF FUNDS BY LEAs
. Coordinated services system . . .300.208(a)(2).
. For school-wide programs . . .300.206.
. For services and aids that also benefit
nondisabled children . . .300.208(a)(1).
. For use in accordance with Part B . . .300.705.
USE OF FUNDS BY STATES (SEAs) (A-C)
. Administering Part B State activities . . .300.704(a)(1).
. Administering Part C (If SEA is Lead Agency) . . .300.704(a)(4).
. Administrative costs of monitoring and complaint investigations . . .300.704(b)(3)(i).
. Allowable costs . . .300.704(b)(3).
. Amount for State administration . . .300.704(a)
. Annual description of use of Part B funds . . .300.171.
. Assist LEAs in meeting personnel shortages . . .300.704(b)(4)(vii).
. Complaint investigations . . .300.704(b)(3)(i).
. Coordination of activities with other
programs . . .300.704(b)(1).
USE OF FUNDS BY STATES (SEAs) (D-Z)
. Direct and support services . . .300.704(b)(4)(i).
. High cost fund . . .300.704(c).
. Mediation process . . .300.704(b)(3)(ii).
. Monitoring . . .300.704(b)(3)(i).
. Personnel preparation, professional development and training (see § 300.704(b)(4)(i), (b)(4)(xi)).
. State plan . . .300.704(c)(3)(i).
. Statewide coordinated services system . . .300.814(d).
. Support and direct services . . .300.704(b)(4)(i).
. Technical assistance:
. To LEAs . . .300.704(b)(4)(xi).
. To other programs that provide services . . .300.704(a)(1).
USE OF FUNDS BY SECRETARY OF THE INTERIOR (see §§ 300.707 through 300.716)
. By Indian tribes:
. For child find for children aged 3
through 5 . . .300.712(d).
. For coordination of assistance for services . . .300.712(a).
. For administrative costs . . .300.710(a).
USE OF SEA ALLOCATIONS . . .300.704.
. Inapplicability of requirements that prohibit commingling and supplanting of funds . . .300.704(d).
VISUAL IMPAIRMENT INCLUDING BLINDNESS
(Definition) . . .300.8(c)(13).
VOCATIONAL EDUCATION
. Definition . . .300.39(b)(5).
. In definition of "Special education" . . .300.39(a)(2)(iii).

. Program options . . .300.110.
. Transition services . . .300.320(b)(1).
VOCATIONAL REHABILITATION (See "Rehabilitation")
VOLUNTARY DEPARTURE OF PERSONNEL (Exception to LEA maintenance of effort) . . .300.204(a).
WAIVER(S)
. For exceptional and uncontrollable circumstances (State maintenance of effort) . . .300.163(c).
. "In whole or in part" . . .300.164(e).
. Public benefits or insurance (Risk of loss of eligibility for home and community-based waivers) . . .300.154(d)(2)(iii)(D).
. State-level nonsupplanting . . .300.162(c).
. State maintenance of effort . . .300.163.
. State's procedures for monitoring . . .300.164(c)(2)(ii)(B).
. Waiver procedures . . .300.164.
WARD OF THE STATE
. Appointment of surrogate parent . . .300.519(c).
. Definition . . .300.45.
. See definition of "Parent" . . .300.30(a)(3).
. See "Surrogate parents" . . .300.519(a)(3).
WEAPON (Definition) . . .300.530(i)(4).
WHEN IEPS MUST BE IN EFFECT . . .300.323.

TITLE 34
EDUCATION

SUBTITLE B   REGULATIONS OF THE OFFICES OF THE DEPARTMENT OF EDUCATION*

CHAPTER III   OFFICE OF SPECIAL EDUCATION AND REHABILITATIVE SERVICES, DEPARTMENT OF EDUCATION

PART 303   EARLY INTERVENTION PROGRAM FOR INFANTS AND TODDLERS WITH DISABILITIES

SUBPART A
GENERAL PURPOSE, ELIGIBILITY, AND OTHER GENERAL PROVISIONS

§ 303.1   Purpose of the early intervention program for infants and toddlers with disabilities.

The purpose of this part is to provide financial assistance to States to —

(a) Maintain and implement a statewide, comprehensive, coordinated, multidisciplinary, interagency system of early intervention services for infants and toddlers with disabilities and their families;

(b) Facilitate the coordination of payment for early intervention services from Federal, State, local, and private sources (including public and private insurance coverage);

(c) Enhance the States' capacity to provide quality early intervention services and expand and improve existing early intervention services being provided to infants and toddlers with disabilities and their families; and

(d) Enhance the capacity of State and local agencies and service providers to identify, evaluate, and meet the needs of historically underrepresented populations, particularly minority, low-income, inner-city, and rural populations.

§ 303.2   Eligible recipients of an award.

Eligible recipients include the 50 States, the Commonwealth of Puerto Rico, the District of Columbia, the Secretary of the Interior, and the following jurisdictions: Guam, American Samoa, the Virgin Islands, the Commonwealth of the Northern Mariana Islands.

§ 303.3   Activities that may be supported under this part.

Funds under this part may be used for the following activities:

(a) To maintain and implement a statewide system of early intervention services for children eligible under this part and their families.

(b) For direct services for eligible children and their families that are not otherwise provided from other public or private sources.

---

* Proposed replacement regulations may be found at 72 Fed. Reg. 26456 (May 9, 2007).

(c) To expand and improve on services for eligible children and their families that are otherwise available, consistent with § 303.527.

(d) To provide a free appropriate public education, in accordance with Part B of the Act, to children with disabilities from their third birthday to the beginning of the following school year.

(e) To strengthen the statewide system by initiating, expanding, or improving collaborative efforts related to at-risk infants and toddlers, including establishing linkages with appropriate public or private community-based organizations, services, and personnel for the purpose of —

(1) Identifying and evaluating at-risk infants and toddlers;

(2) Making referrals of the infants and toddlers identified and evaluated under paragraph (e)(1) of this section; and

(3) Conducting periodic follow-up on each referral under paragraph (e)(2) of this section to determine if the status of the infant or toddler involved has changed with respect to the eligibility of the infant or toddler for services under this part.

§ 303.4 Limitation on eligible children.

This part 303 does not apply to any child with disabilities receiving a free appropriate public education, in accordance with 34 CFR part 300, with funds received under 34 CFR part 301.

§ 303.5 Applicable regulations.

(a) The following regulations apply to this part:

(1) The Education Department General Administrative Regulations (EDGAR), including —

(i) Part 76 (State Administered Programs), except for § 76.103;

(ii) Part 77 (Definitions that Apply to Department Regulations);

(iii) Part 79 (Intergovernmental Review of Department of Education Programs and Activities);

(iv) Part 80 (Uniform Administrative Requirements for Grants and Cooperative Agreements to State and Local Governments);

(v) Part 81 (Grants and Cooperative Agreements under the General Education Provisions Act — Enforcement);

(vi) Part 82 (New Restrictions on Lobbying); and

(vii) Part 85 (Governmentwide Debarment and Suspension (Nonprocurement) and Governmentwide Requirements for Drug-Free Work Place (Grants)).

(2) The regulations in this part 303.

(3) The following regulations in 34 CFR part 300 (Assistance to States for the Education of Children with Disabilities Program): §§ 300.560-300.577, and §§ 300.580-300.585.

(b) In applying the regulations cited in paragraphs (a)(1) and (a)(3) of this section, any reference to —

(1) State educational agencymeans the lead agency under this part;

(2) Special education, related services, free appropriate public education, free public education,or educationmeans "early intervention services" under this part;

(3) Participating agency, when used in reference to a local educational agency or an intermediate educational agency, means a local service provider under this part;

(4) Section 300.128 means §§ 303.164 and 303.321; and

(5) Section 300.129 means § 303.460.

DEFINITIONS

§ 303.6 Act.

As used in this part, Act means the Individuals with Disabilities Education Act.

§ 303.7 Children.

As used in this part, children means "infants and toddlers with disabilities" as that term is defined in § 303.16.

§ 303.8 Council.

As used in this part, Council means the State Interagency Coordinating Council.

§ 303.9 Days.

As used in this part, days means calendar days.

§ 303.10 Developmental delay.

As used in this part, "developmental delay," when used with respect to an individual residing in a State, has the meaning given to that term under § 303.300.

§ 303.11 Early intervention program.

As used in this part, early intervention program means the total effort in a State that is directed at meeting the needs of children eligible under this part and their families.

§ 303.12 Early intervention services.

(a) General. As used in this part, early intervention services means services that —

(1) Are designed to meet the developmental needs of each child eligible under this part and the needs of the family related to enhancing the child's development;

(2) Are selected in collaboration with the parents;

(3) Are provided —

(i) Under public supervision;

(ii) By qualified personnel, as defined in § 303.21, including the types of personnel listed in paragraph (e) of this section;

(iii) In conformity with an individualized family service plan; and

(iv) At no cost, unless, subject to § 303.520(b)(3), Federal or State law provides for a system of payments by families, including a schedule of sliding fees; and

(4) Meet the standards of the State, including the requirements of this part.

(b) Natural environments. To the maximum extent appropriate to the needs of the child, early intervention services must be provided in natural environments, including the home and community settings in which children without disabilities participate.

(c) General role of service providers. To the extent appropriate, service providers in each area of early intervention services included in paragraph (d) of this section are responsible for —

(1) Consulting with parents, other service providers, and representatives of appropriate community agencies to ensure the effective provision of services in that area;

(2) Training parents and others regarding the provision of those services; and

(3) Participating in the multidisciplinary team's assessment of a child and the child's family, and in the development of integrated goals and outcomes for the individualized family service plan.

(d) Types of services; definitions. Following are types of services included under "early intervention services," and, if appropriate, definitions of those services:

(1) Assistive technology device means any item, piece of equipment, or product system, whether acquired commercially off the shelf, modified, or customized, that is used to increase, maintain, or improve the functional capabilities of children with disabilities. Assistive technology service means a service that directly assists a child with a disability in the selection, acquisition, or use of an assistive technology device. Assistive technology services include —

(i) The evaluation of the needs of a child with a disability, including a functional evaluation of the child in the child's customary environment;

(ii) Purchasing, leasing, or otherwise providing for the acquisition of assistive technology devices by children with disabilities;

(iii) Selecting, designing, fitting, customizing, adapting, applying, maintaining, repairing, or replacing assistive technology devices;

(iv) Coordinating and using other therapies, interventions, or services with assistive technology devices, such as those associated with existing education and rehabilitation plans and programs;

(v) Training or technical assistance for a child with disabilities or, if appropriate, that child's family; and

(vi) Training or technical assistance for professionals (including individuals providing early intervention services) or other individuals who provide services to or are otherwise substantially involved in the major life functions of individuals with disabilities.

(2) Audiology includes —

(i) Identification of children with auditory impairment, using at risk criteria and appropriate audiologic screening techniques;

(ii) Determination of the range, nature, and degree of hearing loss and communication functions, by use of audiological evaluation procedures;

(iii) Referral for medical and other services necessary for the habilitation or rehabilitation of children with auditory impairment;

(iv) Provision of auditory training, aural rehabilitation, speech reading and listening device orientation and training, and other services;

(v) Provision of services for prevention of hearing loss; and

(vi) Determination of the child's need for individual amplification, including selecting, fitting, and dispensing appropriate listening and vibrotactile devices, and evaluating the effectiveness of those devices.

(3) Family training, counseling, and home visits means services provided, as appro-

§ 303.12   IDEA REGULATIONS   325

priate, by social workers, psychologists, and other qualified personnel to assist the family of a child eligible under this part in understanding the special needs of the child and enhancing the child's development.

(4) Health services (See § 303.13).

(5) Medical services only for diagnostic or evaluation purposes means services provided by a licensed physician to determine a child's developmental status and need for early intervention services.

(6) Nursing services includes —

(i) The assessment of health status for the purpose of providing nursing care, including the identification of patterns of human response to actual or potential health problems;

(ii) Provision of nursing care to prevent health problems, restore or improve functioning, and promote optimal health and development; and

(iii) Administration of medications, treatments, and regimens prescribed by a licensed physician.

(7) Nutrition services includes —

(i) Conducting individual assessments in —

(A) Nutritional history and dietary intake;

(B) Anthropometric, biochemical, and clinical variables;

(C) Feeding skills and feeding problems; and

(D) Food habits and food preferences;

(ii) Developing and monitoring appropriate plans to address the nutritional needs of children eligible under this part, based on the findings in paragraph (d)(7)(i) of this section; and

(iii) Making referrals to appropriate community resources to carry out nutrition goals.

(8) Occupational therapy includes services to address the functional needs of a child related to adaptive development, adaptive behavior and play, and sensory, motor, and postural development. These services are designed to improve the child's functional ability to perform tasks in home, school, and community settings, and include —

(i) Identification, assessment, and intervention;

(ii) Adaptation of the environment, and selection, design, and fabrication of assistive and orthotic devices to facilitate development and promote the acquisition of functional skills; and

(iii) Prevention or minimization of the impact of initial or future impairment, delay in development, or loss of functional ability.

(9) Physical therapy includes services to address the promotion of sensorimotor function through enhancement of musculoskeletal status, neurobehavioral organization, perceptual and motor development, cardiopulmonary status, and effective environmental adaptation. These services include —

(i) Screening, evaluation, and assessment of infants and toddlers to identify movement dysfunction;

(ii) Obtaining, interpreting, and integrating information appropriate to program planning to prevent, alleviate, or compensate for movement dysfunction and related functional problems; and

(iii) Providing individual and group services or treatment to prevent, alleviate, or compensate for movement dysfunction and related functional problems.

(10) Psychological services includes —

(i) Administering psychological and developmental tests and other assessment procedures;

(ii) Interpreting assessment results;

(iii) Obtaining, integrating, and interpreting information about child behavior, and child and family conditions related to learning, mental health, and development; and

(iv) Planning and managing a program of psychological services, including psychological counseling for children and parents, family counseling, consultation on child development, parent training, and education programs.

(11) Service coordination services means assistance and services provided by a service coordinator to a child eligible under this part and the child's family that are in addition to the functions and activities included under § 303.23.

(12) Social work services includes —

(i) Making home visits to evaluate a child's living conditions and patterns of parent-child interaction;

(ii) Preparing a social or emotional developmental assessment of the child within the family context;

(iii) Providing individual and family-group counseling with parents and other family members, and appropriate social skill-building activities with the child and parents;

(iv) Working with those problems in a child's and family's living situation (home, community, and any center where early intervention services are provided) that affect the child's maximum utilization of early intervention services; and

(v) Identifying, mobilizing, and coordinating community resources and services to enable the child and family to receive maximum benefit from early intervention services.

(13) Special instruction includes —

(i) The design of learning environments and activities that promote the child's acquisition of skills in a variety of developmental areas, including cognitive processes and social interaction;

(ii) Curriculum planning, including the planned interaction of personnel, materials, and time and space, that leads to achieving the outcomes in the child's individualized family service plan;

(iii) Providing families with information, skills, and support related to enhancing the skill development of the child; and

(iv) Working with the child to enhance the child's development.

(14) Speech-language pathology includes —

(i) Identification of children with communicative or oropharyngeal disorders and delays in development of communication skills, including the diagnosis and appraisal of specific disorders and delays in those skills;

(ii) Referral for medical or other professional services necessary for the habilitation or rehabilitation of children with communicative or oropharyngeal disorders and delays in development of communication skills; and

(iii) Provision of services for the habilitation, rehabilitation, or prevention of communicative or oropharyngeal disorders and delays in development of communication skills.

(15) Transportation and related costs includes the cost of travel (e.g., mileage, or

travel by taxi, common carrier, or other means) and other costs (e.g., tolls and parking expenses) that are necessary to enable a child eligible under this part and the child's family to receive early intervention services.

(16) Vision services means —

(i) Evaluation and assessment of visual functioning, including the diagnosis and appraisal of specific visual disorders, delays, and abilities;

(ii) Referral for medical or other professional services necessary for the habilitation or rehabilitation of visual functioning disorders, or both; and

(iii) Communication skills training, orientation and mobility training for all environments, visual training, independent living skills training, and additional training necessary to activate visual motor abilities.

(e) Qualified personnel. Early intervention services must be provided by qualified personnel, including —

(1) Audiologists;

(2) Family therapists;

(3) Nurses;

(4) Nutritionists;

(5) Occupational therapists;

(6) Orientation and mobility specialists;

(7) Pediatricians and other physicians;

(8) Physical therapists;

(9) Psychologists;

(10) Social workers;

(11) Special educators; and

(12) Speech and language pathologists.

§ 303.13 Health services.

(a) As used in this part, health services means services necessary to enable a child to benefit from the other early intervention services under this part during the time that the child is receiving the other early intervention services.

(b) The term includes —

(1) Such services as clean intermittent catheterization, tracheostomy care, tube feeding, the changing of dressings or colostomy collection bags, and other health services; and

(2) Consultation by physicians with other service providers concerning the special health care needs of eligible children that will need to be addressed in the course of providing other early intervention services.

(c) The term does not include the following:

(1) Services that are —

(i) Surgical in nature (such as cleft palate surgery, surgery for club foot, or the shunting of hydrocephalus); or

(ii) Purely medical in nature (such as hospitalization for management of congenital heart ailments, or the prescribing of medicine or drugs for any purpose).

(2) Devices necessary to control or treat a medical condition.

(3) Medical-health services (such as immunizations and regular "well-baby" care) that are routinely recommended for all children.

§ 303.14 IFSP.

As used in this part, IFSP means the individualized family service plan, as that term is defined in § 303.340(b).

§ 303.15 Include; including.

As used in this part, include or including means that the items named are not all of the possible items that are covered whether like or unlike the ones named.

§ 303.16 Infants and toddlers with disabilities.

(a) As used in this part, infants and toddlers with disabilities means individuals from birth through age two who need early intervention services because they —

(1) Are experiencing developmental delays, as measured by appropriate diagnostic instruments and procedures, in one or more of the following areas:

(i) Cognitive development.

(ii) Physical development, including vision and hearing.

(iii) Communication development.

(iv) Social or emotional development.

(v) Adaptive development; or

(2) Have a diagnosed physical or mental condition that has a high probability of resulting in developmental delay.

(b) The term may also include, at a State's discretion, children from birth through age two who are at risk of having substantial developmental delays if early intervention services are not provided.

§ 303.17 Multidisciplinary.

As used in this part, multidisciplinary means the involvement of two or more disciplines or professions in the provision of integrated and coordinated services, including evaluation and assessment activities in § 303.322, and development of the IFSP in § 303.342.

§ 303.18 Natural environments.

As used in this part, natural environments means settings that are natural or normal for the child's age peers who have no disabilities.

§ 303.19 Parent.

(a) General. As used in this part, "parent" means —

(1) A natural or adoptive parent of a child;

(2) A guardian;

(3) A person acting in the place of a parent (such as a grandparent or stepparent with whom the child lives, or a person who is legally responsible for the child's welfare); or

(4) A surrogate parent who has been assigned in accordance with § 303.406.

(b) Foster parent. Unless State law prohibits a foster parent from acting as a parent, a State may allow a foster parent to act as a parent under Part C of the Act if —

(1) The natural parents' authority to make the decisions required of parents under the Act has been extinguished under State law; and

(2) The foster parent —

(i) Has an ongoing, long-term parental relationship with the child;

(ii) Is willing to make the decisions required of parents under the Act; and

(iii) Has no interest that would conflict with the interests of the child.

§ 303.20 Policies.

(a) As used in this part, policiesmeans State statutes, regulations, Governor's orders, directives by the lead agency, or other written documents that represent the State's position concerning any matter covered under this part.

(b) State policies include —

(1) A State's commitment to maintain the statewide system (see § 303.140);

(2) A State's eligibility criteria and procedures (see § 303.300);

(3) A statement that, consistent with § 303.520(b), provides that services under this part will be provided at no cost to parents, except where a system of payments is provided for under Federal or State law.

(4) A State's standards for personnel who provide services to children eligible under this part (see § 303.361);

(5) A State's position and procedures related to contracting or making other arrangements with service providers under subpart F of this part; and

(6) Other positions that the State has adopted related to implementing any of the other requirements under this part.

§ 303.21 Public agency.

As used in this part, public agency includes the lead agency and any other political subdivision of the State that is responsible for providing early intervention services to children eligible under this part and their families.

§ 303.22 Qualified.

As used in this part, qualified means that a person has met State approved or recognized certification, licensing, registration, or other comparable requirements that apply to the area in which the person is providing early intervention services.

§ 303.23 Service coordination (case management).

(a) General.

(1) As used in this part, except in § 303.12(d)(11), service coordination means the activities carried out by a service coordinator to assist and enable a child eligible under this part and the child's family to receive the rights, procedural safeguards, and services that are authorized to be provided under the State's early intervention program.

(2) Each child eligible under this part and the child's family must be provided with one service coordinator who is responsible for —

(i) Coordinating all services across agency lines; and

(ii) Serving as the single point of contact in helping parents to obtain the services and assistance they need.

(3) Service coordination is an active, ongoing process that involves —

(i) Assisting parents of eligible children in gaining access to the early intervention services and other services identified in the individualied family service plan;

(ii) Coordinating the provision of early intervention services and other services (such as medical services for other than diagnostic and evaluation purposes) that the child needs or is being provided;

(iii) Facilitating the timely delivery of available services; and

(iv) Continuously seeking the appropriate services and situations necessary to benefit the development of each child being served for the duration of the child's eligibility.

(b) *Specific service coordination activities.* Service coordination activities include —

(1) Coordinating the performance of evaluations and assessments;

(2) Facilitating and participating in the development, review, and evaluation of individualized family service plans;

(3) Assisting families in identifying available service providers;

(4) Coordinating and monitoring the delivery of available services;

(5) Informing families of the availability of advocacy services;

(6) Coordinating with medical and health providers; and

(7) Facilitating the development of a transition plan to preschool services, if appropriate.

(c) *Employment and assignment of service coordinators.* (1) Service coordinators may be employed or assigned in any way that is permitted under State law, so long as it is consistent with the requirements of this part.

(2) A State's policies and procedures for implementing the statewide system of early intervention services must be designed and implemented to ensure that service coordinators are able to effectively carry out on an interagency basis the functions and services listed under paragraphs (a) and (b) of this section.

(d) *Qualifications of service coordinators.* Service coordinators must be persons who, consistent with § 303.344(g), have demonstrated knowledge and understanding about —

(1) Infants and toddlers who are eligible under this part;

(2) Part C of the Act and the regulations in this part; and

(3) The nature and scope of services available under the State's early intervention program, the system of payments for services in the State, and other pertinent information.

§ 303.24 State.

Except as provided in § 303.200(b)(3), State means each of the 50 States, the Commonwealth of Puerto Rico, the District of Columbia, and the jurisdictions of Guam, American Samoa, the Virgin Islands, the Commonwealth of the Northern Mariana Islands.

§ 303.25 EDGAR definitions that apply.

The following terms used in this part are defined in *34 CFR 77.1*:

Applicant
Award
Contract
Department
EDGAR
Fiscal year
Grant
Grantee
Grant period
Private
Public
Secretary

SUBPART B STATE APPLICATION FOR A GRANT GENERAL REQUIREMENTS

§ 303.100 Conditions of assistance.

(a) In order to receive funds under this part for any fiscal year, a State must have —

(1) An approved application that contains the information required in this part, including —

(i) The information required in §§ 303.140 through 303.148; and

(ii) The information required in §§ 303.161 through 303.176; and

(2) The statement of assurances required under §§ 303.120 through 303.128, on file with the Secretary.

(b) If a State has on file with the Secretary a policy, procedure, or assurance that demonstrates that the State meets an application requirement, including any policy or procedure filed under this part before July 1, 1998, that meets such a requirement, the Secretary considers the State to have met that requirement for purposes of receiving a grant under this part.

(c) An application that meets the requirements of this part remains in effect until the State submits to the Secretary modifications of that application.

(d) The Secretary may require a State to modify its application under this part to the extent necessary to ensure the State's compliance with this part if —

(1) An amendment is made to the Act, or to a regulation under this part;

(2) A new interpretation is made of the Act by a Federal court or the State's highest court; or

(3) An official finding of noncompliance with Federal law or regulations is made with respect to the State.

§ 303.101 How the Secretary disapproves a State's application or statement of assurances.

The Secretary follows the procedures in 34 CFR 300.581 through 300.586 before disapproving a State's application or statement of assurances submitted under this part.

PUBLIC PARTICIPATION

§ 303.110 General requirements and timelines for public participation.

(a) Before submitting to the Secretary its application under this part, and before adopting a new or revised policy that is not in its current application, a State shall —

(1) Publish the application or policy in a manner that will ensure circulation throughout the State for at least a 60-day period, with an opportunity for comment on the application or policy for at least 30 days during that period;

(2) Hold public hearings on the application or policy during the 60-day period required in paragraph (a)(1) of this section; and

(3) Provide adequate notice of the hearings required in paragraph (a)(2) of this section at least 30 days before the dates that the hearings are conducted.

(b) A State may request the Secretary to waive compliance with the timelines in paragraph (a) of this section. The Secretary grants the request if the State demonstrates that —

(1) There are circumstances that would warrant such an exception; and

(2) The timelines that will be followed provide an adequate opportunity for public participation and comment.

§ 303.111 Notice of public hearings and opportunity to comment.

The notice required in § 303.110(a)(3) must —

(a) Be published in newspapers or announced in other media, or both, with coverage adequate to notify the general public, including individuals with disabilities and parents of infants and toddlers with disabilities, throughout the State about the hearings and opportunity to comment on the application or policy; and

(b) Be in sufficient detail to inform the public about —

(1) The purpose and scope of the State application or policy, and its relationship to Part C of the Act;

(2) The length of the comment period and the date, time, and location of each hearing; and

(3) The procedures for providing oral comments or submitting written comments.

§ 303.112 Public hearings.

Each State shall hold public hearings in a sufficient number and at times and places that afford interested parties throughout the State a reasonable opportunity to participate.

§ 303.113 Reviewing public comments received.

(a) Review of comments. Before adopting its application, and before the adoption of a new or revised policy not in the application, the lead agency shall —

(1) Review and consider all public comments; and

(2) Make any modifications it deems necessary in the application or policy.

(b) *Submission to the Secretary.* In submitting the State's application or policy to the Secretary, the lead agency shall include copies of news releases, advertisements, and announcements used to provide notice to the general public, including individuals with disabilities and parents of infants and toddlers with disabilities.

STATEMENT OF ASSURANCES

§ 303.120 General.

(a) A State's statement of assurances must contain the information required in §§ 303.121 through 303.128.

(b) Unless otherwise required by the Secretary, the statement is submitted only once, and remains in effect throughout the term of a State's participation under this part.

(c) A State may submit a revised statement of assurances if the statement is consistent with the requirements in §§ 303.121 through 303.128.

§ 303.121 Reports and records.

The statement must provide for —

(a) Making reports in such form and containing such information as the Secretary may require; and

(b) Keeping such records and affording such access to those records as the Secretary may find necessary to assure compliance with the requirements of this part, the correctness and verification of reports, and the proper disbursement of funds provided under this part.

(Approved by the Office of Management and Budget under control number 1820-0550)

§ 303.122 Control of funds and property.

The statement must provide assurance satisfactory to the Secretary that —

(a) The control of funds provided under this part, and title to property acquired with those funds, will be in a public agency for the uses and purposes provided in this part; and

(b) A public agency will administer the funds and property.

(Approved by the Office of Management and Budget under control number 1820-0550)

§ 303.123 Prohibition against commingling.

The statement must include an assurance satisfactory to the Secretary that funds made available under this part will not be commingled with State funds.

§ 303.124 Prohibition against supplanting.

(a) The statement must include an assurance satisfactory to the Secretary that Federal funds made available under this part will be used to supplement the level of State and local funds expended for children eligible under this part and their families and in no case to supplant those State and local funds.

(b) To meet the requirement in paragraph (a) of this section, the total amount of State and local funds budgeted for expenditures in the current fiscal year for early intervention services for children eligible under this part and their families must be at least equal to the total amount of State and local funds actually expended for early intervention services for these children and their families in the most recent preceding fiscal year for which the information is available. Allowance may be made for —

(1) Decreases in the number of children who are eligible to receive early intervention services under this part; and

(2) Unusually large amounts of funds expended for such long-term purposes as the acquisition of equipment and the construction of facilities.

(Approved by the Office of Management and Budget under control number 1820-0550)

§ 303.125   Fiscal control.

The statement must provide assurance satisfactory to the Secretary that such fiscal control and fund accounting procedures will be adopted as may be necessary to assure proper disbursement of, and accounting for, Federal funds paid under this part.

§ 303.126   Payor of last resort.

The statement must include an assurance satisfactory to the Secretary that the State will comply with the provisions in § 303.527, including the requirements on —

(a) Nonsubstitution of funds; and

(b) Non-reduction of other benefits.

(Approved by the Office of Management and Budget under control number 1820-0550)

§ 303.127   Assurance regarding expenditure of funds.

The statement must include an assurance satisfactory to the Secretary that the funds paid to the State under this part will be expended in accordance with the provisions of this part, including the requirements in § 303.3.

(Approved by the Office of Management and Budget under control number 1820-0550)

§ 303.128   Traditionally underserved groups.

The statement must include an assurance satisfactory to the Secretary that policies and practices have been adopted to ensure —

(a) That traditionally underserved groups, including minority, low-income, and rural families, are meaningfully involved in the planning and implementation of all the requirements of this part; and

(b) That these families have access to culturally competent services within their local geographical areas.

(Approved by the Office of Management and Budget under control number 1820-0550)

GENERAL REQUIREMENTS FOR A STATE APPLICATION

§ 303.140   General.

A State's application under this part must contain information and assurances demonstrating to the satisfaction of the Secretary that —

(a) The statewide system of early intervention services required in this part is in effect; and

(b) A State policy is in effect that ensures that appropriate early intervention services are available to all infants and toddlers with disabilities in the State and their families, including Indian infants and toddlers with disabilities and their families residing on a reservation geographically located in the State.

§ 303.141 Information about the Council.

Each application must include information demonstrating that the State has established a State Interagency Coordinating Council that meets the requirements of Subpart G of this part.

(Approved by the Office of Management and Budget under control number 1820-0550)

§ 303.142 Designation of lead agency.

Each application must include a designation of the lead agency in the State that will be responsible for the administration of funds provided under this part.

(Approved by the Office of Management and Budget under control number 1820-0550)

§ 303.143 Designation regarding financial responsibility.

Each application must include a designation by the State of an individual or entity responsible for assigning financial responsibility among appropriate agencies.

(Approved by the Office of Management and Budget under control number 1820-0550)

§ 303.144 Assurance regarding use of funds.

Each application must include an assurance that funds received under this part will be used to assist the State to maintain and implement the statewide system required under subparts D through F of this part.

(Approved by the Office of Management and Budget under control number 1820-0550)

§ 303.145 Description of use of funds.

(a) *General.* Each application must include a description of how a State proposes to use its funds under this part for the fiscal year or years covered by the application. The description must be presented separately for the lead agency and the Council, and include the information required in paragraphs (b) through (e) of this section.

(b) *Administrative positions.* Each application must include —

(1) A list of administrative positions, with salaries, and a description of the duties for each person whose salary is paid in whole or in part with funds awarded under this part; and

(2) For each position, the percentage of salary paid with those funds.

(c) *Maintenance and implementation activities.* Each application must include —

(1) A description of the nature and scope of each major activity to be carried out under this part in maintaining, and implementing the statewide system of early intervention services; and

(2) The approximate amount of funds to be spent for each activity.

(d) *Direct services.*

(1) Each application must include a description of any direct services that the State

expects to provide to eligible children and their families with funds under this part, including a description of any services provided to at-risk infants and toddlers as defined in § 303.16(b), and their families, consistent with §§ 303.521 and 303.527.

(2) The description must include information about each type of service to be provided, including —

(i) A summary of the methods to be used to provide the service (e.g., contracts or other arrangements with specified public or private organizations); and

(ii) The approximate amount of funds under this part to be used for the service.

(e) At-risk infants and toddlers. For any State that does not provide direct services for at-risk infants and toddlers described in paragraph (d)(1) of this section, but chooses to use funds as described in § 303.3(e), each application must include a description of how those funds will be used.

(f) Activities by other agencies. If other agencies are to receive funds under this part, the application must include —

(1) The name of each agency expected to receive funds;

(2) The approximate amount of funds each agency will receive; and

(3) A summary of the purposes for which the funds will be used.

(Approved by the Office of Management and Budget under control number 1820-0550)

§ 303.146 Information about public participation.

Each application must include the information on public participation that is required in § 303.113(b).

(Approved by the Office of Management and Budget under control number 1820-0550)

§ 303.147 Services to all geographic areas.

Each application must include a description of the procedure used to ensure that resources are made available under this part for all geographic areas within the State.

§ 303.148 Transition to preschool programs. [For effective date, see Publisher's Note.]

[PUBLISHER'S NOTE: *63 FR 18290, 18294*, Apr. 14, 1998, which amended this section, provides: "These regulations take effect on July 1, 1998. However, affected parties do not have to comply with the information collection requirements in §§ 303.100, 303.145, 303.148, 303.167, 303.344, 303.361, 303.426, 303.601, 303.650, and 303.653 until the Department of Education publishes in the Federal Register the control numbers assigned by the Office of Management and Budget (OMB) to these information collection requirements. Publication of the control numbers in a separate final regulation notifies the public that OMB has approved these information collection requirements under the Paperwork Reduction Act of 1995." For the convenience of the user, this section has been set out twice. The version incorporating the amendments at *63 FR 18290, 18294*, Apr. 14, 1998, immediately follows this note. For the version of this section prior to the amendments, see the other version of this section, also numbered § 303.148.]

Each application must include a description of the policies and procedures to be used to ensure a smooth transition for children receiving early intervention services under this part to preschool or other appropriate services, including —

(a) A description of how the families will be included in the transition plans;

(b) A description of how the lead agency under this part will-

(1) Notify the local educational agency for the area in which the child resides that the child will shortly reach the age of eligibility for preschool services under Part B of the Act, as determined in accordance with State law;

(2)

(i) In the case of a child who may be eligible for preschool services under Part B of the Act, with the approval of the family of the child, convene a conference among the lead agency, the family, and the local educational agency at least 90 days, and at the discretion of the parties, up to 6 months, before the child is eligible for the preschool services, to discuss any services that the child may receive; or

(ii) In the case of a child who may not be eligible for preschool services under Part B of the Act, with the approval of the family, make reasonable efforts to convene a conference among the lead agency, the family, and providers of other appropriate services for children who are not eligible for preschool services under Part B, to discuss the appropriate services that the child may receive;

(3) Review the child's program options for the period from the child's third birthday through the remainder of the school year; and

(4) Establish a transition plan; and

(c) If the State educational agency, which is responsible for administering preschool programs under Part B of the Act, is not the lead agency under this part, an interagency agreement between the two agencies to ensure coordination on transition matters.

(Approved by the Office of Management and Budget under control number 1820-0550)

§ 303.148 Transition to preschool programs. [For effective date see Publisher's Note.]

[PUBLISHER'S NOTE: *63 FR 18290, 18294*, Apr. 14, 1998, which amended this section, provides: "These regulations take effect on July 1, 1998. However, affected parties do not have to comply with the information collection requirements in §§ 303.100, 303.145, 303.148, 303.167, 303.344, 303.361, 303.426, 303.601, 303.650, and 303.653 until the Department of Education publishes in the Federal Register the control numbers assigned by the Office of Management and Budget (OMB) to these information collection requirements. Publication of the control numbers in a separate final regulation notifies the public that OMB has approved these information collection requirements under the Paperwork Reduction Act of 1995." For the convenience of the user, this section has been set out twice. The version of this section prior to the amendments at *63 FR 18290, 18294*, Apr. 14, 1998, immediately follows this note. For the version of this section which incorporates the amendments at *63 FR 18290, 18294*, Apr. 14, 1998, see the other version of this section, also numbered § 303.148.]

Each application must include the policies and procedures used to ensure a smooth transition for individuals participating in the early intervention program under this part who are eligible for participation in preschool programs under Part B of the Act, including —

(a) A description of how the families will be included in the transitional plans;

(b) A description of how the lead agency under this part will —

(1) Notify the appropriate local educational agency or intermediate educational unit in which the child resides; and

(2) Convene, with the approval of the family, a conference among the lead agency, the family, and the local educational agency or unit at least 90 days before the child's third birthday or, if earlier, the date on which the child is eligible for the preschool program under Part B of the Act in accordance with State law, to —

(i) Review the child's program options for the period from the child's third birthday through the remainder of the school year; and

(ii) Establish a transition plan; and

(c) If the State educational agency, which is responsible for administering preschool programs under Part B of the Act, is not the lead agency under this part, an interagency agreement between the two agencies to ensure coordination on transition matters.

(Approved by the Office of Management and Budget under control number 1820-0550)

COMPONENTS OF A STATEWIDE SYSTEM — APPLICATION REQUIREMENTS

§ 303.160 Minimum components of a statewide system.

Each application must address the minimum components of a statewide system of coordinated, comprehensive, multidisciplinary, interagency programs providing appropriate early intervention services to all infants and toddlers with disabilities and their families, including Indian infants and toddlers with disabilities and their families residing on a reservation geographically located in the State. The minimum components of a statewide system are described in §§ 303.161 through 303.176.

(Approved by the Office of Management and Budget under control number 1820-0550)

§ 303.161 State definition of developmental delay.

Each application must include the State's definition of "developmental delay," as described in § 303.300.

(Approved by the Office of Management and Budget under control number 1820-0550)

§ 303.162 Central directory.

Each application must include information and assurances demonstrating to the satisfaction of the Secretary that the State has developed a central directory of information that meets the requirements in § 303.301.

(Approved by the Office of Management and Budget under control number 1820-0550)

§ 303.163 [Reserved]

§ 303.164 Public awareness program.

Each application must include information and assurances demonstrating to the satisfaction of the Secretary that the State has established a public awareness program that meets the requirements in § 303.320.

(Approved by the Office of Management and Budget under control number 1820-0550)

§ 303.165 Comprehensive child find system.

Each application must include —

(a) The poliices and procedures required in § 303.321(b);

(b) Information demonstrating that the requirements on coordination in § 303.321(c) are met;

(c) The referral procedures required in § 303.321(d), and either —

(1) A description of how the referral sources are informed about the procedures; or

(2) A copy of any memorandum or other document used by the lead agency to transmit the procedures to the referral sources; and

(d) The timelines in § 303.321(e).

(Approved by the Office of Management and Budget under control number 1820-0550)

§ 303.166 Evaluation, assessment, and nondiscriminatory procedures.

Each application must include information to demonstrate that the requirements in §§ 303.322 and 303.323 are met.

(Approved by the Office of Management and Budget under control number 1820-0550)

§ 303.167 Individualized family service plans.

Each application must include —

(a) An assurance that a current IFSP is in effect and implemented for each eligible child and the child's family;

(b) Information demonstrating that —

(1) The State's procedures for developing, reviewing, and evaluating IFSPs are consistent with the requirements in §§ 303.340, 303.342, 303.343 and 303.345; and

(2) The content of IFSPs used in the State is consistent with the requirements in § 303.344; and

(c) Policies and procedures to ensure that —

(1) To the maximum extent appropriate, early intervention services are provided in natural environments; and

(2) The provision of early intervention services for any infant or toddler occurs in a setting other than a natural environment only if early intervention cannot be achieved satisfactorily for the infant or toddler in a natural environment.

(Approved by the Office of Management and Budget under control number 1820-0550)

§ 303.168 Comprehensive system of personnel development (CSPD).

Each application must include information to show that the requirements in § 303.360(b) are met.

(Approved by the Office of Management and Budget under control number 1820-0550)

§ 303.169 Personnel standards.

(a) Each application must include policies and procedures that are consistent with the requirements in § 303.361.

(Approved by the Office of Management and Budget under control number 1820-0550)

§ 303.170 Procedural safeguards.

Each application must include procedural safeguards that —

(a) Are consistent with §§ 303.400 through 303.406, 303.419 through 303.425 and 303.460; and

(b) Incorporate either —

(1) The due process procedures in *34 CFR 300.506* through *300.512*; or

(2) The procedures that the State has developed to meet the requirements in §§ 303.419, 303.420(b) and 303.421 through 303.425.

(Approved by the Office of Management and Budget under control number 1820-0550)

§ 303.171 Supervision and monitoring of programs.

Each application must include information to show that the requirements in § 303.501 are met.

(Approved by the Office of Management and Budget under control number 1820-0550)

§ 303.172 Lead agency procedures for resolving complaints.

Each application must include procedures that are consistent with the requirements in §§ 303.510 through 303.512.

(Approved by the Office of Management and Budget under control number 1820-0550)

§ 303.173 Policies and procedures related to financial matters.

Each application must include —

(a) Funding policies that meet the requirements in §§ 303.520 and 303.521;

(b) Information about funding sources, as required in § 303.522;

(c) Procedures to ensure the timely delivery of services, in accordance with § 303.525; and

(d) A procedure related to the timely reimbursement of funds under this part, in accordance with §§ 303.527(b) and 303.528.

(Approved by the Office of Management and Budget under control number 1820-0550)

§ 303.174 Interagency agreements; resolution of individual disputes.

Each application must include —

(a) A copy of each interagency agreement that has been developed under § 303.523; and

(b) Information to show that the requirements in § 303.524 are met.

(Approved by the Office of Management and Budget under control number 1820-0550)

§ 303.175 Policy for contracting or otherwise arranging for services.

Each application must include a policy that meets the requirements in § 303.526.

(Approved by the Office of Management and Budget under control number 1820-0550)

§ 303.176 Data collection.

Each application must include procedures that meet the requirements in § 303.540.

(Approved by the Office of Management and Budget under control number 1820-0550)

PARTICIPATION BY THE SECRETARY OF THE INTERIOR

§ 303.180 Payments to the Secretary of the Interior for Indian tribes and tribal organizations.

(a) The Secretary makes payments to the Secretary of the Interior for the coordination of assistance in the provision of early intervention services by the States to infants and toddlers with disabilities and their families on reservations served by elementary and secondary schools for Indian children operated or funded by the Department of the Interior.

(b)

(1) The Secretary of the Interior shall distribute payments under this part to tribes or tribal organizations (as defined under section 4 of the Indian Self-Determination and Education Assistance Act), or combinations of those entities, in accordance with section 684(b) of the Act.

(2) A tribe or tribal organization is eligible to receive a payment under this section if the tribe is on a reservation that is served by an elementary or secondary school operated or funded by the Bureau of Indian Affairs ("BIA").

(c)

(1) Within 90 days after the end of each fiscal year the Secretary of the Interior shall provide the Secretary with a report on the payments distributed under this section.

(2) The report must include —

(i) The name of each tribe, tribal organization, or combination of those entities that received a payment for the fiscal year;

(ii) The amount of each payment; and

(iii) The date of each payment.

(Approved by the Office of Management and Budget under control number 1820-0550)

SUBPART C PROCEDURES FOR MAKING GRANTS TO STATES

§ 303.200 Formula for State allocations.

(a) For each fiscal year, from the aggregate amount of funds available under this part for distribution to the States, the Secretary allots to each State an amount that bears the same ratio to the aggregate amount as the number of infants and toddlers in the State bears to the number of infants and toddlers in all States.

(b) For the purpose of allotting funds to the States under paragraph (a) of this section —

(1) Aggregate amount means the amount available for distribution to the States after the Secretary determines the amount of payments to be made to the Secretary of the Interior under § 303.203 and to the jurisdictions under § 303.204;

(2) Infants and toddlers means children from birth through age two in the general population, based on the most recent satisfactory data as determined by the Secretary; and

(3) State means each of the 50 States, the District of Columbia, and the Commonwealth of Puerto Rico.

§ 303.201 Distribution of allotments from non-participating States.

If a State elects not to receive its allotment, the Secretary reallots those funds among the remaining States, in accordance with § 303.200(a).

§ 303.202 Minimum grant that a State may receive.

No State receives less than 0.5 percent of the aggregate amount available under § 303.200 or $ 500,000, whichever is greater.

§ 303.203 Payments to the Secretary of the Interior.

The amount of the payment to the Secretary of the Interior under § 303.180 for any fiscal year is 1.25 percent of the aggregate amount available to States after the Secretary determines the amount of payments to be made to the jurisdictions under § 303.204.

§ 303.204 Payments to the jurisdictions.

(a) From the sums appropriated to carry out this part for any fiscal year, the Secretary may reserve up to 1 percent for payments to the jurisdictions listed in § 303.2 in accordance with their respective needs.

(b) The provisions of Pub. L. 95-134, permitting the consolidation of grants to the outlying areas, do not apply to funds provided under paragraph (a) of this section.

SUBPART D   PROGRAM AND SERVICE COMPONENTS OF A STATEWIDE SYSTEM OF EARLY INTERVENTION SERVICES
GENERAL

§ 303.300 State eligibility criteria and procedures.

Each statewide system of early intervention services must include the eligibility criteria and procedures, consistent with § 303.16, that will be used by the State in carrying out programs under this part.

(a) The State shall define developmental delay by —

(1) Describing, for each of the areas listed in § 303.16(a)(1), the procedures, including the use of informed clinical opinion, that will be used to measure a child's development; and

(2) Stating the levels of functioning or other criteria that constitute a developmental delay in each of those areas.

(b) The State shall describe the criteria and procedures, including the use of informed clinical opinion, that will be used to determine the existence of a condition that has a high probability of resulting in developmental delay under § 303.16(a)(2).

(c) If the State elects to include in its system children who are at risk under § 303.16(b), the State shall describe the criteria and procedures, including the use of informed clinical opinion, that will be used to identify those children.

(Approved by the Office of Management and Budget under control number 1820-0550)

§ 303.301 Central directory.

(a) Each system must include a central directory of information about —

(1) Public and private early intervention services, resources, and experts available in the State;

(2) Research and demonstration projects being conducted in the State; and

(3) Professional and other groups that provide assistance to children eligible under this part and their families.

(b) The information required in paragraph (a) of this section must be in sufficient detail to —

(1) Ensure that the general public will be able to determine the nature and scope of the services and assistance available from each of the sources listed in the directory; and

(2) Enable the parent of a child eligible under this part to contact, by telephone or letter, any of the sources listed in the directory.

(c) The central directory must be —

(1) Updated at least annually; and

(2) Accessible to the general public.

(d) To meet the requirements in paragraph (c)(2) of this section, the lead agency shall arrange for copies of the directory to be available —

(1) In each geographic region of the State, including rural areas; and

(2) In places and a manner that ensure accessibility by persons with disabilities.

(Approved by the Office of Management and Budget under control number 1820-0550)

IDENTIFICATION AND EVALUATION

§ 303.320 Public awareness program.

Each system must include a public awareness program that focuses on the early identification of children who are eligible to receive early intervention services under this part and includes the preparation and dissemination by the lead agency to all primary referral sources, especially hospitals and physicians, of materials for parents on the availability of early intervention services. The public awareness program must provide for informing the public about —

(a) The State's early intervention program;

(b) The child find system, including —

(1) The purpose and scope of the system;

(2) How to make referrals; and

(3) How to gain access to a comprehensive, multidisciplinary evaluation and other early intervention services; and

(c) The central directory.

(Approved by the Office of Management and Budget under control number 1820-0550)

§ 303.321 Comprehensive child find system.

(a) General.

(1) Each system must include a comprehensive child find system that is consistent

with Part B of the Act (see *34 CFR 300.128*), and meets the requirements of paragraphs (b) through (e) of this section.

(2) The lead agency, with the advice and assistance of the Council, shall be responsible for implementing the child find system.

(b) Procedures. The child find system must include the policies and procedures that the State will follow to ensure that —

(1) All infants and toddlers in the State who are eligible for services under this part are identified, located, and evaluated; and

(2) An effective method is developed and implemented to determine which children are receiving needed early intervention services.

(c) Coordination.

(1) The lead agency, with the assistance of the Council, shall ensure that the child find system under this part is coordinated with all other major efforts to locate and identify children conducted by other State agencies responsible for administering the various education, health, and social service programs relevant to this part, tribes and tribal organizations that receive payments under this part, and other tribes and tribal organizations as appropriate, including efforts in the —

(i) Program authorized under Part B of the Act;

(ii) Maternal and Child Health program under Title V of the Social Security Act;

(iii) Early Periodic Screening, Diagnosis and Treatment (EPSDT) program under Title XIX of the Social Security Act;

(iv) Developmental Disabilities Assistance and Bill of Rights Act;

(v) Head Start Act; and

(vi) Supplemental Security Income program under Title XVI of the Social Security Act.

(2) The lead agency, with the advice and assistance of the Council, shall take steps to ensure that —

(i) There will not be unnecessary duplication of effort by the various agencies involved in the State's child find system under this part; and

(ii) The State will make use of the resources available through each public agency in the State to implement the child find system in an effective manner.

(d) Referral procedures.

(1) The child find system must include procedures for use by primary referral sources for referring a child to the appropriate public agency within the system for —

(i) Evaluation and assessment, in accordance with §§ 303.322 and 303.323; or

(ii) As appropriate, the provision of services, in accordance with § 303.342(a) or § 303.345.

(2) The procedures required in paragraph (b)(1) of this section must —

(i) Provide for an effective method of making referrals by primary referral sources;

(ii) Ensure that referrals are made no more than two working days after a child has been identified; and

(iii) Include procedures for determining the extent to which primary referral sources, especially hospitals and physicians, disseminate the information, as described in § 303.320, prepared by the lead agency on the availability of early intervention services to parents of infants and toddlers with disabilities.

(3) As used in paragraph (d)(1) of this section, primary referral sources includes —

(i) Hospitals, including prenatal and postnatal care facilities;

(ii) Physicians;

(iii) Parents;

(iv) Day care programs;

(v) Local educational agencies;

(vi) Public health facilities;

(vii) Other social service agencies; and

(viii) Other health care providers.

(e) Timelines for public agencies to act on referrals. (1) Once the public agency receives a referral, it shall appoint a service coordinator as soon as possible.

(2) Within 45 days after it receives a referral, the public agency shall —

(i) Complete the evaluation and assessment activities in § 303.322; and

(ii) Hold an IFSP meeting, in accordance with § 303.342.

(Approved by the Office of Management and Budget under control number 1820-0550)

§ 303.322 Evaluation and assessment.

(a) General.

(1) Each system must include the performance of a timely, comprehensive, multidisciplinary evaluation of each child, birth through age two, referred for evaluation, and a family-directed identification of the needs of each child's family to appropriately assist in the development of the child.

(2) The lead agency shall be responsible for ensuring that the requirements of this section are implemented by all affected public agencies and service providers in the State.

(b) Definitions of evaluation and assessment. As used in this part —

(1) Evaluation means the procedures used by appropriate qualified personnel to determine a child's initial and continuing eligibility under this part, consistent with the definition of "infants and toddlers with disabilities" in § 303.16, including determining the status of the child in each of the developmental areas in paragraph (c)(3)(ii) of this section.

(2) Assessment means the ongoing procedures used by appropriate qualified personnel throughout the period of a child's eligibility under this part to identify —

(i) The child's unique strengths and needs and the services appropriate to meet those needs; and

(ii) The resources, priorities, and concerns of the family and the supports and services necessary to enhance the family's capacity to meet the developmental needs of their infant or toddler with a disability.

(c) Evaluation and assessment of the child. The evaluation and assessment of each child must —

(1) Be conducted by personnel trained to utilize appropriate methods and procedures;

(2) Be based on informed clinical opinion; and

(3) Include the following:

(i) A review of pertinent records related to the child's current health status and medical history.

(ii) An evaluation of the child's level of functioning in each of the following developmental areas:

(A) Cognitive development.

(B) Physical development, including vision and hearing.

(C) Communication development.

(D) Social or emotional development.

(E) Adaptive development.

(iii) An assessment of the unique needs of the child in terms of each of the developmental areas in paragraph (c)(3)(ii) of this section, including the identification of services appropriate to meet those needs.

(d) *Family assessment.*

(1) Family assessments under this part must be family-directed and designed to determine the resources, priorities, and concerns of the family and the identification of the supports and services necessary to enhance the family's capacity to meet the developmental needs of the child.

(2) Any assessment that is conducted must be voluntary on the part of the family.

(3) If an assessment of the family is carried out, the assessment must —

(i) Be conducted by personnel trained to utilize appropriate methods and procedures;

(ii) Be based on information provided by the family through a personal interview; and

(iii) Incorporate the family's description of its resources, priorities, and concerns related to enhancing the child's development.

(e) *Timelines.*

(1) Except as provided in paragraph (e)(2) of this section, the evaluation and initial assessment of each child (including the family assessment) must be completed within the 45-day time period required in § 303.321(e).

(2) The lead agency shall develop procedures to ensure that in the event of exceptional circumstances that make it impossible to complete the evaluation and assessment within 45 days (e.g., if a child is ill), public agencies will —

(i) Document those circumstances; and

(ii) Develop and implement an interim IFSP, to the extent appropriate and consistent with § 303.345 (b)(1) and (b)(2).

(Approved by the Office of Management and Budget under control number 1820-0550)

§ 303.323 Nondiscriminatory procedures.

Each lead agency shall adopt nondiscriminatory evaluation and assessment procedures. The procedures must provide that public agencies responsible for the evaluation and assessment of children and families under this part shall ensure, at a minimum, that —

(a) Tests and other evaluation materials and procedures are administered in the native language of the parents or other mode of communication, unless it is clearly not feasible to do so;

(b) Any assessment and evaluation procedures and materials that are used are selected and administered so as not to be racially or culturally discriminatory;

(c) No single procedure is used as the sole criterion for determining a child's eligibility under this part; and

(d) Evaluations and assessments are conducted by qualified personnel.

(Approved by the Office of Management and Budget under control number 1820-0550)

INDIVIDUALIZED FAMILY SERVICE PLANS (IFSPS)

§ 303.340 General.

(a) Each system must include policies and procedures regarding individualized family service plans (IFSPs) that meet the requirements of this section and §§ 303.341 through 303.346.

(b) As used in this part, individualized family service plan and IFSP mean a written plan for providing early intervention services to a child eligible under this part and the child's family. The plan must —

(1) Be developed in accordance with §§ 303.342 and 303.343;

(2) Be based on the evaluation and assessment described in § 303.322; and

(3) Include the matters specified in § 303.344.

(c) Lead agency responsibility. The lead agency shall ensure that an IFSP is developed and implemented for each eligible child, in accordance with the requirements of this part. If there is a dispute between agencies as to who has responsibility for developing or implementing an IFSP, the lead agency shall resolve the dispute or assign responsibility.

(Approved by the Office of Management and Budget under control number 1820-0550)

§ 303.341 [Reserved]

§ 303.342 Procedures for IFSP development, review, and evaluation.

(a) Meeting to develop initial IFSP-timelines. For a child who has been evaluated for the first time and determined to be eligible, a meeting to develop the initial IFSP must be conducted within the 45-day time period in § 303.321(e).

(b) Periodic review.

(1) A review of the IFSP for a child and the child's family must be conducted every six months, or more frequently if conditions warrant, or if the family requests such a review. The purpose of the periodic review is to determine —

(i) The degree to which progress toward achieving the outcomes is being made; and

(ii) Whether modification or revision of the outcomes or services is necessary.

(2) The review may be carried out by a meeting or by another means that is acceptable to the parents and other participants.

(c) Annual meeting to evaluate the IFSP. A meeting must be conducted on at least an annual basis to evaluate the IFSP for a child and the child's family, and, as appropriate, to revise its provisions. The results of any current evaluations conducted under § 303.322(c), and other information available from the ongoing assessment of the child and family, must be used in determining what services are needed and will be provided.

(d) Accessibility and convenience of meetings.

(1) IFSP meetings must be conducted —

(i) In settings and at times that are convenient to families; and

(ii) In the native language of the family or other mode of communication used by the family, unless it is clearly not feasible to do so.

(2) Meeting arrangements must be made with, and written notice provided to, the family and other participants early enough before the meeting date to ensure that they will be able to attend.

(e) Parental consent. The contents of the IFSP must be fully explained to the parents and informed written consent from the parents must be obtained prior to the provision of early intervention services described in the plan. If the parents do not provide consent with respect to a particular early intervention service or withdraw consent after first providing it, that service may not be provided. The early intervention services to which parental consent is obtained must be provided.

(Approved by the Office of Management and Budget under control number 1820-0550)

§ 303.343 Participants in IFSP meetings and periodic reviews.

(a) Initial and annual IFSP meetings.

(1) Each initial meeting and each annual meeting to evaluate the IFSP must include the following participants:

(i) The parent or parents of the child.

(ii) Other family members, as requested by the parent, if feasible to do so;

(iii) An advocate or person outside of the family, if the parent requests that the person participate.

(iv) The service coordinator who has been working with the family since the initial referral of the child for evaluation, or who has been designated by the public agency to be responsible for implementation of the IFSP.

(v) A person or persons directly involved in conducting the evaluations and assessments in § 303.322.

(vi) As appropriate, persons who will be providing services to the child or family.

(2) If a person listed in paragraph (a)(1)(v) of this section is unable to attend a meeting, arrangements must be made for the person's involvement through other means, including —

(i) Participating in a telephone conference call;

(ii) Having a knowledgeable authorized representative attend the meeting; or

(iii) Making pertinent records available at the meeting.

(b) Periodic review. Each periodic review must provide for the participation of persons in paragraphs (a)(1)(i) through (a)(1)(iv) of this section. If conditions warrant, provisions must be made for the participation of other representatives identified in paragraph (a) of this section.

(Approved by the Office of Management and Budget under control number 1820-0550)

§ 303.344 Content of an IFSP.

(a) Information about the child's status.

(1) The IFSP must include a statement of the child's present levels of physical development (including vision, hearing, and health status), cognitive development, communication development, social or emotional development, and adaptive development.

(2) The statement in paragraph (a)(1) of this section must be based on professionally acceptable objective criteria.

(b) Family information. With the concurrence of the family, the IFS must include a statement of the family's resources, priorities, and concerns related to enhancing the development of the child.

(c) Outcomes. The IFSP must include a statement of the major outcomes expected to be achieved for the child and family, and the criteria, procedures, and timeliness used to determine —

(1) The degree to which progress toward achieving the outcomes is being made; and

(2) Whether modifications or revisions of the outcomes or services are necessary.

(d) Early intervention services.

(1) The IFSP must include a statement of the specific early intervention services necessary to meet the unique needs of the child and the family to achieve the outcomes identified in paragraph (c) of this section, including —

(i) The frequency, intensity, and method of delivering the services;

(ii) The natural environments, as described in § 303.12(b), and § 303.18 in which early intervention services will be provided, and a justification of the extent, if any, to which the services will not be provided in a natural environment;

(iii) The location of the services; and

(iv) The payment arrangements, if any.

(2) As used in paragraph (d)(1)(i) of this section —

(i) Frequency and intensity mean the number of days or sessions that a service will be provided, the length of time the service is provided during each session, and whether the service is provided on an individual or group basis; and

(ii) Method means how a service is provided.

(3) As used in paragraph (d)(1)(iii) of this section, location means the actual place or places where a service will be provided.

(e) Other services.

(1) To the extent appropriate, the IFSP must include —

(i) Medical and other services that the child needs, but that are not required under this part; and

(ii) The funding sources to be used in paying for those services or the steps that will be taken to secure those services through public or private sources.

(2) The requirement in paragraph (e)(1) of this section does not apply to routine medical services (e.g., immunizations and "well-baby" care), unless a child needs those services and the services are not otherwise available or being provided.

(f) Dates; duration of services. The IFSP must include —

(1) The projected dates for initiation of the services in paragraph (d)(1) of this section as soon as possible after the IFSP meetings described in § 303.342; and

(2) The anticipated duration of those services.

(g) *Service coordinator.*

(1) The IFSP must include the name of the service coordinator from the profession most immediately relevant to the child's or family's needs (or who is otherwise qualified to carry out all applicable responsibilities under this part), who will be responsible for the implementation of the IFSP and coordination with other agencies and persons.

(2) In meeting the requirements in paragraph (g)(1) of this section, the public agency may —

(i) Assign the same service coordinator who was appointed at the time that the child was initially referred for evaluation to be responsible for implementing a child's and family's IFSP; or

(ii) Appoint a new service coordinator.

(3) As used in paragraph (g)(1) of this section, the term "profession" includes "service coordination."

(h) *Transition from Part C services.*

(1) The IFSP must include the steps to be taken to support the transition of the child, in accordance with § 303.148, to —

(i) Preschool services under Part B of the Act, to the extent that those services are appropriate; or

(ii) Other services that may be available, if appropriate.

(2) The steps required in paragraph (h)(1) of this section include —

(i) Discussions with, and training of, parents regarding future placements and other matters related to the child's transition;

(ii) Procedures to prepare the child for changes in service delivery, including steps to help the child adjust to, and function in, a new setting; and

(iii) With parental consent, the transmission of information about the child to the local educational agency, to ensure continuity of services, including evaluation and assessment information required in § 303.322, and copies of IFSPs that have been developed and implemented in accordance with §§ 303.340 through 303.346.

(Approved by the Office of Management and Budget under control number 1820-0550)

§ 303.345 Provision of services before evaluation and assessment are completed.

Early intervention services for an eligible child and the child's family may commence before the completion of the evaluation and assessment in § 303.322, if the following conditions are met:

(a) Parental consent is obtained.

(b) An interim IFSP is developed that includes —

(1) The name of the service coordinator who will be responsible, consistent with § 303.344(g), for implementation of the interim IFSP and coordination with other agencies and persons; and

(2) The early intervention services that have been determined to be needed immediately by the child and the child's family.

(c) The evaluation and assessment are completed within the time period required in § 303.322(e).

(Approved by the Office of Management and Budget under control number 1820-0550)

§ 303.346 Responsibility and accountability.

Each agency or person who has a direct role in the provision of early intervention services is responsible for making a good faith effort to assist each eligible child in achieving the outcomes in the child's IFSP. However, Part C of the Act does not require that any agency or person be held accountable if an eligible child does not achieve the growth projected in the child's IFSP.

(Approved by the Office of Management and Budget under control number 1820-0550)

PERSONNEL TRAINING AND STANDARDS

§ 303.360 Comprehensive system of personnel development.

(a) Each system must include a comprehensive system of personnel development.

(b) The personnel development system under this part must —

(1) Be consistent with the comprehensive system of personnel development required under Part B of the Act (*34 CFR 300.380* through 300.387);

(2) Provide for preservice and inservice training to be conducted on an interdisciplinary basis, to the extent appropriate;

(3) Provide for the training of a variety of personnel needed to meet the requirements of this part, including public and private providers, primary referral sources, paraprofessionals, and persons who will serve as service coordinators; and

(4) Ensure that the training provided relates specifically to —

(i) Understanding the basic components of early intervention services available in the State;

(ii) Meeting the interrelated social or emotional, health, developmental, and educational needs of eligible children under this part; and

(iii) Assisting families in enhancing the development of their children, and in participating fully in the development and implementation of IFSPs.

(c) A personnel development system under this part may include —

(1) Implementing innovative strategies and activities for the recruitment and retention of early intervention service providers;

(2) Promoting the preparation of early intervention providers who are fully and appropriately qualified to provide early intervention services under this part;

(3) Training personnel to work in rural and inner-city areas; and

(4) Training personnel to coordinate transition services for infants and toddlers with disabilities from an early intervention program under this part to a preschool program under Part B of the Act or to other preschool or other appropriate services.

(Approved by the Office of Management and Budget under control number 1820-0550)

§ 303.361 Personnel standards.

(a) As used in this part —

(1) Appropriate professional requirements in the State means entry level requirements that —

(i) Are based on the highest requirements in the State applicable to the profession or discipline in which a person is providing early intervention services; and

(ii) Establish suitable qualifications for personnel providing early intervention services under this part to eligible children and their families who are served by State, local, and private agencies.

(2) Highest requirements in the State applicable to a specific profession or discipline means the highest entry-level academic degree needed for any State approved or recognized certification, licensing, registration, or other comparable requirements that apply to that profession or discipline.

(3) Profession or discipline means a specific occupational category that —

(i) Provides early intervention services to children eligible under this part and their families;

(ii) Has been established or designated by the State; and

(iii) Has a required scope of responsibility and degree of supervision.

(4) State approved or recognized certification, licensing, registration, or other comparable requirements means the requirements that a State legislature either has enacted or has authorized a State agency to promulgate through rules to establish the entry-level standards for employment in a specific profession or discipline in that State.

(b)

(1) Each statewide system must have policies and procedures relating to the establishment and maintenance of standards to ensure that personnel necessary to carry out the purposes of this part are appropriately and adequately prepared and trained.

(2) The policies and procedures required in paragraph (b)(1) of this section must provide for the establishment and maintenance of standards that are consistent with any State-approved or State-recognized certification, licensing, registration, or other comparable requirements that apply to the profession or discipline in which a person is providing early intervention services.

(c) To the extent that a State's standards for a profession or discipline, including standards for temporary or emergency certification, are not based on the highest requirements in the State applicable to a specific profession or discipline, the State's application for assistance under this part must include the steps the State is taking, the procedures for notifying public agencies and personnel of those steps, and the timelines it has established for the retraining or hiring of personnel that meet appropriate professional requirements in the State.

(d)

(1) In meeting the requirements in paragraphs (b) and (c) of this section, a determination must be made about the status of personnel standards in the State. That determination must be based on current information that accurately describes, for each profession or discipline in which personnel are providing early intervention services, whether the applicable standards are consistent with the highest requirements in the State for that profession or discipline.

(2) The information required in paragraph (d)(1) of this section must be on file in the lead agency, and available to the public.

(e) In identifying the "highest requirements in the State" for purposes of this section, the requirements of all State statutes and the rules of all State agencies applicable to serving children eligible under this part and their families must be considered.

(f) A State may allow paraprofessionals and assistants who are appropriately trained and supervised, in accordance with State law, regulations, or written policy, to assist in the provision of early intervention services to eligible children under this part.

(g) In implementing this section, a State may adopt a policy that includes making ongoing good-faith efforts to recruit and hire appropriately and adequately trained personnel to provide early intervention services to eligible children, including, in a geographic area of the State where there is a shortage of personnel that meet these qualifications, the most qualified individuals available who are making satisfactory progress toward completing applicable course work necessary to meet the standards described in paragraph (b)(2) of this section, consistent with State law, within three years.

(Approved by the Office of Management and Budget under control number 1820-0550)

SUBPART E   PROCEDURAL SAFEGUARDS
GENERAL

§ 303.400   General responsibility of lead agency for procedural safeguards.

Each lead agency shall be responsible for —

(a) Establishing or adopting procedural safeguards that meet the requirements of this subpart; and

(b) Ensuring effective implementation of the safeguards by each public agency in the State that is involved in the provision of early intervention services under this part.

§ 303.401   Definitions of consent, native language, and personally identifiable information.

As used in this subpart —

(a) Consent means that —

(1) The parent has been fully informed of all information relevant to the activity for which consent is sought, in the parent's native language or other mode of communication;

(2) The parent understands and agrees in writing to the carrying out of the activity for which consent is sought, and the consent describes that activity and lists the records (if any) that will be released and to whom; and

(3) The parent understands that the granting of consent is voluntary on the part of the parent and may be revoked at any time;

(b) Native language, where used with reference to persons of limited English proficiency, means the language or mode of communication normally used by the parent of a child eligible under this part;

(c) Personally identifiable means that information includes —

(1) The name of the child, the child's parent, or other family member;

(2) The address of the child;

(3) A personal identifier, such as the child's or parent's social security number; or

(4) A list of personal characteristics or other information that would make it possible

to identify the child with reasonable certainty.

§ 303.402 Opportunity to examine records.

In accordance with the confidentiality procedures in the regulations under Part B of the Act (34 CFR 300.560 through 300.576), the parents of a child eligible under this part must be afforded the opportunity to inspect and review records relating to evaluations and assessments, eligibility determinations, development and implementation of IFSPs, individual complaints dealing with the child, and any other area under this part involving records about the child and the child's family.

§ 303.403 Prior notice; native language.

(a) General. Written prior notice must be given to the parents of a child eligible under this part a reasonable time before a public agency or service provider proposes, or refuses, to initiate or change the identification, evaluation, or placement of the child, or the provision of appropriate early intervention services to the child and the child's family.

(b) Content of notice. The notice must be in sufficient detail to inform the parents about —

(1) The action that is being proposed or refused;

(2) The reasons for taking the action;

(3) All procedural safeguards that are available under §§ 303.401-303.460 of this part; and

(4) The State complaint procedures under §§ 303.510-303.512, including a description of how to file a complaint and the timelines under those procedures.

(c) Native language.

(1) The notice must be —

(i) Written in language understandable to the general public; and

(ii) Provided in the native language of the parents, unless it is clearly not feasible to do so.

(2) If the native language or other mode of communication of the parent is not a written language, the public agency, or designated service provider, shall take steps to ensure that —

(i) The notice is translated orally or by other means to the parent in the parent's native language or other mode of communication;

(ii) The parent understands the notice; and

(iii) There is written evidence that the requirements of this paragraph have been met.

(3) If a parent is deaf or blind, or has no written language, the mode of communication must be that normally used by the parent (such as sign language, braille, or oral communication).

§ 303.404 Parent consent.

(a) Written parental consent must be obtained before —

(1) Conducting the initial evaluation and assessment of a child under § 303.322; and

(2) Initiating the provision of early intervention services (see § 303.342(e)).

(b) If consent is not given, the public agency shall make reasonable efforts to ensure that the parent —

(1) Is fully aware of the nature of the evaluation and assessment or the services that would be available; and

(2) Understands that the child will not be able to receive the evaluation and assessment or services unless consent is given.

§ 303.405 Parent right to decline service.

The parents of a child eligible under this part may determine whether they, their child, or other family members will accept or decline any early intervention service under this part in accordance with State law, and may decline such a service after first accepting it, without jeopardizing other early intervention services under this part.

§ 303.406 Surrogate parents.

(a) General. Each lead agency shall ensure that the rights of children eligible under this part are protected if —

(1) No parent (as defined in § 303.18) can be identified;

(2) The public agency, after reasonable efforts, cannot discover the whereabouts of a parent; or

(3) The child is a ward of the State under the laws of that State.

(b) Duty of lead agency and other public agencies. The duty of the lead agency, or other public agency under paragraph (a) of this section, includes the assignment of an individual to act as a surrogate for the parent. This must include a method for —

(1) Determining whether a child needs a surrogate parent; and

(2) Assigning a surrogate parent to the child.

(c) Criteria for selecting surrogates. (1) The lead agency or other public agency may select a surrogate parent in any way permitted under State law.

(2) Public agencies shall ensure that a person selected as a surrogate parent —

(i) Has no interest that conflicts with the interests of the child he or she represents; and

(ii) Has knowledge and skills that ensure adequate representation of the child.

(d) Non-employee requirement; compensation.

(1) A person assigned as a surrogate parent may not be —

(i) An employee of any State agency; or

(ii) A person or an employee of a person providing early intervention services to the child or to any family member of the child.

(2) A person who otherwise qualifies to be a surrogate parent under paragraph (d)(1) of this section is not an employee solely because he or she is paid by a public agency to serve as a surrogate parent.

(e) Responsibilities. A surrogate parent may represent a child in all matters related to —

(1) The evaluation and assessment of the child;

(2) Development and implementation of the child's IFSPs, including annual evaluations and periodic reviews;

(3) The ongoing provision of early intervention services to the child; and

(4) Any other rights established under this part.

MEDIATION AND DUE PROCESS PROCEDURES FOR PARENTS AND CHILDREN

§ 303.419 Mediation.

(a) General. Each State shall ensure that procedures are established and implemented to allow parties to disputes involving any matter described in § 303.403(a) to resolve the disputes through a mediation process which, at a minimum, must be available whenever a hearing is requested under § 303.420. The lead agency may either use the mediation system established under Part B of the Act or establish its own system.

(b) Requirements. The procedures must meet the following requirements:

(1) The procedures must ensure that the mediation process —

(i) Is voluntary on the part of the parties;

(ii) Is not used to deny or delay a parent's right to a due process hearing under § 303.420, or to deny any other rights afforded under Part C of the Act; and

(iii) Is conducted by a qualified and impartial mediator who is trained in effective mediation techniques.

(2) The State shall maintain a list of individuals who are qualified mediators and knowledgeable in laws and regulations relating to the provision of special education and related services.

(3) The State shall bear the cost of the mediation process, including the costs of meetings described in paragraph (c) of this section.

(4) Each session in the mediation process must be scheduled in a timely manner and must be held in a location that is convenient to the parties to the dispute.

(5) An agreement reached by the parties to the dispute in the mediation process must be set forth in a written mediation agreement.

(6) Discussions that occur during the mediation process must be confidential and may not be used as evidence in any subsequent due process hearings or civil proceedings, and the parties to the mediation process may be required to sign a confidentiality pledge prior to the commencement of the process.

(c) Meeting to encourage mediation. A State may establish procedures to require parents who elect not to use the mediation process to meet, at a time and location convenient to the parents, with a disinterested party —

(1) Who is under contract with a parent training and information center or community parent resource center in the State established under sections 682 or 683 of the Act, or an appropriate alternative dispute resolution entity; and

(2) Who would explain the benefits of the mediation process and encourage the parents to use the process.

§ 303.420 Due process procedures.

Each system must include written procedures including procedures for mediation as described in § 303.419, for the timely administrative resolution of individual child complaints by parents concerning any of the matters in § 303.403(a). A State may meet this requirement by —

(a) Adopting the mediation and due process procedures in *34 CFR 300.506* through *300.512* and developing procedures that meet the requirements of § 303.425; or

(b) Developing procedures that —

(1) Meet the requirements in § 303.419 and §§ 303.421 through 303.425; and

(2) Provide parents a means of filing a complaint.

(Approved by the Office of Management and Budget under control number 1820-0550)

§ 303.421 Appointment of an impartial person.

(a) Qualifications and duties. An impartial person must be appointed to implement the complaint resolution process in this subpart. The person must —

(1) Have knowledge about the provisions of this part and the needs of, and services available for, eligible children and their families; and

(2) Perform the following duties:

(i) Listen to the presentation of relevant viewpoints about the complaint, examine all information relevant to the issues, and seek to reach a timely resolution of the complaint.

(ii) Provide a record of the proceedings, including a written decision.

(b) Definition of impartial.

(1) As used in this section, impartial means that the person appointed to implement the complaint resolution process —

(i) Is not an employee of any agency or other entity involved in the provision of early intervention services or care of the child; and

(ii) Does not have a personal or professional interest that would conflict with his or her objectivity in implementing the process.

(2) A person who otherwise qualifies under paragraph (b)(1) of this section is not an employee of an agency solely because the person is paid by the agency to implement the complaint resolution process.

(Approved by the Office of Management and Budget under control number 1820-0550)

§ 303.422 Parent rights in administrative proceedings.

(a) General. Each lead agency shall ensure that the parents of children eligible under this part are afforded the rights in paragraph (b) of this section in any administrative proceedings carried out under § 303.420.

(b) Rights. Any parent involved in an administrative proceeding has the right to —

(1) Be accompanied and advised by counsel and by individuals with special knowledge or training with respect to early intervention services for children eligible under this part;

(2) Present evidence and confront, cross-examine, and compel the attendance of witnesses;

(3) Prohibit the introduction of any evidence at the proceeding that has not been disclosed to the parent at least five days before the proceeding;

(4) Obtain a written or electronic verbatim transcription of the proceeding; and

(5) Obtain written findings of fact and decisions.

(Approved by the Office of Management and Budget under control number 1820-0550)

§ 303.423 Convenience of proceedings; timelines.

(a) Any proceeding for implementing the complaint resolution process in this subpart must be carried out at a time and place that is reasonably convenient to the parents.

(b) Each lead agency shall ensure that, not later than 30 days after the receipt of a parent's complaint, the impartial proceeding required under this subpart is completed and a written decision mailed to each of the parties.

(Approved by the Office of Management and Budget under control number 1820-0550)

§ 303.424 Civil action.

Any party aggrieved by the findings and decision regarding an administrative complaint has the right to bring a civil action in State or Federal court under section 639(a)(1) of the Act.

(Approved by the Office of Management and Budget under control number 1820-0550)

§ 303.425 Status of a child during proceedings.

(a) During the pendency of any proceeding involving a complaint under this subpart, unless the public agency and parents of a child otherwise agree, the child must continue to receive the appropriate early intervention services currently being provided.

(b) If the complaint involves an application for initial services under this part, the child must receive those services that are not in dispute.

(Approved by the Office of Management and Budget under control number 1820-0550)

CONFIDENTIALITY

§ 303.460 Confidentiality of information.

(a) Each State shall adopt or develop policies and procedures that the State will follow in order to ensure the protection of any personally identifiable information collected, used, or maintained under this part, including the right of parents to written notice of and written consent to the exchange of this information among agencies consistent with Federal and State law.

(b) These policies and procedures must meet the requirements in 34 CFR 300.560 through 300.576, with the modifications specified in § 303.5(b).

(Approved by the Office of Management and Budget under control number 1820-0550)

SUBPART F STATE ADMINISTRATION
GENERAL

§ 303.500 Lead agency establishment or designation.

Each system must include a single line of responsibility in a lead agency that —

(a) Is established or designated by the Governor; and

(b) Is responsible for the administration of the system, in accordance with the requirements of this part.

(Approved by the Office of Management and Budget under control number 1820-0550)

§ 303.501 Supervision and monitoring of programs.

(a) General. Each lead agency is responsible for —

(1) The general administration and supervision of programs and activities receiving assistance under this part; and

(2) The monitoring of programs and activities used by the State to carry out this part, whether or not these programs or activities are receiving assistance under this part, to ensure that the State complies with this part.

(b) Methods of administering programs. In meeting the requirement in paragraph (a) of this section, the lead agency shall adopt and use proper methods of administering each program, including —

(1) Monitoring agencies, institutions, and organizations used by the State to carry out this part;

(2) Enforcing any obligations imposed on those agencies under Part C of the Act and these regulations;

(3) Providing technical assistance, if necessary, to those agencies, institutions, and organizations; and

(4) Correcting deficiencies that are identified through monitoring.

(Approved by the Office of Management and Budget under control number 1820-0550)

LEAD AGENCY PROCEDURES FOR RESOLVING COMPLAINTS

§ 303.510 Adopting complaint procedures.

(a) General. Each lead agency shall adopt written procedures for —

(1) Resolving any complaint, including a complaint filed by an organization or individual from another State, that any public agency or private service provider is violating a requirement of Part C of the Act or this Part by —

(i) Providing for the filing of a complaint with the lead agency; and

(ii) At the lead agency's discretion, providing for the filing of a complaint with a public agency and the right to have the lead agency review the public agency's decision on the complaint; and

(2) Widely disseminating to parents and other interested individuals, including parent training centers, protection and advocacy agencies, independent living centers, and other appropriate entities, the State's procedures under §§ 303.510-303.512.

(b) Remedies for denial of appropriate services. In resolving a complaint in which it finds a failure to provide appropriate services, a lead agency, pursuant to its general supervisory authority under Part C of the Act, must address:

(1) How to remediate the denial of those services, including, as appropriate, the awarding of monetary reimbursement or other corrective action appropriate to the needs of the child and the child's family; and

(2) Appropriate future provision of services for all infants and toddlers with disabilities and their families.

§ 303.511 An organization or individual may file a complaint.

(a) *General.* An individual or organization may file a written signed complaint under § 303.510. The complaint must include —

(1) A statement that the State has violated a requirement of part C of the Act or the regulations in this part; and

(2) The facts on which the complaint is based.

(b) *Limitations.* The alleged violation must have occurred not more than one year before the date that the complaint is received by the public agency unless a longer period is reasonable because —

(1) The alleged violation continues for that child or other children; or

(2) The complainant is requesting reimbursement or corrective action for a violation that occurred not more than three years before the date on which the complaint is received by the public agency.

§ 303.512 Minimum State complaint procedures.

(a) *Time limit, minimum procedures.* Each lead agency shall include in its complaint procedures a time limit of 60 calendar days after a complaint is filed under § 303.510(a) to —

(1) Carry out an independent on-site investigation, if the lead agency determines that such an investigation is necessary;

(2) Give the complainant the opportunity to submit additional information, either orally or in writing, about the allegations in the complaint;

(3) Review all relevant information and make an independent determination as to whether the public agency is violating a requirement of Part C of the Act or of this Part; and

(4) Issue a written decision to the complainant that addresses each allegation in the complaint and contains —

(i) Findings of fact and conclusions; and

(ii) The reasons for the lead agency's final decision.

(b) *Time extension; final decisions; implementation.* The lead agency's procedures described in paragraph (a) of this section also must —

(1) Permit an extension of the time limit under paragraph (a) of this section only if exceptional circumstances exist with respect to a particular complaint; and

(2) Include procedures for effective implementation of the lead agency's final decision, if needed, including —

(i) Technical assistance activities;

(ii) Negotiations; and

(iii) Corrective actions to achieve compliance.

(c) *Complaints filed under this section, and due process hearings under § 303.420.* (1) If a written complaint is received that is also the subject of a due process hearing under § 303.420, or contains multiple issues, of which one or more are part of that hearing, the State must set aside any part of the complaint that is being addressed in the due process hearing until the conclusion of the hearing. However, any issue in the complaint that is not a part of the due process action must be resolved within the 60-calendar-day timeline using the complaint procedures described in paragraphs (a) and (b) of this section.

(2) If an issue is raised in a complaint filed under this section that has previously been decided in a due process hearing involving the same parties —

(i) The hearing decision is binding; and

(ii) The lead agency must inform the complainant to that effect.

(3) A complaint alleging a public agency's or private service provider's failure to implement a due process decision must be resolved by the lead agency.

POLICIES AND PROCEDURES RELATED TO FINANCIAL MATTERS

§ 303.520 Policies related to payment for services.

(a) General. Each lead agency is responsible for establishing State policies related to how services to children eligible under this part and their families will be paid for under the State's early intervention program. The policies must —

(1) Meet the requirements in paragraph (b) of this section; and

(2) Be reflected in the interagency agreements required in § 303.523.

(b) Specific funding policies. A State's policies must —

(1) Specify which functions and services will be provided at no cost to all parents;

(2) Specify which functions or services, if any, will be subject to a system of payments, and include —

(i) Information about the payment system and schedule of sliding fees that will be used; and

(ii) The basis and amount of payments; and

(3) Include an assurance that —

(i) Fees will not be charged for the services that a child is otherwise entitled to receive at no cost to parents; and

(ii) The inability of the parents of an eligible child to pay for services will not result in the denial of services to the child or the child's family; and

(4) Set out any fees that will be charged for early intervention services and the basis for those fees.

(c) Procedures to ensure the timely provision of services. No later than the beginning of the fifth year of a State's participation under this part, the State shall implement a mechanism to ensure that no services that a child is entitled to receive are delayed or denied because of disputes between agencies regarding financial or other responsibilities.

(d) Proceeds from public or private insurance. (1) Proceeds from public or private insurance are not treated as program income for purposes of *34 CFR 80.25*.

(2) If a public agency spends reimbursements from Federal funds (e.g., Medicaid) for services under this part, those funds are not considered State or local funds for purposes of the provisions contained in § 303.124.

(Approved by the Office of Management and Budget under control number 1820-0550)

§ 303.521 Fees.

(a) *General.* A State may establish, consistent with § 303.12(a)(3)(iv), a system of payments for early intervention services, including a schedule of sliding fees.

(b) *Functions not subject to fees.* The following are required functions that must be carried out at public expense by a State, and for which no fees may be charged to parents:

(1) Implementing the child find requirements in § 303.321.

(2) Evaluation and assessment, as included in § 303.322, and including the functions related to evaluation and assessment in § 303.12.

(3) Service coordination, as included in §§ 303.22 and 303.344(g).

(4) Administrative and coordinative activities related to —

(i) The development, review, and evaluation of IFSPs in §§ 303.340 through 303.346; and

(ii) Implementation of the procedural safeguards in subpart E of this part and the other components of the statewide system of early intervention services in subparts D and F of this part.

(c) *States with mandates to serve children from birth.* If a State has in effect a State law requiring the provision of a free appropriate public education to children with disabilities from birth, the State may not charge parents for any services (e.g., physical or occupational therapy) required under that law that are provided to children eligible under this part and their families.

(Approved by the Office of Management and Budget under control number 1820-0550)

§ 303.522 Identification and coordination of resources.

(a) Each lead agency is responsible for —

(1) The identification and coordination of all available resources for early intervention services within the State, including those from Federal, State, local, and private sources; and

(2) Updating the information on the funding sources in paragraph (a)(1) of this section, if a legislative or policy change is made under any of those sources.

(b) The Federal funding sources in paragraph (a)(1) of this section include —

(1) Title V of the Social Security Act (relating to Maternal and Child Health);

(2) Title XIX of the Social Security Act (relating to the general Medicaid Program, and EPSDT);

(3) The Head Start Act;

(4) Parts B and H of the Act;

(5) The Developmental Disabilities Assistance and Bill of Rights Act (Pub. L. 94-103); and

(6) Other Federal programs.

(Approved by the Office of Management and Budget under control number 1820-0550)

§ 303.523 Interagency agreements.

(a) *General.* Each lead agency is responsible for entering into formal interagency agreements with other State-level agencies involved in the State's early intervention program. Each agreement must meet the requirements in paragraphs (b) through (d) of this section.

(b) *Financial responsibility.* Each agreement must define the financial responsibility, in accordance with § 303.143, of the agency for paying for early intervention services (consistent with State law and the requirements of this part).

(c) *Procedures for resolving disputes.* (1) Each agreement must include procedures for achieving a timely resolution of intra-agency and interagency disputes about payments for a given service, or disputes about other matters related to the State's early intervention program. Those procedures must include a mechanism for making a final determination that is binding upon the agencies involved.

(2) The agreement with each agency must —

(i) Permit the agency to resolve its own internal disputes (based on the agency's procedures that are included in the agreement), so long as the agency acts in a timely manner; and

(ii) Include the process that the lead agency will follow in achieving resolution of intra-agency disputes, if a given agency is unable to resolve its own internal disputes in a timely manner.

(d) *Additional components.* Each agreement must include any additional components necessary to ensure effective cooperation and coordination among all agencies involved in the State's early intervention program.

(Approved by the Office of Management and Budget under control number 1820-0550)

§ 303.524   Resolution of disputes.

(a) Each lead agency is responsible for resolving individual disputes, in accordance with the procedures in § 303.523(c)(2)(ii).

(b)

(1) During a dispute, the individual or entity responsible for assigning financial responsibility among appropriate agencies under § 303.143 ("financial designee") shall assign financial responsibility to —

(i) An agency, subject to the provisions in paragraph (b)(2) of this section; or

(ii) The lead agency, in accordance with the "payor of last resort" provisions in § 303.527.

(2) If, during the lead agency's resolution of the dispute, the financial designee determines that the assignment of financial responsibility under paragraph (b)(1)(i) of this section was inappropriately made —

(i) The financial designee shall reassign the responsibility to the appropriate agency; and

(ii) The lead agency shall make arrangements for reimbursement of any expenditures incurred by the agency originally assigned responsibility.

(c) To the extent necessary to ensure compliance with its action in paragraph (b)(2) of this section, the lead agency shall —

(1) Refer the dispute to the Council or the Governor; and

(2) Implement the procedures to ensure the delivery of services in a timely manner in accordance with § 303.525.

(Approved by the Office of Management and Budget under control number 1820-0550)

§ 303.525 Delivery of services in a timely manner.

Each lead agency is responsible for the development of procedures to ensure that services are provided to eligible children and their families in a timely manner, pending the resolution of disputes among public agencies or service providers.

(Approved by the Office of Management and Budget under control number 1820-0550)

§ 303.526 Policy for contracting or otherwise arranging for services.

Each system must include a policy pertaining to contracting or making other arrangements with public or private service providers to provide early intervention services. The policy must include —

(a) A requirement that all early intervention services must meet State standards and be consistent with the provisions of this part;

(b) The mechanisms that the lead agency will use in arranging for these services, including the process by which awards or other arrangements are made; and

(c) The basic requirements that must be met by any individual or organization seeking to provide these services for the lead agency.

(Approved by the Office of Management and Budget under control number 1820-0550)

§ 303.527 Payor of last resort.

(a) Nonsubstitution of funds. Except as provided in paragraph (b)(1) of this section, funds under this part may not be used to satisfy a financial commitment for services that would otherwise have been paid for from another public or private source, including any medical program administered by the Secretary of Defense, including any medical program administered by the Secretary of Defense, but for the enactment of Part C of the Act.Therefore, funds under this part may be used only for early intervention services that an eligible child needs but is not currently entitled to under any other Federal, State, local, or private source.

(b) Interim payments — reimbursement. (1) If necessary to prevent a delay in the timely provision of services to an eligible child or the child's family, funds under this part may be used to pay the provider of services, pending reimbursement from the agency or entity that has ultimate responsibility for the payment.

(2) Payments under paragraph (b)(1) of this section may be made for —

(i) Early intervention services, as described in § 303.12;

(ii) Eligible health services (see § 303.13); and

(iii) Other functions and services authorized under this part, including child find and evaluation and assessment.

(3) The provisions of paragraph (b)(1) of this section do not apply to medical services or "well-baby" health care (see § 303.13(c)(1)).

(c) Non-reduction of benefits. Nothing in this part may be construed to permit a State to reduce medical or other assistance available or to alter eligibility under Title V of the Social Security Act (SSA) (relating to maternal and child health) or Title XIX of the SSA (relating to Medicaid for children eligible under this part) within the State.

(Approved by the Office of Management and Budget under control number 1820-0550)

§ 303.528 Reimbursement procedure.

Each system must include a procedure for securing the timely reimbursement of funds used under this part, in accordance with § 303.527(b).

(Approved by the Office of Management and Budget under control number 1820-0550)

REPORTING REQUIREMENTS

§ 303.540 Data collection.

(a) Each system must include the procedures that the State uses to compile data on the statewide system. The procedures must —

(1) Include a process for —

(i) Collecting data from various agencies and service providers in the State;

(ii) Making use of appropriate sampling methods, if sampling is permitted; and

(iii) Describing the sampling methods used, if reporting to the Secretary; and

(2) Provide for reporting data required under section 618 of the Act that relates to this part.

(b) The information required in paragraph (a)(2) of this section must be provided at the time and in the manner specified by the Secretary.

(Approved by the Office of Management and Budget under control number 1820-0550)

USE OF FUNDS FOR STATE ADMINISTRATION

§ 303.560 Use of funds by the lead agency.

A lead agency may use funds under this part that are reasonable and necessary for administering the State's early intervention program for infants and toddlers with disabilities.

SUBPART G STATE INTERAGENCY COORDINATING COUNCIL
GENERAL

§ 303.600 Establishment of Council.

(a) A State that desires to receive financial assistance under this part shall establish a State Interagency Coordinating Council.

(b) The Council must be appointed by the Governor. The Governor shall ensure that the membership of the Council reasonably represents the population of the State.

(c) The Governor shall designate a member of the Council to serve as the chairperson of the Council or require the Council to do so. Any member of the Council who is a representative of the lead agency designated under § 303.500 may not serve as the chairperson of the Council.

(Approved by the Office of Management and Budget under control number 1820-0550)

§ 303.601 Composition.

(a) The Council must be composed as follows:

(1)

(i) At least 20 percent of the members must be parents, including minority parents, of infants or toddlers with disabilities or children with disabilities aged 12 or younger, with knowledge of, or experience with, programs for infants and toddlers with disabilities.

(ii) At least one member must be a parent of an infant or toddler with a disability or a child with a disability aged six or younger.

(2) At least 20 percent of the members must be public or private providers of early intervention services.

(3) At least one member must be from the State legislature.

(4) At least one member must be involved in personnel preparation.

(5) At least one member must —

(i) Be from each of the State agencies involved in the provisions of, or payment for, early intervention services to infants and toddlers with disabilities and their families; and

(ii) Have sufficient authority to engage in policy planning and implementation on behalf of these agencies.

(6) At least one member must —

(i) Be from the State educational agency responsible for preschool services to children with disabilities; and

(ii) Have sufficient authority to engage in policy planning and implementation on behalf of that agency.

(7) At least one member must be from the agency responsible for the State governance of health insurance.

(8) At least one member must be from a Head Start agency or program in the State.

(9) At least one member must be from a State agency responsible for child care.

(b) The Council may include other members selected by the Governor, including a representative from the BIA or, where there is no school operated or funded by the BIA, from the Indian Health Service or the tribe or tribal council.

(Approved by the Office of Management and Budget under control number 1820-0550)

§ 303.602 Use of funds by the Council.

(a) General. Subject to the approval of the Governor, the Council may use funds under this part —

(1) To conduct hearings and forums;

(2) To reimburse members of the Council for reasonable and necessary expenses for attending Council meetings and performing Council duties (including child care for parent representatives);

(3) To pay compensation to a member of the Council if the member is not employed or must forfeit wages from other employment when performing official Council business;

(4) To hire staff; and

(5) To obtain the services of professional, technical, and clerical personnel, as may be necessary to carry out the performance of its functions under this part.

(b) Compensation and expenses of Council members. Except as provided in paragraph

(a) of this section, Council members shall serve without compensation from funds available under this part.

(Approved by the Office of Management and Budget under control number 1820-0550)

§ 303.603 Meetings.

(a) The Council shall meet at least quarterly and in such places as it deems necessary.

(b) The meetings must —

(1) Be publicly announced sufficiently in advance of the dates they are to be held to ensure that all interested parties have an opportunity to attend; and

(2) To the extent appropriate, be open and accessible to the general public.

(c) Interpreters for persons who are deaf and other necessary services must be provided at Council meetings, both for Council members and participants. The Council may use funds under this part to pay for those services.

(Approved by the Office of Management and Budget under control number 1820-0550)

§ 303.604 Conflict of interest.

No member of the Council may cast a vote on any matter that would provide direct financial benefit to that member or otherwise give the appearance of a conflict of interest.

(Approved by the Office of Management and Budget under control number 1820-0550)

FUNCTIONS OF THE COUNCIL

§ 303.650 General.

(a) Each Council shall —

(1) Advise and assist the lead agency in the development and implementation of the policies that constitute the statewide system;

(2) Assist the lead agency in achieving the full participation, coordination, and cooperation of all appropriate public agencies in the State;

(3) Assist the lead agency in the effective implementation of the statewide system, by establishing a process that includes —

(i) Seeking information from service providers, service coordinators, parents, and others about any Federal, State, or local policies that impede timely service delivery; and

(ii) Taking steps to ensure that any policy problems identified under paragraph (a)(3)(i) of this section are resolved; and

(4) To the extent appropriate, assist the lead agency in the resolution of disputes.

(b) Each Council may advise and assist the lead agency and the State educational agency regarding the provision of appropriate services for children aged birth to five, inclusive.

(c) Each Council may advise appropriate agencies in the State with respect to the integration of services for infants and toddlers with disabilities and at-risk infants and toddlers and their families, regardless of whether at-risk infants and toddlers are eligible for early intervention services in the State.

(Approved by the Office of Management and Budget under control number 1820-0550)

§ 303.651 Advising and assisting the lead agency in its administrative duties.

Each Council shall advise and assist the lead agency in the —

(a) Identification of sources of fiscal and other support for services for early intervention programs under this part;

(b) Assignment of financial responsibility to the appropriate agency; and

(c) Promotion of the interagency agreements under § 303.523.

(Approved by the Office of Management and Budget under control number 1820-0550)

§ 303.652 Applications.

Each Council shall advise and assist the lead agency in the preparation of applications under this part and amendments to those applications.

(Approved by the Office of Management and Budget under control number 1820-0550)

§ 303.653 Transitional services.

Each Council shall advise and assist the State educational agency regarding the transition of toddlers with disabilities to preschool and other appropriate services.

(Approved by the Office of Management and Budget under control number 1820-0578)

§ 303.654 Annual report to the Secretary.

(a) Each Council shall —

(1) Prepare an annual report to the Governor and to the Secretary on the status of early intervention programs operated within the State for children eligible under this part and their families; and

(2) Submit the report to the Secretary by a date that the Secretary establishes.

(b) Each annual report must contain the information required by the Secretary for the year for which the report is made.

(Approved by the Office of Management and Budget under control number 1820-0550)

TITLE 20.
EDUCATION

CHAPTER 70 STRENGTHENING AND IMPROVEMENT OF ELEMENTARY AND SECONDARY SCHOOLS

IMPROVING THE ACADEMIC ACHIEVEMENT OF THE DISADVANTAGED

§ 6301. Statement of purpose

The purpose of this *title [20 USCS §§ 6301 et seq.]* is to ensure that all children have a fair, equal, and significant opportunity to obtain a high-quality education and reach, at a minimum, proficiency on challenging State academic achievement standards and state academic assessments. This purpose can be accomplished by—

(1) ensuring that high-quality academic assessments, accountability systems, teacher preparation and training, curriculum, and instructional materials are aligned with challenging State academic standards so that students, teachers, parents, and administrators can measure progress against common expectations for student academic achievement;

(2) meeting the educational needs of low-achieving children in our Nation's highest-poverty schools, limited English proficient children, migratory children, children with disabilities, Indian children, neglected or delinquent children, and young children in need of reading assistance;

(3) closing the achievement gap between high- and low-performing children, especially the achievement gaps between minority and nonminority students, and between disadvantaged children and their more advantaged peers;

(4) holding schools, local educational agencies, and States accountable for improving the academic achievement of all students, and identifying and turning around low-performing schools that have failed to provide a high-quality education to their students, while providing alternatives to students in such schools to enable the students to receive a high-quality education;

(5) distributing and targeting resources sufficiently to make a difference to local educational agencies and schools where needs are greatest;

(6) improving and strengthening accountability, teaching, and learning by using State assessment systems designed to ensure that students are meeting challenging State academic achievement and content standards and increasing achievement overall, but especially for the disadvantaged;

(7) providing greater decisionmaking authority and flexibility to schools and teachers in exchange for greater responsibility for student performance;

(8) providing children an enriched and accelerated educational program, including the use of schoolwide programs or additional services that increase the amount and quality of instructional time;

(9) promoting schoolwide reform and ensuring the access of children to effective, scientifically based instructional strategies and challenging academic content;

(10) significantly elevating the quality of instruction by providing staff in participating schools with substantial opportunities for professional development;

(11) coordinating services under all parts of this *title [20 USCS §§ 6301 et seq.]* with each other, with other educational services, and, to the extent feasible, with other agencies providing services to youth, children, and families; and

(12) affording parents substantial and meaningful opportunities to participate in the education of their children.

§ 6302. Authorization of appropriations

(a) Local educational agency grants. For the purpose of carrying out part A [20 USCS §§ 6311 et seq.], there are authorized to be appropriated—

(1) $ 13,500,000,000 for fiscal year 2002;

(2) $ 16,000,000,000 for fiscal year 2003;

(3) $ 18,500,000,000 for fiscal year 2004;

(4) $ 20,500,000,000 for fiscal year 2005;

(5) $ 22,750,000,000 for fiscal year 2006; and

(6) $ 25,000,000,000 for fiscal year 2007.

(b) Reading First.

(1) Reading First. For the purpose of carrying out subpart 1 of part B [20 USCS §§ 6361 et seq.], there are authorized to be appropriated $ 900,000,000 for fiscal year 2002 and such sums as may be necessary for each of the 5 succeeding fiscal years.

(2) Early Reading First. For the purpose of carrying out subpart 2 of part B [20 USCS §§ 6371 et seq.], there are authorized to be appropriated $ 75,000,000 for fiscal year 2002 and such sums as may be necessary for each of the 5 succeeding fiscal years.

(3) Even Start. For the purpose of carrying out subpart 3 of part B [20 USCS §§ 6381 et seq.], there are authorized to be appropriated $ 260,000,000 for fiscal year 2002 and such sums as may be necessary for each of the 5 succeeding fiscal years.

(4) Improving literacy through school libraries. For the purpose of carrying out subpart 4 of part B [20 USCS § 6383], there are authorized to be appropriated $ 250,000,000 for fiscal year 2002 and such sums as may be necessary for each of the 5 succeeding fiscal years.

(c) Education of migratory children. For the purpose of carrying out part C [20 USCS §§ 6391 et seq.], there are authorized to be appropriated $ 410,000,000 for fiscal year 2002 and such sums as may be necessary for each of the 5 succeeding fiscal years.

(d) Prevention and intervention programs for youth who are neglected, delinquent, or at risk. For the purpose of carrying out part D [20 USCS §§ 6421 et seq.], there are authorized to be appropriated $ 50,000,000 for fiscal year 2002 and such sums as may be necessary for each of the 5 succeeding fiscal years.

(e) Federal activities.

(1) Sections 1501 and 1502. For the purpose of carrying out sections 1501 and 1502 [20 USCS §§ 6491, 6492], there are authorized to be appropriated such sums as may be necessary for fiscal year 2002 and each of the 5 succeeding fiscal years.

(2) Section 1504.

(A) In general. For the purpose of carrying out section 1504 [20 USCS § 6494], there are authorized to be appropriated such sums as may be necessary for fiscal year 2002 and for each of the 5 succeeding fiscal years.

(B) Special rule. Of the funds appropriated pursuant to subparagraph (A), not more than 30 percent may be used for teachers associated with students participating in the programs described in subsections (a)(1), (b)(1), and (c)(1).

(f) Comprehensive school reform. For the purpose of carrying out part F [20 USCS §§ 6511 et seq.], there are authorized to be appropriated such sums as may be necessary for fiscal year 2002 and each of the 5 succeeding fiscal years.

(g) Advanced placement. For the purposes of carrying out part G [20 USCS §§ 6531 et seq.], there are authorized to be appropriated such sums for fiscal year 2002 and each 5 succeeding fiscal year.

(h) School dropout prevention. For the purpose of carrying out part H [20 USCS §§ 6551 et seq.], there are authorized to be appropriated $ 125,000,000 for fiscal year 2002 and such sums as may be necessary for each of the 5 succeeding fiscal years, of which—

(1) up to 10 percent shall be available to carry out subpart 1 of part H [20 USCS § 6555] for each fiscal year; and

(2) the remainder shall be available to carry out subpart 2 of part H [20 USCS §§ 6561 et seq.] for each fiscal year.

(i) School improvement. For the purpose of carrying out section 1003(g) [20 USCS § 6303(g)], there are authorized to be appropriated $ 500,000,000 for fiscal year 2002 and such sums as may be necessary for each of the 5 succeeding fiscal years.

§ 6303. School improvement

(a) State reservations. Each State shall reserve 2 percent of the amount the State receives under subpart 2 of part A [20 USCS §§ 6331 et seq.] for fiscal years 2002 and 2003, and 4 percent of the amount received under such subpart for fiscal years 2004 through 2007, to carry out subsection (b) and to carry out the State's responsibilities under sections 1116 and 1117 [20 USCS §§ 6316, 6317], including carrying out the State educational agency's statewide system of technical assistance and support for local educational agencies.

(b) Uses. Of the amount reserved under subsection (a) for any fiscal year, the State educational agency—

(1) shall allocate not less than 95 percent of that amount directly to local educational agencies for schools identified for school improvement, corrective action, and restructuring, for activities under section 1116(b) [20 USCS § 6316(b)]; or

(2) may, with the approval of the local educational agency, directly provide for these activities or arrange for their provision through other entities such as school support teams or educational service agencies.

(c) Priority. The State educational agency, in allocating funds to local educational agencies under this section, shall give priority to local educational agencies that—

(1) serve the lowest-achieving schools;

(2) demonstrate the greatest need for such funds; and

(3) demonstrate the strongest commitment to ensuring that such funds are used to enable the lowest-achieving schools to meet the progress goals in school improvement plans under section 1116(b)(3)(A)(v) [20 USCS § 6316(b)(3)(A)(v)].

(d) Unused funds. If, after consultation with local educational agencies in the State, the State educational agency determines that the amount of funds reserved to carry out subsection (b) is greater than the amount needed to provide the assistance described in that subsection, the State educational agency shall allocate the excess amount to local educational agencies in accordance with—

(1) the relative allocations the State educational agency made to those agencies for that fiscal year under subpart 2 of part A [20 USCS §§ 6331 et seq.]; or

(2) section 1126(c) [20 USCS § 6338(c)].

(e) Special rule. Notwithstanding any other provision of this section, the amount of funds reserved by the State educational agency under subsection (a) in any fiscal year shall not decrease the amount of funds each local educational agency receives under subpart 2 below the amount received by such local educational agency under such subpart for the preceding fiscal year.

(f) Reporting. The State educational agency shall make publicly available a list of those schools that have received funds or services pursuant to subsection (b) and the percentage of students from each school from families with incomes below the poverty line.

(g) Assistance for local school improvement.

(1) Program authorized. The Secretary shall award grants to States to enable the States to provide subgrants to local educational agencies for the purpose of providing assistance for school improvement consistent with section 1116 [20 USCS § 6316].

(2) State allotments. Such grants shall be allotted among States, the Bureau of Indian Affairs, and the outlying areas, in proportion to the funds received by the States, the Bureau of Indian Affairs, and the outlying areas, respectively, for the fiscal year under parts A, C, and D of this *title [20 USCS §§ 6311 et seq., 6391 et seq., 6421 et seq.]*. The Secretary shall expeditiously allot a portion of such funds to States for the purpose of assisting local educational agencies and schools that were in school improvement status on the date preceding the date of enactment of the No Child Left Behind Act of 2001 [enacted Jan. 8, 2002].

(3) Reallocations. If a State does not receive funds under this subsection, the Secretary shall reallocate such funds to other States in the same proportion funds are allocated under paragraph (2).

(4) State applications. Each State educational agency that desires to receive funds under this subsection shall submit an application to the Secretary at such time, and containing such information, as the Secretary shall reasonably require, except that such requirement shall be waived if a State educational agency submitted such information as part of its State plan under this part. Each State application shall describe how the State educational agency will allocate such funds in order to assist the State educational agency and local educational agencies in complying with school improvement, corrective action, and restructuring requirements of section 1116 [20 USCS § 6316].

(5) Local educational agency grants. A grant to a local educational agency under this subsection shall be—

(A) of sufficient size and scope to support the activities required under sections 1116 and 1117 [20 USCS §§ 6316, 6317], but not less than $ 50,000 and not more than $ 500,000 for each participating school;

(B) integrated with other funds awarded by the State under this Act [20 USCS §§ 6301 et seq.]; and

(C) renewable for two additional 1-year periods if schools are meeting the goals in their school improvement plans developed under section 1116 [20 USCS § 6316].

(6) Priority. The State, in awarding such grants, shall give priority to local educational agencies with the lowest-achieving schools that demonstrate—

(A) the greatest need for such funds; and

(B) the strongest commitment to ensuring that such funds are used to provide adequate resources to enable the lowest-achieving schools to meet the goals under school and local educational agency improvement, corrective action, and restructuring plans under section 1116 [20 USCS § 6316].

(7) Allocation. A State educational agency that receives a grant under this subsection

shall allocate at least 95 percent of the grant funds directly to local educational agencies for schools identified for school improvement, corrective action, or restructuring to carry out activities under section 1116(b) [20 USCS § 6316(b)], or may, with the approval of the local educational agency, directly provide for these activities or arrange for their provision through other entities such as school support teams or educational service agencies.

(8) Administrative costs. A State educational agency that receives a grant award under this subsection may reserve not more than 5 percent of such grant funds for administration, evaluation, and technical assistance expenses.

(9) Local awards. Each local educational agency that applies for assistance under this subsection shall describe how it will provide the lowest-achieving schools the resources necessary to meet goals under school and local educational agency improvement, corrective action, and restructuring plans under section 1116 [20 USCS § 6316].

§ 6304. State administration

(a) In general. Except as provided in subsection (b), to carry out administrative duties assigned under parts A, C, and D of this title [20 USCS §§ 6311 et seq., 6391 et seq., 6421 et seq.], each State may reserve the greater of—

(1) 1 percent of the amounts received under such parts; or

(2) $ 400,000 ($ 50,000 in the case of each outlying area).

(b) Exception. If the sum of the amounts appropriated for parts A, C, and D of this title [20 USCS §§ 6311 et seq., 6391 et seq., 6421 et seq.] is equal to or greater than $ 14,000,000,000, then the reservation described in subsection (a)(1) shall not exceed 1 percent of the amount the State would receive, if $ 14,000,000,000 were allocated among the States for parts A, C, and D of this title [20 USCS §§ 6311 et seq., 6391 et seq., 6421 et seq.].

IMPROVING BASIC PROGRAMS OPERATED BY LOCAL EDUCATIONAL AGENCIES

Basic Program Requirements

§ 6311. State plans

(a) Plans required.

(1) In general. For any State desiring to receive a grant under this part [20 USCS §§ 6311 et seq.], the State educational agency shall submit to the Secretary a plan, developed by the State educational agency, in consultation with local educational agencies, teachers, principals, pupil services personnel, administrators (including administrators of programs described in other parts of this title [20 USCS §§ 6301 et seq.]), other staff, and parents, that satisfies the requirements of this section and that is coordinated with other programs under this Act [20 USCS §§ 6301 et seq.], the Individuals with Disabilities Education Act [20 USCS §§ 1400 et seq.], the Carl D. Perkins Career and Technical Education Act of 2006 [20 USCS §§ 2301 et seq.], the Head Start Act [42 USCS §§ 9831 et seq.], the Adult Education and Family Literacy Act, and the McKinney-Vento Homeless Assistance Act [42 USCS §§ 11301 et seq.].

(2) Consolidated plan. A State plan submitted under paragraph (1) may be submitted as part of a consolidated plan under section 9302 [20 USCS § 7842].

(b) Academic standards, academic assessments, and accountability.

(1) Challenging academic standards.

(A) In general. Each State plan shall demonstrate that the State has adopted challenging academic content standards and challenging student academic achievement standards that will be used by the State, its local educational agencies, and its schools to carry out this part [20 USCS §§ 6311 et seq.], except that a State shall not be required to submit such standards to the Secretary.

(B) Same standards. The academic standards required by subparagraph (A) shall be the same academic standards that the State applies to all schools and children in the State.

(C) Subjects. The State shall have such academic standards for all public elementary school and secondary school children, including children served under this part [20 USCS §§ 6311 et seq.], in subjects determined by the State, but including at least mathematics, reading or language arts, and (beginning in the 2005-2006 school year) science, which shall include the same knowledge, skills, and levels of achievement expected of all children.

(D) Challenging academic standards. Standards under this paragraph shall include—

(i) challenging academic content standards in academic subjects that—

(I) specify what children are expected to know and be able to do;

(II) contain coherent and rigorous content; and

(III) encourage the teaching of advanced skills; and

(ii) challenging student academic achievement standards that—

(I) are aligned with the State's academic content standards;

(II) describe two levels of high achievement (proficient and advanced) that determine how well children are mastering the material in the State academic content standards; and

(III) describe a third level of achievement (basic) to provide complete information about the progress of the lower-achieving children toward mastering the proficient and advanced levels of achievement.

(E) Information. For the subjects in which students will be served under this part [20 USCS §§ 6311 et seq.], but for which a State is not required by subparagraphs (A), (B), and (C) to develop, and has not otherwise developed, such academic standards, the State plan shall describe a strategy for ensuring that students are taught the same knowledge and skills in such subjects and held to the same expectations as are all children.

(F) Existing standards. Nothing in this part [20 USCS §§ 6311 et seq.] shall prohibit a State from revising, consistent with this section, any standard adopted under this part [20 USCS §§ 6311 et seq.] before or after the date of enactment of the No Child Left Behind Act of 2001 [enacted Jan. 8, 2002].

(2) Accountability.

(A) In general. Each State plan shall demonstrate that the State has developed and is implementing a single, statewide State accountability system that will be effective in ensuring that all local educational agencies, public elementary schools, and public secondary schools make adequate yearly progress as defined under this paragraph. Each State accountability system shall—

(i) be based on the academic standards and academic assessments adopted under paragraphs (1) and (3), and other academic indicators consistent with subparagraph (C)(vi) and (vii), and shall take into account the achievement of all public elementary school and secondary school students;

(ii) be the same accountability system the State uses for all public elementary schools and secondary schools or all local educational agencies in the State, except that public elementary schools, secondary schools, and local educational agencies not participating under this part [20 USCS §§ 6311 et seq.] are not subject to the requirements of section 1116 [20 USCS § 6316]; and

(iii) include sanctions and rewards, such as bonuses and recognition, the State will use to hold local educational agencies and public elementary schools and secondary schools accountable for student achievement and for ensuring that they make adequate yearly progress in accordance with the State's definition under subparagraphs (B) and (C).

(B) Adequate yearly progress. Each State plan shall demonstrate, based on academic assessments described in paragraph (3), and in accordance with this paragraph, what constitutes adequate yearly progress of the State, and of all public elementary schools, secondary schools, and local educational agencies in the State, toward enabling all public elementary school and secondary school students to meet the State's student academic achievement standards, while working toward the goal of narrowing the achievement gaps in the State, local educational agencies, and schools.

(C) Definition. "Adequate yearly progress" shall be defined by the State in a manner that—

(i) applies the same high standards of academic achievement to all public elementary school and secondary school students in the State;

(ii) is statistically valid and reliable;

(iii) results in continuous and substantial academic improvement for all students;

(iv) measures the progress of public elementary schools, secondary schools and local educational agencies and the State based primarily on the academic assessments described in paragraph (3);

(v) includes separate measurable annual objectives for continuous and substantial improvement for each of the following:

(I) The achievement of all public elementary school and secondary school students.

(II) The achievement of—

(aa) economically disadvantaged students;

(bb) students from major racial and ethnic groups;

(cc) students with disabilities; and

(dd) students with limited English proficiency; except that disaggregation of data under subclause (II) shall not be required in a case in which the number of students in a category is insufficient to yield statistically reliable information or the results would reveal personally identifiable information about an individual student;

(vi) in accordance with subparagraph (D), includes graduation rates for public secondary school students (defined as the percentage of students who graduate from secondary school with a regular diploma in the standard number of years) and at least one other academic indicator, as determined by the State for all public elementary school students; and

(vii) in accordance with subparagraph (D), at the State's discretion, may also include other academic indicators, as determined by the State for all public school students, measured separately for each group described in clause (v), such as achievement on additional State or locally administered assessments, decreases in grade-to-grade retention rates, attendance rates, and changes in the percentages of students completing gifted and talented, advanced placement, and college preparatory courses.

(D) Requirements for other indicators. In carrying out subparagraph (C)(vi) and (vii), the State—

(i) shall ensure that the indicators described in those provisions are valid and reliable, and are consistent with relevant, nationally recognized professional and technical standards, if any; and

(ii) except as provided in subparagraph (I)(i), may not use those indicators to reduce the number of, or change, the schools that would otherwise be subject to school improvement, corrective action, or restructuring under section 1116 [*20 USCS § 6316*] if those additional indicators were not used, but may use them to identify additional schools for school improvement or in need of corrective action or restructuring.

(E) Starting point. Each State, using data for the 2001-2002 school year, shall establish the starting point for measuring, under subparagraphs (G) and (H), the percentage of students meeting or exceeding the State's proficient level of academic achievement on the State assessments under paragraph (3) and pursuant to the timeline described in subparagraph (F). The starting point shall be, at a minimum, based on the higher of the percentage of students at the proficient level who are in—

(i) the State's lowest achieving group of students described in subparagraph (C)(v)(II); or

(ii) the school at the 20th percentile in the State, based on enrollment, among all schools ranked by the percentage of students at the proficient level.

(F) Timeline. Each State shall establish a timeline for adequate yearly progress. The timeline shall ensure that not later than 12 years after the end of the 2001-2002 school year, all students in each group described in subparagraph (C)(v) will meet or exceed the State's proficient level of academic achievement on the State assessments under paragraph (3).

(G) Measurable objectives. Each State shall establish statewide annual measurable objectives, pursuant to subparagraph (C)(v), for meeting the requirements of this paragraph, and which—

(i) shall be set separately for the assessments of mathematics and reading or language arts under subsection (a)(3);

(ii) shall be the same for all schools and local educational agencies in the State;

(iii) shall identify a single minimum percentage of students who are required to meet or exceed the proficient level on the academic assessments that applies separately to each group of students described in subparagraph (C)(v);

(iv) shall ensure that all students will meet or exceed the State's proficient level of academic achievement on the State assessments within the State's timeline under subparagraph (F); and

(v) may be the same for more than 1 year, subject to the requirements of subparagraph (H).

(H) Intermediate goals for annual yearly progress. Each State shall establish intermediate goals for meeting the requirements, including the measurable objectives in subparagraph (G), of this paragraph and that shall—

(i) increase in equal increments over the period covered by the State's timeline under subparagraph (F);

(ii) provide for the first increase to occur in not more than 2 years; and

(iii) provide for each following increase to occur in not more than 3 years.

(I) Annual improvement for schools. Each year, for a school to make adequate yearly progress under this paragraph—

(i) each group of students described in subparagraph (C)(v) must meet or exceed the objectives set by the State under subparagraph (G), except that if any group described in subparagraph (C)(v) does not meet those objectives in any particular year, the school shall be considered to have made adequate yearly progress if the percentage of students in that group who did not meet or exceed the proficient level of academic achievement on the State assessments under paragraph (3) for that year decreased by 10 percent of that percentage from the preceding school year and that group made progress on one or more of the academic indicators described in subparagraph (C)(vi) or (vii); and

(ii) not less than 95 percent of each group of students described in subparagraph (C)(v) who are enrolled in the school are required to take the assessments, consistent with paragraph (3)(C)(xi) and with accommodations, guidelines, and alternative assessments provided in the same manner as those provided under section 612(a)(16)(A) of the Individuals with Disabilities Education Act [*20 USCS § 1412(a)(16)(A)*] and paragraph (3), on which adequate yearly progress is based (except that the 95 percent requirement described in this clause shall not apply in a case in which the number of students in a category is insufficient to yield statistically reliable information or the results would reveal personally identifiable information about an individual student).

(J) Uniform averaging procedure. For the purpose of determining whether schools are making adequate yearly progress, the State may establish a uniform procedure for averaging data which includes one or more of the following:

(i) The State may average data from the school year for which the determination is made with data from one or two school years immediately preceding that school year.

(ii) Until the assessments described in paragraph (3) are administered in such manner and time to allow for the implementation of the uniform procedure for averaging data described in clause (i), the State may use the academic assessments that were required under paragraph (3) as that paragraph was in effect on the day preceding the date of enactment of the No Child Left Behind Act of 2001 [enacted Jan. 8, 2002], provided that nothing in this clause shall be construed to undermine or delay the determination of adequate yearly progress, the requirements of section 1116 [*20 USCS § 6316*], or the implementation of assessments under this section.

(iii) The State may use data across grades in a school.

(K) Accountability for charter schools. The accountability provisions under this Act [*20 USCS §§ 6301* et seq.] shall be overseen for charter schools in accordance with State charter school law.

(3) Academic assessments.

(A) In general. Each State plan shall demonstrate that the State educational agency, in consultation with local educational agencies, has implemented a set of high-quality, yearly student academic assessments that include, at a minimum, academic assessments in mathematics, reading or language arts, and science that will be used as the primary means of determining the yearly performance of the State and of each local educational agency and school in the State in enabling all children to meet the State's challenging student academic achievement standards, except that no State shall be required to meet the requirements of this part [*20 USCS §§ 6311* et seq.] relating to science assessments until the beginning of the 2007-2008 school year.

(B) Use of assessments. Each State educational agency may incorporate the data from the assessments under this paragraph into a State-developed longitudinal data system that links student test scores, length of enrollment, and graduation records over time.

(C) Requirements. Such assessments shall—

(i) be the same academic assessments used to measure the achievement of all children;

(ii) be aligned with the State's challenging academic content and student academic achievement standards, and provide coherent information about student attainment of such standards;

(iii) be used for purposes for which such assessments are valid and reliable, and be consistent with relevant, nationally recognized professional and technical standards;

(iv) be used only if the State educational agency provides to the Secretary evidence from the test publisher or other relevant sources that the assessments used are of adequate technical quality for each purpose required under this Act [20 USCS §§ 6301 et seq.] and are consistent with the requirements of this section, and such evidence is made public by the Secretary upon request;

(v)

(I) except as otherwise provided for grades 3 through 8 under clause vii, measure the proficiency of students in, at a minimum, mathematics and reading or language arts, and be administered not less than once during—

(aa) grades 3 through 5;

(bb) grades 6 through 9; and

(cc) grades 10 through 12;

(II) beginning not later than school year 2007-2008, measure the proficiency of all students in science and be administered not less than one time during—

(aa) grades 3 through 5;

(bb) grades 6 through 9; and

(cc) grades 10 through 12;

(vi) involve multiple up-to-date measures of student academic achievement, including measures that assess higher-order thinking skills and understanding;

(vii) beginning not later than school year 2005-2006, measure the achievement of students against the challenging State academic content and student academic achievement standards in each of grades 3 through 8 in, at a minimum, mathematics, and reading or language arts, except that the Secretary may provide the State 1 additional year if the State demonstrates that exceptional or uncontrollable circumstances, such as a natural disaster or a precipitous and unforeseen decline in the financial resources of the State, prevented full implementation of the academic assessments by that deadline and that the State will complete implementation within the additional 1-year period;

(viii) at the discretion of the State, measure the proficiency of students in academic subjects not described in clauses (v), (vi), (vii) in which the State has adopted challenging academic content and academic achievement standards;

(ix) provide for—

(I) the participation in such assessments of all students;

(II) the reasonable adaptations and accommodations for students with disabilities (as defined under section 602(3) of the Individuals with Disabilities Education Act [20 USCS § 1401(3)]) necessary to measure the academic achievement of such students relative to State academic content and State student academic achievement standards; and

(III) the inclusion of limited English proficient students, who shall be assessed in a valid and reliable manner and provided reasonable accommodations on assessments administered to such students under this paragraph, including, to the extent practicable, assessments in the language and form most likely to yield accurate data on what such students know and can do in academic content areas, until such students have achieved English language proficiency as determined under paragraph (7);

(x) notwithstanding subclause (III), the academic assessment (using tests written in English) of reading or language arts of any student who has attended school in the United States (not including Puerto Rico) for three or more consecutive school years, except that if the local educational agency determines, on a case-by-case individual basis, that academic assessments in another language or form would likely yield more accurate and reliable information on what such student knows and can do, the local educational agency may make a determination to assess such student in the appropriate language other than English for a period that does not exceed two additional consecutive years, provided that such student has not yet reached a level of English language proficiency sufficient to yield valid and reliable information on what such student knows and can do on tests (written in English) of reading or language arts;

(xi) include students who have attended schools in a local educational agency for a full academic year but have not attended a single school for a full academic year, except that the performance of students who have attended more than 1 school in the local educational agency in any academic year shall be used only in determining the progress of the local educational agency;

(xii) produce individual student interpretive, descriptive, and diagnostic reports, consistent with clause (iii) that allow parents, teachers, and principals to understand and address the specific academic needs of students, and include information regarding achievement on academic assessments aligned with State academic achievement standards, and that are provided to parents, teachers, and principals, as soon as is practicably possible after the assessment is given, in an understandable and uniform format, and to the extent practicable, in a language that parents can understand;

(xiii) enable results to be disaggregated within each State, local educational agency, and school by gender, by each major racial and ethnic group, by English proficiency status, by migrant status, by students with disabilities as compared to nondisabled students, and by economically disadvantaged students as compared to students who are not economically disadvantaged, except that, in the case of a local educational agency or a school, such disaggregation shall not be required in a case in which the number of students in a category is insufficient to yield statistically reliable information or the results would reveal personally identifiable information about an individual student;

(xiv) be consistent with widely accepted professional testing standards, objectively measure academic achievement, knowledge, and skills, and be tests that do not evaluate or assess personal or family beliefs and attitudes, or publicly disclose personally identifiable information; and

(xv) enable itemized score analyses to be produced and reported, consistent with clause (iii), to local educational agencies and schools, so that parents, teachers, principals, and administrators can interpret and address the specific academic needs of students as indicated by the students' achievement on assessment items.

(D) Deferral. A State may defer the commencement, or suspend the administration, but not cease the development, of the assessments described in this paragraph, that were not required prior to the date of enactment of the No Child Left Behind Act of 2001 [enacted Jan. 8, 2002], for 1 year for each year for which the amount appropriated for grants under section 6113(a)(2) [20 USCS § 7301b(a)(2)] is less than—

(i) $ 370,000,000 for fiscal year 2002;

(ii) $ 380,000,000 for fiscal year 2003;

(iii) $ 390,000,000 for fiscal year 2004; and

(iv) $ 400,000,000 for fiscal years 2005 through 2007.

(4) Special rule. Academic assessment measures in addition to those in paragraph (3) that do not meet the requirements of such paragraph may be included in the assessment under paragraph (3) as additional measures, but may not be used in lieu of the academic

assessments required under paragraph (3). Such additional assessment measures may not be used to reduce the number of or change, the schools that would otherwise be subject to school improvement, corrective action, or restructuring under section 1116 [20 USCS § 6316] if such additional indicators were not used, but may be used to identify additional schools for school improvement or in need of corrective action or restructuring except as provided in paragraph (2)(I)(i).

(5) State authority. If a State educational agency provides evidence, which is satisfactory to the Secretary, that neither the State educational agency nor any other State government official, agency, or entity has sufficient authority, under State law, to adopt curriculum content and student academic achievement standards, and academic assessments aligned with such academic standards, which will be applicable to all students enrolled in the State's public elementary schools and secondary schools, then the State educational agency may meet the requirements of this subsection by—

(A) adopting academic standards and academic assessments that meet the requirements of this subsection, on a statewide basis, and limiting their applicability to students served under this part [20 USCS §§ 6311 et seq.]; or

(B) adopting and implementing policies that ensure that each local educational agency in the State that receives grants under this part [20 USCS §§ 6311 et seq.] will adopt curriculum content and student academic achievement standards, and academic assessments aligned with such standards, which—

(i) meet all of the criteria in this subsection and any regulations regarding such standards and assessments that the Secretary may publish; and

(ii) are applicable to all students served by each such local educational agency.

(6) Language assessments. Each State plan shall identify the languages other than English that are present in the participating student population and indicate the languages for which yearly student academic assessments are not available and are needed. The State shall make every effort to develop such assessments and may request assistance from the Secretary if linguistically accessible academic assessment measures are needed. Upon request, the Secretary shall assist with the identification of appropriate academic assessment measures in the needed languages, but shall not mandate a specific academic assessment or mode of instruction.

(7) Academic assessments of English language proficiency. Each State plan shall demonstrate that local educational agencies in the State will, beginning not later than school year 2002-2003, provide for an annual assessment of English proficiency (measuring students' oral language, reading, and writing skills in English) of all students with limited English proficiency in the schools served by the State educational agency, except that the Secretary may provide the State 1 additional year if the State demonstrates that exceptional or uncontrollable circumstances, such as a natural disaster or a precipitous and unforeseen decline in the financial resources of the State, prevented full implementation of this paragraph by that deadline and that the State will complete implementation within the additional 1-year period.

(8) Requirement. Each State plan shall describe—

(A) how the State educational agency will assist each local educational agency and school affected by the State plan to develop the capacity to comply with each of the requirements of sections 1112(c)(1)(D), 1114(b), and 1115(c) [20 USCS §§ 6312(c)(1)(D), 6314(b), 6315(c)] that is applicable to such agency or school;

(B) how the State educational agency will assist each local educational agency and school affected by the State plan to provide additional educational assistance to individual students assessed as needing help to achieve the State's challenging academic achievement standards;

(C) the specific steps the State educational agency will take to ensure that both schoolwide programs and targeted assistance schools provide instruction by highly qualified instructional staff as required by sections 1114(b)(1)(C) and 1115(c)(1)(E) [20 USCS §§ 6314(b)(1)(C), 6315(c)(1)(E)], including steps that the State educational agency will take to ensure that poor and minority children are not taught at higher rates than other children by inexperienced, unqualified, or out-of-field teachers, and the measures that the State educational agency will use to evaluate and publicly report the progress of the State educational agency with respect to such steps;

(D) an assurance that the State educational agency will assist local educational agencies in developing or identifying high-quality effective curricula aligned with State academic achievement standards and how the State educational agency will disseminate such curricula to each local educational agency and school within the State; and

(E) such other factors the State educational agency determines appropriate to provide students an opportunity to achieve the knowledge and skills described in the challenging academic content standards adopted by the State.

(9) Factors affecting student achievement. Each State plan shall include an assurance that the State educational agency will coordinate and collaborate, to the extent feasible and necessary as determined by the State educational agency, with agencies providing services to children, youth, and families, with respect to local educational agencies within the State that are identified under section 1116 [20 USCS § 6316] and that request assistance with addressing major factors that have significantly affected the academic achievement of students in the local educational agency or schools served by such agency.

(10) Use of academic assessment results to improve student academic achievement. Each State plan shall describe how the State educational agency will ensure that the results of the State assessments described in paragraph (3)—

(A) will be promptly provided to local educational agencies, schools, and teachers in a manner that is clear and easy to understand, but not later than before the beginning of the next school year; and

(B) be used by those local educational agencies, schools, and teachers to improve the educational achievement of individual students.

(c) Other provisions to support teaching and learning. Each State plan shall contain assurances that—

(1) the State educational agency will meet the requirements of subsection (h)(1) and, beginning with the 2002-2003 school year, will produce the annual State report cards described in such subsection, except that the Secretary may provide the State educational agency 1 additional year if the State educational agency demonstrates that exceptional or uncontrollable circumstances, such as a natural disaster or a precipitous and unforeseen decline in the financial resources of the State, prevented full implementation of this paragraph by that deadline and that the State will complete implementation within the additional 1-year period;

(2) the State will, beginning in school year 2002-2003, participate in biennial State academic assessments of 4th and 8th grade reading and mathematics under the National Assessment of Educational Progress carried out under section 303(b)(2) of the National Assessment of Educational Progress Authorization Act [20 USCS § 9622] if the Secretary pays the costs of administering such assessments;

(3) the State educational agency, in consultation with the Governor, will include, as a component of the State plan, a plan to carry out the responsibilities of the State under sections 1116 and 1117 [20 USCS §§ 6316, 6317], including carrying out the State educational agency's statewide system of technical assistance and support for local educational agencies;

(4) the State educational agency will work with other agencies, including educational

service agencies or other local consortia, and institutions to provide technical assistance to local educational agencies and schools, including technical assistance in providing professional development under section 1119 [20 USCS § 6319], technical assistance under section 1117 [20 USCS § 6317], and technical assistance relating to parental involvement under section 1118 [20 USCS § 6318];

(5)

(A) where educational service agencies exist, the State educational agency will consider providing professional development and technical assistance through such agencies; and

(B) where educational service agencies do not exist, the State educational agency will consider providing professional development and technical assistance through other cooperative agreements such as through a consortium of local educational agencies;

(6) the State educational agency will notify local educational agencies and the public of the content and student academic achievement standards and academic assessments developed under this section, and of the authority to operate schoolwide programs, and will fulfill the State educational agency's responsibilities regarding local educational agency improvement and school improvement under section 1116 [20 USCS § 6316], including such corrective actions as are necessary;

(7) the State educational agency will provide the least restrictive and burdensome regulations for local educational agencies and individual schools participating in a program assisted under this part [20 USCS §§ 6311 et seq.];

(8) the State educational agency will inform the Secretary and the public of how Federal laws, if at all, hinder the ability of States to hold local educational agencies and schools accountable for student academic achievement;

(9) the State educational agency will encourage schools to consolidate funds from other Federal, State, and local sources for schoolwide reform in schoolwide programs under section 1114 [20 USCS § 6314];

(10) the State educational agency will modify or eliminate State fiscal and accounting barriers so that schools can easily consolidate funds from other Federal, State, and local sources for schoolwide programs under section 1114 [20 USCS § 6314];

(11) the State educational agency has involved the committee of practitioners established under section 1903(b) [20 USCS § 6573(b)] in developing the plan and monitoring its implementation;

(12) the State educational agency will inform local educational agencies in the State of the local educational agency's authority to transfer funds under title VI [20 USCS §§ 7301 et seq.], to obtain waivers under part D of title IX [20 USCS § 7861], and, if the State is an Ed-Flex Partnership State, to obtain waivers under the Education Flexibility Partnership Act of 1999;

(13) the State educational agency will coordinate activities funded under this part [20 USCS §§ 6311 et seq.] with other Federal activities as appropriate; and

(14) the State educational agency will encourage local educational agencies and individual schools participating in a program assisted under this part [20 USCS §§ 6311 et seq.] to offer family literacy services (using funds under this part [20 USCS §§ 6311 et seq.]), if the agency or school determines that a substantial number of students served under this part [20 USCS §§ 6311 et seq.] by the agency or school have parents who do not have a secondary school diploma or its recognized equivalent or who have low levels of literacy.

(d) Parental involvement. Each State plan shall describe how the State educational agency will support the collection and dissemination to local educational agencies and schools of effective parental involvement practices. Such practices shall—

(1) be based on the most current research that meets the highest professional and technical standards, on effective parental involvement that fosters achievement to high standards for all children; and

(2) be geared toward lowering barriers to greater participation by parents in school planning, review, and improvement experienced.

(e) Peer review and secretarial approval.

(1) Secretarial duties. The Secretary shall—

(A) establish a peer-review process to assist in the review of State plans;

(B) appoint individuals to the peer-review process who are representative of parents, teachers, State educational agencies, and local educational agencies, and who are familiar with educational standards, assessments, accountability, the needs of low-performing schools, and other educational needs of students;

(C) approve a State plan within 120 days of its submission unless the Secretary determines that the plan does not meet the requirements of this section;

(D) if the Secretary determines that the State plan does not meet the requirements of subsection (a), (b), or (c), immediately notify the State of such determination and the reasons for such determination;

(E) not decline to approve a State's plan before—

(i) offering the State an opportunity to revise its plan;

(ii) providing technical assistance in order to assist the State to meet the requirements of subsections (a), (b), and (c); and

(iii) providing a hearing; and

(F) have the authority to disapprove a State plan for not meeting the requirements of this part [20 USCS §§ 6311 et seq.], but shall not have the authority to require a State, as a condition of approval of the State plan, to include in, or delete from, such plan one or more specific elements of the State's academic content standards or to use specific academic assessment instruments or items.

(2) State revisions. A State plan shall be revised by the State educational agency if it is necessary to satisfy the requirements of this section.

(f) Duration of the plan.

(1) In general. Each State plan shall—

(A) remain in effect for the duration of the State's participation under this part [20 USCS §§ 6311 et seq.]; and

(B) be periodically reviewed and revised as necessary by the State educational agency to reflect changes in the State's strategies and programs under this part [20 USCS §§ 6311 et seq.].

(2) Additional information. If significant changes are made to a State's plan, such as the adoption of new State academic content standards and State student achievement standards, new academic assessments, or a new definition of adequate yearly progress, such information shall be submitted to the Secretary.

(g) Penalties.

(1) Failure to meet deadlines enacted in 1994.

(A) In general. If a State fails to meet the deadlines established by the Improving America's Schools Act of 1994 (or under any waiver granted by the Secretary or under any compliance agreement with the Secretary) for demonstrating that the State has in place challenging academic content standards and student achievement standards, and a system for measuring and monitoring adequate yearly progress, the Secretary shall withhold 25 percent of the funds that would otherwise be available to the State for State administration and activities under this part [20 USCS §§ 6311 et seq.] in each year until the Secretary determines that the State meets those requirements.

(B) No extension. Notwithstanding any other provision of law, 90 days after the date of enactment of the No Child Left Behind Act of 2001 [enacted Jan. 8, 2002] the Secretary shall not grant any additional waivers of, or enter into any additional compliance agreements to extend, the deadlines described in subparagraph (A) for any State.

(2) Failure to meet requirements enacted in 2001. If a State fails to meet any of the requirements of this section, other than the requirements described in paragraph (1), then the Secretary may withhold funds for State administration under this part [20 USCS §§ 6311 et seq.] until the Secretary determines that the State has fulfilled those requirements.

(h) Reports.

(1) Annual State report card.

(A) In general. Not later than the beginning of the 2002-2003 school year, unless the State has received a 1-year extension pursuant to subsection (c)(1), a State that receives assistance under this part [20 USCS §§ 6311 et seq.] shall prepare and disseminate an annual State report card.

(B) Implementation. The State report card shall be—

(i) concise; and

(ii) presented in an understandable and uniform format and, to the extent practicable, provided in a language that the parents can understand.

(C) Required information. The State shall include in its annual State report card—

(i) information, in the aggregate, on student achievement at each proficiency level on the State academic assessments described in subsection (b)(3) (disaggregated by race, ethnicity, gender, disability status, migrant status, English proficiency, and status as economically disadvantaged, except that such disaggregation shall not be required in a case in which the number of students in a category is insufficient to yield statistically reliable information or the results would reveal personally identifiable information about an individual student);

(ii) information that provides a comparison between the actual achievement levels of each group of students described in subsection (b)(2)(C)(v) and the State's annual measurable objectives for each such group of students on each of the academic assessments required under this part [20 USCS §§ 6311 et seq.];

(iii) the percentage of students not tested (disaggregated by the same categories and subject to the same exception described in clause (i));

(iv) the most recent 2-year trend in student achievement in each subject area, and for each grade level, for which assessments under this section are required;

(v) aggregate information on any other indicators used by the State to determine the adequate yearly progress of students in achieving State academic achievement standards;

(vi) graduation rates for secondary school students consistent with subsection (b)(2)(C)(vi);

(vii) information on the performance of local educational agencies in the State regarding making adequate yearly progress, including the number and names of each school identified for school improvement under section 1116 [20 USCS § 6316]; and

(viii) the professional qualifications of teachers in the State, the percentage of such teachers teaching with emergency or provisional credentials, and the percentage of classes in the State not taught by highly qualified teachers, in the aggregate and disaggregated by high-poverty compared to low-poverty schools which, for the purpose of this clause, means schools in the top quartile of poverty and the bottom quartile of poverty in the State.

(D) Optional information. The State may include in its annual State report card such other information as the State believes will best provide parents, students, and other members of the public with information regarding the progress of each of the State's public elementary schools and public secondary schools. Such information may include information regarding—

(i) school attendance rates;

(ii) average class size in each grade;

(iii) academic achievement and gains in English proficiency of limited English proficient students;

(iv) the incidence of school violence, drug abuse, alcohol abuse, student suspensions, and student expulsions;

(v) the extent and type of parental involvement in the schools;

(vi) the percentage of students completing advanced placement courses, and the rate of passing of advanced placement tests; and

(vii) a clear and concise description of the State's accountability system, including a description of the criteria by which the State evaluates school performance, and the criteria that the State has established, consistent with subsection (b)(2), to determine the status of schools regarding school improvement, corrective action, and restructuring.

(2) Annual local educational agency report cards.

(A) Report cards.

(i) In general. Not later than the beginning of the 2002-2003 school year, a local educational agency that receives assistance under this part [20 USCS §§ 6311 et seq.] shall prepare and disseminate an annual local educational agency report card, except that the State educational agency may provide the local educational agency 1 additional year if the local educational agency demonstrates that exceptional or uncontrollable circumstances, such as a natural disaster or a precipitous and unforeseen decline in the financial resources of the local educational agency, prevented full implementation of this paragraph by that deadline and that the local educational agency will complete implementation within the additional 1-year period.

(ii) Special rule. If a State educational agency has received an extension pursuant to subsection (c)(1), then a local educational agency within that State shall not be required to include the information required under paragraph (1)(C) in such report card during such extension.

(B) Minimum requirements. The State educational agency shall ensure that each local educational agency collects appropriate data and includes in the local educational agency's annual report the information described in paragraph (1)(C) as applied to the local educational agency and each school served by the local educational agency, and—

(i) in the case of a local educational agency—

(I) the number and percentage of schools identified for school improvement under section 1116(c) [20 USCS § 6316(c)] and how long the schools have been so identified; and

(II) information that shows how students served by the local educational agency achieved on the statewide academic assessment compared to students in the State as a whole; and

(ii) in the case of a school—

(I) whether the school has been identified for school improvement; and

(II) information that shows how the school's students achievement on the statewide academic assessments and other indicators of adequate yearly progress compared to students in the local educational agency and the State as a whole.

(C) Other information. A local educational agency may include in its annual local educational agency report card any other appropriate information, whether or not such information is included in the annual State report card.

(D) Data. A local educational agency or school shall only include in its annual local educational agency report card data that are sufficient to yield statistically reliable information, as determined by the State, and that do not reveal personally identifiable information about an individual student.

(E) Public dissemination. The local educational agency shall, not later than the beginning of the 2002-2003 school year, unless the local educational agency has received a 1-year extension pursuant to subparagraph (A), publicly disseminate the information described in this paragraph to all schools in the school district served by the local educational agency and to all parents of students attending those schools in an understandable and uniform format and, to the extent practicable, provided in a language that the parents can understand, and make the information widely available through public means, such as posting on the Internet, distribution to the media, and distribution through public agencies, except that if a local educational agency issues a report card for all students, the local educational agency may include the information under this section as part of such report.

(3) Preexisting report cards. A State educational agency or local educational agency that was providing public report cards on the performance of students, schools, local educational agencies, or the State prior to the enactment of the No Child Left Behind Act of 2001 [enacted Jan. 8, 2002] may use those report cards for the purpose of this subsection, so long as any such report card is modified, as may be needed, to contain the information required by this subsection.

(4) Annual State report to the Secretary. Each State educational agency receiving assistance under this part [*20 USCS §§ 6311* et seq.] shall report annually to the Secretary, and make widely available within the State—

(A) beginning with school year 2002-2003, information on the State's progress in developing and implementing the academic assessments described in subsection (b)(3);

(B) beginning not later than school year 2002-2003, information on the achievement of students on the academic assessments required by subsection (b)(3), including the disaggregated results for the categories of students identified in subsection (b)(2)(C)(v);

(C) in any year before the State begins to provide the information described in subparagraph (B), information on the results of student academic assessments (including disaggregated results) required under this section;

(D) beginning not later than school year 2002-2003, unless the State has received an extension pursuant to subsection (c)(1), information on the acquisition of English proficiency by children with limited English proficiency;

(E) the number and names of each school identified for school improvement under section 1116(c) [*20 USCS § 6316(c)*], the reason why each school was so identified, and the measures taken to address the achievement problems of such schools;

(F) the number of students and schools that participated in public school choice and supplemental service programs and activities under this *title [20 USCS §§ 6301 et seq.]*; and

(G) beginning not later than the 2002-2003 school year, information on the quality of teachers and the percentage of classes being taught by highly qualified teachers in the State, local educational agency, and school.

(5) Report to Congress. The Secretary shall transmit annually to the Committee on Education and the Workforce of the House of Representatives and the Committee on Health, Education, Labor, and Pensions of the Senate a report that provides national and State-level data on the information collected under paragraph (4).

(6) Parents right-to-know.

(A) Qualifications. At the beginning of each school year, a local educational agency that receives funds under this part *[20 USCS §§ 6311 et seq.]* shall notify the parents of each student attending any school receiving funds under this part *[20 USCS §§ 6311 et seq.]* that the parents may request, and the agency will provide the parents on request (and in a timely manner), information regarding the professional qualifications of the student's classroom teachers, including, at a minimum, the following:

(i) Whether the teacher has met State qualification and licensing criteria for the grade levels and subject areas in which the teacher provides instruction.

(ii) Whether the teacher is teaching under emergency or other provisional status through which State qualification or licensing criteria have been waived.

(iii) The baccalaureate degree major of the teacher and any other graduate certification or degree held by the teacher, and the field of discipline of the certification or degree.

(iv) Whether the child is provided services by paraprofessionals and, if so, their qualifications.

(B) Additional information. In addition to the information that parents may request under subparagraph (A), a school that receives funds under this part *[20 USCS §§ 6311 et seq.]* shall provide to each individual parent—

(i) information on the level of achievement of the parent's child in each of the State academic assessments as required under this part *[20 USCS §§ 6311 et seq.]*; and

(ii) timely notice that the parent's child has been assigned, or has been taught for four or more consecutive weeks by, a teacher who is not highly qualified.

(C) Format. The notice and information provided to parents under this paragraph shall be in an understandable and uniform format and, to the extent practicable, provided in a language that the parents can understand.

(i) Privacy. Information collected under this section shall be collected and disseminated in a manner that protects the privacy of individuals.

(j) Technical assistance. The Secretary shall provide a State educational agency, at the State educational agency's request, technical assistance in meeting the requirements of this section, including the provision of advice by experts in the development of high-quality academic assessments, the setting of State standards, the development of measures of adequate yearly progress that are valid and reliable, and other relevant areas.

(k) Voluntary partnerships. A State may enter into a voluntary partnership with another State to develop and implement the academic assessments and standards required under this section.

(l) Construction. Nothing in this part *[20 USCS §§ 6311 et seq.]* shall be construed to prescribe the use of the academic assessments described in this part [20 USCS §§ 6311 et seq.] for student promotion or graduation purposes.

(m) Special rule with respect to Bureau-funded schools. In determining the assessments to be used by each operated or funded by BIA school receiving funds under this part [20 USCS §§ 6311 et seq.], the following shall apply:

(1) Each such school that is accredited by the State in which it is operating shall use the assessments the State has developed and implemented to meet the requirements of this section, or such other appropriate assessment as approved by the Secretary of the Interior.

(2) Each such school that is accredited by a regional accrediting organization shall adopt an appropriate assessment, in consultation with and with the approval of, the Secretary of the Interior and consistent with assessments adopted by other schools in the same State or region, that meets the requirements of this section.

(3) Each such school that is accredited by a tribal accrediting agency or tribal division of education shall use an assessment developed by such agency or division, except that the Secretary of the Interior shall ensure that such assessment meets the requirements of this section.

§ 6312. Local educational agency plans

(a) Plans required.

(1) Subgrants. A local educational agency may receive a subgrant under this part [20 USCS §§ 6311 et seq.] for any fiscal year only if such agency has on file with the State educational agency a plan, approved by the State educational agency, that is coordinated with other programs under this Act [20 USCS §§ 6301 et seq.], the Individuals with Disabilities Education Act [20 USCS §§ 1400 et seq.], the Carl D. Perkins Career and Technical Education Act of 2006 [20 USCS §§ 2301 et seq.], the McKinney-Vento Homeless Assistance Act [42 USCS §§ 11301 et seq.], and other Acts, as appropriate.

(2) Consolidated application. The plan may be submitted as part of a consolidated application under section 9305 [20 USCS § 7845].

(b) Plan provisions.

(1) In general. In order to help low-achieving children meet challenging achievement academic standards, each local educational agency plan shall include—

(A) a description of high-quality student academic assessments, if any, that are in addition to the academic assessments described in the State plan under section 1111(b)(3) [20 USCS § 6311(b)(3)], that the local educational agency and schools served under this part [20 USCS §§ 6311 et seq.] will use—

(i) to determine the success of children served under this part [20 USCS §§ 6311 et seq.] in meeting the State student academic achievement standards, and to provide information to teachers, parents, and students on the progress being made toward meeting the State student academic achievement standards described in section 1111(b)(1)(D)(ii) [20 USCS § 6311(b)(1)(D)(ii)];

(ii) to assist in diagnosis, teaching, and learning in the classroom in ways that best enable low-achieving children served under this part [20 USCS §§ 6311 et seq.] to meet State student achievement academic standards and do well in the local curriculum;

(iii) to determine what revisions are needed to projects under this part [20 USCS §§ 6311 et seq.] so that such children meet the State student academic achievement standards; and

(iv) to identify effectively students who may be at risk for reading failure or who are having difficulty reading, through the use of screening, diagnostic, and classroom-based instructional reading assessments, as defined under section 1208 [*20 USCS § 6368*];

(B) at the local educational agency's discretion, a description of any other indicators that will be used in addition to the academic indicators described in section 1111 [*20 USCS § 6311*] for the uses described in such section;

(C) a description of how the local educational agency will provide additional educational assistance to individual students assessed as needing help in meeting the State's challenging student academic achievement standards;

(D) a description of the strategy the local educational agency will use to coordinate programs under this part [*20 USCS §§ 6311* et seq.] with programs under title II [*20 USCS §§ 6601* et seq.] to provide professional development for teachers and principals, and, if appropriate, pupil services personnel, administrators, parents and other staff, including local educational agency level staff in accordance with sections 1118 and 1119 [*20 USCS §§ 6318, 6319*];

(E) a description of how the local educational agency will coordinate and integrate services provided under this part [*20 USCS §§ 6311* et seq.] with other educational services at the local educational agency or individual school level, such as—

(i) Even Start, Head Start, Reading First, Early Reading First, and other preschool programs, including plans for the transition of participants in such programs to local elementary school programs; and

(ii) services for children with limited English proficiency, children with disabilities, migratory children, neglected or delinquent youth, Indian children served under part A of title VII [*20 USCS §§ 7401* et seq.], homeless children, and immigrant children in order to increase program effectiveness, eliminate duplication, and reduce fragmentation of the instructional program;

(F) an assurance that the local educational agency will participate, if selected, in the State National Assessment of Educational Progress in 4th and 8th grade reading and mathematics carried out under section 303(b)(2) of the National Assessment of Educational Progress Authorization Act [*20 USCS § 9622(b)(2)*];

(G) a description of the poverty criteria that will be used to select school attendance areas under section 1113 [*20 USCS § 6313*];

(H) a description of how teachers, in consultation with parents, administrators, and pupil services personnel, in targeted assistance schools under section 1115 [*20 USCS § 6315*], will identify the eligible children most in need of services under this part [*20 USCS §§ 6311* et seq.];

(I) a general description of the nature of the programs to be conducted by such agency's schools under sections 1114 and 1115 [*20 USCS §§ 6314, 6315*] and, where appropriate, educational services outside such schools for children living in local institutions for neglected or delinquent children, and for neglected and delinquent children in community day school programs;

(J) a description of how the local educational agency will ensure that migratory children and formerly migratory children who are eligible to receive services under this part [*20 USCS §§ 6311* et seq.] are selected to receive such services on the same basis as other children who are selected to receive services under this part [*20 USCS §§ 6311* et seq.];

(K) if appropriate, a description of how the local educational agency will use funds under this part [*20 USCS §§ 6311* et seq.] to support preschool programs for children, particularly children participating in Early Reading First, or in a Head Start or Even Start program, which services may be provided directly by the local educational agency or through a subcontract with the local Head Start agency designated by the Secretary of Health and Human Services under section 641 of the Head Start Act [*42 USCS § 9836*], or an agency operating an Even Start program, an Early Reading First program, or another comparable public early childhood development program;

(L) a description of the actions the local educational agency will take to assist its low-achieving schools identified under section 1116 [20 USCS § 6316] as in need of improvement;

(M) a description of the actions the local educational agency will take to implement public school choice and supplemental services, consistent with the requirements of section 1116 [20 USCS § 6316];

(N) a description of how the local educational agency will meet the requirements of section 1119 [20 USCS § 6319];

(O) a description of the services the local educational agency will provide homeless children, including services provided with funds reserved under section 1113(c)(3)(A) [20 USCS § 6313(c)(3)(A)];

(P) a description of the strategy the local educational agency will use to implement effective parental involvement under section 1118 [20 USCS § 6318]; and

(Q) where appropriate, a description of how the local educational agency will use funds under this part [20 USCS §§ 6311 et seq.] to support after school (including before school and summer school) and school-year extension programs.

(2) Exception. The academic assessments and indicators described in subparagraphs (A) and (B) of paragraph (1) shall not be used—

(A) in lieu of the academic assessments required under section 1111(b)(3) [20 USCS § 6311(b)(3)] and other State academic indicators under section 1111(b)(2) [20 USCS § 6311(b)(2)]; or

(B) to reduce the number of, or change which, schools would otherwise be subject to school improvement, corrective action, or restructuring under section 1116 [20 USCS § 6316], if such additional assessments or indicators described in such subparagraphs were not used, but such assessments and indicators may be used to identify additional schools for school improvement or in need of corrective action or restructuring.

(c) Assurances.

(1) In general. Each local educational agency plan shall provide assurances that the local educational agency will—

(A) inform eligible schools and parents of schoolwide program authority and the ability of such schools to consolidate funds from Federal, State, and local sources;

(B) provide technical assistance and support to schoolwide programs;

(C) work in consultation with schools as the schools develop the schools' plans pursuant to section 1114 [20 USCS § 6314] and assist schools as the schools implement such plans or undertake activities pursuant to section 1115 [20 USCS § 6315] so that each school can make adequate yearly progress toward meeting the State student academic achievement standards;

(D) fulfill such agency's school improvement responsibilities under section 1116 [20 USCS § 6316], including taking actions under paragraphs (7) and (8) of section 1116(b) [20 USCS § 6316(b)];

(E) provide services to eligible children attending private elementary schools and secondary schools in accordance with section 1120 [20 USCS § 6320], and timely and meaningful consultation with private school officials regarding such services;

(F) take into account the experience of model programs for the educationally disadvantaged, and the findings of relevant scientifically based research indicating that services may be most effective if focused on students in the earliest grades at schools that receive funds under this part [20 USCS §§ 6311 et seq.];

§ 6312. TITLE 20 — EDUCATION 391

(G) in the case of a local educational agency that chooses to use funds under this part [20 USCS §§ 6311 et seq.] to provide early childhood development services to low-income children below the age of compulsory school attendance, ensure that such services comply with the performance standards established under section 641A(a) of the Head Start Act [42 USCS § 9836a(a)];

(H) work in consultation with schools as the schools develop and implement their plans or activities under sections 1118 and 1119 [20 USCS §§ 6318, 6319];

(I) comply with the requirements of section 1119 [20 USCS § 6319] regarding the qualifications of teachers and paraprofessionals and professional development;

(J) inform eligible schools of the local educational agency's authority to obtain waivers on the school's behalf under title IX [20 USCS §§ 7801 et seq.] and, if the State is an Ed-Flex Partnership State, to obtain waivers under the Education Flexibility Partnership Act of 1999;

(K) coordinate and collaborate, to the extent feasible and necessary as determined by the local educational agency, with the State educational agency and other agencies providing services to children, youth, and families with respect to a school in school improvement, corrective action, or restructuring under section 1116 [20 USCS § 6316] if such a school requests assistance from the local educational agency in addressing major factors that have significantly affected student achievement at the school;

(L) ensure, through incentives for voluntary transfers, the provision of professional development, recruitment programs, or other effective strategies, that low-income students and minority students are not taught at higher rates than other students by unqualified, out-of-field, or inexperienced teachers;

(M) use the results of the student academic assessments required under section 1111(b)(3) [20 USCS § 6311(b)(3)], and other measures or indicators available to the agency, to review annually the progress of each school served by the agency and receiving funds under this part [20 USCS §§ 6311 et seq.] to determine whether all of the schools are making the progress necessary to ensure that all students will meet the State's proficient level of achievement on the State academic assessments described in section 1111(b)(3) [20 USCS § 6311(b)(3)] within 12 years from the end of the 2001-2002 school year;

(N) ensure that the results from the academic assessments required under section 1111(b)(3) [20 USCS § 6311(b)(3)] will be provided to parents and teachers as soon as is practicably possible after the test is taken, in an understandable and uniform format and, to the extent practicable, provided in a language that the parents can understand; and

(O) assist each school served by the agency and assisted under this part [20 USCS §§ 6311 et seq.] in developing or identifying examples of high-quality, effective curricula consistent with section 1111(b)(8)(D) [20 USCS § 6311(b)(8)(D)].

(2) Special rule. In carrying out subparagraph (G) of paragraph (1), the Secretary—

(A) shall consult with the Secretary of Health and Human Services and shall establish procedures (taking into consideration existing State and local laws, and local teacher contracts) to assist local educational agencies to comply with such subparagraph; and

(B) shall disseminate to local educational agencies the Head Start performance standards as in effect under section 641A(a) of the Head Start Act [42 USCS § 9836a(a)], and such agencies affected by such subparagraph shall plan for the implementation of such subparagraph (taking into consideration existing State and local laws, and local teacher contracts), including pursuing the availability of other Federal, State, and local funding sources to assist in compliance with such subparagraph.

(3) Inapplicability. Paragraph (1)(G) of this subsection shall not apply to preschool programs using the Even Start model or to Even Start programs that are expanded

through the use of funds under this part [*20 USCS §§ 6311* et seq.].

(d) Plan development and duration.

(1) Consultation. Each local educational agency plan shall be developed in consultation with teachers, principals, administrators (including administrators of programs described in other parts of this *title [20 USCS §§ 6301* et seq.]), and other appropriate school personnel, and with parents of children in schools served under this part [*20 USCS §§ 6311* et seq.].

(2) Duration. Each such plan shall be submitted for the first year for which this part [*20 USCS §§ 6311* et seq.] is in effect following the date of enactment of the No Child Left Behind Act of 2001 [enacted Jan. 8, 2002] and shall remain in effect for the duration of the agency's participation under this part [*20 USCS §§ 6311* et seq.].

(3) Review. Each local educational agency shall periodically review and, as necessary, revise its plan.

(e) State approval.

(1) In general. Each local educational agency plan shall be filed according to a schedule established by the State educational agency.

(2) Approval. The State educational agency shall approve a local educational agency's plan only if the State educational agency determines that the local educational agency's plan—

(A) enables schools served under this part [*20 USCS §§ 6311* et seq.] to substantially help children served under this part [*20 USCS §§ 6311* et seq.] meet the academic standards expected of all children described in section 1111(b)(1) [*20 USCS § 6311(b)(1)*]; and

(B) meets the requirements of this section.

(3) Review. The State educational agency shall review the local educational agency's plan to determine if such agencies activities are in accordance with sections 1118 and 1119 [*20 USCS §§ 6318, 6319*].

(f) Program responsibility. The local educational agency plan shall reflect the shared responsibility of schools, teachers, and the local educational agency in making decisions regarding activities under sections 1114 and 1115 [*20 USCS §§ 6314, 6315*].

(g) Parental notification.

(1) In general.

(A) Notice. Each local educational agency using funds under this part [*20 USCS §§ 6311* et seq.] to provide a language instruction educational program as determined in part C of title III [*20 USCS §§ 7011* et seq.] shall, not later than 30 days after the beginning of the school year, inform a parent or parents of a limited English proficient child identified for participation or participating in, such a program of—

(i) the reasons for the identification of their child as limited English proficient and in need of placement in a language instruction educational program;

(ii) the child's level of English proficiency, how such level was assessed, and the status of the child's academic achievement;

(iii) the methods of instruction used in the program in which their child is, or will be participating, and the methods of instruction used in other available programs, including how such programs differ in content, instructional goals, and the use of English and a native language in instruction;

(iv) how the program in which their child is, or will be participating, will meet the educational strengths and needs of their child;

(v) how such program will specifically help their child learn English, and meet age-appropriate academic achievement standards for grade promotion and graduation;

(vi) the specific exit requirements for the program, including the expected rate of transition from such program into classrooms that are not tailored for limited English proficient children, and the expected rate of graduation from secondary school for such program if funds under this part [20 USCS §§ 6311 et seq.] are used for children in secondary schools;

(vii) in the case of a child with a disability, how such program meets the objectives of the individualized education program of the child;

(viii) information pertaining to parental rights that includes written guidance—

(I) detailing—

(aa) the right that parents have to have their child immediately removed from such program upon their request; and

(bb) the options that parents have to decline to enroll their child in such program or to choose another program or method of instruction, if available; and

(II) assisting parents in selecting among various programs and methods of instruction, if more than one program or method is offered by the eligible entity.

(B) Separate notification. In addition to providing the information required to be provided under paragraph (1), each eligible entity that is using funds provided under this part [20 USCS §§ 6311 et seq.] to provide a language instruction educational program, and that has failed to make progress on the annual measurable achievement objectives described in section 3122 [20 USCS § 6842] for any fiscal year for which part A [20 USCS §§ 6311 et seq.] is in effect, shall separately inform a parent or the parents of a child identified for participation in such program, or participating in such program, of such failure not later than 30 days after such failure occurs.

(2) Notice. The notice and information provided in paragraph (1) to a parent or parents of a child identified for participation in a language instruction educational program for limited English proficient children shall be in an understandable and uniform format and, to the extent practicable, provided in a language that the parents can understand.

(3) Special rule applicable during the school year. For those children who have not been identified as limited English proficient prior to the beginning of the school year the local educational agency shall notify parents within the first 2 weeks of the child being placed in a language instruction educational program consistent with paragraphs (1) and (2).

(4) Parental participation. Each local educational agency receiving funds under this part [20 USCS §§ 6311 et seq.] shall implement an effective means of outreach to parents of limited English proficient students to inform the parents regarding how the parents can be involved in the education of their children, and be active participants in assisting their children to attain English proficiency, achieve at high levels in core academic subjects, and meet challenging State academic achievement standards and State academic content standards expected of all students, including holding, and sending notice of opportunities for, regular meetings for the purpose of formulating and responding to recommendations from parents of students assisted under this part [20 USCS §§ 6311 et seq.].

(5) Basis for admission or exclusion. A student shall not be admitted to, or excluded from, any federally assisted education program on the basis of a surname or language-minority status.

§ 6313. Eligible school attendance areas

(a) Determination.

(1) In general. A local educational agency shall use funds received under this part [20 USCS §§ 6311 et seq.] only in eligible school attendance areas.

(2) Eligible school attendance areas. For the purposes of this part [20 USCS §§ 6311 et seq.]—

(A) the term "school attendance area" means, in relation to a particular school, the geographical area in which the children who are normally served by that school reside; and

(B) the term "eligible school attendance area" means a school attendance area in which the percentage of children from low-income families is at least as high as the percentage of children from low-income families served by the local educational agency as a whole.

(3) Ranking order. If funds allocated in accordance with subsection (c) are insufficient to serve all eligible school attendance areas, a local educational agency shall—

(A) annually rank, without regard to grade spans, such agency's eligible school attendance areas in which the concentration of children from low-income families exceeds 75 percent from highest to lowest according to the percentage of children from low-income families; and

(B) serve such eligible school attendance areas in rank order.

(4) Remaining funds. If funds remain after serving all eligible school attendance areas under paragraph (3), a local educational agency shall—

(A) annually rank such agency's remaining eligible school attendance areas from highest to lowest either by grade span or for the entire local educational agency according to the percentage of children from low-income families; and

(B) serve such eligible school attendance areas in rank order either within each grade-span grouping or within the local educational agency as a whole.

(5) Measures. The local educational agency shall use the same measure of poverty, which measure shall be the number of children ages 5 through 17 in poverty counted in the most recent census data approved by the Secretary, the number of children eligible for free and reduced priced lunches under the Richard B. Russell National School Lunch Act [42 USCS §§ 1751 et seq.], the number of children in families receiving assistance under the State program funded under part A of title IV of the Social Security Act [42 USCS §§ 601 et seq.], or the number of children eligible to receive medical assistance under the Medicaid program, or a composite of such indicators, with respect to all school attendance areas in the local educational agency—

(A) to identify eligible school attendance areas;

(B) to determine the ranking of each area; and

(C) to determine allocations under subsection (c).

(6) Exception. This subsection shall not apply to a local educational agency with a total enrollment of less than 1,000 children.

(7) Waiver for desegregation plans. The Secretary may approve a local educational agency's written request for a waiver of the requirements of subsections (a) and (c), and permit such agency to treat as eligible, and serve, any school that children attend with a State-ordered, court-ordered school desegregation plan or a plan that continues to be

implemented in accordance with a State-ordered or court-ordered desegregation plan, if—

(A) the number of economically disadvantaged children enrolled in the school is at least 25 percent of the school's total enrollment; and

(B) the Secretary determines on the basis of a written request from such agency and in accordance with such criteria as the Secretary establishes, that approval of that request would further the purposes of this part [20 USCS §§ 6311 et seq.].

(b) Local educational agency discretion.

(1) In general. Notwithstanding subsection (a)(2), a local educational agency may—

(A) designate as eligible any school attendance area or school in which at least 35 percent of the children are from low-income families;

(B) use funds received under this part [20 USCS §§ 6311 et seq.] in a school that is not in an eligible school attendance area, if the percentage of children from low-income families enrolled in the school is equal to or greater than the percentage of such children in a participating school attendance area of such agency;

(C) designate and serve a school attendance area or school that is not eligible under this section, but that was eligible and that was served in the preceding fiscal year, but only for 1 additional fiscal year; and

(D) elect not to serve an eligible school attendance area or eligible school that has a higher percentage of children from low-income families if—

(i) the school meets the comparability requirements of section 1120A(c) [20 USCS § 6321(c)];

(ii) the school is receiving supplemental funds from other State or local sources that are spent according to the requirements of section 1114 or 1115 [20 USCS § 6314 or 6315]; and

(iii) the funds expended from such other sources equal or exceed the amount that would be provided under this part [20 USCS §§ 6311 et seq.].

(2) Special rule. Notwithstanding paragraph (1)(D), the number of children attending private elementary schools and secondary schools who are to receive services, and the assistance such children are to receive under this part [20 USCS §§ 6311 et seq.], shall be determined without regard to whether the public school attendance area in which such children reside is assisted under subparagraph (A).

(c) Allocations.

(1) In general. A local educational agency shall allocate funds received under this part [20 USCS §§ 6311 et seq.] to eligible school attendance areas or eligible schools, identified under subsections (a) and (b), in rank order, on the basis of the total number of children from low-income families in each area or school.

(2) Special rule.

(A) In general. Except as provided in subparagraph (B), the per-pupil amount of funds allocated to each school attendance area or school under paragraph (1) shall be at least 125 percent of the per-pupil amount of funds a local educational agency received for that year under the poverty criteria described by the local educational agency in the plan submitted under section 1112 [20 USCS § 6312], except that this paragraph shall not apply to a local educational agency that only serves schools in which the percentage of such children is 35 percent or greater.

(B) Exception. A local educational agency may reduce the amount of funds allocated under subparagraph (A) for a school attendance area or school by the amount of any supplemental State and local funds expended in that school attendance area or school for programs that meet the requirements of section 1114 or 1115 [20 USCS § 6314 or 6315].

(3) Reservation. A local educational agency shall reserve such funds as are necessary under this part [20 USCS §§ 6311 et seq.] to provide services comparable to those provided to children in schools funded under this part [20 USCS §§ 6311 et seq.] to serve—

(A) homeless children who do not attend participating schools, including providing educationally related support services to children in shelters and other locations where children may live;

(B) children in local institutions for neglected children; and

(C) if appropriate, children in local institutions for delinquent children, and neglected or delinquent children in community day school programs.

(4) Financial incentives and rewards reservation. A local educational agency may reserve such funds as are necessary from those funds received by the local educational agency under title II [20 USCS §§ 6601 et seq.], and not more than 5 percent of those funds received by the local educational agency under subpart 2 [20 USCS §§ 6331 et seq.], to provide financial incentives and rewards to teachers who serve in schools eligible under this section and identified for school improvement, corrective action, and restructuring under section 1116(b) [20 USCS § 6316(b)] for the purpose of attracting and retaining qualified and effective teachers.

§ 6314. Schoolwide programs

(a) Use of funds for schoolwide programs.

(1) In general. A local educational agency may consolidate and use funds under this part [20 USCS §§ 6311 et seq.], together with other Federal, State, and local funds, in order to upgrade the entire educational program of a school that serves an eligible school attendance area in which not less than 40 percent of the children are from low-income families, or not less than 40 percent of the children enrolled in the school are from such families.

(2) Identification of students not required.

(A) In general. No school participating in a schoolwide program shall be required—

(i) to identify particular children under this part [20 USCS §§ 6311 et seq.] as eligible to participate in a schoolwide program; or

(ii) to provide services to such children that are supplementary, as otherwise required by section 1120A(b) [20 USCS § 6321(b)].

(B) Supplemental funds. A school participating in a schoolwide program shall use funds available to carry out this section only to supplement the amount of funds that would, in the absence of funds under this part [20 USCS §§ 6311 et seq.], be made available from non-Federal sources for the school, including funds needed to provide services that are required by law for children with disabilities and children with limited English proficiency.

(3) Exemption from statutory and regulatory requirements.

(A) Exemption. Except as provided in subsection (b), the Secretary may, through publication of a notice in the Federal Register, exempt schoolwide programs under this section from statutory or regulatory provisions of any other noncompetitive formula grant program administered by the Secretary (other than formula or discretionary grant programs under the Individuals with Disabilities Education Act [20 USCS §§ 1400 et seq.], except as provided in section 613(a)(2)(D) of such Act [20 USCS § 1413(a)(2)(D)]), or any discretionary grant program administered by the Secretary, to support schoolwide programs if the intent and purposes of such other programs are met.

(B) Requirements. A school that chooses to use funds from such other programs shall not be relieved of the requirements relating to health, safety, civil rights, student and parental participation and involvement, services to private school children, maintenance of effort, comparability of services, uses of Federal funds to supplement, not supplant non-Federal funds, or the distribution of funds to State educational agencies or local educational agencies that apply to the receipt of funds from such programs.

(C) Records. A school that consolidates and uses funds from different Federal programs under this section shall not be required to maintain separate fiscal accounting records, by program, that identify the specific activities supported by those particular funds as long as the school maintains records that demonstrate that the schoolwide program, considered as a whole, addresses the intent and purposes of each of the Federal programs that were consolidated to support the schoolwide program.

(4) Professional development. Each school receiving funds under this part [20 USCS §§ 6311 et seq.] for any fiscal year shall devote sufficient resources to effectively carry out the activities described in subsection (b)(1)(D) in accordance with section 1119 [20 USCS § 6319] for such fiscal year, except that a school may enter into a consortium with another school to carry out such activities.

(b) Components of a schoolwide program.

(1) In general. A schoolwide program shall include the following components:

(A) A comprehensive needs assessment of the entire school (including taking into account the needs of migratory children as defined in section 1309(2) [20 USCS § 6399(2)]) that is based on information which includes the achievement of children in relation to the State academic content standards and the State student academic achievement standards described in section 1111(b)(1) [20 USCS § 6311(b)(1)].

(B) Schoolwide reform strategies that—

(i) provide opportunities for all children to meet the State's proficient and advanced levels of student academic achievement described in section 1111(b)(1)(D) [20 USCS § 6311(b)(1)(D)];

(ii) use effective methods and instructional strategies that are based on scientifically based research that—

(I) strengthen the core academic program in the school;

(II) increase the amount and quality of learning time, such as providing an extended school year and before- and after-school and summer programs and opportunities, and help provide an enriched and accelerated curriculum; and

(III) include strategies for meeting the educational needs of historically underserved populations;

(iii)

(I) include strategies to address the needs of all children in the school, but particularly the needs of low-achieving children and those at risk of not meeting the State student academic achievement standards who are members of the target population of any program that is included in the schoolwide program, which may include—

(aa) counseling, pupil services, and mentoring services;

(bb) college and career awareness and preparation, such as college and career guidance, personal finance education, and innovative teaching methods, which may include applied learning and team-teaching strategies; and

(cc) the integration of vocational and technical education programs; and

(II) address how the school will determine if such needs have been met; and

(iv) are consistent with, and are designed to implement, the State and local improvement plans, if any.

(C) Instruction by highly qualified teachers.

(D) In accordance with section 1119 [20 USCS § 6319] and subsection (a)(4), high-quality and ongoing professional development for teachers, principals, and paraprofessionals and, if appropriate, pupil services personnel, parents, and other staff to enable all children in the school to meet the State's student academic achievement standards.

(E) Strategies to attract high-quality highly qualified teachers to high-need schools.

(F) Strategies to increase parental involvement in accordance with section 1118 [20 USCS § 6318], such as family literary services.

(G) Plans for assisting preschool children in the transition from early childhood programs, such as Head Start, Even Start, Early Reading First, or a State-run preschool program, to local elementary school programs.

(H) Measures to include teachers in the decisions regarding the use of academic assessments described in section 1111(b)(3) [20 USCS § 6311(b)(3)] in order to provide information on, and to improve, the achievement of individual students and the overall instructional program.

(I) Activities to ensure that students who experience difficulty mastering the proficient or advanced levels of academic achievement standards required by section 1111(b)(1) [20 USCS § 6311(b)(1)] shall be provided with effective, timely additional assistance which shall include measures to ensure that students' difficulties are identified on a timely basis and to provide sufficient information on which to base effective assistance.

(J) Coordination and integration of Federal, State, and local services and programs, including programs supported under this Act [20 USCS §§ 6301 et seq.], violence prevention programs, nutrition programs, housing programs, Head Start, adult education, vocational and technical education, and job training.

(2) Plan.

(A) In general. Any eligible school that desires to operate a schoolwide program shall first develop (or amend a plan for such a program that was in existence on the day before the date of enactment of the No Child Left Behind Act of 2001 [enacted Jan. 8, 2002]), in consultation with the local educational agency and its school support team or other technical assistance provider under section 1117 [20 USCS § 6317], a comprehensive plan for reforming the total instructional program in the school that—

(i) describes how the school will implement the components described in paragraph (1);

(ii) describes how the school will use resources under this part [20 USCS §§ 6311 et seq.] and from other sources to implement those components;

(iii) includes a list of State educational agency and local educational agency programs and other Federal programs under subsection (a)(3) that will be consolidated in the schoolwide program; and

(iv) describes how the school will provide individual student academic assessment results in a language the parents can understand, including an interpretation of those results, to the parents of a child who participates in the academic assessments required by section 1111(b)(3) [20 USCS § 6311(b)(3)].

(B) Plan development. The comprehensive plan shall be—

(i) developed during a one-year period, unless—

(I) the local educational agency, after considering the recommendation of the technical assistance providers under section 1117 [20 USCS § 6317], determines that less time is needed to develop and implement the schoolwide program; or

(II) the school is operating a schoolwide program on the day preceding the date of enactment of the No Child Left Behind Act of 2001 [enacted Jan. 8, 2002], in which case such school may continue to operate such program, but shall develop amendments to its existing plan during the first year of assistance after that date to reflect the provisions of this section;

(ii) developed with the involvement of parents and other members of the community to be served and individuals who will carry out such plan, including teachers, principals, and administrators (including administrators of programs described in other parts of this *title [20 USCS §§ 6301* et seq.]), and, if appropriate, pupil services personnel, technical assistance providers, school staff, and, if the plan relates to a secondary school, students from such school;

(iii) in effect for the duration of the school's participation under this part [*20 USCS §§ 6311* et seq.] and reviewed and revised, as necessary, by the school;

(iv) available to the local educational agency, parents, and the public, and the information contained in such plan shall be in an understandable and uniform format and, to the extent practicable, provided in a language that the parents can understand; and

(v) if appropriate, developed in coordination with programs under Reading First, Early Reading First, Even Start, Carl D. Perkins Career and Technical Education Act of 2006 [*20 USCS §§ 2301* et seq.], and the Head Start Act [*42 USCS §§ 9831* et seq.].

(c) Prekindergarten program. A school that is eligible for a schoolwide program under this section may use funds made available under this part [*20 USCS §§ 6311* et seq.] to establish or enhance prekindergarten programs for children below the age of 6, such as Even Start programs or Early Reading First programs.

§ 6315. Targeted assistance schools

(a) In general. In all schools selected to receive funds under section 1113(c) [*20 USCS § 6313(c)*] that are ineligible for a schoolwide program under section 1114 [*20 USCS § 6314*], or that choose not to operate such a schoolwide program, a local educational agency serving such school may use funds received under this part [*20 USCS §§ 6311* et seq.] only for programs that provide services to eligible children under subsection (b) identified as having the greatest need for special assistance.

(b) Eligible children.

(1) Eligible population.

(A) In general. The eligible population for services under this section is—

(i) children not older than age 21 who are entitled to a free public education through grade 12; and

(ii) children who are not yet at a grade level at which the local educational agency provides a free public education.

(B) Eligible children from eligible population. From the population described in subparagraph (A), eligible children are children identified by the school as failing, or most at risk of failing, to meet the State's challenging student academic achievement standards on the basis of multiple, educationally related, objective criteria established by the local educational agency and supplemented by the school, except that children from preschool through grade 2 shall be selected solely on the basis of such criteria as teacher judgment, interviews with parents, and developmentally appropriate measures.

(2) Children included.

(A) In general. Children who are economically disadvantaged, children with disabilities, migrant children or limited English proficient children, are eligible for services under this part [20 USCS §§ 6311 et seq.] on the same basis as other children selected to receive services under this part [20 USCS §§ 6311 et seq.].

(B) Head Start, Even Start, or Early Reading First children. A child who, at any time in the 2 years preceding the year for which the determination is made, participated in a Head Start, Even Start, or Early Reading First program, or in preschool services under this *title* [20 USCS §§ 6301 et seq.], is eligible for services under this part [20 USCS §§ 6311 et seq.].

(C) Part C children. A child who, at any time in the 2 years preceding the year for which the determination is made, received services under part C [20 USCS §§ 6391 et seq.] is eligible for services under this part [20 USCS §§ 6311 et seq.].

(D) Neglected or delinquent children. A child in a local institution for neglected or delinquent children and youth or attending a community day program for such children is eligible for services under this part [20 USCS §§ 6311 et seq.].

(E) Homeless children. A child who is homeless and attending any school served by the local educational agency is eligible for services under this part [20 USCS §§ 6311 et seq.].

(3) Special rule. Funds received under this part [20 USCS §§ 6311 et seq.] may not be used to provide services that are otherwise required by law to be made available to children described in paragraph (2) but may be used to coordinate or supplement such services.

(c) Components of a targeted assistance school program.

(1) In general. To assist targeted assistance schools and local educational agencies to meet their responsibility to provide for all their students served under this part [20 USCS §§ 6311 et seq.] the opportunity to meet the State's challenging student academic achievement standards in subjects as determined by the State, each targeted assistance program under this section shall—

(A) use such program's resources under this part [20 USCS §§ 6311 et seq.] to help participating children meet such State's challenging student academic achievement standards expected for all children;

(B) ensure that planning for students served under this part [20 USCS §§ 6311 et seq.] is incorporated into existing school planning;

(C) use effective methods and instructional strategies that are based on scientifically based research that strengthens the core academic program of the school and that—

(i) give primary consideration to providing extended learning time, such as an extended school year, before- and after-school, and summer programs and opportunities;

(ii) help provide an accelerated, high-quality curriculum, including applied learning; and

(iii) minimize removing children from the regular classroom during regular school hours for instruction provided under this part [20 USCS §§ 6311 et seq.];

(D) coordinate with and support the regular education program, which may include services to assist preschool children in the transition from early childhood programs such as Head Start, Even Start, Early Reading First or State-run preschool programs to elementary school programs;

(E) provide instruction by highly qualified teachers;

(F) in accordance with subsection (e)(3) and section 1119 [20 USCS § 6319], provide opportunities for professional development with resources provided under this part [20 USCS §§ 6311 et seq.], and, to the extent practicable, from other sources, for teachers, principals, and paraprofessionals, including, if appropriate, pupil services personnel, parents, and other staff, who work with participating children in programs under this section or in the regular education program;

(G) provide strategies to increase parental involvement in accordance with section 1118 [20 USCS § 6318], such as family literacy services; and

(H) coordinate and integrate Federal, State, and local services and programs, including programs supported under this Act [20 USCS §§ 6301 et seq.], violence prevention programs, nutrition programs, housing programs, Head Start, adult education, vocational and technical education, and job training.

(2) Requirements. Each school conducting a program under this section shall assist participating children selected in accordance with subsection (b) to meet the State's proficient and advanced levels of achievement by—

(A) the coordinating of resources provided under this part [20 USCS §§ 6311 et seq.] with other resources; and

(B) reviewing, on an ongoing basis, the progress of participating children and revising the targeted assistance program, if necessary, to provide additional assistance to enable such children to meet the State's challenging student academic achievement standards, such as an extended school year, before- and after-school, and summer programs and opportunities, training for teachers regarding how to identify students who need additional assistance, and training for teachers regarding how to implement student academic achievement standards in the classroom.

(d) Integration of professional development. To promote the integration of staff supported with funds under this part [20 USCS §§ 6311 et seq.] into the regular school program and overall school planning and improvement efforts, public school personnel who are paid with funds received under this part [20 USCS §§ 6311 et seq.] may—

(1) participate in general professional development and school planning activities; and

(2) assume limited duties that are assigned to similar personnel who are not so paid, including duties beyond classroom instruction or that do not benefit participating children, so long as the amount of time spent on such duties is the same proportion of total work time as prevails with respect to similar personnel at the same school.

(e) Special rules.

(1) Simultaneous service. Nothing in this section shall be construed to prohibit a school from serving students under this section simultaneously with students with similar educational needs, in the same educational settings where appropriate.

(2) Comprehensive services. If—

(A) health, nutrition, and other social services are not otherwise available to eligible children in a targeted assistance school and such school, if appropriate, has engaged in a comprehensive needs assessment and established a collaborative partnership with local service providers; and

(B) funds are not reasonably available from other public or private sources to provide such services, then a portion of the funds provided under this part [20 USCS §§ 6311 et seq.] may be used as a last resort to provide such services, including—

(i) the provision of basic medical equipment, such as eyeglasses and hearing aids;

(ii) compensation of a coordinator; and

(iii) professional development necessary to assist teachers, pupil services personnel, other staff, and parents in identifying and meeting the comprehensive needs of eligible children.

(3) Professional development. Each school receiving funds under this part [20 USCS §§ 6311 et seq.] for any fiscal year shall devote sufficient resources to carry out effectively the professional development activities described in subparagraph (F) of subsection (c)(1) in accordance with section 1119 [20 USCS § 6319] for such fiscal year, and a school may enter into a consortium with another school to carry out such activities.

§ 6316. Academic assessment and local educational agency and school improvement

(a) Local review.

(1) In general. Each local educational agency receiving funds under this part [20 USCS §§ 6311 et seq.] shall—

(A) use the State academic assessments and other indicators described in the State plan to review annually the progress of each school served under this part [20 USCS §§ 6311 et seq.] to determine whether the school is making adequate yearly progress as defined in section 1111(b)(2) [20 USCS § 6311(b)(2)];

(B) at the local educational agency's discretion, use any academic assessments or any other academic indicators described in the local educational agency's plan under section 1112(b)(1)(A) and (B) [20 USCS § 6312(b)(1)(A), (B)] to review annually the progress of each school served under this part [20 USCS §§ 6311 et seq.] to determine whether the school is making adequate yearly progress as defined in section 1111(b)(2) [20 USCS § 6311(b)(2)], except that the local educational agency may not use such indicators (other than as provided for in section 1111(b)(2)(I) [20 USCS § 6311(b)(2)(I)]) if the indicators reduce the number or change the schools that would otherwise be subject to school improvement, corrective action, or restructuring under section 1116 [this section] if such additional indicators were not used, but may identify additional schools for school improvement or in need of corrective action or restructuring;

(C) publicize and disseminate the results of the local annual review described in paragraph (1) to parents, teachers, principals, schools, and the community so that the teachers, principals, other staff, and schools can continually refine, in an instructionally useful manner, the program of instruction to help all children served under this part [20 USCS §§ 6311 et seq.] meet the challenging State student academic achievement standards established under section 1111(b)(1) [20 USCS § 6311(b)(1)]; and

(D) review the effectiveness of the actions and activities the schools are carrying out under this part [20 USCS §§ 6311 et seq.] with respect to parental involvement, professional development, and other activities assisted under this part [20 USCS §§ 6311 et seq.].

(2) Available results. The State educational agency shall ensure that the results of State academic assessments administered in that school year are available to the local educational agency before the beginning of the next school year.

(b) School improvement.

(1) General requirements.

(A) Identification. Subject to subparagraph (C), a local educational agency shall identify for school improvement any elementary school or secondary school served under this part [20 USCS §§ 6311 et seq.] that fails, for 2 consecutive years, to make adequate yearly progress as defined in the State's plan under section 1111(b)(2) [20 USCS § 6311(b)(2)].

(B) Deadline. The identification described in subparagraph (A) shall take place before the beginning of the school year following such failure to make adequate yearly progress.

(C) Application. Subparagraph (A) shall not apply to a school if almost every student in each group specified in section 1111(b)(2)(C)(v) [*20 USCS § 6311(b)(2)(C)(v)*] enrolled in such school is meeting or exceeding the State's proficient level of academic achievement.

(D) Targeted assistance schools. To determine if an elementary school or a secondary school that is conducting a targeted assistance program under section 1115 [*20 USCS § 6315*] should be identified for school improvement, corrective action, or restructuring under this section, a local educational agency may choose to review the progress of only the students in the school who are served, or are eligible for services, under this part [*20 USCS §§ 6311* et seq.].

(E) Public school choice.

(i) In general. In the case of a school identified for school improvement under this paragraph, the local educational agency shall, not later than the first day of the school year following such identification, provide all students enrolled in the school with the option to transfer to another public school served by the local educational agency, which may include a public charter school, that has not been identified for school improvement under this paragraph, unless such an option is prohibited by State law.

(ii) Rule. In providing students the option to transfer to another public school, the local educational agency shall give priority to the lowest achieving children from low-income families, as determined by the local educational agency for purposes of allocating funds to schools under section 1113(c)(1) [*20 USCS § 6313(c)(1)*].

(F) Transfer. Students who use the option to transfer under subparagraph (E) and paragraph (5)(A), (7)(C)(i), or (8)(A)(i) or subsection (c)(10)(C)(vii) shall be enrolled in classes and other activities in the public school to which the students transfer in the same manner as all other children at the public school.

(2) Opportunity to review and present evidence; time limit.

(A) Identification. Before identifying an elementary school or a secondary school for school improvement under paragraphs (1) or (5)(A), for corrective action under paragraph (7), or for restructuring under paragraph (8), the local educational agency shall provide the school with an opportunity to review the school-level data, including academic assessment data, on which the proposed identification is based.

(B) Evidence. If the principal of a school proposed for identification under paragraph (1), (5)(A), (7), or (8) believes, or a majority of the parents of the students enrolled in such school believe, that the proposed identification is in error for statistical or other substantive reasons, the principal may provide supporting evidence to the local educational agency, which shall consider that evidence before making a final determination.

(C) Final determination. Not later than 30 days after a local educational agency provides the school with the opportunity to review such school-level data, the local educational agency shall make public a final determination on the status of the school with respect to the identification.

(3) School plan.

(A) Revised plan. After the resolution of a review under paragraph (2), each school identified under paragraph (1) for school improvement shall, not later than 3 months after being so identified, develop or revise a school plan, in consultation with parents, school staff, the local educational agency serving the school, and outside experts, for approval by such local educational agency. The school plan shall cover a 2-year period and—

(i) incorporate strategies based on scientifically based research that will strengthen the core academic subjects in the school and address the specific academic issues that caused the school to be identified for school improvement, and may include a strategy for the implementation of a comprehensive school reform model that includes each of the components described in part F;

(ii) adopt policies and practices concerning the school's core academic subjects that have the greatest likelihood of ensuring that all groups of students specified in section 1111(b)(2)(C)(v) [20 USCS § 6311(b)(2)(C)(v)] and enrolled in the school will meet the State's proficient level of achievement on the State academic assessment described in section 1111(b)(3) [20 USCS § 6311(b)(3)] not later than 12 years after the end of the 2001-2002 school year;

(iii) provide an assurance that the school will spend not less than 10 percent of the funds made available to the school under section 1113 [20 USCS § 6313] for each fiscal year that the school is in school improvement status, for the purpose of providing to the school's teachers and principal high-quality professional development that—

(I) directly addresses the academic achievement problem that caused the school to be identified for school improvement;

(II) meets the requirements for professional development activities under section 1119 [20 USCS § 6319]; and

(III) is provided in a manner that affords increased opportunity for participating in that professional development;

(iv) specify how the funds described in clause (iii) will be used to remove the school from school improvement status;

(v) establish specific annual, measurable objectives for continuous and substantial progress by each group of students specified in section 1111(b)(2)(C)(v) [20 USCS § 6311(b)(2)(C)(v)] and enrolled in the school that will ensure that all such groups of students will, in accordance with adequate yearly progress as defined in section 1111(b)(2) [20 USCS § 6311(b)(2)], meet the State's proficient level of achievement on the State academic assessment described in section 1111(b)(3) [20 USCS § 6311(b)(3)] not later than 12 years after the end of the 2001-2002 school year;

(vi) describe how the school will provide written notice about the identification to parents of each student enrolled in such school, in a format and, to the extent practicable, in a language that the parents can understand;

(vii) specify the responsibilities of the school, the local educational agency, and the State educational agency serving the school under the plan, including the technical assistance to be provided by the local educational agency under paragraph (4) and the local educational agency's responsibilities under section 1120A [20 USCS § 6321];

(viii) include strategies to promote effective parental involvement in the school;

(ix) incorporate, as appropriate, activities before school, after school, during the summer, and during any extension of the school year; and

(x) incorporate a teacher mentoring program.

(B) Conditional approval. The local educational agency may condition approval of a school plan under this paragraph on—

(i) inclusion of one or more of the corrective actions specified in paragraph (7)(C)(iv); or

(ii) feedback on the school improvement plan from parents and community leaders.

(C) Plan implementation. Except as provided in subparagraph (D), a school shall implement the school plan (including a revised plan) expeditiously, but not later than the beginning of the next full school year following the identification under paragraph (1).

(D) Plan approved during school year. Notwithstanding subparagraph (C), if a plan is not approved prior to the beginning of a school year, such plan shall be implemented immediately upon approval.

(E) Local educational agency approval. The local educational agency, within 45 days of receiving a school plan, shall—

(i) establish a peer review process to assist with review of the school plan; and

(ii) promptly review the school plan, work with the school as necessary, and approve the school plan if the plan meets the requirements of this paragraph.

(4) Technical assistance.

(A) In general. For each school identified for school improvement under paragraph (1), the local educational agency serving the school shall ensure the provision of technical assistance as the school develops and implements the school plan under paragraph (3) throughout the plan's duration.

(B) Specific assistance. Such technical assistance—

(i) shall include assistance in analyzing data from the assessments required under section 1111(b)(3) [20 USCS § 6311(b)(3)], and other examples of student work, to identify and address problems in instruction, and problems if any, in implementing the parental involvement requirements described in section 1118 [20 USCS § 6318], the professional development requirements described in section 1119 [20 USCS § 6319], and the responsibilities of the school and local educational agency under the school plan, and to identify and address solutions to such problems;

(ii) shall include assistance in identifying and implementing professional development, instructional strategies, and methods of instruction that are based on scientifically based research and that have proven effective in addressing the specific instructional issues that caused the school to be identified for school improvement;

(iii) shall include assistance in analyzing and revising the school's budget so that the school's resources are more effectively allocated to the activities most likely to increase student academic achievement and to remove the school from school improvement status; and

(iv) may be provided—

(I) by the local educational agency, through mechanisms authorized under section 1117 [20 USCS § 6317]; or

(II) by the State educational agency, an institution of higher education (that is in full compliance with all the reporting provisions of title II of the Higher Education Act of 1965 [20 USCS §§ 1021 et seq.]), a private not-for-profit organization or for-profit organization, an educational service agency, or another entity with experience in helping schools improve academic achievement.

(C) Scientifically based research. Technical assistance provided under this section by a local educational agency or an entity approved by that agency shall be based on scientifically based research.

(5) Failure to make adequate yearly progress after identification. In the case of any school served under this part [20 USCS §§ 6311 et seq.] that fails to make adequate yearly progress, as set out in the State's plan under section 1111(b)(2) [20 USCS § 6311(b)(2)], by the end of the first full school year after identification under paragraph (1), the local educational agency serving such school—

(A) shall continue to provide all students enrolled in the school with the option to transfer to another public school served by the local educational agency in accordance with subparagraphs (E) and (F);

(B) shall make supplemental educational services available consistent with subsection (e)(1); and

(C) shall continue to provide technical assistance.

(6) Notice to parents. A local educational agency shall promptly provide to a parent or parents (in an understandable and uniform format and, to the extent practicable, in a language the parents can understand) of each student enrolled in an elementary school or a secondary school identified for school improvement under paragraph (1), for corrective action under paragraph (7), or for restructuring under paragraph (8)—

(A) an explanation of what the identification means, and how the school compares in terms of academic achievement to other elementary schools or secondary schools served by the local educational agency and the State educational agency involved;

(B) the reasons for the identification;

(C) an explanation of what the school identified for school improvement is doing to address the problem of low achievement;

(D) an explanation of what the local educational agency or State educational agency is doing to help the school address the achievement problem;

(E) an explanation of how the parents can become involved in addressing the academic issues that caused the school to be identified for school improvement; and

(F) an explanation of the parents' option to transfer their child to another public school under paragraphs (1)(E), (5)(A), (7)(C)(i), (8)(A)(i), and subsection (c)(10)(C)(vii) (with transportation provided by the agency when required by paragraph (9)) or to obtain supplemental educational services for the child, in accordance with subsection (e).

(7) Corrective action.

(A) In general. In this subsection, the term "corrective action" means action, consistent with State law, that—

(i) substantially and directly responds to—

(I) the consistent academic failure of a school that caused the local educational agency to take such action; and

(II) any underlying staffing, curriculum, or other problems in the school; and

(ii) is designed to increase substantially the likelihood that each group of students described in 1111(b)(2)(C) [*20 USCS § 6311(b)(2)(C)*] enrolled in the school identified for corrective action will meet or exceed the State's proficient levels of achievement on the State academic assessments described in section 1111(b)(3) [*20 USCS § 6311(b)(3)*].

(B) System. In order to help students served under this part [*20 USCS §§ 6311* et seq.] meet challenging State student academic achievement standards, each local educational agency shall implement a system of corrective action in accordance with subparagraphs (C) through (E).

(C) Role of local educational agency. In the case of any school served by a local educational agency under this part [*20 USCS §§ 6311* et seq.] that fails to make adequate yearly progress, as defined by the State under section 1111(b)(2) [*20 USCS § 6311(b)(2)*], by the end of the second full school year after the identification under paragraph (1), the local educational agency shall—

(i) continue to provide all students enrolled in the school with the option to transfer to another public school served by the local educational agency, in accordance with paragraph (1)(E) and (F);

(ii) continue to provide technical assistance consistent with paragraph (4) while instituting any corrective action under clause (iv);

(iii) continue to make supplemental educational services available, in accordance with subsection (e), to children who remain in the school; and

(iv) identify the school for corrective action and take at least one of the following corrective actions:

(I) Replace the school staff who are relevant to the failure to make adequate yearly progress.

(II) Institute and fully implement a new curriculum, including providing appropriate professional development for all relevant staff, that is based on scientifically based research and offers substantial promise of improving educational achievement for low-achieving students and enabling the school to make adequate yearly progress.

(III) Significantly decrease management authority at the school level.

(IV) Appoint an outside expert to advise the school on its progress toward making adequate yearly progress, based on its school plan under paragraph (3).

(V) Extend the school year or school day for the school.

(VI) Restructure the internal organizational structure of the school.

(D) Delay. Notwithstanding any other provision of this paragraph, the local educational agency may delay, for a period not to exceed 1 year, implementation of the requirements under paragraph (5), corrective action under this paragraph, or restructuring under paragraph (8) if the school makes adequate yearly progress for 1 year or if its failure to make adequate yearly progress is due to exceptional or uncontrollable circumstances, such as a natural disaster or a precipitous and unforeseen decline in the financial resources of the local educational agency or school. No such period shall be taken into account in determining the number of consecutive years of failure to make adequate yearly progress.

(E) Publication and dissemination. The local educational agency shall publish and disseminate information regarding any corrective action the local educational agency takes under this paragraph at a school—

(i) to the public and to the parents of each student enrolled in the school subject to corrective action;

(ii) in an understandable and uniform format and, to the extent practicable, provided in a language that the parents can understand; and

(iii) through such means as the Internet, the media, and public agencies.

(8) Restructuring.

(A) Failure to make adequate yearly progress. If, after 1 full school year of corrective action under paragraph (7), a school subject to such corrective action continues to fail to make adequate yearly progress, then the local educational agency shall—

(i) continue to provide all students enrolled in the school with the option to transfer to another public school served by the local educational agency, in accordance with paragraph (1)(E) and (F);

(ii) continue to make supplemental educational services available, in accordance with subsection (e), to children who remain in the school; and

(iii) prepare a plan and make necessary arrangements to carry out subparagraph (B).

(B) Alternative governance. Not later than the beginning of the school year following the year in which the local educational agency implements subparagraph (A), the local educational agency shall implement one of the following alternative governance arrangements for the school consistent with State law:

(i) Reopening the school as a public charter school.

(ii) Replacing all or most of the school staff (which may include the principal) who are relevant to the failure to make adequate yearly progress.

(iii) Entering into a contract with an entity, such as a private management company, with a demonstrated record of effectiveness, to operate the public school.

(iv) Turning the operation of the school over to the State educational agency, if permitted under State law and agreed to by the State.

(v) Any other major restructuring of the school's governance arrangement that makes fundamental reforms, such as significant changes in the school's staffing and governance, to improve student academic achievement in the school and that has substantial promise of enabling the school to make adequate yearly progress as defined in the State plan under section 1111(b)(2) [*20 USCS § 6311(b)(2)*]. In the case of a rural local educational agency with a total of less than 600 students in average daily attendance at the schools that are served by the agency and all of whose schools have a School Locale Code of 7 or 8, as determined by the Secretary, the Secretary shall, at such agency's request, provide technical assistance to such agency for the purpose of implementing this clause.

(C) Prompt notice. The local educational agency shall—

(i) provide prompt notice to teachers and parents whenever subparagraph (A) or (B) applies; and

(ii) provide the teachers and parents with an adequate opportunity to—

(I) comment before taking any action under those subparagraphs; and

(II) participate in developing any plan under subparagraph (A)(iii).

(9) Transportation. In any case described in paragraph (1)(E) for schools described in paragraphs (1)(A), (5), (7)(C)(i), and (8)(A), and subsection (c)(10)(C)(vii), the local educational agency shall provide, or shall pay for the provision of, transportation for the student to the public school the student attends.

(10) Funds for transportation and supplemental educational services.

(A) In general. Unless a lesser amount is needed to comply with paragraph (9) and to satisfy all requests for supplemental educational services under subsection (e), a local educational agency shall spend an amount equal to 20 percent of its allocation under subpart 2 [*20 USCS §§ 6331 et seq.*], from which the agency shall spend—

(i) an amount equal to 5 percent of its allocation under subpart 2 [*20 USCS §§ 6331 et seq.*] to provide, or pay for, transportation under paragraph (9);

(ii) an amount equal to 5 percent of its allocation under subpart 2 [*20 USCS §§ 6331 et seq.*] to provide supplemental educational services under subsection (e); and

(iii) an amount equal to the remaining 10 percent of its allocation under subpart 2 [*20 USCS §§ 6331 et seq.*] for transportation under paragraph (9), supplemental educational services under subsection (e), or both, as the agency determines.

(B) Total amount. The total amount described in subparagraph (A)(ii) is the maximum amount the local educational agency shall be required to spend under this part [*20 USCS §§ 6311 et seq.*] on supplemental educational services described in subsection (e).

(C) Insufficient funds. If the amount of funds described in subparagraph (A)(ii) or (iii) and available to provide services under this subsection is insufficient to provide supplemental educational services to each child whose parents request the services, the local educational agency shall give priority to providing the services to the lowest-achieving children.

(D) Prohibition. A local educational agency shall not, as a result of the application of this paragraph, reduce by more than 15 percent the total amount made available under section 1113(c) [20 USCS § 6313(c)] to a school described in paragraph (7)(C) or (8)(A) of subsection (b).

(11) Cooperative agreement. In any case described in paragraph (1)(E), (5)(A), (7)(C)(i), or (8)(A)(i), or subsection (c)(10)(C)(vii) if all public schools served by the local educational agency to which a child may transfer are identified for school improvement, corrective action or restructuring, the agency shall, to the extent practicable, establish a cooperative agreement with other local educational agencies in the area for a transfer.

(12) Duration. If any school identified for school improvement, corrective action, or restructuring makes adequate yearly progress for two consecutive school years, the local educational agency shall no longer subject the school to the requirements of school improvement, corrective action, or restructuring or identify the school for school improvement for the succeeding school year.

(13) Special rule. A local educational agency shall permit a child who transferred to another school under this subsection to remain in that school until the child has completed the highest grade in that school. The obligation of the local educational agency to provide, or to provide for, transportation for the child ends at the end of a school year if the local educational agency determines that the school from which the child transferred is no longer identified for school improvement or subject to corrective action or restructuring.

(14) State educational agency responsibilities. The State educational agency shall—

(A) make technical assistance under section 1117 [20 USCS § 6317] available to schools identified for school improvement, corrective action, or restructuring under this subsection consistent with section 1117(a)(2) [20 USCS § 6317(a)(2)];

(B) if the State educational agency determines that a local educational agency failed to carry out its responsibilities under this subsection, take such corrective actions as the State educational agency determines to be appropriate and in compliance with State law;

(C) ensure that academic assessment results under this part [20 USCS §§ 6311 et seq.] are provided to schools before any identification of a school may take place under this subsection; and

(D) for local educational agencies or schools identified for improvement under this subsection, notify the Secretary of major factors that were brought to the attention of the State educational agency under section 1111(b)(9) [20 USCS § 6311(b)(9)] that have significantly affected student academic achievement.

(c) State review and local educational agency improvement.

(1) In general. A State shall—

(A) annually review the progress of each local educational agency receiving funds under this part [20 USCS §§ 6311 et seq.] to determine whether schools receiving assistance under this part [20 USCS §§ 6311 et seq.] are making adequate yearly progress as defined in section 1111(b)(2) [20 USCS § 6311(b)(2)] toward meeting the State's student academic achievement standards and to determine if each local educational agency is carrying out its responsibilities under this section and sections 1117, 1118, and 1119 [20 USCS §§ 6317, 6318, 6319]; and

(B) publicize and disseminate to local educational agencies, teachers and other staff, parents, students, and the community the results of the State review, including statistically sound disaggregated results, as required by section 1111(b)(2) [20 USCS § 6311(b)(2)].

(2) Rewards. In the case of a local educational agency that, for 2 consecutive years, has exceeded adequate yearly progress as defined in the State plan under section 1111(b)(2) [20 USCS § 6311(b)(2)], the State may make rewards of the kinds described under section 1117 [20 USCS § 6317] to the agency.

(3) Identification of local educational agency for improvement. A State shall identify for improvement any local educational agency that, for 2 consecutive years, including the period immediately prior to the date of enactment of the No Child Left Behind Act of 2001 [enacted Jan. 8, 2002], failed to make adequate yearly progress as defined in the State's plan under section 1111(b)(2) [20 USCS § 6311(b)(2)].

(4) Targeted assistance schools. When reviewing targeted assistance schools served by a local educational agency, a State educational agency may choose to review the progress of only the students in such schools who are served, or are eligible for services, under this part [20 USCS §§ 6311 et seq.].

(5) Opportunity to review and present evidence.

(A) Review. Before identifying a local educational agency for improvement under paragraph (3) or corrective action under paragraph (10), a State educational agency shall provide the local educational agency with an opportunity to review the data, including academic assessment data, on which the proposed identification is based.

(B) Evidence. If the local educational agency believes that the proposed identification is in error for statistical or other substantive reasons, the agency may provide supporting evidence to the State educational agency, which shall consider the evidence before making a final determination not later than 30 days after the State educational agency provides the local educational agency with the opportunity to review such data under subparagraph (A).

(6) Notification to parents. The State educational agency shall promptly provide to the parents (in a format and, to the extent practicable, in a language the parents can understand) of each student enrolled in a school served by a local educational agency identified for improvement, the results of the review under paragraph (1) and, if the agency is identified for improvement, the reasons for that identification and how parents can participate in upgrading the quality of the local educational agency.

(7) Local educational agency revisions.

(A) Plan. Each local educational agency identified under paragraph (3) shall, not later than 3 months after being so identified, develop or revise a local educational agency plan, in consultation with parents, school staff, and others. Such plan shall—

(i) incorporate scientifically based research strategies that strengthen the core academic program in schools served by the local educational agency;

(ii) identify actions that have the greatest likelihood of improving the achievement of participating children in meeting the State's student academic achievement standards;

(iii) address the professional development needs of the instructional staff serving the agency by committing to spend not less than 10 percent of the funds received by the local educational agency under subpart 2 [20 USCS §§ 6331 et seq.] for each fiscal year in which the agency is identified for improvement for professional development (including funds reserved for professional development under subsection (b)(3)(A)(iii)), but excluding funds reserved for professional development under section 1119 [20 USCS § 6319];

(iv) include specific measurable achievement goals and targets for each of the groups of students identified in the disaggregated data pursuant to section 1111(b)(2)(C)(v) [20 USCS § 6311(b)(2)(C)(v)], consistent with adequate yearly progress as defined under section 1111(b)(2) [20 USCS § 6311(b)(2)];

(v) address the fundamental teaching and learning needs in the schools of that agency, and the specific academic problems of low-achieving students, including a determination of why the local educational agency's prior plan failed to bring about increased student academic achievement;

(vi) incorporate, as appropriate, activities before school, after school, during the summer, and during an extension of the school year;

(vii) specify the responsibilities of the State educational agency and the local educational agency under the plan, including specifying the technical assistance to be provided by the State educational agency under paragraph (9) and the local educational agency's responsibilities under section 1120A [20 USCS § 6321]; and

(viii) include strategies to promote effective parental involvement in the school.

(B) Implementation. The local educational agency shall implement the plan (including a revised plan) expeditiously, but not later than the beginning of the next school year after the school year in which the agency was identified for improvement.

[(8)](9) State educational agency responsibility.

(A) Technical or other assistance. For each local educational agency identified under paragraph (3), the State educational agency shall provide technical or other assistance if requested, as authorized under section 1117 [20 USCS § 6317], to better enable the local educational agency to—

(i) develop and implement the local educational agency's plan; and

(ii) work with schools needing improvement.

(B) Methods and strategies. Technical assistance provided under this section by the State educational agency or an entity authorized by such agency shall be supported by effective methods and instructional strategies based on scientifically based research. Such technical assistance shall address problems, if any, in implementing the parental involvement activities described in section 1118 [20 USCS § 6318] and the professional development activities described in section 1119 [20 USCS § 6319].

[(9)](10) Corrective action. In order to help students served under this part [20 USCS §§ 6311 et seq.] meet challenging State student academic achievement standards, each State shall implement a system of corrective action in accordance with the following:

(A) Definition. As used in this paragraph, the term "corrective action" means action, consistent with State law, that—

(i) substantially and directly responds to the consistent academic failure that caused the State to take such action and to any underlying staffing, curricular, or other problems in the agency; and

(ii) is designed to meet the goal of having all students served under this part [20 USCS §§ 6311 et seq.] achieve at the proficient and advanced student academic achievement levels.

(B) General requirements. After providing technical assistance under paragraph (9) and subject to subparagraph (E), the State—

(i) may take corrective action at any time with respect to a local educational agency that has been identified under paragraph (3);

(ii) shall take corrective action with respect to any local educational agency that fails to make adequate yearly progress, as defined by the State, by the end of the second full school year after the identification of the agency under paragraph (3); and

(iii) shall continue to provide technical assistance while instituting any corrective action under clause (i) or (ii).

(C) Certain corrective actions required. In the case of a local educational agency identified for corrective action, the State educational agency shall take at least one of the following corrective actions:

(i) Deferring programmatic funds or reducing administrative funds.

(ii) Instituting and fully implementing a new curriculum that is based on State and local academic content and achievement standards, including providing appropriate professional development based on scientifically based research for all relevant staff, that offers substantial promise of improving educational achievement for low-achieving students.

(iii) Replacing the local educational agency personnel who are relevant to the failure to make adequate yearly progress.

(iv) Removing particular schools from the jurisdiction of the local educational agency and establishing alternative arrangements for public governance and supervision of such schools.

(v) Appointing, through the State educational agency, a receiver or trustee to administer the affairs of the local educational agency in place of the superintendent and school board.

(vi) Abolishing or restructuring the local educational agency.

(vii) Authorizing students to transfer from a school operated by the local educational agency to a higher-performing public school operated by another local educational agency in accordance with subsections [subsection] (b)(1)(E) and (F), and providing to such students transportation (or the costs of transportation) to such schools consistent with subsection (b)(9), in conjunction with carrying out not less than one additional action described under this subparagraph.

(D) Hearing. Prior to implementing any corrective action under this paragraph, the State educational agency shall provide notice and a hearing to the affected local educational agency, if State law provides for such notice and hearing. The hearing shall take place not later than 45 days following the decision to implement corrective action.

(E) Notice to parents. The State educational agency shall publish, and disseminate to parents and the public, information on any corrective action the State educational agency takes under this paragraph through such means as the Internet, the media, and public agencies.

(F) Delay. Notwithstanding subparagraph (B)(ii), a State educational agency may delay, for a period not to exceed 1 year, implementation of corrective action under this paragraph if the local educational agency makes adequate yearly progress for 1 year or its failure to make adequate yearly progress is due to exceptional or uncontrollable circumstances, such as a natural disaster or a precipitous and unforeseen decline in the financial resources of the local educational agency. No such period shall be taken into account in determining the number of consecutive years of failure to make adequate yearly progress.

[(10)](11) Special rule. If a local educational agency makes adequate yearly progress for two consecutive school years beginning after the date of identification of the agency under paragraph (3), the State educational agency need no longer identify the local educational agency for improvement or subject the local educational agency to corrective action for the succeeding school year.

(d) Construction. Nothing in this section shall be construed to alter or otherwise affect the rights, remedies, and procedures afforded school or school district employees under Federal, State, or local laws (including applicable regulations or court orders) or under the terms of collective bargaining agreements, memoranda of understanding, or other agreements between such employees and their employers.

(e) Supplemental educational services.

(1) Supplemental educational services. In the case of any school described in paragraph (5), (7), or (8) of subsection (b), the local educational agency serving such school shall, subject to this subsection, arrange for the provision of supplemental educational services to eligible children in the school from a provider with a demonstrated record of effectiveness, that is selected by the parents and approved for that purpose by the State educational agency in accordance with reasonable criteria, consistent with paragraph (5), that the State educational agency shall adopt.

(2) Local educational agency responsibilities. Each local educational agency subject to this subsection shall—

(A) provide, at a minimum, annual notice to parents (in an understandable and uniform format and, to the extent practicable, in a language the parents can understand) of—

(i) the availability of services under this subsection;

(ii) the identity of approved providers of those services that are within the local educational agency or whose services are reasonably available in neighboring local educational agencies; and

(iii) a brief description of the services, qualifications, and demonstrated effectiveness of each such provider;

(B) if requested, assist parents in choosing a provider from the list of approved providers maintained by the State;

(C) apply fair and equitable procedures for serving students if the number of spaces at approved providers is not sufficient to serve all students; and

(D) not disclose to the public the identity of any student who is eligible for, or receiving, supplemental educational services under this subsection without the written permission of the parents of the student.

(3) Agreement. In the case of the selection of an approved provider by a parent, the local educational agency shall enter into an agreement with such provider. Such agreement shall—

(A) require the local educational agency to develop, in consultation with parents (and the provider chosen by the parents), a statement of specific achievement goals for the student, how the student's progress will be measured, and a timetable for improving achievement that, in the case of a student with disabilities, is consistent with the student's individualized education program under section 614(d) of the Individuals with Disabilities Education Act [*20 USCS § 1414(d)*];

(B) describe how the student's parents and the student's teacher or teachers will be regularly informed of the student's progress;

(C) provide for the termination of such agreement if the provider is unable to meet such goals and timetables;

(D) contain provisions with respect to the making of payments to the provider by the local educational agency; and

(E) prohibit the provider from disclosing to the public the identity of any student eligible for, or receiving, supplemental educational services under this subsection without the written permission of the parents of such student.

(4) State educational agency responsibilities. A State educational agency shall—

(A) in consultation with local educational agencies, parents, teachers, and other interested members of the public, promote maximum participation by providers to ensure, to the extent practicable, that parents have as many choices as possible;

(B) develop and apply objective criteria, consistent with paragraph (5), to potential providers that are based on a demonstrated record of effectiveness in increasing the academic proficiency of students in subjects relevant to meeting the State academic content and student achievement standards adopted under section 1111(b)(1) [*20 USCS § 6311(b)(1)*];

(C) maintain an updated list of approved providers across the State, by school district, from which parents may select;

(D) develop, implement, and publicly report on standards and techniques for monitoring the quality and effectiveness of the services offered by approved providers under this subsection, and for withdrawing approval from providers that fail, for 2 consecutive years, to contribute to increasing the academic proficiency of students served under this subsection as described in subparagraph (B); and

(E) provide annual notice to potential providers of supplemental educational services of the opportunity to provide services under this subsection and of the applicable procedures for obtaining approval from the State educational agency to be an approved provider of those services.

(5) Criteria for providers. In order for a provider to be included on the State list under paragraph (4)(C), a provider shall agree to carry out the following:

(A) Provide parents of children receiving supplemental educational services under this subsection and the appropriate local educational agency with information on the progress of the children in increasing achievement, in a format and, to the extent practicable, a language that such parents can understand.

(B) Ensure that instruction provided and content used by the provider are consistent with the instruction provided and content used by the local educational agency and State, and are aligned with State student academic achievement standards.

(C) Meet all applicable Federal, State, and local health, safety, and civil rights laws.

(D) Ensure that all instruction and content under this subsection are secular, neutral, and nonideological.

(6) Amounts for supplemental educational services. The amount that a local educational agency shall make available for supplemental educational services for each child receiving those services under this subsection shall be the lesser of—

(A) the amount of the agency's allocation under subpart 2 [*20 USCS §§ 6331 et seq.*], divided by the number of children from families below the poverty level counted under section 1124(c)(1)(A) [*20 USCS § 6333(c)(1)(A)*]; or

(B) the actual costs of the supplemental educational services received by the child.

(7) Funds provided by state educational agency. Each State educational agency may use funds that the agency reserves under this part [*20 USCS §§ 6311 et seq.*], and part A of title V [*20 USCS §§ 7201 et seq.*], to assist local educational agencies that do not have sufficient funds to provide services under this subsection for all eligible students requesting such services.

(8) Duration. The local educational agency shall continue to provide supplemental educational services to a child receiving such services under this subsection until the end of the school year in which such services were first received.

(9) Prohibition. Nothing contained in this subsection shall permit the making of any payment for religious worship or instruction.

(10) Waiver.

(A) Requirement. At the request of a local educational agency, a State educational agency may waive, in whole or in part, the requirement of this subsection to provide supplemental educational services if the State educational agency determines that—

(i) none of the providers of those services on the list approved by the State educational agency under paragraph (4)(C) makes those services available in the area served by the local educational agency or within a reasonable distance of that area; and

(ii) the local educational agency provides evidence that it is not able to provide those services.

(B) Notification. The State educational agency shall notify the local educational agency, within 30 days of receiving the local educational agency's request for a waiver under subparagraph (A), whether the request is approved or disapproved and, if disapproved, the reasons for the disapproval, in writing.

(11) Special rule. If State law prohibits a State educational agency from carrying out one or more of its responsibilities under paragraph (4) with respect to those who provide, or seek approval to provide, supplemental educational services, each local educational agency in the State shall carry out those responsibilities with respect to its students who are eligible for those services.

(12) Definitions. In this subsection—

(A) the term "eligible child" means a child from a low-income family, as determined by the local educational agency for purposes of allocating funds to schools under section 1113(c)(1) [20 USCS § 6313(c)(1)];

(B) the term "provider" means a non-profit entity, a for-profit entity, or a local educational agency that—

(i) has a demonstrated record of effectiveness in increasing student academic achievement;

(ii) is capable of providing supplemental educational services that are consistent with the instructional program of the local educational agency and the academic standards described under section 1111 [20 USCS § 6311]; and

(iii) is financially sound; and

(C) the term "supplemental educational services" means tutoring and other supplemental academic enrichment services that are—

(i) in addition to instruction provided during the school day; and

(ii) are of high quality, research-based, and specifically designed to increase the academic achievement of eligible children on the academic assessments required under section 1111 [20 USCS § 6311] and attain proficiency in meeting the State's academic achievement standards.

(f) Schools and LEAs previously identified for improvement or corrective action.

(1) Schools.

(A) School improvement.

(i) Schools in school-improvement status before date of enactment. Any school that was in the first year of school improvement status under this section on the day preceding the date of enactment of the No Child Left Behind Act of 2001 [enacted Jan. 8, 2002] (as this section was in effect on such day) shall be treated by the local educational agency as a school that is in the first year of school improvement status under paragraph (1).

(ii) Schools in school-improvement status for 2 or more years before date of enactment. Any school that was in school improvement status under this section for two or more consecutive school years preceding the date of enactment of the No Child Left Behind Act of 2001 [enacted Jan. 8, 2002] (as this section was in effect on such day) shall be treated by the local educational agency as a school described in subsection (b)(5).

(B) Corrective action. Any school that was in corrective action status under this section on the day preceding the date of enactment of the No Child Left Behind Act of 2001 [enacted Jan. 8, 2002] (as this section was in effect on such day) shall be treated by the local educational agency as a school described in paragraph (7).

(2) LEAs.

(A) LEA improvement. A State shall identify for improvement under subsection (c)(3) any local educational agency that was in improvement status under this section as this section was in effect on the day preceding the date of enactment of the No Child Left Behind Act of 2001 [enacted Jan. 8, 2002].

(B) Corrective action. A State shall identify for corrective action under subsection (c)(10) any local educational agency that was in corrective action status under this section as this section was in effect on the day preceding the date of enactment of the No Child Left Behind Act of 2001 [enacted Jan. 8, 2002].

(C) Special rule. For the schools and other local educational agencies described under paragraphs (1) and (2), as required, the State shall ensure that public school choice in accordance with subparagraphs (b)(1)(E) and (F) and supplemental education services in accordance with subsection (e) are provided not later than the first day of the 2002-2003 school year.

(D) Transition. With respect to a determination that a local educational agency has for 2 consecutive years failed to make adequate yearly progress as defined in the State plan under section 1111(b)(2) [20 USCS § 6311(b)(2)], such determination shall include in such 2-year period any continuous period of time immediately preceding the date of enactment of the No Child Left Behind Act of 2001 [enacted Jan. 8, 2002] during which the agency has failed to make such progress.

(g) Schools funded by the Bureau of Indian Affairs.

(1) Adequate yearly progress for Bureau funded schools.

(A) Development of definition.

(i) Definition. The Secretary of the Interior, in consultation with the Secretary if the Secretary of Interior requests the consultation, using the process set out in section 1138(b) of the Education Amendments of 1978 [25 USCS § 2018(b)], shall define adequate yearly progress, consistent with section 1111(b) [20 USCS § 6311(b)], for the schools funded by the Bureau of Indian Affairs on a regional or tribal basis, as appropriate, taking into account the unique circumstances and needs of such schools and the students served by such schools.

(ii) Use of definition. The Secretary of the Interior, consistent with clause (i), may use the definition of adequate yearly progress that the State in which the school that is funded by the Bureau is located uses consistent with section 1111(b) [20 USCS § 6311(b)], or in the case of schools that are located in more than one State, the Secretary of the Interior may use whichever State definition of adequate yearly progress that best meets the unique circumstances and needs of such school or schools and the students the schools serve.

(B) Waiver. The tribal governing body or school board of a school funded by the Bureau of Indian Affairs may waive, in part or in whole, the definition of adequate yearly progress established pursuant to paragraph (A) where such definition is determined by such body or school board to be inappropriate. If such definition is waived, the tribal governing body or school board shall, within 60 days thereafter, submit to the Secretary of Interior a proposal for an alternative definition of adequate yearly progress, consistent with section 1111(b) [20 USCS § 6311(b)], that takes into account the unique circumstances and needs of such school or schools and the students served. The Secretary of the Interior, in consultation with the Secretary if the Secretary of Interior requests the consultation, shall approve such alternative definition unless the Secretary determines that the definition does not meet the requirements of section 1111(b) [*20 USCS § 6311(b)*], taking into account the unique circumstances and needs of such school or schools and the students served.

(C) Technical assistance. The Secretary of Interior shall, in consultation with the Secretary if the Secretary of Interior requests the consultation, either directly or through a contract, provide technical assistance, upon request, to a tribal governing body or school board of a school funded by the Bureau of Indian Affairs that seeks to develop an alternative definition of adequate yearly progress.

(2) Accountability for BIA schools. For the purposes of this section, schools funded by the Bureau of Indian Affairs shall be considered schools subject to subsection (b), as specifically provided for in this subsection, except that such schools shall not be subject to subsection (c), or the requirements to provide public school choice and supplemental educational services under subsections (b) and (e).

(3) School improvement for Bureau schools.

(A) Contract and grant schools. For a school funded by the Bureau of Indian Affairs which is operated under a contract issued by the Secretary of the Interior pursuant to the Indian Self-Determination Act (*25 U.S.C. 450* et seq.) or under a grant issued by the Secretary of the Interior pursuant to the Tribally Controlled Schools Act of 1988 (*25 U.S.C. 2501* et seq.), the school board of such school shall be responsible for meeting the requirements of subsection (b) relating to development and implementation of any school improvement plan as described in subsections (b)(1) through (b)(3), and subsection (b)(5), other than subsection (b)(1)(E). The Bureau of Indian Affairs shall be responsible for meeting the requirements of subsection (b)(4) relating to technical assistance.

(B) Bureau operated schools. For schools operated by the Bureau of Indian Affairs, the Bureau shall be responsible for meeting the requirements of subsection (b) relating to development and implementation of any school improvement plan as described in subsections (b)(1) through (b)(5), other than subsection (b)(1)(E).

(4) Corrective action and restructuring for Bureau-funded schools.

(A) Contract and grant schools. For a school funded by the Bureau of Indian Affairs which is operated under a contract issued by the Secretary of the Interior pursuant to the Indian Self-Determination Act (*25 U.S.C. 450* et seq.) or under a grant issued by the Secretary of the Interior pursuant to the Tribally Controlled Schools Act of 1988 (*25 U.S.C. 2501* et seq.), the school board of such school shall be responsible for meeting the requirements of subsection (b) relating to corrective action and restructuring as described in subsection (b)(7) and (b)(8). Any action taken by such school board under subsection (b)(7) or (b)(8) shall take into account the unique circumstances and structure of the Bureau of Indian Affairs-funded school system and the laws governing that system.

(B) Bureau operated schools. For schools operated by the Bureau of Indian Affairs, the Bureau shall be responsible for meeting the requirements of subsection (b) relating to corrective action and restructuring as described in subsection (b)(7) and (b)(8). Any action taken by the Bureau under subsection (b)(7) or (b)(8) shall take into account the unique circumstances and structure of the Bureau of Indian Affairs-funded school system and the laws governing that system.

(5) Annual report. On an annual basis, the Secretary of the Interior shall report to the Secretary of Education and to the appropriate committees of Congress regarding any schools funded by the Bureau of Indian Affairs which have been identified for school improvement. Such report shall include—

(A) the identity of each school;

(B) a statement from each affected school board regarding the factors that lead to such identification; and

(C) an analysis by the Secretary of the Interior, in consultation with the Secretary if the Secretary of Interior requests the consultation, as to whether sufficient resources were available to enable such school to achieve adequate yearly progress.

(h) Other agencies. After receiving the notice described in subsection (b)(14)(D), the Secretary may notify, to the extent feasible and necessary as determined by the Secretary, other relevant Federal agencies regarding the major factors that were determined by the State educational agency to have significantly affected student academic achievement.

§ 6317. School support and recognition

(a) System for support.

(1) In general. Each State shall establish a statewide system of intensive and sustained support and improvement for local educational agencies and schools receiving funds under this part [20 USCS §§ 6311 et seq.], in order to increase the opportunity for all students served by those agencies and schools to meet the State's academic content standards and student academic achievement standards.

(2) Priorities. In carrying out this subsection, a State shall—

(A) first, provide support and assistance to local educational agencies with schools subject to corrective action under section 1116 [20 USCS § 6316] and assist those schools, in accordance with section 1116(b)(11) [20 USCS § 6316(b)(11)], for which a local educational agency has failed to carry out its responsibilities under paragraphs (7) and (8) of section 1116(b) [20 USCS § 6316(b)];

(B) second, provide support and assistance to other local educational agencies with schools identified as in need of improvement under section 1116(b) [20 USCS § 6316(b)]; and

(C) third, provide support and assistance to other local educational agencies and schools participating under this part [20 USCS §§ 6311 et seq.] that need that support and assistance in order to achieve the purpose of this part [20 USCS §§ 6311 et seq.].

(3) Regional centers. Such a statewide system shall, to the extent practicable, work with and receive support and assistance from regional educational laboratories established under part D of the Education Sciences Reform Act of 2002 [20 USCS §§ 9561 et seq.] and comprehensive centers established under the Educational Technical Assistance Act of 2002 [20 USCS §§ 9601 et seq.] and the comprehensive regional technical assistance centers and the regional educational laboratories under section 941(h) of the Educational Research, Development, Dissemination, and Improvement Act of 1994 [20 USCS § 6041(h)] (as such section existed on the day before the date of enactment of the Education Sciences Reform Act of 2002 [enacted Nov. 5, 2002]), or other providers of technical assistance.

(4) Statewide system.

(A) In order to achieve the purpose described in paragraph (1), the statewide system shall include, at a minimum, the following approaches:

(i) Establishing school support teams in accordance with subparagraph (C) for assignment to, and working in, schools in the State that are described in paragraph (2).

(ii) Providing such support as the State educational agency determines necessary and available in order to ensure the effectiveness of such teams.

(iii) Designating and using distinguished teachers and principals who are chosen from schools served under this part [20 USCS §§ 6311 et seq.] that have been especially successful in improving academic achievement.

(iv) Devising additional approaches to providing the assistance described in paragraph (1), such as providing assistance through institutions of higher education and educational service agencies or other local consortia, and private providers of scientifically based technical assistance.

(B) Priority. The State educational agency shall give priority to the approach described in clause (i) of subparagraph (A).

(5) School support teams.

(A) Composition. Each school support team established under this section shall be composed of persons knowledgeable about scientifically based research and practice on teaching and learning and about successful schoolwide projects, school reform, and improving educational opportunities for low-achieving students, including—

(i) highly qualified or distinguished teachers and principals;

(ii) pupil services personnel;

(iii) parents;

(iv) representatives of institutions of higher education;

(v) representatives of regional educational laboratories or comprehensive regional technical assistance centers;

(vi) representatives of outside consultant groups; or

(vii) other individuals as the State educational agency, in consultation with the local educational agency, may determine appropriate.

(B) Functions. Each school support team assigned to a school under this section shall—

(i) review and analyze all facets of the school's operation, including the design and operation of the instructional program, and assist the school in developing recommendations for improving student performance in that school;

(ii) collaborate with parents and school staff and the local educational agency serving the school in the design, implementation, and monitoring of a plan that, if fully implemented, can reasonably be expected to improve student performance and help the school meet its goals for improvement, including adequate yearly progress under section 1111(b)(2)(B) [20 USCS § 6311(b)(2)(B)];

(iii) evaluate, at least semiannually, the effectiveness of school personnel assigned to the school, including identifying outstanding teachers and principals, and make findings and recommendations to the school, the local educational agency, and, where appropriate, the State educational agency; and

(iv) make additional recommendations as the school implements the plan described in clause (ii) to the local educational agency and the State educational agency concerning additional assistance that is needed by the school or the school support team.

(C) Continuation of assistance. After one school year, from the beginning of the activities, such school support team, in consultation with the local educational agency, may recommend that the school support team continue to provide assistance to the school, or that the local educational agency or the State educational agency, as appropriate, take alternative actions with regard to the school.

(b) State recognition.

(1) Academic achievement awards program.

(A) In general. Each State receiving a grant under this part [20 USCS §§ 6311 et seq.]—

(i) shall establish a program for making academic achievement awards to recognize schools that meet the criteria described in subparagraph (B); and

(ii) as appropriate and as funds are available under subsection (c)(2)(A), may financially reward schools served under this part [20 USCS §§ 6311 et seq.] that meet the criteria described in clause (ii).

(B) Criteria. The criteria referred to in subparagraph (A) are that a school—

(i) significantly closed the achievement gap between the groups of students described in section 1111(b)(2) [20 USCS § 6311(b)(2)]; or

(ii) exceeded their adequate yearly progress, consistent with section 1111(b)(2) [20 USCS § 6311(b)(2)], for 2 or more consecutive years.

(2) Distinguished schools. Of those schools meeting the criteria described in paragraph (2), each State shall designate as distinguished schools those schools that have made the greatest gains in closing the achievement gap as described in subparagraph (B)(i) or exceeding adequate yearly progress as described in subparagraph (B)(ii). Such distinguished schools may serve as models for and provide support to other schools, especially schools identified for improvement under section 1116 [20 USCS § 6316], to assist such schools in meeting the State's academic content standards and student academic achievement standards.

(3) Awards to teachers. A State program under paragraph (1) may also recognize and provide financial awards to teachers teaching in a school described in such paragraph that consistently makes significant gains in academic achievement in the areas in which the teacher provides instruction, or to teachers or principals designated as distinguished under subsection (a)(4)(A)(iii).

(c) Funding.

(1) In general. Each State—

(A) shall use funds reserved under section 1003(a) [20 USCS § 6303(a)] and may use funds made available under section 1003(g) [20 USCS § 6303(g)] for the approaches described under subsection (a)(4)(A); and

(B) shall use State administrative funds authorized under section 1004(a) [20 USCS § 6304(a)] to establish the statewide system of support described under subsection (a).

(2) Reservations of funds by State.

(A) Awards program. For the purpose of carrying out subsection (b)(1), each State receiving a grant under this part [20 USCS §§ 6311 et seq.] may reserve, from the amount (if any) by which the funds received by the State under subpart 2 [20 USCS §§ 6331 et seq.] for a fiscal year exceed the amount received by the State under that subpart for the preceding fiscal year, not more than 5 percent of such excess amount.

(B) Teacher awards. For the purpose of carrying out subsection (b)(3), a State educational agency may reserve such funds as necessary from funds made available under section 2113 [20 USCS § 6613].

(3) Use within 3 years. Notwithstanding any other provision of law, the amount reserved under subparagraph (A) by a State for each fiscal year shall remain available to the State until expended for a period not exceeding 3 years receipt of funds.

(4) Special allocation rule for schools in high-poverty areas.

(A) In general. Each State shall distribute not less than 75 percent of any amount reserved under paragraph (2)(A) for each fiscal year to schools described in subparagraph (B), or to teachers in those schools consistent with subsection (b)(3).

(B) School described. A school described in subparagraph (A) is a school whose student population is in the highest quartile of schools statewide in terms of the percentage of children from low income families.

§ 6318. Parental involvement

(a) Local educational agency policy.

(1) In general. A local educational agency may receive funds under this part [20 USCS §§ 6311 et seq.] only if such agency implements programs, activities, and procedures for the involvement of parents in programs assisted under this part [20 USCS §§ 6311 et seq.] consistent with this section. Such programs, activities, and procedures shall be planned and implemented with meaningful consultation with parents of participating children.

(2) Written policy. Each local educational agency that receives funds under this part [20 USCS §§ 6311 et seq.] shall develop jointly with, agree on with, and distribute to, parents of participating children a written parent involvement policy. The policy shall be incorporated into the local educational agency's plan developed under section 1112 [20 USCS § 6312], establish the agency's expectations for parent involvement, and describe how the agency will—

(A) involve parents in the joint development of the plan under section 1112 [20 USCS § 6312], and the process of school review and improvement under section 1116 [20 USCS § 6316];

(B) provide the coordination, technical assistance, and other support necessary to assist participating schools in planning and implementing effective parent involvement activities to improve student academic achievement and school performance;

(C) build the schools' and parents' capacity for strong parental involvement as described in subsection (e);

(D) coordinate and integrate parental involvement strategies under this part [20 USCS §§ 6311 et seq.] with parental involvement strategies under other programs, such as the Head Start program, Reading First program, Early Reading First program, Even Start program, Parents as Teachers program, and Home Instruction Program for Preschool Youngsters, and State-run preschool programs;

(E) conduct, with the involvement of parents, an annual evaluation of the content and effectiveness of the parental involvement policy in improving the academic quality of the schools served under this part [20 USCS §§ 6311 et seq.], including identifying barriers to greater participation by parents in activities authorized by this section (with particular attention to parents who are economically disadvantaged, are disabled, have limited English proficiency, have limited literacy, or are of any racial or ethnic minority background), and use the findings of such evaluation to design strategies for more effective parental involvement, and to revise, if necessary, the parental involvement policies described in this section; and

(F) involve parents in the activities of the schools served under this part [20 USCS §§ 6311 et seq.].

(3) Reservation.

(A) In general. Each local educational agency shall reserve not less than 1 percent of such agency's allocation under subpart 2 of this part [20 USCS §§ 6331 et seq.] to carry out this section, including promoting family literacy and parenting skills, except that this paragraph shall not apply if 1 percent of such agency's allocation under subpart 2 of this part [20 USCS §§ 6331 et seq.] for the fiscal year for which the determination is made is $ 5,000 or less.

(B) Parental input. Parents of children receiving services under this part [20 USCS

§§ 6311 et seq.] shall be involved in the decisions regarding how funds reserved under subparagraph (A) are allotted for parental involvement activities.

(C) Distribution of funds. Not less than 95 percent of the funds reserved under subparagraph (A) shall be distributed to schools served under this part [*20 USCS §§ 6311* et seq.].

(b) School parental involvement policy.

(1) In general. Each school served under this part [*20 USCS §§ 6311* et seq.] shall jointly develop with, and distribute to, parents of participating children a written parental involvement policy, agreed on by such parents, that shall describe the means for carrying out the requirements of subsections (c) through (f). Parents shall be notified of the policy in an understandable and uniform format and, to the extent practicable, provided in a language the parents can understand. Such policy shall be made available to the local community and updated periodically to meet the changing needs of parents and the school.

(2) Special rule. If the school has a parental involvement policy that applies to all parents, such school may amend that policy, if necessary, to meet the requirements of this subsection.

(3) Amendment. If the local educational agency involved has a school district-level parental involvement policy that applies to all parents, such agency may amend that policy, if necessary, to meet the requirements of this subsection.

(4) Parental comments. If the plan under section 1112 [*20 USCS § 6312*] is not satisfactory to the parents of participating children, the local educational agency shall submit any parent comments with such plan when such local educational agency submits the plan to the State.

(c) Policy involvement. Each school served under this part [*20 USCS §§ 6311* et seq.] shall—

(1) convene an annual meeting, at a convenient time, to which all parents of participating children shall be invited and encouraged to attend, to inform parents of their school's participation under this part [*20 USCS §§ 6311* et seq.] and to explain the requirements of this part [*20 USCS §§ 6311* et seq.], and the right of the parents to be involved;

(2) offer a flexible number of meetings, such as meetings in the morning or evening, and may provide, with funds provided under this part [*20 USCS §§ 6311* et seq.], transportation, child care, or home visits, as such services relate to parental involvement;

(3) involve parents, in an organized, ongoing, and timely way, in the planning, review, and improvement of programs under this part [*20 USCS §§ 6311* et seq.], including the planning, review, and improvement of the school parental involvement policy and the joint development of the schoolwide program plan under section 1114(b)(2) [*20 USCS § 6314(b)(2)*], except that if a school has in place a process for involving parents in the joint planning and design of the school's programs, the school may use that process, if such process includes an adequate representation of parents of participating children;

(4) provide parents of participating children—

(A) timely information about programs under this part [*20 USCS §§ 6311* et seq.];

(B) a description and explanation of the curriculum in use at the school, the forms of academic assessment used to measure student progress, and the proficiency levels students are expected to meet; and

(C) if requested by parents, opportunities for regular meetings to formulate suggestions and to participate, as appropriate, in decisions relating to the education of their children, and respond to any such suggestions as soon as practicably possible; and

(5) if the schoolwide program plan under section 1114(b)(2) [20 USCS § 6314(b)(2)] is not satisfactory to the parents of participating children, submit any parent comments on the plan when the school makes the plan available to the local educational agency.

(d) Shared responsibilities for high student academic achievement. As a component of the school-level parental involvement policy developed under subsection (b), each school served under this part [20 USCS §§ 6311 et seq.] shall jointly develop with parents for all children served under this part [20 USCS §§ 6311 et seq.] a school-parent compact that outlines how parents, the entire school staff, and students will share the responsibility for improved student academic achievement and the means by which the school and parents will build and develop a partnership to help children achieve the State's high standards. Such compact shall—

(1) describe the school's responsibility to provide high-quality curriculum and instruction in a supportive and effective learning environment that enables the children served under this part [20 USCS §§ 6311 et seq.] to meet the State's student academic achievement standards, and the ways in which each parent will be responsible for supporting their children's learning, such as monitoring attendance, homework completion, and television watching; volunteering in their child's classroom; and participating, as appropriate, in decisions relating to the education of their children and positive use of extracurricular time; and

(2) address the importance of communication between teachers and parents on an ongoing basis through, at a minimum—

(A) parent-teacher conferences in elementary schools, at least annually, during which the compact shall be discussed as the compact relates to the individual child's achievement;

(B) frequent reports to parents on their children's progress; and

(C) reasonable access to staff, opportunities to volunteer and participate in their child's class, and observation of classroom activities.

(e) Building capacity for involvement. To ensure effective involvement of parents and to support a partnership among the school involved, parents, and the community to improve student academic achievement, each school and local educational agency assisted under this part [20 USCS §§ 6311 et seq.]—

(1) shall provide assistance to parents of children served by the school or local educational agency, as appropriate, in understanding such topics as the State's academic content standards and State student academic achievement standards, State and local academic assessments, the requirements of this part [20 USCS §§ 6311 et seq.], and how to monitor a child's progress and work with educators to improve the achievement of their children;

(2) shall provide materials and training to help parents to work with their children to improve their children's achievement, such as literacy training and using technology, as appropriate, to foster parental involvement;

(3) shall educate teachers, pupil services personnel, principals, and other staff, with the assistance of parents, in the value and utility of contributions of parents, and in how to reach out to, communicate with, and work with parents as equal partners, implement and coordinate parent programs, and build ties between parents and the school;

(4) shall, to the extent feasible and appropriate, coordinate and integrate parent involvement programs and activities with Head Start, Reading First, Early Reading First, Even Start, the Home Instruction Programs for Preschool Youngsters, the Parents as Teachers Program, and public preschool and other programs, and conduct other activities, such as parent resource centers, that encourage and support parents in more fully participating in the education of their children;

(5) shall ensure that information related to school and parent programs, meetings, and other activities is sent to the parents of participating children in a format and, to the extent practicable, in a language the parents can understand;

(6) may involve parents in the development of training for teachers, principals, and other educators to improve the effectiveness of such training;

(7) may provide necessary literacy training from funds received under this part [20 USCS §§ 6311 et seq.] if the local educational agency has exhausted all other reasonably available sources of funding for such training;

(8) may pay reasonable and necessary expenses associated with local parental involvement activities, including transportation and child care costs, to enable parents to participate in school-related meetings and training sessions;

(9) may train parents to enhance the involvement of other parents;

(10) may arrange school meetings at a variety of times, or conduct in-home conferences between teachers or other educators, who work directly with participating children, with parents who are unable to attend such conferences at school, in order to maximize parental involvement and participation;

(11) may adopt and implement model approaches to improving parental involvement;

(12) may establish a districtwide parent advisory council to provide advice on all matters related to parental involvement in programs supported under this section;

(13) may develop appropriate roles for community-based organizations and businesses in parent involvement activities; and

(14) shall provide such other reasonable support for parental involvement activities under this section as parents may request.

(f) Accessibility. In carrying out the parental involvement requirements of this part [20 USCS §§ 6311 et seq.], local educational agencies and schools, to the extent practicable, shall provide full opportunities for the participation of parents with limited English proficiency, parents with disabilities, and parents of migratory children, including providing information and school reports required under section 1111 [20 USCS § 6311] in a format and, to the extent practicable, in a language such parents understand.

(g) Information from parental information and resource centers. In a State where a parental information and resource center is established to provide training, information, and support to parents and individuals who work with local parents, local educational agencies, and schools receiving assistance under this part [20 USCS §§ 6311 et seq.], each local educational agency or school that receives assistance under this part [20 USCS §§ 6311 et seq.] and is located in the State shall assist parents and parental organizations by informing such parents and organizations of the existence and purpose of such centers.

(h) Review. The State educational agency shall review the local educational agency's parental involvement policies and practices to determine if the policies and practices meet the requirements of this section.

§ 6319. Qualifications for teachers and paraprofessionals

(a) Teacher qualifications and measurable objectives.

(1) In general. Beginning with the first day of the first school year after the date of enactment of the No Child Left Behind Act of 2001 [enacted Jan. 8, 2002], each local educational agency receiving assistance under this part [20 USCS §§ 6311 et seq.] shall ensure that all teachers hired after such day and teaching in a program supported with funds under this part are highly qualified.

(2) State plan. As part of the plan described in section 1111 [*20 USCS § 6311*], each State educational agency receiving assistance under this part [*20 USCS §§ 6311 et seq.*] shall develop a plan to ensure that all teachers teaching in core academic subjects within the State are highly qualified not later than the end of the 2005-2006 school year. Such plan shall establish annual measurable objectives for each local educational agency and school that, at a minimum—

(A) shall include an annual increase in the percentage of highly qualified teachers at each local educational agency and school, to ensure that all teachers teaching in core academic subjects in each public elementary school and secondary school are highly qualified not later than the end of the 2005-2006 school year;

(B) shall include an annual increase in the percentage of teachers who are receiving high-quality professional development to enable such teachers to become highly qualified and successful classroom teachers; and

(C) may include such other measures as the State educational agency determines to be appropriate to increase teacher qualifications.

(3) Local plan. As part of the plan described in section 1112 [*20 USCS § 6312*], each local educational agency receiving assistance under this part [*20 USCS §§ 6311 et seq.*]shall develop a plan to ensure that all teachers teaching within the school district served by the local educational agency are highly qualified not later than the end of the 2005-2006 school year.

(b) Reports.

(1) Annual State and local reports.

(A) Local reports. Each State educational agency described in subsection (a)(2) shall require each local educational agency receiving funds under this part [*20 USCS §§ 6311 et seq.*] to publicly report, each year, beginning with the 2002-2003 school year, the annual progress of the local educational agency as a whole and of each of the schools served by the agency, in meeting the measurable objectives described in subsection (a)(2).

(B) State reports. Each State educational agency receiving assistance under this part [*20 USCS §§ 6311 et seq.*] shall prepare and submit each year, beginning with the 2002-2003 school year, a report to the Secretary, describing the State educational agency's progress in meeting the measurable objectives described in subsection (a)(2).

(C) Information from other reports. A State educational agency or local educational agency may submit information from the reports described in section 1111(h) [*20 USCS § 6311(h)*] for the purposes of this subsection, if such report is modified, as may be necessary, to contain the information required by this subsection, and may submit such information as a part of the reports required under section 1111(h) [*20 USCS § 6311(h)*].

(2) Annual reports by the Secretary. Each year, beginning with the 2002-2003 school year, the Secretary shall publicly report the annual progress of State educational agencies, local educational agencies, and schools, in meeting the measurable objectives described in subsection (a)(2).

(c) New paraprofessionals.

(1) In general. Each local educational agency receiving assistance under this part [*20 USCS §§ 6311 et seq.*] shall ensure that all paraprofessionals hired after the date of enactment of the No Child Left Behind Act of 2001 [enacted Jan. 8, 2002] and working in a program supported with funds under this part [*20 USCS §§ 6311 et seq.*] shall have—

(A) completed at least 2 years of study at an institution of higher education;

(B) obtained an associate's (or higher) degree; or

(C) met a rigorous standard of quality and can demonstrate, through a formal State or local academic assessment—

(i) knowledge of, and the ability to assist in instructing, reading, writing, and mathematics; or

(ii) knowledge of, and the ability to assist in instructing, reading readiness, writing readiness, and mathematics readiness, as appropriate.

(2) Clarification. The receipt of a secondary school diploma (or its recognized equivalent) shall be necessary but not sufficient to satisfy the requirements of paragraph (1)(C).

(d) Existing paraprofessionals. Each local educational agency receiving assistance under this part [20 USCS §§ 6311 et seq.] shall ensure that all paraprofessionals hired before the date of enactment of the No Child Left Behind Act of 2001 [enacted Jan. 8, 2002], and working in a program supported with funds under this part [20 USCS §§ 6311 et seq.] shall, not later than 4 years after the date of enactment [enacted Jan. 8, 2002] satisfy the requirements of subsection (c).

(e) Exceptions for translation and parental involvement activities. Subsections (c) and (d) shall not apply to a paraprofessional—

(1) who is proficient in English and a language other than English and who provides services primarily to enhance the participation of children in programs under this part [20 USCS §§ 6311 et seq.] by acting as a translator; or

(2) whose duties consist solely of conducting parental involvement activities consistent with section 1118 [20 USCS § 6318].

(f) General requirement for all paraprofessionals. Each local educational agency receiving assistance under this part [20 USCS §§ 6311 et seq.] shall ensure that all paraprofessionals working in a program supported with funds under this part [20 USCS §§ 6311 et seq.], regardless of the paraprofessionals' hiring date, have earned a secondary school diploma or its recognized equivalent.

(g) Duties of paraprofessionals.

(1) In general. Each local educational agency receiving assistance under this part [20 USCS §§ 6311 et seq.] shall ensure that a paraprofessional working in a program supported with funds under this part [20 USCS §§ 6311 et seq.] is not assigned a duty inconsistent with this subsection.

(2) Responsibilities paraprofessionals may be assigned. A paraprofessional described in paragraph (1) may be assigned—

(A) to provide one-on-one tutoring for eligible students, if the tutoring is scheduled at a time when a student would not otherwise receive instruction from a teacher;

(B) to assist with classroom management, such as organizing instructional and other materials;

(C) to provide assistance in a computer laboratory;

(D) to conduct parental involvement activities;

(E) to provide support in a library or media center;

(F) to act as a translator; or

(G) to provide instructional services to students in accordance with paragraph (3).

(3) Additional limitations. A paraprofessional described in paragraph (1)—

(A) may not provide any instructional service to a student unless the paraprofessional is working under the direct supervision of a teacher consistent with section 1119 [this section]; and

(B) may assume limited duties that are assigned to similar personnel who are not working in a program supported with funds under this part [20 USCS §§ 6311 et seq.], including duties beyond classroom instruction or that do not benefit participating children, so long as the amount of time spent on such duties is the same proportion of total work time as prevails with respect to similar personnel at the same school.

(h) Use of funds. A local educational agency receiving funds under this part [20 USCS §§ 6311 et seq.] may use such funds to support ongoing training and professional development to assist teachers and paraprofessionals in satisfying the requirements of this section.

(i) Verification of compliance.

(1) In general. In verifying compliance with this section, each local educational agency, at a minimum, shall require that the principal of each school operating a program under section 1114 or 1115 [20 USCS § 6314 or 6315] attest annually in writing as to whether such school is in compliance with the requirements of this section.

(2) Availability of information. Copies of attestations under paragraph (1)—

(A) shall be maintained at each school operating a program under section 1114 or 1115 [20 USCS § 6314 or 6315] and at the main office of the local educational agency; and

(B) shall be available to any member of the general public on request.

(j) Combinations of funds. Funds provided under this part [20 USCS §§ 6311 et seq.] that are used for professional development purposes may be combined with funds provided under title II of this Act [20 USCS §§ 6601 et seq.], other Acts, and other sources.

(k) Special rule. Except as provided in subsection (l), no State educational agency shall require a school or a local educational agency to expend a specific amount of funds for professional development activities under this part [20 USCS §§ 6311 et seq.], except that this paragraph shall not apply with respect to requirements under section 1116(c)(3) [20 USCS § 6316(c)(3)].

(l) Minimum expenditures. Each local educational agency that receives funds under this part [20 USCS §§ 6311 et seq.] shall use not less than 5 percent, or more than 10 percent, of such funds for each of fiscal years 2002 and 2003, and not less than 5 percent of the funds for each subsequent fiscal year, for professional development activities to ensure that teachers who are not highly qualified become highly qualified not later than the end of the 2005-2006 school year.

§ 6320. Participation of children enrolled in private schools

(a) General requirement.

(1) In general. To the extent consistent with the number of eligible children identified under section 1115(b) [20 USCS § 6315(b)] in the school district served by a local educational agency who are enrolled in private elementary schools and secondary schools, a local educational agency shall, after timely and meaningful consultation with appropriate private school officials, provide such children, on an equitable basis, special educational services or other benefits under this part [20 USCS §§ 6311 et seq.] (such as dual enrollment, educational radio and television, computer equipment and materials, other technology, and mobile educational services and equipment) that address their needs, and shall ensure that teachers and families of the children participate, on an equitable basis, in services and activities developed pursuant to sections 1118 and 1119 [20 USCS §§ 6318, 6319].

(2) Secular, neutral, nonideological. Such educational services or other benefits,

including materials and equipment, shall be secular, neutral, and nonideological.

(3) Equity. Educational services and other benefits for such private school children shall be equitable in comparison to services and other benefits for public school children participating under this part [20 USCS §§ 6311 et seq.], and shall be provided in a timely manner.

(4) Expenditures. Expenditures for educational services and other benefits to eligible private school children shall be equal to the proportion of funds allocated to participating school attendance areas based on the number of children from low-income families who attend private schools, which the local educational agency may determine each year or every 2 years.

(5) Provision of services. The local educational agency may provide services under this section directly or through contracts with public and private agencies, organizations, and institutions.

(b) Consultation.

(1) In general. To ensure timely and meaningful consultation, a local educational agency shall consult with appropriate private school officials during the design and development of such agency's programs under this part [20 USCS §§ 6311 et seq.], on issues such as—

(A) how the children's needs will be identified;

(B) what services will be offered;

(C) how, where, and by whom the services will be provided;

(D) how the services will be academically assessed and how the results of that assessment will be used to improve those services;

(E) the size and scope of the equitable services to be provided to the eligible private school children, and the proportion of funds that is allocated under subsection (a)(4) for such services;

(F) the method or sources of data that are used under subsection (c) and section 1113(c)(1) [20 USCS § 6313(c)(1)] to determine the number of children from low-income families in participating school attendance areas who attend private schools;

(G) how and when the agency will make decisions about the delivery of services to such children, including a thorough consideration and analysis of the views of the private school officials on the provision of services through a contract with potential third-party providers; and

(H) how, if the agency disagrees with the views of the private school officials on the provision of services through a contract, the local educational agency will provide in writing to such private school officials an analysis of the reasons why the local educational agency has chosen not to use a contractor.

(2) Timing. Such consultation shall include meetings of agency and private school officials and shall occur before the local educational agency makes any decision that affects the opportunities of eligible private school children to participate in programs under this part [20 USCS §§ 6311 et seq.]. Such meetings shall continue throughout implementation and assessment of services provided under this section.

(3) Discussion. Such consultation shall include a discussion of service delivery mechanisms a local educational agency can use to provide equitable services to eligible private school children.

(4) Documentation. Each local educational agency shall maintain in the agency's records and provide to the State educational agency involved a written affirmation signed by officials of each participating private school that the consultation required by

this section has occurred. If such officials do not provide such affirmation within a reasonable period of time, the local educational agency shall forward the documentation that such consultation has taken place to the State educational agency.

(5) Compliance.

(A) In general. A private school official shall have the right to complain to the State educational agency that the local educational agency did not engage in consultation that was meaningful and timely, or did not give due consideration to the views of the private school official.

(B) Procedure. If the private school official wishes to complain, the official shall provide the basis of the noncompliance with this section by the local educational agency to the State educational agency, and the local educational agency shall forward the appropriate documentation to the State educational agency.

(c) Allocation for equitable service to private school students.

(1) Calculation. A local educational agency shall have the final authority, consistent with this section, to calculate the number of children, ages 5 through 17, who are from low-income families and attend private schools by—

(A) using the same measure of low income used to count public school children;

(B) using the results of a survey that, to the extent possible, protects the identity of families of private school students, and allowing such survey results to be extrapolated if complete actual data are unavailable;

(C) applying the low-income percentage of each participating public school attendance area, determined pursuant to this section, to the number of private school children who reside in that school attendance area; or

(D) using an equated measure of low income correlated with the measure of low income used to count public school children.

(2) Complaint process. Any dispute regarding low-income data for private school students shall be subject to the complaint process authorized in section 9505 [20 USCS § 7885].

(d) Public control of funds.

(1) In general. The control of funds provided under this part [20 USCS §§ 6311 et seq.], and title to materials, equipment, and property purchased with such funds, shall be in a public agency, and a public agency shall administer such funds, materials, equipment, and property.

(2) Provision of services.

(A) Provider. The provision of services under this section shall be provided—

(i) by employees of a public agency; or

(ii) through contract by such public agency with an individual, association, agency, or organization.

(B) Requirement. In the provision of such services, such employee, individual, association, agency, or organization shall be independent of such private school and of any religious organization, and such employment or contract shall be under the control and supervision of such public agency.

(e) Standards for a bypass. If a local educational agency is prohibited by law from providing for the participation in programs on an equitable basis of eligible children enrolled in private elementary schools and secondary schools, or if the Secretary determines that a local educational agency has substantially failed or is unwilling, to provide for such participation, as required by this section, the Secretary shall—

(1) waive the requirements of this section for such local educational agency;

(2) arrange for the provision of services to such children through arrangements that shall be subject to the requirements of this section and sections 9503 and 9504 [20 USCS §§ 7883, 7884]; and

(3) in making the determination under this subsection, consider one or more factors, including the quality, size, scope, and location of the program and the opportunity of eligible children to participate.

§ 6321. Fiscal requirements

(a) Maintenance of effort. A local educational agency may receive funds under this part [20 USCS §§ 6311 et seq.] for any fiscal year only if the State educational agency involved finds that the local educational agency has maintained the agency's fiscal effort in accordance with section 9521 [20 USCS § 7901].

(b) Federal funds to supplement, not supplant, non-Federal funds.

(1) In general. A State educational agency or local educational agency shall use Federal funds received under this part [20 USCS §§ 6311 et seq.] only to supplement the funds that would, in the absence of such Federal funds, be made available from non-Federal sources for the education of pupils participating in programs assisted under this part [20 USCS §§ 6311 et seq.], and not to supplant such funds.

(2) Special rule. No local educational agency shall be required to provide services under this part [20 USCS §§ 6311 et seq.] through a particular instructional method or in a particular instructional setting in order to demonstrate such agency's compliance with paragraph (1).

(c) Comparability of services.

(1) In general.

(A) Comparable services. Except as provided in paragraphs (4) and (5), a local educational agency may receive funds under this part [20 USCS §§ 6311 et seq.] only if State and local funds will be used in schools served under this part [20 USCS §§ 6311 et seq.] to provide services that, taken as a whole, are at least comparable to services in schools that are not receiving funds under this part [20 USCS §§ 6311 et seq.].

(B) Substantially comparable services. If the local educational agency is serving all of such agency's schools under this part [20 USCS §§ 6311 et seq.], such agency may receive funds under this part [20 USCS §§ 6311 et seq.] only if such agency will use State and local funds to provide services that, taken as a whole, are substantially comparable in each school.

(C) Basis. A local educational agency may meet the requirements of subparagraphs (A) and (B) on a grade-span by grade-span basis or a school-by-school basis.

(2) Written assurance.

(A) Equivalence. A local educational agency shall be considered to have met the requirements of paragraph (1) if such agency has filed with the State educational agency a written assurance that such agency has established and implemented—

(i) a local educational agency-wide salary schedule;

(ii) a policy to ensure equivalence among schools in teachers, administrators, and other staff; and

(iii) a policy to ensure equivalence among schools in the provision of curriculum materials and instructional supplies.

(B) Determinations. For the purpose of this subsection, in the determination of expenditures per pupil from State and local funds, or instructional salaries per pupil from State and local funds, staff salary differentials for years of employment shall not be included in such determinations.

(C) Exclusions. A local educational agency need not include unpredictable changes in student enrollment or personnel assignments that occur after the beginning of a school year in determining comparability of services under this subsection.

(3) Procedures and records. Each local educational agency assisted under this part [*20 USCS §§ 6311* et seq.] shall—

(A) develop procedures for compliance with this subsection; and

(B) maintain records that are updated biennially documenting such agency's compliance with this subsection.

(4) Inapplicability. This subsection shall not apply to a local educational agency that does not have more than one building for each grade span.

(5) Compliance. For the purpose of determining compliance with paragraph (1), a local educational agency may exclude State and local funds expended for—

(A) language instruction educational programs; and

(B) the excess costs of providing services to children with disabilities as determined by the local educational agency.

(d) Exclusion of funds. For the purpose of complying with subsections (b) and (c), a State educational agency or local educational agency may exclude supplemental State or local funds expended in any school attendance area or school for programs that meet the intent and purposes of this part [*20 USCS §§ 6311* et seq.].

§ 6322. Coordination requirements

(a) In general. Each local educational agency receiving assistance under this part [*20 USCS §§ 6311* et seq.] shall carry out the activities described in subsection (b) with Head Start agencies and, if feasible, other entities carrying out early childhood development programs such as the Early Reading First program.

(b) Activities. The activities referred to in subsection (a) are activities that increase coordination between the local educational agency and a Head Start agency and, if feasible, other entities carrying out early childhood development programs, such as the Early Reading First program, serving children who will attend the schools of the local educational agency, including—

(1) developing and implementing a systematic procedure for receiving records regarding such children, transferred with parental consent from a Head Start program or, where applicable, another early childhood development program such as the Early Reading First program;

(2) establishing channels of communication between school staff and their counterparts (including teachers, social workers, and health staff) in such Head Start agencies or other entities carrying out early childhood development programs such as the Early Reading First program, as appropriate, to facilitate coordination of programs;

(3) conducting meetings involving parents, kindergarten or elementary school teachers, and Head Start teachers or, if appropriate, teachers from other early childhood development programs such as the Early Reading First program, to discuss the developmental and other needs of individual children;

(4) organizing and participating in joint transition-related training of school staff, Head Start program staff, Early Reading First program staff, and, where appropriate, other early childhood development program staff; and

(5) linking the educational services provided by such local educational agency with the services provided by local Head Start agencies and entities carrying out Early Reading First programs.

(c) Coordination of regulations. The Secretary shall work with the Secretary of Health and Human Services to coordinate regulations promulgated under this part [20 USCS §§ 6311 et seq.] with regulations promulgated under the Head Start Act [42 USCS §§ 9831 et seq.].

GENERAL PROVISIONS
Definitions

§ 7801. Definitions

Except as otherwise provided, in this Act [20 USCS §§ 6301 et seq.]:

(1) Average daily attendance.

(A) In general. Except as provided otherwise by State law or this paragraph, the term "average daily attendance" means—

(i) the aggregate number of days of attendance of all students during a school year; divided by

(ii) the number of days school is in session during that year.

(B) Conversion. The Secretary shall permit the conversion of average daily membership (or other similar data) to average daily attendance for local educational agencies in States that provide State aid to local educational agencies on the basis of average daily membership (or other similar data).

(C) Special rule. If the local educational agency in which a child resides makes a tuition or other payment for the free public education of the child in a school located in another school district, the Secretary shall, for the purpose of this Act [20 USCS §§ 6301 et seq.]—

(i) consider the child to be in attendance at a school of the agency making the payment; and

(ii) not consider the child to be in attendance at a school of the agency receiving the payment.

(D) Children with disabilities. If a local educational agency makes a tuition payment to a private school or to a public school of another local educational agency for a child with a disability, as defined in section 602 of the Individuals with Disabilities Education Act [20 USCS § 1401], the Secretary shall, for the purpose of this Act [20 USCS §§ 6301 et seq.], consider the child to be in attendance at a school of the agency making the payment.

(2) Average per-pupil expenditure. The term "average per-pupil expenditure" means, in the case of a State or of the United States—

(A) without regard to the source of funds—

(i) the aggregate current expenditures, during the third fiscal year preceding the fiscal year for which the determination is made (or, if satisfactory data for that year are not available, during the most recent preceding fiscal year for which satisfactory data are available) of all local educational agencies in the State or, in the case of the United

States, for all States (which, for the purpose of this paragraph, means the 50 States and the District of Columbia); plus

(ii) any direct current expenditures by the State for the operation of those agencies; divided by

(B) the aggregate number of children in average daily attendance to whom those agencies provided free public education during that preceding year.

(3) Beginning teacher. The term "beginning teacher" means a teacher in a public school who has been teaching less than a total of three complete school years.

(4) Child. The term "child" means any person within the age limits for which the State provides free public education.

(5) Child with a disability. The term "child with a disability" has the same meaning given that term in section 602 of the Individuals with Disabilities Education Act [20 USCS § 1401].

(6) Community-based organization. The term "community-based organization" means a public or private nonprofit organization of demonstrated effectiveness that—

(A) is representative of a community or significant segments of a community; and

(B) provides educational or related services to individuals in the community.

(7) Consolidated local application. The term "consolidated local application" means an application submitted by a local educational agency pursuant to section 9305 [20 USCS § 7845].

(8) Consolidated local plan. The term "consolidated local plan" means a plan submitted by a local educational agency pursuant to section 9305 [20 USCS § 7845].

(9) Consolidated State application. The term "consolidated State application" means an application submitted by a State educational agency pursuant to section 9302 [20 USCS § 7842].

(10) Consolidated State plan. The term "consolidated State plan" means a plan submitted by a State educational agency pursuant to section 9302 [20 USCS § 7842].

(11) Core academic subjects. The term "core academic subjects" means English, reading or language arts, mathematics, science, foreign languages, civics and government, economics, arts, history, and geography.

(12) County. The term "county" means one of the divisions of a State used by the Secretary of Commerce in compiling and reporting data regarding counties.

(13) Covered program. The term "covered program" means each of the programs authorized by—

(A) part A of title I [20 USCS §§ 6311 et seq.];

(B) subpart 3 of part B of title I [20 USCS §§ 6381 et seq.];

(C) part C of title I [20 USCS §§ 6391 et seq.];

(D) part D of title I [20 USCS §§ 6421 et seq.];

(E) part F of title I [20 USCS §§ 6511 et seq.];

(F) part A of title II [20 USCS §§ 6601 et seq.];

(G) part D of title II [20 USCS §§ 6751 et seq.];

(H) part A of title III [20 USCS §§ 6811 et seq.];

(I) part A of title IV [20 USCS §§ 7101 et seq.];

(J) part B of title IV [*20 USCS §§ 7171* et seq.];

(K) part A of title V [*20 USCS §§ 7201* et seq.]; and

(L) subpart 2 of part B of title VI [*20 USCS §§ 7351* et seq.].

(14) Current expenditures. The term "current expenditures" means expenditures for free public education—

(A) including expenditures for administration, instruction, attendance and health services, pupil transportation services, operation and maintenance of plant, fixed charges, and net expenditures to cover deficits for food services and student body activities; but

(B) not including expenditures for community services, capital outlay, and debt service, or any expenditures made from funds received under title I and part A of title V [*20 USCS §§ 6301* et seq., *7201* et seq.].

(15) Department. The term "Department" means the Department of Education.

(16) Distance learning. The term "distance learning" means the transmission of educational or instructional programming to geographically dispersed individuals and groups via telecommunications.

(17) Educational service agency. The term "educational service agency" means a regional public multiservice agency authorized by State statute to develop, manage, and provide services or programs to local educational agencies.

(18) Elementary school. The term "elementary school" means a nonprofit institutional day or residential school, including a public elementary charter school, that provides elementary education, as determined under State law.

(19) Exemplary teacher. The term "exemplary teacher" means a teacher who—

(A) is a highly qualified teacher such as a master teacher;

(B) has been teaching for at least 5 years in a public or private school or institution of higher education;

(C) is recommended to be an exemplary teacher by administrators and other teachers who are knowledgeable about the individual's performance;

(D) is currently teaching and based in a public school; and

(E) assists other teachers in improving instructional strategies, improves the skills of other teachers, performs teacher mentoring, develops curricula, and offers other professional development.

(20) Family literacy services. The term "family literacy services" means services provided to participants on a voluntary basis that are of sufficient intensity in terms of hours, and of sufficient duration, to make sustainable changes in a family, and that integrate all of the following activities:

(A) Interactive literacy activities between parents and their children.

(B) Training for parents regarding how to be the primary teacher for their children and full partners in the education of their children.

(C) Parent literacy training that leads to economic self-sufficiency.

(D) An age-appropriate education to prepare children for success in school and life experiences.

(21) Free public education. The term "free public education" means education that is provided—

(A) at public expense, under public supervision and direction, and without tuition charge; and

(B) as elementary school or secondary school education as determined under applicable State law, except that the term does not include any education provided beyond grade 12.

(22) Gifted and talented. The term "gifted and talented", when used with respect to students, children, or youth, means students, children, or youth who give evidence of high achievement capability in areas such as intellectual, creative, artistic, or leadership capacity, or in specific academic fields, and who need services or activities not ordinarily provided by the school in order to fully develop those capabilities.

(23) Highly qualified. The term "highly qualified"—

(A) when used with respect to any public elementary school or secondary school teacher teaching in a State, means that—

(i) the teacher has obtained full State certification as a teacher (including certification obtained through alternative routes to certification) or passed the State teacher licensing examination, and holds a license to teach in such State, except that when used with respect to any teacher teaching in a public charter school, the term means that the teacher meets the requirements set forth in the State's public charter school law; and

(ii) the teacher has not had certification or licensure requirements waived on an emergency, temporary, or provisional basis;

(B) when used with respect to—

(i) an elementary school teacher who is new to the profession, means that the teacher—

(I) holds at least a bachelor's degree; and

(II) has demonstrated, by passing a rigorous State test, subject knowledge and teaching skills in reading, writing, mathematics, and other areas of the basic elementary school curriculum (which may consist of passing a State-required certification or licensing test or tests in reading, writing, mathematics, and other areas of the basic elementary school curriculum); or

(ii) a middle or secondary school teacher who is new to the profession, means that the teacher holds at least a bachelor's degree and has demonstrated a high level of competency in each of the academic subjects in which the teacher teaches by—

(I) passing a rigorous State academic subject test in each of the academic subjects in which the teacher teaches (which may consist of a passing level of performance on a State-required certification or licensing test or tests in each of the academic subjects in which the teacher teaches); or

(II) successful completion, in each of the academic subjects in which the teacher teaches, of an academic major, a graduate degree, coursework equivalent to an undergraduate academic major, or advanced certification or credentialing; and

(C) when used with respect to an elementary, middle, or secondary school teacher who is not new to the profession, means that the teacher holds at least a bachelor's degree and—

(i) has met the applicable standard in clause (i) or (ii) of subparagraph (B), which includes an option for a test; or

(ii) demonstrates competence in all the academic subjects in which the teacher teaches based on a high objective uniform State standard of evaluation that—

(I) is set by the State for both grade appropriate academic subject matter knowledge and teaching skills;

(II) is aligned with challenging State academic content and student academic achievement standards and developed in consultation with core content specialists, teachers, principals, and school administrators;

(III) provides objective, coherent information about the teacher's attainment of core content knowledge in the academic subjects in which a teacher teaches;

(IV) is applied uniformly to all teachers in the same academic subject and the same grade level throughout the State;

(V) takes into consideration, but not be based primarily on, the time the teacher has been teaching in the academic subject;

(VI) is made available to the public upon request; and

(VII) may involve multiple, objective measures of teacher competency.

(24) Institution of higher education. The term "institution of higher education" has the meaning given that term in section 101(a) of the Higher Education Act of 1965 [*20 USCS § 1001(a)*].

(25) Limited english proficient. The term "limited English proficient", when used with respect to an individual, means an individual—

(A) who is aged 3 through 21;

(B) who is enrolled or preparing to enroll in an elementary school or secondary school;

(C)

(i) who was not born in the United States or whose native language is a language other than English;

(ii)

(I) who is a Native American or Alaska Native, or a native resident of the outlying areas; and

(II) who comes from an environment where a language other than English has had a significant impact on the individual's level of English language proficiency; or

(iii) who is migratory, whose native language is a language other than English, and who comes from an environment where a language other than English is dominant; and

(D) whose difficulties in speaking, reading, writing, or understanding the English language may be sufficient to deny the individual—

(i) the ability to meet the State's proficient level of achievement on State assessments described in section 1111(b)(3) [*20 USCS § 6311(b)(3)*];

(ii) the ability to successfully achieve in classrooms where the language of instruction is English; or

(iii) the opportunity to participate fully in society.

(26) Local educational agency.

(A) In general. The term "local educational agency" means a public board of education or other public authority legally constituted within a State for either administrative control or direction of, or to perform a service function for, public elementary schools or secondary schools in a city, county, township, school district, or other political subdivision of a State, or of or for a combination of school districts or counties that is recognized in a State as an administrative agency for its public elementary schools or secondary schools.

(B) Administrative control and direction. The term includes any other public institution or agency having administrative control and direction of a public elementary school or secondary school.

(C) BIA schools. The term includes an elementary school or secondary school funded by the Bureau of Indian Affairs but only to the extent that including the school makes the school eligible for programs for which specific eligibility is not provided to the school in another provision of law and the school does not have a student population that is smaller than the student population of the local educational agency receiving assistance under this Act [20 USCS §§ 6301 et seq.] with the smallest student population, except that the school shall not be subject to the jurisdiction of any State educational agency other than the Bureau of Indian Affairs.

(D) Educational service agencies. The term includes educational service agencies and consortia of those agencies.

(E) State educational agency. The term includes the State educational agency in a State in which the State educational agency is the sole educational agency for all public schools.

(27) Mentoring. The term "mentoring", except when used to refer to teacher mentoring, means a process by which a responsible adult, postsecondary student, or secondary school student works with a child to provide a positive role model for the child, to establish a supportive relationship with the child, and to provide the child with academic assistance and exposure to new experiences and examples of opportunity that enhance the ability of the child to become a responsible adult.

(28) Native American and Native American language. The terms "Native American" and "Native American language" have the same meaning given those terms in section 103 of the Native American Languages Act of 1990 [25 USCS § 2902].

(29) Other staff. The term "other staff" means pupil services personnel, librarians, career guidance and counseling personnel, education aides, and other instructional and administrative personnel.

(30) Outlying area. The term "outlying area" means the United States Virgin Islands, Guam, American Samoa, and the Commonwealth of the Northern Mariana Islands, and for the purpose of section 1121(b) [20 USCS § 6331(b)] and any other discretionary grant program under this Act [20 USCS §§ 6301 et seq.], includes the freely associated states of the Republic of the Marshall Islands, the Federated States of Micronesia, and the Republic of Palau until an agreement for the extension of United States education assistance under the Compact of Free Association for each of the freely associated states becomes effective after the date of enactment of the No Child Left Behind Act of 2001 [enacted Jan. 8, 2002].

(31) Parent. The term "parent" includes a legal guardian or other person standing in loco parentis (such as a grandparent or stepparent with whom the child lives, or a person who is legally responsible for the child's welfare).

(32) Parental involvement. The term "parental involvement" means the participation of parents in regular, two-way, and meaningful communication involving student academic learning and other school activities, including ensuring—

(A) that parents play an integral role in assisting their child's learning;

(B) that parents are encouraged to be actively involved in their child's education at school;

(C) that parents are full partners in their child's education and are included, as appropriate, in decisionmaking and on advisory committees to assist in the education of their child;

(D) the carrying out of other activities, such as those described in section 1118 [20 USCS § 6318].

(33) Poverty line. The term "poverty line" means the poverty line (as defined by the Office of Management and Budget and revised annually in accordance with section 673(2) of the Community Services Block Grant Act [*42 USCS § 9902(2)*]) applicable to a family of the size involved.

(34) Professional development. The term "professional development"—

(A) includes activities that—

(i) improve and increase teachers' knowledge of the academic subjects the teachers teach, and enable teachers to become highly qualified;

(ii) are an integral part of broad schoolwide and districtwide educational improvement plans;

(iii) give teachers, principals, and administrators the knowledge and skills to provide students with the opportunity to meet challenging State academic content standards and student academic achievement standards;

(iv) improve classroom management skills;

(v)

(I) are high quality, sustained, intensive, and classroom-focused in order to have a positive and lasting impact on classroom instruction and the teacher's performance in the classroom; and

(II) are not 1-day or short-term workshops or conferences;

(vi) support the recruiting, hiring, and training of highly qualified teachers, including teachers who became highly qualified through State and local alternative routes to certification;

(vii) advance teacher understanding of effective instructional strategies that are—

(I) based on scientifically based research (except that this subclause shall not apply to activities carried out under part D of title II [*20 USCS §§ 6751* et seq.]); and

(II) strategies for improving student academic achievement or substantially increasing the knowledge and teaching skills of teachers; and

(viii) are aligned with and directly related to—

(I) State academic content standards, student academic achievement standards, and assessments; and

(II) the curricula and programs tied to the standards described in subclause (I) except that this subclause shall not apply to activities described in clauses (ii) and (iii) of section 2123(3)(B) [*20 USCS § 6623(3)(B)*];

(ix) are developed with extensive participation of teachers, principals, parents, and administrators of schools to be served under this Act [*20 USCS §§ 6301* et seq.];

(x) are designed to give teachers of limited English proficient children, and other teachers and instructional staff, the knowledge and skills to provide instruction and appropriate language and academic support services to those children, including the appropriate use of curricula and assessments;

(xi) to the extent appropriate, provide training for teachers and principals in the use of technology so that technology and technology applications are effectively used in the classroom to improve teaching and learning in the curricula and core academic subjects in which the teachers teach;

(xii) as a whole, are regularly evaluated for their impact on increased teacher effectiveness and improved student academic achievement, with the findings of the evaluations used to improve the quality of professional development;

(xiii) provide instruction in methods of teaching children with special needs;

(xiv) include instruction in the use of data and assessments to inform and instruct classroom practice; and

(xv) include instruction in ways that teachers, principals, pupil services personnel, and school administrators may work more effectively with parents; and

(B) may include activities that—

(i) involve the forming of partnerships with institutions of higher education to establish school-based teacher training programs that provide prospective teachers and beginning teachers with an opportunity to work under the guidance of experienced teachers and college faculty;

(ii) create programs to enable paraprofessionals (assisting teachers employed by a local educational agency receiving assistance under part A of title I [20 USCS §§ 6311 et seq.]) to obtain the education necessary for those paraprofessionals to become certified and licensed teachers; and

(iii) provide follow-up training to teachers who have participated in activities described in subparagraph (A) or another clause of this subparagraph that are designed to ensure that the knowledge and skills learned by the teachers are implemented in the classroom.

(35) Public telecommunications entity. The term "public telecommunications entity" has the meaning given that term in section 397(12) of the Communications Act of 1934 [47 USCS § 397(12)].

(36) Pupil services personnel; pupil services.

(A) Pupil services personnel. The term "pupil services personnel" means school counselors, school social workers, school psychologists, and other qualified professional personnel involved in providing assessment, diagnosis, counseling, educational, therapeutic, and other necessary services (including related services as that term is defined in section 602 of the Individuals with Disabilities Education Act [20 USCS § 1401]) as part of a comprehensive program to meet student needs.

(B) Pupil services. The term "pupil services" means the services provided by pupil services personnel.

(37) Scientifically based research. The term "scientifically based research"—

(A) means research that involves the application of rigorous, systematic, and objective procedures to obtain reliable and valid knowledge relevant to education activities and programs; and

(B) includes research that—

(i) employs systematic, empirical methods that draw on observation or experiment;

(ii) involves rigorous data analyses that are adequate to test the stated hypotheses and justify the general conclusions drawn;

(iii) relies on measurements or observational methods that provide reliable and valid data across evaluators and observers, across multiple measurements and observations, and across studies by the same or different investigators;

(iv) is evaluated using experimental or quasi-experimental designs in which individuals, entities, programs, or activities are assigned to different conditions and with appropriate controls to evaluate the effects of the condition of interest, with a preference for random-assignment experiments, or other designs to the extent that those designs contain within-condition or across-condition controls;

(v) ensures that experimental studies are presented in sufficient detail and clarity to allow for replication or, at a minimum, offer the opportunity to build systematically on their findings; and

(vi) has been accepted by a peer-reviewed journal or approved by a panel of independent experts through a comparably rigorous, objective, and scientific review.

(38) Secondary school. The term "secondary school" means a nonprofit institutional day or residential school, including a public secondary charter school, that provides secondary education, as determined under State law, except that the term does not include any education beyond grade 12.

(39) Secretary. The term "Secretary" means the Secretary of Education.

[(40)] State. The term "State" means each of the 50 States, the District of Columbia, the Commonwealth of Puerto Rico, and each of the outlying areas.

(41) State educational agency. The term "State educational agency" means the agency primarily responsible for the State supervision of public elementary schools and secondary schools.

(42) Teacher mentoring. The term "teacher mentoring" means activities that—

(A) consist of structured guidance and regular and ongoing support for teachers, especially beginning teachers, that—

(i) are designed to help the teachers continue to improve their practice of teaching and to develop their instructional skills; and

[(ii)] [are] part of an ongoing developmental induction process—

(I) involve the assistance of an exemplary teacher and other appropriate individuals from a school, local educational agency, or institution of higher education; and

(II) may include coaching, classroom observation, team teaching, and reduced teaching loads; and

(B) may include the establishment of a partnership by a local educational agency with an institution of higher education, another local educational agency, a teacher organization, or another organization.

(43) Technology. The term "technology" means state-of-the-art technology products and services.

§ 7802. Applicability of title

Parts B, C, D, and E of this *title [20 USCS §§ 7821 et seq., 7841 et seq., 7861 et seq., 7881 et seq.]* do not apply to title VIII of this Act *[20 USCS §§ 7701 et seq.].*

§ 7803. Applicability to Bureau of Indian Affairs operated schools

For the purpose of any competitive program under this Act *[20 USCS §§ 6301 et seq.]*—

(1) a consortium of schools operated by the Bureau of Indian Affairs;

(2) a school operated under a contract or grant with the Bureau of Indian Affairs in consortium with another contract or grant school or a tribal or community organization; or

(3) a Bureau of Indian Affairs school in consortium with an institution of higher education, a contract or grant school, or a tribal or community organization,

shall be given the same consideration as a local educational agency.

TITLE 29.
LABOR

CHAPTER 16 VOCATIONAL REHABILITATION AND OTHER REHABILITATION SERVICES

GENERAL PROVISIONS

§ 705 Definitions

For the purposes of this Act:

(1) Administrative costs. The term means expenditures incurred in the performance of administrative functions under the vocational rehabilitation program carried out under title I [29 USCS §§ 720 et seq.], including expenses related to program planning, development, monitoring, and evaluation, including expenses for—

(A) quality assurance;

(B) budgeting, accounting, financial management, information systems, and related data processing;

(C) providing information about the program to the public;

(D) technical assistance and support services to other State agencies, private nonprofit organizations, and businesses and industries, except for technical assistance and support services described in section 103(b)(5) [29 USCS § 723(b)(5)];

(E) the State Rehabilitation Council and other advisory committees;

(F) professional organization membership dues for designated State unit employees;

(G) the removal of architectural barriers in State vocational rehabilitation agency offices and State operated rehabilitation facilities;

(H) operating and maintaining designated State unit facilities, equipment, and grounds;

(I) supplies;

(J) administration of the comprehensive system of personnel development described in section 101(a)(7) [29 USCS § 721(a)(7)], including personnel administration, administration of affirmative action plans, and training and staff development;

(K) administrative salaries, including clerical and other support staff salaries, in support of these administrative functions;

(L) travel costs related to carrying out the program, other than travel costs related to the provision of services;

(M) costs incurred in conducting reviews of rehabilitation counselor or coordinator determinations under section 102(c) [29 USCS § 722(c)]; and

(N) legal expenses required in the administration of the program.

(2) Assessment for determining eligibility and vocational rehabilitation needs. The term "assessment for determining eligibility and vocational rehabilitation needs" means, as appropriate in each case—

(A) (i) a review of existing data—

(I) to determine whether an individual is eligible for vocational rehabilitation services; and

(II) to assign priority for an order of selection described in section 101(a)(5)(A) [*29 USCS § 721(a)(5)(A)*] in the States that use an order of selection pursuant to section 101(a)(5)(A) [*29 USCS § 721(a)(5)(A)*]; and

(ii) to the extent necessary, the provision of appropriate assessment activities to obtain necessary additional data to make such determination and assignment;

(B) to the extent additional data is necessary to make a determination of the employment outcomes, and the nature and scope of vocational rehabilitation services, to be included in the individualized plan for employment of an eligible individual, a comprehensive assessment to determine the unique strengths, resources, priorities, concerns, abilities, capabilities, interests, and informed choice, including the need for supported employment, of the eligible individual, which comprehensive assessment—

(i) is limited to information that is necessary to identify the rehabilitation needs of the individual and to develop the individualized plan for employment of the eligible individual;

(ii) uses, as a primary source of such information, to the maximum extent possible and appropriate and in accordance with confidentiality requirements—

(I) existing information obtained for the purposes of determining the eligibility of the individual and assigning priority for an order of selection described in section 101(a)(5)(A) [*29 USCS § 721(a)(5)(A)*] for the individual; and

(II) such information as can be provided by the individual and, where appropriate, by the family of the individual;

(iii) may include, to the degree needed to make such a determination, an assessment of the personality, interests, interpersonal skills, intelligence and related functional capacities, educational achievements, work experience, vocational aptitudes, personal and social adjustments, and employment opportunities of the individual, and the medical, psychiatric, psychological, and other pertinent vocational, educational, cultural, social, recreational, and environmental factors, that affect the employment and rehabilitation needs of the individual; and

(iv) may include, to the degree needed, an appraisal of the patterns of work behavior of the individual and services needed for the individual to acquire occupational skills, and to develop work attitudes, work habits, work tolerance, and social and behavior patterns necessary for successful job performance, including the utilization of work in real job situations to assess and develop the capacities of the individual to perform adequately in a work environment;

(C) referral, for the provision of rehabilitation technology services to the individual, to assess and develop the capacities of the individual to perform in a work environment; and

(D) an exploration of the individual's abilities, capabilities, and capacity to perform in work situations, which shall be assessed periodically during trial work experiences, including experiences in which the individual is provided appropriate supports and training.

(3) Assistive technology device. The term "assistive technology device" has the meaning given such term in section 3 of the Assistive Technology Act of 1998 [*29 USCS § 3002*], except that the reference in such section to the term "individuals with disabilities" shall be deemed to mean more than one individual with a disability as defined in paragraph (20)(A).

(4) Assistive technology service. The term "assistive technology service" has the meaning given such term in section 3 of the Assistive Technology Act of 1998 [*29 USCS § 3002*], except that the reference in such section—

(A) to the term "individual with a disability" shall be deemed to mean an individual with a disability, as defined in paragraph (20)(A); and

(B) to the term "individuals with disabilities" shall be deemed to mean more than one such individual.

(5) Community rehabilitation program. The term "community rehabilitation program" means a program that provides directly or facilitates the provision of vocational rehabilitation services to individuals with disabilities, and that provides, singly or in combination, for an individual with a disability to enable the individual to maximize opportunities for employment, including career advancement—

(A) medical, psychiatric, psychological, social, and vocational services that are provided under one management;

(B) testing, fitting, or training in the use of prosthetic and orthotic devices;

(C) recreational therapy;

(D) physical and occupational therapy;

(E) speech, language, and hearing therapy;

(F) psychiatric, psychological, and social services, including positive behavior management;

(G) assessment for determining eligibility and vocational rehabilitation needs;

(H) rehabilitation technology;

(I) job development, placement, and retention services;

(J) evaluation or control of specific disabilities;

(K) orientation and mobility services for individuals who are blind;

(L) extended employment;

(M) psychosocial rehabilitation services;

(N) supported employment services and extended services;

(O) services to family members when necessary to the vocational rehabilitation of the individual;

(P) personal assistance services; or

(Q) services similar to the services described in one of subparagraphs (A) through (P).

(6) Construction; cost of construction.

(A) Construction. The term "construction" means—

(i) the construction of new buildings;

(ii) the acquisition, expansion, remodeling, alteration, and renovation of existing buildings; and

(iii) initial equipment of buildings described in clauses (i) and (ii).

(B) Cost of construction. The term "cost of construction" includes architects" fees and the cost of acquisition of land in connection with construction but does not include the cost of offsite improvements.

(7) [Deleted]

(8) Designated State agency; designated State unit.

(A) Designated State agency. The term "designated State agency" means an agency designated under section 101(a)(2)(A) [29 USCS § 721(a)(2)(A)].

(B) Designated State unit. The term "designated State unit" means—

(i) any State agency unit required under section 101(a)(2)(B)(ii) [*29 USCS § 721(a)(2)(B)(ii)*]; or

(ii) in cases in which no such unit is so required, the State agency described in section 101(a)(2)(B)(i) [*29 USCS § 721(a)(2)(B)(i)*].

(9) Disability. The term "disability" means—

(A) except as otherwise provided in subparagraph (B), a physical or mental impairment that constitutes or results in a substantial impediment to employment; or

(B) for purposes of sections 2, 14, and 15, and titles II, IV, V, and VII [*29 USCS §§ 701, 713, 714, 760 et seq., 780 et seq., 791 et seq., 796 et seq.*], a physical or mental impairment that substantially limits one or more major life activities.

(10) Drug and illegal use of drugs.

(A) Drug. The term "drug" means a controlled substance, as defined in schedules I through V of section 202 of the Controlled Substances Act (*21 U.S.C. 812*).

(B) Illegal use of drugs. The term "illegal use of drugs" means the use of drugs, the possession or distribution of which is unlawful under the Controlled Substances Act [*21 USCS §§ 801 et seq.*]. Such term does not include the use of a drug taken under supervision by a licensed health care professional, or other uses authorized by the Controlled Substances Act [*21 USCS §§ 801 et seq.*] or other provisions of Federal law.

(11) Employment outcome. The term "employment outcome" means, with respect to an individual—

(A) entering or retaining full-time or, if appropriate, part-time competitive employment in the integrated labor market;

(B) satisfying the vocational outcome of supported employment; or

(C) satisfying any other vocational outcome the Secretary may determine to be appropriate (including satisfying the vocational outcome of self-employment, telecommuting, or business ownership), in a manner consistent with this Act.

(12) Establishment of a community rehabilitation program. The term "establishment of a community rehabilitation program" includes the acquisition, expansion, remodeling, or alteration of existing buildings necessary to adapt them to community rehabilitation program purposes or to increase their effectiveness for such purposes (subject, however, to such limitations as the Secretary may determine, in accordance with regulations the Secretary shall prescribe, in order to prevent impairment of the objectives of, or duplication of, other Federal laws providing Federal assistance in the construction of facilities for community rehabilitation programs), and may include such additional equipment and staffing as the Commissioner considers appropriate.

(13) Extended services. The term "extended services" means ongoing support services and other appropriate services, needed to support and maintain an individual with a most significant disability in supported employment, that—

(A) are provided singly or in combination and are organized and made available in such a way as to assist an eligible individual in maintaining supported employment;

(B) are based on a determination of the needs of an eligible individual, as specified in an individualized plan for employment; and

(C) are provided by a State agency, a nonprofit private organization, employer, or any other appropriate resource, after an individual has made the transition from support provided by the designated State unit.

(14) Federal share.

(A) In general. Subject to subparagraph (B), the term "Federal share" means 78.7 percent.

(B) Exception. The term "Federal share" means the share specifically set forth in section 111(a)(3) [29 USCS § 731(a)(3)], except that with respect to payments pursuant to part B of title I [29 USCS §§ 730 et seq.] to any State that are used to meet the costs of construction of those rehabilitation facilities identified in section 103(b)(2) [29 USCS § 723(b)(2)] in such State, the Federal share shall be the percentages determined in accordance with the provisions of section 111(a)(3) [29 USCS § 731(a)(3)] applicable with respect to the State.

(C) Relationship to expenditures by a political subdivision. For the purpose of determining the non-Federal share with respect to a State, expenditures by a political subdivision thereof or by a local agency shall be regarded as expenditures by such State, subject to such limitations and conditions as the Secretary shall by regulation prescribe.

(15) Governor. The term "Governor" means a chief executive officer of a State.

(16) Impartial hearing officer.

(A) In general. The term "impartial hearing officer" means an individual—

(i) who is not an employee of a public agency (other than an administrative law judge, hearing examiner, or employee of an institution of higher education);

(ii) who is not a member of the State Rehabilitation Council described in section 105 [29 USCS § 725];

(iii) who has not been involved previously in the vocational rehabilitation of the applicant or eligible individual;

(iv) who has knowledge of the delivery of vocational rehabilitation services, the State plan under section 101 [29 USCS § 721], and the Federal and State rules governing the provision of such services and training with respect to the performance of official duties; and

(v) who has no personal or financial interest that would be in conflict with the objectivity of the individual.

(B) Construction. An individual shall not be considered to be an employee of a public agency for purposes of subparagraph (A)(i) solely because the individual is paid by the agency to serve as a hearing officer.

(17) Independent living core services. The term "independent living core services" means—

(A) information and referral services;

(B) independent living skills training;

(C) peer counseling (including cross-disability peer counseling); and

(D) individual and systems advocacy.

(18) Independent living services. The term "independent living services" includes—

(A) independent living core services; and

(B) (i) counseling services, including psychological, psychotherapeutic, and related services;

(ii) services related to securing housing or shelter, including services related to community group living, and supportive of the purposes of this Act and of the titles of this Act, and adaptive housing services (including appropriate accommodations to and modifications of any space used to serve, or occupied by, individuals with disabilities);

(iii) rehabilitation technology;

(iv) mobility training;

(v) services and training for individuals with cognitive and sensory disabilities, including life skills training, and interpreter and reader services;

(vi) personal assistance services, including attendant care and the training of personnel providing such services;

(vii) surveys, directories, and other activities to identify appropriate housing, recreation opportunities, and accessible transportation, and other support services;

(viii) consumer information programs on rehabilitation and independent living services available under this Act, especially for minorities and other individuals with disabilities who have traditionally been unserved or underserved by programs under this Act;

(ix) education and training necessary for living in a community and participating in community activities;

(x) supported living;

(xi) transportation, including referral and assistance for such transportation and training in the use of public transportation vehicles and systems;

(xii) physical rehabilitation;

(xiii) therapeutic treatment;

(xiv) provision of needed prostheses and other appliances and devices;

(xv) individual and group social and recreational services;

(xvi) training to develop skills specifically designed for youths who are individuals with disabilities to promote self-awareness and esteem, develop advocacy and self-empowerment skills, and explore career options;

(xvii) services for children;

(xviii) services under other Federal, State, or local programs designed to provide resources, training, counseling, or other assistance, of substantial benefit in enhancing the independence, productivity, and quality of life of individuals with disabilities;

(xix) appropriate preventive services to decrease the need of individuals assisted under this Act for similar services in the future;

(xx) community awareness programs to enhance the understanding and integration into society of individuals with disabilities; and

(xxi) such other services as may be necessary and not inconsistent with the provisions of this Act.

(19) Indian; American Indian; Indian American; Indian tribe.

(A) In general. The terms "Indian", "American Indian", and "Indian American" mean an individual who is a member of an Indian tribe.

(B) Indian tribe. The term "Indian tribe" means any Federal or State Indian tribe, band, rancheria, pueblo, colony, or community, including any Alaskan native village or regional village corporation (as defined in or established pursuant to the Alaska Native Claims Settlement Act [*43 USCS §§ 1601* et seq.]).

(20) Individual with a disability.

(A) In general. Except as otherwise provided in subparagraph (B), the term "individual with a disability" means any individual who—

(i) has a physical or mental impairment which for such individual constitutes or results in a substantial impediment to employment; and

(ii) can benefit in terms of an employment outcome from vocational rehabilitation services provided pursuant to title I, III, or VI [29 USCS §§ 720 et seq., 771 et seq., or 795 et seq.].

(B) Certain programs; limitations on major life activities. Subject to subparagraphs (C), (D), (E), and (F), the term "individual with a disability" means, for purposes of sections 2, 14, and 15, and titles II, IV, V, and VII of this Act [29 USCS §§ 701, 714, 715, 760 et seq., 780 et seq., 791 et seq., 796 et seq.], any person who—

(i) has a physical or mental impairment which substantially limits one or more of such person's major life activities;

(ii) has a record of such an impairment; or

(iii) is regarded as having such an impairment.

(C) Rights and advocacy provisions.

(i) In general; exclusion of individuals engaging in drug use. For purposes of title V [29 USCS §§ 791 et seq.], the term "individual with a disability" does not include an individual who is currently engaging in the illegal use of drugs, when a covered entity acts on the basis of such use.

(ii) Exception for individuals no longer engaging in drug use. Nothing in clause (i) shall be construed to exclude as an individual with a disability an individual who—

(I) has successfully completed a supervised drug rehabilitation program and is no longer engaging in the illegal use of drugs, or has otherwise been rehabilitated successfully and is no longer engaging in such use;

(II) is participating in a supervised rehabilitation program and is no longer engaging in such use; or

(III) is erroneously regarded as engaging in such use, but is not engaging in such use; except that it shall not be a violation of this Act for a covered entity to adopt or administer reasonable policies or procedures, including but not limited to drug testing, designed to ensure that an individual described in subclause (I) or (II) is no longer engaging in the illegal use of drugs.

(iii) Exclusion for certain services. Notwithstanding clause (i), for purposes of programs and activities providing health services and services provided under titles I, II, and III [29 USCS §§ 720 et seq., 760 et seq., 771 et seq.], an individual shall not be excluded from the benefits of such programs or activities on the basis of his or her current illegal use of drugs if he or she is otherwise entitled to such services.

(iv) Disciplinary action. For purposes of programs and activities providing educational services, local educational agencies may take disciplinary action pertaining to the use or possession of illegal drugs or alcohol against any student who is an individual with a disability and who currently is engaging in the illegal use of drugs or in the use of alcohol to the same extent that such disciplinary action is taken against students who are not individuals with disabilities. Furthermore, the due process procedures at *section 104.36 of title 34, Code of Federal Regulations* (or any corresponding similar regulation or ruling) shall not apply to such disciplinary actions.

(v) Employment; exclusion of alcoholics. For purposes of sections 503 and 504 [29 USCS §§ 793, 794] as such sections relate to employment, the term "individual with a disability" does not include any individual who is an alcoholic whose current use of alcohol prevents such individual from performing the duties of the job in question or whose employment, by reason of such current alcohol abuse, would constitute a direct threat to property or the safety of others.

(D) Employment; exclusion of individuals with certain diseases or infections. For the purposes of sections 503 and 504 [29 USCS §§ 793, 794], as such sections relate to employment, such term does not include an individual who has a currently contagious disease or infection and who, by reason of such disease or infection, would constitute a direct threat to the health or safety of other individuals or who, by reason of the currently contagious disease or infection, is unable to perform the duties of the job.

(E) Rights provisions; exclusion of individuals on basis of homosexuality or bisexuality. For the purposes of sections 501, 503, and 504 [29 USCS §§ 791, 793, 794]—

(i) for purposes of the application of subparagraph (B) to such sections, the term "impairment" does not include homosexuality or bisexuality; and

(ii) therefore the term "individual with a disability" does not include an individual on the basis of homosexuality or bisexuality.

(F) Rights provisions; exclusion of individuals on basis of certain disorders. For the purposes of sections 501, 503, and 504 [29 USCS §§ 791, 793, 794], the term "individual with a disability" does not include an individual on the basis of—

(i) transvestism, transsexualism, pedophilia, exhibitionism, voyeurism, gender identity disorders not resulting from physical impairments, or other sexual behavior disorders;

(ii) compulsive gambling, kleptomania, or pyromania; or

(iii) psychoactive substance use disorders resulting from current illegal use of drugs.

(G) Individuals with disabilities. The term "individuals with disabilities" means more than one individual with a disability.

(21) Individual with a significant disability.

(A) In general. Except as provided in subparagraph (B) or (C), the term "individual with a significant disability" means an individual with a disability—

(i) who has a severe physical or mental impairment which seriously limits one or more functional capacities (such as mobility, communication, self-care, self-direction, interpersonal skills, work tolerance, or work skills) in terms of an employment outcome;

(ii) whose vocational rehabilitation can be expected to require multiple vocational rehabilitation services over an extended period of time; and

(iii) who has one or more physical or mental disabilities resulting from amputation, arthritis, autism, blindness, burn injury, cancer, cerebral palsy, cystic fibrosis, deafness, head injury, heart disease, hemiplegia, hemophilia, respiratory or pulmonary dysfunction, mental retardation, mental illness, multiple sclerosis, muscular dystrophy, musculo-skeletal disorders, neurological disorders (including stroke and epilepsy), paraplegia, quadriplegia, and other spinal cord conditions, sickle cell anemia, specific learning disability, end-stage renal disease, or another disability or combination of disabilities determined on the basis of an assessment for determining eligibility and vocational rehabilitation needs described in subparagraphs (A) and (B) of paragraph (2) to cause comparable substantial functional limitation.

(B) Independent living services and centers for independent living. For purposes of title VII [29 USCS §§ 796 et seq.], the term "individual with a significant disability" means an individual with a severe physical or mental impairment whose ability to function independently in the family or community or whose ability to obtain, maintain, or advance in employment is substantially limited and for whom the delivery of independent living services will improve the ability to function, continue functioning, or move toward functioning independently in the family or community or to continue in employment, respectively.

(C) Research and training. For purposes of title II [*29 USCS §§ 760* et seq.], the term "individual with a significant disability" includes an individual described in subparagraph (A) or (B).

(D) Individuals with significant disabilities. The term "individuals with significant disabilities" means more than one individual with a significant disability.

(E) Individual with a most significant disability.

(i) In general. The term "individual with a most significant disability", used with respect to an individual in a State, means an individual with a significant disability who meets criteria established by the State under section 101(a)(5)(C) [*29 USCS § 721(a)(5)(C)*].

(ii) Individuals with the most significant disabilities. The term "individuals with the most significant disabilities" means more than one individual with a most significant disability.

(22) Individual's representative; applicant's representative. The terms "individual's representative" and "applicant's representative" mean a parent, a family member, a guardian, an advocate, or an authorized representative of an individual or applicant, respectively.

(23) Institution of higher education. The term "institution of higher education" has the meaning given the term in section 101 of the Higher Education Act of 1965 [*20 USCS § 1001*].

(24) Local agency. The term "local agency" means an agency of a unit of general local government or of an Indian tribe (or combination of such units or tribes) which has an agreement with the designated State agency to conduct a vocational rehabilitation program under the supervision of such State agency in accordance with the State plan approved under section 101 [*29 USCS § 721*]. Nothing in the preceding sentence of this paragraph or in section 101 shall be construed to prevent the local agency from arranging to utilize another local public or nonprofit agency to provide vocational rehabilitation services if such an arrangement is made part of the agreement specified in this paragraph.

(25) Local workforce investment board. The term "local workforce investment board" means a local workforce investment board established under section 117 of the Workforce Investment Act of 1998 [*29 USCS § 2832*].

(26) Nonprofit. The term "nonprofit", when used with respect to a community rehabilitation program, means a community rehabilitation program carried out by a corporation or association, no part of the net earnings of which inures, or may lawfully inure, to the benefit of any private shareholder or individual and the income of which is exempt from taxation under *section 501(c)(3) of the Internal Revenue Code of 1986* [*26 USCS § 501(c)(3)*].

(27) Ongoing support services. The term "ongoing support services" means services—

(A) provided to individuals with the most significant disabilities;

(B) provided, at a minimum, twice monthly—

(i) to make an assessment, regarding the employment situation, at the worksite of each such individual in supported employment, or, under special circumstances, especially at the request of the client, off site; and

(ii) based on the assessment, to provide for the coordination or provision of specific intensive services, at or away from the worksite, that are needed to maintain employment stability; and

(C) consisting of—

(i) a particularized assessment supplementary to the comprehensive assessment described in paragraph (2)(B);

(ii) the provision of skilled job trainers who accompany the individual for intensive job skill training at the worksite;

(iii) job development, job retention, and placement services;

(iv) social skills training;

(v) regular observation or supervision of the individual;

(vi) followup services such as regular contact with the employers, the individuals, the individuals" representatives, and other appropriate individuals, in order to reinforce and stabilize the job placement;

(vii) facilitation of natural supports at the worksite;

(viii) any other service identified in section 103; or

(ix) a service similar to another service described in this subparagraph.

(28) Personal assistance services. The term "personal assistance services" means a range of services, provided by one or more persons, designed to assist an individual with a disability to perform daily living activities on or off the job that the individual would typically perform if the individual did not have a disability. Such services shall be designed to increase the individual's control in life and ability to perform everyday activities on or off the job.

(29) Public or nonprofit. The term "public or nonprofit", used with respect to an agency or organization, includes an Indian tribe.

(30) Rehabilitation technology. The term "rehabilitation technology" means the systematic application of technologies, engineering methodologies, or scientific principles to meet the needs of and address the barriers confronted by individuals with disabilities in areas which include education, rehabilitation, employment, transportation, independent living, and recreation. The term includes rehabilitation engineering, assistive technology devices, and assistive technology services.

(31) Secretary. The term "Secretary", except when the context otherwise requires, means the Secretary of Education.

(32) State. The term "State" includes, in addition to each of the several States of the United States, the District of Columbia, the Commonwealth of Puerto Rico, the United States Virgin Islands, Guam, American Samoa, and the Commonwealth of the Northern Mariana Islands.

(33) State workforce investment board. The term "State workforce investment board" means a State workforce investment board established under section 111 of the Workforce Investment Act of 1998 [*29 USCS § 2821*].

(34) Statewide workforce investment system. The term "statewide workforce investment system" means a system described in section 111(d)(2) of the Workforce Investment Act of 1998 [*29 USCS § 2821(d)(2)*].

(35) Supported employment.

(A) In general. The term "supported employment" means competitive work in integrated work settings, or employment in integrated work settings in which individuals are working toward competitive work, consistent with the strengths, resources, priorities, concerns, abilities, capabilities, interests, and informed choice of the individuals, for individuals with the most significant disabilities—

(i) (I) for whom competitive employment has not traditionally occurred; or

(II) for whom competitive employment has been interrupted or intermittent as a result of a significant disability; and

(ii) who, because of the nature and severity of their disability, need intensive supported employment services for the period, and any extension, described in paragraph (36)(C) and extended services after the transition described in paragraph (13)(C) in order to perform such work.

(B) Certain transitional employment. Such term includes transitional employment for persons who are individuals with the most significant disabilities due to mental illness.

(36) Supported employment services. The term "supported employment services" means ongoing support services and other appropriate services needed to support and maintain an individual with a most significant disability in supported employment, that—

(A) are provided singly or in combination and are organized and made available in such a way as to assist an eligible individual to achieve competitive employment;

(B) are based on a determination of the needs of an eligible individual, as specified in an individualized plan for employment; and

(C) are provided by the designated State unit for a period of time not to extend beyond 18 months, unless under special circumstances the eligible individual and the rehabilitation counselor or coordinator involved jointly agree to extend the time in order to achieve the employment outcome identified in the individualized plan for employment.

(37) Transition services. The term "transition services" means a coordinated set of activities for a student, designed within an outcome-oriented process, that promotes movement from school to post school activities, including postsecondary education, vocational training, integrated employment (including supported employment), continuing and adult education, adult services, independent living, or community participation. The coordinated set of activities shall be based upon the individual student's needs, taking into account the student's preferences and interests, and shall include instruction, community experiences, the development of employment and other post school adult living objectives, and, when appropriate, acquisition of daily living skills and functional vocational evaluation.

(38) Vocational rehabilitation services. The term "vocational rehabilitation services" means those services identified in section 103 [29 USCS § 723] which are provided to individuals with disabilities under this Act.

(39) Workforce investment activities. The term "workforce investment activities" means workforce investment activities, as defined in section 101 of the Workforce Investment Act of 1998 [29 USCS § 2801], that are carried out under that Act.

RIGHTS AND ADVOCACY

§ 794 Nondiscrimination under Federal grants and programs

(a) Promulgation of rules and regulations. No otherwise qualified individual with a disability in the United States, as defined in section 7(20) [29 USCS § 705(20)], shall, solely by reason of her or his disability, be excluded from the participation in, be denied the benefits of, or be subjected to discrimination under any program or activity receiving Federal financial assistance or under any program or activity conducted by any Executive agency or by the United States Postal Service. The head of each such agency shall promulgate such regulations as may be necessary to carry out the amendments to this section made by the Rehabilitation, Comprehensive Services, and Developmental Disabilities Act of 1978. Copies of any proposed regulation shall be submitted to appropriate authorizing committees of the Congress, and such regulation may take effect no earlier than the thirtieth day after the date on which such regulation is so submitted to such committees.

(b) "Program or activity" defined. For the purposes of this section, the term "program or activity" means all of the operations of—

(1) (A) a department, agency, special purpose district, or other instrumentality of a State or of a local government; or

(B) the entity of such State or local government that distributes such assistance and each such department or agency (and each other State or local government entity) to which the assistance is extended, in the case of assistance to a State or local government;

(2) (A) a college, university, or other postsecondary institution, or a public system of higher education; or

(B) a local educational agency (as defined in section 9101 of the Elementary and Secondary Education Act of 1965 [*20 USCS § 7801*]), system of vocational education, or other school system;

(3)

(A) an entire corporation, partnership, or other private organization, or an entire sole proprietorship—

(i) if assistance is extended to such corporation, partnership, private organization, or sole proprietorship as a whole; or

(ii) which is principally engaged in the business of providing education, health care, housing, social services, or parks and recreation; or

(B) the entire plant or other comparable, geographically separate facility to which Federal financial assistance is extended, in the case of any other corporation, partnership, private organization, or sole proprietorship; or

(4) any other entity which is established by two or more of the entities described in paragraph (1), (2), or (3); any part of which is extended Federal financial assistance.

(c) Significant structural alterations by small providers. Small providers are not required by subsection (a) to make significant structural alterations to their existing facilities for the purpose of assuring program accessibility, if alternative means of providing the services are available. The terms used in this subsection shall be construed with reference to the regulations existing on the date of the enactment of this subsection [enacted March 22, 1988].

(d) Standards used in determining violation of section. The standards used to determine whether this section has been violated in a complaint alleging employment discrimination under this section shall be the standards applied under title I of the Americans with Disabilities Act of 1990 (*42 U.S.C. 12111* et seq.) and the provisions of sections 501 through 504, and 510, of the Americans with Disabilities Act of 1990 (*42 U.S.C. 12201–12204* and *12210*), as such sections relate to employment.

Review expert commentary from The National Institute for Trial Advocacy following 42 USCS § 1981a (relating to damages in cases of intentional discrimination in employment).

§ 794a Nondiscrimination under Federal grants and programs Remedies and attorney's fees

(a)

(1) The remedies, procedures, and rights set forth in section 717 of the Civil Rights Act of 1964 (*42 U.S.C. 2000e-16*), including the application of sections 706(f) through

706(k) (*42 U.S.C. 2000e-5 (f)* through (k)), shall be available, with respect to any complaint under section 501 of this Act [*29 USCS § 791*], to any employee or applicant for employment aggrieved by the final disposition of such complaint, or by the failure to take final action on such complaint. In fashioning an equitable or affirmative action remedy under such section, a court may take into account the reasonableness of the cost of any necessary work place accommodation, and the availability of alternatives therefor or other appropriate relief in order to achieve an equitable and appropriate remedy.

(2) The remedies, procedures, and rights set forth in title VI of the Civil Rights Act of 1964 [*42 USCS §§ 2000d* et seq.] shall be available to any person aggrieved by any act or failure to act by any recipient of Federal assistance or Federal provider of such assistance under section 504 of this Act [*29 USCS § 794*].

(b) In any action or proceeding to enforce or charge a violation of a provision of this *title [29 USCS §§ 790* et seq.], the court, in its discretion, may allow the prevailing party, other than the United States, a reasonable attorney's fee as part of the costs.

TITLE 34. EDUCATION

SUBTITLE B REGULATIONS OF THE OFFICES OF THE DEPARTMENT OF EDUCATION

CHAPTER I OFFICE FOR CIVIL RIGHTS, DEPARTMENT OF EDUCATION

PART 104 NONDISCRIMINATION ON THE BASIS OF HANDICAP IN PROGRAMS OR ACTIVITIES RECEIVING FEDERAL FINANCIAL ASSISTANCE

SUBPART A GENERAL PROVISIONS

§ 104.1 Purpose.

The purpose of this part is to effectuate section 504 of the Rehabilitation Act of 1973, which is designed to eliminate discrimination on the basis of handicap in any program or activity receiving Federal financial assistance.

§ 104.2 Application.

This part applies to each recipient of Federal financial assistance from the Department of Education and to the program or activity that receives such assistance.

§ 104.3 Definitions.

As used in this part, the term:

(a) The Act means the Rehabilitation Act of 1973, Pub. L. 93-112, as amended by the Rehabilitation Act Amendments of 1974, Pub. L. 93-516, *29 U.S.C. 794.*

(b) Section 504 means section 504 of the Act.

(c) Education of the Handicapped Act means that statute as amended by the Education for all Handicapped Children Act of 1975, Pub. L. 94-142, *20 U.S.C. 1401* et seq.

(d) Department means the Department of Education.

(e) Assistant Secretary means the Assistant Secretary for Civil Rights of the Department of Education.

(f) Recipient means any state or its political subdivision, any instrumentality of a state or its political subdivision, any public or private agency, institution, organization, or other entity, or any person to which Federal financial assistance is extended directly or through another recipient, including any successor, assignee, or transferee of a recipient, but excluding the ultimate beneficiary of the assistance.

(g) Applicant for assistance means one who submits an application, request, or plan required to be approved by a Department official or by a recipient as a condition to becoming a recipient.

(h) Federal financial assistance means any grant, loan, contract (other than a procurement contract or a contract of insurance or guaranty), or any other arrangement by which the Department provides or otherwise makes available assistance in the form of:

(1) Funds;

(2) Services of Federal personnel; or

(3) Real and personal property or any interest in or use of such property, including:

(i) Transfers or leases of such property for less than fair market value or for reduced consideration; and

(ii) Proceeds from a subsequent transfer or lease of such property if the Federal share of its fair market value is not returned to the Federal Government.

(i) Facility means all or any portion of buildings, structures, equipment, roads, walks, parking lots, or other real or personal property or interest in such property.

(j) Handicapped person — (1) Handicapped persons means any person who (i) has a physical or mental impairment which substantially limits one or more major life activities, (ii) has a record of such an impairment, or (iii) is regarded as having such an impairment.

(2) As used in paragraph (j)(1) of this section, the phrase:

(i) Physical or mental impairment means (A) any physiological disorder or condition, cosmetic disfigurement, or anatomical loss affecting one or more of the following body systems: neurological; musculoskeletal; special sense organs; respiratory, including speech organs; cardiovascular; reproductive, digestive, genito-urinary; hemic and lymphatic; skin; and endocrine; or (B) any mental or psychological disorder, such as mental retardation, organic brain syndrome, emotional or mental illness, and specific learning disabilities.

(ii) Major life activities means functions such as caring for one's self, performing manual tasks, walking, seeing, hearing, speaking, breathing, learning, and working.

(iii) Has a record of such an impairment means has a history of, or has been misclassified as having, a mental or physical impairment that substantially limits one or more major life activities.

(iv) Is regarded as having an impairment means (A) has a physical or mental impairment that does not substantially limit major life activities but that is treated by a recipient as constituting such a limitation; (B) has a physical or mental impairment that substantially limits major life activities only as a result of the attitudes of others toward such impairment; or (C) has none of the impairments defined in paragraph (j)(2)(i) of this section but is treated by a recipient as having such an impairment.

(k) Program or activity means all of the operations of —

(1)(i) A department, agency, special purpose district, or other instrumentality of a State or of a local government; or

(ii) The entity of such State or local government that distributes such assistance and each such department or agency (and each other State or local government entity) to which the assistance is extended, in the case of assistance to a State or local government;

(2)(i) A college, university, or other postsecondary institution, or a public system of higher education; or

(ii) A local educational agency (as defined in *20 U.S.C. 8801*), system of vocational education, or other school system;

(3)(i) An entire corporation, partnership, or other private organization, or an entire sole proprietorship —

(A) If assistance is extended to such corporation, partnership, private organization, or sole proprietorship as a whole; or

(B) Which is principally engaged in the business of providing education, health care, housing, social services, or parks and recreation; or

(ii) The entire plant or other comparable, geographically separate facility to which Federal financial assistance is extended, in the case of any other corporation, partnership, private organization, or sole proprietorship; or

(4) Any other entity which is established by two or more of the entities described in paragraph (k)(1), (2), or (3) of this section; any part of which is extended Federal financial assistance.

(Authority: *29 U.S.C. 794*(b))

(l) Qualified handicapped person means:

(1) With respect to employment, a handicapped person who, with reasonable accommodation, can perform the essential functions of the job in question;

(2) With respect to public preschool elementary, secondary, or adult educational services, a handicappped person (i) of an age during which nonhandicapped persons are provided such services, (ii) of any age during which it is mandatory under state law to provide such services to handicapped persons, or (iii) to whom a state is required to provide a free appropriate public education under section 612 of the Education of the Handicapped Act; and

(3) With respect to postsecondary and vocational education services, a handicapped person who meets the academic and technical standards requisite to admission or participation in the recipient's education program or activity;

(4) With respect to other services, a handicapped person who meets the essential eligibility requirements for the receipt of such services.

(m) Handicap means any condition or characteristic that renders a person a handicapped person as defined in paragraph (j) of this section.

§ 104.4 Discrimination prohibited.

(a) General. No qualified handicapped person shall, on the basis of handicap, be excluded from participation in, be denied the benefits of, or otherwise be subjected to discrimination under any program or activitiy which receives Federal financial assistance.

(b) Discriminatory actions prohibited. (1) A recipient, in providing any aid, benefit, or service, may not, directly or through contractual, licensing, or other arrangements, on the basis of handicap:

(i) Deny a qualified handicapped person the opportunity to participate in or benefit from the aid, benefit, or service;

(ii) Afford a qualified handicapped person an opportunity to participate in or benefit from the aid, benefit, or service that is not equal to that afforded others;

(iii) Provide a qualified handicapped person with an aid, benefit, or service that is not as effective as that provided to others;

(iv) Provide different or separate aid, benefits, or services to handicapped persons or to any class of handicapped persons unless such action is necessary to provide qualified handicapped persons with aid, benefits, or services that are as effective as those provided to others;

(v) Aid or perpetuate discrimination against a qualified handicapped person by providing significant assistance to an agency, organization, or person that discriminates on the basis of handicap in providing any aid, benefit, or service to beneficiaries of the recipients program or activity;

(vi) Deny a qualified handicapped person the opportunity to participate as a member of planning or advisory boards; or

(vii) Otherwise limit a qualified handicapped person in the enjoyment of any right, privilege, advantage, or opportunity enjoyed by others receiving an aid, benefit, or service.

(2) For purposes of this part, aids, benefits, and services, to be equally effective, are not required to produce the identical result or level of achievement for handicapped and nonhandicapped persons, but must afford handicapped persons equal opportunity to obtain the same result, to gain the same benefit, or to reach the same level of achievement, in the most integrated setting appropriate to the person's needs.

(3) Despite the existence of separate or different aid, benefits, or services provided in accordance with this part, a recipient may not deny a qualified handicapped person the opportunity to participate in such aid, benefits, or services that are not separate or different.

(4) A recipient may not, directly or through contractual or other arrangements, utilize criteria or methods of administration (i) that have the effect of subjecting qualified handicapped persons to discrimination on the basis of handicap, (ii) that have the purpose or effect of defeating or substantially impairing accomplishment of the objectives of the recipient's program or activity with respect to handicapped persons, or (iii) that perpetuate the discrimination of another recipient if both recipients are subject to common administrative control or are agencies of the same State.

(5) In determining the site or location of a facility, an applicant for assistance or a recipient may not make selections (i) that have the effect of excluding handicapped persons from, denying them the benefits of, or otherwise subjecting them to discrimination under any program or activity that receives Federal financial assistance or (ii) that have the purpose or effect of defeating or substantially impairing the accomplishment of the objectives of the program or activity with respect to handicapped persons.

(6) As used in this section, the aid, benefit, or service provided under a program or activity receiving Federal financial assistance includes any aid, benefit, or service provided in or through a facility that has been constructed, expanded, altered, leased or rented, or otherwise acquired, in whole or in part, with Federal financial assistance.

(c) Aid, benefits, or services limited by Federal law. The exclusion of nonhandicapped persons from aid, benefits, or services limited by Federal statute or executive order to handicapped persons or the exclusion of a specific class of handicapped persons from aid, benefits, or services limited by Federal statute or executive order to a different class of handicapped persons is not prohibited by this part.

§ 104.5 Assurances required.

(a) Assurances. An applicant for Federal financial assistance to which this part applies shall submit an assurance, on a form specified by the Assistant Secretary, that the program or activity will be operated in compliance with this part. An applicant may incorporate these assurances by reference in subsequent applications to the Department.

(b) Duration of obligation. (1) In the case of Federal financial assistance extended in the form of real property or to provide real property or structures on the property, the assurance will obligate the recipient or, in the case of a subsequent transfer, the transferee, for the period during which the real property or structures are used for the purpose for which Federal financial assistance is extended or for another purpose involving the provision of similar services or benefits.

(2) In the case of Federal financial assistance extended to provide personal property, the assurance will obligate the recipient for the period during which it retains ownership or possession of the property.

(3) In all other cases the assurance will obligate the recipient for the period during which Federal financial assistance is extended.

(c) *Covenants.* (1) Where Federal financial assistance is provided in the form of real property or interest in the property from the Department, the instrument effecting or recording this transfer shall contain a covenant running with the land to assure nondiscrimination for the period during which the real property is used for a purpose for which the Federal financial assistance is extended or for another purpose involving the provision of similar services or benefits.

(2) Where no transfer of property is involved but property is purchased or improved with Federal financial assistance, the recipient shall agree to include the covenant described in paragraph (b)(2) of this section in the instrument effecting or recording any subsequent transfer of the property.

(3) Where Federal financial assistance is provided in the form of real property or interest in the property from the Department, the covenant shall also include a condition coupled with a right to be reserved by the Department to revert title to the property in the event of a breach of the covenant. If a transferee of real property proposes to mortgage or otherwise encumber the real property as security for financing construction of new, or improvement of existing, facilities on the property for the purposes for which the property was transferred, the Assistant Secretary may, upon request of the transferee and if necessary to accomplish such financing and upon such conditions as he or she deems appropriate, agree to forbear the exercise of such right to revert title for so long as the lien of such mortgage or other encumbrance remains effective.

§ 104.6 Remedial action, voluntary action, and self-evaluation.

(a) *Remedial action.* (1) If the Assistant Secretary finds that a recipient has discriminated against persons on the basis of handicap in violation of section 504 or this part, the recipient shall take such remedial action as the Assistant Secretary deems necessary to overcome the effects of the discrimination.

(2) Where a recipient is found to have discriminated against persons on the basis of handicap in violation of section 504 or this part and where another recipient exercises control over the recipient that has discriminated, the Assistant Secretary, where appropriate, may require either or both recipients to take remedial action.

(3) The Assistant Secretary may, where necessary to overcome the effects of discrimination in violation of section 504 or this part, require a recipient to take remedial action (i) with respect to handicapped persons who are no longer participants in the recipient's program or activity but who were participants in the program or activity when such discrimination occurred or (ii) with respect to handicapped persons who would have been participants in the program or activity had the discrimination not occurred.

(b) *Voluntary action.* A recipient may take steps, in addition to any action that is required by this part, to overcome the effects of conditions that resulted in limited participation in the recipient's program or activity by qualified handicapped persons.

(c) *Self-evaluation.* (1) A recipient shall, within one year of the effective date of this part:

(i) Evaluate, with the assistance of interested persons, including handicapped persons or organizations representing handicapped persons, its current policies and practices and the effects thereof that do not or may not meet the requirements of this part;

(ii) Modify, after consultation with interested persons, including handicapped persons or organizations representing handicapped persons, any policies and practices that do not meet the requirements of this part; and

(iii) Take, after consultation with interested persons, including handicapped persons or organizations representing handicapped persons, appropriate remedial steps to eliminate the effects of any discrimination that resulted from adherence to these policies and practices.

(2) A recipient that employs fifteen or more persons shall, for at least three years following completion of the evaluation required under paragraph (c)(1) of this section, maintain on file, make available for public inspection, and provide to the Assistant Secretary upon request:

(i) A list of the interested persons consulted,

(ii) A description of areas examined and any problems identified, and

(iii) A description of any modifications made and of any remedial steps taken.

§ 104.7 Designation of responsible employee and adoption of grievance procedures.

(a) *Designation of responsible employee.* A recipient that employs fifteen or more persons shall designate at least one person to coordinate its efforts to comply with this part.

(b) *Adoption of grievance procedures.* A recipient that employs fifteen or more persons shall adopt grievance procedures that incorporate appropriate due process standards and that provide for the prompt and equitable resolution of complaints alleging any action prohibited by this part. Such procedures need not be established with respect to complaints from applicants for employment or from applicants for admission to postsecondary educational institutions.

§ 104.8 Notice.

(a) A recipient that employs fifteen or more persons shall take appropriate initial and continuing steps to notify participants, beneficiaries, applicants, and employees, including those with impaired vision or hearing, and unions or professional organizations holding collective bargaining or professional agreements with the recipient that it does not discriminate on the basis of handicap in violation of section 504 and this part. The notification shall state, where appropriate, that the recipient does not discriminate in admission or access to, or treatment or employment in, its program or activity. The notification shall also include an identification of the responsible employee designated pursuant to § 104.7(a). A recipient shall make the initial notification required by this paragraph within 90 days of the effective date of this part. Methods of initial and continuing notification may include the posting of notices, publication in newspapers and magazines, placement of notices in recipients' publication, and distribution of memoranda or other written communications.

(b) If a recipient publishes or uses recruitment materials or publications containing general information that it makes available to participants, beneficiaries, applicants, or employees, it shall include in those materials or publications a statement of the policy described in paragraph (a) of this section. A recipient may meet the requirement of this paragraph either by including appropriate inserts in existing materials and publications or by revising and reprinting the materials and publications.

§ 104.9 Administrative requirements for small recipients.

The Assistant Secretary may require any recipient with fewer than fifteen employees, or any class of such recipients, to comply with §§ 104.7 and 104.8, in whole or in part, when the Assistant Secretary finds a violation of this part or finds that such compliance will not significantly impair the ability of the recipient or class of recipients to provide benefits or services.

§ 104.10 Effect of state or local law or other requirements and effect of employment opportunities.

(a) The obligation to comply with this part is not obviated or alleviated by the existence of any state or local law or other requirement that, on the basis of handicap, imposes prohibitions or limits upon the eligibility of qualified handicapped persons to receive services or to practice any occupation or profession.

(b) The obligation to comply with this part is not obviated or alleviated because employment opportunities in any occupation or profession are or may be more limited for handicapped persons than for nonhandicapped persons.

SUBPART B EMPLOYMENT PRACTICES

§ 104.11 Discrimination prohibited.

(a) General. (1) No qualified handicapped person shall, on the basis of handicap, be subjected to discrimination in employment under any program or activity to which this part applies.

(2) A recipient that receives assistance under the Education of the Handicapped Act shall take positive steps to employ and advance in employment qualified handicapped persons in programs or activities assisted under that Act.

(3) A recipient shall make all decisions concerning employment under any program or activity to which this part applies in a manner which ensures that discrimination on the basis of handicap does not occur and may not limit, segregate, or classify applicants or employees in any way that adversely affects their opportunities or status because of handicap.

(4) A recipient may not participate in a contractual or other relationship that has the effect of subjecting qualified handicapped applicants or employees to discrimination prohibited by this subpart. The relationships referred to in this paragraph include relationships with employment and referral agencies, with labor unions, with organizations providing or administering fringe benefits to employees of the recipient, and with organizations providing training and apprenticeships.

(b) Specific activities. The provisions of this subpart apply to:

(1) Recruitment, advertising, and the processing of applications for employment;

(2) Hiring, upgrading, promotion, award of tenure, demotion, transfer, layoff, termination, right of return from layoff and rehiring;

(3) Rates of pay or any other form of compensation and changes in compensation;

(4) Job assignments, job classifications, organizational structures, position descriptions, lines of progression, and seniority lists;

(5) Leaves of absense, sick leave, or any other leave;

(6) Fringe benefits available by virtue of employment, whether or not administered by the recipient;

(7) Selection and financial support for training, including apprenticeship, professional meetings, conferences, and other related activities, and selection for leaves of absence to pursue training;

(8) Employer sponsored activities, including those that are social or recreational; and

(9) Any other term, condition, or privilege of employment.

(c) A recipient's obligation to comply with this subpart is not affected by any inconsistent term of any collective bargaining agreement to which it is a party.

§ 104.12   Reasonable accommodation.

(a) A recipient shall make reasonable accommodation to the known physical or mental limitations of an otherwise qualified handicapped applicant or employee unless the recipient can demonstrate that the accommodation would impose an undue hardship on the operation of its program or activity.

(b) Reasonable accommodation may include:

(1) Making facilities used by employees readily accessible to and usable by handicapped persons, and

(2) Job restructuring, part-time or modified work schedules, acquisition or modification of equipment or devices, the provision of readers or interpreters, and other similar actions.

(c) In determining pursuant to paragraph (a) of this section whether an accommodation would impose an undue hardship on the operation of a recipient's program or activity, factors to be considered include:

(1) The overall size of the recipient's program or activity with respect to number of employees, number and type of facilities, and size of budget;

(2) The type of the recipient's operation, including the composition and structure of the recipient's workforce; and

(3) The nature and cost of the accommodation needed.

(d) A recipient may not deny any employment opportunity to a qualified handicapped employee or applicant if the basis for the denial is the need to make reasonable accommodation to the physical or mental limitations of the employee or applicant.

§ 104.13   Employment criteria.

(a) A recipient may not make use of any employment test or other selection criterion that screens out or tends to screen out handicapped persons or any class of handicapped persons unless:

(1) The test score or other selection criterion, as used by the recipient, is shown to be job-related for the position in question, and

(2) Alternative job-related tests or criteria that do not screen out or tend to screen out as many handicapped persons are not shown by the Director to be available.

(b) A recipient shall select and administer tests concerning employment so as best to ensure that, when administered to an applicant or employee who has a handicap that impairs sensory, manual, or speaking skills, the test results accurately reflect the applicant's or employee's job skills, aptitude, or whatever other factor the test purports to measure, rather than reflecting the applicant's or employee's impaired sensory, manual, or speaking skills (except where those skills are the factors that the test purports to measure).

§ 104.14   Preemployment inquiries.

(a) Except as provided in paragraphs (b) and (c) of this section, a recipient may not conduct a preemployment medical examination or may not make preemployment inquiry of an applicant as to whether the applicant is a handicapped person or as to the nature or severity of a handicap. A recipient may, however, make preemployment inquiry into an applicant's ability to perform job-related functions.

(b) When a recipient is taking remedial action to correct the effects of past discrimination pursuant to § 104.6 (a), when a recipient is taking voluntary action to overcome the effects of conditions that resulted in limited participation in its federally assisted program or activity pursuant to § 104.6(b), or when a recipient is taking affirmative action pursuant to section 503 of the Act, the recipient may invite applicants for employment to indicate whether and to what extent they are handicapped, Provided, That:

(1) The recipient states clearly on any written questionnaire used for this purpose or makes clear orally if no written questionnaire is used that the information requested is intended for use solely in connection with its remedial action obligations or its voluntary or affirmative action efforts; and

(2) The recipient states clearly that the information is being requested on a voluntary basis, that it will be kept confidential as provided in paragraph (d) of this section, that refusal to provide it will not subject the applicant or employee to any adverse treatment, and that it will be used only in accordance with this part.

(c) Nothing in this section shall prohibit a recipient from conditioning an offer of employment on the results of a medical examination conducted prior to the employee's entrance on duty, Provided, That:

(1) All entering employees are subjected to such an examination regardless of handicap, and

(2) The results of such an examination are used only in accordance with the requirements of this part.

(d) Information obtained in accordance with this section as to the medical condition or history of the applicant shall be collected and maintained on separate forms that shall be accorded confidentiality as medical records, except that:

(1) Supervisors and managers may be informed regarding restrictions on the work or duties of handicapped persons and regarding necessary accommodations;

(2) First aid and safety personnel may be informed, where appropriate, if the condition might require emergency treatment; and

(3) Government officials investigating compliance with the Act shall be provided relevant information upon request.

SUBPART C   ACCESSIBILITY

§ 104.21   Discrimination prohibited.

No qualified handicapped person shall, because a recipient's facilities are inaccessible to or unusable by handicapped persons, be denied the benefits of, be excluded from participation in, or otherwise be subjected to discrimination under any program or activity to which this part applies.

§ 104.22   Existing facilities.

(a) *Accessibility.* A recipient shall operate its program or activity so that when each part is viewed in its entirety, it is readily accessible to handicapped persons. This paragraph does not require a recipient to make each of its existing facilities or every part of a facility accessible to and usable by handicapped persons.

(b) *Methods.* A recipient may comply with the requirements of paragraph (a) of this section through such means as redesign of equipment, reassignment of classes or other services to accessible buildings, assignment of aides to beneficiaries, home visits, delivery of health, welfare, or other social services at alternate accessible sites, alteration of existing facilities and construction of new facilities in conformance with the requirements of § 104.23, or any other methods that result in making its program or activity accessible to handicapped persons. A recipient is not required to make structural changes in existing facilities where other methods are effective in achieving compliance with paragraph (a) of this section. In choosing among available methods for meeting the requirement of paragraph (a) of this section, a recipient shall give priority to those methods that serve handicapped persons in the most integrated setting appropriate.

(c) Small health, welfare, or other social service providers. If a recipient with fewer than fifteen employees that provides health, welfare, or other social services finds, after consultation with a handicapped person seeking its services, that there is no method of complying with paragraph (a) of this section other than making a significant alteration in its existing facilities, the recipient may, as an alternative, refer the handicapped person to other providers of those services that are accessible.

(d) Time period. A recipient shall comply with the requirement of paragraph (a) of this section within sixty days of the effective date of this part except that where structural changes in facilities are necessary, such changes shall be made within three years of the effective date of this part, but in any event as expeditiously as possible.

(e) Transition plan. In the event that structural changes to facilities are necessary to meet the requirement of paragraph (a) of this section, a recipient shall develop, within six months of the effective date of this part, a transition plan setting forth the steps necessary to complete such changes. The plan shall be developed with the assistance of interested persons, including handicapped persons or organizations representing handicapped persons. A copy of the transition plan shall be made available for public inspection. The plan shall, at a minimum:

(1) Identify physical obstacles in the recipient's facilities that limit the accessibility of its program or activity to handicappped persons;

(2) Describe in detail the methods that will be used to make the facilities accessible;

(3) Specify the schedule for taking the steps necessary to achieve full accessibility in order to comply with paragraph (a) of this section and, if the time period of the transition plan is longer than one year, identify the steps of that will be taken during each year of the transition period; and

(4) Indicate the person responsible for implementation of the plan.

(f) Notice. The recipient shall adopt and implement procedures to ensure that interested persons, including persons with impaired vision or hearing, can obtain information as to the existence and location of services, activities, and facilities that are accessible to and usuable by handicapped persons.

§ 104.23 New construction.

(a) Design and construction. Each facility or part of a facility constructed by, on behalf of, or for the use of a recipient shall be designed and constructed in such manner that the facility or part of the facility is readily accessible to and usable by handicapped persons, if the construction was commenced after the effective date of this part.

(b) Alteration. Each facility or part of a facility which is altered by, on behalf of, or for the use of a recipient after the effective date of this part in a manner that affects or could affect the usability of the facility or part of the facility shall, to the maximum extent feasible, be altered in such manner that the altered portion of the facility is readily accessible to and usable by handicapped persons.

(c) Conformance with Uniform Federal Accessibility Standards. (1) Effective as of January 18, 1991, design, construction, or alteration of buildings in conformance with sections 3-8 of the Uniform Federal Accessibility Standards (UFAS) (Appendix A to 41 CFR subpart 101-19.6) shall be deemed to comply with the requirements of this section with respect to those buildings. Departures from particular technical and scoping requirements of UFAS by the use of other methods are permitted where substantially equivalent or greater access to and usability of the building is provided.

(2) For purposes of this section, section 4.1.6(1)(g) of UFAS shall be interpreted to exempt from the requirements of UFAS onlu mechanical rooms and other spaces that, because of their intended use, will not require accessibility to the public or beneficiaries or result in the employment or residence therein of persons with phusical handicaps.

(3) This section does not require recipients to make building alterations that have little likelihood of being accomplished without removing or altering a load-bearing structural member.

SUBPART D PRESCHOOL, ELEMENTARY, AND SECONDARY EDUCATION

§ 104.31 Application of this subpart.

Subpart D applies to preschool, elementary, secondary, and adult education programs or activities that receive Federal financial assistance and to recipients that operate, or that receive Federal financial assistance for the operation of, such programs or activities.

§ 104.32 Location and notification.

A recipient that operates a public elementary or secondary education program or activity shall annually:

(a) Undertake to identify and locate every qualified handicapped person residing in the recipient's jurisdiction who is not receiving a public education; and

(b) Take appropriate steps to notify handicapped persons and their parents or guardians of the recipient's duty under this subpart.

§ 104.33 Free appropriate public education.

(a) General. A recipient that operates a public elementary or secondary education program or activity shall provide a free appropriate public education to each qualified handicapped person who is in the recipient's jurisdiction, regardless of the nature or severity of the person's handicap.

(b) Appropriate education. (1) For the purpose of this subpart, the provision of an appropriate education is the provision of regular or special education and related aids and services that (i) are designed to meet individual educational needs of handicapped persons as adequately as the needs of nonhandicapped persons are met and (ii) are based upon adherence to procedures that satisfy the requirements of §§ 104.34, 104.35, and 104.36.

(2) Implementation of an Individualized Education Program developed in accordance with the Education of the Handicapped Act is one means of meeting the standard established in paragraph (b)(1)(i) of this section.

(3) A recipient may place a handicapped person or refer such a person for aid, benefits, or services other than those that it operates or provides as its means of carrying out the requirements of this subpart. If so, the recipient remains responsible for ensuring that the requirements of this subpart are met with respect to any handicapped person so placed or referred.

(c) Free education — (1) General. For the purpose of this section, the provision of a free education is the provision of educational and related services without cost to the handicapped person or to his or her parents or guardian, except for those fees that are imposed on non-handicapped persons or their parents or guardian. It may consist either of the provision of free services or, if a recipient places a handicapped person or refers such person for aid, benefits, or services not operated or provided by the recipient as its means of carrying out the requirements of this subpart, of payment for the costs of the aid, benefits, or services. Funds available from any public or private agency may be used to meet the requirements of this subpart. Nothing in this section shall be construed to relieve an insurer or similar third party from an otherwise valid obligation to provide or pay for services provided to a handicapped person.

(2) Transportation. If a recipient places a handicapped person or refers such person for aid, benefits, or services not operated or provided by the recipient as its means of carrying out the requirements of this subpart, the recipient shall ensure that adequate transportation to and from the aid, benefits, or services is provided at no greater cost than would be incurred by the person or his or her parents or guardian if the person were placed in the aid, benefits, or services operated by the recipient.

(3) Residential placement. If a public or private residential placement is necessary to provide a free appropriate public education to a handicapped person because of his or her handicap, the placement, including non-medical care and room and board, shall be provided at no cost to the person or his or her parents or guardian.

(4) Placement of handicapped persons by parents. If a recipient has made available, in conformance with the requirements of this section and § 104.34, a free appropriate public education to a handicapped person and the person's parents or guardian choose to place the person in a private school, the recipient is not required to pay for the person's education in the private school. Disagreements between a parent or guardian and a recipient regarding whether the recipient has made a free appropriate public education available or otherwise regarding the question of financial responsibility are subject to the due process procedures of § 104.36.

(d) Compliance. A recipient may not exclude any qualified handicapped person from a public elementary or secondary education after the effective date of this part. A recipient that is not, on the effective date of this regulation, in full compliance with the other requirements of the preceding paragraphs of this section shall meet such requirements at the earliest practicable time and in no event later than September 1, 1978.

§ 104.34 Educational setting.

(a) Academic setting. A recipient to which this subpart applies shall educate, or shall provide for the education of, each qualified handicapped person in its jurisdiction with persons who are not handicapped to the maximum extent appropriate to the needs of the handicapped person. A recipient shall place a handicapped person in the regular educational environment operated by the recipient unless it is demonstrated by the recipient that the education of the person in the regular environment with the use of supplementary aids and services cannot be achieved satisfactorily. Whenever a recipient places a person in a setting other than the regular educational environment pursuant to this paragraph, it shall take into account the proximity of the alternate setting to the person's home.

(b) Nonacademic settings. In providing or arranging for the provision of nonacademic and extracurricular services and activities, including meals, recess periods, and the services and activities set forth in § 104.37(a)(2), a recipient shall ensure that handicapped persons participate with nonhandicapped persons in such activities and services to the maximum extent appropriate to the needs of the handicapped person in question.

(c) Comparable facilities. If a recipient, in compliance with paragraph (a) of this section, operates a facility that is identifiable as being for handicapped persons, the recipient shall ensure that the facility and the services and activities provided therein are comparable to the other facilities, services, and activities of the recipient.

§ 104.35 Evaluation and placement.

(a) *Preplacement evaluation.* A recipient that operates a public elementary or secondary education program or activity shall shall conduct an evaluation in accordance with the requirements of paragraph (b) of this section of any person who, because of handicap, needs or is belived to need special education or related services before taking any action with respect to the initial placement of the person in regular or special education and any subsequent significant change in placement.

(b) *Evaluation procedures.* A recipient to which this subpart applies shall establish standards and procedures for the evaluation and placement of persons who, because of handicap, need or are believed to need special education or related services which ensure that:

(1) Tests and other evaluation materials have been validated for the specific purpose for which they are used and are administered by trained personnel in conformance with the instructions provided by their producer;

(2) Tests and other evaluation materials include those tailored to assess specific areas of educational need and not merely those which are designed to provide a single general intelligence quotient; and

(3) Tests are selected and administered so as best to ensure that, when a test is administered to a student with impaired sensory, manual, or speaking skills, the test results accurately reflect the student's aptitude or achievement level or whatever other factor the test purports to measure, rather than reflecting the student's impaired sensory, manual, or speaking skills (except where those skills are the factors that the test purports to measure).

(c) *Placement procedures.* In interpreting evaluation data and in making placement decisions, a recipient shall (1) draw upon information from a variety of sources, including aptitude and achievement tests, teacher recommendations, physical condition, social or cultural background, and adaptive behavior, (2) establish procedures to ensure that information obtained from all such sources is documented and carefully considered, (3) ensure that the placement decision is made by a group of persons, including persons knowledgeable about the child, the meaning of the evaluation data, and the placement options, and (4) ensure that the placement decision is made in conformity with § 104.34.

(d) *Reevaluation.* A recipient to which this section applies shall establish procedures, in accordance with paragraph (b) of this section, for periodic reevaluation of students who have been provided special education and related services. A reevaluation procedure consistent with the Education for the Handicapped Act is one means of meeting this requirement.

§ 104.36 Procedural safeguards.

A recipient that operates a public elementary or secondary education program or activity shall establish and implement, with respect to actions regarding the identification, evaluation, or educational placement of persons who, because of handicap, need or are believed to need special instruction or related services, a system of procedural safeguards that includes notice, an opportunity for the parents or guardian of the person to examine relevant records, an impartial hearing with opportunity for participation by the person's parents or guardian and representation by counsel, and a review procedure. Compliance with the procedural safeguards of section 615 of the Education of the Handicapped Act is one means of meeting this requirement.

§ 104.37 Nonacademic services.

(a) *General.* (1) A recipient to which this subpart applies shall provide non-academic and extracurricular services and activities in such manner as is necessary to afford handicapped students an equal opportunity for participation in such services and activities.

(2) Nonacademic and extracurricular services and activities may include counseling services, physical recreational athletics, transportation, health services, recreational activities, special interest groups or clubs sponsored by the recipients, referrals to agencies which provide assistance to handicapped persons, and employment of students, including both employment by the recipient and assistance in making available outside employment.

(b) Counseling services. A recipient to which this subpart applies that provides personal, academic, or vocational counseling, guidance, or placement services to its students shall provide these services without discrimination on the basis of handicap. The recipient shall ensure that qualified handicapped students are not counseled toward more restrictive career objectives than are nonhandicapped students with similar interests and abilities.

(c) Physical education and athletics. (1) In providing physical education courses and athletics and similar aid, benefits, or services to any of its students, a recipient to which this subpart applies may not discriminate on the basis of handicap. A recipient that offers physical education courses or that operates or sponsors interscholastic, club, or intramural athletics shall provide to qualified handicapped students an equal opportunity for participation.

(2) A recipient may offer to handicapped students physical education and athletic activities that are separate or different from those offered to nonhandicapped students only if separation or differentiation is consistent with the requirements of § 104.34 and only if no qualified handicapped student is denied the opportunity to compete for teams or to participate in courses that are not separate or different.

§ 104.38 Preschool and adult education.

A recipient to which this subpart applies that provides preschool education or day care or adult education may not, on the basis of handicap, exclude qualified handicapped persons and shall take into account the needs of such persons in determining the aid, benefits or services to be provided.

§ 104.39 Private education.

(a) A recipient that provides private elementary or secondary education may not, on the basis of handicap, exclude a qualified handicapped person if the person can, with minor adjustments, be provided an appropriate education, as defined in § 104.33(b)(1), within that recipient's program or activity.

(b) A recipient to which this section applies may not charge more for the provision of an appropriate education to handicapped persons than to nonhandicapped persons except to the extent that any additional charge is justified by a substantial increase in cost to the recipient.

(c) A recipient to which this section applies that provides special education shall do so in accordance with the provisions of §§ 104.35 and 104.36. Each recipient to which this section applies is subject to the provisions of §§ 104.34, 104.37, and 104.38.

SUBPART E POSTSECONDARY EDUCATION

§ 104.41 Application of this subpart.

Subpart E applies to postsecondary education programs or activities, including postsecondary vocational education programs or activities, that receive Federal financial assistance and to recipients that operate, or that receive Federal financial assistance for the operation of, such programs or activities.

§ 104.42 Admissions and recruitment.

(a) *General.* Qualified handicapped persons may not, on the basis of handicap, be denied admission or be subjected to discrimination in admission or recruitment by a recipient to which this subpart applies.

(b) *Admissions.* In administering its admission policies, a recipient to which this subpart applies:

(1) May not apply limitations upon the number or proportion of handicapped persons who may be admitted;

(2) May not make use of any test or criterion for admission that has a disproportionate, adverse effect on handicapped persons or any class of handicapped persons unless (i) the test or criterion, as used by the recipient, has been validated as a predictor of success in the education program or activity in question and (ii) alternate tests or criteria that have a less disproportionate, adverse effect are not shown by the Assistant Secretary to be available.

(3) Shall assure itself that (i) admissions tests are selected and administered so as best to ensure that, when a test is administered to an applicant who has a handicap that impairs sensory, manual, or speaking skills, the test results accurately reflect the applicant's aptitude or achievement level or whatever other factor the test purports to measure, rather than reflecting the applicant's impaired sensory, manual, or speaking skills (except where those skills are the factors that the test purports to measure); (ii) admissions tests that are designed for persons with impaired sensory, manual, or speaking skills are offered as often and in as timely a manner as are other admissions tests; and (iii) admissions tests are administered in facilities that, on the whole, are accessible to handicapped persons; and

(4) Except as provided in paragraph (c) of this section, may not make preadmission inquiry as to whether an applicant for admission is a handicapped person but, after admission, may make inquiries on a confidential basis as to handicaps that may require accommodation.

(c) *Preadmission inquiry exception.* When a recipient is taking remedial action to correct the effects of past discrimination pursuant to § 104.6(a) or when a recipient is taking voluntary action to overcome the effects of conditions that resulted in limited participation in its federally assisted program or activity pursuant to § 104.6(b), the recipient may invite applicants for admission to indicate whether and to what extent they are handicapped, *Provided,* That:

(1) The recipient states clearly on any written questionnaire used for this purpose or makes clear orally if no written questionnaire is used that the information requested is intended for use solely in connection with its remedial action obligations or its voluntary action efforts; and

(2) The recipient states clearly that the information is being requested on a voluntary basis, that it will be kept confidential, that refusal to provide it will not subject the applicant to any adverse treatment, and that it will be used only in accordance with this part.

(d) *Validity studies.* For the purpose of paragraph (b)(2) of this section, a recipient may base prediction equations on first year grades, but shall conduct periodic validity studies against the criterion of overall success in the education program or activity in question in order to monitor the general validity of the test scores.

§ 104.43 Treatment of students; general.

(a) No qualified handicapped student shall, on the basis of handicap, be excluded from participation in, be denied the benefits of, or otherwise be subjected to discrimination under any academic, research, occupational training, housing, health insurance, counseling, financial aid, physical education, athletics, recreation, transportation, other extracurricular, or other postsecondary education aid, benefits, or services to which this subpart applies.

(b) A recipient to which this subpart applies that considers participation by students in education programs or activities not operated wholly by the recipient as part of, or equivalent to, and education program or activity operated by the recipient shall assure itself that the other education program or activity, as a whole, provides an equal opportunity for the participation of qualified handicapped persons.

(c) A recipient to which this subpart applies may not, on the basis of handicap, exclude any qualified handicapped student from any course, course of study, or other part of its education program or activity.

(d) A recipient to which this subpart applies shall operate its program or activity in the most integrated setting appropriate.

§ 104.44 Academic adjustments.

(a) *Academic requirements.* A recipient to which this subpart applies shall make such modifications to its academic requirements as are necessary to ensure that such requirements do not discriminate or have the effect of discriminatiing, on the basis of handicap, against a qualified handicapped applicant or student. Academic requirements that the recipient can demonstrate are essential to the instruction being pursued by such student or to any directly related licensing requirement will not be regarded as discriminatory within the meaning of this section. Modifications may include changes in the length of time permitted for the completion of degree requirements, substitution of specific courses required for the completion of degree requirements, and adaptation of the manner in which specific courses are conducted.

(b) *Other rules.* A recipient to which this subpart applies may not impose upon handicapped students other rules, such as the prohibition of tape recorders in classrooms or of dog guides in campus buildings, that have the effect of limiting the participation of handicapped students in the recipient's education program or activity.

(c) *Course examinations.* In its course examinations or other procedures for evaluating students' academic achievement, a recipient to which this subpart applies shall provide such methods for evaluating the achievement of students who have a handicap that impairs sensory, manual, or speaking skills as will best ensure that the results of the evaluation represents the student's achievement in the course, rather than reflecting the student's impaired sensory, manual, or speaking skills (except where such skills are the factors that the test purports to measure).

(d) *Auxiliary aids.* (1) A recipient to which this subpart applies shall take such steps as are necessary to ensure that no handicapped student is denied the benefits of, excluded from participation in, or otherwise subjected to discrimination because of the absence of educational auxiliary aids for students with impaired sensory, manual, or speaking skills.

(2) Auxiliary aids may include taped texts, interpreters or other effective methods of making orally delivered materials available to students with hearing impairments, readers in libraries for students with visual impairments, classroom equipment adapted for use by students with manual impairments, and other similar services and actions. Recipients need not provide attendants, individually prescribed devices, readers for personal use or study, or other devices or services of a personal nature.

§ 104.45 Housing.

(a) *Housing provided by the recipient.* A recipient that provides housing to its nonhandicapped students shall provide comparable, convenient, and accessible housing to handicapped students at the same cost as to others. At the end of the transition period provided for in Subpart C, such housing shall be available in sufficient quantity and variety so that the scope of handicapped students' choice of living accommodations is, as a whole, comparable to that of nonhandicapped students.

(b) *Other housing.* A recipient that assists any agency, organization, or person in making housing available to any of its students shall take such action as may be necessary to assure itself that such housing is, as a whole, made available in a manner that does not result in discrimination on the basis of handicap.

§ 104.46 Financial and employment assistance to students.

(a) *Provision of financial assistance.* (1) In providing financial assistance to qualified handicapped persons, a recipient to which this subpart applies may not,

(i) On the basis of handicap, provide less assistance than is provided to nonhandicapped persons, limit eligibility for assistance, or otherwise discriminate or

(ii) Assist any entity or person that provides assistance to any of the recipient's students in a manner that discriminates against qualified handicapped persons on the basis of handicap.

(2) A recipient may administer or assist in the administration of scholarships, fellowships, or other forms of financial assistance established under wills, trusts, bequests, or similar legal instruments that require awards to be made on the basis of factors that discriminate or have the effect of discriminating on the basis of handicap only if the overall effect of the award of scholarships, fellowships, and other forms of financial assistance is not discriminatory on the basis of handicap.

(b) *Assistance in making available outside employment.* A recipient that assists any agency, organization, or person in providing employment opportunities to any of its students shall assure itself that such employment opportunities, as a whole, are made available in a manner that would not violate subpart B if they were provided by the recipient.

(c) *Employment of students by recipients.* A recipient that employs any of its students may not do so in a manner that violates subpart B.

§ 104.47 Nonacademic services.

(a) *Physical education and athletics.* (1) In providing physical education courses and athletics and similar aid, benefits, or services to any of its students, a recipient to which this subpart applies may not disariminate on the basis of handicap. A recipient that offers physical education courses or that operates or sponsors intercollegiate, club, or intramural athletics shall provide to qualified handicapped students an equal opportunity for participation in these activities.

(2) A recipient may offer to handicapped students physical education and athletic activities that are separate or different only if separation or differentiation is consistent with the requirements of § 104.43(d) and only if no qualified handicapped student is denied the opportunity to compete for teams or to participate in courses that are not separate or different.

(b) *Counseling and placement services.* A recipient to which this subpart applies that provides personal, academic, or vocational counseling, guidance, or placement services to its students shall provide these services without discrimination on the basis of handicap. The recipient shall ensure that qualified handicapped students are not counseled toward more restrictive career objectives than are nonhandicapped students with similar interests and abilities. This requirement does not preclude a recipient from providing factual information about licensing and certification requirements that may present obstacles to handicapped persons in their pursuit of particular careers.

(c) Social organizations. A recipient that provides significant assistance to fraternities, sororities, or similar organizations shall assure itself that the membership practices of such organizations do not permit discrimination otherwise prohibited by this subpart.

TITLE 42.
THE PUBLIC HEALTH AND WELFARE

CHAPTER 126

§ 12101. Congressional findings and purposes

(a) Findings. The Congress finds that—

(1) some 43,000,000 Americans have one or more physical or mental disabilities, and this number is increasing as the population as a whole is growing older;

(2) historically, society has tended to isolate and segregate individuals with disabilities, and, despite some improvements, such forms of discrimination against individuals with disabilities continue to be a serious and pervasive social problem;

(3) discrimination against individuals with disabilities persists in such critical areas as employment, housing, public accommodations, education, transportation, communication, recreation, institutionalization, health services, voting, and access to public services;

(4) unlike individuals who have experienced discrimination on the basis of race, color, sex, national origin, religion, or age, individuals who have experienced discrimination on the basis of disability have often had no legal recourse to redress such discrimination;

(5) individuals with disabilities continually encounter various forms of discrimination, including outright intentional exclusion, the discriminatory effects of architectural, transportation, and communication barriers, overprotective rules and policies, failure to make modifications to existing facilities and practices, exclusionary qualification standards and criteria, segregation, and relegation to lesser services, programs, activities, benefits, jobs, or other opportunities;

(6) census data, national polls, and other studies have documented that people with disabilities, as a group, occupy an inferior status in our society, and are severely disadvantaged socially, vocationally, economically, and educationally;

(7) individuals with disabilities are a discrete and insular minority who have been faced with restrictions and limitations, subjected to a history of purposeful unequal treatment, and relegated to a position of political powerlessness in our society, based on characteristics that are beyond the control of such individuals and resulting from stereotypic assumptions not truly indicative of the individual ability of such individuals to participate in, and contribute to, society;

(8) the Nation's proper goals regarding individuals with disabilities are to assure equality of opportunity, full participation, independent living, and economic self-sufficiency for such individuals; and

(9) the continuing existence of unfair and unnecessary discrimination and prejudice denies people with disabilities the opportunity to compete on an equal basis and to pursue those opportunities for which our free society is justifiably famous, and costs the United States billions of dollars in unnecessary expenses resulting from dependency and non-productivity.

(b) Purpose. It is the purpose of this Act—

(1) to provide a clear and comprehensive national mandate for the elimination of discrimination against individuals with disabilities;

(2) to provide clear, strong, consistent, enforceable standards addressing discrimination against individuals with disabilities;

(3) to ensure that the Federal Government plays a central role in enforcing the standards established in this Act on behalf of individuals with disabilities; and

(4) to invoke the sweep of congressional authority, including the power to enforce the fourteenth amendment and to regulate commerce, in order to address the major areas of discrimination faced day-to-day by people with disabilities.

§ 12102. Definitions

As used in this Act:

(1) Auxiliary aids and services. The term "auxiliary aids and services" includes—

(A) qualified interpreters or other effective methods of making aurally delivered materials available to individuals with hearing impairments;

(B) qualified readers, taped texts, or other effective methods of making visually delivered materials available to individuals with visual impairments;

(C) acquisition or modification of equipment or devices; and

(D) other similar services and actions.

(2) Disability. The term "disability" means, with respect to an individual—

(A) a physical or mental impairment that substantially limits one or more of the major life activities of such individual;

(B) a record of such an impairment; or

(C) being regarded as having such an impairment.

(3) State. The term "State" means each of the several States, the District of Columbia, the Commonwealth of Puerto Rico, Guam, American Samoa, the Virgin Islands, the Trust Territory of the Pacific Islands, and the Commonwealth of the Northern Mariana Islands.

TITLE 42.
THE PUBLIC HEALTH AND WELFARE

CHAPTER 126 EQUAL OPPORTUNITY FOR INDIVIDUALS WITH DISABILITIES

PUBLIC SERVICES
PROHIBITION AGAINST DISCRIMINATION AND OTHER GENERALLY APPLICABLE PROVISIONS

§ 12131 Definition

As used in this title:

(1) Public entity. The term "public entity" means—

(A) any State or local government;

(B) any department, agency, special purpose district, or other instrumentality of a State or States or local government; and

(C) the National Railroad Passenger Corporation, and any commuter authority (as defined in section 103(8) of the Rail Passenger Service Act [*49 USCS § 24102(4)*]).

(2) Qualified individual with a disability. The term "qualified individual with a disability" means an individual with a disability who, with or without reasonable modifications to rules, policies, or practices, the removal of architectural, communication, or transportation barriers, or the provision of auxiliary aids and services, meets the essential eligibility requirements for the receipt of services or the participation in programs or activities provided by a public entity.

§ 12132 Discrimination.

Subject to the provisions of this title, no qualified individual with a disability shall, by reason of such disability, be excluded from participation in or be denied the benefits of the services, programs, or activities of a public entity, or be subjected to discrimination by any such entity.

§ 12133 Enforcement.

The remedies, procedures, and rights set forth in section 505 of the Rehabilitation Act of 1973 (*29 U.S.C. 794a*) shall be the remedies, procedures, and rights this title provides to any person alleging discrimination on the basis of disability in violation of section 202 [*42 USCS § 12132*].

§ 12134 Regulations.

(a) In general. Not later than 1 year after the date of enactment of this Act [enacted July 26, 1990], the Attorney General shall promulgate regulations in an accessible format that implement this subtitle. Such regulations shall not include any matter within the scope of the authority of the Secretary of Transportation under section 223, 229, or 244 [*42 USCS § 12143, 12149*, or *12164*].

(b) Relationship to other regulations. Except for "program accessibility, existing facilities", and "communications", regulations under subsection (a) shall be consistent with this Act and with the coordination regulations under part 41 of title 28, Code of Federal Regulations (as promulgated by the Department of Health, Education, and Welfare on January 13, 1978), applicable to recipients of Federal financial assistance under section 504 of the Rehabilitation Act of 1973 (*29 U.S.C. 794*). With respect to "program accessibility, existing facilities", and "communications", such regulations shall be consistent with regulations and analysis as in part 39 of title 28 of the Code of Federal Regulations, applicable to federally conducted activities under such section 504.

(c) Standards. Regulations under subsection (a) shall include standards applicable to facilities and vehicles covered by this subtitle, other than facilities, stations, rail passenger cars, and vehicles covered by subtitle B. Such standards shall be consistent with the minimum guidelines and requirements issued by the Architectural and Transportation Barriers Compliance Board in accordance with section 504(a) of this Act [*42 USCS § 12204(a)*].

ACTIONS APPLICABLE TO PUBLIC TRANSPORTATION PROVIDED BY PUBLIC ENTITIES CONSIDERED DISCRIMINATORY

Public Transportation other than by Aircraft or Certain Rail Operations

§ 12141 Definitions.

As used in this part:

(1) Demand responsive system. The term "demand responsive system" means any system of providing designated public transportation which is not a fixed route system.

(2) Designated public transportation. The term "designated public transportation" means transportation (other than public school transportation) by bus, rail, or any other conveyance (other than transportation by aircraft or intercity or commuter rail transportation (as defined in section 241 [*42 USCS § 12161*])) that provides the general public with general or special service (including charter service) on a regular and continuing basis.

(3) Fixed route system. The term "fixed route system" means a system of providing designated public transportation on which a vehicle is operated along a prescribed route according to a fixed schedule.

(4) Operates. The term "operates", as used with respect to a fixed route system or demand responsive system, includes operation of such system by a person under a contractual or other arrangement or relationship with a public entity.

(5) Public school transportation. The term "public school transportation" means transportation by schoolbus vehicles of schoolchildren, personnel, and equipment to and from a public elementary or secondary school and school-related activities.

(6) Secretary. The term "Secretary" means the Secretary of Transportation.

§ 12142 Public entities operating fixed route systems.

(a) Purchase and lease of new vehicles. It shall be considered discrimination for purposes of section 202 of this Act [*42 USCS § 12132*] and *section 504 of the Rehabilitation Act of 1973 (29 U.S.C. 794)* for a public entity which operates a fixed route system to purchase or lease a new bus, a new rapid rail vehicle, a new light rail vehicle, or any other new vehicle to be used on such system, if the solicitation for such purchase or lease is made after the 30th day following the effective date of this subsection [effective July 26, 1990] and if such bus, rail vehicle, or other vehicle is not readily accessible to and usable by individuals with disabilities, including individuals who use wheelchairs.

(b) Purchase and lease of used vehicles. Subject to subsection (c)(1), it shall be considered discrimination for purposes of section 202 of this Act [*42 USCS § 12132*] and *section 504* of the Rehabilitation Act of 1973 (*29 U.S.C. 794*) for a public entity which operates a fixed route system to purchase or lease, after the 30th day following the effective date of this subsection [effective July 26, 1990], a used vehicle for use on such system unless such entity makes demonstrated good faith efforts to purchase or lease a used vehicle for use on such system that is readily accessible to and usable by individuals with disabilities, including individuals who use wheelchairs.

(c) Remanufactured vehicles.

(1) General rule. Except as provided in paragraph (2), it shall be considered discrimination for purposes of section 202 of this Act [*42 USCS § 12132*] and *section 504* of the Rehabilitation Act of 1973 (*29 U.S.C. 794*) for a public entity which operates a fixed route system—

(A) to remanufacture a vehicle for use on such system so as to extend its usable life for 5 years or more, which remanufacture begins (or for which the solicitation is made) after the 30th day following the effective date of this subsection [effective July 26, 1990]; or

(B) to purchase or lease for use on such system a remanufactured vehicle which has been remanufactured so as to extend its usable life for 5 years or more, which purchase or lease occurs after such 30th day and during the period in which the usable life is extended;

unless, after remanufacture, the vehicle is, to the maximum extent feasible, readily accessible to and usable by individuals with disabilities, including individuals who use wheelchairs.

(2) Exception for historic vehicles.

(A) General rule. If a public entity operates a fixed route system any segment of which is included on the National Register of Historic Places and if making a vehicle of historic character to be used solely on such segment readily accessible to and usable by individuals with disabilities would significantly alter the historic character of such vehicle, the public entity only has to make (or to purchase or lease a remanufactured vehicle with) those modifications which are necessary to meet the requirements of paragraph (1) and which do not significantly alter the historic character of such vehicle.

(B) Vehicles of historic character defined by regulations. For purposes of this paragraph and section 228(b) [*42 USCS § 12148(b)*], a vehicle of historic character shall be defined by the regulations issued by the Secretary to carry out this subsection.

§ 12143 Paratransit as a complement to fixed route service.

(a) General rule. It shall be considered discrimination for purposes of section 202 of this Act [*42 USCS § 12132*] and *section 504* of the Rehabilitation Act of 1973 (*29 U.S.C. 794*) for a public entity which operates a fixed route system (other than a system which provides solely commuter bus service) to fail to provide with respect to the operations of its fixed route system, in accordance with this section, paratransit and other special transportation services to individuals with disabilities, including individuals who use wheelchairs, that are sufficient to provide to such individuals a level of service (1) which is comparable to the level of designated public transportation services provided to individuals without disabilities using such system; or (2) in the case of response time, which is comparable, to the extent practicable, to the level of designated public transportation services provided to individuals without disabilities using such system.

(b) Issuance of regulations. Not later than 1 year after the effective date of this subsection [effective July 26, 1990], the Secretary shall issue final regulations to carry out this section.

(c) Required contents of regulations.

(1) Eligible recipients of service. The regulations issued under this section shall require each public entity which operates a fixed route system to provide the paratransit and other special transportation services required under this section—

(A) (i) to any individual with a disability who is unable, as a result of a physical or mental impairment (including a vision impairment) and without the assistance of another individual (except an operator of a wheelchair lift or other boarding assistance device), to board, ride, or disembark from any vehicle on the system which is readily accessible to and usable by individuals with disabilities;

(ii) to any individual with a disability who needs the assistance of a wheelchair lift or other boarding assistance device (and is able with such assistance) to board, ride, and disembark from any vehicle which is readily accessible to and usable by individuals with disabilities if the individual wants to travel on a route on the system during the hours of operation of the system at a time (or within a reasonable period of such time) when such a vehicle is not being used to provide designated public transportation on the route; and

(iii) to any individual with a disability who has a specific impairment-related condition which prevents such individual from traveling to a boarding location or from a disembarking location on such system;

(B) to one other individual accompanying the individual with the disability; and

(C) to other individuals, in addition to the one individual described in subparagraph (B), accompanying the individual with a disability provided that space for these additional individuals is available on the paratransit vehicle carrying the individual with a disability and that the transportation of such additional individuals will not result in a denial of service to individuals with disabilities.

For purposes of clauses (i) and (ii) of subparagraph (A), boarding or disembarking from a vehicle does not include travel to the boarding location or from the disembarking location.

(2) Service area. The regulations issued under this section shall require the provision of paratransit and special transportation services required under this section in the service area of each public entity which operates a fixed route system, other than any portion of the service area in which the public entity solely provides commuter bus service.

(3) Service criteria. Subject to paragraphs (1) and (2), the regulations issued under this section shall establish minimum service criteria for determining the level of services to be required under this section.

(4) Undue financial burden limitation. The regulations issued under this section shall provide that, if the public entity is able to demonstrate to the satisfaction of the Secretary that the provision of paratransit and other special transportation services otherwise required under this section would impose an undue financial burden on the public entity, the public entity, notwithstanding any other provision of this section (other than paragraph (5)), shall only be required to provide such services to the extent that providing such services would not impose such a burden.

(5) Additional services. The regulations issued under this section shall establish circumstances under which the Secretary may require a public entity to provide, notwithstanding paragraph (4), paratransit and other special transportation services under this section beyond the level of paratransit and other special transportation services which would otherwise be required under paragraph (4).

(6) Public participation. The regulations issued under this section shall require that each public entity which operates a fixed route system hold a public hearing, provide an opportunity for public comment, and consult with individuals with disabilities in preparing its plan under paragraph (7).

(7) Plans. The regulations issued under this section shall require that each public

entity which operates a fixed route system—

(A) within 18 months after the effective date of this subsection [effective July 26, 1990], submit to the Secretary, and commence implementation of, a plan for providing paratransit and other special transportation services which meets the requirements of this section; and

(B) on an annual basis thereafter, submit to the Secretary, and commence implementation of, a plan for providing such services.

(8) Provision of services by others. The regulations issued under this section shall—

(A) require that a public entity submitting a plan to the Secretary under this section identify in the plan any person or other public entity which is providing a paratransit or other special transportation service for individuals with disabilities in the service area to which the plan applies; and

(B) provide that the public entity submitting the plan does not have to provide under the plan such service for individuals with disabilities.

(9) Other provisions. The regulations issued under this section shall include such other provisions and requirements as the Secretary determines are necessary to carry out the objectives of this section.

(d) Review of plan.

(1) General rule. The Secretary shall review a plan submitted under this section for the purpose of determining whether or not such plan meets the requirements of this section, including the regulations issued under this section.

(2) Disapproval. If the Secretary determines that a plan reviewed under this subsection fails to meet the requirements of this section, the Secretary shall disapprove the plan and notify the public entity which submitted the plan of such disapproval and the reasons therefor.

(3) Modification of disapproved plan. Not later than 90 days after the date of disapproval of a plan under this subsection, the public entity which submitted the plan shall modify the plan to meet the requirements of this section and shall submit to the Secretary, and commence implementation of, such modified plan.

(e) Discrimination defined. As used in subsection (a), the term "discrimination" includes—

(1) a failure of a public entity to which the regulations issued under this section apply to submit, or commence implementation of, a plan in accordance with subsections (c)(6) and (c)(7);

(2) a failure of such entity to submit, or commence implementation of, a modified plan in accordance with subsection (d)(3);

(3) submission to the Secretary of a modified plan under subsection (d)(3) which does not meet the requirements of this section; or

(4) a failure of such entity to provide paratransit or other special transportation services in accordance with the plan or modified plan the public entity submitted to the Secretary under this section.

(f) Statutory construction. Nothing in this section shall be construed as preventing a public entity—

(1) from providing paratransit or other special transportation services at a level which is greater than the level of such services which are required by this section,

(2) from providing paratransit or other special transportation services in addition to those paratransit and special transportation services required by this section, or

(3) from providing such services to individuals in addition to those individuals to whom such services are required to be provided by this section.

§ 12144 Public entity operating a demand responsive system

If a public entity operates a demand responsive system, it shall be considered discrimination, for purposes of section 202 of this Act [42 USCS § 12132] and *section 504 of the Rehabilitation Act of 1973 (29 U.S.C. 794)*, for such entity to purchase or lease a new vehicle for use on such system, for which a solicitation is made after the 30th day following the effective date of this section [effective July 26, 1990], that is not readily accessible to and usable by individuals with disabilities, including individuals who use wheelchairs, unless such system, when viewed in its entirety, provides a level of service to such individuals equivalent to the level of service such system provides to individuals without disabilities.

§ 12145 Temporary relief where lifts are unavailable

(a) Granting. With respect to the purchase of new buses, a public entity may apply for, and the Secretary may temporarily relieve such public entity from the obligation under section 222(a) or 224 [42 USCS § 12142(a) or 12144] to purchase new buses that are readily accessible to and usable by individuals with disabilities if such public entity demonstrates to the satisfaction of the Secretary—

(1) that the initial solicitation for new buses made by the public entity specified that all new buses were to be lift-equipped and were to be otherwise accessible to and usable by individuals with disabilities;

(2) the unavailability from any qualified manufacturer of hydraulic, electromechanical, or other lifts for such new buses;

(3) that the public entity seeking temporary relief has made good faith efforts to locate a qualified manufacturer to supply the lifts to the manufacturer of such buses in sufficient time to comply with such solicitation; and

(4) that any further delay in purchasing new buses necessary to obtain such lifts would significantly impair transportation services in the community served by the public entity.

(b) Duration and notice to Congress. Any relief granted under subsection (a) shall be limited in duration by a specified date, and the appropriate committees of Congress shall be notified of any such relief granted.

(c) Fraudulent application. If, at any time, the Secretary has reasonable cause to believe that any relief granted under subsection (a) was fraudulently applied for, the Secretary shall—

(1) cancel such relief if such relief is still in effect; and

(2) take such other action as the Secretary considers appropriate.

§ 12146 New facilities

For purposes of section 202 of this Act [42 USCS § 12132] and *section 504 of the Rehabilitation Act of 1973 (29 U.S.C. 794)*, it shall be considered discrimination for a public entity to construct a new facility to be used in the provision of designated public transportation services unless such facility is readily accessible to and usable by individuals with disabilities, including individuals who use wheelchairs.

§ 12147 Alterations of existing facilities

(a) General rule. With respect to alterations of an existing facility or part thereof used in the provision of designated public transportation services that affect or could affect the usability of the facility or part thereof, it shall be considered discrimination, for purposes of section 202 of this Act [42 USCS § 12132] and *section 504* of the Rehabilitation Act of 1973 (*29 U.S.C. 794*), for a public entity to fail to make such alterations (or to ensure that the alterations are made) in such a manner that, to the maximum extent feasible, the altered portions of the facility are readily accessible to and usable by individuals with disabilities, including individuals who use wheelchairs, upon the completion of such alterations. Where the public entity is undertaking an alteration that affects or could affect usability of or access to an area of the facility containing a primary function, the entity shall also make the alterations in such a manner that, to the maximum extent feasible, the path of travel to the altered area and the bathrooms, telephones, and drinking fountains serving the altered area, are readily accessible to and usable by individuals with disabilities, including individuals who use wheelchairs, upon completion of such alterations, where such alterations to the path of travel or the bathrooms, telephones, and drinking fountains serving the altered area are not disproportionate to the overall alterations in terms of cost and scope (as determined under criteria established by the Attorney General).

(b) Special rule for stations.

(1) General rule. For purposes of section 202 of this Act [42 USCS § 12132] and *section 504* of the Rehabilitation Act of 1973 (*29 U.S.C. 794*), it shall be considered discrimination for a public entity that provides designated public transportation to fail, in accordance with the provisions of this subsection, to make key stations (as determined under criteria established by the Secretary by regulation) in rapid rail and light rail systems readily accessible to and usable by individuals with disabilities, including individuals who use wheelchairs.

(2) Rapid rail and light rail key stations.

(A) Accessibility. Except as otherwise provided in this paragraph, all key stations (as determined under criteria established by the Secretary by regulation) in rapid rail and light rail systems shall be made readily accessible to and usable by individuals with disabilities, including individuals who use wheelchairs, as soon as practicable but in no event later than the last day of the 3-year period beginning on the effective date of this paragraph [effective July 26, 1990].

(B) Extension for extraordinarily expensive structural changes. The Secretary may extend the 3-year period under subparagraph (A) up to a 30-year period for key stations in a rapid rail or light rail system which stations need extraordinarily expensive structural changes to, or replacement of, existing facilities; except that by the last day of the 20th year following the date of the enactment of this Act [enacted July 26, 1990] at least 2/3 of such key stations must be readily accessible to and usable by individuals with disabilities.

(3) Plans and milestones. The Secretary shall require the appropriate public entity to develop and submit to the Secretary a plan for compliance with this subsection—

(A) that reflects consultation with individuals with disabilities affected by such plan and the results of a public hearing and public comments on such plan, and

(B) that establishes milestones for achievement of the requirements of this subsection.

§ 12148 Public transportation programs and activities in existing facilities and one car per train rule

(a) Public transportation programs and activities in existing facilities.

(1) In general. With respect to existing facilities used in the provision of designated public transportation services, it shall be considered discrimination, for purposes of section 202 of this Act [42 USCS § 12132] and *section 504* of the Rehabilitation Act of

1973 (*29 U.S.C. 794*), for a public entity to fail to operate a designated public transportation program or activity conducted in such facilities so that, when viewed in the entirety, the program or activity is readily accessible to and usable by individuals with disabilities.

(2) Exception. Paragraph (1) shall not require a public entity to make structural changes to existing facilities in order to make such facilities accessible to individuals who use wheelchairs, unless and to the extent required by section 227(a) [*42 USCS § 12147(a)*] (relating to key alterations) or section 227(b) [*42 USCS § 12147(b)*] (relating to key stations).

(3) Utilization. Paragraph (1) shall not require a public entity to which paragraph (2) applies, to provide to individuals who use wheelchairs services made available to the general public at such facilities when such individuals could not utilize or benefit from such services provided at such facilities.

(b) One car per train rule.

(1) General rule. Subject to paragraph (2), with respect to 2 or more vehicles operated as a train by a light or rapid rail system, for purposes of section 202 of this Act [*42 USCS § 12132*] and *section 504* of the Rehabilitation Act of 1973 (*29 U.S.C. 794*), it shall be considered discrimination for a public entity to fail to have at least 1 vehicle per train that is accessible to individuals with disabilities, including individuals who use wheelchairs, as soon as practicable but in no event later than the last day of the 5-year period beginning on the effective date of this section.

(2) Historic trains. In order to comply with paragraph (1) with respect to the remanufacture of a vehicle of historic character which is to be used on a segment of a light or rapid rail system which is included on the National Register of Historic Places, if making such vehicle readily accessible to and usable by individuals with disabilities would significantly alter the historic character of such vehicle, the public entity which operates such system only has to make (or to purchase or lease a remanufactured vehicle with) those modifications which are necessary to meet the requirements of section 222(c)(1) [*42 USCS § 14142(c)(1)*] and which do not significantly alter the historic character of such vehicle.

§ 12149 Regulations

(a) In general. Not later than 1 year after the date of enactment of this Act [enacted July 26, 1990], the Secretary of Transportation shall issue regulations, in an accessible format, necessary for carrying out this part [*42 USCS §§ 12141* et seq.] (other than section 223).

(b) Standards. The regulations issued under this section and section 223 [*42 USCS § 12143*] shall include standards applicable to facilities and vehicles covered by this subtitle [*42 USCS §§ 12141* et seq.]. The standards shall be consistent with the minimum guidelines and requirements issued by the Architectural and Transportation Barriers Compliance Board in accordance with section 504 of this Act [*42 USCS § 12204*].

§ 12150 Interim accessibility requirements

If final regulations have not been issued pursuant to section 229 [*42 USCS § 12149*] for new construction or alterations for which a valid and appropriate State or local building permit is obtained prior to the issuance of final regulations under such section, and for which the construction or alteration authorized by such permit begins within one year of the receipt of such permit and is completed under the terms of such permit, compliance with the Uniform Federal Accessibility Standards in effect at the time the building permit is issued shall suffice to satisfy the requirement that facilities be readily accessible to and usable by persons with disabilities as required under sections 226 and 227 [*42 USCS §§ 12146, 12147*], except that, if such final regulations have not been issued one year after the Architectural and Transportation Barriers Compliance Board has issued the supplemental minimum guidelines required under section 504(a) of this Act [*42 USCS § 12204(a)*], compliance with such supplemental minimum guidelines shall be necessary to satisfy the requirement that facilities be readily accessible to and usable by persons with disabilities prior to issuance of the final regulations.

TITLE 28.
JUDICIAL ADMINISTRATION

CHAPTER I   DEPARTMENT OF JUSTICE

PART 35   NONDISCRIMINATION ON THE BASIS OF DISABILITY IN STATE AND LOCAL GOVERNMENT SERVICES

SUBPART A   GENERAL

§ 35.101   Purpose.

The purpose of this part is to effectuate subtitle A of title II of the Americans with Disabilities Act of 1990 *(42 U.S.C. 12131)*, which prohibits discrimination on the basis of disability by public entities.

§ 35.102   Application.

(a) Except as provided in paragraph (b) of this section, this part applies to all services, programs, and activities provided or made available by public entities.

(b) To the extent that public transportation services, programs, and activities of public entities are covered by subtitle B of title II of the ADA *(42 U.S.C. 12141)*, they are not subject to the requirements of this part.

§ 35.103   Relationship to other laws.

(a) Rule of interpretation. Except as otherwise provided in this part, this part shall not be construed to apply a lesser standard than the standards applied under title V of the Rehabilitation Act of 1973 *(29 U.S.C. 791)* or the regulations issued by Federal agencies pursuant to that title.

(b) Other laws. This part does not invalidate or limit the remedies, rights, and procedures of any other Federal laws, or State or local laws (including State common law) that provide greater or equal protection for the rights of individuals with disabilities or individuals associated with them.

§ 35.104   Definitions.

For purposes of this part, the term —

Act means the Americans with Disabilities Act (Pub. L. 101-336, *104 Stat. 327, 42 U.S.C. 12101*-12213 and *47 U.S.C. 225* and 611).

Assistant Attorney General means the Assistant Attorney General, Civil Rights Division, United States Department of Justice.

Auxiliary aids and services includes —

(1) Qualified interpreters, notetakers, transcription services, written materials, telephone handset amplifiers, assistive listening devices, assistive listening systems, telephones compatible with hearing aids, closed caption decoders, open and closed captioning, telecommunications devices for deaf persons (TDD's), videotext displays, or other effective methods of making aurally delivered materials available to individuals with hearing impairments;

(2) Qualified readers, taped texts, audio recordings, Brailled materials, large print

materials, or other effective methods of making visually delivered materials available to individuals with visual impairments;

(3) Acquisition or modification of equipment or devices; and

(4) Other similar services and actions.

Complete complaint means a written statement that contains the complainant's name and address and describes the public entity's alleged discriminatory action in sufficient detail to inform the agency of the nature and date of the alleged violation of this part. It shall be signed by the complainant or by someone authorized to do so on his or her behalf. Complaints filed on behalf of classes or third parties shall describe or identify (by name, if possible) the alleged victims of discrimination.

Current illegal use of drugs means illegal use of drugs that occurred recently enough to justify a reasonable belief that a person's drug use is current or that continuing use is a real and ongoing problem.

Designated agency means the Federal agency designated under subpart G of this part to oversee compliance activities under this part for particular components of State and local governments.

Disability means, with respect to an individual, a physical or mental impairment that substantially limits one or more of the major life activities of such individual; a record of such an impairment; or being regarded as having such an impairment.

(1)(i) The phrase physical or mental impairment means —

(A) Any physiological disorder or condition, cosmetic disfigurement, or anatomical loss affecting one or more of the following body systems: Neurological, musculoskeletal, special sense organs, respiratory (including speech organs), cardiovascular, reproductive, digestive, genitourinary, hemic and lymphatic, skin, and endocrine;

(B) Any mental or psychological disorder such as mental retardation, organic brain syndrome, emotional or mental illness, and specific learning disabilities.

(ii) The phrase physical or mental impairment includes, but is not limited to, such contagious and noncontagious diseases and conditions as orthopedic, visual, speech and hearing impairments, cerebral palsy, epilepsy, muscular dystrophy, multiple sclerosis, cancer, heart disease, diabetes, mental retardation, emotional illness, specific learning disabilities, HIV disease (whether symptomatic or asymptomatic), tuberculosis, drug addiction, and alcoholism.

(iii) The phrase physical or mental impairment does not include homosexuality or bisexuality.

(2) The phrase major life activities means functions such as caring for one's self, performing manual tasks, walking, seeing, hearing, speaking, breathing, learning, and working.

(3) The phrase has a record of such an impairment means has a history of, or has been misclassified as having, a mental or physical impairment that substantially limits one or more major life activities.

(4) The phrase is regarded as having an impairment means —

(i) Has a physical or mental impairment that does not substantially limit major life activities but that is treated by a public entity as constituting such a limitation;

(ii) Has a physical or mental impairment that substantially limits major life activities only as a result of the attitudes of others toward such impairment; or

(iii) Has none of the impairments defined in paragraph (1) of this definition but is treated by a public entity as having such an impairment.

(5) The term disability does not include —

(i) Transvestism, transsexualism, pedophilia, exhibitionism, voyeurism, gender identity disorders not resulting from physical impairments, or other sexual behavior disorders;

(ii) Compulsive gambling, kleptomania, or pyromania; or

(iii) Psychoactive substance use disorders resulting from current illegal use of drugs.

Drug means a controlled substance, as defined in schedules I through V of section 202 of the Controlled Substances Act *(21 U.S.C. 812)*.

Facility means all or any portion of buildings, structures, sites, complexes, equipment, rolling stock or other conveyances, roads, walks, passageways, parking lots, or other real or personal property, including the site where the building, property, structure, or equipment is located.

Historic preservation programs means programs conducted by a public entity that have preservation of historic properties as a primary purpose.

Historic Properties means those properties that are listed or eligible for listing in the National Register of Historic Places or properties designated as historic under State or local law.

Illegal use of drugs means the use of one or more drugs, the possession or distribution of which is unlawful under the Controlled Substances Act *(21 U.S.C. 812)*. The term illegal use of drugs does not include the use of a drug taken under supervision by a licensed health care professional, or other uses authorized by the Controlled Substances Act or other provisions of Federal law.

Individual with a disability means a person who has a disability. The term individual with a disability does not include an individual who is currently engaging in the illegal use of drugs, when the public entity acts on the basis of such use.

Public entity means —

(1) Any State or local government;

(2) Any department, agency, special purpose district, or other instrumentality of a State or States or local government; and

(3) The National Railroad Passenger Corporation, and any commuter authority (as defined in section 103(8) of the Rail Passenger Service Act).

Qualified individual with a disability means an individual with a disability who, with or without reasonable modifications to rules, policies, or practices, the removal of architectural, communication, or transportation barriers, or the provision of auxiliary aids and services, meets the essential eligibility requirements for the receipt of services or the participation in programs or activities provided by a public entity.

Qualified interpreter means an interpreter who is able to interpret effectively, accurately, and impartially both receptively and expressively, using any necessary specialized vocabulary.

Section 504 means section 504 of the Rehabilitation Act of 1973 (Pub. L. 93-112, *87 Stat. 394 (29 U.S.C. 794))*, as amended.

State means each of the several States, the District of Columbia, the Commonwealth of Puerto Rico, Guam, American Samoa, the Virgin Islands, the Trust Territory of the Pacific Islands, and the Commonwealth of the Northern Mariana Islands.

§ 35.105 Self-evaluation.

(a) A public entity shall, within one year of the effective date of this part, evaluate its current services, policies, and practices, and the effects thereof, that do not or may not meet the requirements of this part and, to the extent modification of any such services, policies, and practices is required, the public entity shall proceed to make the necessary modifications.

(b) A public entity shall provide an opportunity to interested persons, including individuals with disabilities or organizations representing individuals with disabilities, to participate in the self-evaluation process by submitting comments.

(c) A public entity that employs 50 or more persons shall, for at least three years following completion of the self-evaluation, maintain on file and make available for public inspection:

(1) A list of the interested persons consulted;

(2) A description of areas examined and any problems identified; and

(3) A description of any modifications made.

(d) If a public entity has already complied with the self-evaluation requirement of a regulation implementing section 504 of the Rehabilitation Act of 1973, then the requirements of this section shall apply only to those policies and practices that were not included in the previous self-evaluation.

(Approved by the Office of Management and Budget under control number 1190-0006)

§ 35.106 Notice.

A public entity shall make available to applicants, participants, beneficiaries, and other interested persons information regarding the provisions of this part and its applicability to the services, programs, or activities of the public entity, and make such information available to them in such manner as the head of the entity finds necessary to apprise such persons of the protections against discrimination assured them by the Act and this part.

SUBPART B GENERAL REQUIREMENTS

§ 35.130 General prohibitions against discrimination.

(a) No qualified individual with a disability shall, on the basis of disability, be excluded from participation in or be denied the benefits of the services, programs, or activities of a public entity, or be subjected to discrimination by any public entity.

(b) (1) A public entity, in providing any aid, benefit, or service, may not, directly or through contractual, licensing, or other arrangements, on the basis of disability —

(i) Deny a qualified individual with a disability the opportunity to participate in or benefit from the aid, benefit, or service;

(ii) Afford a qualified individual with a disability an opportunity to participate in or benefit from the aid, benefit, or service that is not equal to that afforded others;

(iii) Provide a qualified individual with a disability with an aid, benefit, or service that is not as effective in affording equal opportunity to obtain the same result, to gain the same benefit, or to reach the same level of achievement as that provided to others;

(iv) Provide different or separate aids, benefits, or services to individuals with disabilities or to any class of individuals with disabilities than is provided to others unless such action is necessary to provide qualified individuals with disabilities with aids, benefits, or services that are as effective as those provided to others;

(v) Aid or perpetuate discrimination against a qualified individual with a disability by providing significant assistance to an agency, organization, or person that discriminates on the basis of disability in providing any aid, benefit, or service to beneficiaries of the public entity's program;

(vi) Deny a qualified individual with a disability the opportunity to participate as a member of planning or advisory boards;

(vii) Otherwise limit a qualified individual with a disability in the enjoyment of any right, privilege, advantage, or opportunity enjoyed by others receiving the aid, benefit, or service.

(2) A public entity may not deny a qualified individual with a disability the opportunity to participate in services, programs, or activities that are not separate or different, despite the existence of permissibly separate or different programs or activities.

(3) A public entity may not, directly or through contractual or other arrangements, utilize criteria or methods of administration:

(i) That have the effect of subjecting qualified individuals with disabilities to discrimination on the basis of disability;

(ii) That have the purpose or effect of defeating or substantially impairing accomplishment of the objectives of the public entity's program with respect to individuals with disabilities; or

(iii) That perpetuate the discrimination of another public entity if both public entities are subject to common administrative control or are agencies of the same State.

(4) A public entity may not, in determining the site or location of a facility, make selections —

(i) That have the effect of excluding individuals with disabilities from, denying them the benefits of, or otherwise subjecting them to discrimination; or

(ii) That have the purpose or effect of defeating or substantially impairing the accomplishment of the objectives of the service, program, or activity with respect to individuals with disabilities.

(5) A public entity, in the selection of procurement contractors, may not use criteria that subject qualified individuals with disabilities to discrimination on the basis of disability.

(6) A public entity may not administer a licensing or certification program in a manner that subjects qualified individuals with disabilities to discrimination on the basis of disability, nor may a public entity establish requirements for the programs or activities of licensees or certified entities that subject qualified individuals with disabilities to discrimination on the basis of disability. The programs or activities of entities that are licensed or certified by a public entity are not, themselves, covered by this part.

(7) A public entity shall make reasonable modifications in policies, practices, or procedures when the modifications are necessary to avoid discrimination on the basis of disability, unless the public entity can demonstrate that making the modifications would fundamentally alter the nature of the service, program, or activity.

(8) A public entity shall not impose or apply eligibility criteria that screen out or tend to screen out an individual with a disability or any class of individuals with disabilities from fully and equally enjoying any service, program, or activity, unless such criteria can be shown to be necessary for the provision of the service, program, or activity being offered.

(c) Nothing in this part prohibits a public entity from providing benefits, services, or advantages to individuals with disabilities, or to a particular class of individuals with disabilities beyond those required by this part.

(d) A public entity shall administer services, programs, and activities in the most integrated setting appropriate to the needs of qualified individuals with disabilities.

(e)(1) Nothing in this part shall be construed to require an individual with a disability to accept an accommodation, aid, service, opportunity, or benefit provided under the ADA or this part which such individual chooses not to accept.

(2) Nothing in the Act or this part authorizes the representative or guardian of an individual with a disability to decline food, water, medical treatment, or medical services for that individual.

(f) A public entity may not place a surcharge on a particular individual with a disability or any group of individuals with disabilities to cover the costs of measures, such as the provision of auxiliary aids or program accessibility, that are required to provide that individual or group with the nondiscriminatory treatment required by the Act or this part.

(g) A public entity shall not exclude or otherwise deny equal services, programs, or activities to an individual or entity because of the known disability of an individual with whom the individual or entity is known to have a relationship or association.

§ 35.131 Illegal use of drugs.

(a) General. (1) Except as provided in paragraph (b) of this section, this part does not prohibit discrimination against an individual based on that individual's current illegal use of drugs.

(2) A public entity shall not discriminate on the basis of illegal use of drugs against an individual who is not engaging in current illegal use of drugs and who —

(i) Has successfully completed a supervised drug rehabilitation program or has otherwise been rehabilitated successfully;

(ii) Is participating in a supervised rehabilitation program; or

(iii) Is erroneously regarded as engaging in such use.

(b) Health and drug rehabilitation services. (1) A public entity shall not deny health services, or services provided in connection with drug rehabilitation, to an individual on the basis of that individual's current illegal use of drugs, if the individual is otherwise entitled to such services.

(2) A drug rehabilitation or treatment program may deny participation to individuals who engage in illegal use of drugs while they are in the program.

(c) Drug testing. (1) This part does not prohibit a public entity from adopting or administering reasonable policies or procedures, including but not limited to drug testing, designed to ensure that an individual who formerly engaged in the illegal use of drugs is not now engaging in current illegal use of drugs.

(2) Nothing in paragraph (c) of this section shall be construed to encourage, prohibit, restrict, or authorize the conduct of testing for the illegal use of drugs.

§ 35.132 Smoking.

This part does not preclude the prohibition of, or the imposition of restrictions on, smoking in transportation covered by this part.

§ 35.133 Maintenance of accessible features.

(a) A public entity shall maintain in operable working condition those features of facilities and equipment that are required to be readily accessible to and usable by persons with disabilities by the Act or this part.

(b) This section does not prohibit isolated or temporary interruptions in service or access due to maintenance or repairs.

§ 35.134 Retaliation or coercion.

(a) No private or public entity shall discriminate against any individual because that individual has opposed any act or practice made unlawful by this part, or because that individual made a charge, testified, assisted, or participated in any manner in an investigation, proceeding, or hearing under the Act or this part.

(b) No private or public entity shall coerce, intimidate, threaten, or interfere with any individual in the exercise or enjoyment of, or on account of his or her having exercised or enjoyed, or on account of his or her having aided or encouraged any other individual in the exercise or enjoyment of, any right granted or protected by the Act or this part.

§ 35.135 Personal devices and services.

This part does not require a public entity to provide to individuals with disabilities personal devices, such as wheelchairs; individually prescribed devices, such as prescription eyeglasses or hearing aids; readers for personal use or study; or services of a personal nature including assistance in eating, toileting, or dressing.

SUBPART C EMPLOYMENT

§ 35.140 Employment discrimination prohibited.

(a) No qualified individual with a disability shall, on the basis of disability, be subjected to discrimination in employment under any service, program, or activity conducted by a public entity.

(b)(1) For purposes of this part, the requirements of title I of the Act, as established by the regulations of the Equal Employment Opportunity Commission in 29 CFR part 1630, apply to employment in any service, program, or activity conducted by a public entity if that public entity is also subject to the jurisdiction of title I.

(2) For the purposes of this part, the requirements of section 504 of the Rehabilitation Act of 1973, as established by the regulations of the Department of Justice in 28 CFR part 41, as those requirements pertain to employment, apply to employment in any service, program, or activity conducted by a public entity if that public entity is not also subject to the jurisdiction of title I.

SUBPART D PROGRAM ACCESSIBILITY

§ 35.149 Discrimination prohibited.

Except as otherwise provided in § 35.150, no qualified individual with a disability shall, because a public entity's facilities are inaccessible to or unusable by individuals with disabilities, be excluded from participation in, or be denied the benefits of the services, programs, or activities of a public entity, or be subjected to discrimination by any public entity.

§ 35.150 Existing facilities.

(a) General. A public entity shall operate each service, program, or activity so that the service, program, or activity, when viewed in its entirety, is readily accessible to and usable by individuals with disabilities. This paragraph does not—

(1) Necessarily require a public entity to make each of its existing facilities accessible to and usable by individuals with disabilities;

(2) Require a public entity to take any action that would threaten or destroy the historic significance of an historic property; or

(3) Require a public entity to take any action that it can demonstrate would result in a fundamental alteration in the nature of a service, program, or activity or in undue financial and administrative burdens. In those circumstances where personnel of the public entity believe that the proposed action would fundamentally alter the service, program, or activity or would result in undue financial and administrative burdens, a public entity has the burden of proving that compliance with § 35.150(a) of this part would result in such alteration or burdens. The decision that compliance would result in such alteration or burdens must be made by the head of a public entity or his or her designee after considering all resources available for use in the funding and operation of the service, program, or activity, and must be accompanied by a written statement of the reasons for reaching that conclusion. If an action would result in such an alteration or such burdens, a public entity shall take any other action that would not result in such an alteration or such burdens but would nevertheless ensure that individuals with disabilities receive the benefits or services provided by the public entity.

(b) Methods— (1) General. A public entity may comply with the requirements of this section through such means as redesign of equipment, reassignment of services to accessible buildings, assignment of aides to beneficiaries, home visits, delivery of services at alternate accessible sites, alteration of existing facilities and construction of new facilities, use of accessible rolling stock or other conveyances, or any other methods that result in making its services, programs, or activities readily accessible to and usable by individuals with disabilities. A public entity is not required to make structural changes in existing facilities where other methods are effective in achieving compliance with this section. A public entity, in making alterations to existing buildings, shall meet the accessibility requirements of § 35.151. In choosing among available methods for meeting the requirements of this section, a public entity shall give priority to those methods that offer services, programs, and activities to qualified individuals with disabilities in the most integrated setting appropriate.

(2) Historic preservation programs. In meeting the requirements of § 35.150(a) in historic preservation programs, a public entity shall give priority to methods that provide physical access to individuals with disabilities. In cases where a physical alteration to an historic property is not required because of paragraph (a)(2) or (a)(3) of this section, alternative methods of achieving program accessibility include—

(i) Using audio-visual materials and devices to depict those portions of an historic property that cannot otherwise be made accessible;

(ii) Assigning persons to guide individuals with handicaps into or through portions of historic properties that cannot otherwise be made accessible; or

(iii) Adopting other innovative methods.

(c) Time period for compliance. Where structural changes in facilities are undertaken to comply with the obligations established under this section, such changes shall be made within three years of January 26, 1992, but in any event as expeditiously as possible.

(d) Transition plan. (1) In the event that structural changes to facilities will be undertaken to achieve program accessibility, a public entity that employs 50 or more persons shall develop, within six months of January 26, 1992, a transition plan setting forth the steps necessary to complete such changes. A public entity shall provide an opportunity to interested persons, including individuals with disabilities or organizations representing individuals with disabilities, to participate in the development of the transition plan by submitting comments. A copy of the transition plan shall be made available for public inspection.

(2) If a public entity has responsibility or authority over streets, roads, or walkways, its transition plan shall include a schedule for providing curb ramps or other sloped areas where pedestrian walks cross curbs, giving priority to walkways serving entities covered by the Act, including State and local government offices and facilities, transportation, places of public accommodation, and employers, followed by walkways serving other areas.

(3) The plan shall, at a minimum—

(i) Identify physical obstacles in the public entity's facilities that limit the accessibility of its programs or activities to individuals with disabilities;

(ii) Describe in detail the methods that will be used to make the facilities accessible;

(iii) Specify the schedule for taking the steps necessary to achieve compliance with this section and, if the time period of the transition plan is longer than one year, identify steps that will be taken during each year of the transition period; and

(iv) Indicate the official responsible for implementation of the plan.

(4) If a public entity has already complied with the transition plan requirement of a Federal agency regulation implementing section 504 of the Rehabilitation Act of 1973, then the requirements of this paragraph (d) shall apply only to those policies and practices that were not included in the previous transition plan.

(Approved by the Office of Management and Budget under control number 1190-0004)

§ 35.151 New construction and alterations.

(a) Design and construction. Each facility or part of a facility constructed by, on behalf of, or for the use of a public entity shall be designed and constructed in such manner that the facility or part of the facility is readily accessible to and usable by individuals with disabilities, if the construction was commenced after January 26, 1992.

(b) Alteration. Each facility or part of a facility altered by, on behalf of, or for the use of a public entity in a manner that affects or could affect the usability of the facility or part of the facility shall, to the maximum extent feasible, be altered in such manner that the altered portion of the facility is readily accessible to and usable by individuals with disabilities, if the alteration was commenced after January 26, 1992.

(c) Accessibility standards. Design, construction, or alteration of facilities in conformance with the Uniform Federal Accessibility Standards (UFAS) (appendix A to 41 CFR part 101-19.6) or with the Americans with Disabilities Act Accessibility Guidelines for Buildings and Facilities (ADAAG) (appendix A to 28 CFR part 36) shall be deemed to comply with the requirements of this section with respect to those facilities, except that the elevator exemption contained at section 4.1.3(5) and section 4.1.6(1)(k) of ADAAG shall not apply. Departures from particular requirements of either standard by the use of other methods shall be permitted when it is clearly evident that equivalent access to the facility or part of the facility is thereby provided.

(d) Alterations: Historic properties. (1) Alterations to historic properties shall comply, to the maximum extent feasible, with section 4.1.7 of UFAS or section 4.1.7 of ADAAG.

(2) If it is not feasible to provide physical access to an historic property in a manner

that will not threaten or destroy the historic significance of the building or facility, alternative methods of access shall be provided pursuant to the requirements of § 35.150.

(e) Curb ramps. (1) Newly constructed or altered streets, roads, and highways must contain curb ramps or other sloped areas at any intersection having curbs or other barriers to entry from a street level pedestrian walkway.

(2) Newly constructed or altered street level pedestrian walkways must contain curb ramps or other sloped areas at intersections to streets, roads, or highways.

SUBPART E COMMUNICATIONS

§ 35.160 General.

(a) A public entity shall take appropriate steps to ensure that communications with applicants, participants, and members of the public with disabilities are as effective as communications with others.

(b)(1) A public entity shall furnish appropriate auxiliary aids and services where necessary to afford an individual with a disability an equal opportunity to participate in, and enjoy the benefits of, a service, program, or activity conducted by a public entity.

(2) In determining what type of auxiliary aid and service is necessary, a public entity shall give primary consideration to the requests of the individual with disabilities.

§ 35.161 Telecommunication devices for the deaf (TDD's).

Where a public entity communicates by telephone with applicants and beneficiaries, TDD's or equally effective telecommunication systems shall be used to communicate with individuals with impaired hearing or speech.

§ 35.162 Telephone emergency services.

Telephone emergency services, including 911 services, shall provide direct access to individuals who use TDD's and computer modems.

§ 35.163 Information and signage.

(a) A public entity shall ensure that interested persons, including persons with impaired vision or hearing, can obtain information as to the existence and location of accessible services, activities, and facilities.

(b) A public entity shall provide signage at all inaccessible entrances to each of its facilities, directing users to an accessible entrance or to a location at which they can obtain information about accessible facilities. The international symbol for accessibility shall be used at each accessible entrance of a facility.

§ 35.164 Duties.

This subpart does not require a public entity to take any action that it can demonstrate would result in a fundamental alteration in the nature of a service, program, or activity or in undue financial and administrative burdens. In those circumstances where personnel of the public entity believe that the proposed action would fundamentally alter the service, program, or activity or would result in undue financial and administrative burdens, a public entity has the burden of proving that compliance with this subpart would result in such alteration or burdens. The decision that compliance would result in such alteration or burdens must be made by the head of the public entity or his or her designee after considering all resources available for use in the funding and operation of the service, program, or activity and must be accompanied by a written statement of the reasons for reaching that conclusion. If an action required to comply with this subpart would result in such an alteration or such burdens, a public entity shall take any other action that would not result in such an alteration or such burdens but would nevertheless ensure that, to the maximum extent possible, individuals with disabilities receive the benefits or services provided by the public entity.

SUBPART F COMPLIANCE PROCEDURES

§ 35.170 Complaints.

(a) Who may file. An individual who believes that he or she or a specific class of individuals has been subjected to discrimination on the basis of disability by a public entity may, by himself or herself or by an authorized representative, file a complaint under this part.

(b) Time for filing. A complaint must be filed not later than 180 days from the date of the alleged discrimination, unless the time for filing is extended by the designated agency for good cause shown. A complaint is deemed to be filed under this section on the date it is first filed with any Federal agency.

(c) Where to file. An individual may file a complaint with any agency that he or she believes to be the appropriate agency designated under subpart G of this part, or with any agency that provides funding to the public entity that is the subject of the complaint, or with the Department of Justice for referral as provided in § 35.171(a)(2).

§ 35.171 Acceptance of complaints.

(a) Receipt of complaints. (1)(i) Any Federal agency that receives a complaint of discrimination on the basis of disability by a public entity shall promptly review the complaint to determine whether it has jurisdiction over the complaint under section 504.

(ii) If the agency does not have section 504 jurisdiction, it shall promptly determine whether it is the designated agency under subpart G of this part responsible for complaints filed against that public entity.

(2)(i) If an agency other than the Department of Justice determines that it does not have section 504 jurisdiction and is not the designated agency, it shall promptly refer the complaint, and notify the complainant that it is referring the complaint to the Department of Justice.

(ii) When the Department of Justice receives a complaint for which it does not have jurisdiction under section 504 and is not the designated agency, it shall refer the complaint to an agency that does have jurisdiction under section 504 or to the appropriate agency designated in subpart G of this part or, in the case of an employment complaint that is also subject to title I of the Act, to the Equal Employment Opportunity Commission.

(3)(i) If the agency that receives a complaint has section 504 jurisdiction, it shall process the complaint according to its procedures for enforcing section 504.

(ii) If the agency that receives a complaint does not have section 504 jurisdiction, but is the designated agency, it shall process the complaint according to the procedures established by this subpart.

(b) Employment complaints. (1) If a complaint alleges employment discrimination subject to title I of the Act, and the agency has section 504 jurisdiction, the agency shall follow the procedures issued by the Department of Justice and the Equal Employment Opportunity Commission under section 107(b) of the Act.

(2) If a complaint alleges employment discrimination subject to title I of the Act, and the designated agency does not have section 504 jurisdiction, the agency shall refer the complaint to the Equal Employment Opportunity Commission for processing under title I of the Act.

(3) Complaints alleging employment discrimination subject to this part, but not to title I of the Act shall be processed in accordance with the procedures established by this subpart.

(c) *Complete complaints.* (1) A designated agency shall accept all complete complaints under this section and shall promptly notify the complainant and the public entity of the receipt and acceptance of the complaint.

(2) If the designated agency receives a complaint that is not complete, it shall notify the complainant and specify the additional information that is needed to make the complaint a complete complaint. If the complainant fails to complete the complaint, the designated agency shall close the complaint without prejudice.

§ 35.172   Resolution of complaints.

(a) The designated agency shall investigate each complete complaint, attempt informal resolution, and, if resolution is not achieved, issue to the complainant and the public entity a Letter of Findings that shall include—

(1) Findings of fact and conclusions of law;

(2) A description of a remedy for each violation found; and

(3) Notice of the rights available under paragraph (b) of this section.

(b) If the designated agency finds noncompliance, the procedures in §§ 35.173 and 35.174 shall be followed. At any time, the complainant may file a private suit pursuant to section 203 of the Act, whether or not the designated agency finds a violation.

§ 35.173   Voluntary compliance agreements.

(a) When the designated agency issues a noncompliance Letter of Findings, the designated agency shall—

(1) Notify the Assistant Attorney General by forwarding a copy of the Letter of Findings to the Assistant Attorney General; and

(2) Initiate negotiations with the public entity to secure compliance by voluntary means.

(b) Where the designated agency is able to secure voluntary compliance, the voluntary compliance agreement shall—

(1) Be in writing and signed by the parties;

(2) Address each cited violation;

(3) Specify the corrective or remedial action to be taken, within a stated period of time, to come into compliance;

(4) Provide assurance that discrimination will not recur; and

(5) Provide for enforcement by the Attorney General.

§ 35.174   Referral.

If the public entity declines to enter into voluntary compliance negotiations or if negotiations are unsuccessful, the designated agency shall refer the matter to the Attorney General with a recommendation for appropriate action.

§ 35.175 Attorney's fees.

In any action or administrative proceeding commenced pursuant to the Act or this part, the court or agency, in its discretion, may allow the prevailing party, other than the United States, a reasonable attorney's fee, including litigation expenses, and costs, and the United States shall be liable for the foregoing the same as a private individual.

§ 35.176 Alternative means of dispute resolution.

Where appropriate and to the extent authorized by law, the use of alternative means of dispute resolution, including settlement negotiations, conciliation, facilitation, mediation, factfinding, minitrials, and arbitration, is encouraged to resolve disputes arising under the Act and this part.

§ 35.177 Effect of unavailability of technical assistance.

A public entity shall not be excused from compliance with the requirements of this part because of any failure to receive technical assistance, including any failure in the development or dissemination of any technical assistance manual authorized by the Act.

§ 35.178 State immunity.

A State shall not be immune under the eleventh amendment to the Constitution of the United States from an action in Federal or State court of competent jurisdiction for a violation of this Act. In any action against a State for a violation of the requirements of this Act, remedies (including remedies both at law and in equity) are available for such a violation to the same extent as such remedies are available for such a violation in an action against any public or private entity other than a State.

TITLE 42.
THE PUBLIC HEALTH AND WELFARE

CHAPTER 126. EQUAL OPPORTUNITY FOR INDIVIDUALS WITH DISABILITIES

PUBLIC ACCOMMODATIONS AND SERVICES OPERATED BY PRIVATE ENTITIES

§ 12181. Definitions

As used in this *title [42 USCS §§ 12181* et seq.]:

(1) Commerce. The term "commerce" means travel, trade, traffic, commerce, transportation, or communication—

(A) among the several States;

(B) between any foreign country or any territory or possession and any State; or

(C) between points in the same State but through another State or foreign country.

(2) Commercial facilities. The term "commercial facilities" means facilities—

(A) that are intended for nonresidential use; and

(B) whose operations will affect commerce. Such term shall not include railroad locomotives, railroad freight cars, railroad cabooses, railroad cars described in section 242 [*42 USCS § 12162*] or covered under this *title [42 USCS §§ 12181* et seq.], railroad rights-of-way, or facilities that are covered or expressly exempted from coverage under the Fair Housing Act of 1968 (*42 U.S.C. 3601* et seq.).

(3) Demand responsive system. The term "demand responsive system" means any system of providing transportation of individuals by a vehicle, other than a system which is a fixed route system.

(4) Fixed route system. The term "fixed route system" means a system of providing transportation of individuals (other than by aircraft) on which a vehicle is operated along a prescribed route according to a fixed schedule.

(5) Over-the-road bus. The term "over-the-road bus" means a bus characterized by an elevated passenger deck located over a baggage compartment.

(6) Private entity. The term "private entity" means any entity other than a public entity (as defined in section 201(1) [*42 USCS § 12131(1)*]).

(7) Public accommodation. The following private entities are considered public accommodations for purposes of this *title [42 USCS §§ 12181* et seq.], if the operations of such entities affect commerce—

(A) an inn, hotel, motel, or other place of lodging, except for an establishment located within a building that contains not more than five rooms for rent or hire and that is actually occupied by the proprietor of such establishment as the residence of such proprietor;

(B) a restaurant, bar, or other establishment serving food or drink;

(C) a motion picture house, theater, concert hall, stadium, or other place of exhibition or entertainment;

(D) an auditorium, convention center, lecture hall, or other place of public gathering;

(E) a bakery, grocery store, clothing store, hardware store, shopping center, or other sales or rental establishment;

(F) a laundromat, dry-cleaner, bank, barber shop, beauty shop, travel service, shoe repair service, funeral parlor, gas station, office of an accountant or lawyer, pharmacy, insurance office, professional office of a health care provider, hospital, or other service establishment;

(G) a terminal, depot, or other station used for specified public transportation;

(H) a museum, library, gallery, or other place of public display or collection;

(I) a park, zoo, amusement park, or other place of recreation;

(J) a nursery, elementary, secondary, undergraduate, or postgraduate private school, or other place of education;

(K) a day care center, senior citizen center, homeless shelter, food bank, adoption agency, or other social service center establishment; and

(L) a gymnasium, health spa, bowling alley, golf course, or other place of exercise or recreation.

(8) Rail and railroad. The terms "rail" and "railroad" have the meaning given the term "railroad" in section 202(e) of the Federal Railroad Safety Act of 1970 (*45 U.S.C. 431(e)*) [*49 USCS § 20102(1)*].

(9) Readily achievable. The term "readily achievable" means easily accomplishable and able to be carried out without much difficulty or expense. In determining whether an action is readily achievable, factors to be considered include—

(A) the nature and cost of the action needed under this Act;

(B) the overall financial resources of the facility or facilities involved in the action; the number of persons employed at such facility; the effect on expenses and resources, or the impact otherwise of such action upon the operation of the facility;

(C) the overall financial resources of the covered entity; the overall size of the business of a covered entity with respect to the number of its employees; the number, type, and location of its facilities; and

(D) the type of operation or operations of the covered entity, including the composition, structure, and functions of the workforce of such entity; the geographic separateness, administrative or fiscal relationship of the facility or facilities in question to the covered entity.

(10) Specified public transportation. The term "specified public transportation" means transportation by bus, rail, or any other conveyance (other than by aircraft) that provides the general public with general or special service (including charter service) on a regular and continuing basis.

(11) Vehicle. The term "vehicle" does not include a rail passenger car, railroad locomotive, railroad freight car, railroad caboose, or a railroad car described in section 242 [*42 USCS § 12162*] or covered under this *title [42 USCS §§ 12181* et seq.].

§ 12182. Prohibition of discrimination by public accommodations

(a) General rule. No individual shall be discriminated against on the basis of disability in the full and equal enjoyment of the goods, services, facilities, privileges, advantages, or accommodations of any place of public accommodation by any person who owns, leases (or leases to), or operates a place of public accommodation.

(b) Construction.

(1) General prohibition.

(A) Activities.

(i) Denial of participation. It shall be discriminatory to subject an individual or class of individuals on the basis of a disability or disabilities of such individual or class, directly, or through contractual, licensing, or other arrangements, to a denial of the opportunity of the individual or class to participate in or benefit from the goods, services, facilities, privileges, advantages, or accommodations of an entity.

(ii) Participation in unequal benefit. It shall be discriminatory to afford an individual or class of individuals, on the basis of a disability or disabilities of such individual or class, directly, or through contractual, licensing, or other arrangements with the opportunity to participate in or benefit from a good, service, facility, privilege, advantage, or accommodation that is not equal to that afforded to other individuals.

(iii) Separate benefit. It shall be discriminatory to provide an individual or class of individuals, on the basis of a disability or disabilities of such individual or class, directly, or through contractual, licensing, or other arrangements with a good, service, facility, privilege, advantage, or accommodation that is different or separate from that provided to other individuals, unless such action is necessary to provide the individual or class of individuals with a good, service, facility, privilege, advantage, or accommodation, or other opportunity that is as effective as that provided to others.

(iv) Individual or class of individuals. For purposes of clauses (i) through (iii) of this subparagraph, the term "individual or class of individuals" refers to the clients or customers of the covered public accommodation that enters into the contractual, licensing or other arrangement.

(B) Integrated settings. Goods, services, facilities, privileges, advantages, and accommodations shall be afforded to an individual with a disability in the most integrated setting appropriate to the needs of the individual.

(C) Opportunity to participate. Notwithstanding the existence of separate or different programs or activities provided in accordance with this section, an individual with a disability shall not be denied the opportunity to participate in such programs or activities that are not separate or different.

(D) Administrative methods. An individual or entity shall not, directly or through contractual or other arrangements, utilize standards or criteria or methods of administration—

(i) that have the effect of discriminating on the basis of disability; or

(ii) that perpetuate the discrimination of others who are subject to common administrative control.

(E) Association. It shall be discriminatory to exclude or otherwise deny equal goods, services, facilities, privileges, advantages, accommodations, or other opportunities to an individual or entity because of the known disability of an individual with whom the individual or entity is known to have a relationship or association.

(2) Specific prohibitions.

(A) Discrimination. For purposes of subsection (a), discrimination includes—

(i) the imposition or application of eligibility criteria that screen out or tend to screen out an individual with a disability or any class of individuals with disabilities from fully and equally enjoying any goods, services, facilities, privileges, advantages, or accommodations, unless such criteria can be shown to be necessary for the provision of the goods, services, facilities, privileges, advantages, or accommodations being offered;

(ii) a failure to make reasonable modifications in policies, practices, or procedures, when such modifications are necessary to afford such goods, services, facilities, privileges, advantages, or accommodations to individuals with disabilities, unless the entity can demonstrate that making such modifications would fundamentally alter the nature of such goods, services, facilities, privileges, advantages, or accommodations;

(iii) a failure to take such steps as may be necessary to ensure that no individual with a disability is excluded, denied services, segregated or otherwise treated differently than other individuals because of the absence of auxiliary aids and services, unless the entity can demonstrate that taking such steps would fundamentally alter the nature of the good, service, facility, privilege, advantage, or accommodation being offered or would result in an undue burden;

(iv) a failure to remove architectural barriers, and communication barriers that are structural in nature, in existing facilities, and transportation barriers in existing vehicles and rail passenger cars used by an establishment for transporting individuals (not including barriers that can only be removed through the retrofitting of vehicles or rail passenger cars by the installation of a hydraulic or other lift), where such removal is readily achievable; and

(v) where an entity can demonstrate that the removal of a barrier under clause (iv) is not readily achievable, a failure to make such goods, services, facilities, privileges, advantages, or accommodations available through alternative methods if such methods are readily achievable.

(B) Fixed route system.

(i) Accessibility. It shall be considered discrimination for a private entity which operates a fixed route system and which is not subject to section 304 [*42 USCS § 12184*] to purchase or lease a vehicle with a seating capacity in excess of 16 passengers (including the driver) for use on such system, for which a solicitation is made after the 30th day following the effective date of this subparagraph, that is not readily accessible to and usable by individuals with disabilities, including individuals who use wheelchairs.

(ii) Equivalent service. If a private entity which operates a fixed route system and which is not subject to section 304 [*42 USCS § 12184*] purchases or leases a vehicle with a seating capacity of 16 passengers or less (including the driver) for use on such system after the effective date of this subparagraph that is not readily accessible to or usable by individuals with disabilities, it shall be considered discrimination for such entity to fail to operate such system so that, when viewed in its entirety, such system ensures a level of service to individuals with disabilities, including individuals who use wheelchairs, equivalent to the level of service provided to individuals without disabilities.

(C) Demand responsive system. For purposes of subsection (a), discrimination includes—

(i) a failure of a private entity which operates a demand responsive system and which is not subject to section 304 [*42 USCS § 12184*] to operate such system so that, when viewed in its entirety, such system ensures a level of service to individuals with disabilities, including individuals who use wheelchairs, equivalent to the level of service provided to individuals without disabilities; and

(ii) the purchase or lease by such entity for use on such system of a vehicle with a seating capacity in excess of 16 passengers (including the driver), for which solicitations are made after the 30th day following the effective date of this subparagraph, that is not readily accessible to and usable by individuals with disabilities (including individuals who use wheelchairs) unless such entity can demonstrate that such system, when viewed in its entirety, provides a level of service to individuals with disabilities equivalent to that provided to individuals without disabilities.

(D) Over-the-road buses.

(i) Limitation on applicability. Subparagraphs (B) and (C) do not apply to over-the-road buses.

(ii) Accessibility requirements. For purposes of subsection (a), discrimination includes

(I) the purchase or lease of an over-the-road bus which does not comply with the regulations issued under section 306(a)(2) [42 USCS § 12186(a)(2)] by a private entity which provides transportation of individuals and which is not primarily engaged in the business of transporting people, and (II) any other failure of such entity to comply with such regulations.

(3) Specific construction. Nothing in this *title [42 USCS §§ 12181* et seq.] shall require an entity to permit an individual to participate in or benefit from the goods, services, facilities, privileges, advantages and accommodations of such entity where such individual poses a direct threat to the health or safety of others. The term "direct threat" means a significant risk to the health or safety of others that cannot be eliminated by a modification of policies, practices, or procedures or by the provision of auxiliary aids or services.

§ 12183. New construction and alterations in public accommodations and commercial facilities

(a) Application of term. Except as provided in subsection (b), as applied to public accommodations and commercial facilities, discrimination for purposes of section 302(a) [42 USCS § 12182(a)] includes—

(1) a failure to design and construct facilities for first occupancy later than 30 months after the date of enactment of this Act [enacted July 26, 1990] that are readily accessible to and usable by individuals with disabilities, except where an entity can demonstrate that it is structurally impracticable to meet the requirements of such subsection in accordance with standards set forth or incorporated by reference in regulations issued under this *title [42 USCS §§ 12181* et seq.]; and

(2) with respect to a facility or part thereof that is altered by, on behalf of, or for the use of an establishment in a manner that affects or could affect the usability of the facility or part thereof, a failure to make alterations in such a manner that, to the maximum extent feasible, the altered portions of the facility are readily accessible to and usable by individuals with disabilities, including individuals who use wheelchairs. Where the entity is undertaking an alteration that affects or could affect usability of or access to an area of the facility containing a primary function, the entity shall also make the alterations in such a manner that, to the maximum extent feasible, the path of travel to the altered area and the bathrooms, telephones, and drinking fountains serving the altered area, are readily accessible to and usable by individuals with disabilities where such alterations to the path of travel or the bathrooms, telephones, and drinking fountains serving the altered area are not disproportionate to the overall alterations in terms of cost and scope (as determined under criteria established by the Attorney General).

(b) Elevator. Subsection (a) shall not be construed to require the installation of an elevator for facilities that are less than three stories or have less than 3,000 square feet per story unless the building is a shopping center, a shopping mall, or the professional office of a health care provider or unless the Attorney General determines that a particular category of such facilities requires the installation of elevators based on the usage of such facilities.

§ 12184. Prohibition of discrimination in specified public transportation services provided by private entities

(a) General rule. No individual shall be discriminated against on the basis of disability in the full and equal enjoyment of specified public transportation services provided by a private entity that is primarily engaged in the business of transporting people and whose operations affect commerce.

(b) Construction. For purposes of subsection (a), discrimination includes—

(1) the imposition or application by a [an] entity described in subsection (a) of eligibility criteria that screen out or tend to screen out an individual with a disability or any class of individuals with disabilities from fully enjoying the specified public transportation services provided by the entity, unless such criteria can be shown to be necessary for the provision of the services being offered;

(2) the failure of such entity to—

(A) make reasonable modifications consistent with those required under section 302(b)(2)(A)(ii) [*42 USCS § 12182(b)(2)(A)(ii)*];

(B) provide auxiliary aids and services consistent with the requirements of section 302(b)(2)(A)(iii) [*42 USCS § 12182(b)(2)(A)(iii)*]; and

(C) remove barriers consistent with the requirements of section 302(b)(2)(A) [*42 USCS § 12182(b)(2)(A)*] and with the requirements of section 303(a)(2) [*42 USCS § 12183(a)(2)*];

(3) the purchase or lease by such entity of a new vehicle (other than an automobile, a van with a seating capacity of less than 8 passengers, including the driver, or an over-the-road bus) which is to be used to provide specified public transportation and for which a solicitation is made after the 30th day following the effective date of this section, that is not readily accessible to and usable by individuals with disabilities, including individuals who use wheelchairs; except that the new vehicle need not be readily accessible to and usable by such individuals if the new vehicle is to be used solely in a demand responsive system and if the entity can demonstrate that such system, when viewed in its entirety, provides a level of service to such individuals equivalent to the level of service provided to the general public;

(4) (A) the purchase or lease by such entity of an over-the-road bus which does not comply with the regulations issued under section 306(a)(2) [*42 USCS § 12186(a)(2)*]; and

(B) any other failure of such entity to comply with such regulations; and

(5) the purchase or lease by such entity of a new van with a seating capacity of less than 8 passengers, including the driver, which is to be used to provide specified public transportation and for which a solicitation is made after the 30th day following the effective date of this section that is not readily accessible to or usable by individuals with disabilities, including individuals who use wheelchairs; except that the new van need not be readily accessible to and usable by such individuals if the entity can demonstrate that the system for which the van is being purchased or leased, when viewed in its entirety, provides a level of service to such individuals equivalent to the level of service provided to the general public;

(6) the purchase or lease by such entity of a new rail passenger car that is to be used to provide specified public transportation, and for which a solicitation is made later than 30 days after the effective date of this paragraph, that is not readily accessible to and usable by individuals with disabilities, including individuals who use wheelchairs; and

(7) the remanufacture by such entity of a rail passenger car that is to be used to provide specified public transportation so as to extend its usable life for 10 years or more, or the purchase or lease by such entity of such a rail car, unless the rail car, to the maximum extent feasible, is made readily accessible to and usable by individuals with disabilities, including individuals who use wheelchairs.

(c) Historical or antiquated cars.

(1) Exception. To the extent that compliance with subsection (b)(2)(C) or (b)(7) would significantly alter the historic or antiquated character of a historical or antiquated rail passenger car, or a rail station served exclusively by such cars, or would result in violation of any rule, regulation, standard, or order issued by the Secretary of Transportation under the Federal Railroad Safety Act of 1970 [*45 USCS §§ 431 et seq.*], such compliance shall not be required.

(2) Definition. As used in this subsection, the term "historical or antiquated rail passenger car" means a rail passenger car—

(A) which is not less than 30 years old at the time of its use for transporting individuals;

(B) the manufacturer of which is no longer in the business of manufacturing rail passenger cars; and

(C) which—

(i) has a consequential association with events or persons significant to the past; or

(ii) embodies, or is being restored to embody, the distinctive characteristics of a type of rail passenger car used in the past, or to represent a time period which has passed.

§ 12185. Study

(a) Purposes. The Office of Technology Assessment shall undertake a study to determine—

(1) the access needs of individuals with disabilities to over-the-road buses and over-the-road bus service; and

(2) the most cost-effective methods for providing access to over-the-road buses and over-the-road bus service to individuals with disabilities, particularly individuals who use wheelchairs, through all forms of boarding options.

(b) Contents. The study shall include, at a minimum, an analysis of the following:

(1) The anticipated demand by individuals with disabilities for accessible over-the-road buses and over-the-road bus service.

(2) The degree to which such buses and service, including any service required under sections 304(b)(4) and 306(a)(2) [42 USCS §§ 12184(b)(4), 12186(a)(2)], are readily accessible to and usable by individuals with disabilities.

(3) The effectiveness of various methods of providing accessibility to such buses and service to individuals with disabilities.

(4) The cost of providing accessible over-the-road buses and bus service to individuals with disabilities, including consideration of recent technological and cost saving developments in equipment and devices.

(5) Possible design changes in over-the-road buses that could enhance accessibility, including the installation of accessible restrooms which do not result in a loss of seating capacity.

(6) The impact of accessibility requirements on the continuation of over-the-road bus service, with particular consideration of the impact of such requirements on such service to rural communities.

(c) Advisory committee. In conducting the study required by subsection (a), the Office of Technology Assessment shall establish an advisory committee, which shall consist of—

(1) members selected from among private operators and manufacturers of over-the-road buses;

(2) members selected from among individuals with disabilities, particularly individuals who use wheelchairs, who are potential riders of such buses; and

(3) members selected for their technical expertise on issues included in the study, including manufacturers of boarding assistance equipment and devices.

The number of members selected under each of paragraphs (1) and (2) shall be equal, and the total number of members selected under paragraphs (1) and (2) shall exceed the number of members selected under paragraph (3).

(d) Deadline. The study required by subsection (a), along with recommendations by the Office of Technology Assessment, including any policy options for legislative action, shall be submitted to the President and Congress within 36 months after the date of the enactment of this Act [enacted July 26, 1990]. If the President determines that compliance with the regulations issued pursuant to section 306(a)(2)(B) [*42 USCS § 12186(a)(2)(B)*] on or before the applicable deadlines specified in section 306(a)(2)(B) [*42 USCS § 12186(a)(2)(B)*] will result in a significant reduction in intercity over-the-road bus service, the President shall extend each such deadline by 1 year.

(e) Review. In developing the study required by subsection (a), the Office of Technology Assessment shall provide a preliminary draft of such study to the Architectural and Transportation Barriers Compliance Board established under section 502 of the Rehabilitation Act of 1973 (*29 U.S.C. 792*). The Board shall have an opportunity to comment on such draft study, and any such comments by the Board made in writing within 120 days after the Board's receipt of the draft study shall be incorporated as part of the final study required to be submitted under subsection (d).

§ 12186. Regulations

(a) Transportation provisions.

(1) General rule. Not later than 1 year after the date of the enactment of this Act [enacted July 26, 1990], the Secretary of Transportation shall issue regulations in an accessible format to carry out sections 302(b)(2)(B) and (C) [*42 USCS § 12182(b)(2)(B), (C)*] and to carry out section 304 [*42 USCS § 12184*] (other than subsection (b)(4)).

(2) Special rules for providing access to over-the-road buses.

(A) Interim requirements.

(i) Issuance. Not later than 1 year after the date of the enactment of this Act [enacted July 26, 1990], the Secretary of Transportation shall issue regulations in an accessible format to carry out sections 304(b)(4) and 302(b)(2)(D)(ii) [*42 USCS §§ 12184(b)(4), 12182(b)(2)(D)(ii)*] that require each private entity which uses an over-the-road bus to provide transportation of individuals to provide accessibility to such bus; except that such regulations shall not require any structural changes in over-the-road buses in order to provide access to individuals who use wheelchairs during the effective period of such regulations and shall not require the purchase of boarding assistance devices to provide access to such individuals.

(ii) Effective period. The regulations issued pursuant to this subparagraph shall be effective until the effective date of the regulations issued under subparagraph (B).

(B) Final requirement.

(i) Review of study and interim requirements. The Secretary shall review the study submitted under section 305 [*42 USCS § 12185*] and the regulations issued pursuant to subparagraph (A).

(ii) Issuance. Not later than 1 year after the date of the submission of the study under section 305 [*42 USCS § 12185*], the Secretary shall issue in an accessible format new regulations to carry out sections 304(b)(4) and 302(b)(2)(D)(ii) [*42 USCS §§ 12184(b)(4), 12182(b)(2)(D)(ii)*] that require, taking into account the purposes of the study under section 305 [*42 USCS § 12185*] and any recommendations resulting from such study, each private entity which uses an over-the-road bus to provide transportation to individuals to provide accessibility to such bus to individuals with disabilities, including individuals who use wheelchairs.

(iii) Effective period. Subject to section 305(d) [*42 USCS § 12185(d)*], the regulations issued pursuant to this subparagraph shall take effect—

(I) with respect to small providers of transportation (as defined by the Secretary), 3 years after the date of issuance of final regulations under clause (ii); and

(II) with respect to other providers of transportation, 2 years after the date of issuance of such final regulations.

(C) Limitation on requiring installation of accessible restrooms. The regulations issued pursuant to this paragraph shall not require the installation of accessible restrooms in over-the-road buses if such installation would result in a loss of seating capacity.

(3) Standards. The regulations issued pursuant to this subsection shall include standards applicable to facilities and vehicles covered by sections 302(b)(2) and 304 [42 USCS §§ 12182(b)(2), 12184].

(b) Other provisions. Not later than 1 year after the date of the enactment of this Act [enacted July 26, 1990], the Attorney General shall issue regulations in an accessible format to carry out the provisions of this *title [42 USCS §§ 12181* et seq.] not referred to in subsection (a) that include standards applicable to facilities and vehicles covered under section 302 [*42 USCS § 12182*].

(c) Consistency with ATBCB guidelines. Standards included in regulations issued under subsections (a) and (b) shall be consistent with the minimum guidelines and requirements issued by the Architectural and Transportation Barriers Compliance Board in accordance with section 504 of this Act [*42 USCS § 12204*].

(d) Interim accessibility standards.

(1) Facilities. If final regulations have not been issued pursuant to this section, for new construction or alterations for which a valid and appropriate State or local building permit is obtained prior to the issuance of final regulations under this section, and for which the construction or alteration authorized by such permit begins within one year of the receipt of such permit and is completed under the terms of such permit, compliance with the Uniform Federal Accessibility Standards in effect at the time the building permit is issued shall suffice to satisfy the requirement that facilities be readily accessible to and usable by persons with disabilities as required under section 303 [*42 USCS § 12183*], except that, if such final regulations have not been issued one year after the Architectural and Transportation Barriers Compliance Board has issued the supplemental minimum guidelines required under section 504(a) of this Act [*42 USCS § 12204(a)*], compliance with such supplemental minimum guidelines shall be necessary to satisfy the requirement that facilities be readily accessible to and usable by persons with disabilities prior to issuance of the final regulations.

(2) Vehicles and rail passenger cars. If final regulations have not been issued pursuant to this section, a private entity shall be considered to have complied with the requirements of this *title [42 USCS §§ 12181* et seq.], if any, that a vehicle or rail passenger car be readily accessible to and usable by individuals with disabilities, if the design for such vehicle or car complies with the laws and regulations (including the Minimum Guidelines and Requirements for Accessible Design and such supplemental minimum guidelines as are issued under section 504(a) of this Act [*42 USCS § 12204(a)*] governing accessibility of such vehicles or cars, to the extent that such laws and regulations are not inconsistent with this *title [42 USCS §§ 12181* et seq.] and are in effect at the time such design is substantially completed.

§ 12187. Exemptions for private clubs and religious organizations

The provisions of this *title [42 USCS §§ 12181* et seq.] shall not apply to private clubs or establishments exempted from coverage under title II of the Civil Rights Act of 1964 *(42 U.S.C. 2000-a(e))* or to religious organizations or entities controlled by religious organizations, including places of worship.

§ 12188. Enforcement

(a) In general.

(1) Availability of remedies and procedures. The remedies and procedures set forth in section 204(a) of the Civil Rights Act of 1964 (*42 U.S.C. 2000a-3(a)*) are the remedies and procedures this *title [42 USCS §§ 12181* et seq.] provides to any person who is being subjected to discrimination on the basis of disability in violation of this *title [42 USCS §§ 12181* et seq.] or who has reasonable grounds for believing that such person is about to be subjected to discrimination in violation of section 303 [*42 USCS § 12183*]. Nothing in this section shall require a person with a disability to engage in a futile gesture if such person has actual notice that a person or organization covered by this *title [42 USCS §§ 12181* et seq.] does not intend to comply with its provisions.

(2) Injunctive relief. In the case of violations of sections 302(b)(2)(A)(iv) and [section] 303(a) [*42 USCS §§ 12182(b)(2)(A)(iv)* and *12183(a)*], injunctive relief shall include an order to alter facilities to make such facilities readily accessible to and usable by individuals with disabilities to the extent required by this *title [42 USCS §§ 12181* et seq.]. Where appropriate, injunctive relief shall also include requiring the provision of an auxiliary aid or service, modification of a policy, or provision of an auxiliary aid or service, modification of a policy, or provision of alternative methods, to the extent required by this *title [42 USCS §§ 12181* et seq.].

(b) Enforcement by the Attorney General.

(1) Denial of rights.

(A) Duty to investigate.

(i) In general. The Attorney General shall investigate alleged violations of this *title [42 USCS §§ 12181* et seq.], and shall undertake periodic reviews of compliance of covered entities under this *title [42 USCS §§ 12181* et seq.].

(ii) Attorney General certification. On the application of a State or local government, the Attorney General may, in consultation with the Architectural and Transportation Barriers Compliance Board, and after prior notice and a public hearing at which persons, including individuals with disabilities, are provided an opportunity to testify against such certification, certify that a State law or local building code or similar ordinance that establishes accessibility requirements meets or exceeds the minimum requirements of this Act for the accessibility and usability of covered facilities under this *title [42 USCS §§ 12181* et seq.]. At any enforcement proceeding under this section, such certification by the Attorney General shall be rebuttable evidence that such State law or local ordinance does meet or exceed the minimum requirements of this Act.

(B) Potential violation. If the Attorney General has reasonable cause to believe that—

(i) any person or group of persons is engaged in a pattern or practice of discrimination under this *title [42 USCS §§ 12181* et seq.]; or

(ii) any person or group of persons has been discriminated against under this *title [42 USCS §§ 12181* et seq.] and such discrimination raises an issue of general public importance, the Attorney General may commence a civil action in any appropriate United States district court.

(2) Authority of court. In a civil action under paragraph (1)(B), the court—

(A) may grant any equitable relief that such court considers to be appropriate, including, to the extent required by this *title [42 USCS §§ 12181* et seq.]—

(i) granting temporary, preliminary, or permanent relief;

(ii) providing an auxiliary aid or service, modification of policy, practice, or procedure, or alternative method; and

(iii) making facilities readily accessible to and usable by individuals with disabilities;

(B) may award such other relief as the court considers to be appropriate, including monetary damages to persons aggrieved when requested by the Attorney General; and

(C) may, to vindicate the public interest, assess a civil penalty against the entity in an amount—

(i) not exceeding $ 50,000 for a first violation; and

(ii) not exceeding $ 100,000 for any subsequent violation.

(3) Single violation. For purposes of paragraph (2)(C), in determining whether a first or subsequent violation has occurred, a determination in a single action, by judgment or settlement, that the covered entity has engaged in more than one discriminatory act shall be counted as a single violation.

(4) Punitive damages. For purposes of subsection (b)(2)(B), the term "monetary damages" and "such other relief" does not include punitive damages.

(5) Judicial consideration. In a civil action under paragraph (1)(B), the court, when considering what amount of civil penalty, if any, is appropriate, shall give consideration to any good faith effort or attempt to comply with this Act by the entity. In evaluating good faith, the court shall consider, among other factors it deems relevant, whether the entity could have reasonably anticipated the need for an appropriate type of auxiliary aid needed to accommodate the unique needs of a particular individual with a disability.

§ 12189. Examinations and courses

Any person that offers examinations or courses related to applications, licensing, certification, or credentialing for secondary or post-secondary education, professional, or trade purposes shall offer such examinations or courses in a place and manner accessible to persons with disabilities or offer alternative accessible arrangements for such individuals.

TITLE 28
JUDICIAL ADMINISTRATION

CHAPTER I DEPARTMENT OF JUSTICE

PART 36 NONDISCRIMINATION ON THE BASIS OF DISABILITY BY PUBLIC ACCOMMODATIONS AND IN COMMERCIAL FACILITIES

SUBPART A GENERAL

§ 36.104 Definitions.

For purposes of this part, the term—

Act means the Americans with Disabilities Act of 1990 (Pub. L. 101-336, *104 Stat. 327, 42 U.S.C. 12101*-12213 and *47 U.S.C. 225* and 611).

Commerce means travel, trade, traffic, commerce, transportation, or communication—

(1) Among the several States;

(2) Between any foreign country or any territory or possession and any State; or

(3) Between points in the same State but through another State or foreign country.

Commercial facilities means facilities—

(1) Whose operations will affect commerce;

(2) That are intended for nonresidential use by a private entity; and

(3) That are not—

(i) Facilities that are covered or expressly exempted from coverage under the Fair Housing Act of 1968, as amended *(42 U.S.C. 3601*-3631);

(ii) Aircraft; or

(iii) Railroad locomotives, railroad freight cars, railroad cabooses, commuter or intercity passenger rail cars (including coaches, dining cars, sleeping cars, lounge cars, and food service cars), any other railroad cars described in section 242 of the Act or covered under title II of the Act, or railroad rights-of-way. For purposes of this definition, "rail" and "railroad" have the meaning given the term "railroad" in section 202(e) of the Federal Railroad Safety Act of 1970 *(45 U.S.C. 431*(e)).

Current illegal use of drugs means illegal use of drugs that occurred recently enough to justify a reasonable belief that a person's drug use is current or that continuing use is a real and ongoing problem.

Disability means, with respect to an individual, a physical or mental impairment that substantially limits one or more of the major life activities of such individual; a record of such an impairment; or being regarded as having such an impairment.

(1) The phrase physical or mental impairment means—

(i) Any physiological disorder or condition, cosmetic disfigurement, or anatomical loss affecting one or more of the following body systems: neurological; musculoskeletal; special sense organs; respiratory, including speech organs; cardiovascular; reproductive; digestive; genitourinary; hemic and lymphatic; skin; and endocrine;

(ii) Any mental or psychological disorder such as mental retardation, organic brain syndrome, emotional or mental illness, and specific learning disabilities;

(iii) The phrase physical or mental impairment includes, but is not limited to, such contagious and noncontagious diseases and conditions as orthopedic, visual, speech, and hearing impairments, cerebral palsy, epilepsy, muscular dystrophy, multiple sclerosis, cancer, heart disease, diabetes, mental retardation, emotional illness, specific learning disabilities, HIV disease (whether symptomatic or asymptomatic), tuberculosis, drug addiction, and alcoholism;

(iv) The phrase physical or mental impairment does not include homosexuality or bisexuality.

(2) The phrase major life activities means functions such as caring for one's self, performing manual tasks, walking, seeing, hearing, speaking, breathing, learning, and working.

(3) The phrase has a record of such an impairment means has a history of, or has been misclassified as having, a mental or physical impairment that substantially limits one or more major life activities.

(4) The phrase is regarded as having an impairment means—

(i) Has a physical or mental impairment that does not substantially limit major life activities but that is treated by a private entity as constituting such a limitation;

(ii) Has a physical or mental impairment that substantially limits major life activities only as a result of the attitudes of others toward such impairment; or

(iii) Has none of the impairments defined in paragraph (1) of this definition but is treated by a private entity as having such an impairment.

(5) The term disability does not include—

(i) Transvestism, transsexualism, pedophilia, exhibitionism, voyeurism, gender identity disorders not resulting from physical impairments, or other sexual behavior disorders;

(ii) Compulsive gambling, kleptomania, or pyromania; or

(iii) Psychoactive substance use disorders resulting from current illegal use of drugs.

Drug means a controlled substance, as defined in schedules I through V of section 202 of the Controlled Substances Act *(21 U.S.C. 812)*.

Facility means all or any portion of buildings, structures, sites, complexes, equipment, rolling stock or other conveyances, roads, walks, passageways, parking lots, or other real or personal property, including the site where the building, property, structure, or equipment is located.

Illegal use of drugs means the use of one or more drugs, the possession or distribution of which is unlawful under the Controlled Substances Act *(21 U.S.C. 812)*. The term "illegal use of drugs" does not include the use of a drug taken under supervision by a licensed health care professional, or other uses authorized by the Controlled Substances Act or other provisions of Federal law.

Individual with a disability means a person who has a disability. The term "individual with a disability" does not include an individual who is currently engaging in the illegal use of drugs, when the private entity acts on the basis of such use.

Place of public accommodation means a facility, operated by a private entity, whose operations affect commerce and fall within at least one of the following categories—

(1) An inn, hotel, motel, or other place of lodging, except for an establishment located within a building that contains not more than five rooms for rent or hire and that is

actually occupied by the proprietor of the establishment as the residence of the proprietor;

(2) A restaurant, bar, or other establishment serving food or drink;

(3) A motion picture house, theater, concert hall, stadium, or other place of exhibition or entertainment;

(4) An auditorium, convention center, lecture hall, or other place of public gathering;

(5) A bakery, grocery store, clothing store, hardware store, shopping center, or other sales or rental establishment;

(6) A laundromat, dry-cleaner, bank, barber shop, beauty shop, travel service, shoe repair service, funeral parlor, gas station, office of an accountant or lawyer, pharmacy, insurance office, professional office of a health care provider, hospital, or other service establishment;

(7) A terminal, depot, or other station used for specified public transportation;

(8) A museum, library, gallery, or other place of public display or collection;

(9) A park, zoo, amusement park, or other place of recreation;

(10) A nursery, elementary, secondary, undergraduate, or postgraduate private school, or other place of education;

(11) A day care center, senior citizen center, homeless shelter, food bank, adoption agency, or other social service center establishment; and

(12) A gymnasium, health spa, bowling alley, golf course, or other place of exercise or recreation.

Private club means a private club or establishment exempted from coverage under title II of the Civil Rights Act of 1964 *(42 U.S.C. 2000a(e))*.

Private entity means a person or entity other than a public entity.

Public accommodation means a private entity that owns, leases (or leases to), or operates a place of public accommodation.

Public entity means—

(1) Any State or local government;

(2) Any department, agency, special purpose district, or other instrumentality of a State or States or local government; and

(3) The National Railroad Passenger Corporation, and any commuter authority (as defined in section 103(8) of the Rail Passenger Service Act). *(45 U.S.C. 541)*

Qualified interpreter means an interpreter who is able to interpret effectively, accurately and impartially both receptively and expressively, using any necessary specialized vocabulary.

Readily achievable means easily accomplishable and able to be carried out without much difficulty or expense. In determining whether an action is readily achievable factors to be considered include—

(1) The nature and cost of the action needed under this part;

(2) The overall financial resources of the site or sites involved in the action; the number of persons employed at the site; the effect on expenses and resources; legitimate safety requirements that are necessary for safe operation, including crime prevention measures; or the impact otherwise of the action upon the operation of the site;

(3) The geographic separateness, and the administrative or fiscal relationship of the

site or sites in question to any parent corporation or entity;

(4) If applicable, the overall financial resources of any parent corporation or entity; the overall size of the parent corporation or entity with respect to the number of its employees; the number, type, and location of its facilities; and

(5) If applicable, the type of operation or operations of any parent corporation or entity, including the composition, structure, and functions of the workforce of the parent corporation or entity.

Religious entity means a religious organization, including a place of worship.

Service animal means any guide dog, signal dog, or other animal individually trained to do work or perform tasks for the benefit of an individual with a disability, including, but not limited to, guiding individuals with impaired vision, alerting individuals with impaired hearing to intruders or sounds, providing minimal protection or rescue work, pulling a wheelchair, or fetching dropped items.

Specified public transportation means transportation by bus, rail, or any other conveyance (other than by aircraft) that provides the general public with general or special service (including charter service) on a regular and continuing basis.

State means each of the several States, the District of Columbia, the Commonwealth of Puerto Rico, Guam, American Samoa, the Virgin Islands, the Trust Territory of the Pacific Islands, and the Commonwealth of the Northern Mariana Islands.

Undue burden means significant difficulty or expense. In determining whether an action would result in an undue burden, factors to be considered include—

(1) The nature and cost of the action needed under this part;

(2) The overall financial resources of the site or sites involved in the action; the number of persons employed at the site; the effect on expenses and resources; legitimate safety requirements that are necessary for safe operation, including crime prevention measures; or the impact otherwise of the action upon the operation of the site;

(3) The geographic separateness, and the administrative or fiscal relationship of the site or sites in question to any parent corporation or entity;

(4) If applicable, the overall financial resources of any parent corporation or entity; the overall size of the parent corporation or entity with respect to the number of its employees; the number, type, and location of its facilities; and

(5) If applicable, the type of operation or operations of any parent corporation or entity, including the composition, structure, and functions of the workforce of the parent corporation or entity.

SUBPART B GENERAL REQUIREMENTS

§ 36.201 General.

(a) Prohibition of discrimination. No individual shall be discriminated against on the basis of disability in the full and equal enjoyment of the goods, services, facilities, privileges, advantages, or accommodations of any place of public accommodation by any private entity who owns, leases (or leases to), or operates a place of public accommodation.

(b) Landlord and tenant responsibilities. Both the landlord who owns the building that houses a place of public accommodation and the tenant who owns or operates the place of public accommodation are public accommodations subject to the requirements of this part. As between the parties, allocation of responsibility for complying with the obligations of this part may be determined by lease or other contract.

§ 36.202 Activities.

(a) Denial of participation. A public accommodation shall not subject an individual or class of individuals on the basis of a disability or disabilities of such individual or class, directly, or through contractual, licensing, or other arrangements, to a denial of the opportunity of the individual or class to participate in or benefit from the goods, services, facilities, privileges, advantages, or accommodations of a place of public accommodation.

(b) Participation in unequal benefit. A public accommodation shall not afford an individual or class of individuals, on the basis of a disability or disabilities of such individual or class, directly, or through contractual, licensing, or other arrangements, with the opportunity to participate in or benefit from a good, service, facility, privilege, advantage, or accommodation that is not equal to that afforded to other individuals.

(c) Separate benefit. A public accommodation shall not provide an individual or class of individuals, on the basis of a disability or disabilities of such individual or class, directly, or through contractual, licensing, or other arrangements with a good, service, facility, privilege, advantage, or accommodation that is different or separate from that provided to other individuals, unless such action is necessary to provide the individual or class of individuals with a good, service, facility, privilege, advantage, or accommodation, or other opportunity that is as effective as that provided to others.

(d) Individual or class of individuals. For purposes of paragraphs (a) through (c) of this section, the term "individual or class of individuals" refers to the clients or customers of the public accommodation that enters into the contractual, licensing, or other arrangement.

§ 36.203 Integrated settings.

(a) General. A public accommodation shall afford goods, services, facilities, privileges, advantages, and accommodations to an individual with a disability in the most integrated setting appropriate to the needs of the individual.

(b) Opportunity to participate. Notwithstanding the existence of separate or different programs or activities provided in accordance with this subpart, a public accommodation shall not deny an individual with a disability an opportunity to participate in such programs or activities that are not separate or different.

(c) Accommodations and services. (1) Nothing in this part shall be construed to require an individual with a disability to accept an accommodation, aid, service, opportunity, or benefit available under this part that such individual chooses not to accept.

(2) Nothing in the Act or this part authorizes the representative or guardian of an individual with a disability to decline food, water, medical treatment, or medical services for that individual.

§ 36.204 Administrative methods.

A public accommodation shall not, directly or through contractual or other arrangements, utilize standards or criteria or methods of administration that have the effect of discriminating on the basis of disability, or that perpetuate the discrimination of others who are subject to common administrative control.

§ 36.205 Association.

A public accommodation shall not exclude or otherwise deny equal goods, services, facilities, privileges, advantages, accommodations, or other opportunities to an individual or entity because of the known disability of an individual with whom the individual or entity is known to have a relationship or association.

§ 36.206 Retaliation or coercion.

(a) No private or public entity shall discriminate against any individual because that individual has opposed any act or practice made unlawful by this part, or because that individual made a charge, testified, assisted, or participated in any manner in an investigation, proceeding, or hearing under the Act or this part.

(b) No private or public entity shall coerce, intimidate, threaten, or interfere with any individual in the exercise or enjoyment of, or on account of his or her having exercised or enjoyed, or on account of his or her having aided or encouraged any other individual in the exercise or enjoyment of, any right granted or protected by the Act or this part.

(c) Illustrations of conduct prohibited by this section include, but are not limited to:

(1) Coercing an individual to deny or limit the benefits, services, or advantages to which he or she is entitled under the Act or this part;

(2) Threatening, intimidating, or interfering with an individual with a disability who is seeking to obtain or use the goods, services, facilities, privileges, advantages, or accommodations of a public accommodation;

(3) Intimidating or threatening any person because that person is assisting or encouraging an individual or group entitled to claim the rights granted or protected by the Act or this part to exercise those rights; or

(4) Retaliating against any person because that person has participated in any investigation or action to enforce the Act or this part.

§ 36.207 Places of public accommodation located in private residences.

(a) When a place of public accommodation is located in a private residence, the portion of the residence used exclusively as a residence is not covered by this part, but that portion used exclusively in the operation of the place of public accommodation or that portion used both for the place of public accommodation and for residential purposes is covered by this part.

(b) The portion of the residence covered under paragraph (a) of this section extends to those elements used to enter the place of public accommodation, including the homeowner's front sidewalk, if any, the door or entryway, and hallways; and those portions of the residence, interior or exterior, available to or used by customers or clients, including restrooms.

§ 36.208 Direct threat.

(a) This part does not require a public accommodation to permit an individual to participate in or benefit from the goods, services, facilities, privileges, advantages and accommodations of that public accommodation when that individual poses a direct threat to the health or safety of others.

(b) Direct threat means a significant risk to the health or safety of others that cannot be eliminated by a modification of policies, practices, or procedures, or by the provision of auxiliary aids or services.

(c) In determining whether an individual poses a direct threat to the health or safety of others, a public accommodation must make an individualized assessment, based on reasonable judgment that relies on current medical knowledge or on the best available objective evidence, to ascertain: the nature, duration, and severity of the risk; the probability that the potential injury will actually occur; and whether reasonable modifications of policies, practices, or procedures will mitigate the risk.

§ 36.209 Illegal use of drugs.

(a) General. (1) Except as provided in paragraph (b) of this section, this part does not prohibit discrimination against an individual based on that individual's current illegal use of drugs.

(2) A public accommodation shall not discriminate on the basis of illegal use of drugs against an individual who is not engaging in current illegal use of drugs and who—

(i) Has successfully completed a supervised drug rehabilitation program or has otherwise been rehabilitated successfully;

(ii) Is participating in a supervised rehabilitation program; or

(iii) Is erroneously regarded as engaging in such use.

(b) Health and drug rehabilitation services. (1) A public accommodation shall not deny health services, or services provided in connection with drug rehabilitation, to an individual on the basis of that individual's current illegal use of drugs, if the individual is otherwise entitled to such services.

(2) A drug rehabilitation or treatment program may deny participation to individuals who engage in illegal use of drugs while they are in the program.

(c) Drug testing. (1) This part does not prohibit a public accommodation from adopting or administering reasonable policies or procedures, including but not limited to drug testing, designed to ensure that an individual who formerly engaged in the illegal use of drugs is not now engaging in current illegal use of drugs.

(2) Nothing in this paragraph (c) shall be construed to encourage, prohibit, restrict, or authorize the conducting of testing for the illegal use of drugs.

§ 36.210 Smoking.

This part does not preclude the prohibition of, or the imposition of restrictions on, smoking in places of public accommodation.

§ 36.211 Maintenance of accessible features.

(a) A public accommodation shall maintain in operable working condition those features of facilities and equipment that are required to be readily accessible to and usable by persons with disabilities by the Act or this part.

(b) This section does not prohibit isolated or temporary interruptions in service or access due to maintenance or repairs.

§ 36.212 Insurance.

(a) This part shall not be construed to prohibit or restrict—

(1) An insurer, hospital or medical service company, health maintenance organization, or any agent, or entity that administers benefit plans, or similar organizations from underwriting risks, classifying risks, or administering such risks that are based on or not inconsistent with State law; or

(2) A person or organization covered by this part from establishing, sponsoring, observing or administering the terms of a bona fide benefit plan that are based on underwriting risks, classifying risks, or administering such risks that are based on or not inconsistent with State law; or

(3) A person or organization covered by this part from establishing, sponsoring,

observing or administering the terms of a bona fide benefit plan that is not subject to State laws that regulate insurance.

(b) Paragraphs (a) (1), (2), and (3) of this section shall not be used as a subterfuge to evade the purposes of the Act or this part.

(c) A public accommodation shall not refuse to serve an individual with a disability because its insurance company conditions coverage or rates on the absence of individuals with disabilities.

SUBPART C   SPECIFIC REQUIREMENTS

§ 36.301   Eligibility criteria.

(a) *General.* A public accommodation shall not impose or apply eligibility criteria that screen out or tend to screen out an individual with a disability or any class of individuals with disabilities from fully and equally enjoying any goods, services, facilities, privileges, advantages, or accommodations, unless such criteria can be shown to be necessary for the provision of the goods, services, facilities, privileges, advantages, or accommodations being offered.

(b) *Safety.* A public accommodation may impose legitimate safety requirements that are necessary for safe operation. Safety requirements must be based on actual risks and not on mere speculation, stereotypes, or generalizations about individuals with disabilities.

(c) *Charges.* A public accommodation may not impose a surcharge on a particular individual with a disability or any group of individuals with disabilities to cover the costs of measures, such as the provision of auxiliary aids, barrier removal, alternatives to barrier removal, and reasonable modifications in policies, practices, or procedures, that are required to provide that individual or group with the nondiscriminatory treatment required by the Act or this part.

§ 36.302   Modifications in policies, practices, or procedures.

(a) *General.* A public accommodation shall make reasonable modifications in policies, practices, or procedures, when the modifications are necessary to afford goods, services, facilities, privileges, advantages, or accommodations to individuals with disabilities, unless the public accommodation can demonstrate that making the modifications would fundamentally alter the nature of the goods, services, facilities, privileges, advantages, or accommodations.

(b) *Specialties*—(1) *General.* A public accommodation may refer an individual with a disability to another public accommodation, if that individual is seeking, or requires, treatment or services outside of the referring public accommodation's area of specialization, and if, in the normal course of its operations, the referring public accommodation would make a similar referral for an individual without a disability who seeks or requires the same treatment or services.

(2) *Illustration—medical specialties.* A health care provider may refer an individual with a disability to another provider, if that individual is seeking, or requires, treatment or services outside of the referring provider's area of specialization, and if the referring provider would make a similar referral for an individual without a disability who seeks or requires the same treatment or services. A physician who specializes in treating only a particular condition cannot refuse to treat an individual with a disability for that condition, but is not required to treat the individual for a different condition.

(c) *Service animals*—(1) *General.* Generally, a public accommodation shall modify policies, practices, or procedures to permit the use of a service animal by an individual with a disability.

(2) *Care or supervision of service animals.* Nothing in this part requires a public accommodation to supervise or care for a service animal.

(d) *Check-out aisles.* A store with check-out aisles shall ensure that an adequate number of accessible check-out aisles are kept open during store hours, or shall otherwise modify its policies and practices, in order to ensure that an equivalent level of convenient service is provided to individuals with disabilities as is provided to others. If only one check-out aisle is accessible, and it is generally used for express service, one way of providing equivalent service is to allow persons with mobility impairments to make all their purchases at that aisle.

§ 36.303 Auxiliary aids and services.

(a) *General.* A public accommodation shall take those steps that may be necessary to ensure that no individual with a disability is excluded, denied services, segregated or otherwise treated differently than other individuals because of the absence of auxiliary aids and services, unless the public accommodation can demonstrate that taking those steps would fundamentally alter the nature of the goods, services, facilities, privileges, advantages, or accommodations being offered or would result in an undue burden, i.e., significant difficulty or expense.

(b) *Examples.* The term "auxiliary aids and services" includes—

(1) Qualified interpreters, notetakers, computer-aided transcription services, written materials, telephone handset amplifiers, assistive listening devices, assistive listening systems, telephones compatible with hearing aids, closed caption decoders, open and closed captioning, telecommunications devices for deaf persons (TDD's), videotext displays, or other effective methods of making aurally delivered materials available to individuals with hearing impairments;

(2) Qualified readers, taped texts, audio recordings, Brailled materials, large print materials, or other effective methods of making visually delivered materials available to individuals with visual impairments;

(3) Acquisition or modification of equipment or devices; and

(4) Other similar services and actions.

(c) *Effective communication.* A public accommodation shall furnish appropriate auxiliary aids and services where necessary to ensure effective communication with individuals with disabilities.

(d) *Telecommunication devices for the deaf (TDD's).* (1) A public accommodation that offers a customer, client, patient, or participant the opportunity to make outgoing telephone calls on more than an incidental convenience basis shall make available, upon request, a TDD for the use of an individual who has impaired hearing or a communication disorder.

(2) This part does not require a public accommodation to use a TDD for receiving or making telephone calls incident to its operations.

(e) *Closed caption decoders.* Places of lodging that provide televisions in five or more guest rooms and hospitals that provide televisions for patient use shall provide, upon request, a means for decoding captions for use by an individual with impaired hearing.

(f) *Alternatives.* If provision of a particular auxiliary aid or service by a public accommodation would result in a fundamental alteration in the nature of the goods, services, facilities, privileges, advantages, or accommodations being offered or in an undue burden, i.e., significant difficulty or expense, the public accommodation shall provide an alternative auxiliary aid or service, if one exists, that would not result in an alteration or such burden but would nevertheless ensure that, to the maximum extent possible, individuals with disabilities receive the goods, services, facilities, privileges, advantages, or accommodations offered by the public accommodation.

§ 36.304 Removal of barriers.

(a) General. A public accommodation shall remove architectural barriers in existing facilities, including communication barriers that are structural in nature, where such removal is readily achievable, i.e., easily accomplishable and able to be carried out without much difficulty or expense.

(b) Examples. Examples of steps to remove barriers include, but are not limited to, the following actions—

(1) Installing ramps;

(2) Making curb cuts in sidewalks and entrances;

(3) Repositioning shelves;

(4) Rearranging tables, chairs, vending machines, display racks, and other furniture;

(5) Repositioning telephones;

(6) Adding raised markings on elevator control buttons;

(7) Installing flashing alarm lights;

(8) Widening doors;

(9) Installing offset hinges to widen doorways;

(10) Eliminating a turnstile or providing an alternative accessible path;

(11) Installing accessible door hardware;

(12) Installing grab bars in toilet stalls;

(13) Rearranging toilet partitions to increase maneuvering space;

(14) Insulating lavatory pipes under sinks to prevent burns;

(15) Installing a raised toilet seat;

(16) Installing a full-length bathroom mirror;

(17) Repositioning the paper towel dispenser in a bathroom;

(18) Creating designated accessible parking spaces;

(19) Installing an accessible paper cup dispenser at an existing inaccessible water fountain;

(20) Removing high pile, low density carpeting; or

(21) Installing vehicle hand controls.

(c) Priorities. A public accommodation is urged to take measures to comply with the barrier removal requirements of this section in accordance with the following order of priorities.

(1) First, a public accommodation should take measures to provide access to a place of public accommodation from public sidewalks, parking, or public transportation. These

measures include, for example, installing an entrance ramp, widening entrances, and providing accessible parking spaces.

(2) Second, a public accommodation should take measures to provide access to those areas of a place of public accommodation where goods and services are made available to the public. These measures include, for example, adjusting the layout of display racks, rearranging tables, providing Brailled and raised character signage, widening doors, providing visual alarms, and installing ramps.

(3) Third, a public accommodation should take measures to provide access to restroom facilities. These measures include, for example, removal of obstructing furniture or vending machines, widening of doors, installation of ramps, providing accessible signage, widening of toilet stalls, and installation of grab bars.

(4) Fourth, a public accommodation should take any other measures necessary to provide access to the goods, services, facilities, privileges, advantages, or accommodations of a place of public accommodation.

(d) Relationship to alterations requirements of subpart D of this part. (1) Except as provided in paragraph (d)(2) of this section, measures taken to comply with the barrier removal requirements of this section shall comply with the applicable requirements for alterations in § 36.402 and §§ 36.404-36.406 of this part for the element being altered. The path of travel requirements of § 36.403 shall not apply to measures taken solely to comply with the barrier removal requirements of this section.

(2) If, as a result of compliance with the alterations requirements specified in paragraph (d)(1) of this section, the measures required to remove a barrier would not be readily achievable, a public accommodation may take other readily achievable measures to remove the barrier that do not fully comply with the specified requirements. Such measures include, for example, providing a ramp with a steeper slope or widening a doorway to a narrower width than that mandated by the alterations requirements. No measure shall be taken, however, that poses a significant risk to the health or safety of individuals with disabilities or others.

(e) Portable ramps. Portable ramps should be used to comply with this section only when installation of a permanent ramp is not readily achievable. In order to avoid any significant risk to the health or safety of individuals with disabilities or others in using portable ramps, due consideration shall be given to safety features such as nonslip surfaces, railings, anchoring, and strength of materials.

(f) Selling or serving space. The rearrangement of temporary or movable structures, such as furniture, equipment, and display racks is not readily achievable to the extent that it results in a significant loss of selling or serving space.

(g) Limitation on barrier removal obligations. (1) The requirements for barrier removal under § 36.304 shall not be interpreted to exceed the standards for alterations in subpart D of this part.

(2) To the extent that relevant standards for alterations are not provided in subpart D of this part, then the requirements of § 36.304 shall not be interpreted to exceed the standards for new construction in subpart D of this part.

(3) This section does not apply to rolling stock and other conveyances to the extent that § 36.310 applies to rolling stock and other conveyances.

§ 36.305 Alternatives to barrier removal.

(a) General. Where a public accommodation can demonstrate that barrier removal is not readily achievable, the public accommodation shall not fail to make its goods, services, facilities, privileges, advantages, or accommodations available through alternative methods, if those methods are readily achievable.

(b) Examples. Examples of alternatives to barrier removal include, but are not limited to, the following actions—

(1) Providing curb service or home delivery;

(2) Retrieving merchandise from inaccessible shelves or racks;

(3) Relocating activities to accessible locations;

(c) Multiscreen cinemas. If it is not readily achievable to remove barriers to provide access by persons with mobility impairments to all of the theaters of a multiscreen cinema, the cinema shall establish a film rotation schedule that provides reasonable access for individuals who use wheelchairs to all films. Reasonable notice shall be provided to the public as to the location and time of accessible showings.

§ 36.306 Personal devices and services.

This part does not require a public accommodation to provide its customers, clients, or participants with personal devices, such as wheelchairs; individually prescribed devices, such as prescription eyeglasses or hearing aids; or services of a personal nature including assistance in eating, toileting, or dressing.

§ 36.307 Accessible or special goods.

(a) This part does not require a public accommodation to alter its inventory to include accessible or special goods that are designed for, or facilitate use by, individuals with disabilities.

(b) A public accommodation shall order accessible or special goods at the request of an individual with disabilities, if, in the normal course of its operation, it makes special orders on request for unstocked goods, and if the accessible or special goods can be obtained from a supplier with whom the public accommodation customarily does business.

(c) Examples of accessible or special goods include items such as Brailled versions of books, books on audio cassettes, closed-captioned video tapes, special sizes or lines of clothing, and special foods to meet particular dietary needs.

§ 36.308 Seating in assembly areas.

(a) Existing facilities.

(1) To the extent that it is readily achievable, a public accommodation in assembly areas shall—

(i) Provide a reasonable number of wheelchair seating spaces and seats with removable aisle-side arm rests; and

(ii) Locate the wheelchair seating spaces so that they—

(A) Are dispersed throughout the seating area;

(B) Provide lines of sight and choice of admission prices comparable to those for members of the general public;

(C) Adjoin an accessible route that also serves as a means of egress in case of emergency; and

(D) Permit individuals who use wheelchairs to sit with family members or other companions.

(2) If removal of seats is not readily achievable, a public accommodation shall provide, to the extent that it is readily achievable to do so, a portable chair or other means to permit a family member or other companion to sit with an individual who uses a wheelchair.

(3) The requirements of paragraph (a) of this section shall not be interpreted to exceed the standards for alterations in subpart D of this part.

(b) *New construction and alterations.* The provision and location of wheelchair seating spaces in newly constructed or altered assembly areas shall be governed by the standards for new construction and alterations in subpart D of this part.

§ 36.309   Examinations and courses.

(a) *General.* Any private entity that offers examinations or courses related to applications, licensing, certification, or credentialing for secondary or postsecondary education, professional, or trade purposes shall offer such examinations or courses in a place and manner accessible to persons with disabilities or offer alternative accessible arrangements for such individuals.

(b) *Examinations.*

(1) Any private entity offering an examination covered by this section must assure that—

(i) The examination is selected and administered so as to best ensure that, when the examination is administered to an individual with a disability that impairs sensory, manual, or speaking skills, the examination results accurately reflect the individual's aptitude or achievement level or whatever other factor the examination purports to measure, rather than reflecting the individual's impaired sensory, manual, or speaking skills (except where those skills are the factors that the examination purports to measure);

(ii) An examination that is designed for individuals with impaired sensory, manual, or speaking skills is offered at equally convenient locations, as often, and in as timely a manner as are other examinations; and

(iii) The examination is administered in facilities that are accessible to individuals with disabilities or alternative accessible arrangements are made.

(2) Required modifications to an examination may include changes in the length of time permitted for completion of the examination and adaptation of the manner in which the examination is given.

(3) A private entity offering an examination covered by this section shall provide appropriate auxiliary aids for persons with impaired sensory, manual, or speaking skills, unless that private entity can demonstrate that offering a particular auxiliary aid would fundamentally alter the measurement of the skills or knowledge the examination is intended to test or would result in an undue burden. Auxiliary aids and services required by this section may include taped examinations, interpreters or other effective methods of making orally delivered materials available to individuals with hearing impairments, Brailled or large print examinations and answer sheets or qualified readers for individuals with visual impairments or learning disabilities, transcribers for individuals with manual impairments, and other similar services and actions.

(4) Alternative accessible arrangements may include, for example, provision of an examination at an individual's home with a proctor if accessible facilities or equipment

are unavailable. Alternative arrangements must provide comparable conditions to those provided for nondisabled individuals.

(c) *Courses.*

(1) Any private entity that offers a course covered by this section must make such modifications to that course as are necessary to ensure that the place and manner in which the course is given are accessible to individuals with disabilities.

(2) Required modifications may include changes in the length of time permitted for the completion of the course, substitution of specific requirements, or adaptation of the manner in which the course is conducted or course materials are distributed.

(3) A private entity that offers a course covered by this section shall provide appropriate auxiliary aids and services for persons with impaired sensory, manual, or speaking skills, unless the private entity can demonstrate that offering a particular auxiliary aid or service would fundamentally alter the course or would result in an undue burden. Auxiliary aids and services required by this section may include taped texts, interpreters or other effective methods of making orally delivered materials available to individuals with hearing impairments, Brailled or large print texts or qualified readers for individuals with visual impairments and learning disabilities, classroom equipment adapted for use by individuals with manual impairments, and other similar services and actions.

(4) Courses must be administered in facilities that are accessible to individuals with disabilities or alternative accessible arrangements must be made.

(5) Alternative accessible arrangements may include, for example, provision of the course through videotape, cassettes, or prepared notes. Alternative arrangements must provide comparable conditions to those provided for nondisabled individuals.

SUBPART D NEW CONSTRUCTION AND ALTERATIONS

§ 36.401 New construction.

(a) *General.*

(1) Except as provided in paragraphs (b) and (c) of this section, discrimination for purposes of this part includes a failure to design and construct facilities for first occupancy after January 26, 1993, that are readily accessible to and usable by individuals with disabilities.

(2) For purposes of this section, a facility is designed and constructed for first occupancy after January 26, 1993, only—

(i) If the last application for a building permit or permit extension for the facility is certified to be complete, by a State, County, or local government after January 26, 1992 (or, in those jurisdictions where the government does not certify completion of applications, if the last application for a building permit or permit extension for the facility is received by the State, County, or local government after January 26, 1992); and

(ii) If the first certificate of occupancy for the facility is issued after January 26, 1993.

(b) *Commercial facilities located in private residences.*

(1) When a commercial facility is located in a private residence, the portion of the residence used exclusively as a residence is not covered by this subpart, but that portion used exclusively in the operation of the commercial facility or that portion used both for the commercial facility and for residential purposes is covered by the new construction

and alterations requirements of this subpart.

(2) The portion of the residence covered under paragraph (b)(1) of this section extends to those elements used to enter the commercial facility, including the homeowner's front sidewalk, if any, the door or entryway, and hallways; and those portions of the residence, interior or exterior, available to or used by employees or visitors of the commercial facility, including restrooms.

(c) *Exception for structural impracticability.*

(1) Full compliance with the requirements of this section is not required where an entity can demonstrate that it is structurally impracticable to meet the requirements. Full compliance will be considered structurally impracticable only in those rare circumstances when the unique characteristics of terrain prevent the incorporation of accessibility features.

(2) If full compliance with this section would be structurally impracticable, compliance with this section is required to the extent that it is not structurally impracticable. In that case, any portion of the facility that can be made accessible shall be made accessible to the extent that it is not structurally impracticable.

(3) If providing accessibility in conformance with this section to individuals with certain disabilities (e.g., those who use wheelchairs) would be structurally impracticable, accessibility shall nonetheless be ensured to persons with other types of disabilities (e.g., those who use crutches or who have sight, hearing, or mental impairments) in accordance with this section.

(d) *Elevator exemption.*

(1) For purposes of this paragraph (d)—

(i) *Professional office of a health care provider* means a location where a person or entity regulated by a State to provide professional services related to the physical or mental health of an individual makes such services available to the public. The facility housing the "professional office of a health care provider" only includes floor levels housing at least one health care provider, or any floor level designed or intended for use by at least one health care provider.

(ii) *Shopping center or shopping mall* means—

(A) A building housing five or more sales or rental establishments; or

(B) A series of buildings on a common site, either under common ownership or common control or developed either as one project or as a series of related projects, housing five or more sales or rental establishments. For purposes of this section, places of public accommodation of the types listed in paragraph (5) of the definition of "place of public accommodation" in section § 36.104 are considered sales or rental establishments. The facility housing a "shopping center or shopping mall" only includes floor levels housing at least one sales or rental establishment, or any floor level designed or intended for use by at least one sales or rental establishment.

(2) This section does not require the installation of an elevator in a facility that is less than three stories or has less than 3000 square feet per story, except with respect to any facility that houses one or more of the following:

(i) A shopping center or shopping mall, or a professional office of a health care provider.

(ii) A terminal, depot, or other station used for specified public transportation, or an airport passenger terminal. In such a facility, any area housing passenger services, including boarding and debarking, loading and unloading, baggage claim, dining facilities, and other common areas open to the public, must be on an accessible route from an accessible entrance.

(3) The elevator exemption set forth in this paragraph (d) does not obviate or limit, in any way the obligation to comply with the other accessibility requirements established in paragraph (a) of this section. For example, in a facility that houses a shopping center or shopping mall, or a professional office of a health care provider, the floors that are above or below an accessible ground floor and that do not house sales or rental establishments or a professional office of a health care provider, must meet the requirements of this section but for the elevator.

§ 36.402 Alterations.

(a) General.

(1) Any alteration to a place of public accommodation or a commercial facility, after January 26, 1992, shall be made so as to ensure that, to the maximum extent feasible, the altered portions of the facility are readily accessible to and usable by individuals with disabilities, including individuals who use wheelchairs.

(2) An alteration is deemed to be undertaken after January 26, 1992, if the physical alteration of the property begins after that date.

(b) Alteration. For the purposes of this part, an alteration is a change to a place of public accommodation or a commercial facility that affects or could affect the usability of the building or facility or any part thereof.

(1) Alterations include, but are not limited to, remodeling, renovation, rehabilitation, reconstruction, historic restoration, changes or rearrangement in structural parts or elements, and changes or rearrangement in the plan configuration of walls and full-height partitions. Normal maintenance, reroofing, painting or wallpapering, asbestos removal, or changes to mechanical and electrical systems are not alterations unless they affect the usability of the building or facility.

(2) If existing elements, spaces, or common areas are altered, then each such altered element, space, or area shall comply with the applicable provisions of appendix A to this part.

(c) To the maximum extent feasible. The phrase "to the maximum extent feasible," as used in this section, applies to the occasional case where the nature of an existing facility makes it virtually impossible to comply fully with applicable accessibility standards through a planned alteration. In these circumstances, the alteration shall provide the maximum physical accessibility feasible. Any altered features of the facility that can be made accessible shall be made accessible. If providing accessibility in conformance with this section to individuals with certain disabilities (e.g., those who use wheelchairs) would not be feasible, the facility shall be made accessible to persons with other types of disabilities (e.g., those who use crutches, those who have impaired vision or hearing, or those who have other impairments).

§ 36.403 Alterations: Path of travel.

(a) General. An alteration that affects or could affect the usability of or access to an area of a facility that contains a primary function shall be made so as to ensure that, to the maximum extent feasible, the path of travel to the altered area and the restrooms, telephones, and drinking fountains serving the altered area, are readily accessible to and usable by individuals with disabilities, including individuals who use wheelchairs, unless the cost and scope of such alterations is disproportionate to the cost of the overall alteration.

(b) Primary function. A "primary function" is a major activity for which the facility is intended. Areas that contain a primary function include, but are not limited to, the customer services lobby of a bank, the dining area of a cafeteria, the meeting rooms in a conference center, as well as offices and other work areas in which the activities of the public accommodation or other private entity using the facility are carried out. Mechanical rooms, boiler rooms, supply storage rooms, employee lounges or locker rooms, janitorial closets, entrances, corridors, and restrooms are not areas containing a primary function.

(c) Alterations to an area containing a primary function.

(1) Alterations that affect the usability of or access to an area containing a primary function include, but are not limited to—

(i) Remodeling merchandise display areas or employee work areas in a department store;

(ii) Replacing an inaccessible floor surface in the customer service or employee work areas of a bank;

(iii) Redesigning the assembly line area of a factory; or

(iv) Installing a computer center in an accounting firm.

(2) For the purposes of this section, alterations to windows, hardware, controls, electrical outlets, and signage shall not be deemed to be alterations that affect the usability of or access to an area containing a primary function.

(d) Landlord/tenant: If a tenant is making alterations as defined in § 36.402 that would trigger the requirements of this section, those alterations by the tenant in areas that only the tenant occupies do not trigger a path of travel obligation upon the landlord with respect to areas of the facility under the landlord's authority, if those areas are not otherwise being altered.

(e) Path of travel.

(1) A "path of travel" includes a continuous, unobstructed way of pedestrian passage by means of which the altered area may be approached, entered, and exited, and which connects the altered area with an exterior approach (including sidewalks, streets, and parking areas), an entrance to the facility, and other parts of the facility.

(2) An accessible path of travel may consist of walks and sidewalks, curb ramps and other interior or exterior pedestrian ramps; clear floor paths through lobbies, corridors, rooms, and other improved areas; parking access aisles; elevators and lifts; or a combination of these elements.

(3) For the purposes of this part, the term "path of travel" also includes the restrooms, telephones, and drinking fountains serving the altered area.

(f) Disproportionality.

(1) Alterations made to provide an accessible path of travel to the altered area will be deemed disproportionate to the overall alteration when the cost exceeds 20% of the cost of the alteration to the primary function area.

(2) Costs that may be counted as expenditures required to provide an accessible path of travel may include:

(i) Costs associated with providing an accessible entrance and an accessible route to the altered area, for example, the cost of widening doorways or installing ramps;

(ii) Costs associated with making restrooms accessible, such as installing grab bars, enlarging toilet stalls, insulating pipes, or installing accessible faucet controls;

(iii) Costs associated with providing accessible telephones, such as relocating the telephone to an accessible height, installing amplification devices, or installing a telecommunications device for deaf persons (TDD);

(iv) Costs associated with relocating an inaccessible drinking fountain.

(g) Duty to provide accessible features in the event of disproportionality.

(1) When the cost of alterations necessary to make the path of travel to the altered area fully accessible is disproportionate to the cost of the overall alteration, the path of travel shall be made accessible to the extent that it can be made accessible without incurring disproportionate costs.

(2) In choosing which accessible elements to provide, priority should be given to those elements that will provide the greatest access, in the following order:

(i) An accessible entrance;

(ii) An accessible route to the altered area;

(iii) At least one accessible restroom for each sex or a single unisex restroom;

(iv) Accessible telephones;

(v) Accessible drinking fountains; and

(vi) When possible, additional accessible elements such as parking, storage, and alarms.

(h) Series of smaller alterations.

(1) The obligation to provide an accessible path of travel may not be evaded by performing a series of small alterations to the area served by a single path of travel if those alterations could have been performed as a single undertaking.

(2)

(i) If an area containing a primary function has been altered without providing an accessible path of travel to that area, and subsequent alterations of that area, or a different area on the same path of travel, are undertaken within three years of the original alteration, the total cost of alterations to the primary function areas on that path of travel during the preceding three year period shall be considered in determining whether the cost of making that path of travel accessible is disproportionate.

(ii) Only alterations undertaken after January 26, 1992, shall be considered in determining if the cost of providing an accessible path of travel is disproportionate to the overall cost of the alterations.

§ 36.404 Alterations: Elevator exemption.

(a) This section does not require the installation of an elevator in an altered facility that is less than three stories or has less than 3,000 square feet per story, except with respect to any facility that houses a shopping center, a shopping mall, the professional office of a health care provider, a terminal, depot, or other station used for specified public transportation, or an airport passenger terminal.

(1) For the purposes of this section, "professional office of a health care provider" means a location where a person or entity regulated by a State to provide professional services related to the physical or mental health of an individual makes such services available to the public. The facility that houses a "professional office of a health care provider" only includes floor levels housing by at least one health care provider, or any floor level designed or intended for use by at least one health care provider.

(2) For the purposes of this section, shopping center or shopping mall means—

(i) A building housing five or more sales or rental establishments; or

(ii) A series of buildings on a common site, connected by a common pedestrian access route above or below the ground floor, that is either under common ownership or common control or developed either as one project or as a series of related projects, housing five or more sales or rental establishments. For purposes of this section, places of public accommodation of the types listed in paragraph (5) of the definition of "place of public accommodation" in § 36.104 are considered sales or rental establishments. The facility housing a "shopping center or shopping mall" only includes floor levels housing at least one sales or rental establishment, or any floor level designed or intended for use by at least one sales or rental establishment.

(b) The exemption provided in paragraph (a) of this section does not obviate or limit in any way the obligation to comply with the other accessibility requirements established in this subpart. For example, alterations to floors above or below the accessible ground floor must be accessible regardless of whether the altered facility has an elevator.

§ 36.405 Alterations: Historic preservation.

(a) Alterations to buildings or facilities that are eligible for listing in the National Register of Historic Places under the National Historic Preservation Act *(16 U.S.C. 470 et seq.)*, or are designated as historic under State or local law, shall comply to the maximum extent feasible with section 4.1.7 of appendix A to this part.

(b) If it is determined under the procedures set out in section 4.1.7 of appendix A that it is not feasible to provide physical access to an historic property that is a place of public accommodation in a manner that will not threaten or destroy the historic significance of the building or facility, alternative methods of access shall be provided pursuant to the requirements of subpart C of this part.

§ 36.406 Standards for new construction and alterations.

(a) New construction and alterations subject to this part shall comply with the standards for accessible design published as appendix A to this part (ADAAG).

(b) The chart in the appendix to this section provides guidance to the user in reading appendix A to this part (ADAAG) together with subparts A through D of this part, when determining requirements for a particular facility.

APPENDIX TO § 36.406

This chart has no effect for purposes of compliance or enforcement. It does not necessarily provide complete or mandatory information.

	Subparts A–D	ADAAG
Application, General.	36.102(b)(3): public accommodations. 36.102(c): commercial facilities. 36.102(e): public entities. 36.103 (other laws) 36.401 ("for first occupancy"). 36.402(a) (alterations).	1, 2, 3, 4.1.1.
Definitions	36.104: commercial facilities, facility, place of public accommodation, private club, public accommodation, public entity, religious entity. 36.401(d)(1)(i), 36.404(a)(2): shopping center or shopping mall. 36.401(d)(1)(i), 36.404(a)(1): professional office of a health care provider. 36.402: alteration; usability. 36.402(c): to the maximum extent feasible.	3.5 Definitions, including: addition, alteration, building, element, facility, space, story. 4.1.6(j), technical infeasibility.
New Construction. General	36.401(a) General 36.401(b) Commercial facilities in private residences. 36.207 Places of public accommodation in private residences.	4.1.2. 4.1.3.
Work Areas Structural Impracticability.	36.401(c)	4.1.1(3). 4.1.1(5)(a).
Elevator Exemption.	36.401(d) 36.404	4.1.3(5).
Other Exceptions.		4.1.1(5), 4.1.3(5) and throughout
Alterations: General.	36.401(b): commercial facilities in private residences. 36.402 36.403	4.1.6(1). 4.1.6(2).
Alterations Affecting an Area Containing A Primary Function; Path of Travel; Disproportionality.		
Alterations: Special Technical Provisions.		4.1.6(3).
Additions	36.401–36.405 36.405	4.1.5. 4.1.7.
Historic Preservation.		
Technical Provisions.		4.2 through 4.35.
Restaurants and Cafeterias.		5.

	Subparts A–D	ADAAG
Medical Care Facilities.		6.
Business and Mercantile.		7.
Libraries		8.
Transient Lodging (Hotels, Homeless Shelters, Etc.).		9.
Transportation Facilities.		10.

[Order No. 1513–91, 56 FR 35592, July 26, 1991, as amended by Order No. 1836–94, 59 FR 2675, Jan. 18, 1994]

SUBPART E ENFORCEMENT

§ 36.501 Private suits.

(a) *General.* Any person who is being subjected to discrimination on the basis of disability in violation of the Act or this part or who has reasonable grounds for believing that such person is about to be subjected to discrimination in violation of section 303 of the Act or subpart D of this part may institute a civil action for preventive relief, including an application for a permanent or temporary injunction, restraining order, or other order. Upon timely application, the court may, in its discretion, permit the Attorney General to intervene in the civil action if the Attorney General or his or her designee certifies that the case is of general public importance. Upon application by the complainant and in such circumstances as the court may deem just, the court may appoint an attorney for such complainant and may authorize the commencement of the civil action without the payment of fees, costs, or security. Nothing in this section shall require a person with a disability to engage in a futile gesture if the person has actual notice that a person or organization covered by title III of the Act or this part does not intend to comply with its provisions.

(b) Injunctive relief. In the case of violations of § 36.304, § 36.308, § 36.310(b), § 36.401, § 36.402, § 36.403, and § 36.405 of this part, injunctive relief shall include an order to alter facilities to make such facilities readily accessible to and usable by individuals with disabilities to the extent required by the Act or this part. Where appropriate, injunctive relief shall also include requiring the provision of an auxiliary aid or service, modification of a policy, or provision of alternative methods, to the extent required by the Act or this part.

§ 36.502 Investigations and compliance reviews.

(a) The Attorney General shall investigate alleged violations of the Act or this part.

(b) Any individual who believes that he or she or a specific class of persons has been subjected to discrimination prohibited by the Act or this part may request the Department to institute an investigation.

(c) Where the Attorney General has reason to believe that there may be a violation of this part, he or she may initiate a compliance review.

§ 36.503 Suit by the Attorney General.

Following a compliance review or investigation under § 36.502, or at any other time in his or her discretion, the Attorney General may commence a civil action in any appropriate United States district court if the Attorney General has reasonable cause to believe that—

(a) Any person or group of persons is engaged in a pattern or practice of discrimination in violation of the Act or this part; or

(b) Any person or group of persons has been discriminated against in violation of the Act or this part and the discrimination raises an issue of general public importance.

§ 36.504 Relief.

(a) Authority of court. In a civil action under § 36.503, the court —

(1) May grant any equitable relief that such court considers to be appropriate, including, to the extent required by the Act or this part —

(i) Granting temporary, preliminary, or permanent relief;

(ii) Providing an auxiliary aid or service, modification of policy, practice, or procedure, or alternative method; and

(iii) Making facilities readily accessible to and usable by individuals with disabilities;

(2) May award other relief as the court considers to be appropriate, including monetary damages to persons aggrieved when requested by the Attorney General; and

(3) May, to vindicate the public interest, assess a civil penalty against the entity in an amount

(i) Not exceeding $ 50,000 for a first violation occurring before September 29, 1999, and not exceeding $ 55,000 for a first violation occurring on or after September 29, 1999; and

(ii) Not exceeding $ 100,000 for any subsequent violation occurring before September 29, 1999, and not exceeding $ 110,000 for any subsequent violation occurring on or after September 29, 1999.

(b) Single violation. For purposes of paragraph (a) (3) of this section, in determining whether a first or subsequent violation has occurred, a determination in a single action, by judgment or settlement, that the covered entity has engaged in more than one discriminatory act shall be counted as a single violation.

(c) Punitive damages. For purposes of paragraph (a)(2) of this section, the terms "monetary damages" and "such other relief" do not include punitive damages.

(d) Judicial consideration. In a civil action under § 36.503, the court, when considering what amount of civil penalty, if any, is appropriate, shall give consideration to any good faith effort or attempt to comply with this part by the entity. In evaluating good faith, the court shall consider, among other factors it deems relevant, whether the entity could have reasonably anticipated the need for an appropriate type of auxiliary aid needed to accommodate the unique needs of a particular individual with a disability.

§ 36.505 Attorneys fees.

In any action or administrative proceeding commenced pursuant to the Act or this part, the court or agency, in its discretion, may allow the prevailing party, other than the United States, a reasonable attorney's fee, including litigation expenses, and costs, and the United States shall be liable for the foregoing the same as a private individual.

TITLE 42.
THE PUBLIC HEALTH AND WELFARE

CHAPTER 126. EQUAL OPPORTUNITY FOR INDIVIDUALS WITH DISABILITIES

MISCELLANEOUS PROVISIONS

§ 12201. Construction

(a) In general. Except as otherwise provided in this Act, nothing in this Act shall be construed to apply a lesser standard than the standards applied under title V of the Rehabilitation Act of 1973 (*29 U.S.C. 790* et seq.) or the regulations issued by Federal agencies pursuant to such title.

(b) Relationship to other laws. Nothing in this Act shall be construed to invalidate or limit the remedies, rights, and procedures of any Federal law or law of any State or political subdivision of any State or jurisdiction that provides greater or equal protection for the rights of individuals with disabilities than are afforded by this Act. Nothing in this Act shall be construed to preclude the prohibition of, or the imposition of restrictions on, smoking in places of employment covered by title I [*42 USCS §§ 12111* et seq.], in transportation covered by title II or III [*42 USCS §§ 12131* et seq. or *12181* et seq.], or in places of public accommodation covered by title III [*42 USCS §§ 12181* et seq.].

(c) Insurance. Titles I through IV of this Act shall not be construed to prohibit or restrict—

(1) an insurer, hospital or medical service company, health maintenance organization, or any agent, or entity that administers benefit plans, or similar organizations from underwriting risks, classifying risks, or administering such risks that are based on or not inconsistent with State law; or

(2) a person or organization covered by this Act from establishing, sponsoring, observing or administering the terms of a bona fide benefit plan that are based on underwriting risks, classifying risks, or administering such risks that are based on or not inconsistent with State law; or

(3) a person or organization covered by this Act from establishing, sponsoring, observing or administering the terms of a bona fide benefit plan that is not subject to State laws that regulate insurance.

Paragraphs (1), (2), and (3) shall not be used as a subterfuge to evade the purposes of title [titles] I and III [*42 USCS §§ 12111* et seq., *12181* et seq.].

(d) Accommodations and services. Nothing in this Act shall be construed to require an individual with a disability to accept an accommodation, aid, service, opportunity, or benefit which such individual chooses not to accept.

§ 12202. State immunity.

A State shall not be immune under the *eleventh amendment to the Constitution of the United States* from an action in Federal or State court of competent jurisdiction for a violation of this Act. In any action against a State for a violation of the requirements of this Act, remedies (including remedies both at law and in equity) are available for such a violation to the same extent as such remedies are available for such a violation in an action against any public or private entity other than a State.

§ 12203. Prohibition against retaliation and coercion

(a) Retaliation. No person shall discriminate against any individual because such individual has opposed any act or practice made unlawful by this Act or because such individual made a charge, testified, assisted, or participated in any manner in an investigation, proceeding, or hearing under this Act.

(b) Interference, coercion, or intimidation. It shall be unlawful to coerce, intimidate, threaten, or interfere with any individual in the exercise or enjoyment of, or on account of his or her having exercised or enjoyed, or on account of his or her having aided or encouraged any other individual in the exercise or enjoyment of, any right granted or protected by this Act.

(c) Remedies and procedures. The remedies and procedures available under sections 107, 203, and 308 of this Act [42 USCS §§ 12117, 12133, 12188] shall be available to aggrieved persons for violations of subsections (a) and (b), with respect to title I, title II and title III [42 USCS §§ 12111 et seq., 12131 et seq., 12181 et seq.], respectively.

§ 12204. Regulations by the Architectural and Transportation Barriers Compliance Board

(a) Issuance of guidelines. Not later than 9 months after the date of enactment of this Act [enacted July 26, 1990], the Architectural and Transportation Barriers Compliance Board shall issue minimum guidelines that shall supplement the existing Minimum Guidelines and Requirements for Accessible Design for purposes of titles II and III of this Act [42 USCS §§ 12131 et seq., 12181 et seq.].

(b) Contents of guidelines. The supplemental guidelines issued under subsection (a) shall establish additional requirements, consistent with this Act, to ensure that buildings, facilities, rail passenger cars, and vehicles are accessible, in terms of architecture and design, transportation, and communication, to individuals with disabilities.

(c) Qualified historic properties.

(1) In general. The supplemental guidelines issued under subsection (a) shall include procedures and requirements for alterations that will threaten or destroy the historic significance of qualified historic buildings and facilities as defined in 4.1.7(1)(a) of the Uniform Federal Accessibility Standards.

(2) Sites eligible for listing in National Register. With respect to alterations of buildings or facilities that are eligible for listing in the National Register of Historic Places under the National Historic Preservation Act (16 U.S.C. 470 et seq.), the guidelines described in paragraph (1) shall, at a minimum, maintain the procedures and requirements established in 4.1.7 (1) and (2) of the Uniform Federal Accessibility Standards.

(3) Other sites. With respect to alterations of buildings or facilities designated as historic under State or local law, the guidelines described in paragraph (1) shall establish procedures equivalent to those established by 4.1.7(1)(b) and (c) of the Uniform Federal Accessibility Standards, and shall require, at a minimum, compliance with the requirements established in 4.1.7(2) of such standards.

§ 12205. Attorney's fees

In any action or administrative proceeding commenced pursuant to this Act, the court or agency, in its discretion, may allow the prevailing party, other than the United States, a reasonable attorney's fee, including litigation expenses, and costs, and the United States shall be liable for the foregoing the same as a private individual.

§ 12206. Technical assistance

(a) Plan for assistance.

(1) In general. Not later than 180 days after the date of enactment of this Act [enacted July 26, 1990], the Attorney General, in consultation with the Chair of the Equal Employment Opportunity Commission, the Secretary of Transportation, the Chair of the Architectural and Transportation Barriers Compliance Board, and the Chairman of the Federal Communications Commission, shall develop a plan to assist entities covered under this Act, and other Federal agencies, in understanding the responsibility of such entities and agencies under this Act.

(2) Publication of plan. The Attorney General shall publish the plan referred to in paragraph (1) for public comment in accordance with subchapter II of chapter 5 of *title 5, United States Code [5* USCS §§ 551 et seq.] (commonly known as the Administrative Procedure Act).

(b) Agency and public assistance. The Attorney General may obtain the assistance of other Federal agencies in carrying out subsection (a), including the National Council on Disability, the President's Committee on Employment of People with Disabilities, the Small Business Administration, and the Department of Commerce.

(c) Implementation.

(1) Rendering assistance. Each Federal agency that has responsibility under paragraph (2) for implementing this Act may render technical assistance to individuals and institutions that have rights or duties under the respective title or titles for which such agency has responsibility.

(2) Implementation of Titles.

(A) Title I. The Equal Employment Opportunity Commission and the Attorney General shall implement the plan for assistance developed under subsection (a), for title I [*42 USCS §§ 12111* et seq.].

(B) Title II.

(i) Subtitle A. The Attorney General shall implement such plan for assistance for subtitle A of title II [*42 USCS §§ 12131* et seq.].

(ii) Subtitle B. The Secretary of Transportation shall implement such plan for assistance for subtitle B of title II [*42 USCS §§ 12141* et seq.].

(C) Title III. The Attorney General, in coordination with the Secretary of Transportation and the Chair of the Architectural Transportation Barriers Compliance Board, shall implement such plan for assistance for title III [*42 USCS §§ 12181* et seq.], except for section 304 [*42 USCS § 12184*], the plan for assistance for which shall be implemented by the Secretary of Transportation.

(D) Title IV. The Chairman of the Federal Communications Commission, in coordination with the Attorney General, shall implement such plan for assistance for title IV.

(3) Technical assistance manuals. Each Federal agency that has responsibility under paragraph (2) for implementing this Act shall, as part of its implementation responsibilities, ensure the availability and provision of appropriate technical assistance manuals to individuals or entities with rights or duties under this Act no later than six months after applicable final regulations are published under titles I, II, III, and IV.

(d) Grants and contracts.

(1) In general. Each Federal agency that has responsibility under subsection (c)(2) for

implementing this Act may make grants or award contracts to effectuate the purposes of this section, subject to the availability of appropriations. Such grants and contracts may be awarded to individuals, institutions not organized for profit and no part of the net earnings of which inures to the benefit of any private shareholder or individual (including educational institutions), and associations representing individuals who have rights or duties under this Act. Contracts may be awarded to entities organized for profit, but such entities may not be the recipients or [of] grants described in this paragraph.

(2) Dissemination of information. Such grants and contracts, among other uses, may be designed to ensure wide dissemination of information about the rights and duties established by this Act and to provide information and technical assistance about techniques for effective compliance with this Act.

(e) Failure to receive assistance. An employer, public accommodation, or other entity covered under this Act shall not be excused from compliance with the requirements of this Act because of any failure to receive technical assistance under this section, including any failure in the development or dissemination of any technical assistance manual authorized by this section.

§ 12207. Federal wilderness areas

(a) Study. The National Council on Disability shall conduct a study and report on the effect that wilderness designations and wilderness land management practices have on the ability of individuals with disabilities to use and enjoy the National Wilderness Preservation System as established under the Wilderness Act (*16 U.S.C. 1131* et seq.).

(b) Submission of report. Not later than 1 year after the enactment of this Act [enacted July 26, 1990], the National Council on Disability shall submit the report required under subsection (a) to Congress.

(c) Specific wilderness access.

(1) In general. Congress reaffirms that nothing in the Wilderness Act is to be construed as prohibiting the use of a wheelchair in a wilderness area by an individual whose disability requires use of a wheelchair, and consistent with the Wilderness Act no agency is required to provide any form of special treatment or accommodation, or to construct any facilities or modify any conditions of lands within a wilderness area in order to facilitate such use.

(2) Definition. For purposes of paragraph (1), the term "wheelchair" means a device designed solely for use by a mobility-impaired person for locomotion, that is suitable for use in an indoor pedestrian area.

§ 12208. Transvestites

For the purposes of this Act, the term "disabled" or "disability" shall not apply to an individual solely because that individual is a transvestite.

§ 12209. Instrumentalities of the Congress

The General Accounting Office [Government Accountability Office], the Government Printing Office, and the Library of Congress shall be covered as follows:

(1) In general. The rights and protections under this Act shall, subject to paragraph (2), apply with respect to the conduct of each instrumentality of the Congress.

(2) Establishment of remedies and procedures by instrumentalities. The chief official of each instrumentality of the Congress shall establish remedies and procedures to be utilized with respect to the rights and protections provided pursuant to paragraph (1).

(3) Report to Congress. The chief official of each instrumentality of the Congress shall,

after establishing remedies and procedures for purposes of paragraph (2), submit to the Congress a report describing the remedies and procedures.

(4) Definition of instrumentalities. For purposes of this section, the term "instrumentality of the Congress" means the following:[,] the General Accounting Office [Government Accountability Office], the Government Printing Office, and the Library of Congress[,].

(5) Enforcement of employment rights. The remedies and procedures set forth in section 717 of the Civil Rights Act of 1964 (*42 U.S.C. 2000e-16*) shall be available to any employee of an instrumentality of the Congress who alleges a violation of the rights and protections under sections 102 through 104 of this Act [*42 USCS §§ 12112-12114*] that are made applicable by this section, except that the authorities of the Equal Employment Opportunity Commission shall be exercised by the chief official of the instrumentality of the Congress.

(6) Enforcement of rights to public services and accommodations. The remedies and procedures set forth in section 717 of the Civil Rights Act of 1964 (*42 U.S.C. 2000e-16*) shall be available to any qualified person with a disability who is a visitor, guest, or patron of an instrumentality of Congress and who alleges a violation of the rights and protections under sections 201 through 230 or section 302 or 303 of this Act [*42 USCS §§ 12131-12150 or § 12182 or 12183*] that are made applicable by this section, except that the authorities of the Equal Employment Opportunity Commission shall be exercised by the chief official of the instrumentality of the Congress.

(7) Construction. Nothing in this section shall alter the enforcement procedures for individuals with disabilities provided in the General Accounting Office Personnel Act of 1980 and regulations promulgated pursuant to that Act.

§ 12210. Illegal use of drugs

(a) In general. For purposes of this Act, the term "individual with a disability" does not include an individual who is currently engaging in the illegal use of drugs, when the covered entity acts on the basis of such use.

(b) Rules of construction. Nothing in subsection (a) shall be construed to exclude as an individual with a disability an individual who—

(1) has successfully completed a supervised drug rehabilitation program and is no longer engaging in the illegal use of drugs, or has otherwise been rehabilitated successfully and is no longer engaging in such use;

(2) is participating in a supervised rehabilitation program and is no longer engaging in such use; or

(3) is erroneously regarded as engaging in such use, but is not engaging in such use; except that it shall not be a violation of this Act for a covered entity to adopt or administer reasonable policies or procedures, including but not limited to drug testing, designed to ensure that an individual described in paragraph (1) or (2) is no longer engaging in the illegal use of drugs; however, nothing in this section shall be construed to encourage, prohibit, restrict, or authorize the conducting of testing for the illegal use of drugs.

(c) Health and other services. Notwithstanding subsection (a) and section 511(b)(3) [*42 USCS § 12211(b)(3)*], an individual shall not be denied health services, or services provided in connection with drug rehabilitation, on the basis of the current illegal use of drugs if the individual is otherwise entitled to such services.

(d) "Illegal use of drugs" defined.

(1) In general. The term "illegal use of drugs" means the use of drugs, the possession or distribution of which is unlawful under the Controlled Substances Act (*21 U.S.C. 812*).

Such term does not include the use of a drug taken under supervision by a licensed health care professional, or other uses authorized by the Controlled Substances Act or other provisions of Federal law.

(2) Drugs. The term "drug" means a controlled substance, as defined in schedules I through V of section 202 of the Controlled Substances Act [21 USCS § 812].

§ 12211. Definitions

(a) Homosexuality and bisexuality. For purposes of the definition of "disability" in section 3(2), [42 USCS § 12102(2)], homosexuality and bisexuality are not impairments and as such are not disabilities under this Act.

(b) Certain conditions. Under this Act, the term "disability" shall not include—

(1) transvestism, transsexualism, pedophilia, exhibitionism, voyeurism, gender identity disorders not resulting from physical impairments, or other sexual behavior disorders;

(2) compulsive gambling, kleptomania, or pyromania; or

(3) psychoactive substance use disorders resulting from current illegal use of drugs.

§ 12212. Alternative means of dispute resolution

Where appropriate and to the extent authorized by law, the use of alternative means of dispute resolution, including settlement negotiations, conciliation, facilitation, mediation, factfinding, minitrials, and arbitration, is encouraged to resolve disputes arising under this Act.

§ 12213. Severability

Should any provision in this Act be found to be unconstitutional by a court of law, such provision shall be severed from the remainder of the Act, and such action shall not affect the enforceability of the remaining provisions of the Act.